THE BOOK

Ford Sierra
Service and Repair Manual

Steve Rendle and Christopher Rogers

Models covered

Saloon (Sapphire and Hatchback), Estate and P100 Pick-up models, including special/limited editions, with four-cylinder SOHC, DOHC & CVH petrol engines and two-wheel-drive

Does not cover V6 or Diesel engine models, four-wheel-drive models, or RS Cosworth

(903 - 368 - 1Y7)

© Haynes Publishing 1996

A book in the **Haynes Service and Repair Manual Series**

AB

2

ISBN 1 85960 090 5

British Library Cataloguing in Publication Data
A catalogue record for this book is available from from the British library.

Printed by **J H Haynes & Co. Ltd, Sparkford, Nr Yeovil, Somerset BA22 7JJ**

Haynes Publishing
Sparkford, Nr Yeovil, Somerset BA22 7JJ England

Haynes North America, Inc
861 Lawrence Drive, Newbury Park, California 91320 USA

Editions Haynes S.A.
147/149, rue Saint Honore, 75001 PARIS, France

Contents

Contents

REPAIRS AND OVERHAUL

Engine and Associated Systems

TRANSMISSION

BRAKES AND SUSPENSION

BODY EQUIPMENT

Wiring Diagrams

Reference

Index

Introduction to the Ford Sierra

The Ford Sierra was first introduced in late 1982 with the option of seven different engines and four different trim levels. This manual covers the four cylinder in-line petrol engines, but other models in the range are fitted with V6 or diesel engines.

The Sierra was introduced by Ford as the successor to the Cortina and initially received a mixed reception as it was one of the first vehicles to make use of the "aeroback" body style designed to reduce the air drag coefficient to a minimum in the interests of fuel economy. Mechanically the Sierra is similar to the Cortina with the exception of all-round independent suspension.

Initially, 1.3, 1.6 and 2.0 litre SOHC carburettor engines were available, with Hatchback and Estate body styles. In late 1984, a 1.8 litre SOHC engine became available and in 1985, a performance orientated 2.0 litre SOHC fuel injection engine was introduced.

Towards the end of 1986, the 1.3 litre engine was phased out. In order to fill a gap in the range, a Saloon body style, designated the Sapphire, was introduced in early 1987 and shortly afterwards, a 1.8 litre CVH engine replaced the previously used 1.8 litre SOHC engine throughout the model range.

A 1.6 litre CVH engine was introduced in September 1991 to replace the 1.6 litre SOHC engine used previously, this engine being broadly similar to the original 1.8 litre CVH engine which was in turn uprated in March, 1992.

A 2.0 litre DOHC (Double OverHead Camshaft) engine was introduced in August 1989 to replace the 2.0 litre SOHC engine.

In early 1988, a Sierra-based P100 pick-up model became available to replace the previous Cortina-based design. The P100 consists of a Sierra-type "cab" and front suspension, and a Ford Transit-type rear suspension and 2.0 litre engine.

A wide range of standard and optional equipment is available within the Sierra range to suit most tastes, including an anti-lock braking system.

For the home mechanic, the Sierra is a straightforward vehicle to maintain and repair since design features have been incorporated to reduce the actual cost of ownership to a minimum, and most of the items requiring frequent attention are easily accessible.

Ford Sierra L

Ford Sierra Ghia Estate

Acknowledgements

Thanks are due to Champion Spark Plug who supplied the illustrations showing spark plug conditions. Certain other illustrations are the copyright of the Ford Motor Company and are used with their permission. Thanks are also due to Sykes-Pickavant Limited, who provided some of the workshop tools, and to all those people at Sparkford who helped in the production of this manual.

We take great pride in the accuracy of information given in this manual, but vehicle manufacturers make alterations and design changes during the production run of a particular vehicle of which they do not inform us. No liability can be accepted by the authors or publishers for loss, damage or injury caused by errors in, or omissions from, the information given.

Working on your car can be dangerous. This page shows just some of the potential risks and hazards, with the aim of creating a safety-conscious attitude.

General hazards

Scalding

• Don't remove the radiator or expansion tank cap while the engine is hot.
• Engine oil, automatic transmission fluid or power steering fluid may also be dangerously hot if the engine has recently been running.

Burning

• Beware of burns from the exhaust system and from any part of the engine. Brake discs and drums can also be extremely hot immediately after use.

Crushing

• When working under or near a raised vehicle, always supplement the jack with axle stands, or use drive-on ramps. *Never venture under a car which is only supported by a jack.*

• Take care if loosening or tightening high-torque nuts when the vehicle is on stands. Initial loosening and final tightening should be done with the wheels on the ground.

Fire

• Fuel is highly flammable; fuel vapour is explosive.
• Don't let fuel spill onto a hot engine.
• Do not smoke or allow naked lights (including pilot lights) anywhere near a vehicle being worked on. Also beware of creating sparks (electrically or by use of tools).
• Fuel vapour is heavier than air, so don't work on the fuel system with the vehicle over an inspection pit.
• Another cause of fire is an electrical overload or short-circuit. Take care when repairing or modifying the vehicle wiring.
• Keep a fire extinguisher handy, of a type suitable for use on fuel and electrical fires.

Electric shock

• Ignition HT voltage can be dangerous, especially to people with heart problems or a pacemaker. Don't work on or near the ignition system with the engine running or the ignition switched on.

• Mains voltage is also dangerous. Make sure that any mains-operated equipment is correctly earthed. Mains power points should be protected by a residual current device (RCD) circuit breaker.

Fume or gas intoxication

• Exhaust fumes are poisonous; they often contain carbon monoxide, which is rapidly fatal if inhaled. Never run the engine in a confined space such as a garage with the doors shut.

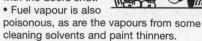

• Fuel vapour is also poisonous, as are the vapours from some cleaning solvents and paint thinners.

Poisonous or irritant substances

• Avoid skin contact with battery acid and with any fuel, fluid or lubricant, especially antifreeze, brake hydraulic fluid and Diesel fuel. Don't syphon them by mouth. If such a substance is swallowed or gets into the eyes, seek medical advice.
• Prolonged contact with used engine oil can cause skin cancer. Wear gloves or use a barrier cream if necessary. Change out of oil-soaked clothes and do not keep oily rags in your pocket.
• Air conditioning refrigerant forms a poisonous gas if exposed to a naked flame (including a cigarette). It can also cause skin burns on contact.

Asbestos

• Asbestos dust can cause cancer if inhaled or swallowed. Asbestos may be found in gaskets and in brake and clutch linings. When dealing with such components it is safest to assume that they contain asbestos.

Special hazards

Hydrofluoric acid

• This extremely corrosive acid is formed when certain types of synthetic rubber, found in some O-rings, oil seals, fuel hoses etc, are exposed to temperatures above 400°C. The rubber changes into a charred or sticky substance containing the acid. *Once formed, the acid remains dangerous for years. If it gets onto the skin, it may be necessary to amputate the limb concerned.*
• When dealing with a vehicle which has suffered a fire, or with components salvaged from such a vehicle, wear protective gloves and discard them after use.

The battery

• Batteries contain sulphuric acid, which attacks clothing, eyes and skin. Take care when topping-up or carrying the battery.
• The hydrogen gas given off by the battery is highly explosive. Never cause a spark or allow a naked light nearby. Be careful when connecting and disconnecting battery chargers or jump leads.

Air bags

• Air bags can cause injury if they go off accidentally. Take care when removing the steering wheel and/or facia. Special storage instructions may apply.

Diesel injection equipment

• Diesel injection pumps supply fuel at very high pressure. Take care when working on the fuel injectors and fuel pipes.

⚠ *Warning: Never expose the hands, face or any other part of the body to injector spray; the fuel can penetrate the skin with potentially fatal results.*

Remember...

DO

• Do use eye protection when using power tools, and when working under the vehicle.

• Do wear gloves or use barrier cream to protect your hands when necessary.

• Do get someone to check periodically that all is well when working alone on the vehicle.

• Do keep loose clothing and long hair well out of the way of moving mechanical parts.

• Do remove rings, wristwatch etc, before working on the vehicle – especially the electrical system.

• Do ensure that any lifting or jacking equipment has a safe working load rating adequate for the job.

DON'T

• Don't attempt to lift a heavy component which may be beyond your capability – get assistance.

• Don't rush to finish a job, or take unverified short cuts.

• Don't use ill-fitting tools which may slip and cause injury.

• Don't leave tools or parts lying around where someone can trip over them. Mop up oil and fuel spills at once.

• Don't allow children or pets to play in or near a vehicle being worked on.

Jacking, vehicle support and wheel changing

The jack supplied with the vehicle tool kit should only be used for changing roadwheels. When carrying out any other kind of work, raise the vehicle using a trolley jack, and always supplement the jack with axle stands positioned under the vehicle jacking points.

To change a roadwheel, first remove the spare wheel and jack from their stowage positions. On Saloon, Hatchback and Estate models, the jack and spare wheel are located in the luggage compartment. On P100 models, the jack is located behind the passenger seat, and the spare wheel is located under the rear of the cargo area. Firmly apply the handbrake and engage first gear on manual gearbox models or "P" on automatic transmission models. Place chocks at the front and rear of the wheel diagonally opposite the one to be changed.

Where applicable, remove the wheel trim and slacken the wheel nuts using the wheel brace provided in the vehicle tool kit. Position the jack head under the jacking point nearest to the wheel to be changed. Raise the jack until the wheel is clear of the ground, then remove the wheel nuts and the wheel. Fit the spare wheel and secure it with the wheel nuts. Lower the jack until the wheel is just touching the ground, and tighten the wheel nuts moderately tight. Now lower the jack fully and tighten the wheel nuts securely in a diagonal sequence. Where applicable, refit the wheel trim , then withdraw the jack and stow the wheel and jack in thier respective locations.

When jacking up the vehicle with a trolley jack, position the jack under one of the relevant jacking point (note that on P100 models, the jackng points for use with a trolley jack are different to those for use with the vehicle jack). Do not jack the vehicle under the sump or or any of the steering or suspension components. Supplement the jack using axle stands. The jacking points and axle stand positions are shown in the accompanying illustrations. Never work under, around or near a raised vehicle unless it is adequately supported in at least two places.

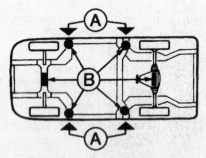

Location of jacking points - Saloon, Hatchback and Estate models
A Jacking points for use with vehicle jack
B Jacking points for use with trolley jack or axle stands

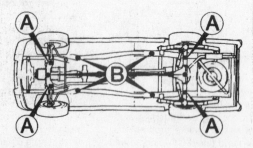

Location of jacking points - P100 models
A Jacking points for use with vehicle jack
B Jacking points for use with trolley jack or axle stands

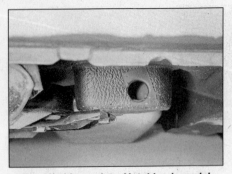

Rear jacking point - Hatchback model

Jack location by front wheel - Hatchback model

Axle stand correctly positioned under front jacking point - Hatchback model

Towing

Towing eyes are fitted to the front and rear of the vehicle for attachment of a tow rope. Always turn the ignition key to position "II" when thew vehicle is being towed, so that the steering lock is released and the direction indicator and brake lamps are operational.

Before being towed, release the handbrake and place the gear lever in neutral. On automatic transmission models, the towing speed must not exceed 25 mph (40 kph), and the towing distance must not exceed 12 miles (20 km). For longer distances, or if transmission damage is suspected, the propellor shaft should be removed, or the rear of the vehicle should be lifted clear of the ground.

Push or tow starting is not possible on vehicles fitted with automatic transmission.

Front towing eye - Hatchback model

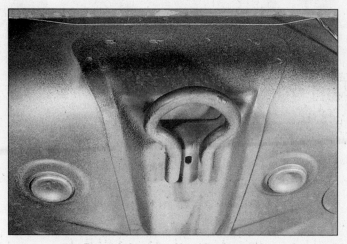

Rear towing eye - Hatchback model

Identifying leaks

Puddles on the garage floor or drive, or obvious wetness under the bonnet or underneath the car, suggest a leak that needs investigating. It can sometimes be difficult to decide where the leak is coming from, especially if the engine bay is very dirty already. Leaking oil or fluid can also be blown rearwards by the passage of air under the car, giving a false impression of where the problem lies.

 Warning: Most automotive oils and fluids are poisonous. Wash them off skin, and change out of contaminated clothing, without delay.

 The smell of a fluid leaking from the car may provide a clue to what's leaking. Some fluids are distinctively coloured. It may help to clean the car carefully and to park it over some clean paper overnight as an aid to locating the source of the leak.
Remember that some leaks may only occur while the engine is running.

Sump oil

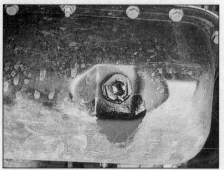

Engine oil may leak from the drain plug...

Oil from filter

...or from the base of the oil filter.

Gearbox oil

Gearbox oil can leak from the seals at the inboard ends of the driveshafts.

Antifreeze

Leaking antifreeze often leaves a crystalline deposit like this.

Brake fluid

A leak occurring at a wheel is almost certainly brake fluid.

Power steering fluid

Power steering fluid may leak from the pipe connectors on the steering rack.

Jump starting

HAYNES HINT *Jump starting will get you out of trouble, but you must correct whatever made the battery go flat in the first place. There are three possibilities:*

1 *The battery has been drained by repeated attempts to start, or by leaving the lights on.*

2 *The charging system is not working properly (alternator drivebelt slack or broken, alternator wiring fault or alternator itself faulty).*

3 *The battery itself is at fault (electrolyte low, or battery worn out).*

When jump-starting a car using a booster battery, observe the following precautions:

✔ Before connecting the booster battery, make sure that the ignition is switched off.

✔ Ensure that all electrical equipment (lights, heater, wipers, etc) is switched off.

✔ Make sure that the booster battery is the same voltage as the discharged one in the vehicle.

✔ If the battery is being jump-started from the battery in another vehicle, the two vehcles MUST NOT TOUCH each other.

✔ Make sure that the transmission is in neutral (or PARK, in the case of automatic transmission).

1 Connect one end of the red jump lead to the positive (+) terminal of the flat battery

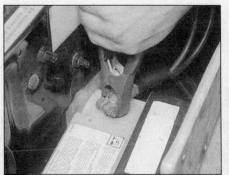

2 Connect the other end of the red lead to the positive (+) terminal of the booster battery.

3 Connect one end of the black jump lead to the negative (-) terminal of the booster battery

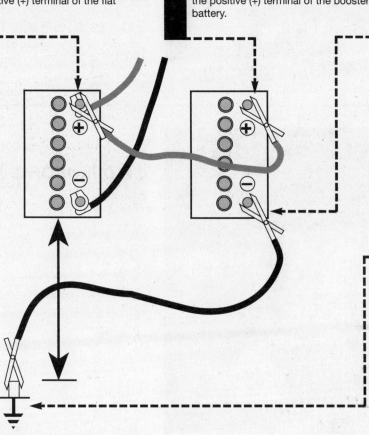

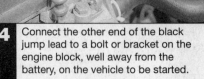

4 Connect the other end of the black jump lead to a bolt or bracket on the engine block, well away from the battery, on the vehicle to be started.

5 Make sure that the jump leads will not come into contact with the fan, drive belts or other moving parts of the engine.

6 Start the engine using the booster battery, then with the engine running at idle speed, disconnect the jump leads in the reverse order of connection.

Introduction

There are some very simple checks which need only take a few minutes to carry out, but which could save you a lot of inconvenience and expense.

These "Weekly checks" require no great skill or special tools, and the small amount of time they take to perform could prove to be very well spent, for example;

☐ Keeping an eye on tyre condition and pressures, will not only help to stop them wearing out prematurely, but could also save your life.

☐ Many breakdowns are caused by electrical problems. Battery-related faults are particularly common, and a quick check on a regular basis will often prevent the majority of these.

☐ If your car develops a brake fluid leak, the first time you might know about it is when your brakes don't work properly. Checking the level regularly will give advance warning of this kind of problem.

☐ If the oil or coolant levels run low, the cost of repairing any engine damage will be far greater than fixing the leak, for example.

Underbonnet check points

◀ 2.0 litre OHC

Carburettor model (air cleaner removed for clarity)

A *Location of oil level dipstick*

B *Engine oil filler cap*

C *Coolant expansion tank*

D *Brake fluid reservoir*

E *Windscreen washer reservoir*

F *Battery*

◀ 2.0 litre OHC

Fuel injection model

A *Oil level dipstick*

B *Engine oil filler cap*

C *Coolant expansion tank*

D *Brake fluid reservoir*

E *Windscreen washer reservoir*

F *Battery*

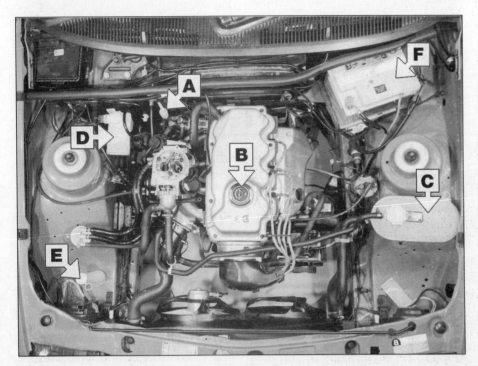

◀ 1.8 litre CVH

Air cleaner removed for clarity

A *Oil level dipstick*
B *Engine oil filler cap*
C *Coolant expansion tank*
D *Brake fluid reservoir*
E *Windscreen washer reservoir*
F *Battery*

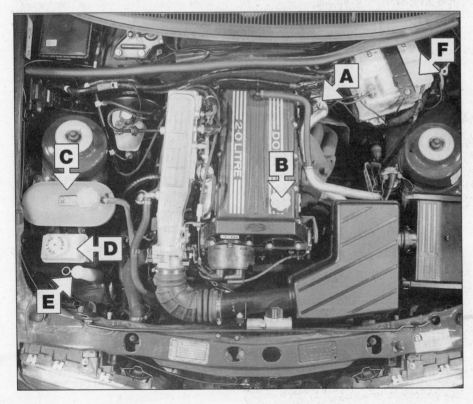

◀ 2.0 litre DOHC

A *Oil level dipstick*
B *Engine oil filler cap*
C *Coolant expansion tank*
D *Power steering fluid reservoir*
E *Windscreen washer reservoir*
F *Battery*

Engine oil level

Before you start

✔ Make sure that your car is on level ground.
✔ Check the oil level before the car is driven, or at least 5 minutes after the engine has been switched off.

 If the oil is checked immediately after driving the vehicle, some of the oil will remain in the upper engine components, resulting in an inaccurate reading on the dipstick!

The correct oil

Modern engines place great demands on their oil. It is very important that the correct oil for your car is used (See "Lubricants and Fluids").

Car Care

● If you have to add oil frequently, you should check whether you have any oil leaks. Place some clean paper under the car overnight, and check for stains in the morning. If there are no leaks, the engine may be burning oil (see "Fault Finding").

● Always maintain the level between the upper and lower dipstick marks (see photo 3). If the level is too low severe engine damage may occur. Oil seal failure may result if the engine is overfilled by adding too much oil.

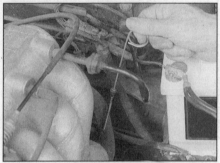

1 On some models, the dipstick is brightly coloured for easy identification. Refer to the photos on pages 0•10 and 0•11 for the exact location for each engine type

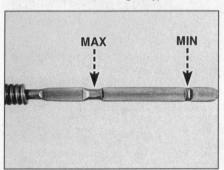

3 Note the oil level on the end of the dipstick, which should be between the upper ("MAX") mark and lower ("MIN") mark. Approximately 1.0 litre of oil will raise the level from the lower mark to the upper mark.

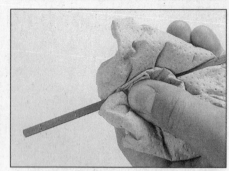

2 Using a clean rag or paper towel remove all oil from the dipstick. Insert the clean dipstick into the tube as far as it will go, then withdraw it again.

4 Oil is added through the filler cap. Unscrew the cap and top-up the level; a funnel may help to reduce spillage . Add the oil slowly, checking the level on the dipstick frequently. Avoid overfilling (see "Car Care").

Coolant level

 Warning: DO NOT attempt to remove the expansion tank pressure cap when the engine is hot, as there is a very great risk of scalding. Do not leave open containers of coolant about, as it is poisonous.

Car Care

● With a sealed-type cooling system, adding coolant should not be necessary on a regular basis. If frequent topping-up is required, it is likely there is a leak. Check the radiator, all hoses and joint faces for signs of staining or wetness, and rectify as necessary.

● It is important that antifreeze is used in the cooling system all year round, not just during the winter months. Don't top-up with water alone, as the antifreeze will become too diluted.

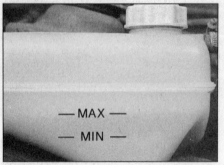

1 The coolant level varies with the temperature of the engine. When the engine is cold, the coolant level should be at the "MAX" mark. When the engine is hot, the level may rise slightly above this mark.

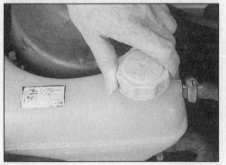

2 If topping-up is necessary, **wait until the engine is cold**. Slowly turn the expansion tank cap anti-clockwise to relieve the system pressure. Once any pressure is released, turn the cap anti-clockwise until it can be lifted off.

3 Add a mixture of water and antifreeze through the expansion tank filler neck until the coolant reaches the "MAX" level mark. Refit the cap, turning it clockwise as far as it will go until it is secure.

Screen washer fluid level

Screenwash additives not only keep the winscreen clean during foul weather, they also prevent the washer system freezing in cold weather - which is when you are likely to need it most. Don't top up using plain water as the screenwash will become too diluted, and will freeze during cold weather. On no account use engine antifreeze in the washer system - this could discolour or damage paintwork.

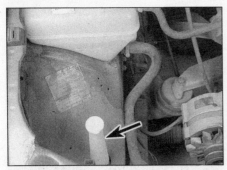

1 Some models have a visible reservoir, whilst others have only the filler nozzle (arrowed) showing. Either way, the location is in the same place.

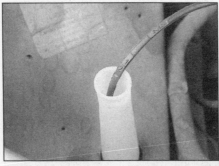

2 On models with only the filler tube fitted, a dipstick is fitted to show the quantity of fluid left in the reservoir

3 Top-up the washer reservoir using a propietary screen wash.

Brake fluid level

Warning:Brake hydraulic fluid can harm your eyes and damage painted surfaces, so use extreme caution when handling and pouring it.

● *Do not use fluid that has been standing open for some time, as it absorbs moisture from the air which can cause a dangerous loss of braking effectiveness.*

HAYNES HiNT

• *Make sure that your car is on level ground.*
• *The fluid level in the master cylinder reservoir will drop slightly as the brake pads wear down, but the fluid level must never be allowed to drop below the 'MIN' mark.*

Safety first

● If the reservoir requires repeated topping-up this is an indication of a fluid leak somewhere in the system, which should be investigated immediately.

● If a leak is suspected, the car should not be driven until the braking system has been checked. Never take any risks where brakes are concerned.

● On ABS models, switch the ignition off and pump the brake pedal at least 20 times or until the pedal feels hard. Open the bonnet. Switch on the ignition: the hydraulic unit pump will be heard running. Wait until the pump stops, then switch off the ignition.

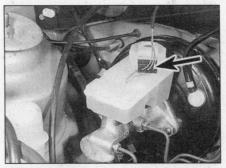

1 The "MAX" and "MIN" marks are indicated on the side of the reservoir. The fluid level must be kept between the marks. Disconnect the wiring plug (arrowed) before removing the cap.

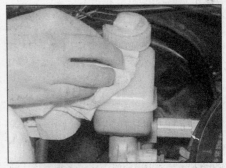

2 If topping-up is necessary, first wipe the area around the filler cap with a clean rag before removing the cap.

3 When adding fluid, It's a good idea to Inspect the reservoir. The system should be drained and refilled if dirt is seen in the fluid (see Chapter 9 for details).

4 Carefully add fluid avoiding spilling it on surrounding paintwork. Use only the specified hydraulic fluid; mixing different types of fluid can cause damage to the system. After filling to the correct level, refit the cap securely, to prevent leaks and the entry of foreign matter. Wipe off any spilt fluid.

Power steering fluid level

Before you start:

✔ Park the vehicle on level ground.

✔ Set the steering wheel pointing straight-ahead.

✔ The system should be at operating temperature and the engine should be turned off.

 For the check to be accurate the steering must not be turned once the engine has been stopped.

Safety First:

● The need for frequent topping-up indicates a leak, which should be investigated immediately.

1 The power steering fluid reservoir is located next to the coolant expansion tank. Clean around the filler cap and then remove it should topping up be required.

2 The fluid level should be up to the "MAX" or upper "HOT" mark

3 Top-up if necessary with clean fluid of the specified type If the level is checked cold, use the "MIN" or "FULL COLD" mark. Recheck the level at operating temperature.

Electrical system

✔ Check all external lights and the horn. Refer to the appropriate Sections of Chapter 13 for details if any of the circuits are found to be inoperative.

✔ Visually check all wiring connectors, harnesses and retaining clips for security, and for signs of chafing or damage.

 If you need to check your brake lights and indicators unaided, back up to a wall or garage door and operate the lights. The reflected light should show if they are working properly.

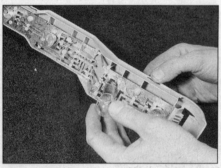

1 If a single indicator light, brake light or headlight has failed it is likely that a bulb has blown and will need to be replaced. Refer to Chapter 12 for details.
If both brake lights have failed, it is possible that the brake light switch above the brake pedal needs adjusting. This simple operation is described in Chapter 9.

2 If more than one indicator light or headlight has failed it is likely that either a fuse has blown or that there is a fault in the circuit (refer to *"Electrical fault-finding"* in Chapter 13).
The fuses are mounted in a box in the engine compartment on the right-hand side of the bulkhead. Remove the loose cover (and spring clip if fitted), pulling the plastic clip, and removing the plastic cover.

3 To replace a blown fuse, simply pull it out. Fit a new fuse of the same rating, available from car accessory shops.
It is important that you find the reason that the fuse blew - a checking procedure is given in Chapter 13.

Battery

Caution: Before carrying out any work on the vehicle battery, read the precautions given in "Safety first" at the start of this manual.

✔ Make sure that the battery tray is in good condition, and that the clamp is tight. Corrosion on the tray, retaining clamp and the battery itself can be removed with a solution of water and baking soda. Thoroughly rinse all cleaned areas with water. Any metal parts damaged by corrosion should be covered with a zinc-based primer, then painted.

✔ Periodically (approximately every three months), check the charge condition of the battery as described in Chapter 5A.

✔ If the battery is flat, and you need to jump start your vehicle, see "*Roadside Repairs*".

1 The battery is located on the left-hand side of the engine compartment. The exterior of the battery should be inspected periodically for damage such as a cracked case or cover.

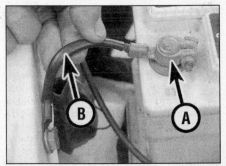

2 Check the tightness of battery clamps (A) to ensure good electrical connections. You should not be able to move them. Also check each cable (B) for cracks and frayed conductors.

Battery corrosion can be kept to a minimum by applying a layer of petroleum jelly to the clamps and terminals after they are reconnected.

3 If corrosion (white, fluffy deposits) is evident, remove the cables from the battery terminals, clean them with a small wire brush, then refit them. Accessory stores sell a useful tool for cleaning the battery post ...

4 ... as well as the battery cable clamps

Wiper blades

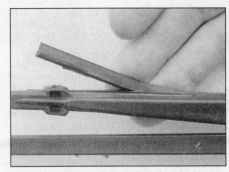

1 Check the condition of the wiper blades; if they are cracked or show any signs of deterioration, or if the glass swept area is smeared, renew them. For maximum clarity of vision, wiper blades should be renewed annually, as a matter of course.

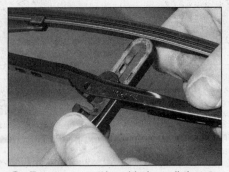

2 To remove a wiper blade, pull the arm fully away from the glass until it locks. Swivel the blade through 90°, press the locking tab(s) with your fingers, and slide the blade out of the arm's hooked end. On refitting, ensure that the blade locks securely into the arm.

Tyre condition and pressure

It is very important that tyres are in good condition, and at the correct pressure - having a tyre failure at any speed is highly dangerous. Tyre wear is influenced by driving style - harsh braking and acceleration, or fast cornering, will all produce more rapid tyre wear. As a general rule, the front tyres wear out faster than the rears. Interchanging the tyres from front to rear ("rotating" the tyres) may result in more even wear. However, if this is completely effective, you may have the expense of replacing all four tyres at once! Remove any nails or stones embedded in the tread before they penetrate the tyre to cause deflation. If removal of a nail does reveal that the tyre has been punctured, refit the nail so that its point of penetration is marked. Then immediately change the wheel, and have the tyre repaired by a tyre dealer.

Regularly check the tyres for damage in the form of cuts or bulges, especially in the sidewalls. Periodically remove the wheels, and clean any dirt or mud from the inside and outside surfaces. Examine the wheel rims for signs of rusting, corrosion or other damage. Light alloy wheels are easily damaged by "kerbing" whilst parking; steel wheels may also become dented or buckled. A new wheel is very often the only way to overcome severe damage.

New tyres should be balanced when they are fitted, but it may become necessary to re-balance them as they wear, or if the balance weights fitted to the wheel rim should fall off. Unbalanced tyres will wear more quickly, as will the steering and suspension components. Wheel imbalance is normally signified by vibration, particularly at a certain speed (typically around 50 mph). If this vibration is felt only through the steering, then it is likely that just the front wheels need balancing. If, however, the vibration is felt through the whole car, the rear wheels could be out of balance. Wheel balancing should be carried out by a tyre dealer or garage.

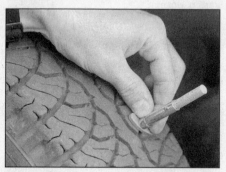

Tread Depth - visual check

1 The original tyres have tread wear safety bands (B), which will appear when the tread depth reaches approximately 1.6 mm. The band positions are indicated by a triangular mark on the tyre sidewall (A).

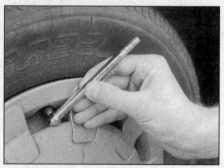

Tread Depth - manual check

2 Alternatively tread wear can be monitored with a simple, inexpensive device known as a tread depth indicator gauge.

Tyre Pressure Check

3 Check the tyre pressures regularly with the tyres cold. Do not adjust the tyre pressures immediately after the vehicle has been used, or an inaccurate setting will result. Tyre pressures are shown on the next page.

4 *Tyre tread wear patterns*

Shoulder Wear

Under-inflation (wear on both sides)
Under-inflation will cause overheating of the tyre, because the tyre will flex too much, and the tread will not sit correctly on the road surface. This will cause a loss of grip and excessive wear, not to mention the danger of sudden tyre failure due to heat build-up.
Check and adjust pressures
Incorrect wheel camber (wear on one side)
Repair or renew suspension parts
Hard cornering
Reduce speed!

Centre Wear

Over-inflation
Over-inflation will cause rapid wear of the centre part of the tyre tread, coupled with reduced grip, harsher ride, and the danger of shock damage occurring in the tyre casing.
Check and adjust pressures

If you sometimes have to inflate your car's tyres to the higher pressures specified for maximum load or sustained high speed, don't forget to reduce the pressures to normal afterwards.

Uneven Wear

Front tyres may wear unevenly as a result of wheel misalignment. Most tyre dealers and garages can check and adjust the wheel alignment (or "tracking") for a modest charge.
Incorrect camber or castor
Repair or renew suspension parts
Malfunctioning suspension
Repair or renew suspension parts
Unbalanced wheel
Balance tyres
Incorrect toe setting
Adjust front wheel alignment
Note: *The feathered edge of the tread which typifies toe wear is best checked by feel.*

Lubricants and fluids

Component or system	Lubricant type/specification
1 Engine	Multigrade engine oil, viscosity range SAE 10W/30 to 20W/50, to API SG/CD or better
2 Manual gearbox	
4-speed (A, B and C type)	Gear oil, viscosity SAE 80EP, to Ford spec SQM-2C 9008-A
5-speed (N type)	Gear oil, viscosity SAE 80EP, to Ford spec ESD-M2C 175-A
5-speed (MT75 type)	Gear oil to Ford spec ESD-M2C 186-A
3 Automatic transmission	ATF to Ford spec SQM-2C 9010-A
4 Final drive	Hypoid gear oil, viscosity SAE 90EP to Ford spec SQM-2C 9002-AA or 9003-AA
5 Power steering	ATF to Ford spec SQM-2C 9010-A
6 Brake hydraulic system	Brake fluid to Ford spec Amber SAM-1C 9103-A Fluid
7 Cooling system:	
SOHC engines	Soft water and antifreeze to Ford spec SSM-97 B-9103-A
CVH engines	Soft water and antifreeze to Ford spec ESD-M97B49-A
DOHC engine	Soft water and antifreeze to Ford spec SDM-M97B49-A

Note: *From 1992, the cooling system on all models is filled with a long-life coolant mixture in production ("4-Year Longlife Engine Coolant"/"Super Plus 40"). The manufacturers do not specify any renewal intervals for this later type of coolant as it is intended to last the lifetime of the vehicle. Provided any topping-up is carried out with a similar coolant mixture of the correct strength, coolant renewal is unnecessary. It is advisable to renew the coolant if the vehicle has covered a particularly high mileage, or if the history of the car is uncertain, but this is up to the discretion of the individual owner.*

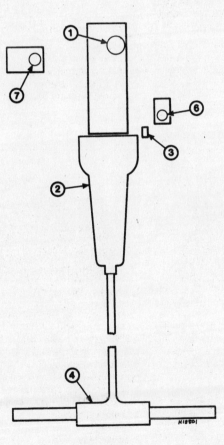

CVH engines

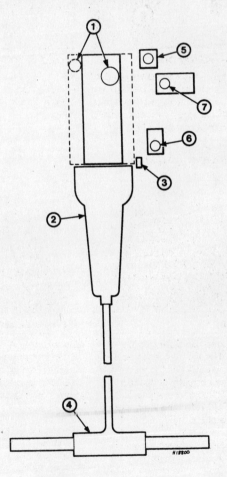

SOHC and DOHC engines

Tyre pressures

Note: *Manufacturers often modify tyre sizes and pressure recommendations. The following is intended as a guide only. Refer to your vehicle handbook or a Ford dealer for the latest recommendations*

Tyre pressures (cold) - lbf/in^2 (bar):	Front	Rear
All Saloon, Hatchback and Estate models with normal load*	26 (1.8)	26 (1.8)
All Saloon and Hatchback models with full load	29 (2.0)	36 (2.5)
Estate models with full load:		
175 R 13H, 175 R 135,175 R 13T, 195/70 R 13H and		
195/65 R 14T tyres	29 (2.0)	48 (2.8)
195/60 R 14H and 195/60 VR 14 tyres	29 (2.0)	36 (2.5)
P100 models with light load	26 (1.8)	36 (2.5)
P100 models with full load	50 (3.5)	65 (4.5)

Normal load is defined as up to three passengers (or equivalent). For sustained high speeds add 1.5 lbf/in^2 (0.1 bar) for every 6 mph (10 km/h) over 100 mph (160 km/h)
A light load is defined as one passenger plus up to 100 kg (220 lb) payload

Chapter 1
Routine maintenance and servicing

Contents

1

Degrees of difficulty

Easy, suitable for novice with little experience	**Fairly easy,** suitable for beginner with some experience	**Fairly difficult,** suitable for competent DIY mechanic	**Difficult,** suitable for experienced DIY mechanic	**Very difficult,** suitable for expert DIY or professional

Specifications

Engine

Oil filter type:
- SOHC and DOHC .... Champion C102
- CVH .... Champion C104

Valve clearances (cold):
- SOHC:
  - Inlet .... 0.20 ± 0.03 mm (0.008 ± 0.001 in)
  - Exhaust .... 0.25 ± 0.03 mm (0.010 ± 0.001 in)
- DOHC and CVH:
  - Inlet .... Not applicable (hydraulic cam followers)
  - Exhaust .... Not applicable (hydraulic cam followers)

Cooling system

Drivebelt tensions:

Air conditioning system compressor .... 10.0 mm (0.4 in) deflection at the midpoint of the belt's longest run under firm thumb pressure

Coolant pump/alternator .... 10.0 mm (0.4 in) deflection midway between coolant pump and alternator (or power steering pump) pulleys under firm thumb pressure

Fuel system

Air filter element:

Carburettor type:

1.3 and 1.6 litre (SOHC - Ford carburettor) .... Champion W110

1.6 litre (SOHC - Weber carburettor) and 1.8 litre SOHC .... Champion W118

1.6 litre (SOHC - 1984-on) and 2.0 litre SOHC .... Champion W152

1.8 litre CVH .... Champion W219

2.0 litre DOHC .... Champion W152

Fuel injection type:

2.0 litre SOHC and DOHC .... Champion U507

1.6 and 1.8 litre (R6A type) CVH .... Champion W219

Fuel filter:

All fuel injection models .... Champion L204

Ignition system

Spark plugs:

Make and type:

All except 1.8 CVH, CVH (R6A), 2.0 DOHC and P100 .... Champion RF7YCC or RF7YC

1.8 litre CVH .... Champion RC7YCC or RC7YC

P100 .... Champion RF7YC or F7YC

1.6 and 1.8 litre (R6A type) CVH .... Champion RC7YCC

2.0 litre DOHC .... Champion RC7YCC

Electrode gap*:

Champion F7YCC or RC7YCC .... 0.8 mm (0.032 in)

Champion RF7YC, F7YC or RC7YC .... 0.7 mm (0.028 in)

Ignition HT leads

Resistance .... 30 k ohms maximum per lead

Type:

All SOHC models .... Champion LS-09 or LS-10 boxed set

1.8 litre CVH .... Champion LS-10 boxed set

1.6 and 1.8 litre (R6A type) CVH .... Champion LS-30 boxed set

2.0 litre DOHC .... Champion LS-29 boxed set

The spark plug gap quoted is that recommended by Champion for their specified plugs listed above. If spark plugs of any other type are to be fitted, refer to their manufacturer's recommendations.

Brakes

Brake pad friction material minimum thickness .... 1.5 mm (0.06 in)

Brake shoe friction material minimum thickness .... 1.0 mm (0.04 in)

Torque wrench settings	Nm	lbf ft
Engine oil drain plug:		
SOHC and DOHC	21 to 28	16 to 21
CVH	20 to 30	15 to 22
Engine block coolant drain plug (where fitted)	21 to 25	16 to 18
Manual gearbox:		
Oil filler/level plug:		
A,B,C and N types	33 to 41	24 to 30
MT75 type	29 to 41	21 to 30
Oil drain plug:		
MT75 type	29 to 41	21 to 30
Final drive oil filler plug	35 to 45	26 to 33
Roadwheel nuts:		
Saloon, Hatchback and Estate models (steel and alloy wheels)	70 to 100	52 to 74
P100 models	85 to 90	63 to 66
Spark plugs:		
SOHC models	20 to 28	15 to 21
CVH models	18 to 33	13 to 24
DOHC models	15 to 21	11 to 15
Brake caliper guide bolts:		
Front	20 to 25	15 to 18
Rear	31 to 35	23 to 26

Capacities

Engine oil

SOHC engines:
With filter	3.75 litres (6.6 pints)
Without filter	3.25 litres (5.7 pints)

DOHC engine:
With filter	4.5 litres (7.9 pints)
Without filter	4.0 litres (7.0 pints)

1.6 litre CVH engine:
With filter	3.5 litres (6.2 pints)
Without filter	3.25 litres (5.7 pints)

1.8 CVH engines:
With filter	4.0 litres (7.0 pints)
Without filter	3.5 litres (6.2 pints)

Cooling system (including heater)

SOHC engines	8.0 litres (14.1 pints)
DOHC engine:	
Carburettor models	7.0 litres (12.3 pints)
Fuel injection models	7.3 litres (12.8 pints)
CVH engines:	
1.6 and 1.8 litre (R2A)	9.5 litres (16.7 pints)
1.8 litre (R6A)	7.9 litres (13.9 pints)

Fuel tank

All models except P100	60.0 litres (13.2 gals)
P100 models	66.0 litres (14.5 gals)

Manual gearbox

A1 and A2 types	0.98 litre (1.72 pints)
B type	1.46 litres (2.57 pints)
C type	1.25 litres (2.20 pints)
N type up to 1987	1.90 litres (3.34 pints)
N type from 1987	1.25 litres (2.20 pints)
MT75 type	1.2 litres (2.1 pints)

Automatic transmission

C3 type	6.3 litres (11.1 pints)
A4LD type	8.5 litres (15.0 pints)

Final drive (from dry)

All models except 1.3 and 1.6 litre Hatchback and P100	0.9 litre (1.6 pints)
1.3 and 1.6 litre Hatchback models	0.8 litre (1.4 pints)
P100 models (rear axle)	1.14 litres (2.0 pints)

Power steering

All models	0.65 litre (1.14 pints)

1 Ford Sierra maintenance schedule

The maintenance intervals in this manual are provided with the assumption that you will be carrying out the work yourself. These are the minimum maintenance intervals recommended by the manufacturer for vehicles driven daily. If you wish to keep your vehicle in peak condition at all times, you may wish to perform some of these procedures more often. We encourage frequent maintenance, because it enhances the efficiency, performance and resale value of your vehicle.

If the vehicle is driven in dusty areas, used to tow a trailer, or driven frequently at slow speeds (idling in traffic) or on short journeys, more frequent maintenance intervals are recommended.

When the vehicle is new, it should be serviced by a factory-authorised dealer service department, in order to preserve the factory warranty.

Every 250 miles (400 km) or weekly

☐ Check the engine oil level (Section 3)
☐ Check the engine coolant level (Section 3)
☐ Check the brake fluid level (Section 3)
☐ Check the power steering fluid level (Section 3)
☐ Check the screen washer fluid level (Section 3)
☐ Visually examine the tyres for tread depth, and wear or damage (Section 4)
☐ Check and if necessary adjust the tyre pressures (Section 4)
☐ Check and if necessary top-up the battery electrolyte level - where applicable (Section 6)
☐ Check the operation of the horn, all lights, and the wipers and washers (Sections 5 and 7)

Every 6000 miles (10 000 km) or 6 months - whichever comes sooner

☐ Renew engine oil and filter (Section 8)
☐ Check brake pads or shoes for wear (front and rear) (Section 9)
☐ Check operation of brake fluid level warning indicator (Section 9)
☐ Inspect engine bay and underside of vehicle for fluid leaks or other signs of damage (Section 10)
☐ Check function and condition of seat belts (Section 11)
☐ Check condition and security of exhaust system (Section 12)
☐ Check tightness of wheel nuts (Section 13)
☐ Clean oil filler cap (Section 14)
☐ Check idle speed (where applicable) (Section 15)
☐ Check mixture adjustment (where applicable) (Section 16)

Every 12 000 miles (20 000 km) or 12 months - whichever comes sooner

☐ Check automatic transmission fluid level (engine hot) (Section 17)
☐ Check manual gearbox oil level (Section 18)
☐ Check operation of latches, check straps and locks; lubricate if necessary (Section 19)
☐ Renew spark plugs (Section 20)
☐ Check condition and tension of auxiliary drivebelt(s); adjust or renew as necessary (Section 21)
☐ Check tightness of battery terminals, clean and neutralise corrosion if necessary (Section 22)
☐ Check engine valve clearances - SOHC only (Section 23)
☐ Check handbrake mechanism (Section 24)

Every 12 000 miles (20 000 km) or 12 months - whichever comes sooner (continued)

☐ Clean radiator matrix and air conditioning condenser fins (where applicable) (Section 25)
☐ Check air conditioning refrigerant charge (where applicable) (Section 26)
☐ Check final drive oil level (Section 27)
☐ Lubricate automatic transmission selector/kickdown linkage (Section 28)
☐ Check security and condition of steering and suspension components, gaiters and boots (Section 29)
☐ Check condition and security of driveshaft joints and gaiters (Section 30)
☐ Inspect underbody and panels for corrosion or other damage (Section 31)
☐ Inspect brake pipes and hoses (Section 32)
☐ Clean idle speed control linkage at throttle (where applicable) (Section 33)
☐ Road test and check operation of ABS (Section 34)
☐ Check crankcase ventilation system (Section 35)

Every 24 000 miles (40 000 km) or 2 years - whichever comes sooner

☐ Check air cleaner inlet air temperature control operation (carburettor models) (Section 36)
☐ Renew pulse air filter element (1.6 litre CVH) (Section 37)
☐ Renew air cleaner element (Section 38)
☐ Clean and inspect distributor cap and HT leads (Section 39)
☐ Check automatic transmission brake band adjustment (Section 40)
☐ Renew fuel filter (fuel-injection models only) (Section 41)
☐ Renew crankcase ventilation vent valve (SOHC and DOHC) (Section 42)

Every 36 000 miles (60 000 km) or 3 years - whichever comes sooner

☐ Renew brake hydraulic system seals and hoses if necessary (Section 43)
☐ Renew brake hydraulic fluid (Section 44)
☐ Renew camshaft drivebelt (optional on SOHC models - compulsory on CVH) (Section 45)
☐ Renew coolant (Section 46)

Underbonnet view of a 1983 2.0 litre SOHC carburettor model (air cleaner removed)

1 Brake fluid reservoir
2 Windscreen wiper motor
3 Battery
4 Ignition coil
5 Carburettor
6 Distributor
7 Fuel pressure regulator
8 Thermostat housing
9 Radiator top hose
10 Upper fan shroud
11 Alternator
12 Windscreen washer reservoir
13 Oil filler cap
14 Cooler expansion tank
15 Suspension strut top
16 VIN plate
17 Fusebox

Underbonnet view of a 1985 2.0 litre SOHC fuel injection model

1 Battery
2 Brake servo non-return valve
3 Ignition coil
4 Suspension strut top
5 Fuel filter
6 Air cleaner
7 Airflow meter
8 Fuel pressure regulator
9 Air inlet hose
10 Throttle body
11 Alternator
12 VIN plate
13 Windscreen washer reservoir
14 Coolant expansion tank
15 Oil filler cap
16 Idle speed control valve
17 Inlet manifold
18 Brake fluid reservoir
19 Fusebox
20 Windscreen wiper motor
21 Engine oil level dipstick

1

Underbonnet view of a 1990 2.0 litre DOHC fuel injection model

1 Battery
2 Braking system deceleration-sensitive valve
3 Ignition coil
4 Suspension strut top
5 Air cleaner
6 Plenum chamber
7 Idle speed control valve
8 Distributor
9 Oil filler cap
10 VIN plate
11 Windscreen washer reservoir filler neck
12 Power steering fluid reservoir
13 Coolant expansion tank
14 Manifold absolute pressure (MAP) sensor
15 Brake fluid reservoir
16 Inlet manifold
17 Fuel pressure regulator
18 Fusebox
19 Windscreen wiper motor

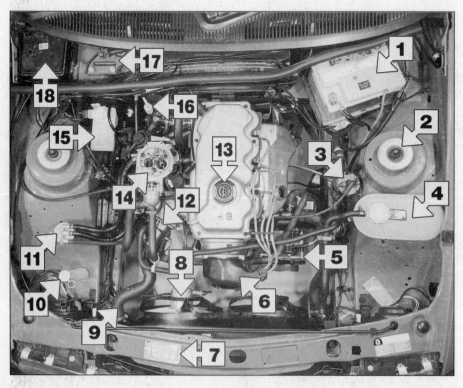

Underbonnet view of a 1989 1.8 litre (R2A) CVH model (air cleaner removed)

1 Battery
2 Suspension strut top
3 Ignition coil
4 Coolant expansion tank
5 Alternator
6 Distributor cap shroud
7 VIN plate
8 Electric cooling fan
9 Radiator top hose
10 Windscreen washer reservoir
11 Fuel vapour separator
12 Thermostat housing
13 Oil filler cap
14 Carburettor
15 Brake fluid reservoir
16 Engine oil level dipstick
17 Windscreen wiper motor
18 Fusebox

Underbonnet view of a 1992 1.6 litre CVH model (air cleaner removed)

1 Battery
2 Braking system deceleration-sensitive valve
3 Suspension strut top
4 Coolant expansion tank
5 Pulse-air filter
6 Vacuum-operated air valve
7 Alternator
8 Cooling fans
9 Oil filler cap
10 Thermostat housing
11 VIN plate
12 Windscreen washer reservoir filler neck
13 Ignition module
14 Pulse-air control solenoid
15 CFI unit
16 Brake fluid reservoir
17 Engine oil level dipstick
18 Manifold absolute pressure (MAP) Sensor
19 Fusebox
20 Windscreen wiper motor

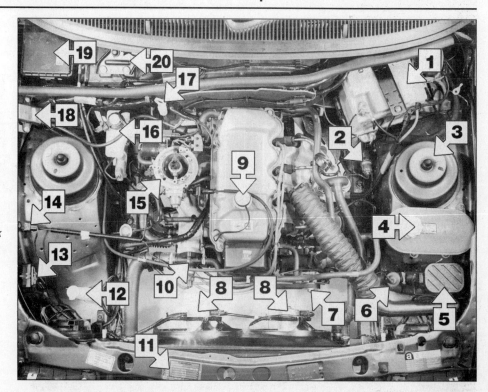

Front underside view of a 1990 2.0 GLS model

1 Horns
2 Tie-rod end
3 Tie-rod
4 Gaiter
5 Coolant pump
6 Suspension lower arm
7 Anti-roll bar
8 Starter motor
9 Exhaust downpipes
10 Crossmember
11 Engine sump
12 Oil filter
13 Power steering fluid pump
14 Windscreen washer reservoir
15 Cooling fans

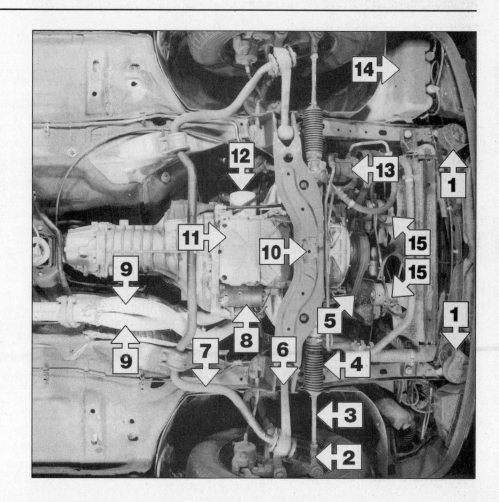

1

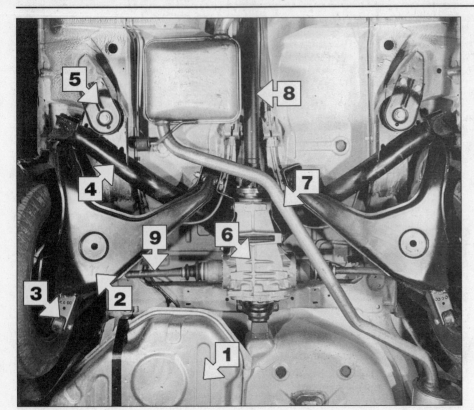

Rear underside view of a Hatchback models

1 Fuel tank
2 Suspension lower arm
3 Lower shock absorber mounting
4 Suspension crossmember
5 Suspension guide plate
6 Final drive unit
7 Exhaust system
8 Propeller shaft
9 Driveshaft

Rear underside view of a P100 model

1 Suspension leaf spring
2 Rear axle
3 Shock absorber
4 Propeller shaft
5 Exhaust system
6 Handbrake cable adjuster
7 Brake load apportioning valve

2 Introduction

General information

This Chapter is designed to help the home mechanic maintain his/her vehicle for safety, economy, long life and peak performance.

The Chapter contains a master maintenance schedule, followed by Sections dealing specifically with each task in the schedule. Visual checks, adjustments, component renewal and other helpful items are included. Refer to the accompanying illustrations of the engine compartment and the underside of the vehicle for the locations of the various components.

Servicing your vehicle in accordance with the mileage/time maintenance schedule and the following Sections will provide a planned maintenance programme, which should result in a long and reliable service life. This is a comprehensive plan, so maintaining some items but not others at the specified service intervals, will not produce the same results.

As you service your vehicle, you will discover that many of the procedures can - and should - be grouped together, because of the particular procedure being performed, or because of the close proximity of two otherwise-unrelated components to one another. For example, if the vehicle is raised for any reason, the exhaust can be inspected at the same time as the suspension and steering components.

The first step in this maintenance programme is to prepare yourself before the actual work begins. Read through all the Sections relevant to the work to be carried out, then make a list and gather together all the parts and tools required. If a problem is encountered, seek advice from a parts specialist, or a dealer service department.

Intensive maintenance

If, from the time the vehicle is new, the routine maintenance schedule is followed closely, and frequent checks are made of fluid levels and high-wear items, as suggested throughout this manual, the engine will be kept in relatively good running condition, and the need for additional work will be minimised.

It is possible that there will be times when the engine is running poorly due to the lack of regular maintenance. This is even more likely if a used vehicle, which has not received regular and frequent maintenance checks, is purchased. In such cases, additional work may need to be carried out, outside of the regular maintenance intervals.

If engine wear is suspected, a compression test will provide valuable information regarding the overall performance of the main internal components. Such a test can be used as a basis to decide on the extent of the work to be carried out. If, for example, a compression test indicates serious internal engine wear, conventional maintenance as described in this Chapter will not greatly improve the performance of the engine, and may prove a waste of time and money, unless extensive overhaul work is carried out first.

The following series of operations are those most often required to improve the performance of a generally poor-running engine:

Primary operations

a) Clean, inspect and test the battery
b) Check all the engine-related fluids
c) Check the condition and tension of the auxiliary drivebelt
d) Renew the spark plugs
e) Inspect the distributor cap and HT leads - as applicable
f) Check the condition of the air cleaner filter element, and renew if necessary
g) Renew the fuel filter
h) Check the condition of all hoses, and check for fluid leaks
i) Check the idle speed and mixture settings - as applicable

If the above operations do not prove fully effective, carry out the following secondary operations:

Secondary operations

a) Check the charging system
b) Check the ignition system
c) Check the fuel system
d) Renew the distributor cap and rotor arm - as applicable
f) Renew the ignition HT leads - as applicable

Every 250 miles (400 km) or weekly

3 Fluid level checks

See "Weekly checks".

4 Tyre checks

See "Weekly checks".

5 Electrical system check

See "Weekly checks".

6 Battery electrolyte level check

See "Weekly checks".

7 Wiper blade check

See "Weekly checks".

Every 6000 miles (10 000 km) or 6 months

8 Engine oil and filter renewal

1 Frequent oil and filter changes are the most important preventative maintenance procedures which can be undertaken by the DIY owner. As engine oil ages, it becomes diluted and contaminated, which leads to premature engine wear.

2 Before starting this procedure, gather together all the necessary tools and materials. Also make sure that you have plenty of clean rags and newspapers handy, to mop up any spills. Ideally, the engine oil should be warm, as it will drain better, and more built-up sludge will be removed with it. Take care, however, not to touch the exhaust or any other hot parts of the engine when working under the vehicle. To avoid any possibility of scalding, and to protect yourself from possible skin irritants and other harmful contaminants in used engine oils, it is advisable to wear gloves when carrying out this work. Access to the underside of the vehicle will be greatly improved if it can be raised on a lift, driven onto ramps, or jacked up and supported on axle stands (see "Jacking and vehicle support"). Whichever method is chosen, make sure that the vehicle remains level, or if it is at an angle, so that the drain plug is at the lowest point **(see illustration)**.

8.2 **Sump drain plug location**

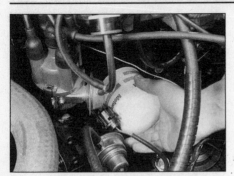

8.7 Unscrewing the oil filter

3 Slacken the drain plug about half a turn. Position the draining container under the drain plug, then remove the plug completely. If possible, try to keep the plug pressed into the sump while unscrewing it by hand the last couple of turns. As the plug releases from the threads, move it away sharply so the stream of oil issuing from the sump runs into the container, not up your sleeve! Recover the sealing washer from the drain plug.

4 Allow some time for the old oil to drain, noting that it may be necessary to reposition the container as the oil flow slows to a trickle.

5 After all the oil has drained, wipe off the drain plug with a clean rag. Check the sealing washer for condition, and renew it if necessary. Clean the area around the drain plug opening, and refit the plug. Tighten the plug to the specified torque.

6 Move the container into position under the oil filter.

7 Using an oil filter removal tool if necessary, slacken the filter initially, then unscrew it by hand the rest of the way (see illustration). Empty the oil from the old filter into the container, and discard the filter.

8 Use a clean rag to remove all oil, dirt and sludge from the filter sealing area on the engine. Check the old filter to make sure that the rubber sealing ring hasn't stuck to the engine. If it has, carefully remove it.

9 Apply a light coating of clean engine oil to the sealing ring on the new filter, then screw it into position on the engine. Tighten the filter firmly by hand only - do not use any tools. Wipe clean the filter and sump drain plug.

10 Remove the old oil and all tools from under the car, then lower the car to the ground (if applicable).

11 Remove the oil filler cap and withdraw the dipstick. Fill the engine, using the correct grade and type of oil (see "Lubricants and fluids"). An oil can spout or funnel may help to reduce spillage. Pour in half the specified quantity of oil first, then wait a few minutes for the oil to fall to the sump. Continue adding oil a small quantity at a time until the level is up to the lower mark on the dipstick. Finally, bring the level up to the upper mark on the dipstick. Insert the dipstick, and refit the filler cap.

12 Start the engine and run it for a few minutes; check for leaks around the oil filter seal and the sump drain plug. Note that there may be a delay of a few seconds before the oil pressure warning light goes out when the engine is first started, as the oil circulates through the engine oil galleries and the new oil filter, before the pressure builds up.

13 Switch off the engine, and wait a few minutes for the oil to settle in the sump once more. With the new oil circulated and the filter completely full, recheck the level on the dipstick, and add more oil as necessary.

14 Dispose of the used engine oil safely, with reference to "General repair procedures" in the Reference section of this manual.

9 Front and rear brake pad/shoe check

1 Firmly apply the handbrake, then jack up the front and rear of the car and support it securely on axle stands (see "Jacking and vehicle support").

2 For a quick check, the front brake disc pads can be inspected without removing the front wheels by inserting a mirror between each caliper and roadwheel (see illustration). If any one pad is worn down to the minimum specified thickness, all four pads (on both front wheels) must be renewed.

3 It is necessary to remove the rear wheels in order to inspect the rear disc pads. The pads can be viewed through the top of the caliper after removing the blanking spring clip (see illustration). If any one pad is worn down to the minimum specified, all four pads (on both rear wheels) must be renewed.

4 For a comprehensive check, the brake disc pads should be removed and cleaned. The operation of the caliper can then also be checked, and the condition of the brake discs can be fully examined on both sides. Refer to Chapter 10 for further information.

5 On rear drum brake models, the brake shoe friction material can be inspected for wear without removing the roadwheels. Working beneath the vehicle, prise the plug from the brake backplate, and using an inspection lamp or torch, check that the friction material thickness is not less than the minimum given in the Specifications (see illustration). If any one of the shoes has worn below the specified limit, the shoes must be renewed as an axle set (4 shoes).

6 At the same interval, check the function of the brake fluid level warning light. Chock the wheels, release the handbrake and switch on the ignition. Unscrew and raise the brake fluid reservoir cap whilst an assistant observes the warning light: it should come on as the level sensor is withdrawn from the fluid. Refit the cap.

7 On completion, refit the wheels and lower the car to the ground.

10 Fluid leak check

1 Visually inspect the engine joint faces, gaskets and seals for any signs of water or oil leaks. Pay particular attention to the areas around the rocker cover, cylinder head, oil filter and sump joint faces. Bear in mind that over a period of time some very slight seepage from these areas is to be expected but what you are really looking for is any indication of a serious leak. Should a leak be found, renew the offending gasket or oil seal by referring to the appropriate Chapter(s) in this manual.

2 Similarly, check the transmission for oil leaks, and investigate and rectify and problems found.

3 Check the security and condition of all the engine related pipes and hoses. Ensure that all cable-ties or securing clips are in place and in good condition. Clips which are broken or missing can lead to chafing of the hoses, pipes or wiring which could cause more serious problems in the future.

9.2 Using a mirror to inspect the disc pad friction material for wear
A Brake disc   B Brake disc pads

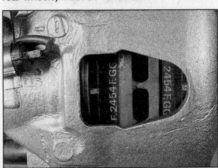

9.3 Disc pads viewed through caliper inspection hole (roadwheel removed)

9.5 Brake shoe inspection hole plug (arrowed)

4 Carefully check the condition of all coolant, fuel, power steering and brake hoses. Renew any hose which is cracked, swollen or deteriorated. Cracks will show up better if the hose is squeezed. Pay close attention to the hose clips that secure the hoses to the system components. Hose clips can pinch and puncture hoses, resulting in leaks. If wire type hose clips are used, it may be a good idea to replace them with screw-type clips.

5 With the vehicle raised, inspect the fuel tank and filler neck for punctures, cracks and other damage. The connection between the filler neck and tank is especially critical. Sometimes a rubber filler neck or connecting hose will leak due to loose retaining clamps or deteriorated rubber.

6 Similarly, inspect all brake hoses and metal pipes. If any damage or deterioration is discovered, do not drive the vehicle until the necessary repair work has been carried out. Renew any damaged sections of hose or pipe.

7 Carefully check all rubber hoses and metal fuel lines leading away from the petrol tank. Check for loose connections, deteriorated hoses, crimped lines and other damage. Pay particular attention to the vent pipes and hoses which often loop up around the filler neck and can become blocked or crimped. Follow the lines to the front of the vehicle carefully inspecting them all the way. Renew damaged sections as necessary.

8 From within the engine compartment, check the security of all fuel hose attachments and pipe unions, and inspect the fuel hoses and vacuum hoses for kinks, chafing and deterioration.

9 Where applicable, check the condition of the oil cooler hoses and pipes.

10 Check the condition of all exposed wiring harnesses.

11 Seat belt check

1 Periodically check the belts for fraying or other damage. If evident, renew the belt.

2 If the belts become dirty, wipe them with a damp cloth using a little detergent only.

3 Check the tightness of the anchor bolts and if they are ever disconnected, make quite sure that the original sequence of fitting of washers, bushes and anchor plates is retained.

12 Exhaust system check

With the vehicle raised on a hoist or supported on axle stands, check the exhaust system for signs of leaks, corrosion or damage and check the rubber mountings for condition and security. Where damage or corrosion are evident, renew the system complete or in sections, as applicable, using the information given in Chapter 4.

13 Roadwheel security check

With the wheels on the ground, slacken each wheel nut by a quarter turn, then retighten it immediately to the specified torque.

14 Oil filler cap check

Remove and clean the oil filler cap of any sludge build-up using paraffin.

Inspect the vent hose for blockage or damage. A blocked hose can cause a build-up of crankcase pressure, which in turn can cause oil leaks.

15 Engine idle speed check

 Caution: Refer to the precautions in Section 1, Chapter 4, Part A or B (as applicable), before proceeding. *Before carrying out any carburettor adjustments, ensure that the ignition timing and spark plug gaps are set as specified. To carry out the adjustments an accurate tachometer and an exhaust gas analyser (CO meter) will be required.*

Ford VV carburettor

1 Ensure that the air cleaner is correctly fitted, and that all vacuum hoses and pipes are securely connected and free from restrictions, then run the engine until it is at normal operating temperature.

2 Stop the engine, and connect a tachometer and an exhaust gas analyser in accordance with the manufacturer's instructions.

3 Start the engine and run it at 3000 rpm for 30 seconds, ensuring that all electrical loads are switched off (headlamps, heater blower etc), then allow the engine to idle and check the idle speed and CO content. Note that the CO reading will initially rise, then fall and finally stabilise after between 5 and 25 seconds.

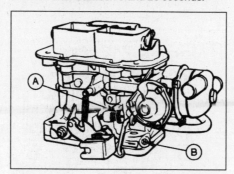

15.7a Weber 2V carburettor adjustment screw locations - 2.0 litre models up to 1985

A Idle speed screw   B Idle mixture screw

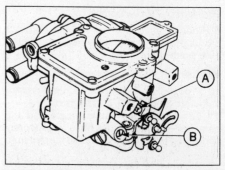

15.4 Ford VV carburettor adjustment screw locations

A Idle speed screw   B Idle mixture screw

4 If necessary, adjust the idle speed screw to give the specified idle speed **(see illustration).**

5 Checking and adjustment should be completed within 30 seconds of the meter readings stabilising. If this has not been possible, repeat paragraphs 3 and 4, ignoring the reference to starting the engine.

Weber 2V carburettor

Models without stepper motor

6 Proceed as described for the Ford VV carburettor but note the following:

7 It is permissible to loosen the air cleaner securing screws to allow easier access to the carburettor adjustment screws but ensure that all vacuum hoses and pipes are securely connected. For adjustment screw location **(see illustrations).**

Models with stepper motor (ESC II system)

8 The idle speed is controlled by the ESC II module via the stepper motor. The only idle speed adjustment possible is provided by the "idle speed adjustment" wire, which can be earthed to raise the idle speed by 75 rpm. No other method of idle speed adjustment should be attempted. If the idle speed is incorrect, the problem should be referred to a Ford dealer, as the problem probably lies in the ESC II module for which special diagnostic equipment is required.

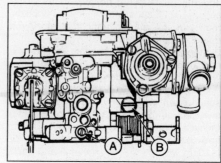

15.7b Weber 2V carburettor adjustment screw locations - 1.6 litre models

A Idle mixture screw   B Idle speed screw

1

Pierburg 2V carburettor

9 Proceed as described for the Ford VV carburettor. For adjustment screw location (see illustration).

Weber 2V TLD carburettor

10 Proceed as described for the Ford VV carburettor, noting the following points:

11 Ensure that the vacuum pipe and the camshaft cover breather hose are securely connected to the air cleaner and are free from restrictions.

12 When warming-up the engine, run the engine until the cooling fan cuts in.

13 For adjustment screw location (see illustration).

Fuel injection

2.0 litre SOHC models

14 Idle speed is controlled by the EEC IV module and the only means of adjustment provided is by the yellow "idle speed adjustment" wire (Chapter 5, Section 17) which allows the idle speed to be raised by 75 rpm.

2.0 litre DOHC models

15 Idle speed is controlled by the EEC IV module, and manual adjustment is not possible.

16 The "base" idle speed can be adjusted, but only by a Ford dealer, using special equipment.

16 Mixture adjustment check

⚠️ *Caution: Refer to the precautions in Section 1, Chapter 4, Part A or B (as applicable), before proceeding.*
Before carrying out any carburettor adjustments, ensure that the ignition timing and spark plug gaps are set as specified. To carry out the adjustments an accurate tachometer and an exhaust gas analyser (CO meter) will be required.

Ford VV carburettor

1 Ensure that the air cleaner is correctly fitted and that all vacuum hoses and pipes are securely connected and free from restrictions, then run the engine until it is at normal operating temperature.

2 Stop the engine, and connect a tachometer and an exhaust gas analyser in accordance with the manufacturer's instructions.

3 Start the engine and run it at 3000 rpm for 30 seconds, ensuring that all electrical loads are switched off (headlamps, heater blower etc), then allow the engine to idle and check the idle speed and CO content. Note that the CO reading will initially rise, then fall and finally stabilise after between 5 and 25 seconds.

4 If the reading noted in paragraph 3 is not as specified, proceed as follows:

5 Using a thin screwdriver, remove the tamperproof seal from the mixture screw.

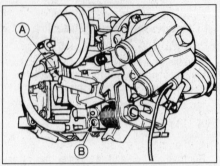

15.9 Pierburg 2V carburettor adjustment screw locations

A Idle speed screw   B Idle mixture screw

6 Run the engine at 3000 rpm for 30 seconds, then allow the engine to idle, and using a small screwdriver or a 4.0 mm Allen key, as applicable, adjust the mixture screw to give the specified CO content.

7 Checking and adjustment should be completed within 30 seconds of the meter readings stabilising. If this has not been possible, then repeat paragraph 6.

8 If necessary adjust the idle speed, then recheck the CO content.

9 On completion of the adjustments, stop the engine and disconnect the tachometer and exhaust gas analyser. Fit a new tamperproof seal to the mixture screw.

Weber 2V carburettor

Models without stepper motor

10 Proceed as described for the Ford VV carburettor but note the following:

11 To remove the mixture screw tamperproof seal, it will be necessary to drill the seal in order to prise it from the mixture screw housing. Alternatively a self-tapping screw can be used to draw out the seal. If the tamperproof seal is to be renewed, ensure that a blue-coloured replacement seal is fitted.

12 It is permissible to loosen the air cleaner securing screws to allow easier access to the carburettor adjustment screws, but ensure that all vacuum hoses and pipes are securely connected.

16.13 Weber 2V carburettor idle mixture adjustment screw location (arrowed) - 2.0 litre models from 1985

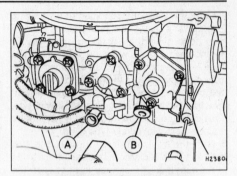

15.13 Weber 2V TLD carburettor adjustment screw locations

A Idle mixture screw   B Idle speed screw

Models with stepper motor (ESC II system)

13 If necessary, the mixture can be adjusted as described for the Ford VV carburettor with reference to paragraphs 11 and 12 of this Section. Do not attempt to adjust the idle speed on completion of mixture adjustment. For adjustment screw location (see illustration).

Pierburg 2V carburettor

14 Proceed as described for the Ford VV carburettor.

Weber 2V TLD carburettor

15 Proceed as described for the Ford VV carburettor, noting the following points:

16 Ensure that the vacuum pipe and the camshaft cover breather hose are securely connected to the air cleaner and are free from restrictions.

17 When warming-up the engine, run the engine until the cooling fan cuts in.

18 If adjustment of the mixture (CO content) is required, the air cleaner must be removed for access to the adjustment screw, as follows.

19 Remove the air cleaner, and prise the tamperproof seal from the mixture screw.

20 Loosely refit the air cleaner, ensuring that the vacuum pipe and the camshaft cover breather hose are securely connected and free from restrictions (there is no need to secure the air cleaner in position).

21 On completion, fit a new tamperproof seal to the mixture screw (the service replacement plug is coloured blue), and refit the air cleaner assembly.

Fuel injection

2.0 litre SOHC models

22 The idle mixture can be checked and if necessary adjusted as follows:

23 Run the engine until it is at normal operating temperature.

24 Stop the engine and connect a tachometer and an exhaust gas analyser in accordance with the manufacturer's instructions.

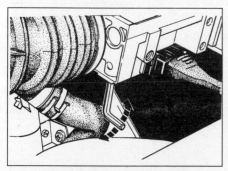

16.26 Adjusting the idle mixture - SOHC models

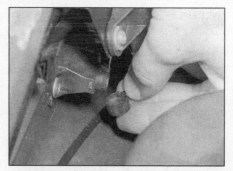

16.34a Remove the cover from the mixture adjustment potentiometer . . .

16.34b . . . to enable mixture adjustment - DOHC models

25 Start the engine and run it at 3000 rpm for 15 seconds, ensuring that all electrical loads (headlamps, heater blower etc) are switched off, then allow the engine to idle and check the CO content. Note that the CO reading will initially rise, then fall and finally stabilise.

26 If adjustment is necessary, remove the tamperproof cap from the base of the airflow meter, and turn the mixture screw using a suitable Allen key to give the specified CO content (see illustration).

27 Checking and adjustment should be completed within 30 seconds of the meter readings stabilising. If this has not been possible, run the engine at 3000 rpm, for 15 seconds, then allow the engine to idle. Re-check the CO content and carry out further adjustment if necessary.

28 On completion of adjustment, stop the engine and disconnect the tachometer and exhaust gas analyser. Fit a new tamperproof cap to the mixture screw.

2.0 litre DOHC models

29 On models with a catalytic converter, the mixture is controlled by the EEC IV module. No manual adjustment is possible.

30 On models without a catalytic converter, the idle mixture can be adjusted as follows:

31 Run the engine until it is at normal operating temperature.

32 Stop the engine, and connect a tachometer and an exhaust gas analyser in accordance with the equipment manufacturer's instructions.

33 Start the engine and run it at 3000 rpm for 15 seconds, ensuring that all electrical loads (headlamps, heater blower, etc) are switched off. Allow the engine to idle, and check the CO content. Note that the reading will initially rise, then fall and finally stabilise.

34 If adjustment is necessary, remove the cover from the mixture adjustment potentiometer (located at the rear right-hand side of the engine compartment, behind the MAP sensor), and turn the screw to give the specified CO content (see illustrations).

35 If adjustment does not produce a change in reading, the potentiometer may be at the extreme of its adjustment range. To centralise the potentiometer, turn the adjustment screw 20 turns clockwise followed by 10 turns anti-clockwise, then repeat the adjustment procedure.

36 Checking and adjustment should be completed within 30 seconds of the meter readings stabilising. If this has not been possible, run the engine at 3000 rpm for 15 seconds, then allow the engine to idle. Re-check the CO content, and carry out further adjustments if necessary.

37 On completion of adjustment, stop the engine, and disconnect the tachometer and the exhaust gas analyser. Refit the cover to the adjustment screw.

1

Every 12 000 miles (20 000 km) or 12 months

17 Automatic transmission fluid level check

1 Fluid level should be checked with the transmission at operating temperature (after a run) and with the vehicle parked on level ground.

2 Open and prop the bonnet. With the engine idling and the handbrake and footbrake applied, move the gear selector through all positions three times, finishing up in position "P".

3 Wait one minute. With the engine still idling, withdraw the transmission dipstick (see illustration). Wipe the dipstick with a clean lint-free rag, re-insert it fully and withdraw it again. Read the fluid level at the end of the dipstick: it should be between the two notches.

4 If topping-up is necessary, do so via the dipstick tube, using clean transmission fluid of the specified type (see illustration). Do not overfill.

5 Stop the engine, refit the dipstick and close the bonnet.

6 Note that if the fluid level was below the minimum mark when checked or is in constant need of topping-up, check around the transmission for any signs of excessive fluid leaks. If present, leaks must be rectified without delay.

7 If the colour of the fluid is dark brown or black this denotes the sign of a worn brake band or transmission clutches, in which case have your Ford dealer check the transmission at the earliest opportunity.

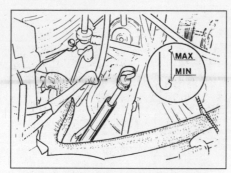
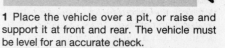

17.3 Automatic transmission dipstick location and markings

18 Manual gearbox oil level check

1 Place the vehicle over a pit, or raise and support it at front and rear. The vehicle must be level for an accurate check.

2 If the gearbox is hot after a run, allow it to cool for a few minutes. This is necessary because the oil can foam when hot and give a false level reading.

17.4 Topping-up the transmission fluid

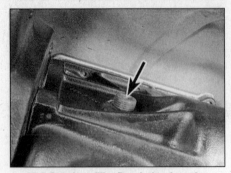

18.3 Gearbox filler/level plug location (arrowed) - N type gearbox

Gearbox type	Oil level
All four-speed gearboxes	0 to 5.0 mm (0 to 0.2 in) below lower edge of filler/level hole
All five-speed gearboxes up to April 1984 (build code E6) except those subsequently fitted with a modified extension housing	Level with bottom edge of filler/level hole
All five-speed gearboxes from May 1984 (build code EC) to end of April 1985 (build code FP) and all vehicles built up to April 1984 (build code E6) subsequently fitted with a modified gearbox extension housing	20.0 to 25.0 mm (0.79 to 0.99 in) below lower edge of filler/level hole
All five-speed gearboxes from May 1985	0 to 5.0 mm (0 to 0.2 in) below lower edge of filler/level hole

Note: *The vehicle build code appears as the twelfth and thirteenth characters of the VIN number on the plate in the engine compartment.*

3 Wipe clean around the filler/level plug. Unscrew the plug and remove it **(see illustration).**

4 Using a suitably marked piece of bent wire as a dipstick, check that the oil level is as shown in the table at the top of this page, according to gearbox type.

5 Top-up the level if necessary, using clean oil of the specified type. Do not overfill, as this can lead to leakage and difficult gear changing. Allow excess oil to drip out of the filler/level hole if necessary. Refit and tighten the filler/level plug on completion.

6 The frequent need for topping-up can only be due to leaks, which should be rectified. The most likely sources of leaks are the rear extension housing and input shaft oil seals.

7 No periodic oil changing is specified, and no drain plug is fitted.

19 Hinge and lock check and lubrication

1 Work around the vehicle, and lubricate the bonnet, door and tailgate hinges with a light machine oil.

2 Lightly lubricate the bonnet release mechanism and exposed sections of inner cable with a smear of grease.

3 Check the security and operation of all hinges, latches and locks, adjusting them where required. Where applicable, check the operation of the central locking system.

4 Check the condition and operation of the tailgate struts, renewing them if either is leaking or is no longer able to support the tailgate securely when raised.

20 Spark plug renewal

1 The correct functioning of the spark plugs is vital for the correct running and efficiency of the engine. It is essential that the plugs fitted are appropriate for the engine.

2 Make sure that the ignition is switched off before inspecting the HT leads to see if they carry their cylinder numbers. Note that the position of No 1 cylinder HT lead in the distributor cap is marked with either a pip, or a number "1 ".

 HAYNES HiNT *Number each HT lead using sticky tape or paint before removal so as to avoid confusion when refitting.*

3 Where necessary, for improved access remove the air cleaner and/or the inlet hose.

4 Disconnect the leads from the plugs by pulling on the connectors, not the leads.

5 On 2.0 litre DOHC carburettor models, the location of the spark plugs and the close proximity of the carburettor makes spark plug access difficult, particularly when removing the plugs from cylinders 2 and 3. It is suggested that a 3/8 inch ratchet drive spark plug socket with rubber insert and long extension bar is used, possibly in conjunction with a universal joint adapter. It is also advisable to disconnect No 3 cylinder HT lead from the distributor first, to allow some slack for disconnection at the spark plug.

6 Clean the area around each spark plug using a small brush, then using a plug spanner (preferably with a rubber insert), unscrew and remove the plugs **(see illustration).** Cover the spark plug holes with a clean rag to prevent the ingress of any foreign matter.

7 Before fitting new spark plugs, check that the threaded connector sleeves are tight. As the plugs incorporate taper seats, make sure that the threads and seats are clean.

20.6 Removing a spark plug - CVH engine

8 On DOHC models before refitting the spark plugs, coat their threads with suitable anti-seize compound, taking care not to contaminate the electrodes.

9 Screw in the spark plugs by hand, then tighten them to the specified torque. *Do not exceed the torque figure.*

10 Push the HT leads firmly onto the spark plugs, and where applicable refit the air cleaner and/or inlet hose.

21 Auxiliary drivebelt check

1 Refer to the Specifications at the beginning of this Chapter and check the tension of each drivebelt at the point stated. Check the full length of each drivebelt for cracks and deterioration. It will be necessary to turn the engine in order to check that portion of the drivebelt in contact with the pulleys. Renew or tension each belt as necessary as follows, according to model type:

SOHC models

2 Note that two drivebelts are fitted to models equipped with power steering and both should be renewed if either one is unserviceable. Where fitted, the air conditioning compressor is driven by a separate belt.

3 Disconnect the battery negative lead.

4 Where applicable, remove the air conditioning compressor drivebelt.

5 Loosen the alternator mounting and adjustment nuts and bolts, and pivot the alternator towards the cylinder block.

6 Slip the drivebelt(s) from the alternator, water pump, crankshaft and (where applicable) the power steering pump pulleys.

7 Fit the new drivebelt(s) over the pulleys, then lever the alternator away from the cylinder block until the specified belt tension is achieved. Lever the alternator using a wooden or plastic lever at the pulley end to prevent damage and straining the brackets. It is helpful to partially tighten the adjustment link bolt before tensioning the drivebelt(s).

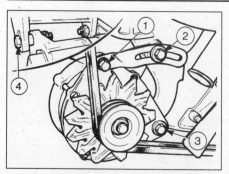

21.8 Alternator mounting tightening sequence - SOHC engines

8 Tighten the alternator mounting and adjustment nuts and bolts in the order shown (see illustration).
9 Where applicable, refit and tension the air conditioning compressor drivebelt.
10 Reconnect the battery negative lead.
11 Drivebelt tension should be rechecked and if necessary adjusted after the engine has been run for a minimum of ten minutes.

DOHC models

12 Three different types of drivebelt arrangement are used, depending on model (see illustrations). On models without power

21.12a Coolant pump/alternator drivebelt arrangement - 2.0 litre DOHC engine without power steering

1 Alternator
2 Coolant pump
3 Crankshaft pulley

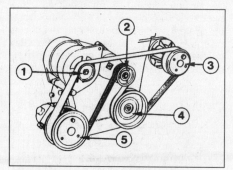

21.12b Coolant pump/alternator drivebelt arrangement - 2.0 litre DOHC engine with power steering

1 Alternator
2 Automatic belt tension
3 Coolant pump
4 Crankshaft pulley
5 Power steering pump

steering, the drivebelt is tensioned by moving the alternator. On models with power steering, the power steering pump is also driven by the coolant pump/alternator drivebelt and an automatic belt tensioner is fitted (see illustration). On models with air conditioning, the drivebelt drives the alternator, coolant pump, power steering pump and air conditioning compressor, and an automatic belt tensioner is fitted.
13 On models without power steering, loosen the alternator mounting and adjustment bolts, and pivot the alternator towards the cylinder block. Slip the drivebelt from the pulleys.
14 On models with power steering, the automatic tensioner can be released using a 17 mm socket and a wrench on the boss in the centre of the pulley. Lever the tensioner assembly clockwise, slide the belt from the pulleys, then slowly release the tensioner.
15 To fit a new belt on models without power steering, slide the belt over the pulleys, then lever the alternator away from the cylinder block until the correct belt tension is achieved. Lever the alternator using a plastic or wooden lever at the pulley end to prevent damage. It is helpful to partially tighten the adjustment link bolt before tensioning the drivebelt. When the correct tension is achieved, tighten all the bolts.
16 To fit a new belt on models with power steering, lever the tensioner clockwise as during removal, then slide the belt over the pulleys, and slowly release the tensioner.

22 Battery terminal check

⚠️ **Caution: Before carrying out any work on the vehicle battery, read through the precautions given in "Safety first!" at the beginning of this manual.**

1 The battery fitted as original equipment is "maintenance-free", and requires no

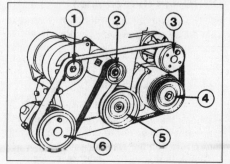

21.12c Coolant pump/alternator drivebelt arrangement - 2.0 litre DOHC engine with power steering and air conditioning

1 Alternator
2 Automatic belt tensioner
3 Coolant pump
4 Air conditioning compressor
5 Crankshaft pulley
6 Power steering pump

maintenance apart from having the case kept clean, and the terminals clean and tight.
2 To clean the battery terminals disconnect them, after having first removed the cover (later models) - negative earth first. Use a wire brush or abrasive paper to clean the terminals. Bad corrosion should be treated with a solution of bicarbonate of soda, applied with an old toothbrush. Do not let this solution get inside the battery.
3 Coat the battery terminals with petroleum jelly or a proprietary anti-corrosive compound before reconnecting them. Reconnect and tighten the positive (live) lead first, followed by the negative (earth) lead. Do not overtighten.
4 Keep the top of the battery clean and dry. Inspect the battery tray for corrosion, and make good as necessary.

23 Engine valve clearance check

HAYNES HINT *It will be easier to turn the engine by hand if the spark plugs are removed but take care not to allow dirt to enter the spark plug holes.*

SOHC engines

1 The valve clearances must be checked with the engine cold. On carburettor models remove the air cleaner.
2 Disconnect the HT leads from the spark plugs and release them from the clips on the camshaft cover.
3 On fuel injection models, unbolt and remove the bracing strut securing the inlet manifold to the right-hand side of the cylinder head.
4 Where applicable, unclip any hoses and wires from the camshaft cover, then unscrew the securing bolts and remove the camshaft cover and gaskets. Take care not to lose the spacer plates which fit under the bolt heads, where applicable.

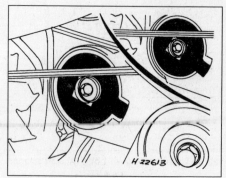

21.12d Alternator/coolant pump drivebelt tensioner indicator position - 2.0 litre DOHC engine

Inset shows tensioner at maximum adjustment

1

23.6 Cam lobe correctly positioned for checking valve clearance. Insert feeler gauge as shown by arrow

23.7a Using a feeler gauge to check a valve clearance

23.7b Adjusting a valve clearance

5 Numbering from the front (camshaft sprocket) end of the engine, the exhaust valves are 1, 3, 5 and 7, and the inlet valves are 2, 4, 6 and 8.

6 Turn the engine clockwise using a suitable socket on the crankshaft pulley bolt, until the exhaust valve of No 1 cylinder (valve No 1) is fully closed; ie the cam lobe is pointing vertically upwards **(see illustration)**.

7 Insert a feeler blade of the correct thickness (see Specifications) between the cam follower and the heel of the No 1 valve cam lobe. The feeler blade should be a firm sliding fit. If not, loosen the locknut and adjust the ball-pin position accordingly by turning the adjuster

nut, then tighten the locknut **(see illustrations)**. Allowance must be made for tightening the locknut, as this tends to decrease the valve clearance. Recheck the adjustment after tightening the locknut.

8 Repeat the procedure given in paragraphs 6 and 7 for the remaining valves. With the carburettor/inlet manifold fitted, some difficulty may be experienced when adjusting the exhaust valve clearances, and a suitable open-ended spanner bent to 90° will be found helpful.

9 Check the condition of the camshaft cover gasket, and renew if necessary. Fit the gasket to the camshaft cover ensuring that the locating tabs and dovetails are correctly located **(see illustration)**, then refit the camshaft cover and tighten the securing bolts in the order shown **(see illustration)**, ensuring that the spacer plates are in position under the bolt heads, where applicable.

10 On fuel injection models, refit the inlet manifold bracing strut.

11 Where applicable refit the spark plugs. Reconnect the HT leads and locate them in the clips on the camshaft cover.

12 Where applicable, refit any wires and hoses to the clips on the camshaft cover and on carburettor models, refit the air cleaner.

DOHC and CVH engines

13 These engines are fitted with hydraulic cam followers therefore no adjustment is necessary.

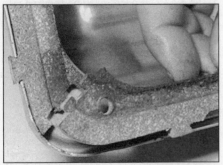

23.9a Camshaft cover gasket dovetails

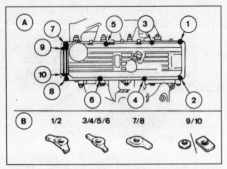

23.9b Camshaft cover bolts (A) and spacer plates (B)

Tighten bolts in following stages:
Stage 1 Bolts 1 to 6
Stage 2 Bolts 7 and 8
Stage 3 Bolts 9 and 10
Stage 4 Bolts 7 and 8 (again)

24 Handbrake check

Chock the front roadwheels and jack the rear wheels clear of the ground, supporting the vehicle with axlestands.

Check that with the handbrake released, the rear wheels are free to rotate and no brake "bind" is evident. The handbrake lever travel should be between two and four clicks of the ratchet. If brake "bind" or excessive lever travel is evident, check the handbrake cable routing and check the self-adjuster mechanism for wear or damage. Refer to Chapter 10 for full service information.

25 Radiator matrix and air conditioner condenser clean

Gain access to the radiator matrix by removing the surrounding body panels, fan shrouds, etc. Clean dirt and debris from the matrix using an air jet or water and a soft brush. Be careful not to damage the fins or cut your fingers.

Remove the protecting grille and clean any leaves, insects etc. from the air conditioner condenser coil and fins. Be very careful not to damage the condenser fins: use a soft brush, or a compressed air jet, along (not across) the fins.

26 Air conditioner refridgerant charge check

1 If applicable, remove the radiator grille being careful not to damage the condenser fins.

2 Check the refrigerant charge as follows. The engine should be cold and the ambient temperature should be between 64° and 77°F (18° and 25°C).

3 Start the engine and allow it to idle. Observe the refrigerant sight glass **(see illustration)** and have an assistant switch on the air conditioning to fan speed III. A few bubbles should be seen in the sight glass as the system starts up, but all bubbles should disappear within 10 seconds. Persistent bubbles, or no bubbles at all, mean that the refrigerant charge is low. Switch off the

26.3 Air conditioning system refrigerant sight glass (arrowed)

system immediately if the charge is low and do not use it again until it has been recharged.

4 Inspect the refrigerant pipes, hoses and unions for security and good condition. Refit the radiator grille.

5 The air conditioning system will lose a proportion of its charge through normal seepage typically up to 100 g (4 oz) per year - so it is as well to regard periodic recharging as a maintenance operation.

27 Final drive oil level check

1 Check the final drive oil level as follows.
2 Position the vehicle over a pit, or raise it at front and rear on ramps or axle stands. The vehicle must be level.
3 Wipe clean around the final drive filler/level plug **(see illustrations)** and unscrew the plug. Using a piece of bent wire as a dipstick, check that the oil is no more than 10 mm (0.4 in) below the plug hole.
4 If topping-up is necessary, use clean gear oil of the specified type. Do not overfill. Frequent need for topping-up can only be due to leaks, which should be rectified.
5 When the level is correct, refit the filler/level plug and tighten it to the specified torque loading.
6 There is no requirement for periodic oil changing, and no drain plug is provided.

28 Automatic transmission selector linkage lubrication

Lubricate the transmission selector and kickdown linkages with engine oil or aerosol lubricant.

29 Steering and suspension security check

1 Check the shock absorbers by bouncing the vehicle up and down at each corner in turn. When released, it should come to rest within one complete oscillation. Continued movement, or squeaking and groaning noises from the shock absorber suggests that renewal is required .
2 Raise and support the vehicle. Examine all steering and suspension components for wear and damage. Pay particular attention to dust covers and gaiters, which if renewed promptly when damaged can save further damage to the component protected.
3 At the same intervals, check the front suspension lower arm balljoints for wear by levering up the arms **(see illustration)**. Balljoint free movement must not exceed 0.5 mm (0.02 in). The track rod end balljoints can be checked in a similar manner, or by observing them whilst an assistant rocks the steering wheel back and forth. If the lower arm balljoint is worn, the complete lower arm must be renewed .

27.3a Final drive unit filler plug location (arrowed) - Saloon, Hatchback and Estate models

4 Wheel bearings can be checked for wear by spinning the relevant roadwheel. Any roughness or excessive noise indicates worn bearings, which must be renewed, as no adjustment is possible. It is unlikely that any wear will be evident unless the vehicle has covered a very high mileage. It should be noted that it is normal for the bearings to exhibit slight endfloat, which is perceptible as wheel rock at the wheel rim.

30 Driveshaft check

1 Position the vehicle over a pit, or raise it at front and rear on ramps or axle stands (see *"Jacking and vehicle support"*).
2 Examine the driveshaft joint rubber gaiters. Flex the gaiters by hand and inspect the folds and clips. Damaged or leaking gaiters must be renewed without delay to avoid damage occurring to the joint itself
3 Check the tightness of the final drive mounting bolts and the driveshaft flange screws.

31 Underbody inspection

1 Except on vehicles with a wax-based underbody protective coating, have the whole of the underframe of the vehicle steam-cleaned, engine compartment included, so that a thorough inspection can be carried out to see what minor repairs and renovations are necessary.

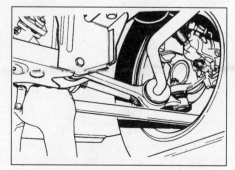

29.3 Levering up lower arm to check balljoint for wear

27.3b Rear axle filler plug location - P100 models

2 Steam-cleaning is available at many garages and is necessary for the removal of the accumulation of oily grime which sometimes is allowed to become thick in certain areas. If steam-cleaning facilities are not available, there are some excellent grease solvents available which can be brush-applied; the dirt can then be simply hosed off.
3 After cleaning, position the vehicle over a pit, or raise it at front and rear on ramps or axle stands (see *"Jacking and vehicle support"*).
4 Using a strong light, work around the underside of the vehicle, inspecting it for corrosion or damage. If either is found, refer to Chapter 12 for details of repair.

32 Brake pipe and hose check

Periodically inspect the rigid brake pipes for rust and other damage, and the flexible hoses for cracks, splits or "ballooning". Have an assistant depress the brake pedal (ignition on) and inspect the hose and pipe unions for leaks. Renew any defective item without delay.

33 Idle speed linkage clean

On carburettor models which incorporate a stepper motor (ie. Weber 2V from 1985), good electrical contact between the motor plunger and the adjusting screw is essential to maintain a regular idle speed.

Clean the plunger and adjusting screw contact faces with abrasive paper followed by switch cleaning fluid. Switch cleaning fluid is available from electronic component shops.

34 Road test

Instruments and electrical equipment

1 Check the operation of all instruments and electrical equipment.
2 Make sure that all instruments read correctly, and switch on all electrical equipment in turn to check that it functions properly.

35.1 Loosening the crankcase ventilation hose clip - CVH models

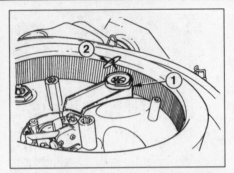

35.3 Oil separator (1) and mushroom valve (2) locations in air cleaner - CVH models

Steering and suspension

3 Check for any abnormalities in the steering, suspension, handling or road "feel".

4 Drive the vehicle, and check that there are no unusual vibrations or noises.

5 Check that the steering feels positive, with no excessive "sloppiness", or roughness, and check for any suspension noises when cornering, or when driving over bumps.

Drivetrain

6 Check the performance of the engine, clutch, transmission and driveshafts.

7 Listen for any unusual noises from the engine, clutch and transmission.

8 Make sure that the engine runs smoothly when idling, and that there is no hesitation when accelerating.

9 Where applicable, check that the clutch action is smooth and progressive, that the drive is taken up smoothly, and that the pedal travel is not excessive. Also listen for any noises when the clutch pedal is depressed.

10 Check that all gears can be engaged smoothly, without noise, and that the gear lever action is not abnormally vague or "notchy".

Check the operation and performance of the braking system

11 Make sure that the vehicle does not pull to one side when braking, and that the wheels do not lock prematurely when braking hard.

12 Check that there is no vibration through the steering when braking.

13 Check that the handbrake operates correctly, without excessive movement of the lever, and that it holds the vehicle stationary on a slope.

14 Test the operation of the brake servo unit as follows. With the engine off, depress the footbrake four or five times to exhaust the vacuum. Start the engine, holding the brake pedal depressed. As the engine starts, there should be a noticeable "give" in the brake pedal as vacuum builds up. Allow the engine to run for at least two minutes, and then switch it off. If the brake pedal is depressed now, it should be possible to detect a hiss from the servo as the pedal is depressed. After about four or five applications, no further hissing should be heard, and the pedal should feel considerably firmer.

35 Crankcase ventilation system check

1 Inspect the crankcase ventilation system for blockage or damage. A blocked hose can cause a build-up of crankcase pressure, which in turn can cause oil leaks (see illustration).

2 On carburettor model SOHC engines, clean the oil filler cap with paraffin and check that the vent valve is not blocked by pulling it from the oil separator and loosening the hose clip (Section 42).

3 On CVH engines, check that the oil separator and mushroom valve are not blocked, and clean if necessary (see illustration).

Every 24 000 miles (40 000 km) or 2 years

36 Air cleaner inlet air temperature control check

SOHC and DOHC carburettor models

1 A vacuum pump will be required to test the control components.

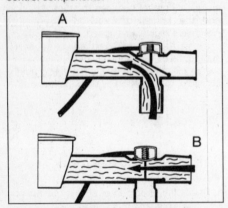

36.2 Air cleaner flap valve operation - OHC models

A Flap fully open to admit hot air
B Flap fully closed to admit cold air

2 To check the operation of the air temperature control, the engine must be cold. First observe the position of the flap valve which should be fully closed prior to starting the engine (see illustration). The position of the flap can be observed by disconnecting the cold air inlet hose from the air cleaner spout and looking into the spout.

3 Start the engine and allow it to idle. Check that the flap is now fully open to admit hot air from the exhaust manifold shroud. If the flap does not fully open, stop the engine and check the vacuum diaphragm unit and heat sensor as follows (see illustrations).

36.3a Air cleaner vacuum diaphragm unit - OHC models

4 Working under the base of the air cleaner body, disconnect the diaphragm unit-to-heat sensor vacuum pipe at the sensor end, and connect a vacuum pump to the diaphragm unit. Apply a vacuum of 100.0 mm (4.0 in) of mercury.

5 If the flap opens, then the heat sensor is faulty and should be renewed. If the flap remains closed, then the diaphragm unit is faulty, and a new air cleaner body will have to be obtained, as the diaphragm unit is not available separately.

6 On completion of the checks, disconnect the vacuum pump, and reconnect the vacuum pipe and cold air inlet hose.

36.3b Air cleaner heat sensor viewed from inside air cleaner - OHC models

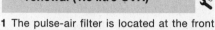

A

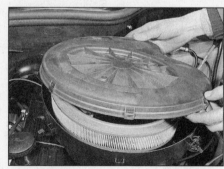

36.7 Air cleaner flap valve operation - CVH models

A Flap fully open to admit hot air	3 Flap valve
B Flap fully closed to admit cold air	4 Link arm
1 Air inlet spout	5 Waxstat
2 Hot air inlet hose	6 Air cleaner body

37 Pulse air filter element renewal (1.6 litre CVH)

1 The pulse-air filter is located at the front left-hand side of the engine compartment.
2 To renew the element, simply unclip the filter cover, then lift out the metal gauze, and withdraw the filter element (see illustration).
3 Refitting is a reversal of removal. Ensure that the holes in the gauze and the filter element are positioned on the engine side of the filter housing.

38 Air cleaner element renewal

Carburettor models

1 Remove the screws from the top of the air cleaner cover (see illustration).
2 Where applicable release the spring clips around the edge of the cover, then lift or prise off the cover (see illustration).
3 Lift out the air cleaner element. Wipe the inside of the air cleaner body clean, taking care not to allow dirt to enter the carburettor throat. Also clean the inside of the cover.
4 Place a new element in position, then refit the air cleaner cover.

Fuel-injection models

All models except 2.0 litre DOHC

5 Disconnect the battery negative lead.
6 Depress the locking clip on the airflow meter wiring plug and disconnect the plug. Pull on the plug, not the wiring (see illustration).
7 Loosen the securing clip and disconnect the air inlet hose from the airflow meter.
8 Release the four securing clips and lift off the air cleaner lid with the airflow meter.
9 Lift out the old air cleaner element (see illustration), then wipe the inside of the air cleaner casing and lid clean.
10 Fit the new element with the sealing lip uppermost.
11 Refit the air cleaner lid and secure with the four clips.
12 Reconnect the air inlet hose to the airflow meter, ensuring that the securing clip is correctly aligned (see illustration). Reconnect the wiring plug.

37.2 Withdrawing the pulse-air filter element and gauze - 1.6 litre CVH models

CVH carburettor models

7 To test the unit the engine must initially be cold. Disconnect the hot air inlet hose from the air cleaner spout and observe the position of the flap which should be fully open to allow only hot air to enter (see illustration).
8 Refit the hose and warm up the engine to normal operating temperature.
9 Disconnect the hot air inlet hose again, and observe the position of the flap which should be fully closed to admit only cold air.
10 If the flap positions are not as described, the waxstat is defective and the complete air cleaner must be renewed as the waxstat is not available separately.
11 On completion of the checks, stop the engine and reconnect the hot air inlet hose.

38.1 Remove the air cleaner cover screws . . .

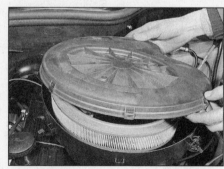

38.2 . . . release the spring clips, and lift off the cover for access to the element

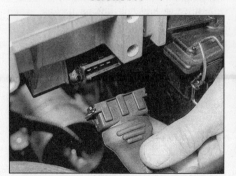

38.6 Disconnecting the airflow meter wiring plug

38.9 Unclip the lid and remove the air cleaner element

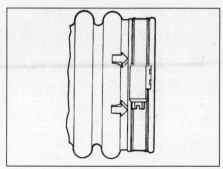

38.12 Air intake hose clip correctly aligned

38.17 Air intake tube securing nut (arrowed)

38.19 Lifting out the air cleaner element

13 Reconnect the battery negative lead.

2.0 litre DOHC models

14 Disconnect the battery negative lead.
15 Disconnect the wiring plug from the idle speed control valve at the front of the plenum chamber.
16 Loosen the clamp, and detach the air inlet hose from the air inlet tubing.
17 Unscrew the securing nut, and release the air inlet tube from the bracket on the engine compartment front panel **(see illustration)**.
18 Release the air cleaner lid securing clips, then lift away the air inlet tube, plenum chamber and air cleaner lid as an assembly, disconnecting the breather hose from the air inlet tube.
19 Lift out the air cleaner element **(see illustration)**, then wipe the inside of the air cleaner lid and casing clean.
20 Fit the new element with the sealing lip uppermost.
21 Further refitting is a reversal of removal.

39 Ignition system component check

1 Before disturbing any part of the ignition system, disconnect the battery negative lead.
2 Identify and clearly mark all HT leads before disconnecting them from the spark plugs.
3 Refer to the appropriate Section in Chapter 5 and, where applicable, remove the distributor cap and rotor arm.
4 Clean the HT leads and distributor cap with a dry cloth. Scrape any corrosion or other

deposits from the connectors and terminals. Also clean the coil tower.
5 Renew the HT leads if they are cracked, burnt or otherwise damaged. If a multi-meter is available, measure the resistance of the leads. The desired value is given in the Specifications of Chapter 5.
6 Renew the distributor cap if it is cracked or badly burnt inside, or if there is evidence of "tracking" (black lines marking the path of HT leakage). If there is a carbon brush at the centre of the cap, make sure that it moves freely, and is not excessively worn **(see illustration)**.
7 Clean the metal track of the rotor arm with fine abrasive paper. Renew the arm if it is cracked or badly burnt.
8 Refit the rotor arm and distributor cap.
9 Reconnect the HT leads to the spark plugs and coil.
10 Reconnect the battery and run the engine.

40 Automatic transmission brake band adjustment

Note: A brake band torque wrench - Ford tool No 17-005, or a conventional torque wrench and a splined socket of suitable size to fit the square section head of the adjuster screw(s) will be required for this operation.

1 For improved access, apply the handbrake, then jack up the front of the vehicle and support on axle stands (see "Jacking and vehicle support").

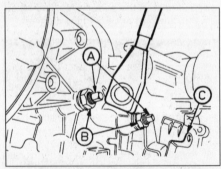

40.2 Brake band adjustment - A4LD type transmission

A Adjuster screws   C Kickdown lever
B Locknuts

2 The brake band adjuster screw(s) is/are situated on the left-hand side of the transmission housing, forward of the kickdown lever. Note that the C3 type transmission has a single adjuster screw for adjustment of the front brake band, whereas the A4LD type transmission has two adjuster screws for adjustment of the front and intermediate brake bands **(see illustration)**.
3 Disconnect the kickdown cable from the kickdown lever on the transmission housing.
4 Loosen the locknut on the front brake band adjuster screw, and back off the adjuster screw several turns.
5 Using the Ford special tool or a suitable equivalent, tighten the adjuster screw to the specified torque, then back off the screw two complete turns, and tighten the locknut. Ensure that the adjuster screw does not turn as the locknut is tightened.
6 Repeat the procedure given in paragraphs 4 and 5 for the remaining adjuster screw on A4LD type transmissions, but on all models where the part number on the transmission identification tag starts with "88" **(see illustration)** and additionally on all 1.8 CVH engine models, the adjuster screw should be backed off two and a half turns after tightening to the specified torque. On all other models, the adjuster screw should be backed off two turns.
7 Reconnect the kickdown cable, and lower the vehicle to the ground on completion.

41 Fuel filter renewal

> ⚠ **Caution: Refer to the precautions in Chapter 4, Part B, Section 1 before proceeding.**

2.0 litre SOHC fuel injection models

1 The fuel filter is located on the left-hand side of the engine compartment **(see illustration)**.
2 Disconnect the battery negative lead.
3 Position a suitable container beneath the filter, then slowly loosen the fuel inlet union to relieve the pressure in the fuel lines.
4 Disconnect the fuel inlet and outlet unions. Be prepared for petrol spillage. If necessary, identify the fuel line unions for use when refitting.
5 Loosen the filter clamp screw, and withdraw the filter from the clamp. Drain the petrol from the filter into the container. Dispose of the filter carefully.

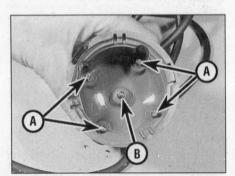

39.6 Bosch distributor cap showing HT segments (A) and carbon brush (B)

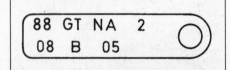

```
88 GT NA   2
08 B  05        ◯
```

40.6 Transmission identification tag with part number starting with "88"

41.1 Fuel filter location - outlet union arrowed

41.10 Fuel filter location (arrowed) under rear of vehicle

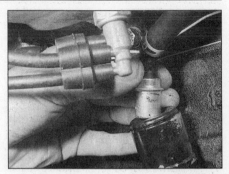

42.1 Removing the crankcase vent valve from the oil separator

6 Fit the new filter, ensuring that the arrows on the filter body point in the direction of fuel flow.
7 Tighten the clamp screw, and reconnect the fuel inlet and outlet unions. Ensure that the unions are correctly connected.
8 Reconnect the battery negative lead, and check the fuel line unions for leaks, pressurising the system by switching the ignition on and off several times.

All models except 2.0 litre SOHC
9 Proceed as described for the 2.0 litre SOHC

models, noting the following points.
10 The fuel filter is located under the rear of the vehicle, above the driveshaft **(see illustration)**. For access to the filter, chock the front wheels, then jack up the rear of the vehicle and support it on axle stands.
11 To remove the filter, the mounting bracket must first be removed from the floor, after unscrewing the securing bolt. The filter can then be removed from the bracket after unscrewing the clamp bolt.

42 Crankcase ventilation vent valve renewal

On carburettor model SOHC engines, renew the crankcase ventilation vent valve by pulling it from the oil separator and loosening the hose clip **(see illustration)**. Fit the new valve, tighten the clip, and insert it into the oil separator grommet.

Every 36 000 miles (60 000 km) or 3 years

43 Brake hydraulic system seal and hose renewal

If in doubt as to the condition of any of the brake system seals and hoses, then renew defective items whilst referring to the relevant Sections of Chapter 10.

44 Brake hydraulic fluid renewal

1 An assistant and bleeding equipment will be needed. A considerable quantity of hydraulic fluid will be required - probably about 2 litres (nearly half a gallon).
2 Slacken the front wheel nuts. Raise and support the front of the vehicle and remove the front wheels.
3 Remove the hydraulic fluid reservoir cap.
4 Open both front bleed screws one full turn. Attach one bleed tube to each screw, placing the free end of each tube in a jar.
5 Pump the brake pedal to expel fluid from the bleed screws. Pause after each upstroke to allow the master cylinder to refill.
6 When air emerges from both bleed screws, stop pumping. Detach the left-hand caliper without disconnecting it and remove the inboard brake pad.
7 Depress the caliper piston, using a purpose-made tool or a blunt item such as a tyre lever, to force more fluid out of the caliper. Hold the piston depressed and have the assistant pump the pedal until air emerges from the bleed screw again.

8 Tighten the bleed screw on the left-hand caliper. Loosely refit the caliper and pad so that the piston is not accidentally ejected.
9 Repeat the purging operation on the right-hand caliper, but do not refit it or tighten the bleed screw yet.
10 Fill the reservoir with fresh hydraulic fluid. Position the bleed jar for the right-hand caliper at least 300 mm (1 foot) above the level of the bleed screw.
11 Have the assistant pump the brake pedal until fluid free of bubbles emerges from the bleed screw. Tighten the bleed screw at the end of a downstroke.
12 Place a piece of wood in the caliper jaws to limit piston travel. Keep your fingers clear of the piston. Have the assistant depress the brake pedal **gently** in order to move the caliper piston out.
13 With the pedal held depressed, slacken the bleed screw on the right-hand caliper and again depress the piston. Tighten the bleed screw when the piston is retracted. The pedal can now be released.
14 Disconnect the bleed tube. Refit the right-hand brake pad and caliper.
15 Remove the left-hand caliper and inboard pad again. Carry out the operations described in paragraphs 10 to 14 on the left-hand caliper.
16 Bleed the rear brakes (Chapter 10).
17 Refit the front wheels, lower the vehicle and tighten the wheel nuts.
18 Pump the brake pedal to bring the pads up to the discs, then make a final check of the hydraulic fluid level. Top-up and refit the reservoir cap.

45 Camshaft drivebelt renewal

Camshaft drivebelt renewal is recommended as a precautionary measure for SOHC engines but is compulsory for CVH engines. Refer to Chapter 2 for the appropriate renewal procedure.

46 Engine coolant renewal

⚠️ *Caution: Before proceeding, note the precautions given in Chapter 3, Section 1.*

1 Disconnect the battery negative lead.
2 It is preferable to drain the cooling system with the engine cold. If this is not possible, take precautions against scalding when removing the expansion tank cap. Place a thick rag over the cap and slacken the cap a little to release any pressure. When all pressure has been released, carry on unscrewing the cap and remove it.
3 Early models have no radiator drain plug, so the radiator must be drained by detaching the bottom coolant hose from the outlet on the right-hand side of the radiator. Later SOHC models have a drain plug located in the base of the left-hand radiator end tank, whilst all CVH models have a drain plug in the right-hand radiator end tank and DOHC models have a plug to the bottom right-hand side of the radiator.

1

46.4 Unscrew the clip and remove the rubber cap from the bleed spigot - SOHC models

46.6a Disconnect the bottom hose from the radiator - early OHC models

46.6b Radiator drain plug (arrowed) - later CVH models

4 Certain SOHC models have a bleed spigot on the thermostat housing, which is covered by a rubber cap. The cap should be removed from the spigot before commencing draining **(see illustration)**.

5 With the expansion tank cap removed, place a suitable container beneath the radiator bottom hose or drain plug as applicable.

6 On early models, loosen the clip and ease the bottom hose away from the radiator outlet. On later models, unscrew the drain plug **(see illustrations)**. Allow the coolant to drain into the container.

7 On SOHC models, place a second container beneath the drain plug on the right-hand side of the cylinder block **(see illustration)**. Unscrew the drain plug and allow the coolant to drain into the container. No cylinder block drain plug is fitted on CVH and DOHC models.

46.7 Cylinder block drain plug (arrowed) - SOHC models (engine removed)

8 Dispose of the drained coolant safely.

9 After some time the radiator and engine waterways may become restricted or even blocked with scale or sediment, which reduces the efficiency of the cooling system. When this occurs, the coolant will appear rusty and dark in colour and the system should then be flushed.

10 Disconnect the top hose from the radiator, then insert a garden hose and allow water to circulate through the radiator until it runs clear from the outlet.

11 Insert the hose in the expansion tank filler neck and allow water to run out of the bottom hose (and cylinder block on SOHC models) until clear. If, after a reasonable period the water still does not run clear, the radiator can be flushed with a good proprietary cleaning agent.

12 Disconnect the inlet hose from the inlet manifold, connect the garden hose and allow water to circulate through the manifold, automatic choke (where applicable), heater and out through the bottom hose until clear.

13 In severe cases of contamination the system should be reverse flushed. To do this, remove the radiator, invert it and insert a hose in the outlet. Continue flushing until clear water runs from the inlet.

14 The engine should also be reverse flushed. To do this, remove the thermostat

and insert the hose into the cylinder head on SOHC models, or into the inlet manifold on CVH and DOHC models. Continue flushing until clear water runs from the bottom hose (and cylinder block on SOHC models).

15 Where applicable, refit the radiator and the thermostat.

16 Reconnect any disturbed hoses and refit and tighten the cylinder block drain plug and/or radiator drain plug, as applicable.

17 On SOHC models fitted with a bleed spigot on the thermostat housing, ensure that the rubber cap is removed before refilling the system.

18 Pour coolant in through the expansion tank filler hole until the level is up to the "MAX" mark.

19 Where applicable, refit the rubber cap to the bleed spigot when coolant starts to emerge from the spigot. Tighten the clip.

20 Squeeze the coolant hoses to help disperse air locks. Top-up the coolant further if necessary, then refit and tighten the expansion tank cap.

21 Run the engine up to operating temperature, checking for coolant leaks. Stop the engine and allow it to cool, then re-check the coolant level. Top-up the level as necessary, taking care to avoid scalding as the expansion tank cap is removed.

Chapter 2 Part A:
SOHC engines

Contents

Degrees of difficulty

Easy, suitable for novice with little experience	**Fairly easy,** suitable for beginner with some experience	**Fairly difficult,** suitable for competent DIY mechanic	**Difficult,** suitable for experienced DIY mechanic	**Very difficult,** suitable for expert DIY or professional

Specifications

1.3 litre engine

General

Engine type	Four-cylinder, in-line, single overhead camshaft
Firing order	1-3-4-2
Engine code	JCT
Bore	79.02 mm
Stroke	66.00 mm
Cubic capacity	1294 cc
Compression ratio	9.0:1
Compression pressure at starter motor speed	11 to 13 bar
Maximum continuous engine speed	5800 rpm
Maximum engine power (DIN)	44 kW at 5700 rpm
Maximum engine torque (DIN)	98 Nm at 3100 rpm

Cylinder bore diameter

Standard class 1	79.000 to 79.010 mm
Standard class 2	79.010 to 79.020 mm
Standard class 3	79.020 to 79.030 mm
Standard class 4	79.030 to 79.040 mm
Oversize class A	79.510 to 79.520 mm
Oversize class B	79.520 to 79.530 mm
Oversize class C	79.530 to 79.540 mm
Standard service	79.030 to 79.040 mm
Oversize 0.5	79.530 to 79.540 mm
Oversize 1.0	80.030 to 80.040 mm

Crankshaft

Endfloat . . . . 0.08 to 0.28 mm (0.003 to 0.011 in)
Main bearing running clearance . . . . 0.010 to 0.064 mm
Main bearing journal diameter:
   Standard . . . . 56.970 to 56.990 mm
   Undersize 0.25 . . . . 56.720 to 56.740 mm
   Undersize 0.50 . . . . 56.470 to 56.490 mm
   Undersize 0.75 . . . . 56.220 to 56.240 mm
   Undersize 1.00 . . . . 55.970 to 55.990 mm
Main bearing thrustwasher thickness:
   Standard . . . . 2.30 to 2.35 mm
   Oversize . . . . 2.50 to 2.55 mm
Big-end bearing running clearance . . . . 0.006 to 0.060 mm
Big-end bearing journal diameter:
   Standard . . . . 51.980 to 52.000 mm
   Undersize 0.25 . . . . 51.730 to 51.750 mm
   Undersize 0.50 . . . . 51.480 to 51.500 mm
   Undersize 0.75 . . . . 51.230 to 51.250 mm
   Undersize 1.00 . . . . 50.980 to 51.000 mm

Pistons and piston rings

Piston diameter:
   Standard class 1 . . . . 78.965 to 78.975 mm
   Standard class 2 . . . . 78.975 to 78.985 mm
   Standard class 3 . . . . 78.985 to 78.995 mm
   Standard class 4 . . . . 78.995 to 79.005 mm
   Standard service . . . . 78.990 to 79.015 mm
   Service oversize 0.5 . . . . 79.490 to 79.515 mm
   Service oversize 1.0 . . . . 79.990 to 80.015 mm
Piston ring end gap:
   Top . . . . 0.300 to 0.500 mm
   Centre . . . . 0.300 to 0.500 mm
   Bottom . . . . 0.400 to 1.400 mm

Auxiliary shaft

Endfloat . . . . 0.050 to 0.204 mm (0.002 to 0.008 in)

Cylinder head

Valve seat angle . . . . 44° 30' to 45° 00'
Service correction cutter*:
   Upper correction angle . . . . 30°
   Lower correction angle:
      Inlet . . . . 75°
      Exhaust . . . . 62.5°
Valve seat width . . . . 1.5 to 2.0 mm
Valve guide bore:
   Standard . . . . 8.063 to 8.088 mm
   Oversize 0.2 . . . . 8.263 to 8.288 mm
   Oversize 0.4 . . . . 8.463 to 8.488 mm
Not for use with hardened valve seats

Camshaft

Endfloat . . . . 0.104 to 0.204 mm (0.004 to 0.008 in)
Thrust plate thickness . . . . 3.98 to 4.01 mm (0.156 to 0.158 in)
Bearing journal diameter:
   Front . . . . 41.987 to 42.013 mm
   Centre . . . . 44.607 to 44.633 mm
   Rear . . . . 44.987 to 45.013 mm

Valves

Valve clearance (cold engine):
   Inlet . . . . 0.20 ± 0.03 mm (0.008 ± 0.001 in)
   Exhaust . . . . 0.25 ± 0.03 mm (0.010 ± 0.001 in)
Valve timing:
   Inlet opens . . . . 22° BTDC
   Inlet closes . . . . 54° ABDC
   Exhaust opens . . . . 64° BBDC
   Exhaust closes . . . . 12° ATDC
Valve spring free length . . . . 47.00 mm (1.85 in)

Inlet valve stem diameter:
Standard	8.025 to 8.043 mm
Oversize 0.2	8.225 to 8.243 mm
Oversize 0.4	8.425 to 8.443 mm
Oversize 0.6	8.625 to 8.643 mm
Oversize 0.8	8.825 to 8.843 mm

Exhaust valve stem diameter:
Standard	7.999 to 8.017 mm
Oversize 0.2	8.199 to 8.217 mm
Oversize 0.4	8.399 to 8.417 mm
Oversize 0.6	8.599 to 8.617 mm
Oversize 0.8	8.799 to 8.817 mm

Lubrication system

Oil type	Multigrade engine oil, viscosity range SAE 10W/30 to 20W/50 to API SG/CD or better

Oil capacity:
With filter	3.75 litres (6.6 pints)
Without filter	3.25 litres (5.7 pints)
Oil filter	Champion C102

Oil pump clearances:
Outer rotor to body	0.153 to 0.304 mm (0.006 to 0.012 in)
Inner rotor to outer rotor	0.050 to 0.200 mm (0.002 to 0.008 in)
Rotor endfloat	0.039 to 0.104 mm (0.002 to 0.004 in)

Torque wrench settings

	Nm	lbf ft
Main bearing cap bolts	88 to 102	65 to 75
Big-end bearing cap nuts	40 to 47	30 to 35
Crankshaft pulley bolt:		
Strength class 8.8	55 to 60	41 to 44
Strength class 10.9	100 to 115	74 to 85
Camshaft sprocket bolt	45 to 50	33 to 37
Auxiliary shaft sprocket bolt	45 to 50	33 to 37
Flywheel bolts	64 to 70	47 to 52
Oil pump bolts	17 to 21	13 to 15
Oil pump cover bolts	9 to 13	7 to 10
Sump bolts:		
Stage 1	1 to 2	0.7 to 1.5
Stage 2	6 to 8	4 to 6
Stage 3 (after running engine for 20 minutes)	8 to 10	6 to 7
Sump drain plug	21 to 28	15 to 21
Oil pressure warning lamp switch	12 to 15	9 to 11
Valve adjustment ball-pin locknuts:		
7 mm thick nuts	45 to 50	33 to 37
8 mm thick nuts	50 to 55	37 to 41
Cylinder head bolts:		
Splined type bolts:		
Stage 1	40 to 55	30 to 41
Stage 2	50 to 70	37 to 52
Stage 3 (after 20 minutes)	73 to 83	54 to 61
Stage 4 (after running engine for 15 minutes at 1000 rpm)	95 to 115	70 to 85
Torx type bolts:		
Stage 1	35 to 40	26 to 30
Stage 2	70 to 75	52 to 55
Stage 3 (after 5 minutes)	Tighten through a further 90°	
Camshaft cover bolts:		
Stage 1	6 to 8	4 to 6
Stage 2	2 to 3	1.5 to 2
Stage 3	6 to 8	4 to 6
Stage 4	6 to 0	4 to 6
Timing cover bolts	13 to 17	10 to 13
Timing belt tensioner bolts:		
Models with tensioner spring:		
Spring bolt	17 to 21	13 to 15
Pivot bolt	20 to 25	15 to 18
Models without tensioner spring	20 to 25	15 to 18
Oil pick-up tube/strainer-to-oil pump bolts	11 to 14	8 to 10
Oil pick-up tube/strainer-to-cylinder block bolts	17 to 21	13 to 15

2A

1.6 litre engine

General

Engine type	Four-cylinder, in-line, single overhead camshaft	
Firing order	1-3-4-2	
Engine codes	LCS, LCT, LSD and LSE	
	LCS and LCT	**LSD and LSE**
Bore	87.67 mm	81.32 mm
Stroke	66.00 mm	76.95 mm
Cubic capacity	1593 cc	1597 cc
Compression ratio	9.2 : 1	9.5 : 1
Compression pressure at starter motor speed	11 to 13 bar	11 to 13 bar
Maximum continuous engine speed	5800 rpm	5950 rpm
Maximum engine power (DIN)	55 kW at 5300 rpm	55 kW at 4900 rpm
Maximum engine torque (DIN)	120 Nm at 2900 rpm	123 Nm at 2900 rpm

Cylinder bore diameter

	LCS and LCT	**LSD and LSE**
Standard class 1	87.650 to 87.660 mm	81.300 to 81.310 mm
Standard class 2	87.660 to 87.670 mm	81.310 to 81.320 mm
Standard class 3	87.670 to 87.680 mm	81.320 to 81.330 mm
Standard class 4	87.680 to 87.690 mm	81.330 to 81.340 mm
Oversize class A	88.160 to 88.170 mm	81.810 to 81.820 mm
Oversize class B	88.170 to 88.180 mm	81.820 to 81.830 mm
Oversize class C	88.180 to 88.190 mm	81.830 to 81.840 mm
Standard service	87.680 to 87.690 mm	81.330 to 81.340 mm
Oversize 0.5	88.180 to 88.190 mm	81.830 to 81.840 mm
Oversize 1.0	88.680 to 88.690 mm	82.330 to 82.340 mm

Crankshaft

Specifications as for 1.3 litre engine except for the following:
Main bearing thrustwasher thickness from 1987:

Standard	2.28 to 2.33 mm
Oversize	2.48 to 2.53 mm

Pistons and piston rings

Piston diameter:	**LCS and LCT**	**LSD and LSE**
Standard class 1	87.615 to 87.625 mm	81.265 to 81.275 mm
Standard class 2	87.625 to 87.635 mm	81.275 to 81.285 mm
Standard class 3	87.635 to 87.645 mm	81.285 to 81.295 mm
Standard class 4	87.645 to 87.655 mm	81.295 to 81.305 mm
Standard service	87.640 to 87.665 mm	81.290 to 81.315 mm
Service oversize 0.5	88.140 to 88.165 mm	81.790 to 81.815 mm
Service oversize 1.0	88.640 to 88.665 mm	82.290 to 82.315 mm
Piston ring end gap:		
Top	0.300 to 0.500 mm	0.300 to 0.500 mm
Centre	0.300 to 0.500 mm	0.300 to 0.500 mm
Bottom	0.400 to 1.400 mm	0.400 to 1.400 mm

Auxiliary shaft

Endfloat	0.050 to 0.204 mm (0.002 to 0.008 in)

Cylinder head

Specifications as for 1.3 litre engine

Camshaft

Specifications as for 1.3 litre engine except for the following:
Endfloat:

Engine codes LCS, LCT and LSE	0.104 to 0.204 mm (0.004 to 0.008 in)
Engine code LSD	0.090 to 0.170 mm (0.003 to 0.007 in)

Valves

Specification as for 1.3 litre engine

Lubrication system

Specifications as for 1.3 litre engine

Torque wrench settings

Specification as for 1.3 litre engine

1.8 litre engine

General

Engine type	Four-cylinder, in line, single overhead camshaft
Firing order	1-3-4-2
Engine codes	REB and RED
Bore	86.20 mm
Stroke	76.95 mm
Cubic capacity	1796 cc
Compression ratio	9.5:1
Compression pressure at starter motor speed	11 to 13 bar
Maximum continuous engine speed	5850 rpm
Maximum engine power (DIN)	66kW at 5400 rpm
Maximum engine torque (DIN)	140 Nm at 3500 rpm

Cylinder bore diameter

Standard class 1	86.180 to 86.190 mm
Standard class 2	86.190 to 86.200 mm
Standard class 3	86.200 to 86.210 mm
Standard class 4	86.210 to 86.220 mm
Oversize class A	86.690 to 86.700 mm
Oversize class B	86.700 to 86.710 mm
Oversize class C	86.710 to 86.720 mm
Standard service	86.210 to 86.220 mm
Oversize 0.5	86.710 to 86.720 mm
Oversize 1.0	87.210 to 87.220 mm

Crankshaft

Specifications as for 1.3 litre engine except for the following:
Main bearing thrustwasher thickness from 1987:

Standard	2.28 to 2.33 mm
Oversize	2.48 to 2.53 mm

Pistons and piston rings

Piston diameter:

Standard class 1	86.145 to 86.155 mm
Standard class 2	86.155 to 86.165 mm
Standard class 3	86.165 to 86.175 mm
Standard class 4	86.175 to 86.185 mm
Standard service	86.170 to 86.195 mm
Service oversize 0.5	86.670 to 86.695 mm
Service oversize 1.0	86.170 to 86.195 mm

Piston ring end gap:

Top	0.300 to 0.500 mm
Centre	0.300 to 0.500 mm
Bottom	0.400 to 1.400 mm

Auxiliary shaft

Endfloat	0.050 to 0.204 mm (0.002 to 0.008 in)

Cylinder head and camshaft

Specifications as for 1.3 litre engine

Valves

Specifications as for 1.3 litre engine except for the following:
Valve clearance (cold engine):

Inlet	0.20 ± 0.03 mm (0.008 ± 0.001 in)
Exhaust	0.25 ± 0.03 mm (0.010 ± 0.001 in)

Valve timing:

Inlet opens	24° BTDC
Inlet closes	64° ABDC
Exhaust opens	70° BBDC
Exhaust closes	18° ATDC

Lubrication system

Specifications as for 1.3 litre engine

Torque wrench settings

Specifications as for 1.3 litre engine

2A

2.0 litre engine

General

Engine type	Four-cylinder, in-line, single overhead camshaft
Firing order	1-3-4-2
Engine codes	NES and NET (carburettor, except P100), NRB and N4A (fuel injection), and NAE (P100)
Bore	90.82 mm
Stroke	76.95 mm
Cubic capacity	1993 cc
Compression ratio:	
All except engine code NAE	9.2:1
Engine code NAE	8.2:1
Compression pressure at starter motor speed:	
All except engine code NAE	11 to 13 bar
Engine code NAE	10 to 12 bar
Maximum continuous engine speed:	
Engine code NES	5850 rpm
Engine codes NET and NAE	5800 rpm
Engine codes NRB and N4A	6050 rpm
Maximum engine power (DIN):	
Engine codes NES and NET	77kW at 5200 rpm
Engine codes NRB and N4A	85kW at 5500 rpm
Engine code NAE	57kW at 4500 rpm
Maximum engine torque (DIN):	
Engine codes NES and NET.	157 Nm at 4000 rpm
Engine codes NRB and N4A	160 Nm at 4000 rpm
Engine code NAE	143 Nm at 2800 rpm

Cylinder bore diameter

Standard class 1	90.800 to 90.810 mm
Standard class 2	90.810 to 90.820 mm
Standard class 3	90.820 to 90.830 mm
Standard class 4	90.830 to 90.840 mm
Oversize class A	91.310 to 91.320 mm
Oversize class B	91.320 to 91.330 mm
Oversize class C	91.330 to 91.340 mm
Standard service	90.830 to 90.840 mm
Oversize 0.5	91.330 to 91.340 mm
Oversize 1.0	91.830 to 91.840 mm

Crankshaft

Specifications as for 1.3 litre engine except for the following:
Main bearing thrustwasher thickness:

All except engine codes NES, NET, NRB and N4A from 1987:	
Standard	2.30 to 2.35 mm
Oversize	2.50 to 2.55 mm
Engine codes NES, NET, NRB and N4A from 1987:	
Standard	2.28 to 2.33 mm
Oversize	2.48 to 2.53 mm

Pistons and piston rings

Piston diameter:

Standard class 1	90.765 to 90.775 mm
Standard class 2	90.775 to 90.785 mm
Standard class 3	90.785 to 90.795 mm
Standard class 4	90.795 to 90.805 mm
Standard service:	
Up to 1985	90.780 to 90.805 mm
From 1985	90.790 to 90.815 mm
Service oversize 0.5:	
Up to 1985	91.280 to 91.305 mm
From 1985	91.290 to 91.315 mm
Service oversize 1.0:	
Up to 1985	91.780 to 91.805 mm
From 1985	91.790 to 91.815 mm

Piston ring end gap:
Top:	
Up to 1985	0.038 to 0.048 mm
From 1985	0.400 to 0.600 mm
Centre:	
Up to 1985	0.038 to 0.048 mm
From 1985	0.400 to 0.600 mm
Bottom	0.400 to 1.400 mm

Auxiliary shaft
Endfloat .... 0.050 to 0.204 mm (0.002 to 0.008 in)

Cylinder head
Specifications as for 1.3 litre engine

Valves
Specifications as for 1.3 litre engine except for the following:

Valve clearance (cold engine):
Inlet .... 0.20 ± 0.03 mm (0.008 ± 0.001 in)
Exhaust .... 0.25 ± 0.003 mm (0.010 ± 0.001 in)

Valve timing:
	All except code NAE	Engine code NAE
Inlet opens	24° BTDC	18° BTDC
Inlet closes	64° ABDC	58° ABDC
Exhaust opens	70° BBDC	70° BBDC
Exhaust closes	18° ATDC	6° ATDC

Lubrication system
Specifications as for 1.3 litre engine

Torque wrench settings
Specifications as for 1.3 litre engine except for the following:

	Nm	lbf ft
Crankshaft pulley bolt:		
Fuel injection models up to 1987	115 to 130	85 to 96
Fuel injection models from 1987	100 to 115	74 to 85

2A

1 General information

The engine is of a four-cylinder, in-line, single overhead camshaft type, mounted at the front of the vehicle and available in 1.3, 1.6, 1.8 and 2.0 litre versions.

The crankshaft incorporates five main bearings. Thrustwashers are fitted to the centre main bearing in order to control crankshaft endfloat.

The camshaft is driven by a toothed belt and operates the slightly angled valves via cam followers which pivot on ball-pins.

The auxiliary shaft which is also driven by the toothed belt, drives the distributor, oil pump and fuel pump.

The cylinder head is of crossflow design with the inlet manifold mounted on the left-hand side and the exhaust manifold mounted on the right-hand side.

Lubrication is by means of a bi-rotor pump which draws oil through a strainer located inside the sump, and forces it through a full-flow filter into the engine oil galleries where it is distributed to the crankshaft, camshaft and auxiliary shaft. The big-end bearings are supplied with oil via internal drillings in the crankshaft. The undersides of the pistons are supplied with oil from drillings in the big-ends. The distributor shaft is intermittently supplied with oil from the drilled auxiliary shaft. The camshaft followers are supplied with oil via a drilled spray tube from the centre camshaft bearing.

A semi-closed crankcase ventilation system is employed whereby piston blow-by gases are drawn into the inlet manifold via an oil separator and control valve.

2 Engine oil and filter - renewal

Refer to Chapter 1, Section 8.

3 Valve clearances - checking and adjustment

Refer to Chapter 1, Section 23.

4 Crankcase ventilation system - inspection and maintenance

Refer to Chapter 1, Section 35.

5 Compression test

1 When engine performance is poor, or if misfiring occurs which cannot be attributed to the ignition or fuel system, a compression test can provide diagnostic clues. If the test is performed regularly it can give warning of trouble before any other symptoms become apparent.

2 The engine must be at operating temperature, the battery must be fully charged and the spark plugs must be removed. The services of an assistant will also be required.

3 Disable the ignition system by disconnecting the coil LT feed. Fit the compression tester to No 1 spark plug hole. (The type of tester which screws into the spark plug hole is to be preferred.)

4 Have the assistant hold the throttle wide open and crank the engine on the starter. Record the highest reading obtained on the compression tester.

5 Repeat the test on the remaining cylinders, recording the pressure developed in each.

6 Desired pressures are given in the Specifications. If the pressure in any cylinder is low, introduce a teaspoonful of clean engine oil into the spark plug hole and repeat the test.

7 If the addition of oil temporarily improves the compression pressure, this indicates that bore, piston or piston ring wear was responsible for the pressure loss. No improvement suggests that leaking or burnt valves, or a blown head gasket, may be to blame.

8 A low reading from the two adjacent cylinders is almost certainly due to the head gasket between them having blown.

9 On completion of the test, refit the spark plugs and reconnect the coil LT feed.

6 Major operations possible with the engine in the vehicle

The following operations can be carried out without removing the engine from the vehicle:
a) *Removal and servicing of the cylinder head*
b) *Removal of the camshaft after removal of the cylinder head*
c) *Removal of the timing belt and sprockets*
d) *Removal of the sump*
e) *Removal of the oil pump*
f) *Removal of the pistons and connecting rods*
g) *Removal of the big-end bearings*
h) *Removal of the engine mountings*
i) *Removal of the clutch and flywheel*
j) *Removal of crankshaft front and rear oil seals*
k) *Removal of the auxiliary shaft*

7 Major operations requiring engine removal

The following operations can only be carried out after removing the engine from the vehicle:
a) *Removal of the crankshaft main bearings*
b) *Removal of the crankshaft*

8 Method of engine removal

 Warning: Vehicles equipped with air conditioning: Components of the air conditioning system may obstruct work being undertaken on the engine, and it is not always possible to unbolt and move them aside sufficiently, within the limits of their flexible connecting pipes. In such a case, the system should be discharged by a Ford dealer or air conditioning specialist. The refrigerant is harmless under normal conditions, but in the presence of a naked flame (or a lighted cigarette) it forms a highly toxic gas. Liquid refrigerant spilled on the skin will cause frostbite. If refrigerant enters the eyes, rinse them with a diluted solution of boric acid and seek medical advice immediately.

The engine may be lifted out either on its own, or together with the manual gearbox/automatic transmission. Unless work is to be carried out on the manual gearbox/automatic transmission, it is recommended that the engine is removed on its own. Where automatic transmission is fitted, the engine should where possible be removed on its own due to the additional weight of the transmission.

9 Engine - removal leaving manual gearbox in vehicle

Note: *The air conditioning system should always be discharged by a Ford dealer or air conditioning specialist.*
Note: *Refer to the warning in Section 8 before proceeding. A suitable hoist and lifting tackle will be required for this operation.*
1 Disconnect the battery negative lead.
2 Remove the bonnet.
3 On carburettor models remove the air cleaner.
4 On fuel injection models, disconnect the crankcase ventilation hose from the air inlet hose, then disconnect the air inlet hose from the throttle body. Depress the locking clip on the airflow meter wiring plug and disconnect the plug (pulling on the plug, not the wiring) then release the four securing clips and lift off the air cleaner lid with the airflow meter and air inlet hose.
5 Remove the four retaining clips and unscrew the two retaining screws, then withdraw the upper section of the cooling fan shroud from the radiator. Unclip and remove the lower section of the shroud.
6 Remove the thermo-viscous cooling fan as described in Chapter 3.
7 Drain the cooling system.
8 Disconnect the upper radiator hose and where applicable, the expansion tank hose from the thermostat housing.
9 Disconnect the coolant hoses from the coolant pump, and where applicable from the inlet manifold and automatic choke. Unclip the coolant hose from the bracket on the exhaust manifold hot air shroud/heat shield, or the camshaft cover, as applicable.
10 On carburettor models, where applicable disconnect the vacuum pipe from the engine management module.
11 Disconnect the brake servo vacuum pipe from the inlet manifold.
12 On carburettor models, disconnect the fuel hoses from the carburettor and where applicable the mechanical fuel pump and plug the ends of the hoses to minimise petrol spillage. Remember to take adequate fire precautions.
13 On fuel injection models, disconnect the fuel feed line from the fuel pressure regulator, then disconnect the fuel supply hose from the

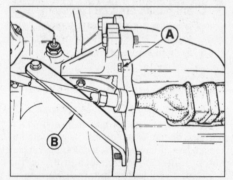

9.25 Engine adapter plate bolt (A) and engine-to-gearbox brace (B)

fuel rail. Position a suitable container beneath the pressure regulator, then slowly loosen the fuel feed union to relieve the pressure in the fuel lines before disconnecting the union. Take adequate fire precautions. Plug the ends of the hoses to minimise petrol spillage.
14 Disconnect the throttle cable, and where applicable remove its bracket.
15 Disconnect the HT lead from the ignition coil.
16 Disconnect the wiring from the following components as applicable depending on model:
Alternator
Starter motor
Distributor
Oil pressure warning lamp switch
Temperature gauge sender
Engine coolant temperature sensor
Automatic choke
Automatic choke pull-down solenoid
Carburettor anti-dieselling valve
Inlet manifold heater
Carburettor stepper motor
Fuel injection harness
Dipstick
17 Where applicable, detach the power steering pump from the cylinder block and move it to one side.
18 Unscrew and remove the top engine-to-gearbox bolts which are accessible from the engine compartment. Note the location of the earth strap on one of the bolts.
19 Note the location of the earth strap on the rear inlet manifold stud, then remove the nut and disconnect the strap.
20 Apply the handbrake (if not already done), jack up the front of the vehicle and support on axle stands (see *"Jacking and Vehicle Support"*).
21 Drain the engine oil into a suitable container.
22 Remove the starter motor.
23 Remove the exhaust downpipe.
24 Unscrew the nuts or bolts, as applicable, securing the engine mountings to the crossmember. Recover the washers.
25 Unscrew and remove the remaining engine-to-gearbox bolts, and remove the bolt from the engine adapter plate **(see illustration)**.
26 Remove the two securing bolts and disconnect the engine-to-gearbox brace from the engine and gearbox.
27 Working inside the vehicle, place a wooden block under the clutch pedal to raise it fully against its stop which will hold the automatic adjuster pawl clear of the toothed quadrant.
28 Disconnect the clutch cable from the clutch release arm, and pass the cable through the bellhousing. Where applicable, remove the clip securing the clutch cable to the right-hand engine mounting bracket. Note the cable routing for use when refitting.
29 Lower the vehicle to the ground, and support the gearbox with a trolley jack, using a block of wood between the jack and the gearbox to spread the load.
30 Make a final check to ensure that all relevant wires, pipes and hoses have been disconnected to facilitate engine removal.

31 Attach a suitable hoist to the engine lifting brackets located at the front and rear of the cylinder head, and carefully take the weight of the engine. The engine should be supported horizontally, ie do not allow it to tilt front to rear.
32 Raise the engine until the engine mountings are clear of the crossmember then pull the engine forwards to disconnect it from the gearbox. Ensure that the gearbox is adequately supported, and take care not to strain the gearbox input shaft. It may be necessary to rock the engine a little to release it from the gearbox.
33 Once clear of the gearbox, lift the engine from the vehicle, taking care not to damage the radiator fins.

10 Engine - removal leaving automatic transmission in vehicle

Note: *Refer to the warning in Section 8 before proceeding. A suitable hoist and lifting tackle will be required for this operation.*

1 Proceed as described in Section 9, paragraphs 1 to 17 inclusive, but additionally, where applicable, disconnect the kickdown cable from the carburettor/inlet manifold.
2 Unscrew and remove the top engine-to-transmission bolts which are accessible from the engine compartment. Note the location of the earth strap, vacuum pipe bracket, and transmission dipstick tube bracket.
3 Proceed as described in Section 9, paragraphs 20 to 24 inclusive.
4 Working through the starter motor aperture, unscrew the four torque converter-to-driveplate nuts. It will be necessary to turn the crankshaft, using a suitable spanner on the crankshaft pulley bolt, in order to gain access to each nut in turn through the aperture.
5 Unscrew and remove the remaining engine-to-transmission bolts, and remove the bolt from the engine adapter plate. Where applicable pull the blanking plug from the adapter plate.
6 Remove the two securing bolts and disconnect the engine-to-transmission brace from the engine and transmission.
7 Lower the vehicle to the ground, and support the transmission with a trolley jack, using a block of wood between the jack and the transmission to spread the load.
8 Proceed as described in Section 9, paragraphs 30 and 31.
9 Raise the engine until the engine mountings are clear of the crossmember, then pull the engine forwards to disconnect it from the transmission. Ensure that the torque converter is held firmly in place in the transmission housing, otherwise it could fall out resulting in fluid spillage and possible damage. It may be necessary to rock the engine a little to release it from the transmission.
10 Once clear of the transmission lift the engine from the vehicle, taking care not to damage the radiator fins.

11 Engine/manual gearbox assembly - removal and separation

Note: *Refer to the warning in Section 8 before proceeding. A suitable hoist and lifting tackle will be required for this operation.*

Removal

1 Proceed as described in Section 9, paragraphs 1 to 17 inclusive.
2 Note the location of the earth strap on the rear inlet manifold stud, then remove the nut and disconnect the strap.
3 Working inside the vehicle, unscrew the gear lever knob and remove the centre console. Where a full length console is fitted, it is only necessary to remove the front tray.
4 Detach the outer gaiter from the retaining frame and withdraw it over the gear lever.
5 Unscrew the securing screws on early models, or release the clips on later models, and remove the gaiter retaining frame and inner gaiter.
6 Using a suitable Torx key, remove the screws securing the gear lever to the gearbox extension housing, and withdraw the gear lever. Note how the base of the gear lever locates over the selector shaft.
7 Jack up the vehicle and support on axle stands (see *"Jacking and Vehicle Support"*). Ensure that there is sufficient working room beneath the vehicle.
8 To improve access, disconnect the exhaust downpipe from the manifold and remove the exhaust system.
9 Remove the propeller shaft.
10 Where applicable bend back the locktabs, then unscrew the two bolts in each case securing the two anti-roll bar U-clamps to the vehicle underbody. Lower the anti-roll bar as far as possible.
11 Proceed as described in Section 9, paragraphs 27 and 28.
12 Drain the engine oil into a container.
13 Unscrew the nuts or bolts, as applicable, securing the engine mountings to the crossmember. Recover the washers.
14 Disconnect the wiring from the reversing lamp switch.
15 Remove the retaining circlip, and withdraw the speedometer cable from the gearbox extension housing.
16 Support the gearbox with a trolley jack, using a block of wood between the jack and the gearbox to spread the load.
17 Unscrew the four bolts securing the gearbox crossmember to the vehicle underbody. Unscrew the central bolt securing the crossmember to the gearbox and remove the crossmember. Note the position of the earth strap, where applicable. Recover the mounting cup and where applicable the exhaust mounting bracket and heat shield.
18 Make a final check to ensure that all relevant wires, pipes and hoses have been disconnected to facilitate removal of the engine/gearbox assembly.

11.20 Lifting the engine/gearbox assembly from the vehicle

19 Attach a suitable hoist to the engine lifting brackets located at the front and rear of the cylinder head. Arrange the lifting tackle so that the engine/gearbox assembly will assume a steep angle of approximately 40° to 45° as it is being removed.
20 Raise the engine/gearbox so that the engine mountings are clear of the crossmember, then ease the assembly forwards, at the same time lowering the trolley jack which is supporting the gearbox. Lift the assembly from the vehicle, taking care not to damage surrounding components **(see illustration)**.
21 With the engine/gearbox assembly removed, temporarily reconnect the anti-roll bar to the underbody if the vehicle is to be moved.

Separation

22 To separate the engine from the gearbox, proceed as follows.
23 Remove the starter motor.
24 Support the engine and gearbox horizontally on blocks of wood.
25 Unscrew the two securing bolts and disconnect the engine-to-gearbox brace from the engine and gearbox.
26 Unscrew and remove the engine-to-gearbox bolts, noting the location of the earth strap, and remove the bolt from the engine adapter plate.
27 Pull the engine and gearbox apart, taking care not to strain the gearbox input shaft. It may be necessary to rock the units slightly to separate them.

12 Engine/automatic transmission assembly - removal and separation

Note: *Refer to the warning in Section 8 before proceeding. A suitable hoist and lifting tackle will be required for this operation. Any suspected faults in the automatic transmission should be referred to a Ford dealer or automatic transmission specialist before removal of the unit, as the specialist fault diagnosis equipment is designed to operate with the transmission in the vehicle.*

Removal

1 Proceed as described in Section 9, paragraphs 1 to 17 inclusive, but additionally,

where applicable disconnect the kickdown cable from the carburettor/inlet manifold.

2 Note the location of the earth strap on the rear inlet manifold stud, then remove the nut and disconnect the strap.

3 Jack up the vehicle and support on axle stands (see "*Jacking and Vehicle Support*"). Ensure that there is sufficient working room beneath the vehicle.

4 To improve access, disconnect the exhaust downpipe from the manifold and remove the exhaust system.

5 Remove the propeller shaft.

6 Where applicable bend back the locktabs, then unscrew the two bolts, in each case securing the two anti-roll bar U-clamps to the vehicle underbody. Lower the anti-roll bar as far as possible.

7 Unscrew the unions and disconnect the fluid cooler pipes from the transmission. Plug the open ends of the pipes and the transmission to prevent dirt ingress and fluid leakage. Remove the fluid cooler pipe bracket from the engine mounting bracket, and place it to one side.

8 Remove the two clips securing the selector rod, and detach the selector rod from the manual selector lever, and the selector lever on the transmission.

9 Disconnect the kickdown cable from the lever on the transmission, and where applicable, detach the cable from the bracket on the transmission. On C3 type transmissions it will be necessary to unscrew the locknut in order to remove the cable from the bracket. Withdraw the cable from the vehicle.

10 Disconnect the wiring from the starter inhibitor/reversing lamp switch and where applicable, on A4LD type transmissions, the kickdown solenoid and the lock-up clutch.

11 Remove the securing screw, and disconnect the speedometer cable from the transmission extension housing. Plug the opening in the transmission to prevent dirt ingress.

12 Disconnect the vacuum pipe from the vacuum diaphragm unit, and unclip the pipe from its securing bracket on the transmission housing where applicable.

13 Drain the engine oil into a suitable container.

14 Unscrew the nuts or bolts, as applicable, securing the engine mountings to the crossmember. Recover the washers.

15 Support the transmission with a trolley jack, using a block of wood to spread the load.

16 Unscrew the four bolts securing the transmission crossmember to the vehicle underbody. Note the position of the earth strap, where applicable. Unscrew the central bolt securing the crossmember to the transmission and remove the crossmember. Recover the mounting cup and where applicable the exhaust mounting bracket.

17 Make a final check to ensure that all relevant wires, pipes and hoses have been disconnected to facilitate removal of the engine/transmission assembly.

18 Attach a suitable hoist to the engine lifting brackets located at the front and rear of the cylinder head. Arrange the lifting tackle so that the engine/transmission assembly will assume a steep angle of approximately 40° to 45° as it is being removed.

19 Raise the engine/transmission so that the engine mountings are clear of the crossmember, then ease the assembly forwards, at the same time lowering the trolley jack which is supporting the transmission. Lift the assembly from the vehicle, taking care not to damage surrounding components.

20 With the engine/transmission assembly removed, temporarily reconnect the anti-roll bar to the underbody if the vehicle is to be moved.

Separation

21 To separate the engine from the transmission, proceed as follows.

22 Remove the starter motor.

23 Support the engine and transmission horizontally on blocks of wood.

24 Working through the starter motor aperture, unscrew the four torque converter-to-driveplate nuts. It will be necessary to turn the crankshaft using a suitable spanner on the crankshaft pulley bolt in order to gain access to each nut in turn through the aperture.

25 Unscrew the two securing bolts and disconnect the engine-to-transmission brace from the engine and transmission.

26 Unscrew and remove the engine-to-transmission bolts, noting the locations of the earth strap, vacuum pipe bracket, and transmission dipstick tube bracket. Remove the bolt from the engine adapter plate, and where applicable pull the blanking plug from the adapter plate.

27 Pull the engine and transmission apart, ensuring that the torque converter is held firmly in place in the transmission housing, otherwise it could fall out resulting in fluid spillage and possible damage. It may be necessary to rock the units slightly to separate them.

13 Engine - refitting (manual gearbox in vehicle)

1 Reverse the procedure described in Section 9, noting the following points:

2 Before attempting to refit the engine, check that the clutch friction disc is centralised. This is necessary to ensure that the gearbox input shaft splines will pass through the splines in the centre of the friction disc.

3 Check that the clutch release arm and bearing are correctly fitted and lightly grease the input shaft splines.

4 Check that the engine adapter plate is correctly positioned on its locating dowels.

5 Refit the exhaust downpipe.

6 Reconnect the clutch cable to the release arm, ensuring that it is routed as noted during removal.

7 Fill the engine with the correct grade and quantity of oil.

8 Fill the cooling system.

9 Check and if necessary adjust the tension of the alternator and where applicable the power steering pump drivebelt(s).

10 Adjust the throttle cable.

14 Engine - refitting (automatic transmission in vehicle)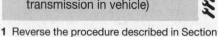

1 Reverse the procedure described in Section 10, noting the following points:

2 Check that the engine adapter plate is correctly positioned on its locating dowels.

3 As the torque converter is only loosely engaged in the transmission, care must be taken to prevent the torque converter from falling out forwards. When the torque converter hub is fully engaged with the fluid pump drivegear in the transmission, distance "A" in illustration 2.24 of Chapter 7B must be as specified. Incorrect installation of the torque converter will result in damage to the transmission.

4 As the engine is installed, guide the torque converter studs through the holes in the driveplate, noting that on the C3 type transmission, the torque converter fluid drain plug must line up with the opening in the driveplate (see illustration 2.25 in Chapter 7B). When the engine is positioned flush with the engine adapter plate and the transmission housing, check that the torque converter is free to move axially a small amount before refitting and tightening the engine-to-transmission bolts.

5 Do not tighten the torque converter-to-driveplate nuts until the lower engine-to-transmission bolts have been fitted and tightened.

6 Refit the exhaust downpipe.

7 Fill the engine with the correct grade and quantity of oil.

8 Fill the cooling system.

9 Check and if necessary adjust the tension of the alternator and where applicable the power steering pump drivebelt(s).

10 Adjust the throttle cable.

11 Where applicable, adjust the kickdown cable.

15 Engine/manual gearbox assembly - reconnection and refitting

1 Reverse the procedure described in Section 11, noting the following points.

2 Before attempting to reconnect the engine to the gearbox, check that the clutch friction disc is centralised. This is to ensure that the gearbox input shaft splines will pass through the splines in the centre of the friction disc.

3 Check that the clutch release arm and bearing are correctly fitted, and lightly grease the input shaft splines.

17.4 Withdrawing an engine mounting

4 Check that the engine adapter plate is correctly positioned on its locating dowels.
5 Refit the propeller shaft.
6 Refit the exhaust system.
7 Reconnect the clutch cable to the release arm, ensuring that it is routed as noted during removal.
8 Fill the engine with the correct grade and quantity of oil.
9 Fill the cooling system.
10 Check and if necessary top-up the gearbox oil level.
11 Check and if necessary adjust the tension of the alternator and where applicable the power steering pump drivebelt(s).
12 Adjust the throttle cable.

16 Engine/automatic transmission assembly - reconnection and refitting

1 Reverse the removal procedure described in Section 12, noting the following points.
2 Check that the engine adapter plate is correctly positioned on its locating dowels.
3 As the torque converter is only loosely engaged in the transmission, care must be taken to prevent the torque converter from falling out forwards. When the torque converter hub is fully engaged with the fluid pump drivegear in the transmission, distance "A" in illustration 2.24 of Chapter 7B must be as shown. Incorrect installation of the torque converter will result in damage to the transmission.
4 As the engine and transmission are reconnected, guide the torque converter studs through the holes in the driveplate, noting that on the C3 type transmission, the torque converter fluid drain plug must line up with the opening in the driveplate (see illustration 2.25 in Chapter 7B). When the engine is positioned flush with the engine adapter plate and the transmission housing, check that the torque converter is free to move axially a small amount before refitting and tightening the engine-to-transmission bolts.
5 Do not tighten the torque converter-to-driveplate nuts until the lower engine-to-transmission bolts have been fitted and tightened.
6 Reconnect and adjust the selector rod.
7 Refit the propeller shaft.

8 Refit the exhaust system.
9 Fill the engine with the correct grade and quantity of oil.
10 Fill the cooling system.
11 Check and if necessary top-up the transmission fluid level.
12 Check and if necessary adjust the tension of the alternator and where applicable the power steering pump drivebelt(s).
13 Adjust the throttle cable.
14 If applicable, adjust the kickdown cable.

17 Engine mountings - renewal

1 The engine mountings incorporate hydraulic dampers and must be renewed if excessive engine movement is evident.
2 Working in the engine compartment, unscrew the central nuts securing the engine mounting brackets to the tops of the mountings. Recover the washers where applicable.
3 Remove the two bolts or the central nut and washer (as applicable) in each case securing the mountings to the crossmember.
4 Raise the engine using a hoist and lifting tackle attached to the engine lifting brackets on the cylinder head, or a jack with an interposed block of wood under the sump, until the mountings can be withdrawn (see illustration).
5 Fit the new mountings, then lower the engine onto them.
6 Fit the bolts or the nuts and washers (as applicable) securing the mountings to the crossmember, and tighten them.
7 Fit and tighten the central nuts, and washers if applicable, securing the engine mounting brackets to the tops of the mountings.

18 Engine dismantling, examination, renovation and reassembly - general information

Dismantling

1 It is best to mount the engine on a dismantling stand but if this is not available, stand the engine on a strong bench at a comfortable working height. Failing this, it will have to be stripped down on the floor.
2 Cleanliness is most important, and if the

engine is dirty, it should be cleaned with paraffin while keeping it in an upright position.
3 Avoid working with the engine directly on a concrete floor, as grit presents a real source of trouble.
4 As parts are removed, clean them in a paraffin bath. However, do not immerse parts with internal oilways in paraffin as it is difficult to remove, usually requiring a high pressure hose. Clean oilways with nylon pipe cleaners.
5 It is advisable to have suitable containers available to hold small items according to their use, as this will help when reassembling the engine and also prevent possible losses.
6 Always obtain a complete set of new gaskets for use during engine reassembly, but retain the old gaskets with a view to using them as a pattern to make a replacement if a new one is not available.
7 Where possible, refit securing nuts, bolts and washers to their locations after removing the relevant components. This will help to protect the threads and will also prevent losses.
8 Retain unserviceable components in order to compare them with the new parts supplied.
9 Suitable splined sockets will be required for removal of the oil pump bolts, the timing belt tensioner bolts on early models (up to mid-1985), and the cylinder head bolts on early models (up to early 1984) and a size T55 Torx socket will be required to remove the cylinder head bolts on later models (from early 1984).
10 Before dismantling the main engine components the following externally mounted ancillary components can be removed, with reference to the relevant Chapters of this Manual and the relevant Sections of this Chapter, where applicable:

Inlet manifold (and carburettor, where applicable)
Exhaust manifold
Fuel pump and operating pushrod (where applicable)
Alternator
Distributor, HT leads and spark plug
Coolant pump, thermostat and housing
Temperature gauge sender and oil pressure warning lamp switch
Oil filter
Dipstick
Engine mounting brackets (see illustration)
Crankcase ventilation valve and oil separator
Clutch
Alternator mounting bracket (see illustration)

2A

18.10a Removing the right-hand engine mounting bracket

18.10b Removing the alternator mounting bracket

19.3 TDC pointer on camshaft sprocket backplate aligned with indentation on cylinder head

19.4 Loosening the timing belt tensioner spring bolt using a splined socket - models up to mid-1985

19.5 Timing belt tensioner bolts (arrowed) - models from mid-1985

Examination and renovation

11 With the engine completely stripped, clean all the components and examine them for wear. Each part should be checked, and where necessary renewed or renovated as described in the relevant Sections. Renew main and big end shell bearings as a matter of course, unless it is known that they have had little wear and are in perfect condition.

12 If in doubt as to whether to renew a component which is still just serviceable, consider the time and effort which will be incurred should it fail at an early date. Obviously the age and expected life of the vehicle must influence the standards applied.

13 Gaskets, oil seals and O-rings must all be renewed as a matter of routine. Flywheel and Torx type cylinder head bolts must be renewed because of the high stresses to which they are subjected.

14 Take the opportunity to renew the engine core plugs while they are easily accessible. Knock out the old plugs with a hammer and chisel or punch. Clean the plug seats, smear the new plugs with sealant and tap them squarely into position.

Reassembly

15 To ensure maximum life with minimum trouble from a rebuilt engine, not only must everything be correctly assembled, but it must also be spotlessly clean. All oilways must be clear, and locking washers and spring washers must be fitted where indicated. Oil all bearings and other working surfaces thoroughly with clean engine oil during assembly.

16 Before assembly begins, renew any bolts or studs with damaged threads.

17 Gather together a torque wrench, oil can, clean rag, and a set of engine gaskets and oil seals, together with a new oil filter.

18 If they have been removed, new Torx type cylinder head bolts and new flywheel bolts will be required.

19 After reassembling the main engine components, refit the ancillary components listed, referring to the appropriate Chapters where necessary. Delicate items such as the alternator and distributor may be left until after the engine has been refitted if preferred.

20 If the crankcase ventilation oil separator was removed, apply a liquid sealing agent to its tube before pressing it into the cylinder block.

19 Timing belt and sprockets - removal and refitting

Note: *Refer to the warning in Section 8 before proceeding. On models from mid-1985 (without a timing belt tensioner spring) the belt tension should be checked using Ford special tool No 21-113 after refitting. On models up to mid-1985 (with a tensioner spring), a suitable splined socket will be required for the tensioner spring bolt. A suitable puller may be required to remove the sprockets.*

Removal

1 If the engine is in the vehicle, carry out the following operations:
   a) *Disconnect the battery negative lead*
   b) *Remove the thermo-viscous cooling fan*
   c) *Remove the coolant pump/alternator/power-steering pump drivebelt(s)*
   d) *For improved access, remove the radiator and disconnect the radiator top hose from the thermostat housing*

2 Unscrew the three securing bolts and washers and withdraw the timing cover. Note the position of the fourth bolt above the crankshaft pulley which can be left in place.

3 Using a socket on the crankshaft pulley bolt, turn the engine clockwise until the TDC (top dead centre) mark on the crankshaft pulley is aligned with the pointer on the crankshaft front oil seal housing (see illustration 16.2a of Chapter 5) and the pointer on the camshaft sprocket backplate is aligned with the indentation on the cylinder head **(see illustration)**.

4 On models up to mid-1985 (with a tensioner spring), loosen the timing belt tensioner spring bolt using the special splined socket **(see illustration)**, then loosen the tensioner pivot bolt. If necessary for improved access, remove the thermostat housing. Press the tensioner against the spring tension and tighten the pivot bolt to retain the tensioner in the released position.

5 On models from mid-1985 (without a tensioner spring), loosen the timing belt tensioner bolts **(see illustration)** and move the tensioner away from the belt. If necessary to improve access, remove the thermostat housing.

6 Mark the running direction of the belt if it is to be re-used, then slip it off the camshaft sprocket.

7 Slacken the crankshaft pulley bolt. Prevent the crankshaft from turning by engaging top gear (manual gearbox only) and having an assistant apply the brake pedal hard, or by removing the starter motor and jamming the ring gear teeth with a lever. Alternatively, if the pulley has peripheral bolt holes, screw in a couple of bolts and use a lever between them to jam it. Do not allow the crankshaft to turn very far, or piston/valve contact may occur.

8 Remove the bolt and washer and withdraw the pulley. If the pulley will not come off easily, refit the bolt part way and use a puller **(see illustration)**. A puller will almost certainly be required on fuel-injection models.

9 Remove the guide washer from in front of the crankshaft sprocket, then remove the timing belt **(see illustration)**. Do not kink it or get oil on it if it is to be re-used.

10 If desired, the sprocket can be removed as follows, otherwise proceed to paragraph 21.

11 Remove the crankshaft sprocket, refitting the bolt part way and using a puller if necessary **(see illustration)**.

12 Unscrew the auxiliary shaft sprocket bolt while holding the sprocket stationary with a screwdriver inserted through one of the holes.

19.8 Using a puller to remove a pressed type crankshaft pulley

19.9 Removing the guide washer from the crankshaft

19.11 Removing the crankshaft sprocket

19.13 Removing the auxiliary shaft sprocket

13 Remove the auxiliary shaft sprocket, refitting the bolt part way and using a puller if necessary **(see illustration)**.

14 Hold the camshaft sprocket stationary using a home-made tool similar to that shown (in illustration 18.17 in Part C of this Chapter) with two bolts engaged in the sprocket holes, and unscrew the bolt and washer. Alternatively, remove the camshaft cover and hold the camshaft using a spanner on the boss behind the No 6 valve cam.

15 Remove the camshaft sprocket, refitting the bolt part way and using a puller if necessary, then remove the backplate, noting which way round it is fitted **(see illustrations)**.

16 If desired, the camshaft oil seal can be removed using self-tapping screws and a pair of grips. A new seal can be fitted using a suitable tube drift to press it into place. Lubricate the seal lips with clean engine oil before installation.

Refitting

17 Refit the sprockets as follows.

18 Fit the camshaft sprocket backplate, as noted during removal, then fit the sprocket. Insert the bolt, hold the camshaft or sprocket

as during removal, and tighten the bolt to the specified torque. Where applicable, refit the camshaft cover.

19 Fit the auxiliary shaft sprocket with the ribs towards the engine. Fit the sprocket bolt and tighten it to the specified torque, counterholding the sprocket with a bar through one of the holes.

20 Fit the crankshaft sprocket, chamfered side inwards.

21 Fit the timing belt over the crankshaft sprocket, but do not engage it with the other sprockets yet. Be careful not to kink the belt. If the old belt is being refitted, observe the previously noted running direction.

22 Refit the guide washer and the crankshaft pulley. Fit the bolt and washer and tighten just enough to seat the pulley, being careful not to turn the crankshaft.

23 Make sure that the TDC pointer on the camshaft sprocket backplate is still aligned with the indentation on the cylinder head.

24 Make sure that the TDC mark on the crankshaft pulley is still aligned with the pointer on the oil seal housing. If necessary, turn the crankshaft by the shortest possible

route to align the marks.

25 If the distributor is fitted, turn the auxiliary shaft sprocket so that the rotor arm points to the No 1 HT segment position in the distributor cap.

26 Fit the timing belt over the sprockets and round the tensioner.

27 On models up to mid-1985 (with a tensioner spring), slacken the pivot bolt, and allow the tensioner roller to rest against the belt. Using a socket on the crankshaft pulley bolt, turn the crankshaft through two complete revolutions in a clockwise direction, to bring No 1 cylinder back to TDC. Tighten the tensioner pivot bolt and then the spring bolt to the specified torque. Do not turn the crankshaft anti-clockwise with the belt tensioner released. Proceed to paragraph 33.

28 On models from mid-1985 (without a tensioner spring), move the tensioner to tension the belt roughly and nip up the tensioner bolts. Using a socket on the crankshaft pulley bolt, turn the crankshaft through two complete revolutions in a clockwise direction (to bring No 1 cylinder back to TDC), then turn the crankshaft 60°

2A

19.15a Removing the camshaft sprocket . . .

19.15b . . . and backplate

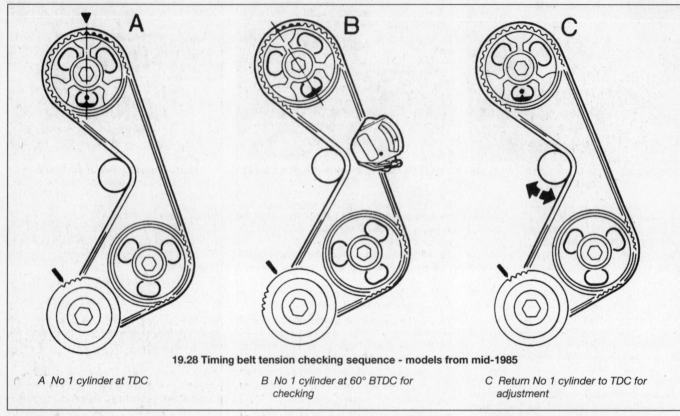

19.28 Timing belt tension checking sequence - models from mid-1985

A No 1 cylinder at TDC	B No 1 cylinder at 60° BTDC for checking	C Return No 1 cylinder to TDC for adjustment

anti-clockwise (No 1 cylinder at 60° BTDC) **(see illustration)**.

29 The belt tension should now be checked by applying Ford tension gauge, tool No 21-113 to the longest belt run. Desired gauge readings are:

Used belt - 4 to 5
New belt - 10 to 11

If the tension gauge is not available, a rough guide is that the belt tension is correct when the belt can be twisted 90° in the middle of the longest run with the fingers, using moderate pressure **(see illustration)**. In this case, the vehicle should be taken to a Ford dealer so that the belt tension can be checked using the special gauge at the earliest opportunity.

30 If adjustment of belt tension is necessary, turn the crankshaft clockwise to bring No 1 cylinder to TDC, then slacken the tensioner

bolts and move the tensioner to increase or decrease the belt tension. Tighten the tensioner bolts to the specified torque.

31 Turn the crankshaft 90° clockwise past TDC, then anti-clockwise back to the 60° BTDC position (No 1 cylinder at 60° BTDC). Check the belt tension again.

32 Repeat the procedure given in paragraphs 30 and 31 until the belt tension is correct.

33 Tighten the crankshaft pulley bolt to the specified torque, preventing the crankshaft from turning as described in paragraph 7 **(see illustration)**.

34 Refit the timing cover and tighten its bolts.

35 If the engine is in the vehicle, reverse the operations described in paragraph 1.

36 When the engine is next started, check the ignition timing is correct.

20 Cylinder head - removal and refitting (engine in vehicle)

Note: *Refer to the warning in Section 8 and the note at the beginning of Section 21 before proceeding.*

Removal

1 Disconnect the battery negative lead.

2 Drain the cooling system.

3 Disconnect the coolant hose from the thermostat housing.

4 Disconnect the wiring from the temperature gauge sender.

5 Disconnect the HT leads from the spark plugs and from the clips on the camshaft cover and remove the spark plugs.

6 On carburettor models, remove the air cleaner.

7 The cylinder head can be removed either with or without the manifolds. If desired, the inlet manifold can be unbolted and moved to one side, leaving the wires, hoses, pipes and cables connected, but care must be taken not to strain any of the wires, hoses, pipes or cables.

8 Unscrew the three securing nuts and disconnect the exhaust downpipe from the manifold flange. Recover the gasket.

9 Disconnect the coolant hose from the clip on the exhaust manifold hot air shroud, and if desired, remove the exhaust manifold.

10 If the inlet manifold is to be removed with the cylinder head, disconnect all relevant

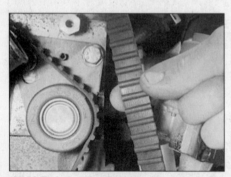

19.29 Twisting the timing belt to assess its tension

19.33 Holding a pressed type crankshaft pulley with two bolts and a lever while tightening the bolt

---

21.11 Fitting a new cylinder head gasket

wires, hoses, pipes and cables, otherwise, unbolt the manifold and move it to one side, ensuring that it is adequately supported.
11 If not already done, unclip any wires and hoses from the camshaft cover, noting their locations for use when refitting, and on fuel injection models unbolt the bracing strut securing the inlet manifold to the right-hand side of the cylinder head.
12 If desired, remove the thermostat and housing, and the temperature gauge sender.
13 Proceed as described in Section 21 for cylinder head removal.

Refitting

14 With the cylinder head refitted as described in Section 21, proceed as follows.
15 Where applicable, refit the temperature gauge sender and the thermostat and housing.
16 Refit the manifolds and/or reconnect all wires, hoses, pipes and cables, as applicable.
17 Reconnect the exhaust downpipe to the manifold, using a new gasket.
18 Refit the coolant hose to the clip on the exhaust manifold hot air shroud.
19 Refit the spark plugs and reconnect the HT leads.
20 Reconnect the temperature gauge sender wiring.
21 Reconnect the coolant hoses to the thermostat housing.
22 Fill the cooling system.
23 If not already done, refit any hoses and wires to the camshaft cover, as noted during removal, and on fuel injection models refit the inlet manifold bracing strut. If splined type cylinder head bolts have been used, leave these operations until the bolts have been finally tightened after running the engine.
24 Refit the air cleaner on carburettor models.
25 Reconnect the battery negative lead.
26 If splined type cylinder head bolts have been used, start the engine and run it at 1000 rpm for 15 minutes, then stop the engine, remove the air cleaner and the camshaft cover as described previously, and finally tighten the cylinder head bolts to the fourth stage (see Specifications). Refit the camshaft cover on completion, then refit any hoses and wires, and on fuel injection models the inlet manifold bracing strut. Refit the air cleaner.

21 Cylinder head - removal and refitting (engine removed)

HAYNES HiNT *Tap a stuck cylinder head free with a wooden mallet. Do not insert a lever into the head joint as this may damage the mating faces.*

Note: *Up to early 1984, splined type cylinder head bolts were used, and from early 1984, size TSS Torx bolts were used. Torx type bolts must always be renewed after slackening. The two types of bolts are interchangeable, but only in complete sets - the two types must not be mixed on the same engine. A suitable special socket will be required for removal of the bolts, and a new cylinder head gasket must be used when refitting.*

Removal

1 With the manifolds removed, proceed as follows.
2 Remove the timing belt.
3 Where applicable, disconnect the breather hose from the camshaft cover.
4 Unscrew the ten securing bolts and remove the camshaft cover and gasket. Take care not to lose the spacer plates which fit under the bolt heads, where applicable.
5 Using the relevant special socket, unscrew the ten cylinder head bolts half a turn at a time in the reverse order to that shown for tightening.
6 With the bolts removed, lift the cylinder head from the block. If the cylinder head is stuck, tap it free with a wooden mallet. Place the cylinder head on blocks of wood to prevent damage to the valves.
7 Recover the gasket.

Refitting

8 Commence refitting as follows.
9 With the cylinder head supported on blocks of wood, check and if necessary adjust the

valve clearances. This work is easier to carry out on the bench rather than in the vehicle.
10 Turn the crankshaft so that No 1 piston is approximately 20 mm (0.8 in) before TDC. This precaution will prevent any damage to open valves.
11 Make sure that the mating faces of the cylinder block and cylinder head are perfectly clean, then locate the new gasket on the block making sure that all the internal holes are aligned **(see illustration)**. *Do not use jointing compound.*
12 Turn the camshaft so that the TDC pointer on the camshaft sprocket backplate is aligned with the indentation on the front of the cylinder head.
13 Lower the cylinder head onto the gasket. The help of an assistant will ensure that the gasket is not dislodged.
14 Lightly oil the cylinder head bolt threads and heads, then insert the bolts into their locations in the cylinder head. Note that if the original bolts were of the Torx type, new bolts must be used when refitting.
15 Using the relevant special socket, tighten the bolts in the correct sequence **(see illustration)** to the stages given in the Specifications. *Note that the bolt tightening stages are different for splined and Torx type bolts. If splined type bolts are used, they must be finally tightened to the fourth stage after the engine has been run for 15 minutes (see Specifications).*
16 Check the condition of the camshaft cover gasket and renew if necessary. Fit the gasket to the camshaft cover, ensuring that the locating tabs and dovetails are correctly located, then refit the camshaft cover and tighten the securing bolts in the order shown (see Chapter 1, Section 23), ensuring that the spacer plates are in position under the bolt heads, where applicable.
17 Where applicable, reconnect the breather hose to the camshaft cover.
18 Refit the timing belt.

2A

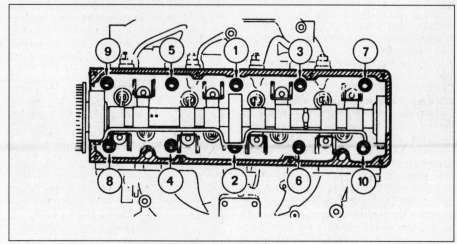

21.15 Cylinder head bolt tightening sequence

22.2a Compressing a valve spring

22.2b Removing a valve spring and cap

22.2c Removing a valve

22 Cylinder head - dismantling and reassembly

Note: *A valve spring compressor will be required during this procedure. New valve stem oil seals should be used on reassembly.*

Dismantling

1 With the cylinder head removed, remove the camshaft.

2 Using a valve spring compressor, compress one of the valve springs until the split collets can be removed from the groove in the valve stem. Release the compressor and remove the cap and spring, identifying them for location. If the cap is difficult to release, do not continue to tighten the compressor, but gently tap the top of the tool with a hammer. Always make sure that the compressor is firmly located on the valve head and the cap. Withdraw the valve **(see illustrations)**.

3 Repeat the procedure given in paragraph 2 for the remaining valves, keeping all components identified for location so that they can be refitted in their original positions.

4 Prise the valve stem oil seals from the tops of the valve guides **(see illustration)**.

5 Unscrew the cam follower ball-pins from the cylinder head, keeping them identified for location.

Reassembly

6 Commence reassembly by refitting the cam follower ball-pins to their original locations, where applicable.

7 Lubricate the valve stems and guides with SAE 80/90 hypoid oil, then insert the valves into their original guides.

8 Wrap a thin layer of adhesive tape over the collet groove of each valve, then smear the new oil seals with a little SAE 80/90 hypoid oil and slide them down the valve stems onto the guides. If necessary use a suitable metal tube to press the oil seals into the guides. Remove the adhesive tape.

9 Working on each valve in turn, fit the valve spring and cap, then compress the spring using the valve spring compressor and fit the split collets to the groove in the valve stem. Release the compressor and tap the end of the valve stem with a soft-faced mallet to

settle the components. If the original components are being refitted, ensure that they are refitted in their original locations.

10 Refit the camshaft.

23 Cylinder head - inspection and renovation

Note: *On engines fitted with hardened valve seats for use with unleaded petrol, valve and valve seat grinding and recutting cannot be carried out without the use of specialist equipment. Consult a Ford dealer for further advice.*

1 This operation will normally only be required at comparatively high mileages. However, if persistent pre-ignition ("pinking") occurs and performance has deteriorated even though the engine adjustments are correct, de-carbonizing and valve grinding may be required.

2 With the cylinder head removed, use a scraper to remove the carbon from the combustion chambers and ports. Remove all traces of gasket from the cylinder head surface, then wash it thoroughly with paraffin.

3 Use a straight edge and feeler blade to check that the cylinder head surface is not distorted. If it is, it must be resurfaced by a suitably equipped engineering works.

4 If the engine is still in the vehicle, clean the piston crowns and cylinder bore upper edges, but make sure that no carbon drops between the pistons and bores. To do this, locate two of the pistons at the top of their bores and seal off the remaining bores with paper and

22.4 Removing a valve stem oil seal

masking tape. Press a little grease between the two pistons and their bores to collect any carbon dust; this can be wiped away when the piston is lowered. To prevent carbon build-up, polish the piston crown with metal polish, but remove all traces of the polish afterwards.

5 Examine the heads of the valves for pitting and burning, especially the exhaust valve heads. Renew any valve which is badly burnt. Examine the valve seats at the same time. If the pitting is very slight, it can be removed by grinding the valve heads and seats together with coarse, then fine, grinding paste.

6 Where excessive pitting has occurred, the valve seats must be recut or renewed by a suitably equipped engineering works.

7 Valve grinding is carried out as follows. Place the cylinder head upside down on a bench on blocks of wood.

8 Smear a trace of coarse carborundum paste on the valve seat face and press a suction grinding tool onto the valve head. With a semi-rotary action, grind the valve head to its seat, lifting the valve occasionally to redistribute the grinding paste. When a dull matt even surface is produced on the mating surface of both the valve seat and the valve, wipe off the paste and repeat the process with fine carborundum paste as before. A light spring placed under the valve head will greatly ease this operation. When a smooth unbroken ring of light grey matt finish is produced on the mating surface of both the valve and seat, the grinding operation is complete.

9 Scrape away all carbon from the valve head and stem, and clean away all traces of grinding compound. Clean the valves and seats with a paraffin soaked rag, then wipe with a clean rag.

10 If the guides are worn they will need reboring for oversize valves or for fitting guide inserts. The valve seats will also need recutting to ensure that they are concentric with the stems. This work should be entrusted to a Ford dealer or local engineering works.

11 Check that the free length of the valve springs is as specified, and renew if necessary. Do not renew individual springs; if any springs are excessively worn, renew all the springs as a set.

24.4 Withdrawing the camshaft oil supply tube

24.5 Note how the cam follower retaining springs are fitted

24.6 Removing a cam follower

24 Camshaft and cam followers - removal, inspection and refitting

Note: *A new camshaft oil seal should be used when refitting the camshaft.*

Removal

1 Remove the cylinder head.
2 Hold the camshaft stationary using a suitable spanner on the cast boss behind the No 6 valve cam, and unscrew the camshaft sprocket bolt and washer.
3 Remove the camshaft sprocket, using a suitable puller if necessary, and withdraw the sprocket backplate, noting which way round it is fitted.
4 Remove the three securing bolts and

24.7 Unscrew the securing bolts and remove the camshaft thrustplate

withdraw the camshaft oil supply tube **(see illustration)**.
5 Note how the cam follower retaining springs are fitted, then unhook them from the cam followers **(see illustration)**.
6 Loosen the locknuts and back off the ball-pin adjuster nuts until the cam followers can be removed **(see illustration)**. Note their locations for use when refitting. It will be necessary to rotate the camshaft during this operation.
7 Unscrew the two bolts and remove the camshaft thrustplate from the rear bearing housing **(see illustration)**.
8 Carefully withdraw the camshaft from the rear of the cylinder head taking care not to damage the bearings **(see illustration)**.
9 Prise the oil seal from the front bearing in the cylinder head **(see illustration)**.

Inspection

10 Examine the surfaces of the camshaft journals and lobes, and the cam followers for wear. If wear is excessive, considerable noise would have been noticed from the top of the engine when running, and a new camshaft and followers must be fitted.
11 Check the camshaft bearings for wear, and if necessary have them renewed by a Ford dealer.
12 Check the camshaft oil supply tube for obstructions, making sure the jet holes are clear.

Refitting

13 Commence refitting by driving a new oil seal into the cylinder head front bearing, using

a suitable tube drift or socket **(see illustration)**. Smear the seal lip with clean engine oil.
14 Lubricate the camshaft, bearings and thrustplate with SAE 80/90 hypoid oil, then carefully insert the camshaft from the rear of the cylinder head, taking care not to damage the bearings.
15 Locate the thrustplate in the camshaft groove, then insert and tighten the bolts.
16 Using a dial test indicator if available, or feeler blades, check that the camshaft endfloat is within the limits given in the Specifications. If not, renew the thrustplate and re-check. If this does not bring the endfloat within limits, the camshaft must be renewed.
17 Lubricate the ball-pins with SAE 80/90 hypoid oil, then refit the cam followers to their original locations, and refit the retaining springs as noted during removal. It will be necessary to rotate the camshaft during this operation.
18 Fit the oil supply tube and tighten the bolts.
19 Fit the camshaft sprocket backplate, as noted during removal.
20 Fit the camshaft sprocket, then insert and tighten the bolt (with washer in place) to the specified torque, holding the camshaft stationary as described in paragraph 2.
21 With the cylinder head supported on blocks of wood, adjust the valve clearances. This work is easier to carry out on the bench rather than in the vehicle.
22 Refit the cylinder head.

2A

24.8 Withdrawing the camshaft

24.9 Prising out the camshaft oil seal

24.13 Fitting a new camshaft oil seal using a socket

25.4 Unscrew the auxiliary shaft cover securing bolts and remove the cover

25.5a Unscrew the auxiliary shaft thrustplate securing screws and remove the thrustplate

25.5b Withdraw the auxiliary shaft

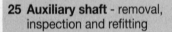
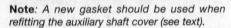

25 Auxiliary shaft - removal, inspection and refitting

Note: *A new gasket should be used when refitting the auxiliary shaft cover (see text).*

Removal

1 Remove the timing belt and the auxiliary shaft sprocket.

2 Remove the distributor.

3 Remove the mechanical fuel pump and operating pushrod (where applicable).

4 Unscrew the three securing bolts and remove the auxiliary shaft cover **(see illustration)**.

5 Unscrew the cross-head screws, using an impact screwdriver if necessary, remove the thrustplate and withdraw the auxiliary shaft from the cylinder block **(see illustrations)**.

6 Cut the cover gasket along the top of the crankshaft front oil seal housing and scrape off the gasket.

Inspection

7 Examine the shaft for wear and damage, and renew it if necessary.

8 If desired, the oil seal in the cover can be renewed as follows.

9 Support the cover on blocks of wood and drive out the old oil seal. Drive the new seal into place using a suitable metal tube or socket **(see illustrations)**. The sealing lip must face towards the cylinder block. Smear the sealing lip with clean engine oil before installation.

Refitting

10 Commence refitting by lubricating the auxiliary shaft journals with clean engine oil, then insert the shaft into the cylinder block.

11 Locate the thrustplate in the shaft groove, then insert the crosshead screws and tighten them with an impact screwdriver.

12 Using a dial test indicator (if available), or feeler blades, check that the auxiliary shaft endfloat is within the limits given in the Specifications. If not, renew the thrustplate and re-check. If this does not bring the endfloat within limits, the auxiliary shaft must be renewed.

13 Cut out the relevant section of a new gasket, and locate it on the cylinder block, then refit the auxiliary shaft cover and tighten the securing bolts.

14 Where applicable, refit the fuel pump.

15 Refit the distributor.

16 Refit the auxiliary shaft sprocket and the timing belt.

26 Flywheel/driveplate - removal, inspection and refitting

Note: *The manufacturers recommend that the flywheel/driveplate securing bolts are renewed after slackening. Suitable thread-locking agent will be required to coat the bolt threads.*

Removal

1 If the engine is in the vehicle, remove the clutch or the automatic transmission, as applicable.

2 Prevent the flywheel/driveplate from turning by jamming the ring gear teeth or by bolting a strap between the flywheel/driveplate and the cylinder block.

3 Make alignment marks on the flywheel/driveplate and the end of the crankshaft, so that the flywheel/driveplate can be refitted in its original position.

4 Unscrew the securing bolts and withdraw the flywheel/driveplate. *Do not drop it, it is very heavy.* Note that on models with A4LD type automatic transmission, the driveplate may be secured with one or two reinforcing plates depending on model.

5 The engine adapter plate may now be withdrawn from the dowels if required **(see illustration)**.

Inspection

6 With the flywheel/driveplate removed, the ring gear can be examined for wear and damage.

7 If the ring gear is badly worn or has missing teeth it should be renewed. The old ring can be removed from the flywheel/driveplate by cutting a notch between two teeth with a hacksaw and then splitting it with a cold chisel. Wear eye protection when doing this.

8 Fitting of a new ring gear requires heating the ring to 400°F (204°C). This can be done by polishing four equally spaced sections of the gear, laying it on a heat resistant surface (such as fire bricks) and heating it evenly with a blow lamp or torch until the polished areas turn a light yellow tinge. Do not overheat, or the hard wearing properties will be lost. The gear has a

25.9a Driving out the auxiliary shaft cover oil seal

25.9b Using a socket to fit a new auxiliary shaft cover oil seal

26.5 Withdrawing the engine adaptor plate

26.10 Flywheel located on crankshaft

26.12 Use a strap to prevent the flywheel turning as its securing bolts are tightened

chamfered inner edge which should fit against the shoulder on the flywheel. When hot enough, place the gear in position quickly, tapping it home if necessary, and let it cool naturally without quenching in any way.

Refitting

9 Commence refitting of the flywheel/driveplate by refitting the engine adapter plate to the dowels on the rear of the cylinder block, where applicable.

10 Ensure that the mating faces are clean, then locate the flywheel/driveplate on the rear of the crankshaft, aligning the previously made marks **(see illustration)**.

11 Coat the threads of the securing bolts with a liquid thread-locking agent, then insert the bolts. Note that the manufacturers recommend the use of new bolts. Where applicable refit the reinforcing plate(s) on models with A4LD type automatics

12 Prevent the flywheel/driveplate from turning as described in paragraph 2, then tighten the securing bolts to the specified torque in a diagonal sequence **(see illustration)**.

13 If the engine is in the vehicle, refit the clutch or the automatic transmission, as applicable.

27 Crankshaft front oil seal - renewal

Note: *A new gasket will be required for refitting if the old seal housing is removed during this procedure.*

1 Remove the timing belt and the crankshaft sprocket.

2 If an oil seal removal tool is available, the oil seal can be removed at this stage. It may also be possible to remove the oil seal by drilling

the outer face and using self-tapping screws and a pair of grips.

3 If the oil seal cannot be removed as described in paragraph 2, remove the sump and the auxiliary shaft sprocket, then unbolt the oil seal housing and the auxiliary shaft front cover. Recover the gasket. The oil seal can then be driven out from the inside of the housing **(see illustrations)**.

4 Clean the oil seal housing, then drive in a new seal using a suitable metal tube or socket. Make sure that the seal lip faces into the engine and lightly smear the lip with clean engine oil **(see illustration)**.

5 Where applicable, refit the oil seal housing and the auxiliary shaft front cover, using a new gasket, and tighten the bolts. Using a straight edge, ensure that the bottom face of the oil seal housing is aligned with the bottom face of the cylinder block before finally tightening the bolts **(see illustrations)**. Refit the auxiliary shaft sprocket and refit the sump.

6 Refit the crankshaft sprocket and timing belt.

28 Crankshaft rear oil seal - renewal

1 Remove the flywheel/driveplate and the engine adapter plate.

2 Extract the oil seal using an oil seal removal tool if available. It may also be possible to remove the oil seal by drilling the outer face and using self-tapping screws and a pair of grips **(see illustration)**.

2A

27.3a Removing the crankshaft front oil seal housing

27.3b Driving the crankshaft front oil seal from the housing

27.4 Using a socket to fit a new crankshaft front oil seal

27.5a Crankshaft front oil seal housing/auxiliary shaft cover gasket located on front of cylinder block

27.5b Checking the alignment of the crankshaft front oil seal housing

28.2 Crankshaft rear oil seal location (arrowed)

29.9a Make up wooden blocks to fit the front suspension turrets and support a metal bar . . .

3 Clean the oil seal housing, then drive in a new seal using a suitable metal tube or socket. Make sure that the seal lip faces into the engine and lightly smear the lip with clean engine oil.
4 Refit the engine adapter plate and the flywheel/driveplate.

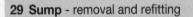

29 Sump - removal and refitting

Note: *New gaskets and sealing strips will be required for refitting, and sealing compound will be required to coat the gasket faces.*

Removal

1 If the engine is in the vehicle, proceed as follows, otherwise proceed to paragraph 12.
2 Disconnect the battery negative lead.

29.11a Lower the suspension . . .

29.12 Unscrew the securing bolts and withdraw the sump

29.9b . . . which will support the engine

3 Apply the handbrake, jack up the front of the vehicle and support on axle stands (see "*Jacking and Vehicle Support*").
4 Drain the engine oil into a container.
5 Remove the starter motor, if necessary.
6 Unscrew the nuts or bolts, as applicable, securing the engine mountings to the crossmember.
7 Working in the engine compartment, unscrew the bolt securing the intermediate shaft to the steering column, swivel the clamp plate to one side, and disconnect the intermediate shaft.
8 Where applicable, detach the brake lines from the crossmember.
9 Support the engine using a hoist, or a bar and blocks of wood resting on the suspension turrets **(see illustrations)**. Attach the lifting tackle to the engine lifting brackets on the cylinder head. If using a support bar, the engine may be lifted slightly by using the bar

29.11b . . . to give sufficient clearance for sump removal

29.15a Apply sealing compound . . .

29.10 Unscrew the front crossmember securing bolts

as a lever before resting it on the wooden blocks.
10 Support the front crossmember with a trolley jack, then unscrew the bolts securing the crossmember to the underbody **(see illustration)**.
11 Lower the crossmember just enough to give sufficient clearance to remove the sump **(see illustrations)**.
12 Unscrew the twenty-three securing bolts and withdraw the sump **(see illustration)**. If the sump is stuck, carefully tap it sideways to free it. Do not prise between the mating faces. Note that if the engine has been removed, it is preferable to keep the engine upright until the sump has been removed to prevent sludge from entering the engine internals.
13 Recover the gaskets and sealing strips.
14 Thoroughly clean the mating faces of the cylinder block and sump.

Refitting

15 Commence refitting by applying sealing compound (available from a Ford dealer) to the corners of the front and rear rubber sealing strip locations in the cylinder block, then press the sealing strips into the grooves in the rear main bearing cap and the crankshaft front oil seal housing **(see illustrations)**.
16 Apply a little sealing compound to the mating face of the cylinder block, then place the sump gaskets in position, ensuring that the end tabs locate correctly beneath the rubber sealing strips **(see illustration)**.
17 Locate the sump on the gaskets and loosely fit the securing bolts.

29.15b . . . then fit the rubber sealing strips

29.16 Locate the sump gasket end tabs beneath the rubber sealing strips

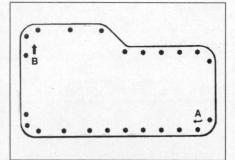

29.18 Sump bolt tightening sequence - refer to text

30.2 Unscrewing the oil pick-up tube securing bolt

30.3 Unscrewing an oil pump securing bolt

30.4 Withdrawing the oil pump driveshaft

2A

18 Tighten the bolts in the correct sequence **(see illustration)** noting the two stages given in the Specifications. Tighten to the first stage in a clockwise sequence starting at point "A", then tighten to the second stage in a clockwise sequence starting at point "B". Tighten to the third stage after the engine has been running for twenty minutes.
19 If the engine is in the vehicle proceed as follows.
20 Carefully lift the crossmember with the jack, then refit the securing bolts and tighten to the specified torque.
21 Withdraw the jack, then lower the engine and remove the lifting tackle.
22 Where applicable, refit the brake lines to the crossmember.
23 Ensure that the front wheels are pointing straight ahead and that the steering wheel is centred, then reconnect the intermediate shaft to the steering column. Secure the clamp plate with the bolt.
24 Refit the engine mounting bolts and

tighten to the specified torque.
25 Refit the starter motor.
26 Lower the vehicle to the ground.
27 Ensure that the sump drain plug is fitted, then fill the engine with the correct quantity and grade of oil. If necessary, renew the oil filter before filling the engine with oil.
28 Reconnect the battery negative lead.
29 Start the engine and check for leaks around the sump, and where applicable the oil filter. When the engine is started, there may be a delay in the extinguishing of the oil pressure warning lamp while the system pressurises.
30 Run the engine for twenty minutes then stop the engine and tighten the sump bolts to the third stage given in the Specifications, starting at the point "A" shown and working clockwise.
31 Check the oil level.
32 Dispose of any old engine oil safely. Do not pour it down a drain - this is illegal and causes pollution.

30 Oil pump - removal and refitting

Removal

1 Remove the sump.
2 Unscrew the bolt securing the pick-up tube and strainer to the cylinder block **(see illustration)**.
3 Using a suitable splined socket, unscrew the two securing bolts and withdraw the oil pump and strainer **(see illustration)**.
4 If desired, the hexagon-shaped driveshaft can be withdrawn, but note which way round

it is fitted **(see illustration)**. The driveshaft engages with the lower end of the distributor driveshaft.
5 Thoroughly clean the mating faces of the oil pump and cylinder block.

Refitting

6 Commence refitting by inserting the oil pump driveshaft into the cylinder block in its previously noted position.
7 Prime the pump by injecting oil into it and turning it by hand.
8 Fit the pump, insert the securing bolts, and tighten them to the specified torque.
9 Fit the pick-up tube securing bolt and tighten it.
10 Refit the sump.

31 Oil pump - dismantling, inspection and reassembly

Note: A new pressure relief valve plug and pick-up tube gasket will be required for reassembly.

Dismantling

1 If oil pump wear is suspected, check the cost and availability of new parts and the cost of a new pump. Examine the pump as described in this Section and then decide whether renewal or repair is the best course of action.
2 Unbolt the pick-up tube and strainer. Recover the gasket.
3 Unscrew the three securing bolts and remove the oil pump cover **(see illustration)**.

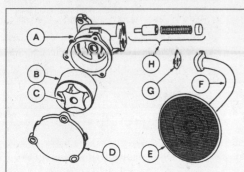

31.3 Exploded view of the oil pump

A Body
B Outer rotor
C Inner rotor
D Cover
E Strainer
F Pick-up tube
G Gasket
H Pressure relief valve

31.10a Checking the oil pump outer rotor-to-body clearance

31.10b Checking the oil pump inner-to-outer rotor clearance

31.11 Checking the oil pump rotor endfloat

4 Mark the rotor faces so that the rotors can be refitted in their original positions, then lift the rotors from the pump body.

5 Remove the pressure relief valve plug by piercing it with a punch and levering it out, then withdraw the spring and plunger.

6 Thoroughly clean all parts in petrol or paraffin and wipe dry using a non-fluffy rag.

Reassembly and inspection

7 Commence reassembly by lubricating the relief valve plunger. Fit the plunger and spring.

8 Fit a new relief valve plug, flat side outwards and seat it with a drift until it is flush with the pick-up mating face.

9 Lubricate the rotors and fit them. Note the marks made when dismantling, if applicable.

10 The necessary clearances may now be checked using a machined straight edge (a good steel rule) and a set of feeler blades. The critical clearances are between the lobes of the centre rotor and convex faces of the outer rotor; between the outer and pump body; and between both rotors and the end cover plate (endfloat). The desired clearances are given in the Specifications **(see illustrations)**.

11 Endfloat can be measured by placing a straight edge across the pump body and measuring the clearance between the two rotors and the straight edge using feeler blades **(see illustration)**.

12 New rotors are only available as a pair. If the rotor-to-body clearance is excessive, a complete new pump should be fitted.

13 Refit the pump cover and tighten the securing bolts.

14 Fit the pick-up tube and strainer, using a new gasket.

15 Temporarily insert the driveshaft into the pump and make sure that the rotors turn freely.

16 Prime the pump before refitting.

32 Pistons and connecting rods
- removal and refitting

Removal

1 Remove the sump and the cylinder head.

2 Check the big-end bearing caps for identification marks and if necessary use a centre-punch to identify the caps and corresponding connecting rods **(see illustration)**.

3 Turn the crankshaft so that No 1 crankpin is at its lowest point, then unscrew the nuts and tap off the bearing cap. Keep the bearing shells in the cap and connecting rod.

4 Using the handle of a hammer, push the piston and connecting rod up the bore and withdraw from the top of the cylinder block. Loosely refit the cap to the connecting rod.

5 Repeat the procedure in paragraphs 3 and 4 on No 4 piston and connecting rod, then turn the crankshaft through half a turn and repeat the procedure on Nos 2 and 3 pistons and connecting rods.

Refitting

6 Commence refitting as follows.

7 Clean the backs of the bearing shells and the recesses in the connecting rods and big-end caps.

8 Press the bearing shells into the connecting rods and caps in their correct positions and oil them liberally. Note that the lugs in corresponding shells must be adjacent to each other **(see illustration)**.

9 Lubricate the cylinder bores with clean engine oil.

10 Fit a piston ring compressor to No 1 piston, then insert the piston and connecting rod into No 1 cylinder **(see illustration)**. With No 1 crankpin at its lowest point, drive the piston carefully into the cylinder with the wooden handle of a hammer, and at the same time guide the connecting rod onto the crankpin. Make sure that the arrow on the piston crown is facing the front of the engine.

11 Oil the crankpin, then fit the big-end bearing cap in its previously noted position, and tighten the nuts to the specified torque.

12 Check that the crankshaft turns freely.

13 Repeat the procedure given in paragraphs 11 to 13 inclusive on the remaining pistons.

14 Refit the cylinder head and the sump.

33 Pistons and connecting rods
- examination and renovation

1 Examine the pistons for ovality, scoring, and scratches. Check the connecting rods for wear and damage. The connecting rods carry a letter indicating their weight class; all the rods fitted must be of the same class.

2 The gudgeon pins are an interference fit in the connecting rods, and if new pistons are to be fitted to the existing connecting rods, the work should be carried out by a Ford dealer who will have the necessary tooling. Note that the oil splash hole in the connecting rod must be located on the right-hand side of the piston (the arrow on the piston crown faces forwards).

3 If new rings are to be fitted to the existing pistons, expand the old rings over the top of the pistons. The use of two or three old feeler blades will be helpful in preventing the rings dropping into empty grooves. Note that the oil control ring is in three sections.

32.2 Big-end cap and connecting rod identification numbers

32.8 The bearing shell lugs (arrowed) must be adjacent to each other

32.10 Fitting a piston ring compressor

33.4 Checking a piston ring gap at the top of the cylinder bore

4 Before fitting the new rings to the pistons, insert them into the cylinder bore and use a feeler blade to check that the end gaps are within the specified limits **(see illustration)**.

5 Clean out the piston ring groove using a piece of old piston ring as a scraper. Be careful not to scratch the aluminium surface of the pistons. Protect your fingers - piston ring edges are sharp.

6 Fit the oil control ring sections with the spreader ends abutted opposite the front of the piston. The side ring gaps should be 25 mm (1.0 in) either side of the spreader gap. Fit the tapered lower compression ring with the "TOP" mark towards the top of the piston and the gap 150° from the spreader gap, then fit the upper compression ring with the gap 150° on the other side of the spreader gap. Note that the compression rings are coated with a molybdenum skin which must not be damaged. Note also that the compression rings are made of cast iron, and will snap if expanded too far.

34 Crankshaft and main bearings - removal and refitting

Removal

1 With the engine removed from the vehicle, remove the timing belt, crankshaft sprocket, auxiliary shaft sprocket and the flywheel/driveplate.

2 Remove the pistons and connecting rods. If no work is to be done on the pistons and connecting rods, there is no need to push the pistons out of the cylinder bores.

3 Unbolt the crankshaft front oil seal housing and the auxiliary shaft front cover and remove the gasket.

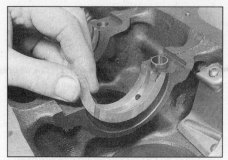

34.8 Removing a thrustwasher from the centre main bearing

4 Remove the oil pump and pick-up tube.

5 Check the main bearing caps for identification marks and if necessary use a centre-punch to identify them **(see illustration)**.

6 Before removing the crankshaft, check that the endfloat is within the specified limits by inserting a feeler blade between the centre crankshaft web and the thrustwashers **(see illustration)**. This will indicate whether or not new thrustwashers are required.

7 Unscrew the bolts and tap off the main bearing caps complete with bearing shells. If the thrustwashers are to be re-used identify them for location. Recover the sealing wedges from either side of the rear bearing cap.

8 Lift the crankshaft from the crankcase and remove the rear oil seal. Recover the remaining thrustwashers **(see illustration)**.

9 Extract the bearing shells, keeping them identified for location **(see illustration)**.

Refitting

10 Commence refitting as follows.

11 Wipe the bearing shell locations in the crankcase with a soft, non-fluffy rag.

12 Wipe the crankshaft journals with a soft, non-fluffy rag.

13 If the old main bearing shells are to be renewed (not to do so is a false economy, unless they are virtually new) fit the five upper halves of the main bearing shells to their location in the crankcase.

14 Identify each main bearing cap and place in order. The number is cast on to the cap and on intermediate caps an arrow is marked which points towards the front of the engine.

15 Wipe each cap bearing shell location with a soft non-fluffy rag.

34.5 Main bearing cap identification marks. The arrow points to the front of the engine

34.9 Extract each main bearing shell

16 Fit the bearing half shell onto each main bearing cap.

17 Apply a little grease to each side of the centre main bearing so as to retain the thrustwashers.

18 Fit the upper halves of the thrustwashers into their grooves either side of the main bearing. The slots must face outwards.

19 Lubricate the crankshaft journals and the upper and lower main bearing shells with clean engine oil and locate the rear oil seal (with lip lubricated) on the rear of the crankshaft.

20 Carefully lower the crankshaft into the crankcase.

21 Lubricate the crankshaft main bearing journals again, and then fit No 1 bearing cap. Fit the two securing bolts but do not tighten yet.

22 Make sure that the mating faces are clean, then apply sealant (Loctite 518 or equivalent) to the areas on the rear main bearing cap shown **(see illustration)**.

23 Fit the rear main bearing cap. Fit the two securing bolts but as before do not tighten yet.

24 Apply a little grease to either side of the centre main bearing cap so as to retain the thrustwashers. Fit the thrustwashers with the tag located in the groove and the slots facing outwards **(see illustration)**.

25 Fit the centre main bearing cap and the two securing bolts, then refit the intermediate main bearing caps. Make sure that the arrows point towards the front of the engine.

26 Lightly tighten all main bearing cap securing bolts and then fully tighten in a progressive manner to the specified torque wrench setting.

27 Check that the crankshaft rotates freely. Some stiffness is to be expected with new

2A

34.6 Checking crankshaft endfloat

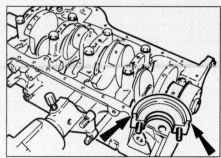

34.22 Coat the arrowed areas of the rear main bearing cap with sealant

34.24 Fitting a thrustwasher to the centre main bearing cap

34.29 Fitting a sealing wedge to the rear main bearing cap

35.5 Checking the width of the filament against the scale of the packet

components, but there must be no tight spots or binding.

28 Check that the crankshaft endfloat is within the specified limits by inserting a feeler blade between the centre crankshaft web and the thrustwashers.

29 Make sure that the rear oil seal is fully located onto its seating. Coat the rear main bearing cap sealing wedges with sealing compound, then press them into position using a blunt screwdriver with the rounded red face towards the cap **(see illustration)**.

30 Refit the oil pump and pick-up tube.

31 Refit the crankshaft front oil seal housing and the auxiliary shaft front cover using a new gasket, and tighten the securing bolts. Smear the lip of the oil seal with clean engine oil before fitting; and using a straight edge, ensure that the bottom face of the oil seal housing is aligned with the bottom face of the cylinder block before finally tightening the bolts.

32 Refit the pistons and connecting rods.

33 Refit the flywheel/driveplate and the auxiliary shaft sprocket, crankshaft sprocket, and timing belt.

35 Crankshaft and bearings - examination and renovation

1 Examine the bearing surfaces of the crankshaft for scratches or scoring and, using a micrometer, check each journal and crankpin for ovality. Where this is found to be in excess of 0.0254 mm (0.001 in) the crankshaft will have to be reground and undersize bearings fitted.

2 Crankshaft regrinding should be carried out by a suitable engineering works, who will normally supply the matching undersize main and big-end shell bearings.

3 Note that undersize bearings may already have been fitted, either in production or by a previous repairer. Check the markings on the backs of the old bearing shells, and if in doubt take them along when buying new ones. Production undersizes are also indicated by paint marks as follows:

White line on main bearing cap - parent bore 0.40 mm oversize

Green line on crankshaft front counterweight - main bearing journals 0.25 mm undersize

Green spot on counterweight - big-end bearing journals 0.25 mm undersize

4 If the crankshaft endfloat is more than the maximum specified amount, new thrustwashers should be fitted to the centre main bearings. These are usually supplied together with the main and big-end bearings on a reground crankshaft.

5 An accurate method of determining bearing wear is by the use of Plastigage. The crankshaft is located in the main bearings (and big-end bearings if necessary) and the Plastigage filament located across the journal which must be dry. The cap is then fitted and the bolts/nuts tightened to the specified torque. On removal of the cap the width of the filaments is checked against a scale which shows the bearing running clearance. This clearance is then compared with that given in the Specifications **(see illustration)**.

6 If the spigot bearing in the rear of the crankshaft requires renewal, extract it with a suitable puller. Alternatively fill it with heavy grease and use a close fitting metal dowel driven into the centre of the bearing. Drive the new bearing into the crankshaft with a soft metal drift.

36 Cylinder block and bores - examination and renovation

1 The cylinder bores must be examined for taper, ovality, scoring and scratches. Start by examining the top of the bores; if these are worn, a slight ridge will be found which marks the top of the piston ring travel. If the wear is excessive, the engine will have had a high oil consumption rate accompanied by blue smoke from the exhaust.

2 If available, use an inside dial gauge to measure the bore diameter just below the ridge and compare it with the diameter at the bottom of the bore, which is not subject to wear. If the difference is more than 0.152 mm (0.006 in), the cylinders will normally require reboring with new oversize pistons fitted.

3 Proprietary oil control rings can be obtained for fitting to the existing pistons if it is felt that the degree of wear does not justify a rebore. However, any improvement brought about by such rings may be short-lived.

4 If new pistons or piston rings are to be fitted to old bores, deglaze the bores with abrasive paper or a "glaze buster" tool. The object is to produce a light cross-hatch pattern to assist

the new rings to bed in.

5 If there is a ridge at the top of the bore and new piston rings are being fitted, either the top piston ring must be stepped ("ridge dodger" pattern) or the ridge must be removed with a ridge reamer. If the ridge is left, the piston ring may hit it and break.

6 Thoroughly examine the crankcase and cylinder block for cracks and damage and use a piece of wire to probe all oilways and waterways to ensure that they are unobstructed.

37 Initial start-up after overhaul or major repair

1 Make a final check to ensure that everything has been reconnected to the engine and that no rags or tools have been left in the engine bay.

2 Check that oil and coolant levels are correct.

3 Start the engine. This may take a little longer than usual as fuel is pumped up to the engine.

4 Check that the oil pressure light goes out when the engine starts.

5 Run the engine at a fast tickover and check for leaks of oil, fuel or coolant. Also check power steering and transmission fluid cooler unions, where applicable. Some smoke and odd smells may be experienced as assembly lubricant burns off the exhaust manifold and other components.

6 Bring the engine to normal operating temperature, then check the ignition timing and the idle speed (where applicable) and mixture.

7 If splined type cylinder head bolts have been used, stop the engine after it has been running for 15 minutes, then remove the crankshaft cover and tighten the cylinder head bolts to the fourth stage given in the Specifications, in the correct order.

8 When the engine has completely cooled, re-check the oil and coolant levels, and check, and if necessary adjust, the valve clearances.

9 If new bearings, pistons etc have been fitted, the engine should be run-in at reduced speeds and loads for the first 500 miles (800 km) or so. It is beneficial to change the engine oil and filter after this mileage.

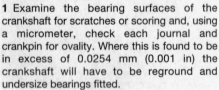

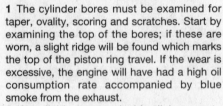

Chapter 2 Part B:
DOHC engine

Unless otherwise stated, procedures are as described for the SOHC engines in Part A of this Chapter.

Contents

Degrees of difficulty

Easy, suitable for novice with little experience	Fairly easy, suitable for beginner with some experience	Fairly difficult, suitable for competent DIY mechanic	Difficult, suitable for experienced DIY mechanic	Very difficult, suitable for expert DIY or professional

2B

Specifications

General

Engine type	Four-cylinder, in-line, double overhead camshaft
Engine code:	
Carburettor engine	N8A
Fuel injection engine without catalyst	N9A
Fuel injection engine with catalyst	N9C
Bore	86.00 mm
Stroke	86.00 mm
Cubic capacity	1998 cc
Compression ratio	10.3 : 1
Compression pressure at starter motor speed	11 to 13 bars
Maximum continuous engine speed:	
N8A engine	6050 rpm
All engines except N8A	5950 rpm
Maximum engine power (DIN):	
N8A engine	80 kW at 5600 rpm
N9A engine	92 kW at 5500 rpm
N9C engine	88 kW at 5500 rpm
Maximum engine torque:	
N8A engine	174 Nm at 3000 rpm
N9A engine	174 Nm at 2500 rpm
N9C engine	171 Nm at 2500 rpm

Cylinder bore diameter

Standard class 1	86.000 to 86.010 mm
Standard class 2	86.010 to 86.020 mm
Oversize 0.15 class A	86.150 to 86.160 mm
Oversize 0.15 class B	86.160 to 86.170 mm
Oversize 0.5	86.500 to 86.510 mm

Crankshaft

Endfloat	0.090 to 0.300 mm (0.004 to 0.012 in)
Main bearing running clearance	0.011 to 0.048 mm
Main bearing journal diameter:	
Standard (yellow)	54.980 to 54.990 mm
Standard (red)	54.990 to 55.000 mm
Undersize 0.25 (green)	54.730 to 54.750 mm
Main bearing thrustwasher thickness:	
Standard	2.301 to 2.351 mm (0.090 to 0.093 in)
Oversize 0.38 (yellow)	2.491 to 2.541 mm (0.098 to 0.100 in)
Big-end bearing running clearance	0.006 to 0.060 mm
Big-end bearing journal diameter:	
Standard	50.890 to 50.910 mm
Undersize 0.25 (green)	50.640 to 50.660 mm

Pistons and piston rings

Piston diameter:	
Standard 1	85.970 to 85.980 mm
Standard 2	85.980 to 85.990 mm
Standard service	85.980 to 85.990 mm
Oversize 0.15	86.130 to 86.150 mm
Oversize 0.50	86.470 to 86.490 mm
Piston ring end gap:	
Top	0.300 to 0.600 mm (0.012 to 0.024 in)
Centre	0.500 to 0.800 mm (0.020 to 0.032 in)
Bottom (oil control)	0.400 to 1.500 mm (0.016 to 0.059 in)

Cylinder head

Valve guide bore	7.063 to 7.094 mm
Camshaft bearing parent bore diameter	26.000 to 26.030 mm

Camshafts

Endfloat	0.020 to 0.260 mm (0.001 to 0.010 in)

Valves

Valve timing:	
Carburettor engines:	
Inlet opens	13° BTDC
Inlet closes	39° ABDC
Exhaust opens	43° BBDC
Exhaust closes	13° ATDC
Fuel injection engines:	
Inlet opens	13° BTDC
Inlet closes	51° ABDC
Exhaust opens	43° BBDC
Exhaust closes	13° ATDC
Valve spring free length:	
Inner spring	48.200 mm (1.899 in)
Outer spring	46.800 mm (1.844 in)
Inlet valve stem diameter:	
Standard	7.025 to 7.043 mm
Oversize 0.2	7.225 to 7.243 mm
Oversize 0.4	7.425 to 7.443 mm
Oversize 0.6	7.625 to 7.643 mm
Oversize 0.8	7.825 to 7.843 mm
Exhaust valve stem diameter:	
Standard	6.999 to 7.017 mm
Oversize 0.2	7.199 to 7.217 mm
Oversize 0.4	7.399 to 7.417 mm
Oversize 0.6	7.599 to 7.617 mm
Oversize 0.8	7.799 to 7.817 mm

Lubrication system

Oil type	Multigrade engine oil, viscosity range SAE 10W/30 to 20W/50, to API SG/CD or better
Oil capacity:	
With filter	4.5 litres (7.9 pints)
Without filter	4.0 litres (7.0 pints)
Oil filter	Champion C102

Torque wrench settings

	Nm	lbf ft
Main bearing cap bolts	90 to 104	66 to 77
Connecting rod (big-end bearing cap) bolts:		
Stage 1	6 to 8	4 to 6
Stage 2	15 to 17	11 to 13
Stage 3	Angle-tighten a further 85°	
Crankshaft pulley bolt:		
Stage 1	45 to 58	33 to 43
Stage 2	Angle-tighten a further 80°	
Camshaft sprocket bolt	55 to 63	41 to 46
Flywheel bolts	82 to 92	61 to 68
Oil pump bolts	9 to 12	7 to 9
Oil pump sprocket bolt	16 to 19	12 to 14
Oil pump chain tensioner bolt	10 to 13	7 to 10
Sump bolts and nuts	8 to 10	6 to 7
Sump studs	6 to 8	4 to 6
Sump drain plug	21 to 28	15 to 21
Sump front mounting plate	23 to 28	17 to 21
Oil baffle nuts	17 to 21	13 to 15
Oil pick-up pipe-to-cylinder block bolts	9 to 13	7 to 10
Oil pressure warning lamp switch	18 to 22	13 to 16
Cylinder head bolts:		
M11 bolts:		
Stage 1	40	30
Stage 2	55	41
Stage 3	Angle-tighten a further 90°	
Stage 4	Angle-tighten a further 90°	
M8 bolts	36 to 39	27 to 29
Camshaft cover bolts	6 to 8	4 to 6
Camshaft bearing cap nuts	22 to 26	16 to 19
Lower timing chain guide upper bolt	10 to 13	7 to 10
Lower timing chain guide lower bolt	24 to 28	18 to 21
Upper and lower timing chain cover bolts	7 to 10	5 to 7
Crankshaft rear oil seal housing bolts	8 to 11	6 to 8
Engine-to-gearbox/transmission bolts	29 to 41	21 to 30

2B

1 General information

The 2.0 litre DOHC (Double OverHead Camshaft) engine was introduced in August 1989 to replace the 2.0 litre SOHC engine used previously in the Sierra range. The engine is of four-cylinder, in-line type.

The crankshaft incorporates five main bearings. Thrustwashers are fitted to the centre main bearing in order to control crankshaft endfloat.

The camshafts are driven by a chain from the crankshaft, and operate the angled valves via hydraulic cam followers. One camshaft operates the inlet valves, and the other operates the exhaust valves. The operation of the cam followers is explained in Chapter 2, Part C, but note that no rollers are fitted and the base of each cam follower is in direct contact with the cam profile.

The distributor is driven directly from the front of the inlet camshaft, and the oil pump is driven by a chain from the crankshaft. An electric fuel pump is mounted in the fuel tank.

Lubrication is by means of a bi-rotor pump which draws oil through a strainer located inside the sump, and forces it through a full-flow filter into the engine oil galleries, from where it is distributed to the crankshaft and camshafts. The big-end bearings are supplied with oil via internal drillings in the crankshaft. The undersides of the pistons are supplied with oil from drillings in the connecting rods. The hydraulic cam followers are supplied with oil from passages in the cylinder head. The camshafts are lubricated by oil from spray tubes mounted above the camshaft bearing caps.

A closed crankcase ventilation system is employed, whereby piston blow-by gases are drawn from the crankcase, through a breather pipe into the inlet manifold, where they are burnt with fresh air/fuel mixture.

2 Crankcase ventilation system - inspection and maintenance

Refer to Chapter 1, Section 35.

3 Major operations possible with the engine in the vehicle

The following operations can be carried out without removing the engine from the vehicle:
a) Removal of the camshafts.
b) Removal and servicing of the cylinder head.
c) Removal of the timing chain and sprockets.
d) Removal of the oil pump.
e) Removal of the sump.
f) Removal of the pistons and connecting rods.
g) Removal of the big-end bearings.
h) Removal of the engine mountings.
i) Removal of the clutch and flywheel.
j) Removal of the crankshaft front and rear oil seals.

4 Major operations requiring engine removal

The following operation can only be carried out after removing the engine from the vehicle:
a) Removal of the crankshaft and main bearings.

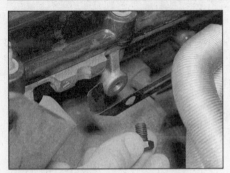

5.5 Removing the hose support bracket bolt from the cylinder head

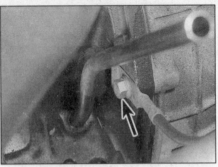

5.22 Earth strap position on top engine-to-gearbox (arrowed)

5.29 Removing the lower steering column clamp bolt

5 Engine - removal leaving manual gearbox in vehicle

Warning: Vehicles equipped with air conditioning: Components of the air conditioning system may obstruct work being undertaken on the engine and it is not always possible to unbolt and move them aside sufficiently, within the limits of their flexible connecting pipes. In such a case, the system should be discharged by a Ford dealer or air conditioning specialist. The refrigerant is harmless under normal conditions but in the presence of a naked flame (or a lighted cigarette) it forms a highly toxic gas. Liquid refrigerant spilled on the skin will cause frostbite. If refrigerant enters the eyes, rinse them with a diluted solution of boric acid and seek medical advice immediately.

Note: A hoist and lifting tackle will be required.

1 Disconnect the battery negative lead.
2 Remove the bonnet.
3 On carburettor models, remove the air cleaner.
4 On fuel injection models, remove the air inlet hose, plenum chamber, and air cleaner lid as an assembly.
5 Disconnect the breather hose from the camshaft cover, and unscrew the bolt securing the hose support bracket to the left-hand side of the cylinder head (see illustration).
6 Drain the cooling system.
7 To provide additional working space, remove the radiator.
8 Disconnect the coolant hoses from the coolant pump housing on the left-hand side of the engine.
9 Disconnect the coolant hoses from the thermostat housing.
10 Disconnect the heater coolant hose from the inlet manifold.
11 Where applicable, release the coolant hose from the bracket under the carburettor automatic choke housing.
12 On carburettor models, disconnect the vacuum pipe from the engine management module.
13 Disconnect the brake servo vacuum hose from the inlet manifold.

14 On fuel injection models, disconnect the vacuum pipes from the MAP sensor (located at the rear right-hand side of the engine compartment) and, where applicable, from the air conditioning system.
15 On carburettor models, disconnect the fuel supply and return hoses at the carburettor, and plug the ends of the hoses to minimise petrol spillage. Take adequate fire precautions.
16 On fuel injection models, slowly loosen the fuel feed union at the fuel rail, to relieve the pressure in the fuel system before disconnecting the union. Be prepared for petrol spillage, and take adequate fire precautions. Disconnect the fuel feed hose, and disconnect the fuel return hose from the fuel pressure regulator. Plug the ends of the hoses to minimise petrol spillage.
17 Disconnect the throttle cable and move it to one side.
18 Disconnect the HT lead from the ignition coil, and unclip it from the timing chain cover.
19 Disconnect the wiring from the following components as applicable, depending on model:
Alternator.
Starter motor.
Oil pressure warning lamp switch.
Temperature gauge sender.
Cooling fan switch.
Anti-dieselling valve (carburettor models).
Automatic choke heater (carburettor models).
Engine coolant temperature sensor.
Crankshaft speed/position sensor.
Air charge temperature sensor.
Throttle position sensor.
Fuel temperature sensor.
Fuel injectors.
20 On models fitted with power steering, unbolt the power steering pump from its mounting bracket and move it clear of the engine. Note that there is no need to disconnect the fluid hoses, but make sure that the pump is adequately supported to avoid straining them.
21 On models fitted with air conditioning, unbolt the air conditioning compressor from its mounting bracket, and move it clear of the engine. Do not disconnect the hoses; make sure that the compressor is adequately supported to avoid straining them.
22 Unscrew and remove the top engine-to-gearbox bolts which are accessible from the

engine compartment. Note the location of the bolts, and note the positions of the earth strap and any wiring clips attached to the bolts (see illustration).
23 Unscrew the securing bolt, and disconnect the earth lead from the rear left-hand side of the cylinder head.
24 Unscrew the nuts securing the engine mountings to the engine mounting brackets.
25 Apply the handbrake, jack up the front of the vehicle and support it securely on axle stands (see "Jacking and Vehicle Support").
26 Drain the engine oil into a suitable container.
27 Remove the starter motor.
28 Remove the exhaust downpipe.
29 Ensure that the steering wheel is positioned in the straight-ahead position, then remove the clamp bolt from the lower steering column clamp, swivel the plate to one side, and disconnect the lower steering column from the lower flexible coupling (see illustration).
30 Working inside the vehicle, place a wooden block under the clutch pedal to raise it fully against its stop, so holding the automatic adjuster pawl clear of the toothed quadrant.
31 Disconnect the clutch cable from the clutch release arm, and pass the cable through the bellhousing.
32 Support the gearbox with a trolley jack, using a block of wood between the jack and the gearbox to spread the load.
33 Unscrew and remove the remaining engine-to-gearbox bolts, and remove the bolt from the engine adapter plate (see illustration). Recover any shims fitted between the sump and the gearbox when removing the lower engine-to-gearbox bolts.

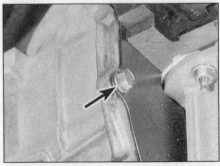

5.33 Engine adapter plate bolt (arrowed)

5.36 Remove the engine mounting brackets to improve clearance

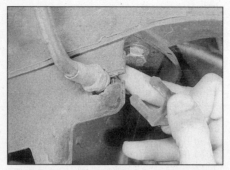

5.37 Removing a brake line securing clip from the suspension crossmember

5.38 Removing a suspension crossmember securing bolt

34 Make a final check to ensure that all relevant wires, pipes and hoses have been disconnected to facilitate engine removal.

35 Attach a suitable hoist to the engine lifting brackets located at the front and rear of the cylinder head, and carefully take the weight of the engine.

36 To improve clearance in the engine compartment when lifting the engine, unbolt the engine mounting brackets from the cylinder block, and remove them **(see illustration)**.

37 Detach the brake lines from the front suspension crossmember **(see illustration)**.

38 Support the crossmember with a jack (*do not remove the jack from under the gearbox*), then loosen the bolts securing the crossmember to the underbody. Remove the bolts from one side **(see illustration)**, and carefully lower the crossmember sufficiently to allow the sump to clear the steering rack and crossmember when pulling the engine forwards from the gearbox.

39 Gently raise the engine, then pull it forwards to disconnect it from the gearbox. Ensure that the gearbox is adequately supported, and take care not to strain the gearbox input shaft. It may be necessary to rock the engine a little to release it from the gearbox.

40 Once clear of the gearbox, lift the engine from the vehicle, taking care not to damage the components in the engine compartment **(see illustration)**.

5.40 Lifting the engine from the vehicle

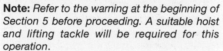

6 Engine - removal leaving automatic transmission in vehicle

Note: *Refer to the warning at the beginning of Section 5 before proceeding. A suitable hoist and lifting tackle will be required for this operation.*

1 Proceed as described in paragraphs 1 to 21 of Section 5.

2 Unscrew and remove the top engine-to-transmission bolts which are accessible from the engine compartment. Note the location of the earth strap, vacuum pipe bracket, and transmission dipstick tube bracket, as applicable.

3 Proceed as described in paragraphs 23 to 29 of Section 5.

4 Where applicable, remove the bolt securing the transmission fluid dipstick tube to the left-hand side of the cylinder block.

5 Working through the starter motor aperture, unscrew the four torque converter-to-driveplate nuts. It will be necessary to turn the crankshaft, using a suitable spanner on the crankshaft pulley bolt, in order to gain access to each bolt in turn through the aperture.

6 Support the transmission with a trolley jack, using a block of wood between the jack and the transmission to spread the load.

7 Unscrew and remove the remaining engine-to-transmission bolts, and remove the bolt from the engine adapter plate. Recover any shims fitted between the sump and the transmission when removing the lower engine-to-transmission bolts. Where applicable, pull the blanking plug from the adapter plate.

8 Proceed as described in paragraphs 34 to 38 of Section 5.

9 Gently raise the engine, then pull the engine forwards to disconnect it from the transmission. Ensure that the torque converter is held firmly in place in the transmission housing, otherwise it could fall out, resulting in fluid spillage and possible damage. It may be necessary to rock the engine a little to release it from the transmission.

10 Once clear of the transmission, lift the engine from the vehicle, taking care not to damage the components in the engine compartment.

7 Engine/manual gearbox assembly - removal and separation

Note: *Refer to the warning at the beginning of Section 5 before proceeding. A suitable hoist and lifting tackle will be required for this operation.*

Removal

1 Proceed as described in paragraphs 1 to 21 of Section 5.

2 Unscrew the securing bolt, and disconnect the earth lead from the rear left-hand side of the cylinder head.

3 Unscrew the nuts securing the engine mountings to the engine mounting brackets.

4 Jack up the vehicle and support it securely on axle stands (see "*Jacking and Vehicle Support*").
Ensure that there is enough working room beneath the vehicle.

5 To improve access, disconnect the exhaust downpipe from the manifold, and remove the exhaust system.

6 Drain the engine oil into a suitable container.

7 On models fitted with a catalytic converter, release the securing clips, and withdraw the exhaust heat shield from under the vehicle for access to the propeller shaft.

8 Remove the propeller shaft.

9 Where applicable, bend back the locktabs, then unscrew the two bolts in each case securing the two anti-roll bar U-clamps to the vehicle underbody. Lower the anti-roll bar as far as possible.

10 Working inside the vehicle, place a wooden block under the clutch pedal to raise it fully against its stop, so holding the automatic adjuster pawl clear of the toothed quadrant.

11 Disconnect the clutch cable from the clutch release arm, and pass the cable through the bellhousing.

12 Support the gearbox with a trolley jack, using a block of wood between the jack and the gearbox to spread the load.

13 Unscrew the four nuts securing gearbox crossmember to the vehicle underbody. Unscrew the central bolt securing the crossmember to the gearbox, and remove the crossmember. Note the position of the earth strap, where applicable. Recover the mounting cup, and where applicable the exhaust mounting bracket and heat shield.

14 Lower the gearbox slightly on the jack, then remove the securing circlip, and disconnect the speedometer drive cable from the gearbox.

15 Disconnect the wiring from the reversing lamp switch. On models with fuel injection, disconnect the wiring from the vehicle speed sensor mounted in the side of the gearbox.

16 Unscrew the two securing bolts, and disconnect the gear linkage support bracket from the gearbox.

17 Using a suitable pin punch, drive out the roll-pin securing the gearchange rod to the gear linkage.

18 Attach a suitable hoist to the engine lifting brackets located at the front and rear of the cylinder head, and carefully take the weight of the engine. Arrange the lifting tackle so that the engine/gearbox assembly will assume a steep angle of approximately 40° to 45° as it is being removed.

19 To improve clearance in the engine compartment when lifting the engine, unbolt the engine mounting brackets from the cylinder block, and remove them.

20 Ensure that the steering wheel is positioned in the straight-ahead position, then remove the clamp bolt from the lower steering column clamp, swivel the plate to one side, and disconnect the lower steering column from the lower flexible coupling.

21 Detach the brake lines from the front suspension crossmember.

22 Support the crossmember with a jack (do not remove the jack from under the gearbox), then loosen the bolts securing the crossmember to the underbody. Remove the crossmember securing bolts, and carefully lower the crossmember sufficiently to allow the engine sump to clear the steering rack and crossmember as the engine/gearbox assembly is removed.

23 Make a final check to ensure that all relevant wires, pipes and hoses have been disconnected to facilitate removal of the engine/gearbox assembly.

24 Raise the engine/gearbox, at the same time lowering the trolley jack which is supporting the gearbox.

25 Place a suitable rod across the vehicle underbody to support the gear linkage support bracket whilst the gearbox is removed.

26 Tilt the engine/gearbox assembly using the hoist and the trolley jack, until the assembly can be lifted from the vehicle. Take care not to damage surrounding components.

27 If the vehicle is to be moved while the engine/gearbox assembly is removed, temporarily refit the suspension crossmember and the anti-roll bar to the underbody, and reconnect the steering column to the intermediate shaft.

Separation

28 To separate the engine from the gearbox, proceed as follows.

29 Remove the starter motor.

30 Support the engine and gearbox horizontally on blocks of wood.

31 Unscrew the engine-to-gearbox bolts, noting the locations of the bolts, and the positions of the earth strap and any wiring clips attached to the bolts. Recover any shims fitted between the sump and the gearbox when removing the lower engine-to-gearbox bolts.

32 Unscrew the bolt from the engine adapter plate.

33 Pull the engine and gearbox apart, taking care not to strain the gearbox input shaft. It may be necessary to rock the units slightly to separate them.

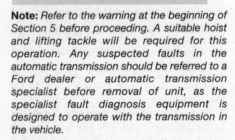

8 Engine/automatic transmission assembly - removal and separation

Note: *Refer to the warning at the beginning of Section 5 before proceeding. A suitable hoist and lifting tackle will be required for this operation. Any suspected faults in the automatic transmission should be referred to a Ford dealer or automatic transmission specialist before removal of unit, as the specialist fault diagnosis equipment is designed to operate with the transmission in the vehicle.*

Removal

1 Proceed as described in paragraphs 1 to 21 of Section 5.

2 Unscrew the securing bolt, and disconnect the earth lead from the rear left-hand side of the cylinder head.

3 Unscrew the nuts securing the engine mountings to the engine mounting brackets.

4 Jack up the vehicle and support it securely on axle stands. (see *"Jacking and Vehicle Support"*).
Ensure that there is enough working room beneath the vehicle.

5 To improve access, disconnect the exhaust downpipe from the manifold, and remove the exhaust system.

6 Drain the engine oil into a suitable container.

7 On models fitted with a catalytic converter, release the securing clips and withdraw the exhaust heat shield from under the vehicle for access to the propeller shaft.

8 Remove the propeller shaft.

9 Where applicable, bend back the locktabs, then unscrew the two bolts in each case securing the two anti-roll bar U-clamps to the vehicle underbody. Lower the anti-roll bar as far as possible.

10 Support the transmission with a trolley jack, using a block of wood between the jack and the transmission to spread the load.

11 Unscrew the four bolts securing the transmission crossmember to the vehicle underbody. Unscrew the central bolt securing the crossmember to the transmission, and remove the crossmember. Note the position of the earth strap, where applicable. Recover the mounting cup, and where applicable, the exhaust mounting bracket and heat shield.

12 Lower the transmission slightly on the jack.

13 Unscrew the unions and disconnect the fluid cooler pipes from the transmission. Plug the open ends of the pipes and the transmission, to prevent dirt ingress and fluid leakage. Where applicable, detach the fluid cooler pipe bracket from the engine mounting bracket, and move it to one side.

14 Remove the two clips securing the selector rod, and detach the selector rod from the manual selector lever, and from the selector lever on the transmission.

15 Disconnect the wiring from the starter inhibitor switch, kickdown solenoid, lock-up clutch, reversing lamp switch, and where applicable, the 3rd/4th gearchange solenoid.

16 Remove the securing screw, and disconnect the speedometer cable from the transmission extension housing. Plug the opening in the transmission to prevent dirt ingress.

17 Proceed as described in paragraphs 18 to 27 of Section 7, substituting transmission for gearbox, and ignoring paragraph 25.

Separation

18 To separate the engine from the transmission, proceed as follows.

19 Remove the starter motor.

20 Support the engine and transmission horizontally on blocks of wood.

21 Working through the starter motor aperture, unscrew the four torque converter-to-driveplate nuts. It will be necessary to turn the crankshaft using a suitable spanner on the crankshaft pulley bolt in order to gain access to each nut in turn through the aperture.

22 Where applicable, remove the bolt securing the transmission fluid dipstick tube to the left-hand side of the cylinder block.

23 Unscrew the engine-to-transmission bolts, noting the locations of the bolts, and the positions of the earth strap and any wiring clips attached to the bolts. Recover any shims fitted between the sump and the transmission when removing the lower engine-to-transmission bolts.

24 Unscrew the bolt from the engine adapter plate and, where applicable, pull the blanking plug from the adapter plate.

25 Pull the engine and the transmission apart, ensuring that the torque converter is held firmly in place in the transmission housing, otherwise it could fall out, resulting in fluid spillage and possible damage. It may be necessary to rock the units slightly to separate them.

9 Engine - refitting (manual gearbox in vehicle)

1 Reverse the procedure described in paragraphs 1 to 40, Section 5, noting the following points.

2 Before attempting to refit the engine, check that the clutch friction disc is centralised.

3 Check that the clutch release arm and bearing are correctly fitted, and lightly grease the input shaft splines.

4 Check that the engine adapter plate is correctly positioned on its locating dowels. If necessary, a cable-tie can be used to temporarily secure the adapter plate in position on the cylinder block using one of the engine-to-gearbox bolt holes.

5 If shims were fitted between the sump and the gearbox, refit them in their original locations when mating the engine to the gearbox. If the engine has been overhauled, where applicable fit the relevant shims as calculated during engine reassembly.

6 Reconnect the clutch cable to the release arm, ensuring that it is routed as noted during removal.

7 Ensure that the roadwheels and the steering wheel are in the straight-ahead position before reconnecting the lower steering column to the intermediate shaft, and tighten the clamp bolt to the specified torque.

8 Fill the engine with the correct grade and quantity of oil.

9 Check the throttle cable adjustment.

10 Fill the cooling system.

11 Tighten all fixings to the specified torque, where applicable.

10 Engine - refitting (automatic transmission in vehicle)

1 Reverse the procedure in paragraphs 1 to 10 of Section 6, noting the following points.

2 Check that the engine adapter plate is correctly positioned on its locating dowels. If necessary, a cable-tie can be used to temporarily secure the adapter plate in position on the cylinder block, using one of the engine-to-transmission bolt holes.

3 As the torque converter is only loosely engaged in the transmission, care must be taken to prevent the torque converter from falling out forwards. When the torque converter hub is fully engaged with the fluid pump drivegear in the transmission, distance "A" in illustration 2.24 of Chapter 7B must be as specified. Incorrect installation of the torque converter will result in damage to the transmission.

4 If shims were fitted between the sump and the transmission, refit them in their original locations when mating the engine to the transmission. If the engine has been overhauled, where applicable fit the relevant shims as calculated during engine reassembly.

5 As the engine is installed, guide the torque converter studs through the holes in the driveplate. When the engine is positioned flush with the engine adapter plate and the transmission housing, check that the torque converter is free to move axially a small amount before refitting and tightening the engine-to-transmission bolts.

6 Do not tighten the torque converter-to-driveplate nuts until the lower engine-to-transmission bolts have been fitted and tightened.

7 Ensure that the roadwheels and the steering wheel are in the straight-ahead position before reconnecting the lower steering column to the intermediate shaft.

8 Fill the engine with the correct grade and quantity of oil.

9 Check the throttle cable adjustment.

10 Fill the cooling system.

11 Tighten all fixings to the specified torque, where applicable.

11 Engine/manual gearbox assembly - reconnection and refitting

1 Reverse the procedure described in paragraphs 1 to 33 of Section 7, noting the following points.

2 Before attempting to reconnect the engine to the gearbox, check that the clutch friction disc is centralised.

3 Check that the clutch release arm and bearing are correctly fitted, and lightly grease the input shaft splines.

4 Check that the engine adapter plate is correctly positioned on its locating dowels. If necessary, a cable-tie can be used to temporarily secure the adapter plate in position on the cylinder block, using one of the engine-to-gearbox bolt holes.

5 If shims were fitted between the sump and the gearbox, refit them in their original locations when mating the engine to the gearbox. If the engine has been overhauled, where applicable fit the relevant shims as calculated during engine reassembly.

6 Ensure that the roadwheels and the steering wheel are in the straight-ahead position before reconnecting the lower steering column to the intermediate shaft.

7 Reconnect the clutch cable to the release arm, ensuring that it is routed as noted during removal.

8 Fill the engine with the correct grade and quantity of oil.

9 Check the throttle cable adjustment.

10 Fill the cooling system.

11 Check and if necessary top-up the gearbox oil level.

12 Tighten all fixings to the specified torque, where applicable.

12 Engine/automatic transmission assembly - reconnection and refitting

1 Reverse the procedure described in paragraphs 1 to 25 of Section 8, noting the following points.

2 Check that the engine adapter plate is correctly positioned on its locating dowels. If necessary, a cable-tie can be used to temporarily secure the adapter plate in position on the cylinder block, using one of the engine-to-transmission bolt holes.

3 As the torque converter is only loosely engaged in the transmission, care must be taken to prevent the torque converter from falling out forwards. When the torque converter hub is fully engaged with the fluid pump drivegear in the transmission, distance "A" in illustration 2.24 of Chapter 7B must be as specified. Incorrect installation of the torque converter will result in damage to the transmission.

4 If shims were fitted between the sump and the transmission, refit them in their original locations when mating the engine to the transmission. If the engine has been overhauled, where applicable fit the relevant shims as calculated during engine reassembly.

5 As the engine and transmission are mated together, guide the torque converter studs through the holes in the driveplate. When the engine is positioned flush with the engine adapter plate and the transmission housing, check that the torque converter is free to move axially a small amount before refitting and tightening the engine-to-transmission bolts.

6 Do not tighten the torque converter-to-driveplate nuts until the lower engine-to-transmission bolts have been fitted and tightened.

7 Ensure that the roadwheels and the steering wheel are in the straight-ahead position before reconnecting the lower steering column to the intermediate shaft.

8 Reconnect the selector rod and check for correct adjustment.

9 Fill the engine with the correct grade and quantity of oil.

10 Check the throttle cable adjustment.

11 Fill the cooling system.

12 Check and if necessary top-up the transmission fluid level.

13 Tighten all fixings to the specified torque, where applicable.

13 Engine mountings - renewal

Proceed as described in Chapter 2, Part C, but note that on certain models it may be necessary to unbolt the engine mounting brackets from the cylinder block to allow sufficient clearance to remove the mountings.

2B

14 Engine dismantling, examination, renovation and reassembly - general information

Dismantling

1 Refer to Chapter 2, Part A, Section 18, paragraphs 1 to 8 inclusive.
2 A suitable selection of splined and Torx sockets will be required to remove many of the bolts when dismantling the engine.
3 Before dismantling the main engine components, the following externally-mounted ancillary components can be removed, with reference to the relevant Chapters of this Manual and the relevant Sections of this Chapter, where applicable.

Inlet manifold (and carburettor, if applicable)
Exhaust manifold
Alternator.
Coolant pump, and thermostat
Alternator/coolant pump drivebelt tensioner
Distributor cap, HT leads and spark plugs
Oil pressure warning lamp switch
Crankshaft speed/position sensor
Oil filter
Dipstick
Engine mounting brackets (if not already done)
Crankcase ventilation pipe and hoses
Clutch
Alternator mounting bracket.
Air conditioning compressor mounting bracket (where applicable).
Engine lifting brackets.

Examination and renovation

4 Refer to Chapter 2, Part A, Section 18, but note that the connecting rod bolts should be renewed on reassembly, and when renewing the cylinder head bolts, the latest type bolts with hexagonal heads should always be used.

Reassembly

5 Proceed as described in Chapter 2, Part A, Section 18, noting the following:
6 If they have been removed, new cylinder head bolts (both M11 and M8, of the latest type with hexagonal heads), flywheel bolts, and connecting rod bolts must be used.

15 Timing chain and sprockets - removal and refitting

Note: Refer to the warning at the beginning of Section 5 before proceeding. A suitable puller will be required to remove the crankshaft pulley. A new crankshaft pulley bolt, a new timing chain tensioner plunger assembly, new upper and lower timing chain cover gaskets, and a new camshaft cover gasket and reinforcing sleeve sealing rings, must be used on refitting.

Removal

1 If the engine is in the car, carry out the following operations:
a) Disconnect the battery negative lead.
b) To improve access, remove the radiator. It will be difficult to remove the crankshaft pulley with the radiator in place.

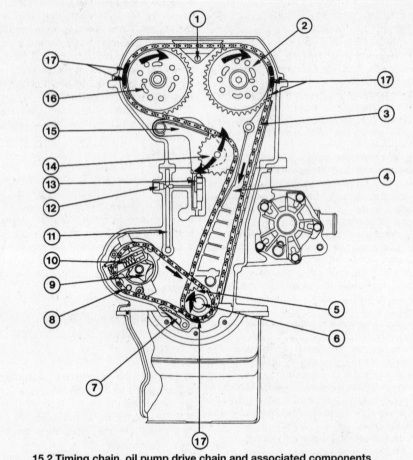

15.2 Timing chain, oil pump drive chain and associated components

1 Upper timing chain guide
2 Exhaust camshaft sprocket
3 Timing chain
4 Lower timing chain guide
5 Crankshaft sprocket (double)
6 Crankshaft
7 Oil pump chain tensioner
8 Oil pump drive chain
9 Oil pump
10 Oil pressure relief valve
11 Oil passage to timing chain tensioner plunger
12 Plug
13 Timing chain tensioner plunger
14 Timing chain tensioner sprocket
15 Timing chain tensioner arm
16 Inlet camshaft sprocket
17 Copper chain links

c) On carburettor models, remove the air cleaner.
d) On fuel injection models, remove the air inlet hose, plenum chamber, and air cleaner lid as an assembly.
e) Disconnect the breather hose from the camshaft cover.
f) Remove the distributor cap and HT leads, and the rotor arm and housing.

2 Proceed as described in paragraphs 2 to 11 inclusive of Section 18 (see illustration).
3 Remove the alternator drivebelt.
4 Slacken the crankshaft pulley bolt. Prevent the crankshaft from turning by engaging top gear (manual gearbox only) and having an assistant press the brake pedal hard, or by removing the starter motor and jamming the ring gear teeth with a lever.
5 Unscrew the bolt part-way, and use a puller to remove the crankshaft pulley. The legs of

the puller must be suitably shaped to enable them to rest on the metal surfaces of the pulley. Do not use a puller on the rubber surface of the pulley (see illustrations).

15.5a Remove the crankshaft pulley using a puller (viewed from under vehicle)

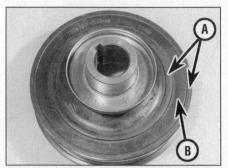

15.5b Position the legs of the puller on the metal surfaces of the pulley (A), not the rubber surface (B)

15.9 Oil pump chain tensioner securing screw (arrowed)

15.11 Withdrawing the lower timing chain guide

6 Loosen the alternator lower mounting through-bolt, then remove the alternator upper mounting bolt, and swing the alternator away from the engine.

7 Unscrew the central securing bolt, and withdraw the drivebelt tensioner assembly.

8 Unscrew the eleven securing bolts, and remove the lower timing chain cover. Recover the rubber gasket.

9 Using a suitable Torx socket, unscrew the securing screw, and carefully withdraw the oil pump chain tensioner **(see illustration)**.

10 Unscrew the Torx type securing bolt, and withdraw the oil pump sprocket, complete with the oil pump drive chain.

11 Unscrew the two lower timing chain guide securing bolts, noting their locations, and withdraw the timing chain guide through the top of the timing case **(see illustration)**.

12 Remove the Woodruff key from the end of the crankshaft, prising it free with a screwdriver if necessary, then slide the double chain sprocket from the end of the crankshaft, and lift the chain from the sprocket **(see illustration)**.

13 Withdraw the timing chain through the top of the timing case and, where applicable, remove the cable-tie from the chain **(see illustration)**.

Refitting

14 Commence refitting as follows. Note that coppered links are provided in the timing chain to assist with refitting, but these can be difficult to see on a chain which has already been in service. If possible, position the

coppered links as described during the following procedure. If the coppered links are not visible, the chain should still be refitted as described, but ignore the references to the coppered links.

15 Make sure that the slot for the Woodruff key in the end of the crankshaft is pointing vertically downwards. If necessary, temporarily refit the crankshaft pulley bolt in order to turn the crankshaft to the required position.

16 Lower the timing chain into the timing case from above, with the single coppered link at the bottom. If desired, use a cable-tie to prevent the chain from dropping into the timing case, as during removal.

17 Locate the double chain sprocket loosely over the end of the crankshaft (larger sprocket nearest the crankcase), with the timing mark pointing vertically down.

18 Fit the chain over the inner, larger sprocket, aligning the coppered link in the chain with the timing mark on the sprocket **(see illustration)**.

19 Coat the threads of the lower timing chain guide lower securing bolt with a suitable thread-locking compound.

20 Introduce the lower timing chain guide through the top of the timing case, manipulating the chain around the guide as necessary, then fit the chain guide lower securing bolt and tighten it finger-tight.

21 Push the double chain sprocket onto the crankshaft, engaging the notch in the sprocket with the groove in the end of the crankshaft.

22 Proceed as shown in paragraphs 34 to 42 of Section 18 but when fitting the chain over the camshaft sprockets, align the timing mark on each sprocket between the two corresponding coppered links in the chain.

23 Coat the threads of the lower timing chain guide upper securing bolt with a suitable thread-locking compound, then fit the bolt and tighten it finger-tight.

24 Proceed as shown in paragraphs 43 to 46 of Section 18.

25 Tighten the two chain guide securing bolts to the specified torque.

26 Proceed as shown in paragraphs 47 to 55 of Section 18.

27 Fit the oil pump drive chain around the outer crankshaft sprocket and the oil pump sprocket, then refit the oil pump sprocket, and tighten the securing bolt to the specified torque. If necessary, a screwdriver can be inserted through one of the holes in the sprocket to prevent it from turning as the securing bolt is tightened.

28 Refit the oil pump drive chain tensioner, and tighten the securing bolt to the specified torque.

29 Refit the Woodruff key to the end of the crankshaft.

30 Inspect the oil seal in the lower timing chain cover. If the oil seal is in good condition, the cover can be refitted as follows, but if the seal is damaged, or has been leaking, a new seal should be fitted to the cover. If necessary, carefully prise the old oil seal from the cover using a screwdriver. The new seal

2B

15.12 Sliding the double chain sprocket from the end of the crankshaft

15.13 Withdrawing the timing chain through the top of the timing case

15.18 Coppered link in timing chain aligned with crankshaft sprocket timing mark (arrowed)

should be fitted dry. Drive in the new seal using a suitable metal tube, making sure that the seal lip faces into the engine, and taking care not to damage the timing chain cover **(see illustration)**.

31 Fit the lower timing chain cover using a new rubber gasket **(see illustration)**.

32 Loosely refit the timing chain cover securing bolts.

33 Refit the crankshaft pulley to the end of the crankshaft, and draw the pulley onto the crankshaft using the original securing bolt, at the same time centring the lower timing chain cover.

34 With the lower timing chain cover centralised, and the pulley fully home on the crankshaft, remove the old securing bolt, then fit a new bolt.

35 Tighten the new crankshaft pulley bolt to the specified torque, in the two stages given in the Specifications at the beginning of this Chapter. Prevent the crankshaft from turning as during removal.

36 Tighten the lower timing chain cover securing bolts.

37 Refit the drivebelt tensioner assembly, ensuring that the lug on the rear of the tensioner bracket engages with the corresponding hole in the cylinder block, and tighten the securing bolt.

38 Swing the alternator into position to align the upper mounting bolt hole with the corresponding hole in the drivebelt tensioner assembly, then refit the upper mounting bolt, and tighten the upper bolt and the lower through-bolt.

39 Refit the alternator drivebelt.

40 If the engine is in the vehicle, reverse the operations described in paragraph 1.

41 If applicable, refill the cooling system.

16 Timing chain, sprockets and tensioner - examination and renovation

1 Examine all the teeth on the camshaft and crankshaft sprockets. If the teeth are "hooked" in appearance, renew the sprockets.

2 Examine the chain tensioner plastic sprocket for wear. If excessive wear is evident, the complete tensioner assembly must be renewed, as the sprocket cannot be renewed independently. Note that the tensioner plunger assembly must be renewed whenever the timing chain is removed.

15.30 Fitting a new lower timing chain cover oil seal

3 Examine the timing chain for wear. If the chain has been in operation for a considerable time, or if when held horizontally (rollers vertical) it takes on a deeply-bowed appearance, renew it.

17 Cylinder head - removal and refitting (engine in vehicle)

Note: *Refer to the warning at the beginning of Section 5 and the note at the beginning of the following Section before proceeding. The cylinder head must not be removed when the engine is warm.*

Removal

1 Disconnect the battery negative lead.

2 On carburettor models, remove the air cleaner.

3 On fuel injection models, remove the air inlet hose, plenum chamber, and air cleaner lid as an assembly.

4 Drain the cooling system.

5 Disconnect the heater coolant hose from the inlet manifold **(see illustration)**.

6 Disconnect the breather hose from the camshaft cover, and unbolt the hose bracket from the left-hand side of the cylinder head **(see illustration)**.

7 Unscrew the securing bolt and disconnect the earth lead from the left-hand rear of the cylinder head **(see illustration)**.

8 Remove the distributor cap and HT leads, and the rotor arm and housing. If necessary, mark the HT leads to aid refitting.

9 The cylinder head can be removed either with or without the manifolds and fuel rail, where applicable (it is easiest to remove the

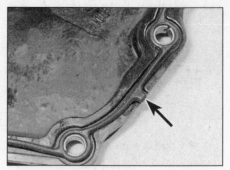
15.31 Lower timing chain cover rubber gasket in position. Ensure that lug on gasket engages with notch in cover (arrowed)

head complete with the manifolds and fuel rail). If desired, the inlet manifold and the fuel rail can be unbolted and moved to one side, leaving the wires, hoses, pipes and cables connected, but care must be taken not to place any strain on them.

10 Unscrew the three securing nuts and disconnect the exhaust downpipe from the manifold. It may be necessary to jack up the front of the vehicle to gain access to the nuts (in which case, apply the handbrake and support the front of the vehicle securely on axle stands). Recover the gasket.

11 If the inlet manifold and the fuel rail (where applicable) are to be removed with the cylinder head, disconnect all relevant wires, hoses, pipes and cables. Otherwise, unbolt the manifold and the fuel rail, and move them to one side, ensuring that they are adequately supported. If the fuel rail is unbolted, be prepared for fuel spillage, and take adequate fire precautions.

12 Proceed as shown in paragraphs 2 to 19 of Section 18.

Refitting

13 Proceed as shown in paragraphs 20 to 55 of Section 18.

14 With the cylinder head refitted, reverse the procedure described in paragraphs 1 to 11, noting the following points.

15 Use a new gasket when reconnecting the exhaust downpipe to the manifold.

16 Ensure that the HT leads are reconnected correctly.

17 Fill the cooling system.

17.5 Disconnecting the heater coolant hose from the inlet manifold

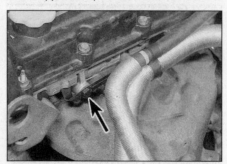
17.6 Hose bracket bolted to cylinder head (arrowed)

17.7 Disconnect the earth lead (arrowed) from the cylinder head

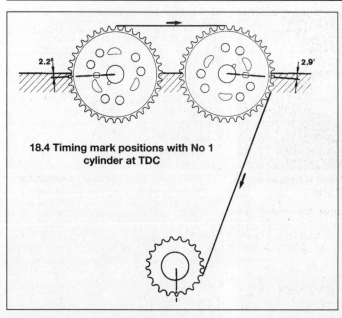

18.4 Timing mark positions with No 1 cylinder at TDC

18.5 Removing the inlet camshaft sprocket bolt and the distributor rotor shaft

18 Cylinder head - removal and refitting (engine removed)

Note: *New cylinder head bolts, a new cylinder head gasket, a new timing chain tensioner plunger assembly, a new upper timing chain cover gasket, and a new camshaft cover gasket and reinforcing sleeve sealing rings, must be used on refitting.*

Removal

1 With the manifolds removed, proceed as follows.

2 Unscrew the eleven bolts and four nuts, and remove the camshaft cover. Recover the gasket.

3 Unscrew the four securing bolts and three studs, and remove the upper timing chain cover. Note the locations of the studs to aid refitting.

4 Using a spanner on the crankshaft pulley, turn the crankshaft to bring No 1 piston to the firing point. With No 1 piston at the firing point, the timing marks on the camshaft sprockets should be pointing away from each other, and should be approximately level with

the top edge of the cylinder head. Timing notches are provided in the camshaft sprockets, and corresponding paint marks are provided on the outside edges of the sprockets **(see illustration)**.

5 Hold the inlet camshaft sprocket stationary using an improvised tool similar to that shown then unscrew the camshaft sprocket bolt and remove the distributor rotor shaft **(see illustration)**.

6 Repeat the procedure given in the previous paragraph for the exhaust camshaft, but note that a spacer is fitted in place of the distributor rotor shaft.

7 Squeeze the upper timing chain guide securing lugs together, using pliers if necessary, and withdraw the guide from the plate at the front of the cylinder head **(see illustrations)**.

8 Mark the position of the timing chain in relation to the camshaft sprockets, so that the chain can be refitted in precisely its original position (ie, make alignment marks between each sprocket and a corresponding link in the chain), then slide the camshaft sprockets from the camshafts. Withdraw the sprockets and lay the timing chain over the exhaust side of the timing case, having eliminated the slack in

the chain. Secure the chain using a cable-tie through two of the chain links, to prevent it from dropping off the crankshaft sprocket.

9 Using a suitable pair of pliers, extract the circlip from the chain tensioner arm pivot pin, taking care not to drop it into the timing case, then withdraw the pivot pin from the tensioner arm **(see illustrations)**. If the pivot pin proves difficult to withdraw, an M6 bolt can be screwed into its end to facilitate removal.

10 Lift the chain tensioner arm from the timing case.

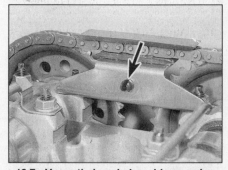

18.7a Upper timing chain guide securing lugs (arrowed)

18.7b Removing the upper timing chain guide

18.9a Removing the chain tensioner arm pivot pin circlip

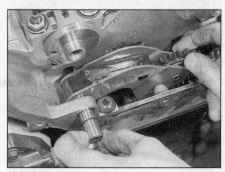

18.9b Withdrawing the pivot pin from the chain tensioner arm

2B

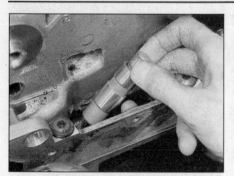

18.11 Lifting the chain tensioner plunger assembly from the cylinder head

11 Lift the chain tensioner plunger assembly from the cylinder head, and discard it **(see illustration)**.

 Warning: Take care when removing the plunger assembly, as there is a risk of injury if the piston flies out.

12 Take note of the markings on the camshaft bearing caps, then progressively unscrew the bearing cap securing nuts.
13 Remove the bearing cap securing nuts, then lift off the camshaft oil spray bars **(see illustration)**, and the timing chain guide plate.
14 Lift off the bearing caps, and then lift out the two camshafts **(see illustrations)**. Note that the inlet camshaft is normally identified by a green paint mark. If necessary, identify the camshafts so that they can be refitted in their correct positions.
15 Withdraw the cam followers from their locations in the cylinder head, keeping them in order so that they can be refitted in their original locations **(see illustration)**. It is advisable to store the cam followers upright in an oil bath until they are to be refitted. Ensure that the depth of oil is sufficient to fully cover the cam followers.
16 Working at the front of the cylinder head, unscrew the three small M8 cylinder head bolts which are accessible through the timing case **(see illustration)**.
17 Working in the reverse order to that shown for the tightening sequence, progressively loosen the remaining cylinder head bolts and withdraw them from the cylinder head.
18 Lift the cylinder head from the block. If the

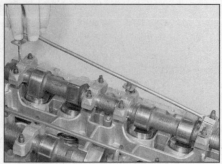

18.13 Lifting off a camshaft oil spray bar

18.14b Lifting out the exhaust camshaft

cylinder head is stuck, tap it free with a soft-faced mallet. Do not insert a lever into the joint between the cylinder head and block, as this may result in damage to the mating faces. Place the cylinder head on blocks of wood to prevent damage to the valves.
19 Recover the gasket, and the locating dowels if they are loose, noting the positions of the locating dowels.

Refitting

20 Commence refitting as follows.
21 Turn the crankshaft so that No 1 piston is approximately 20.0 mm (0.8 in) before TDC. This precaution will prevent possible contact between the valves and pistons.
22 Make sure that the mating faces of the cylinder block and cylinder head are perfectly clean, then refit the locating dowels (where applicable) and locate a new gasket over the dowels. Note that the gasket can only fit in one position **(see illustration)**. Do not use jointing compound.

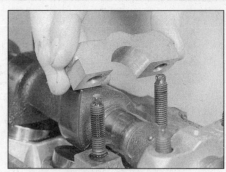

18.14a Lifting off a camshaft bearing cap

18.15 Withdrawing a cam follower

18.16 M8 cylinder head bolts (arrowed) located at front of cylinder head

23 Lower the cylinder head onto the gasket, making sure that the locating dowels engage.
24 Oil the threads of the **new** main cylinder head bolts, and insert them into their locations in the cylinder head.
25 Tighten the bolts in the order shown **(see illustrations)** in the four stages given in the Specifications.

18.22 Fitting a new cylinder head gasket

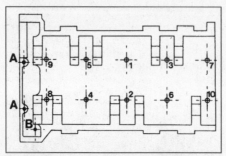

18.25a Cylinder head bolt tightening sequence
A Long M8 bolt   B Short M8 bolt

18.25b Tightening a cylinder head bolt using an angle gauge

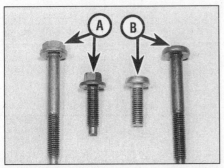

18.26 Use new M8 (auxiliary) cylinder head bolts with hexagonal heads (A), not earlier-type Torx bolts (B)

26 Insert the three smaller M8 cylinder head bolts through the top of the timing case and tighten them to the specified torque. Note that new bolts must be used, and that they should be of the latest type, with hexagonal heads (see illustration).

27 Lubricate the cam follower bores in the cylinder head, and the cam followers themselves, then insert the cam followers into their original locations in the cylinder head.

28 Lubricate the camshaft bearing surfaces in the cylinder head, and the bearing caps.

29 Lubricate the surfaces of the camshafts, then carefully lay the camshafts in their original positions in the cylinder head. Position the camshafts with the slots in their front ends pointing away from each other.

30 Fit and tighten the bearing caps L1, L3, L5, R1, R3, and R5 in the sequence shown (see illustration), then lay the camshaft oil spray bars and the timing chain guide plate in position over the studs (see illustrations).

31 Carefully tighten the bearing cap securing nuts by hand in the following sequence to lower the camshafts into position. Continue to tighten the nuts in the sequence given, in small amounts, until the bearing caps contact the cylinder head.

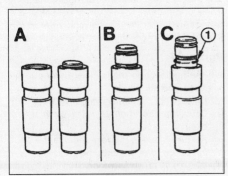

18.34 Timing chain tensioner plunger assembly

A Piston retracted - plunger assembly useable
B Piston partially unlatched - discard plunger assembly
C Latching ring (1) visible - discard plunger assembly

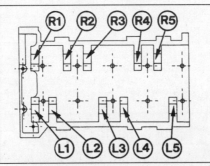

18.30a Camshaft bearing cap tightening sequence (see text)

1 Tighten the nuts for bearing caps L1 and R1 by half-a-turn (180°)
2 Tighten the nuts for bearing caps L5 and R5 by half-a-turn (180°)
3 Tighten the nuts for bearing caps L3 and R3 by half-a-turn (180°)

32 Fit bearing caps L2, L4, R2 and R4, and tap them into position on the cylinder head using light taps from a soft-faced mallet. Tighten the securing nuts evenly by hand.

33 Tighten all the bearing cap nuts to the specified torque in half-turn stages, using the following sequence:

1 L1 and R1
2 L5 and R5
3 L3 and R3
4 L2 and L4
5 R2 and R4

34 Fit a new chain tensioner plunger assembly to the housing in the cylinder head with the piston uppermost. Before fitting the new plunger assembly, take note of position of the piston (see illustration). The assembly is normally supplied with the piston protruding slightly from the cylinder, or slightly below the top surface of the cylinder ("A"). If the new assembly is supplied with the piston partially unlatched ("B"), or fully unlatched with the latching ring visible ("C"), it must not be used (see illustration).

  Warning: Take care when installing the plunger assembly, as there is a risk of injury if the piston flies out.

35 Locate the chain tensioner arm in position, then insert the pivot pin, and secure it with the circlip. Take care not to drop the circlip into the timing-case.

36 Release the cable-tie securing the timing chain (if used), and lay the chain over the exhaust camshaft sprocket, aligning the marks made previously on the chain and sprocket, so that the timing chain is taut on the exhaust side of the engine.

37 Fit the sprocket to the exhaust camshaft, with the camshaft in the TDC position (ie with the exhaust camshaft sprocket timing mark in line with the top edge of the cylinder head, pointing to the exhaust side of the engine - see paragraph 4. If necessary, use a pair of pliers on one of the unmachined sections of the camshaft to turn the camshaft to the TDC

18.30b Camshaft oil spray bars correctly fitted

18.30c Fitting the timing chain guide plate

position. Take care not to damage the machined surfaces of the camshaft.

38 With the sprocket fitted, fit the spacer to the end of the camshaft, and tighten the securing bolt finger-tight (see illustration).

39 Lay the timing chain over the inlet camshaft sprocket, aligning the marks made previously on the chain and the sprocket.

40 Fit the sprocket to the inlet camshaft, with the camshaft in the TDC position (ie with the inlet camshaft sprocket timing mark in line with the top edge of the cylinder head, pointing to the inlet side of the engine - see paragraph 4). Again, turn the camshaft if necessary to enable the sprocket to be fitted.

41 With the sprocket fitted, fit the distributor rotor shaft to the end of the camshaft, and tighten the securing bolt finger-tight. Note that it is acceptable for the timing chain to sag slightly between the two pulleys.

18.38 Spacer and sprocket securing bolt fitted to end of camshaft, with camshaft in TDC position (timing marks arrowed)

2B

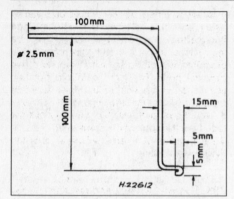

18.45 Fabricated tool used to unlatch
tensioner plunger piston

42 Fit a new upper timing chain guide to the plate at the front of the cylinder head.

43 Turn the crankshaft clockwise until the inlet camshaft begins to turn.

44 If the chain tensioner plunger piston protrudes from the cylinder, unlatch the piston by pressing the chain tensioner arm down by hand.

45 If the plunger piston is below the top surface of the cylinder, a tool similar to that shown **(see illustration)** must be fabricated to unlatch the piston. It is suggested that a 2.5 mm diameter welding rod is used to manufacture the tool. Use the tool to release the piston as follows.

46 Carefully lift the chain tensioner arm with a screwdriver, and insert the tool between the tensioner arm and the piston. Remove the screwdriver, and release the piston by pressing the tensioner arm down by hand. Carefully withdraw the tool once the piston has been released.

47 Tighten the camshaft sprocket securing bolts to the specified torque, holding the sprockets stationary as during removal.

48 Turn the crankshaft clockwise through two complete revolutions, and check that the timing marks on the camshaft sprockets are still aligned with the top face of the cylinder head as described in paragraph 4.

49 Turn the crankshaft clockwise through another complete revolution, and check that the timing marks on the camshaft sprockets are facing each other, directly in line with the top face of the cylinder head.

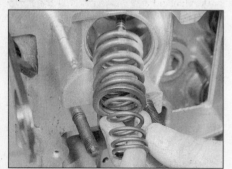

19.1 Withdrawing the double valve springs
from the cylinder head

18.53 Upper timing chain cover securing
stud locations (arrowed)

50 If the timing marks do not align as described, the timing chain has been incorrectly fitted (probably one chain link away from the correct position on one of the camshaft sprockets), and the chain should be removed from the sprockets and refitted again in the correct position as described previously.

51 Inspect the oil seal in the upper timing chain cover. If the oil seal is in good condition, the cover can be refitted as follows, but if the seal is damaged, or has been leaking, a new seal should be fitted to the cover. If necessary, carefully prise the old oil seal from the cover using a screwdriver, and drive in the new seal using a suitable metal tube. Make sure that the seal lip faces into the engine. Take care not to damage the timing chain cover.

52 Fit the upper timing chain cover using a new rubber gasket. Great care must be taken to avoid damage to the oil seal when passing the seal over the end of the inlet camshaft. Careful manipulation will be required (possibly using a thin feeler blade) to avoid damage to the oil seal sealing lip. Note that the oil seal should be fitted dry.

53 Refit the timing chain cover securing bolts and studs in their original locations, and tighten them to the specified torque **(see illustration)**.

54 Remove the reinforcing sleeves from the camshaft cover, and renew the rubber sealing rings. Note that the four short reinforcing sleeves fit at the front of the cover **(see illustration)**.

55 Refit the camshaft cover using a new gasket, and tighten the securing bolts and studs to the specified torque.

19 Cylinder head - dismantling and reassembly

Note: *A valve spring compressor will be required during this procedure. New valve stem oil seals should be used on reassembly.*

1 Proceed as described in Chapter 2, Part C, noting the following points:

a) *Ignore the references to removing and refitting the camshaft.*
b) *Double valve springs are used on all the valves (see illustration).*

18.54 Fitting a camshaft cover reinforcing
sleeve and sealing ring

c) *Ignore the reference to inlet valve dampers.*
d) *Refer to the following Section if the cylinder head is to be inspected and renovated.*

20 Cylinder head - inspection and renovation

1 Refer to Chapter 2, Part A, noting the following points:

a) *Valve and valve seat cutting and regrinding can be carried out using conventional tools.*
b) *The cylinder head cannot be resurfaced, and if the surface distortion exceeds the specified limits, the cylinder head must be renewed.*

21 Camshafts and cam followers - removal, inspection and refitting

Note: *Once the timing chain has been removed from the camshaft sprockets, do not turn the crankshaft until the timing chain has been correctly refitted - this is to prevent contact between the valves and pistons. A new timing chain tensioner plunger assembly, a new upper timing chain cover gasket, and a new camshaft cover gasket and reinforcing sleeve sealing rings, must be used on refitting.*

Removal

1 If the engine is in the vehicle, carry out the following operations:

a) *Disconnect the battery negative lead.*
b) *On carburettor models, remove the air cleaner.*
c) *On fuel injection models, remove the air inlet hose, plenum chamber, and air cleaner lid as an assembly.*
d) *Disconnect the breather hose from the camshaft cover.*
e) *Remove the distributor cap and HT leads, and the rotor arm and housing. If necessary, mark the HT leads to aid refitting.*

2 Proceed as described in paragraphs 2 to 15 inclusive of Section 18.

Inspection

3 Examine the surfaces of the camshaft journals and lobes and the contact surfaces of the cam followers for wear. If wear is excessive considerable noise would have been noticed from the top of the engine when running, and new camshafts and followers must be fitted. It is unlikely that this level of wear will occur unless a considerable mileage has been covered. Note that the cam followers cannot be dismantled for renewal of individual components.

4 Check the camshaft bearing surfaces in the cylinder head and the bearing caps for wear. If excessive wear is evident, the only course of action available is to renew the cylinder head and bearing caps.

5 Check the cam follower bores in the cylinder head for wear. If excessive wear is evident, the cylinder head must be renewed.

6 Check the cam follower oil grooves and the oil ports in the cylinder head for obstructions.

Refitting

7 Refit the cam followers and the camshafts as described in paragraphs 27 to 55 of Section 18.

8 If the engine is in the vehicle, reverse the operations given in paragraph 1.

22 Flywheel/driveplate - removal inspection and refitting

Note: *New flywheel/driveplate securing bolts must be used on refitting.*

1 Refer to Chapter 2, Part A, noting the following points.

2 If the engine is in the car, refer to Chapter 6 when removing and refitting the clutch.

3 There is no need to make alignment marks between the flywheel/driveplate and the end of the crankshaft, as the securing bolt holes are offset, so the flywheel/driveplate can only be fitted to the crankshaft in one position.

4 The flywheel/driveplate securing bolts must be renewed when refitting, and the new bolts are supplied ready-coated with threadlocking compound **(see illustration)**.

5 Check on the availability of new parts before contemplating renewal of the ring gear.

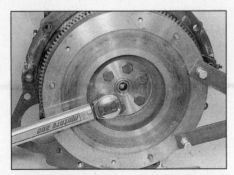

22.4 Improvised tool used to hold flywheel when tightening securing bolts

23 Crankshaft front oil seal - renewal

Note: *A suitable puller will be required to remove the crankshaft pulley. A new crankshaft pulley bolt, and a new lower timing chain cover gasket, must be used on refitting.*

1 The crankshaft front oil seal is located in the lower timing chain cover.

2 If the engine is in the car, carry out the following operations:

a) *Disconnect the battery negative lead.*
b) *To improve access, remove the radiator. It will be difficult to remove the crankshaft pulley with the radiator in place.*
c) *On fuel injection models, remove the air inlet hose, plenum chamber, and air cleaner lid as an assembly.*

3 Proceed as described in paragraphs 3 to 8 of Section 15.

4 With the lower timing chain cover removed, prise the old oil seal from the cover using a screwdriver, and drive in the new seal using a suitable metal tube. Make sure that the seal lip faces into the engine. Take care not to damage the timing chain cover.

5 Refit the lower timing chain cover as described in paragraphs 31 to 39 of Section 15.

6 If the engine is in the vehicle, reverse the operations given in paragraph 2.

24 Crankshaft rear oil seal - renewal

Note: *New flywheel/driveplate bolts must be used on refitting.*

1 Remove the flywheel/driveplate and the engine adapter plate.

2 Extract the seal using an oil seal removal tool if available. It may also be possible to remove the oil seal by drilling the outer face and using self-tapping screws and a pair of grips.

3 Clean the oil seal housing, then carefully wind a thin layer of tape around the edge of the crankshaft to protect the oil seal lip as the seal is installed.

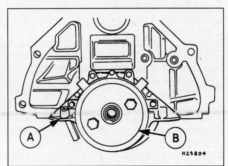

24.4 Tool used to fit crankshaft rear oil seal

A *Rear oil seal housing*
B *Special tool*

4 Ideally, the new oil seal should be installed using a tool similar to that shown **(see illustration)**. A suitable tool can be improvised using a metal tube of suitable diameter, a metal disc or flat bar, and two flywheel bolts. Draw the seal into position using the two flywheel bolts. Make sure that the seal lip faces into the engine.

5 With the oil seal installed, carefully pull the tape from the edge of the crankshaft.

6 Refit the engine adapter plate and the flywheel/driveplate.

25 Sump - removal and refitting

⚠ *Warning: A new sump gasket will be required on refitting, and suitable sealing compound will be required to coat the sump and cylinder block mating faces.* Shims may be required when mating the engine and gearbox/transmission - see text.

Removal

1 Sump removal and refitting is far easier if the engine is removed from the vehicle - if so, proceed to paragraph 9. However, if the engine is in the vehicle, proceed as follows.

2 Remove the gearbox and clutch, or automatic transmission, as applicable.

3 Remove the flywheel/driveplate and the engine adapter plate.

4 Drain the engine oil into a container.

5 Ensure that the steering wheel is positioned in the straight-ahead position, then remove the clamp bolt from the lower steering column clamp, swivel the plate to one side, and disconnect the lower steering column from the lower flexible coupling.

6 Attach a suitable hoist to the engine lifting brackets located at the front and rear of the cylinder head, and carefully take the weight of the engine.

7 Detach the brake lines from the front suspension crossmember.

8 Support the crossmember with a jack, then loosen the bolts securing the crossmember to the underbody. Remove the bolts, and carefully lower the crossmember sufficiently to allow the sump to be removed.

9 If the engine has been removed, it is preferable to keep it upright until the sump has been removed, to prevent sludge in the sump from entering the engine internals.

10 Unscrew the sump securing nuts and bolts, and withdraw the sump from the engine. If the sump is stuck, gently tap it sideways to free it (the sump will not move far sideways, as it locates on studs in the cylinder block). Do not prise between the mating faces of the sump and block. Recover the gasket.

11 Thoroughly clean the mating faces of the cylinder block and sump.

Refitting

12 Commence refitting by locating a new gasket in the grooves in the sump.

2B

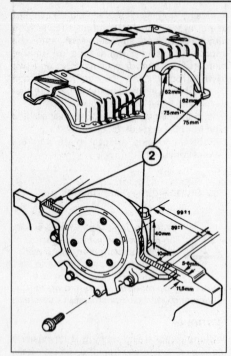

25.13 Apply sealing compound to the sump/cylinder block mating faces at the points indicated (2)
Dimensions are for guidance only

13 Apply a suitable sealing compound to the faces of the cylinder block and sump, at the points indicated **(see illustration)**.
14 Locate the sump on the cylinder block, then apply suitable thread-locking compound to the sump securing studs and bolts. Fit the securing nuts and bolts, but do not fully tighten them at this stage.
15 Align the sump so that its end faces and the cylinder block are flush. To do this, use a straight-edge. If the sump cannot be positioned so that the faces of the cylinder block and sump are flush, measure the difference in height using a feeler blade as shown **(see illustration)**.
16 Tighten the sump securing nuts and bolts to the specified torque, then repeat the measurement made in paragraph 15. If the end faces of the sump and cylinder block are not flush, suitable shims (available from a Ford dealer) must be fitted between the sump and the gearbox/transmission to eliminate the clearance when mating the engine to the gearbox/transmission. Note that shims should be fitted at both sides of the sump, as required. Select suitable shims from those listed in the following table:

Clearance measured	Shims required
0 to 0.25 mm	No shims required
0.25 to 0.29 mm	0.15 mm (silver)
0.30 to 0.44 mm	0.30 mm (light blue)
0.45 to 0.59 mm	0.45 mm (red)
0.60 to 0.75 mm	0.60 mm (black)

17 If the engine is in the vehicle, proceed as follows.
18 Reverse the procedure described in paragraphs 2 to 8, noting the following points.

25.15 Measuring the clearance between the cylinder block and sump end faces

19 Ensure that the roadwheels and the steering wheel are in the straight-ahead position before reconnecting the lower steering column to the intermediate shaft.
20 Fill the engine with the correct grade and quantity of oil.
21 Refit the engine adapter plate and the flywheel/driveplate.
22 Refit the gearbox or automatic transmission, ensuring that the required shims are fitted between the sump and the gearbox/transmission.
23 Tighten all fixings to the specified torque, where applicable.

26 Oil pump - removal and refitting

Note: *A suitable puller will be required to remove the crankshaft pulley. A new crankshaft pulley bolt, a new lower timing chain cover gasket, and a new oil pump gasket, must be used on refitting.*

Removal

1 If the engine is in the car, carry out the following operations:
 a) *Disconnect the battery negative lead.*
 b) *To improve access, remove the radiator. It will be difficult to remove the crankshaft pulley with the radiator in place.*
 c) *On fuel injection models, remove the air inlet hose, plenum chamber, and air cleaner lid as an assembly.*
2 Proceed as described in paragraphs 3 to 10 of Section 15.
3 Unscrew the four securing bolts, and withdraw the oil pump from the cylinder block **(see illustrations)**. Recover the gasket.

Refitting

4 Thoroughly clean the mating faces of the pump and the cylinder block.
5 Prime the pump by injecting clean engine oil into it and turning it by hand.
6 Place a new gasket on the oil pump flange, ensuring that the gasket is correctly located so that its holes align with the oil passages in the pump.
7 Fit the oil pump, and tighten the securing bolts to the specified torque.

26.3a Oil pump securing bolts (arrowed)

26.3b Withdrawing the oil pump

8 Proceed as shown in paragraphs 27 to 39 of Section 15.
9 If the engine is in the vehicle, reverse the operations described in paragraph 1.

27 Oil pump - dismantling, inspection and reassembly

Dismantling

1 The oil pump can be dismantled for cleaning, but if any of the components are worn, the pump must be renewed as an assembly.
2 To dismantle the pump, proceed as follows.
3 Unscrew the two securing bolts, and remove the pump cover **(see illustration)**.
4 Lift the inner and outer rotors from the pump casing.

27.3 Removing the oil pump cover

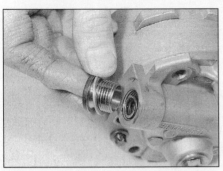

27.5a Unscrew the pressure relief valve plug and washer . . .

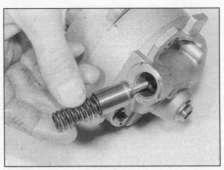

27.5b . . . and withdraw the spring and plunger

27.9 The punch marks (arrowed) on the oil pump rotors must face the pump cover

5 Unscrew the pressure relief valve plug from the pump cover, recover the washer, and withdraw the spring and plunger **(see illustrations)**.

Inspection

6 Thoroughly clean all components in petrol or paraffin, and wipe dry using a non-fluffy rag.
7 Examine the rotors and the pump casing for signs of excessive wear on the machined surfaces. If wear is evident, the complete pump assembly must be renewed, as spare parts are not available individually.

Reassembly

8 Commence reassembly by lubricating the relief valve plunger. Fit the plunger and the spring, and screw the plug into place, ensuring that the washer is in place under the plug.
9 Lubricate the rotors, and fit them to the pump casing with the punch marks facing the pump cover **(see illustration)**.
10 Refit the pump cover and tighten the securing bolts.
11 Prime the pump before refitting.

28 Oil pump drive chain and sprockets - examination and renovation

1 Examine all the teeth on the sprockets. If the teeth are "hooked" in appearance, renew the sprockets.
2 Examine the chain tensioner for wear, and renew it if necessary.

3 Examine the chain for wear. If it has been in operation for a considerable time, or if when held horizontally (rollers vertical) it takes on a deeply-bowed appearance, renew it.

29 Pistons and connecting rods - removal and refitting

Note: *New connecting rod bolts and a new oil pick-up pipe gasket must be used on refitting.*

Removal

1 Remove the sump and the cylinder head.
2 Unscrew the two securing bolts, and remove the oil pick-up pipe **(see illustration)**. Recover the gasket.
3 Unscrew the four securing nuts, and withdraw the oil baffle from the studs on the main bearing caps **(see illustration)**.
4 Proceed as described in Chapter 2, Part A, Section 32, paragraphs 2 to 5.

Refitting

5 Proceed as described in Chapter 2, Part A, Section 32, paragraphs 6 to 13, noting the following points:
6 Take note of the orientation of the bearing shells during dismantling, and ensure that they are fitted correctly during reassembly.
7 When fitting the pistons, ensure that the arrow on the piston crown and the letter "F" on the face of the connecting rod are pointing towards the front of the engine.
8 Use new connecting rod bolts on reassembly, and before fitting, oil the threads and the contact faces of the bolts. Tighten the

bolts in the three stages given in the Specifications at the beginning of this Chapter.
9 Refit the oil baffle, and tighten the securing nuts.
10 Clean the mating faces of the cylinder block and the oil pick-up pipe, and refit the pick-up pipe using a new gasket.
11 Refit the cylinder head and the sump.

30 Crankshaft and main bearings - removal and refitting

Note: *A new crankshaft rear oil seal and a new rear oil seal housing gasket should be used on refitting.*

Removal

1 With the engine removed from the vehicle, remove the timing chain and crankshaft sprocket, and the flywheel/driveplate.
2 Remove the pistons and connecting rods. If no work is to be done on the pistons and connecting rods, there is no need to push the pistons out of the cylinder bores.
3 Unbolt the crankshaft rear oil seal housing, and remove it from the rear of the cylinder block. Recover the gasket.
4 Unscrew the two securing bolts, and remove the sump mounting plate from the front of the cylinder block **(see illustration)**.
5 Check the main bearing caps for identification marks, and if necessary, use a centre-punch to identify them **(see illustration)**.

2B

29.2 Removing the oil pick-up pipe

29.3 Withdrawing the oil baffle

30.4 Unscrewing a sump mounting plate securing bolt

30.5 Main bearing cap identification mark (arrowed)

6 Before removing the crankshaft, check that the endfloat is within the specified limits by inserting a feeler blade between the centre crankshaft web and one of the thrustwashers (the thrustwashers are fitted to the crankcase, not the bearing cap). This will indicate whether or not new thrustwashers are required.
7 Unscrew the bolts, and tap off the main bearing caps complete with bearing shells.
8 Lift the crankshaft from the cylinder block, and remove the rear oil seal if it is still in place on the crankshaft.
9 Extract the bearing shells, and recover the thrustwashers, keeping them identified for location.

Refitting

10 Commence refitting as follows **(see illustration)**.
11 Wipe the bearing shell locations in the crankcase, and the crankshaft journals with a soft non-fluffy rag.
12 If the old main bearing shells are to be renewed (not to do so is a false economy, unless they are virtually new) fit the five upper halves of the main bearing shells to their locations in the crankcase.
13 Fit the thrustwashers to the centre main bearing location, using a little grease to retain them if necessary. The oil grooves in the thrustwashers must face outwards (ie facing the crankshaft webs). Note that where standard thrustwashers have been fitted in production, the centre main bearing is unmarked. If oversize (0.38 mm) thrustwashers have been fitted, the centre main bearing will carry a yellow paint mark.
14 Lubricate the crankshaft journals and the upper and lower main bearing shells with clean engine oil, then carefully lower the crankshaft into the crankcase.
15 Lubricate the crankshaft main bearing journals again, and then fit the main bearing caps in their correct locations, with the arrows on the caps pointing to the front of the engine.

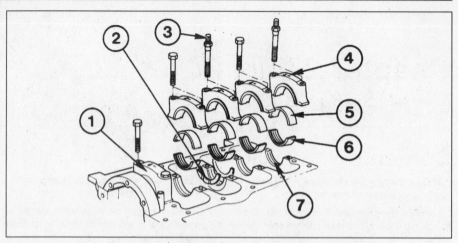

30.10 Crankshaft main bearings and associated components

1 *Bearing cap*
2 *Thrustwasher*
3 *Stud for oil baffle*
4 *Identification markings*
5 *Bearing shell without oil groove*
6 *Bearing shell with oil groove*
7 *Bearing seat in cylinder block*

16 Fit the main bearing cap bolts, noting that the studded bolts secure bearing caps Nos 3 and 5.
17 Lightly tighten all the securing bolts, then progressively tighten all bolts to the specified torque.
18 Check that the crankshaft rotates freely. Some stiffness is to be expected with new components, but there must be no tight spots or binding.
19 Check that the crankshaft endfloat is within the specified limits by inserting a feeler blade between the centre crankshaft web and the thrustwashers.
20 Refit the sump mounting plate to the front of the cylinder block, and tighten the securing bolts to the specified torque.
21 Carefully wind a thin layer of tape around the rear edge of the crankshaft, to protect the oil seal lips as the rear oil seal is installed.
22 Refit the crankshaft rear oil seal housing, using a new gasket, and tighten the securing bolts to the specified torque.
23 Ideally, the new oil seal should be installed using a tool similar to that used for fitting the crankshaft rear oil seal. A suitable tool can be improvised using a metal tube of suitable diameter, a metal disc or flat bar, and two flywheel bolts. Draw the seal into position using the two flywheel bolts. Make sure that the seal lip faces into the engine.
24 With the oil seal installed, carefully pull the tape from the edge of the crankshaft.
25 Refit the pistons and connecting rods.
26 Refit the flywheel/driveplate, and the timing chain and crankshaft sprocket.

31 Crankshaft and bearings - examination and renovation

1 Proceed as described in Chapter 2, Part A, noting the following.
2 Production bearing undersizes are indicated as follows:
Yellow or red paint marks on crankshaft - standard-diameter main bearing journals.
Green line on crankshaft front counterweight - main bearing journals 0.25 mm undersize.
Green spot on counterweight - big-end bearing journals 25 mm undersize.

32 Initial start-up after overhaul or major repair

1 Refer to Chapter 2, Part A, but note that when the engine is first started, a metallic tapping noise may be heard. This is due to the timing chain tensioner plunger assembly taking time to pressurise with oil, resulting in a temporarily slack chain. The noise should stop after a short time, once oil pressure has built up.

Chapter 2 Part C:
CVH engines

Contents

Degrees of difficulty

| **Easy,** suitable for novice with little experience | | **Fairly easy,** suitable for beginner with some experience | | **Fairly difficult,** suitable for competent DIY mechanic | | **Difficult,** suitable for experienced DIY mechanic | | **Very difficult,** suitable for expert DIY or professional | |

Specifications

1.6 litre engine

Note: *Unless otherwise stated, the Specifications for the 1.6 litre CVH engine are as given for the 1.8 litre (R2A type) which follow.*

General

Engine code	L6B
Bore	79.960 mm
Stroke	79.520 mm
Cubic capacity	1596 cc
Compression ratio	9.0 :1
Compression pressure at starter motor speed	12.2 to 14.3 bars
Maximum continuous engine speed	6000 rpm
Maximum engine power (DIN)	59 kW at 5500 rpm
Maximum engine torque (DIN)	121 Nm at 3500 rpm

Cylinder bore diameter

Standard class 1	79.940 to 79.950 mm
Standard class 2	79.950 to 79.960 mm
Standard class 3	79.960 to 79.970 mm
Standard class 4	79.970 to 79.980 mm
Oversize class A	80.230 to 80.240 mm
Oversize class B	80.240 to 80.250 mm
Oversize class C	80.250 to 80.260 mm

Crankshaft

Endfloat	0.09 to 0.30 mm (0.004 to 0.012 in)
Main bearing running clearance	0.011 to 0.058 mm
Main bearing journal diameter:	
Standard	57.980 to 58.000 mm
Undersize 0.25	57.730 to 57.750 mm
Undersize 0.50	57.480 mm
Undersize 0.75	57.230 to 57.250 mm
Main bearing thrustwasher thickness:	
Standard	2.301 to 2.351 mm
Oversize	2.491 to 2.541 mm
Big-end bearing running clearance	0.006 to 0.060 mm
Big-end bearing journal diameter:	
Standard	47.890 to 47.910 mm
Undersize 0.25	47.640 to 47.660 mm
Undersize 0.50	47.390 to 47.410 mm
Undersize 0.75	47.140 to 47.160 mm
Undersize 1.00	46.890 to 46.910 mm

Pistons and piston rings

Piston diameter:	
Standard class 1	79.915 to 79.925 mm
Standard class 2	79.925 to 79.935 mm
Standard class 3	79.935 to 79.945 mm
Standard class 4	79.945 to 79.955 mm
Oversize class A	80.205 to 80.215 mm
Oversize class B	80.215 to 80.225 mm
Oversize class C	80.225 to 80.235 mm
Piston ring end gap:	
Top and centre rings	0.300 to 0.500 mm (0.012 to 0.020 in)
Bottom (oil control) ring	0.250 to 0.400 mm (0.010 to 0.016 in)

Camshaft

Endfloat	0.050 to 0.150 mm (0.002 to 0.006 in)
Thrustplate thickness	4.990 to 5.010 mm (0.1966 to 0.1974 in)
Bearing journal diameter:	
Bearing No 1	44.750 mm
Bearing No 2	45.000 mm
Bearing No 3	45.250 mm
Bearing No 4	45.500 mm
Bearing No 5	45.750 mm

Valves

Valve timing:	
Inlet opens	4° ATDC
Inlet closes	32° ABDC
Exhaust opens	38° BBDC
Exhaust closes	10° BTDC
Valve spring free length:	
Colour code blue/blue	47.200 mm
Colour code white/blue	45.400 mm
Inlet valve stem diameter:	
Standard	8.025 to 8.043 mm
Oversize 0.20	8.225 to 8.243 mm
Oversize 0.40	8.425 to 8.443 mm
Exhaust valve stem diameter:	
Standard	7.999 to 8.017 mm
Oversize 0.20	8.199 to 8.217 mm
Oversize 0.40	8.399 to 8.417 mm

Lubrication system

Oil type	Multigrade engine oil, viscosity range SAE 10W/30 to 20W/50, to API SG/CD or better
Oil capacity:	
With filter	3.5 litres (6.2 pints)
Without filter	3.25 litres (5.7 pints)
Oil pump clearances:	
Outer rotor-to-body	0.060 to 0.190 mm (0.002 to 0.007 in)
Inner rotor-to-outer rotor	0.050 to 0.180 mm (0.002 to 0.007 in)
Rotor endfloat	0.014 to 0.100 mm (0.001 to 0.004 in)

Torque wrench settings

	Nm	lbf ft
Main bearing cap bolts	90 to 100	66 to 74
Connecting rod (big-end bearing cap) bolts	30 to 36	22 to 27
Crankshaft pulley bolt	100 to 115	74 to 85
Camshaft sprocket bolt	54 to 59	40 to 44
Flywheel bolts	82 to 92	61 to 68
Oil pump bolts	8 to 11	6 to 8
Oil pump cover bolts	8 to 12	6 to 9
Sump bolts (in two stages)	5 to 8	4 to 6
Rocker arm nuts	25 to 29	18 to 21
Cylinder head bolts:		
Stage 1	20 to 40	15 to 30
Stage 2	40 to 60	30 to 44
Stage 3	Angle-tighten a further 90°	
Stage 4	Angle-tighten a further 90°	
Camshaft cover bolts	6 to 8	4 to 6
Timing cover bolts	9 to 11	7 to 8
Timing belt tensioner bolts	16 to 20	12 to 15
Oil pick-up tube/strainer-to-oil pump bolts	8 to 12	6 to 9
Oil pick-up tube/strainer-to-cylinder block bolt	17 to 23	13 to 17
Camshaft thrustplate bolts	9 to 13	7 to 10
Crankshaft rear oil seal housing bolts	8 to 11	6 to 8

1.8 litre (R2A type) engine

General

Engine type	Four-cylinder, in-line, single overhead camshaft
Firing order	1-3-4-2
Engine code	R2A
Bore	80.00 mm
Stroke	88.00 mm
Cubic capacity	1769 cc
Compression ratio	9.3:1
Compression pressure at starter motor speed	11 to 13 bar
Maximum continuous engine speed	5850 rpm
Maximum engine power (DIN)	66 kW at 5250 rpm
Maximum engine torque (DIN)	147 Nm at 3000 rpm

Cylinder bore diameter

Standard class 1	79.940 to 79.950 mm
Standard class 2	79.950 to 79.960 mm
Standard class 3	79.960 to 79.970 mm
Standard class 4	79.970 to 79.980 mm
Standard class 5	79.980 to 79.990 mm
Standard class 6	79.990 to 80.000 mm
Oversize class A	80.000 to 80.010 mm
Oversize class B	80.010 to 80.020 mm
Oversize class C	80.020 to 80.030 mm

Crankshaft

Endfloat	0.10 to 0.20 mm (0.004 to 0.008 in)
Main bearing running clearance	0.028 to 0.067 mm
Main bearing journal diameter:	
Standard	53.980 to 54.000 mm
Undersize 0.25	53.730 to 54.750 mm
Undersize 0.50	53.480 to 53.500 mm
Undersize 0.75	53.230 to 53.250 mm
Centre main thrust bearing shell width:	
Standard	28.825 to 28.875 mm
Undersize 0.15	28.675 to 28.725 mm
Big-end bearing running clearance	0.020 to 0.065 mm
Big-end bearing journal diameter:	
Standard	43.890 to 43.910 mm
Undersize 0.25	43.640 to 43.660 mm
Undersize 0.50	43.390 to 43.410 mm
Undersize 0.75	43.140 to 43.160 mm
Undersize 1.00	42.890 to 42.910 mm

Pistons and piston rings

Piston diameter:
Standard class 1	79.910 to 79.920 mm
Standard class 2	79.920 to 79.930 mm
Standard class 3	79.930 to 79.940 mm
Standard class 4	79.940 to 79.950 mm
Standard class 5	79.950 to 79.960 mm
Standard class 6	79.960 to 79.970 mm
Oversize class A	79.970 to 79.980 mm
Oversize class B	79.980 to 79.990 mm
Oversize class C	79.990 to 80.000 mm

Camshaft

Endfloat	0.15 to 0.20 mm (0.006 to 0.008 in)
Thrustplate thickness	4.99 to 5.01 mm (0.1966 to 0.1974 in)
Bearing journal diameter	45.7625 to 45.7375 mm

Valves

Valve timing:
Inlet opens	22° BTDC
Inlet closes	54° ABDC
Exhaust opens	64° BBDC
Exhaust closes	12° ATDC
Valve spring free length	47.20 mm (1.86 in)

Inlet valve stem diameter:
Standard	8.025 to 8.043 mm
Oversize 0.38	8.405 to 8.423 mm
Oversize 0.76	8.825 to 8.843 mm
Exhaust valve stem diameter (standard)	7.996 to 8.017 mm

Lubrication system

Oil type	Multigrade engine oil, viscosity range SAE 10W/30 to 20W/50, to API SG/CD or better

Oil capacity:
With filter	4.0 litres (7.0 pints)
Without filter	3.5 litres (6.2 pints)
Oil filter	Champion C104

Oil pump clearances:
Outer rotor to body	0.074 to 0.161 mm (0.003 to 0.006 in)
Inner rotor to outer rotor	0.050 to 0.180 mm (0.002 to 0.007 in)
Rotor endfloat	0.013 to 0.070 mm (0.0005 to 0.0028 in)

Torque wrench settings

	Nm	lbf ft
Main bearing cap bolts	90 to 108	66 to 80
Big-end bearing caps:		
With retaining nuts	26 to 34	19 to 25
With retaining bolts	35 to 41	26 to 30
Crankshaft pulley bolt	110 to 130	81 to 96
Camshaft sprocket bolt	95 to 115	70 to 85
Flywheel bolts	73 to 91	54 to 67
Oil pump bolts	11 to 16	8 to 12
Oil pump cover bolts	9 to 12	7 to 9
Sump bolts:		
M6 bolts	8 to 11	6 to 8
M8 bolts	20 to 30	15 to 22
Sump drain plug	20 to 30	15 to 22
Rocker arm bolts	23 to 30	17 to 22
Cylinder head bolts:		
Stage 1	40 to 60	30 to 44
Stage 2	Slacken bolts by half a turn	
Stage 3	40 to 60	30 to 44
Stage 4	Tighten through a further 90°	
Stage 5	Tighten through a further 90°	
Camshaft cover bolts	8 to 11	6 to 8
Timing cover bolts	8 to 11	6 to 8
Timing cover nuts	5 to 7	4 to 5
Timing belt tensioner bolts	23 to 30	17 to 22
Oil pick-up tube/strainer-to-oil pump bolts	10 to 13	7 to 9
Camshaft thrustplate bolts	9 to 13	6 to 9
Crankshaft rear oil seal housing bolts	20 to 30	15 to 22

1.8 litre (R6A type) engine

Note: *Unless otherwise stated, the Specifications for this later version of the 1.8 litre CVH engine are as given for the earlier R2A type above.*

General

Engine code R6A
Maximum continuous engine speed . . . . 5700 rpm
Maximum engine power (DIN) . . . . 64 kW at 5200 rpm
Maximum engine torque (DIN) . . . . 145 Nm at 3000 rpm

Valve timing

Inlet opens . . . . 24° BTDC
Inlet closes . . . . 116° BTDC
Exhaust opens . . . . 110° ATDC
Exhaust closes . . . . 18° ATDC

1 General information

1.6 litre engine

The 1.6 litre CVH engine was introduced in September 1991, to replace the 1.6 litre SOHC engine used previously in the Sierra range. The engine is broadly similar to the 1.8 litre (R2A type) CVH engine described below. The main differences are outlined in the following paragraphs.

The centre main bearing is fitted with thrustwashers to control crankshaft endfloat, instead of a flanged bearing shell.

The hydraulic cam followers operate in a similar manner to those described for the 1.8 litre (R2A) engine but no rollers are fitted, and the base of each cam follower is in direct contact with the cam profile.

A distributorless ignition system is used and a blanking plate is therefore fitted to the cylinder head in place of the distributor drive. The electric fuel pump is mounted in the fuel tank.

A comprehensive emissions control system is fitted, comprising Central Fuel Injection (CFI), a sophisticated engine management system, a crankcase ventilation system, a catalytic converter, and a pulseair system (to reduce exhaust gas emissions).

Unless otherwise stated, all procedures are as described for the 1.8 litre (R2A) engine.

1.8 litre (R2A type) engine

The CVH (Compound Valve angle, Hemispherical combustion chambers) engine is of four-cylinder, in-line, single overhead camshaft type. The engine was introduced to replace the 1.8 SOHC engine previously used in the range.

The crankshaft incorporates five main bearings. The centre main bearing has a flanged bearing shell (thrust bearing) fitted to the cylinder block to control crankshaft endfloat

The camshaft is driven by a toothed belt and operates the compound angled valves via roller type hydraulic cam followers, which eliminates the need for valve clearance adjustment. The cam followers operate in the following way. When the valve is closed, pressurised engine oil passes through ports in the body of the cam follower and the plunger into the cylinder feed chamber. From this chamber, oil flows through a ball type non-return valve into the pressure

chamber. The tension of the coil spring causes the plunger to press the rocker arm against the valve and to eliminate any free play.

As the cam lifts the cam follower, the oil pressure in the pressure chamber increases and causes the non-return valve to close the port to the feed chamber. As oil cannot be compressed, it forms a rigid link between the body of the cam follower, the cylinder and the plunger which then rise as one component to open the valve.

The clearance between the body of the cam follower and the cylinder is accurately designed to meter a specific quantity of oil as it escapes from the pressure chamber. Oil will only pass along the cylinder bore when pressure is high during the moment of valve opening. Once the valve has closed, the escape of oil will produce a small amount of free play and no pressure will exist in the pressure chamber. Oil from the feed chamber can then flow through the non-return valve into the pressure chamber so that the cam follower cylinder can be raised by the pressure of the coil spring, thus eliminating any play in the arrangement until the valve is operated again.

As wear occurs between rocker arm and valve stem, the quantity of oil which flows into the pressure chamber will be slightly more than the quantity lost during the expansion cycle of the cam follower. Conversely, when the cam follower is compressed by the expansion of the valve, a slightly smaller quantity of oil will flow into the pressure chamber than was lost.

To reduce valve clatter when the engine is started, a small plastic stand pipe retains oil inside the plunger. When the engine is started, the reservoir in the plunger (and via the non-return valve, the pressure chamber) are immediately filled with oil. This reduces the noise often associated with hydraulic cam followers as they pressurise with oil after engine start-up.

The cam follower rollers run in needle bearings, which greatly reduces friction as the rollers follow the cam profile.

The distributor and fuel pump are driven directly from the camshaft and the oil pump is driven directly from the front of the crankshaft.

The cylinder head is of crossflow design, with the inlet manifold mounted on the right-hand side and the exhaust manifold mounted on the left-hand side.

Lubrication is by means of a bi-rotor pump

which draws oil through a strainer located inside the sump and forces it through a full-flow filter into the oil galleries where it is distributed to the crankshaft and camshaft. The big-end bearings are supplied with oil via internal drillings in the crankshaft. The undersides of the pistons are supplied with oil from drillings in the big-ends. The hydraulic cam followers are supplied with oil from the camshaft bearings via short passages in the cylinder head.

A semi-closed crankcase ventilation system is employed whereby piston blow-by gases are drawn from the crankcase, through the camshaft cover via an external vent hose, out to an oil separator built into the base of the air cleaner.

1.8 litre (R6A type) engine

The 1.8 litre (R6A type) CVH engine, introduced in March 1992, is a further development of the earlier 1.8 litre (R2A type) unit described above. Apart from minor engineering modifications to provide increased fuel economy, reliability and power output, the engine is mechanically identical to the earlier version.

In common with the 1.6 litre unit, a distributorless ignition system is used, together with a comprehensive emissions control system comprising Central Fuel Injection (CFI), a sophisticated engine management system, a crankcase ventilation system, a catalytic converter, and additionally, an exhaust gas recirculation (EGR) system.

Unless otherwise stated, all procedures are as described for the 1.8 litre (R2A type) engine.

2 Engine oil and filter - renewal

Refer to Section 2, Chapter 2, Part A.

3 Crankcase ventilation system - inspection and maintenance

Refer to Chapter 1, Section 35.

4 Compression test

Refer to Section 5, Chapter 2, Part A.

2C

5 Major operations possible with the engine in the vehicle

1.8 litre (R2A type)

a) Removal of the cylinder head
b) Removal of the camshaft
c) Removal of the timing belt and sprockets
d) Removal of the engine mountings
e) Removal of the clutch and flywheel
f) Removal of the crankshaft oil seals

1.6 and 1.8 litre (R6A type)

Add the following procedures to those listed above:
a) Removal of the sump.
b) Removal of the oil pump.
c) Removal of the pistons/connecting rods.
d) Removal of the big-end bearings.

6 Major operations requiring engine removal

1.8 litre (R2A type)

a) Removal of the sump
b) Removal of the oil pump
c) Removal of the pistons/connecting rods
d) Removal of the big-end bearings
e) Removal of the crankshaft main bearings
f) Removal of the crankshaft

1.6 and 1.8 litre (R6A type)

a) Removal of the crankshaft main bearings
b) Removal of the crankshaft

7 Method of engine removal

Refer to Section 8, Chapter 2, Part A.

8 Engine - removal leaving manual gearbox in vehicle

Note: A suitable hoist and lifting tackle will be required for this operation.

1.8 litre (R2A type)

1 Disconnect the battery negative lead.
2 Remove the bonnet.
3 Remove the air cleaner.

8.22a Earth strap location under engine-to-gearbox bolt - 1.8 litre (R2A)

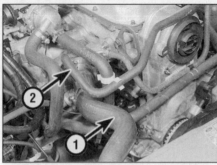

8.7 Disconnect the upper radiator hose (1) and the expansion tank hose (2) from the thermostat housing - 1.8 litre (R2A)

4 Disconnect the cooling fan wiring plug, then unscrew the retaining nuts and washers and withdraw the fan shroud and cooling fan assembly.
5 Drain the cooling system.
6 Disconnect the coolant hoses from the coolant pump elbow, and detach the heater hose from the clip on the front of the timing cover.
7 Disconnect the upper radiator hose and the expansion tank hose from the thermostat housing **(see illustration)**.
8 Disconnect the heater hose from the automatic choke.
9 Disconnect the brake servo vacuum hose from the inlet manifold **(see illustration)**.
10 Disconnect the throttle damper solenoid vacuum pipes (noting their locations) from the throttle damper and the carburettor "T"-piece connector.
11 Disconnect the engine management module vacuum pipe from the inlet manifold.
12 Disconnect the fuel hoses from the carburettor and fuel pump, and plug the ends of the hoses to minimise petrol spillage. Take adequate fire precautions.
13 Disconnect the throttle cable.
14 Disconnect the HT leads from the coil and spark plugs, unclip the leads from the camshaft cover, and remove the distributor cap, rotor arm and housing.
15 Disconnect the wiring from the following components:
Alternator
Starter motor
Oil pressure warning lamp switch
Temperature gauge sender
Engine coolant temperature sensor

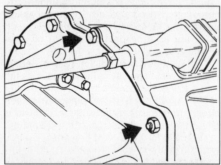

8.22b Remove the two bolts (arrowed) from the engine adapter plate - 1.8 litre (R2A)

8.9 Disconnecting the brake servo vacuum hose from the inlet manifold - 1.8 litre (R2A)

Automatic choke
Cooling fan switch
Crankshaft speed/position sensor
Engine earth strap to battery tray

16 Unscrew and remove the top engine-to-gearbox bolts which are accessible from the engine compartment.
17 Apply the handbrake (if not already done), jack up the front of the vehicle and support on axle stands (see "*Jacking and Vehicle Support*").
18 Drain the engine oil into a container.
19 Remove the starter motor.
20 Remove the exhaust downpipe.
21 Unscrew the two nuts securing the engine mountings to the crossmember. Recover the washers.
22 Unscrew and remove the remaining engine-to-gearbox bolts, noting the location of the earth strap **(see illustration)**, and remove the two bolts from the engine adapter plate **(see illustration)**.
23 Working inside the vehicle, place a wooden block under the clutch pedal to raise it fully against its stop which will hold the automatic adjuster pawl clear of the toothed quadrant.
24 Disconnect the clutch cable from the release arm, and pass the cable through the bellhousing. Remove the clip securing the clutch cable to the right-hand engine mounting bracket. Note the cable routing for use when refitting.
25 Lower the vehicle to the ground, and support the gearbox with a trolley jack using a block of wood between the jack and the gearbox to spread the load.
26 Make a final check to ensure that all relevant wires, pipes and hoses have been disconnected to facilitate engine removal.
27 Attach a suitable hoist to the engine lifting brackets located at the front and rear of the cylinder head, and carefully take the weight of the engine. The engine should be supported horizontally, ie do not allow it to tilt front to rear.
28 Raise the engine until the engine mounting studs are clear of the crossmember, then pull the engine forwards to disconnect it from the gearbox. Ensure that the gearbox is adequately supported, and take care not to strain the gearbox input shaft. It may be necessary to rock the engine a little to release it from the gearbox.

8.29 Lifting the engine from the vehicle - 1.8 litre (R2A)

29 Once clear of the gearbox, lift the engine from the vehicle, taking care not to damage the radiator fins (see illustration).

1.6 and 1.8 litre (R6A type)

30 Proceed as described in paragraphs 1 to 5.
31 Disconnect the coolant hoses from the thermostat housing, noting their locations.
32 Disconnect the lower radiator hose from the coolant pump elbow and, where applicable, disconnect the heater hose from the T-piece on the lower radiator hose.
33 On 1.6 engines, disconnect the coolant hose from the central fuel injection (CFI) unit.
34 Disconnect the brake servo vacuum hose from the inlet manifold by carefully pressing the clip on the inlet manifold connector into the manifold using a screwdriver, and withdrawing the hose.
35 Disconnect the vacuum hoses from the inlet manifold, noting their locations.
36 On 1.6 litre engines, disconnect the two hoses from the pulse-air system check valves (see illustration).
37 Gradually loosen the fuel inlet pipe union on the CFI unit, to relieve the pressure in the fuel system. Be prepared for fuel spray, and take adequate fire precautions. Once the pressure has reduced, disconnect the fuel inlet and return hoses. Plug the ends of the hoses to minimise petrol spillage.
38 Disconnect the throttle cable, if necessary.
39 Disconnect the wiring from the following components, as applicable.

Alternator
Starter motor
Oil pressure warning lamp switch
Temperature gauge sender
Engine coolant temperature sensor
Inlet air temperature sensor
Ignition coil
Throttle stepper motor
Throttle position sensor
Fuel injector
Cooling fan switch
Air charge temperature sensor
Engine earth strap to battery tray

40 On 1.8 litre engine models with power steering, slacken the power steering pump pulley bolts, then remove the alternator/power steering pump drivebelt. Remove the pulley, unbolt the power steering pump from its bracket, and move it clear of the engine.

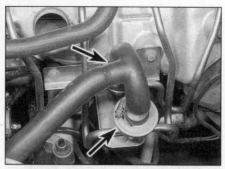

8.36 Pulse-air system check valves (arrowed) - 1.6/1.8 litre (R6A)

41 Unscrew and remove the top engine-to-gearbox bolts which are accessible from the engine compartment.
42 Apply the handbrake (if not already done), jack up the front of the vehicle and support it on axle stands (see "Jacking and Vehicle Support").
43 Drain the engine oil into a suitable container.
44 Remove the starter motor.
45 Disconnect the exhaust gas oxygen sensor wiring connector, then remove the exhaust downpipe.
46 Disconnect the wiring plug from the crankshaft speed/position sensor.
47 Unscrew the two nuts securing the engine mountings to the crossmember. Recover the washers.
48 Unscrew and remove the remaining engine-to-gearbox bolts, noting the location of the earth strap and any wiring brackets, and remove the two bolts from the engine adapter plate (see illustration).
49 Unscrew the securing bolt, and remove the crankshaft speed/position sensor shroud (where fitted).
50 On 1.6 litre engines, working inside the vehicle, place a wooden block under the clutch pedal to raise it fully against its stop. This will hold the automatic adjuster pawl clear of the toothed quadrant. Disconnect the clutch cable from the release arm, and pass the cable through the bellhousing. Note the cable routing for use when refitting.
51 Proceed as shown in paragraphs 25 to 29.

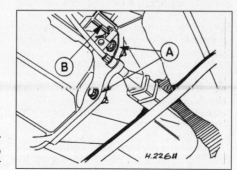

8.48 Engine adapter plate bolts (A) and crankshaft speed/position sensor shroud (B) - 1.6 litre

9 Engine - removal leaving automatic transmission in vehicle

Note: *A suitable hoist and lifting tackle will be required for this operation.*

1 Proceed as described in Section 8, paragraphs 1 to 15 inclusive. Additionally, if applicable disconnect the kickdown cable from the carburettor.
2 Unscrew and remove the top engine-to-transmission bolts which are accessible from the engine compartment. Note the location of the vacuum pipe bracket and transmission dipstick tube bracket.
3 Proceed as described in Section 8, paragraphs 17 to 21 inclusive.
4 Working through the starter motor aperture, unscrew the four torque converter-to-driveplate nuts. It will be necessary to turn the crankshaft using a suitable spanner on the crankshaft pulley bolt in order to gain access to each nut in turn through the aperture.
5 Unscrew and remove the remaining engine-to-transmission bolts, noting the location of the earth strap, and remove the two bolts from the engine adapter plate. Where applicable pull the blanking plug from the adapter plate.
6 Lower the vehicle to the ground and support the transmission with a trolley jack, using a block of wood between the jack and the transmission to spread the load.
7 Make a final check to ensure that all relevant wires, pipes and hoses have been disconnected to facilitate engine removal.
8 Attach a suitable hoist to the engine lifting brackets located at the front and rear of the cylinder head, and carefully take the weight of the engine. The engine should be supported horizontally, ie do not allow it to tilt front to rear.
9 Raise the engine until the engine mounting studs are clear of the crossmember, then pull the engine forwards to disconnect it from the transmission. Ensure that the torque converter is held firmly in place in the transmission housing, otherwise it could fall out resulting in fluid spillage and possible damage. It may be necessary to rock the engine a little to release it from the transmission.
10 Once clear of the transmission, lift the engine from the vehicle, taking care not to damage the radiator fins.

10 Engine/manual gearbox assembly - removal and separation

Note: *A suitable hoist and lifting tackle will be required for this operation.*

1.8 litre (R2A type)

Removal

1 Proceed as described in Section 8, paragraphs 1 to 15 inclusive.
2 Working inside the vehicle, unscrew the gear lever knob and remove the centre

2C

console. Where a full-length console is fitted, it is only necessary to remove the front tray.

3 Detach the outer gaiter from the retaining frame and withdraw it over the gear lever.

4 Release the clips and remove the gaiter retaining frame and inner gaiter.

5 Using a suitable Torx key, remove the screws securing the gear lever to the gearbox extension housing, and withdraw the gear lever. Note how the base of the gear lever locates over the selector shaft.

6 Jack up the vehicle and support on axle stands (see "*Jacking and Vehicle Support*"). Ensure that there is sufficient working room beneath the vehicle.

7 To improve access, disconnect the exhaust downpipe from the manifold and remove the exhaust system.

8 Remove the propeller shaft.

9 Where applicable bend back the locktabs, then unscrew the two bolts securing each of the two anti-roll bar U-clamps to the vehicle underbody. Lower the anti-roll bar as far as possible.

10 Proceed as described in Section 8, paragraphs 23 and 24.

11 Drain the engine oil into a container.

12 Unscrew the two nuts securing the engine mountings to the crossmember. Recover the washers.

13 Disconnect the wiring from the reversing lamp switch.

14 Remove the retaining circlip, and withdraw the speedometer cable from the gearbox extension housing.

15 Support the gearbox with a trolley jack, using a block of wood between the jack and the gearbox to spread the load.

16 Unscrew the four bolts securing the gearbox crossmember to the vehicle underbody. Unscrew the central bolt securing the crossmember to the gearbox and remove the crossmember. Note the position of the earth strap, where applicable. Recover the mounting cup and where applicable the exhaust mounting bracket and heat shield.

17 Make a final check to ensure that all relevant wires, pipes and hoses have been disconnected to facilitate removal of the engine/gearbox assembly.

18 Attach a hoist to the engine lifting brackets located at the front and rear of the cylinder head. Arrange the lifting tackle so that the engine/gearbox assembly will assume a steep angle of approximately 40° to 45° as it is being removed.

19 Raise the engine/gearbox so that the engine mounting studs are clear of the crossmember, then ease the assembly forwards, at the same time lowering the trolley jack which is supporting the gearbox. Lift the assembly from the vehicle, taking care not to damage the surrounding components.

20 With the engine/gearbox assembly removed, temporarily reconnect the anti-roll bar to the underbody if the vehicle is to be moved.

Separation

21 To separate the engine from the gearbox, proceed as follows.

22 Remove the starter motor.

23 Support the engine and gearbox horizontally on blocks of wood.

24 Unscrew and remove the engine-to-gearbox bolts, noting the location of the earth strap, and remove the two bolts from the engine adapter plate.

25 Pull the engine and gearbox apart, taking care not to strain the gearbox input shaft. It may be necessary to rock the units slightly to separate them.

1.6 and 1.8 litre (R6A type)

26 Proceed as described in paragraphs 30 to 40 inclusive of Section 8.

27 Proceed as described in paragraphs 2 to 25 inclusive of Section 10, noting the following points.

28 Disconnect the wiring from the vehicle speed sensor mounted on the gearbox before removing the engine/gearbox assembly.

29 Note that on 1.6 litre engines, the crankshaft speed/position sensor shroud (which is secured by a single bolt) must be removed before separating the engine from the gearbox.

11 Engine/automatic transmission assembly - removal and separation

Note: *A suitable hoist and lifting tackle will be required for this operation. Any suspected faults in the automatic transmission should be referred to a Ford dealer or automatic transmission specialist before removal of the unit, as the specialist fault diagnosis equipment is designed to operate with the transmission in the vehicle.*

Removal

1 Proceed as described in Section 8, paragraphs 1 to 15 inclusive, but additionally, where applicable disconnect the kickdown cable from the carburettor.

2 Jack up the vehicle and support on axle stands (see "*Jacking and Vehicle Support*"). Ensure that there is sufficient working room beneath the vehicle.

3 To improve access, disconnect the exhaust downpipe from the manifold and remove the exhaust system.

4 Remove the propeller shaft.

5 Where applicable bend back the locktabs, then unscrew the two bolts securing each of the two anti-roll bar U-clamps to the vehicle underbody. Lower the anti-roll bar as far as possible.

6 Unscrew the unions and disconnect the fluid cooler pipes from the transmission. Plug the open ends of the pipes and the transmission to prevent dirt ingress and fluid leakage. Remove the fluid cooler pipe bracket from the engine mounting bracket and place it to one side.

7 Remove the two clips securing the selector rod, and detach the selector rod from the manual selector lever, and the selector lever on the transmission.

8 If applicable, disconnect the kickdown cable from the transmission and withdraw the cable.

9 Disconnect the wiring from the starter inhibitor/reversing lamp switch, the lock-up clutch and where applicable the kickdown solenoid.

10 Remove the securing screw, and disconnect the speedometer cable from the transmission extension housing. Plug the opening in the transmission to prevent dirt ingress.

11 Disconnect the vacuum pipe from the vacuum diaphragm unit, and unclip the pipe from its securing bracket on the transmission housing.

12 Drain the engine oil into a container.

13 Unscrew the two nuts securing the engine mountings to the crossmember. Recover the washers.

14 Support the transmission with a trolley jack using a block of wood between the jack and the transmission to spread the load.

15 Unscrew the four bolts securing the transmission crossmember to the vehicle underbody. Note the position of the earth strap, where applicable. Unscrew the central bolt securing the crossmember to the transmission and remove the crossmember. Recover the mounting cup and the exhaust mounting bracket.

16 Make a final check to ensure that all relevant wires, pipes and hoses have been disconnected to facilitate removal of the engine/transmission assembly.

17 Attach a suitable hoist to the engine lifting brackets located at the front and rear of the cylinder head. Arrange the lifting tackle so that the engine/transmission assembly will assume a steep angle of approximately 40° to 45° as it is being removed.

18 Raise the engine/transmission so that the engine mounting studs are clear of the crossmember, then ease the assembly forwards, at the same time lowering the trolley jack which is supporting the transmission. Lift the assembly from the vehicle, taking care not to damage surrounding components.

19 With the engine/transmission assembly removed, temporarily reconnect the anti-roll bar to the underbody if the vehicle is to be moved.

Separation

20 To separate the engine from the transmission, proceed as follows.

21 Remove the starter motor.

22 Support the engine and transmission horizontally on blocks of wood.

23 Working through the starter motor aperture, unscrew the four torque converter-to-driveplate nuts. It will be necessary to turn the crankshaft using a suitable spanner on the crankshaft pulley bolt in order to gain access to each nut in turn through the aperture.

24 Unscrew and remove the engine-to-transmission bolts, noting the locations of the earth strap, vacuum pipe bracket, and transmission dipstick tube bracket. Remove the two bolts from the engine adapter plate, and where applicable pull the blanking plug from the adapter plate.

25 Pull the engine and transmission apart, ensuring that the torque converter is held

firmly in place in the transmission housing, otherwise it could fall out resulting in fluid spillage and possible damage. It may be necessary to rock the units slightly to separate them.

12 Engine - refitting (manual gearbox in vehicle)

1.8 litre (R2A type)

1 Reverse the procedure described in Section 8, noting the following points.
2 Before attempting to refit the engine, check that the clutch friction disc is centralised. This is necessary to ensure that the gearbox input shaft splines will pass through the splines in the centre of the friction disc.
3 Check that the clutch release arm and bearing are correctly fitted, and lightly grease the input shaft splines.
4 Check that the engine adapter plate is correctly positioned on its locating dowels.
5 Reconnect the clutch cable to the release arm, ensuring that it is routed as noted during removal.
6 Fill the engine with the correct grade and quantity of oil.
7 Fill the cooling system.
8 Check and if necessary adjust the tension of the alternator drivebelt.
9 Adjust the throttle cable.

1.6 and 1.8 litre (R6A type)

10 Reverse the procedure described in Section 8, noting the points made above.

13 Engine - refitting (automatic transmission in vehicle)

1 Reverse the procedure described in Section 9, noting the following points.
2 Check that the engine adapter plate is correctly positioned on its locating dowels.
3 As the torque converter is only loosely engaged in the transmission, care must be taken to prevent the torque converter from falling out forwards. When the torque converter hub is fully engaged with the fluid pump drivegear in the transmission, distance "A" in illustration 2.24 of Chapter 7B must be as specified. Incorrect installation of the torque converter will result in damage to the transmission.
4 As the engine is installed, guide the torque converter studs through the holes in the driveplate. When the engine is positioned flush with the engine adapter plate and the transmission housing, check that the torque converter is free to move axially a small amount before refitting and tightening the engine-to-transmission bolts.
5 Do not tighten the torque converter-to-driveplate nuts until the lower engine-to-transmission bolts have been fitted and tightened.
6 Fill the engine with the correct grade and quantity of oil.

7 Fill the cooling system.
8 Check and if necessary adjust the tension of the alternator drivebelt.
9 Adjust the throttle cable.
10 If applicable, adjust the kickdown cable.

14 Engine/manual gearbox assembly - reconnection and refitting

1.8 litre (R2A type)

1 Reverse the procedure described in Section 10, noting the following points.
2 Before attempting to reconnect the engine to the gearbox, check that the clutch friction disc is centralised. This is necessary to ensure that the gearbox input shaft splines will pass through the splines in the centre of the friction disc.
3 Check that the clutch release arm and bearing are correctly fitted, and lightly grease the input shaft splines.
4 Check that the engine adapter plate is correctly positioned on its locating dowels.
5 Reconnect the clutch cable to the release arm, ensuring that it is routed as noted during removal.
6 Fill the engine with the correct grade and quantity of oil.
7 Fill the cooling system.
8 Check and if necessary top-up the gearbox oil level.
9 Check and if necessary adjust the tension of the alternator drivebelt.
10 Adjust the throttle cable.

1.6 and 1.8 litre (R6A type)

11 Reverse the procedure described in Section 10, noting the points made above. Ensure that the vehicle speed sensor wiring plug is reconnected.

15 Engine/automatic transmission assembly - reconnection and refitting

1 Reverse the procedure described in Section 11, noting the following points.
2 Check that the engine adapter plate is correctly positioned on its locating dowels.
3 As the torque converter is only loosely engaged in the transmission, care must be taken to prevent the torque converter from falling out forwards. When the torque converter hub is fully engaged with the fluid pump drivegear in the transmission, distance "A" in illustration 2.24 of Chapter 7B must be as specified. Incorrect installation of the torque converter will result in damage to the transmission.
4 As the engine and transmission are reconnected, guide the torque converter studs through the holes in the driveplate. When the engine is positioned flush with the engine adapter plate and the transmission housing, check that the torque converter is free to move axially a small amount before

refitting and tightening the engine-to-transmission bolts.
5 Do not tighten the torque converter-to-driveplate nuts until the lower engine-to-transmission bolts have been fitted and tightened.
6 Reconnect and adjust the selector rod.
7 Fill the engine with the correct grade and quantity of oil.
8 Fill the cooling system.
9 Check and if necessary top-up the transmission fluid level.
10 Check and if necessary adjust the tension of the alternator drivebelt.
11 Adjust the throttle cable.
12 Where applicable, adjust the kickdown cable.

16 Engine mountings - renewal

1 The engine mountings incorporate hydraulic dampers and must be renewed if excessive engine movement is evident.
2 Working in the engine compartment, unscrew the central nuts securing the engine mounting brackets to the tops of the mountings. Recover the washers.
3 Apply the handbrake, jack up the front of the vehicle and support on axle stands (see "Jacking and Vehicle Support").
4 Working underneath the vehicle, remove the central nuts securing the mountings to the crossmember. Recover the washers.
5 Raise the engine using a suitable hoist and lifting tackle attached to the engine lifting brackets on the cylinder head, or a jack and interposed block of wood under the sump, until the mountings can be withdrawn.
6 Fit the new mountings, then lower the engine onto them. Note that the locating pins on the mountings must engage with the corresponding holes in the engine mounting brackets (see illustration).
7 Fit the nuts and washers securing the mountings to the crossmember and tighten the nuts.
8 Lower the vehicle to the ground and fit the nuts and washers securing the engine mounting brackets to the mountings. Tighten the nuts.

16.6 Locating pin on mounting must engage with hole (arrowed) in engine mounting bracket

2C

17 Engine dismantling, examination, renovation and reassembly - general information

1.8 litre (R2A type)

Dismantling

1 It is best to mount the engine on a dismantling stand, but if this is not available, stand the engine on a strong bench at a comfortable working height. Failing this, it will have to stripped down on the floor.

2 Cleanliness is most important, and if the engine is dirty, it should be cleaned with paraffin while keeping it in an upright position.

3 Avoid working with the engine directly on a concrete floor, as grit presents a real source of trouble.

4 As parts are removed, clean them in a paraffin bath. However, do not immerse parts with internal oilways in paraffin as it is difficult to remove, usually requiring a high pressure hose. Clean oilways with nylon pipe cleaners.

5 It is advisable to have suitable containers available to hold small items according to their use, as this will help when reassembling the engine and also prevent possible losses.

6 Always obtain a complete set of new gaskets for use during engine reassembly, but retain the old gaskets with a view to using them as a pattern to make a replacement if a new one is not available.

7 Where possible, refit securing nuts, bolts and washers to their locations after removing the relevant components. This will help to protect the threads and will also prevent possible losses.

8 Retain unserviceable components in order to compare them with the new components supplied.

9 A suitable Torx socket will be required to remove the oil pump cover securing screws.

10 Before dismantling the main engine components, the following externally mounted ancillary components can be removed:

> Inlet manifold and carburettor
> Exhaust manifold
> Fuel pump and operating pushrod
> Alternator
> Spark plugs
> Oil pressure warning lamp switch **(see illustration)**
> Oil filter
> Dipstick
> Engine mounting brackets
> Clutch
> Alternator mounting bracket
> Crankshaft speed/position sensor
> Engine lifting brackets

Examination and renovation

11 Refer to Section 18 in Chapter 2, Part A.

Reassembly

12 To ensure maximum life with minimum trouble from a rebuilt engine, not only must everything be correctly assembled, but it must

17.10 Removing the oil pressure warning lamp switch - 1.8 litre (R2A)

also be spotlessly clean. All oilways must be clear, and locking washers and spring washers must be fitted where indicated. Oil all bearings and other working surfaces thoroughly with engine oil during assembly.

13 Before assembly begins, renew any bolts or studs with damaged threads.

14 Gather together a torque wrench, oil can, clean rag, and a set of engine gaskets and oil seals, together with a new oil filter.

15 If they have been removed, new cylinder head bolts, big-end bolts/nuts and new flywheel bolts will be required.

16 After reassembling the main engine components, refer to paragraph 10 and refit the ancillary components listed. Delicate items such as the alternator may be left until after the engine has been refitted.

1.6 and 1.8 litre (R6A type)

Dismantling

17 Refer to paragraphs 1 to 9 inclusive.

18 Before dismantling the main engine components, the following ancillary components can be removed:

> Inlet manifold and CFI unit.
> Exhaust manifold .
> Alternator.
> Spark plugs and HT leads.
> Ignition coil and mounting bracket.
> Oil pressure warning lamp switch.
> Oil filter.
> Dipstick and tube.
> Engine mounting brackets.
> Clutch.
> Alternator mounting bracket.

18.3 Withdrawing the crankshaft pulley - 1.8 litre (R2A)

> Crankshaft speed/position sensor.
> Engine lifting brackets.
> Crankcase ventilation hose.

Examination and renovation

19 Refer to Section 18 in Chapter 2, Part A.

Reassembly

20 Refer to paragraphs 12 to 16 but note that new rocker arm nuts will be required, if they have been removed.

18 Timing belt and sprockets - removal and refitting

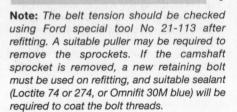

Note: *The belt tension should be checked using Ford special tool No 21-113 after refitting. A suitable puller may be required to remove the sprockets. If the camshaft sprocket is removed, a new retaining bolt must be used on refitting, and suitable sealant (Loctite 74 or 274, or Omnifit 30M blue) will be required to coat the bolt threads.*

1.8 litre (R2A type)

Removal

1 If the engine is in the vehicle, carry out the following operations:
   a) Disconnect the battery negative lead
   b) Remove the alternator drivebelt
   c) Remove the distributor cap, rotor arm and housing
   d) Disconnect the wiring plug from the crankshaft speed/position sensor
   e) Unclip the coolant hoses from the timing cover, and position them across the top of the camshaft cover out of the way
   f) If desired for improved access, remove the fan shroud and cooling fan assembly, although this is not essential

2 Slacken the crankshaft pulley bolt. Prevent the crankshaft from turning by engaging top gear (manual gearbox only) and having an assistant apply the brake pedal hard, or by removing the starter motor and jamming the ring gear teeth with a lever.

3 Remove the bolt and washer and withdraw the pulley **(see illustration)**. If the pulley will not come off easily, refit the bolt part way and use a puller, but take care not to damage the sensor toothed disc.

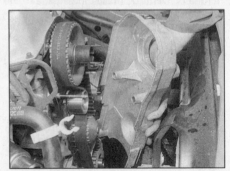

18.5 Withdrawing the timing cover - 1.8 litre (R2A)

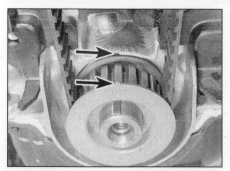

18.6a TDC lug on crankshaft sprocket aligned with notch in oil pump flange - 1.8 litre (R2A)

18.6b TDC pointer on camshaft sprocket aligned with dot on cylinder head - 1.8 litre (R2A)

18.8 Withdrawing the timing belt - 1.8 litre (R2A)

4 Unscrew the two timing cover securing nuts, and recover the earth tag and the coolant hose clip.

5 Unscrew the two securing bolts and withdraw the timing cover **(see illustration)**.

6 Refit the crankshaft pulley bolt, and using a socket on the bolt, turn the engine clockwise until the TDC (top dead centre) lug on the crankshaft sprocket is uppermost, and in line with the notch in the oil pump flange, and the pointer on the camshaft sprocket is aligned with the dot on the cylinder head front face **(see illustrations)**.

7 Loosen the two timing belt tensioner bolts, press the tensioner to the left against the spring tension, and tighten the two bolts to retain the tensioner in the released position.

8 Mark the running direction of the belt if it is to be re-used, then slip it off the sprockets,

and withdraw the belt **(see illustration)**.

9 If desired, the camshaft and crankshaft sprockets can be removed as follows, otherwise proceed to paragraph 19. The coolant pump sprocket is integral with the pump and cannot be removed separately.

10 Unscrew the crankshaft pulley bolt, preventing the crankshaft from turning as before if necessary, then remove the crankshaft sprocket. Refit the bolt part way and use a puller if necessary. Recover the Woodruff key from the end of the crankshaft and remove the thrustwasher **(see illustrations)**.

11 Unscrew the camshaft sprocket bolt while holding the sprocket stationary with a 41 mm ring spanner. Alternatively, make up a tool similar to that shown for tightening the bolt and hold the sprocket using two bolts

engaged in the sprockets holes. Recover the distributor rotor shaft which is held in place by the camshaft sprocket bolt **(see illustration)**.

12 Remove the camshaft sprocket, refitting the bolt part way and using a puller if necessary **(see illustration)**.

13 If desired, the timing belt backplate can be removed by lifting it from the studs **(see illustration)** and the timing belt tensioner and coolant pump can be removed.

14 If required, the camshaft oil seal can be removed using self-tapping screws and a pair of grips. A new seal can be fitted using a suitable tube drift to press it into place. Lubricate the seal lips with clean engine oil before installation.

Refitting

15 Refit the sprockets as follows.

2C

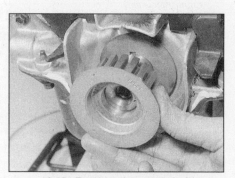

18.10a Remove the crankshaft sprocket . . .

18.10b . . . the Woodruff key . . .

18.10c . . . and the thrustwasher - 1.8 litre (R2A)

18.11 Removing the camshaft sprocket bolt and distributor rotor shaft - 1.8 litre (R2A)

18.12 Using a puller to remove the camshaft sprocket - 1.8 litre (R2A)

18.13 Removing the timing belt backplate - 1.8 litre (R2A)

18.17 Tightening the camshaft sprocket bolt. Hold the sprocket stationary using an improvised tool with two bolts engaged in the sprocket holes - 1.8 litre (R2A)

16 Where applicable, refit the timing belt tensioner and coolant pump, locate the timing belt backplate over the studs, then fit the camshaft sprocket and the distributor rotor shaft.

17 The camshaft sprocket bolt must be coated with sealant before installation. The manufacturers recommend Loctite 74 or 274, or Omnifit 30M blue. With the sealant applied, insert the bolt, hold the camshaft sprocket stationary as during removal, and tighten the bolt to the specified torque (see illustration).

18 Refit the thrustwasher with the convex side facing forwards, and refit the Woodruff key, then refit the crankshaft sprocket with the "FRONT" mark facing forwards.

19 Fit the timing belt over the crankshaft sprocket, but do not engage it with the other sprockets yet. Be careful not to kink the belt, and if the old belt is being refitted, observe the previously noted running direction.

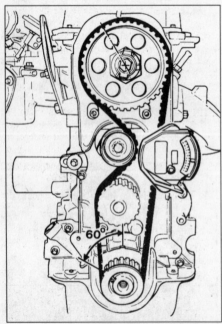

18.27 No 1 cylinder at 60° BTDC for checking of timing belt tension - 1.8 litre (R2A)

18.25 Twisting the timing belt to assess its tension - 1.8 litre (R2A)

20 Make sure that the TDC pointer on the camshaft sprocket is still aligned with the dot on the cylinder head front face.

21 Check that the TDC lug on the crankshaft sprocket is still in line with the notch in the oil pump flange. If necessary, refit the crankshaft pulley bolt, if not already done, and using a socket on the bolt, turn the crankshaft by the shortest possible route to align the lug and notch.

22 Starting at the crankshaft and working in an anti-clockwise direction, fit the timing belt over the camshaft sprocket, round the tensioner roller, and over the coolant pump sprocket.

23 Slacken the tensioner bolts, allow the tensioner roller to rest against the belt, then tighten the tensioner bolts.

24 Refit the crankshaft pulley bolt, if not already done, and using a socket on the bolt, turn the engine through two revolutions in a clockwise direction (to bring No 1 cylinder back to TDC), then turn the crankshaft 60° anti-clockwise (No 1 cylinder at 60° BTDC).

25 The belt tension should now be checked by applying Ford tension gauge, tool No 21-113 to the longest belt run. Desired gauge readings are:

  Used belt - 4 to 6
  New belt - 10 to 11

If the tension gauge is not available, a rough guide is that the belt tension is correct when the belt can be twisted 90° in the middle of the longest run with the fingers using moderate pressure (see illustration). In this case, the vehicle should be taken to a Ford dealer so that the belt tension can be checked using the special gauge at the earliest opportunity.

26 If adjustment of belt tension is necessary, turn the crankshaft clockwise to bring No 1 cylinder to TDC, then slacken the tensioner bolts and move the tensioner to increase or decrease the belt tension. Tighten the tensioner bolts to the specified torque.

27 Turn the crankshaft 90° clockwise past TDC, then anti-clockwise back to the 60° BTDC position (No 1 cylinder at 60° BTDC). Check the belt tension again (see illustration).

28 Repeat the procedure given in paragraphs 26 and 27 until the belt tension is correct.

29 Refit the timing cover and secure with the two bolts and nuts. Ensure that the earth tag and the coolant hose clip are fitted under the relevant nuts (see illustration).

30 Unscrew the crankshaft pulley bolt, then refit the crankshaft pulley and the bolt and washer. Tighten the crankshaft pulley bolt to the specified torque, preventing the crankshaft from turning as described in paragraph 2.

31 If the engine is in the vehicle, reverse the operations described in paragraph 1.

1.6 and 1.8 litre (R6A type)

32 If the engine is in the vehicle, carry out the following operations.

  a) Disconnect the battery negative lead.
  b) Remove the alternator drivebelt.
  c) Disconnect the HT leads from the spark plugs, noting their locations; detach the HT lead bracket from the camshaft cover, and position the leads out of the way.
  d) Move the coolant hoses from the front of the timing cover, and position them across the top of the camshaft cover out of the way.
  e) If desired for improved access, remove the fan shroud and the cooling fan assembly, although this is not essential.

33 Proceed as described in paragraphs 2 to 30 inclusive, noting the following differences for the 1.6 litre engine (see illustrations).

  a) There is no sensor toothed disc on the crankshaft pulley.
  b) A two-piece timing cover is fitted, consisting of upper and lower sections, each secured by two bolts. No earth tag or coolant hose clip is fitted to the bolts.
  c) The TDC datum on the oil pump takes the form of a lug instead of a notch.
  d) There is no distributor rotor shaft fitted to the camshaft sprocket bolt.
  e) There is no timing belt backplate.

34 On completion, if the engine is in the vehicle, reverse the operations given in paragraph 32.

18.29 Earth tag (1) and coolant hose clip (2) locations on timing cover - 1.8 litre (R2A)

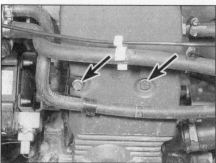

18.33a Upper timing cover securing bolts (arrowed) - 1.6/1.8 litre (R6A)

18.33b Removing the upper timing cover - 1.6/1.8 litre (R6A)

18.33c Removing the lower timing cover - 1.6/1.8 litre (R6A)

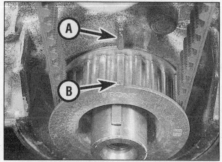

18.33d Oil pump TDC lug (A) and crankshaft sprocket lug (B) - 1.6/1.8 litre (R6A)

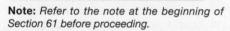

19 Cylinder head - removal and refitting (engine in vehicle)

Note: *Refer to the note at the beginning of Section 61 before proceeding.*

1.8 litre (R2A type)

Removal

1 Disconnect the battery negative lead.
2 Drain the cooling system.
3 Disconnect the heater coolant hose from the coolant pump elbow, and the coolant bypass hose from the left-hand side of cylinder head, then unclip the hoses from the timing cover and move them to one side out of the way **(see illustrations)**.
4 Remove the air cleaner.

5 Disconnect the HT leads from the spark plugs and coil, identifying them for position if necessary, unclip the leads from the camshaft cover, then remove the distributor cap, rotor arm and housing. Remove the spark plugs.
6 Disconnect the cylinder head earth lead from the battery tray.
7 The cylinder head can be removed either with or without the manifolds. If desired, the inlet manifold can be unbolted and moved to one side, leaving the wires, hoses, pipes and cables connected, but care must be taken not to strain any of the wires, hoses, pipes or cables.
8 Unscrew the three securing nuts and disconnect the exhaust downpipe from the manifold flange. Recover the gasket.
9 If desired, remove the exhaust manifold.
10 If the inlet manifold is to be removed with the cylinder head, disconnect all relevant

wires, hoses, pipes and cables, otherwise unbolt the manifold and move it to one side, ensuring that it is adequately supported **(see illustration)**.
11 If desired, remove the fuel pump and operating pushrod.
12 Proceed as described in Section 20 to complete cylinder head removal.

Refitting

13 With the cylinder head refitted as described in Section 20, proceed as follows.
14 Where applicable, refit the fuel pump and operating pushrod.
15 Refit the manifolds and/or reconnect all wires, hoses, pipes and cables, as applicable.
16 Reconnect the exhaust downpipe to the manifold, using a new gasket.
17 Reconnect the earth lead to the battery tray.
18 Refit the spark plugs, then refit the distributor cap, rotor arm and housing, and reconnect the HT leads.
19 Refit the air cleaner.
20 Reconnect the coolant hoses to the coolant pump elbow and the cylinder head, and locate them in the clip on the timing cover.
21 Fill the cooling system.
22 Reconnect the battery negative lead.

1.6 and 1.8 litre (R6A type)

Removal

23 Disconnect the battery negative lead.
24 Drain the cooling system.
25 Disconnect the coolant hoses from the thermostat housing, and the bypass hose from the left-hand side of the cylinder head, then move them to one side out of the way.
26 Remove the air cleaner.
27 Disconnect the HT leads from the spark plugs, identifying them for position if necessary. Unclip them from the camshaft cover, and move them to one side out of the way.
28 Remove the spark plugs.
29 Disconnect the cylinder head earth lead from the battery tray.
30 The cylinder head can be removed either with or without the manifolds. If desired, the inlet manifold can be unbolted and moved to one side (after unbolting the dipstick tube),

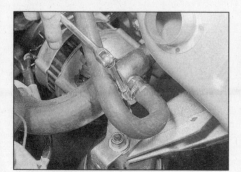

19.3a Disconnecting the heater coolant hose from the coolant pump elbow - 1.8 litre (R2A)

19.3b Coolant bypass hose connection at cylinder head - 1.8 litre (R2A)

19.10 Withdraw the inlet manifold - 1.8 litre (R2A)

2C

19.31 Disconnecting the exhaust gas oxygen sensor wiring connector - 1.6/1.8 litre (R6A)

20.4 Remove the camshaft cover and gasket - 1.8 litre (R2A)

20.6 Withdraw the cylinder head bolts and lift the cylinder head from the block - 1.8 litre (R2A)

leaving the wires, hoses, pipes and cables connected. However, care must be taken not to strain any of the wires, hoses or cables.

31 Disconnect the exhaust gas oxygen sensor wiring connector **(see illustration)** then unscrew the three securing bolts and disconnect the exhaust downpipe from the manifold flange. Recover the gasket.

32 If desired, remove the exhaust manifold.

33 If the inlet manifold is to be removed with the cylinder head, disconnect all relevant wires, hoses, pipes and cables, otherwise unbolt the manifold and move it to one side, ensuring that it is adequately supported.

34 Note the information given in paragraphs 18 to 21 inclusive of Section 20.

Refitting

35 With the cylinder head refitted, proceed as follows.

36 Refit the manifolds and/or reconnect all wires, hoses, pipes and cables as applicable.

37 Reconnect the exhaust downpipe to the manifold using a new gasket, and reconnect the exhaust gas oxygen sensor wiring connector.

38 Reconnect the earth lead to the battery tray.

39 Refit the spark plugs and reconnect the HT leads.

40 Refit the air cleaner.

41 Reconnect the coolant hoses to the thermostat housing and cylinder head.

42 Fill the cooling system.

43 Reconnect the battery negative lead.

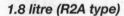

20 Cylinder head - removal and refitting (engine removed)

Note: The cylinder head bolts must always be renewed after slackening, and a new cylinder head gasket and camshaft cover gasket must be used on refitting. If the engine has recently run, the cylinder head must be allowed to cool to room temperature before it is removed.

1.8 litre (R2A type)

Removal

1 With the manifolds removed, proceed as follows.

2 Remove the timing belt, camshaft sprocket, and timing belt backplate.

3 Disconnect the crankcase ventilation hose from the camshaft cover.

4 Unscrew the nine securing bolts and remove the camshaft cover and gasket **(see illustration)**.

5 Unscrew the ten cylinder head bolts half a turn at a time in the reverse order to that shown for tightening.

6 With the bolts removed, lift the cylinder head from the block **(see illustration)**. If the cylinder head is stuck, tap it free with a wooden mallet. Do not insert a lever into the joint between the cylinder head and block as this may result in damage to the mating faces. Place the cylinder head on blocks of wood to prevent damage to the valves.

7 Recover the gasket, and the locating dowels if they are loose **(see illustration)**.

Refitting

8 Commence refitting as follows.

9 Turn the crankshaft so that No 1 piston is approximately 20.0 mm (0.8 in) before TDC. This precaution will prevent any damage to open valves.

10 Make sure that the mating faces of the cylinder block and cylinder head are perfectly clean, then refit the locating dowels to the block where applicable, and locate a new gasket over the dowels with the red sealing bead and the "1.8" mark uppermost **(see illustrations)**. *Do not use jointing compound.*

11 Turn the camshaft so that the TDC pointer on the camshaft sprocket is aligned with the dot on the cylinder head front face.

12 Lower the cylinder head onto the gasket, making sure that the locating dowels engage.

13 Insert the new cylinder head bolts into their locations in the cylinder head, then tighten the bolts in the order shown to the five stages given in the Specifications **(see illustrations)**.

14 Fit a new camshaft cover gasket to the cylinder head, ensuring that the gasket locates correctly over the edges of the cylinder head **(see illustration)**.

15 Refit the camshaft cover and tighten the bolts evenly, ensuring that the studded bolts which retain the HT lead clips are refitted to their correct positions **(see illustration)**.

20.7 Recover the cylinder head gasket - 1.8 litre (R2A)

20.10a Fit the locating dowels (arrowed) to the block . . .

20.10b . . . then locate a new gasket with the red sealing bead and "1.8" mark uppermost - 1.8 litre (R2A)

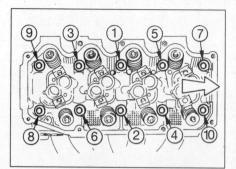

20.13a Cylinder head bolt tightening
sequence - 1.8 litre (R2A)

20.13b Tighten the cylinder head bolts
using an angle gauge - 1.8 litre (R2A)

20.14 Ensure that the camshaft cover
gasket locates over the edges of the
cylinder head - 1.8 litre (R2A)

20.15 Fit the camshaft cover, ensuring that
the studded bolts (arrowed) are correctly
located - 1.8 litre (R2A)

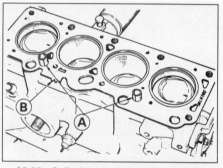
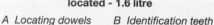

20.20a Cylinder head gasket correctly
located - 1.6 litre

A Locating dowels   B Identification teeth

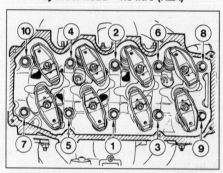

20.20b Cylinder head bolt tightening
sequence - 1.6 litre

2C

16 Reconnect the crankcase ventilation hose
to the camshaft cover.
17 Refit the timing belt backplate, camshaft
sprocket and timing belt.

1.6 and 1.8 litre (R6A type)

18 With the manifolds removed, proceed as
follows.
19 Remove the timing belt.
20 Proceed as shown in paragraphs 3 to 16
inclusive, noting the following differences for
the 1.6 litre engine only:
a) Unscrew the cylinder head bolts in the
reverse order to that shown for tightening.
b) The cylinder head gasket is identified by a
single tooth on its edge, and the gasket
must be fitted with the tooth nearest the

oil filter end of the engine, as shown **(see
illustration)**.
c) Tighten the cylinder head bolts in the
order shown **(see illustration)**, to the four
stages given in the Specifications at the
beginning of this Chapter.
d) Ignore the reference to the studded
camshaft cover bolts.
21 On completion, refit the timing belt.

21 Cylinder head - dismantling and reassembly

Note: *A valve spring compressor will be
required during this procedure. New valve
stem oil seals should be used on
reassembly.*

1.8 litre (R2A type)

Dismantling

1 With the cylinder head removed, remove
the camshaft.
2 Using a valve spring compressor, compress
one of the valve springs until the split collets
can be removed from the grooves in the valve
stem. Release the compressor and remove
the cap and spring, identifying them for
location. If the cap is difficult to release, do
not continue to tighten the compressor, but
gently tap the top of the tool with a hammer.
Always make sure that the compressor is
firmly located on the valve head and the cap
(see illustrations).
3 Prise the oil seal from the valve stem, and
remove the spring seat, then withdraw the
valve **(see illustrations)**.

21.2a Compress the valve spring . . .

21.2b . . . to free the split collets . . .

21.2c . . . then remove the cap and spring -
1.8 litre (R2A)

21.3a Remove the spring seat . . .

21.3b . . . and valve - 1.8 litre (R2A)

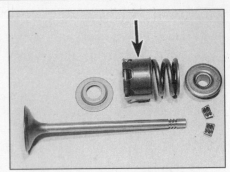

21.4 Inlet valve components. Spring damper arrowed - 1.8 litre (R2A)

4 Repeat the procedure given in paragraphs 2 and 3 for the remaining valves, keeping all components identified for location so that they can be refitted in their original positions. Note that the inlet valve springs are fitted with metal dampers. The damper is an integral part of the spring and cannot be removed (see illustration).

Reassembly

5 Commence reassembly by lubricating the valve stems and guides with SAE 80/90 hypoid oil, then insert the valves into their original guides.
6 Refit the spring seats over the valve stems.
7 Wrap a thin layer of adhesive tape over the collet grooves of each valve, then smear the new oil seals with a little hypoid oil and slide them down the valve stems onto the spring seats. Use a suitable metal tube to seat the seals, then remove the adhesive tape from the valves (see illustration).
8 Working on each valve in turn, fit the valve spring and cap, then compress the spring using the valve spring compressor and fit the split collets to the groove in the valve stem. Release the compressor and tap the end of the valve stem with a soft-faced mallet to settle the components. If the original components are being refitted, ensure that they are refitted in their original locations.
9 Refit the camshaft.

1.6 and 1.8 litre (R6A type)

10 Proceed as described in paragraphs 1 to 9 inclusive, but note that no dampers are fitted to the inlet valve springs on the 1.6 litre engine.

22 Cylinder head - inspection and renovation

Refer to Section 23, Chapter 2, Part A but pay particular attention to the note at the beginning of the Section as all CVH engines are fitted with hardened valve seats.

23 Camshaft and cam followers - removal, inspection and refitting

Note: *A new camshaft oil seal and new rocker arm securing nuts should be used when refitting.*

1.8 litre (R2A type)

Removal

1 Remove the cylinder head.
2 Unscrew the securing bolts and remove the rocker arm guides, rocker arms, and cam follower guide retainers, then lift out the cam follower guides and the cam followers. Keep all components in the correct order so that each component can be refitted in the original position if it is to be re-used. It is advisable to store the cam followers upright in an oil bath until they are to be refitted. Ensure that the depth of oil is sufficient to fully cover the cam followers.
3 Prise out the camshaft oil seal, taking care not to damage the surface of the camshaft. If necessary use self-tapping screws and a suitable pair of grips to withdraw the seal.

4 Unscrew the two securing bolts and withdraw the camshaft thrustplate from the front of the cylinder head.
5 Carefully withdraw the camshaft from the front of the cylinder head, taking care not to damage the bearings. If necessary, loosely refit the camshaft sprocket and bolt to aid removal.

Inspection

6 Examine the surfaces of the camshaft journals and lobes, and the cam follower rollers for wear. If wear is excessive, considerable noise would have been noticed from the top of the engine when running, and a new camshaft and followers must be fitted. It is unlikely that this level of wear will occur unless a considerable mileage has been covered. Note that the cam followers cannot be dismantled for renewal of individual components.
7 Check the camshaft bearings in the cylinder head for wear. If excessive wear is evident, it may be possible to have the head machined by a suitably equipped engineering workshop to enable a camshaft with oversize bearing journals to be fitted. The only other course of action available is renewal of the cylinder head.
8 Check the cam follower bores in the cylinder head for wear. If excessive wear is evident, the cylinder head must be renewed.
9 Check the cam follower oil ports and the oil holes in the cylinder head for obstructions (see illustrations).

Refitting

10 Commence refitting by lubricating the camshaft, bearings and thrustplate with

21.7 Seat each new valve seal using a metal tube - 1.8 litre (R2A)

23.9a Hydraulic cam follower oil port (arrowed) - 1.8 litre (R2A)

23.9b Cam follower supply hole (arrowed) in cylinder head - 1.8 litre (R2A)

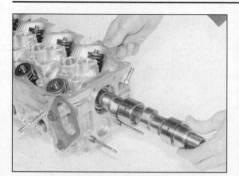

23.10 Refitting the camshaft - 1.8 litre (R2A)

23.11a Refit the camshaft thrustplate . . .

23.11b . . . and tighten the securing bolts - 1.8 litre (R2A)

23.14 Using a special tool to fit the camshaft oil seal - 1.8 litre (R2A)

hypoid oil, then carefully insert the camshaft from the front of the cylinder head, taking care not to damage the bearings (see illustration).

11 Locate the thrustplate in the camshaft groove, then refit the bolts and tighten them. Note that the stamped number on the thrustplate should face forwards (see illustrations).

12 Using a dial test indicator if available, or feeler blades, check that the camshaft endfloat is within the limits given in the Specifications. If not, renew the thrustplate and re-check. If this does not bring the endfloat within limits, the camshaft must be renewed.

13 Remove the thrustplate bolts, coat the threads with sealing compound, then refit and tighten the bolts.

14 Smear the lip of the new camshaft oil seal with clean engine oil, then fit the seal using the camshaft sprocket bolt and a suitable tool

similar to that shown (see illustration).Draw the seal into position so that it rests on the shoulder.

> **HAYNES HiNT** *The tool can be improvised using a metal tube of suitable diameter and a large washer or metal disc.*

15 Lubricate the cam followers with hypoid oil, refit them to their original locations, with the colour marking pointing to the oil feed hole in the cylinder head. The oil feed port in the cam follower should be opposite the oil feed hole in the cylinder head (see illustrations).

16 Lubricate the tops of the cam followers, then refit the four cam follower guides to their

2C

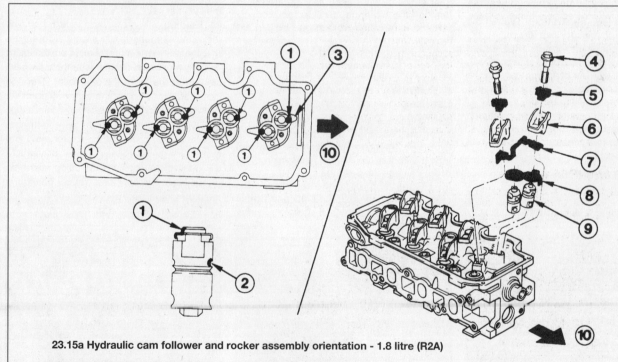

23.15a Hydraulic cam follower and rocker assembly orientation - 1.8 litre (R2A)

1 Cam follower colour markings
2 Oil port in cam follower
3 Oil supply hole in cylinder head
4 Securing bolt
5 Rocker arm guide
6 Rocker arm
7 Cam follower guide retainer - stepped end to inlet side
8 Cam follower guide - stepped end to exhaust side
9 Cam follower
10 Front of engine

23.15b Refit the cam followers . . .

23.16 . . . guides . . .

23.17 . . . and retainers - 1.8 litre (R2A)

original locations with their "stepped" ends pointing towards the exhaust side of the cylinder head (see illustration).

17 Refit the four cam follower guide retainers to their original locations with their "stepped" ends pointing towards the inlet side of the cylinder head (see illustration).

18 Temporarily refit the camshaft sprocket, and turn the camshaft so that the TDC pointer on the sprocket is aligned with the dot on the cylinder head front face (ie the pointer is at the 12 o'clock position).

19 Refit rocker arms Nos 1, 2, 4 and 5 together with their rocker arm guides and securing bolts, to their original locations (see illustration). Lubricate the contact faces of the rocker arms and guides and the valve stems with hypoid oil, and ensure that the guides seat correctly in their locations in the cylinder head (see illustration). Tighten the securing bolts to the specified torque.

20 Turn the camshaft through 180° so that the camshaft sprocket keyway is aligned with the dot on the cylinder head front face (ie the TDC pointer on the sprocket is at the 6 o'clock position) (see illustration).

21 Repeat the procedure given in paragraph 19 for rocker arms Nos 3, 6, 7 and 8.

22 Remove the camshaft sprocket and refit the cylinder head.

1.6 and 1.8 litre (R6A type)

Removal

23 Remove the cylinder head.

24 Unscrew the securing nuts and remove the rocker arm guides, rocker arms, and spacer plates, then lift out the cam followers. Keep all components in the correct order so that they can be refitted in their original locations on reassembly. It is advisable to store the cam followers upright in an oil bath until they are to be refitted. Ensure that the depth of oil is sufficient to fully cover the cam followers.

25 Prise out the camshaft oil seal, taking care not to damage the surface of the camshaft. If necessary, use self-tapping screws and a suitable pair of grips to withdraw the seal.

26 Unscrew the two securing bolts, and withdraw the camshaft thrustplate from the front of the cylinder head.

27 Carefully withdraw the camshaft from the front of the cylinder head, taking care not to damage the bearings. If necessary, loosely refit the camshaft sprocket and bolt to aid removal.

Inspection

28 Proceed as described in paragraphs 6 to 9 inclusive.

Refitting

29 Commence refitting by lubricating the camshaft, bearings and thrustplate with hypoid oil, then carefully insert the camshaft from the front of the cylinder head, taking care not to damage the bearings.

30 Locate the thrustplate in position in the cylinder head, then refit the bolts and tighten them. Note that the oil groove in the

thrustplate must face the front of the engine.

31 Using a dial test indicator (if available) or feeler blades, check that the camshaft endfloat is within the limits given in the Specifications. If not, renew the thrustplate and re-check. If this does not bring the endfloat within limits, the camshaft must be renewed.

32 Smear the lip of the new camshaft oil seal with clean engine oil, then refit the seal using the camshaft sprocket bolt and a suitable tool. The tool can be improvised using a metal tube of suitable diameter and a large washer or metal disc. Draw the seal into position so that it rests on the shoulder.

33 Lubricate the cam followers with hypoid oil, then refit them to their original locations in the cylinder head.

34 Before each rocker arm is fitted and its (new) nut tightened, it is essential to ensure that the relevant cam follower is positioned at its lowest point (in contact with the cam base circle, not the tip of the cam lobe). Turn the camshaft (by means of the camshaft sprocket bolt if necessary) as necessary to achieve this.

35 Lubricate the tops of the cam followers, then refit the spacer plates, rocker arms and rocker arm guides to their original locations.

36 Secure the rocker arms using new nuts tightened to the specified torque, bearing in mind the point made in paragraph 34.

37 Refit the cylinder head.

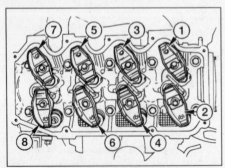

23.19a Rocker arm numbering sequence - 1.8 litre (R2A)

23.19b Lubricate the valve stem contact faces and refit the rocker arms and guides - 1.8 litre (R2A)

23.20 Camshaft sprocket keyway aligned with dot on cylinder head - 1.8 litre (R2A)

24 Flywheel/driveplate - removal, inspection and refitting

Note: *New flywheel securing bolts must be used on refitting.*

1.8 litre (R2A type)

1 Refer to Section 26, Chapter 2, Part A but also note the following points.
2 The flywheel/driveplate securing bolts must be renewed when refitting, and the new bolts are supplied ready-coated with threadlocking compound **(see illustration)**.
3 The ring gear cannot be renewed independently of the flywheel/driveplate. If the ring gear is badly worn or has missing teeth, a new flywheel/driveplate must be fitted.

1.6 and 1.8 litre (R6A type)

4 Refer to Section 26, Chapter 2, Part A, noting the following points.
5 If the engine is in the vehicle, refer to Chapter 6 when removing the clutch.
6 The flywheel securing bolts must be renewed when refitting, and the new bolts are supplied ready-coated with thread-locking compound.
7 The ring gear cannot be renewed independently of the flywheel. If the ring gear is badly worn or has missing teeth, a new flywheel must be fitted. Similarly, the flywheel must be renewed if the crankshaft speed/position sensor toothed disc is damaged.

25 Crankshaft front oil seal - renewal

1.8 litre (R2A type)

1 Remove the timing belt and the crankshaft sprocket and thrustwasher.
2 Withdraw the oil seal using an oil seal removal tool or by drilling the oil seal outer face and using self-tapping screws and a pair of grips.
3 Clean the oil seal housing, then smear the lip of a new oil seal with clean engine oil.
4 Fit the oil seal using the crankshaft pulley bolt and a suitable tool similar to that shown **(see illustration)**.

24.2 Using an improvised tool to hold the flywheel stationary while tightening the securing bolts - 1.8 litre (R2A)

 HAYNES HINT *A tool can be improvised to fit the crankshaft front oil seal by using a metal tube of suitable diameter and a large washer or metal disc. Do not attempt to drive the seal home using a tube drift.*

5 As the seal is drawn into position, the inner edge of the seal may be damaged as it passes over the end of the shaft. To prevent this, as soon as the seal begins to locate in the housing remove the tools being used to fit the seal, and carefully work the inner edge of the seal over the end of the crankshaft, using a small screwdriver or similar blunt tool. The seal can then be pushed home using the tools described previously **(see illustration)**.
6 Refit the thrustwasher, crankshaft sprocket and timing belt.

1.6 and 1.8 litre (R6A type)

7 Remove the timing belt, and the crankshaft sprocket and thrustwasher.
8 Proceed as described in paragraphs 2 to 4 inclusive.
9 Refit the thrustwasher, crankshaft sprocket and timing belt.

26 Crankshaft rear oil seal - renewal

1 Remove the flywheel/driveplate.
2 Prise out the oil seal. If necessary, drill the outer face of the oil seal and use self-tapping

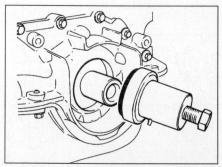

25.4 Using a special tool to fit the crankshaft front oil seal - 1.8 litre (R2A)

screws and a pair of grips to withdraw the seal **(see illustration)**.
3 Clean the oil seal housing, then fit the new oil seal using two flywheel/driveplate securing bolts and a tool similar to that shown **(see illustration)**. A suitable tool can be improvised using a narrow strip of metal sheet bent to form a circle of the correct diameter, and a large metal disc with appropriate holes drilled to allow the flywheel/driveplate securing bolts to pass through. Make sure that the seal lip faces into the engine and lightly smear the lip with clean engine oil.
4 Refit the flywheel/driveplate.

27 Sump - removal and refitting

Note: *A new gasket and new sump bolts must be used when refitting, and suitable sealant will be required (available from a Ford dealer). Note that it is preferable to keep the engine upright until the sump has been removed to prevent sludge from entering the engine internals.*

1.8 litre (R2A type)

Removal

1 With the engine removed, proceed as follows.
2 Remove the flywheel/driveplate and the engine adapter plate.
3 Unscrew the fourteen securing bolts and withdraw the two reinforcing strips and the sump. If the sump is stuck, carefully tap it sideways to free it. Do not prise between the mating faces.

2C

25.5 Crankshaft front oil seal (arrowed) located in oil pump housing - 1.8 litre (R2A)

26.2 Crankshaft rear oil seal location (arrowed)

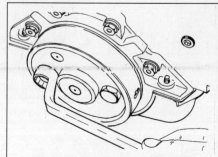

26.3 Using a special tool to fit the crankshaft rear oil seal - 1.8 litre (R2A)

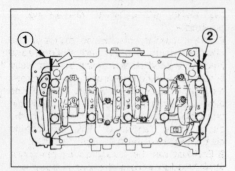

27.6 Apply sealing compound to the areas shown before fitting the sump gasket - 1.8 litre (R2A)

4 Recover the gasket.
5 Thoroughly clean the mating faces of the cylinder block and sump.

Refitting

6 Commence refitting by applying sealing compound (available from a Ford dealer) to the cylinder block, oil pump housing and crankshaft rear oil seal housing mating faces at the points shown **(see illustration)**. Note that the sump must be fitted within ten minutes of applying the sealing compound.
7 Fit a new gasket, ensuring that it engages correctly in the grooves in the crankshaft rear oil seal carrier and the oil pump housing **(see illustration)**.
8 Locate the sump on the gasket and loosely fit the securing bolts.
9 Tighten all the bolts slightly to obtain a light and even gasket preload.
10 Tighten the bolts to the specified torque in the sequence shown **(see illustration)**. Note that the ten M8 bolts and the four M6 bolts are tightened to different torques.
11 Refit the engine adapter plate and the flywheel/driveplate.

1.6 and 1.8 litre (R6A type)

Note: The following procedure applies to the 1.6 litre CVH engine. For the 1.8 litre (R6A type) engine, proceed as described above for the 1.8 litre (R2A type).

Removal

12 Sump removal and refitting is easier if the engine is removed from the vehicle. However, if the engine is in the vehicle, proceed as follows. If the engine has been removed from the vehicle, proceed to paragraph 15.
13 Remove the clutch.
14 Drain the engine oil into a suitable container.
15 Remove the flywheel and the engine adapter plate.
16 Unscrew the eighteen securing bolts and withdraw the sump. If the sump is stuck, carefully tap it sideways to free it. Do not prise between the mating faces. Recover the gasket.
17 Thoroughly clean the mating faces of cylinder block and sump.

Refitting

18 Apply sealing compound to the joints between the oil pump and the cylinder block, and the crankshaft rear oil seal housing and the cylinder block, as shown **(see illustration)**.
19 Without applying any further sealer, locate the gasket into the grooves of the oil pump and the rear oil seal housing. To hold the gasket in position, studs can be inserted temporarily in the bolt hole positions circled in the illustration indicating the bolt tightening sequence. Make sure that the gasket spacing pips are seated correctly.

27.7 Ensure that the gasket locates correctly on the oil pump housing - 1.8 litre (R2A)

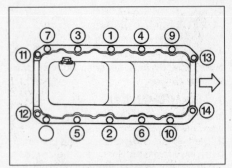

27.10 Sump bolt tightening sequence - 1.8 litre (R2A)

20 Locate the sump on the gasket, taking care not to displace the gasket, then loosely fit the securing bolts. With the sump in position, where applicable remove the studs from the bolt holes, and loosely fit the remaining securing bolts.
21 Tighten the bolts to the torque given in the Specifications at the beginning of this Chapter, in two stages, and in the sequence shown **(see illustration)**.
22 Refit the engine adapter plate and the flywheel.
23 If the engine is in the vehicle, refit the clutch. Refill the engine with oil.

28 Oil pump - removal and refitting

Note: New oil pump and oil pick-up tube gaskets should be used when refitting.

Removal

1 With the engine removed, proceed as follows.
2 Remove the timing belt, crankshaft sprocket and thrustwasher.
3 Remove the sump.
4 Unscrew and remove the nut securing the oil strainer/pick-up tube to No 4 main bearing cap **(see illustration)**.
5 Using a suitable Allen key, unscrew the two bolts securing the oil pick-up tube to the oil pump, and withdraw the oil strainer/pick-up tube. Recover the washers and gasket **(see illustration)**.

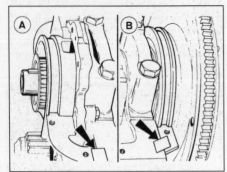

27.18 Apply sealing compound at the points arrowed before refitting the sump - 1.6 litre

A Oil pump/cylinder block joint
B Crankshaft rear oil seal housing/cylinder block joint

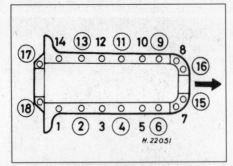

27.21 Sump bolt tightening sequence - 1.6 litre
Arrow indicates front of engine

28.4 Oil strainer/pick-up tube securing nut (arrowed) on No 4 main bearing cap

28.5 Removing the oil pick-up tube from the oil pump

6 Unscrew and remove the six securing bolts, and withdraw the oil pump over the front of the crankshaft. Recover the gasket.

Refitting

7 Commence refitting by prising the crankshaft front oil seal from the pump housing.
8 Prime the pump by injecting clean engine oil into it and turning it by hand.
9 Using a new gasket, fit the oil pump over the front of the crankshaft, ensuring that the central rotor engages with the flats on the crankshaft (see illustration). Fit the securing bolts, and using a straight-edge, ensure that the bottom face of the oil pump is aligned with the bottom face of the cylinder block before finally tightening the bolts.
10 Using a new gasket, fit the oil pick-up tube to the oil pump and secure with the two bolts.

29.2 Remove the oil pump cover

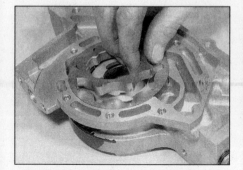

29.3 Lifting out the oil pump inner rotor

28.9 Refitting the oil pump

11 Refit the oil strainer/pick-up tube securing nut to No 4 main bearing cap.
12 Refit the sump.
13 Fit the crankshaft front oil seal using a suitable tool.
14 Refit the thrustwasher, crankshaft sprocket and timing belt.

29 Oil pump - dismantling, inspection and reassembly

1.8 litre (R2A type)

1 If oil pump wear is suspected, check the cost and availability of new parts and the cost of a new pump. Examine the pump as described in this Section and then decide whether renewal or repair is the best course of action.
2 Using a suitable Torx socket, unscrew the seven securing bolts and remove the oil pump cover (see illustration).
3 Mark the rotor faces so that the rotors can be refitted in their original positions, then lift the rotors from the pump housing (see illustration).
4 Unscrew the pressure relief valve plug and withdraw the spring and plunger (see illustration).
5 Thoroughly clean all parts in petrol or paraffin and wipe dry using a non-fluffy rag.
6 Commence reassembly by lubricating the relief valve plunger. Fit the plunger and spring, and screw the plug into place.
7 Lubricate the rotors and fit them, observing

29.4 Unscrew the pressure relief valve plug and withdraw the spring and plunger

the marks made when dismantling, if applicable.
8 The necessary clearances may now be checked using a machined straight-edge (such as a good steel rule) and a set of feeler blades. The critical clearances are between the lobes of the centre rotor and convex faces of the outer rotor; between the outer rotor and pump body; and between both rotors and the cover plate (endfloat). The serviceable clearances are given in the Specifications.
9 Endfloat can be measured by placing a straight-edge across the pump body and measuring the clearance between the two rotors and the straight-edge using feeler blades.
10 Refit the pump cover and tighten the securing bolts.
11 Prime the pump before refitting.

1.6 and 1.8 litre (R6A type)

12 The procedure is as described above but refer to the Specifications at the beginning of this Chapter for the rotor clearances.

30 Pistons and connecting rods - removal and refitting

1.8 litre (R2A type)

Removal

1 With the engine removed from the vehicle, remove the sump and the cylinder head.
2 Check the big-end caps for identification marks and if necessary use a centre-punch to identify the caps and connecting rods (see illustration).
3 Turn the crankshaft so that No 1 crankpin is at its lowest point, then unscrew the nuts or bolts and tap off the cap. Keep the bearing shells in the cap and connecting rod.
4 Using the handle of a hammer, push the piston and connecting rod up the bore and withdraw from the top of the cylinder block. Loosely refit the cap to the connecting rod.
5 Repeat the procedure in paragraphs 3 and 4 on No 4 piston and connecting rod, then turn the crankshaft through half a turn and repeat the procedure on Nos 2 and 3 pistons and connecting rods.

2C

30.2 Big-end cap and connecting rod identification marks (arrowed) - 1.8 litre (R2A)

30.8 Bearing shell lug (arrowed) must engage with groove in big-end cap - 1.8 litre (R2A)

30.10a Cut-out (arrowed) in piston crown . . .

30.10b . . . and lug (arrowed) on piston skirt must face the front of the engine

Refitting

6 Commence refitting as follows.

7 Clean the backs of the bearing shells and the recesses in the connecting rods and big-end caps.

8 Press the bearing shells into the connecting rods and caps in their correct positions and oil them liberally. Note that the lugs must be adjacent to each other (see illustration).

9 Lubricate the cylinder bores with engine oil.

10 Fit a ring compressor to No 1 piston then insert the piston and connecting rod into No 1 cylinder. With No 1 crankpin at its lowest point, drive the piston carefully into the cylinder with the wooden handle of a hammer, and at the same time guide the connecting rod onto the crankpin. The piston must be fitted with the cut-out in the piston crown (and the lug on the piston skirt) facing the front of the engine, with the oil hole in the connecting rod on the inlet manifold side of the engine (see illustrations).

11 Oil the crankpin, then fit the big-end bearing cap in its previously noted position, and tighten the nuts or bolts to the specified torque.

12 Check that the crankshaft turns freely.

13 Repeat the procedure given in paragraphs 11 to 12 inclusive on the remaining pistons.

14 Refit the cylinder head and the sump.

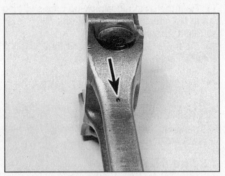

30.10c Connecting rod oil hole (arrowed) must face inlet manifold side of engine - 1.8 litre (R2A)

1.6 and 1.8 litre (R6A type)

15 The procedure is as described above, noting the following points:

a) On the 1.6 litre engine, when refitting a piston/connecting rod assembly, the piston must be fitted with the arrow on the piston crown and the cast pip on the piston skirt facing the front (timing belt end) of the engine (see illustration).

b) On the 1.6 litre engine, the big-end bearing caps locate on dowels in the connecting rods, and can only be fitted in one position.

31 Pistons and connecting rods - examination and renovation

1.8 litre (R2A type)

1 Examine the pistons for ovality, scoring, and scratches. Check the connecting rods for wear or damage.

2 The gudgeon pins are an interference fit in the connecting rods, and if new pistons are to be fitted to the existing connecting rods the work should be carried out by a Ford dealer who will have the necessary tooling. Note that the oil hole in the connecting rod must be located on the right-hand side of the piston (the cut-out in the piston crown and the lug on the piston skirt face forwards).

3 If new rings are to be fitted to the existing pistons, expand the old rings over the top of

30.10d Fitting a piston and connecting rod into the cylinder bore - 1.8 litre (R2A)

the pistons (see illustration). Note that the oil control ring is in three sections.

> **HAYNES HiNT** *The use of two or three old feeler blades will be helpful in preventing the rings dropping into empty grooves.*

4 Before fitting the piston rings, clean out the piston ring grooves using a piece of old piston ring as a scraper. Be careful not to scratch the aluminium surface of the pistons. Protect your fingers - piston ring edges are sharp. Then probe the groove oil return holes.

5 Fit the oil control ring sections with the spreader ends abutted opposite the front of the piston. The side ring gaps should be 25 mm (1.0 in) either side of the spreader gap. Fit

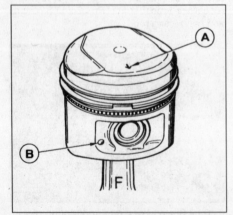

30.15 The arrow (A) and the cast pip (B) must face the front of the engine - 1.6 litre

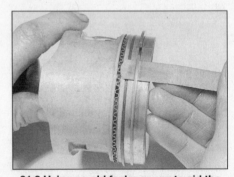

31.3 Using an old feeler gauge to aid the fitting of a piston ring - 1.8 litre (R2A)

32.6 Checking crankshaft endfloat - 1.8 litre (R2A)

the tapered lower compression ring with the "TOP" mark towards the top of the piston and the gap 150° from the spreader gap, then fit the upper compression ring with the gap 150° on the other side of the spreader gap. Note that the compression rings are coated with a molybdenum skin which must not be damaged.

1.6 and 1.8 litre (R6A type)

6 Proceed as described in paragraphs 1 to 5 inclusive, but note the following differences for the 1.6 litre engine.

7 Before fitting the new rings to the pistons, insert them into the relevant cylinder bore and use a feeler blade to check that the end gaps are within the limits given in the Specifications at the beginning of this Chapter. Check the end gaps with the ring at the top and the bottom of the cylinder bore.

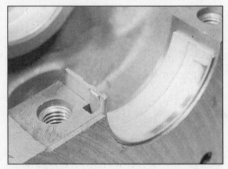

32.13a Rear main bearing shell in cylinder block - 1.8 litre (R2A)

32.18 Lowering the crankshaft into the crankcase - 1.8 litre (R2A)

8 Fit the oil control ring sections with the spreader ends abutted opposite the front of the piston, making sure that the ends do not overlap. The side ring gaps should be offset 120° either side of the spreader gap. Fit the tapered lower compression ring with the "TOP" mark uppermost and the gap 120° from the spreader gap, then fit the upper compression ring with the gap 120° on the other side of the spreader gap. Note that the compression rings are coated with a molybdenum disulphide skin, which must not be damaged.

32 Crankshaft and main bearings - removal and refitting

1.8 litre (R2A type)

Removal

1 With the engine removed from the vehicle, remove the timing belt, crankshaft sprocket and thrustwasher.

2 Remove the pistons and connecting rods. If no work is to be done on the pistons and connecting rods, there is no need to push the pistons out of the cylinder bores.

3 Remove the oil pump and pick-up tube.

4 Unscrew the four securing bolts and remove the crankshaft rear oil seal housing.

5 Check the main bearing caps for identification marks and if necessary use a centre-punch to identify them.

6 Before removing the crankshaft, check that the endfloat is within the specified limits by

32.13b Centre main thrust bearing shell in cylinder block - 1.8 litre (R2A)

32.22a The arrows on the bearing caps must point towards the front of the engine - 1.8 litre (R2A)

inserting a feeler blade between the centre crankshaft web and the thrust bearing shell **(see illustration)**. This will indicate whether a new thrust bearing shell is required.

7 Unscrew the bolts and tap off the main bearing caps complete with bearing shells.

8 Lift the crankshaft from the crankcase.

9 Extract the bearing shells, keeping them identified for location.

Refitting

10 Commence refitting as follows.

11 Wipe the bearing shell locations in the crankcase with a soft, non-fluffy rag.

12 Wipe the crankshaft journals with a soft, non-fluffy rag.

13 If the old main bearing shells are to be renewed (not to do so is a false economy, unless they are virtually new) fit the five upper halves of the main bearing shells to their location in the crankcase. Note the flanged thrust bearing shell should be fitted to the centre bearing location **(see illustrations)**.

14 Identify each main bearing cap and place in order. The number is cast on to the cap and an arrow is also marked which should point towards the front of the engine.

15 Wipe the cap bearing shell location with a soft non-fluffy rag.

16 Fit the bearing half shell onto each main bearing cap.

17 Lubricate the crankshaft journals and the upper and lower main bearing shells with clean engine oil.

18 Carefully lower the crankshaft into the crankcase **(see illustration)**.

19 Lubricate the crankshaft main bearing journals again, then fit No 1 bearing cap. Fit the two securing bolts but do not tighten yet.

20 Fit the rear bearing cap, then the centre bearing cap, but as before do not tighten the bolts yet.

21 Fit the intermediate bearing caps and securing bolts, noting that the studded bolt which retains the oil strainer/pick-up tube fits on the inlet manifold side of No 4 bearing cap. Again, do not tighten the bolts yet.

22 Check that the arrows on the bearing caps all point towards the front of the engine, and lightly tighten all the bearing cap bolts, then finally tighten the bolts in a progressive manner to the specified torque **(see illustrations)**.

2C

32.22b Tightening a main bearing cap bolt. Note studded bolt location (arrowed) on No 4 bearing cap - 1.8 litre (R2A)

32.25 Fit the crankshaft rear oil seal housing and tighten the securing bolts - 1.8 litre (R2A)

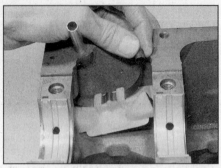

34.1 Removing the crankcase ventilation baffle

23 Check that the crankshaft rotates freely. Some stiffness is to be expected with new components, but there must be no tight spots or binding.

24 Check that the crankshaft endfloat is within the specified limits by inserting a feeler blade between the centre crankshaft web and the thrust bearing cap.

25 Lubricate the oil seal lip with clean engine oil, then carefully fit the crankshaft rear oil seal housing. Using a straight-edge, ensure that the bottom face of the oil seal housing is aligned with the bottom face of the cylinder block before finally tightening the securing bolts **(see illustration)**.

26 Carefully prise the crankshaft front oil seal from the oil pump housing, then refit the oil pump, oil strainer/pick-up tube and crankshaft front oil seal.

27 Refit the pistons and connecting rods.

28 Refit the thrustwasher, crankshaft sprocket and timing belt.

1.6 and 1.8 litre (R6A type)

29 Proceed as described above, noting the following point:

On the 1.6 litre engine, note that thrustwashers are used at the centre main bearing (one each side of the bearing) instead of a thrust bearing shell to control crankshaft endfloat. Oversize thrustwashers are available to compensate for wear if necessary. The thrustwashers should be fitted with the oil grooves visible

33 Crankshaft and bearings - examination and renovation

1.8 litre (R2A type)

1 Examine the bearing surfaces of the crankshaft for scratches or scoring and, using a micrometer, check each journal and crankpin for ovality. Where this is found to be in excess of 0.0254 mm (0.001 in) the crankshaft will have to be reground and undersize bearings fitted.

2 Crankshaft regrinding should be carried out by a suitable engineering works, who will normally supply the matching undersize main and big-end shell bearings.

3 Note that undersize bearings may already have been fitted either in production or by a previous repairer. Check the markings on the backs of the old bearing shells, and if in doubt take them along when buying new ones.

4 If the crankshaft endfloat is more than the maximum specified amount, a new thrust bearing shell should be fitted to the centre main bearing.

5 An accurate method of determining bearing wear is by the use of Plastigage. The crankshaft is located in the main bearings (and big-end bearings if necessary) and the Plastigage filament located across the journal which must be dry. The cap is then fitted and the bolts/nuts tightened to the specified torque. On removal of the cap the width of the filament is checked with a plastic gauge and

the running clearance compared with that given in the Specifications.

6 If the spigot bearing in the rear of the crankshaft requires renewal extract it with a suitable puller. Alternatively fill it with heavy grease and use a close fitting metal dowel driven into the centre of the bearing. Drive the new bearing into the crankshaft with a soft metal drift.

1.6 and 1.8 litre (R6A type)

7 Proceed as described above but note that if the crankshaft endfloat is more than the maximum specified amount, new thrustwashers should be fitted to the centre main bearing.

34 Cylinder block and bores - examination and renovation

Refer to Section 36, Chapter 2, Part A but note that the crankcase ventilation baffle should be removed from its location at the rear of the cylinder block and cleaned if necessary **(see illustration)**.

35 Initial start-up after overhaul or major repair

Refer to Section 37, Chapter 2, Part A.

Chapter 3
Cooling, heating and air conditioning systems

Contents

Degrees of difficulty

| Easy, suitable for novice with little experience | | Fairly easy, suitable for beginner with some experience | | Fairly difficult, suitable for competent DIY mechanic | 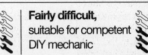 | Difficult, suitable for experienced DIY mechanic | | Very difficult, suitable for expert DIY or professional | |

Specifications

System type
SOHC models ....   Pressurised, with belt-driven coolant pump, crossflow radiator, thermo-viscous fan, thermostat, and expansion tank

CVH and DOHC models ....   Pressurised, with belt-driven coolant pump, crossflow radiator, electric fan, thermostat, and expansion tank

Thermostat
Nominal temperature rating (fully open):
  SOHC models ....   88°C (190° F)
  CVH models ....   100°C (212°F)
  DOHC models ....   102°C (216°F)
Opening temperature:
  SOHC models ....   85 to 89°C (185 to 192°F)
  CVH models ....   88°C (190°F)
  CVH (R6A type) models ....   85 to 89°C (185 to 192°F)
  DOHC models ....   85 to 89°C (185 to 192°F)

Expansion tank cap opening pressure
SOHC models:
  Up to 1987 ....   0.85 to 1.1 bar (12 to 16 lbf/in2)
  From 1987 ....   1.0 to 1.25 bar (15 to 18 lbf/in2)
CVH models ....   1.0 to 1.25 bar (15 to 18 lbf/in2)
DOHC models ....   1.0 to 1.4 bar (15 to 20 lbf/in2)

Coolant mixture ....   See Chapter 1 Specifications
System capacity ....   See Chapter 1 Specifications

Drivebelt tensions
Air conditioning system compressor ....   10.0 mm (0.4 in) deflection at the midpoint of the belt's longest run under firm thumb pressure

Coolant pump/alternator ....   10.0 mm (0.4 in) deflection midway between coolant pump and alternator (or power steering pump) pulleys under firm thumb pressure

3

Torque wrench settings

	Nm	lbf ft
Radiator upper mounting nuts	21 to 25	15 to 18
Radiator lower mounting bolts	8 to 12	6 to 9
Coolant pump bolts:		
SOHC models:		
M8 bolts	17 to 21	13 to 15
M10 bolts	35 to 42	26 to 31
CVH models	8 to 11	6 to 8
CVH (R6A type) models	7 to 10	5 to 7
DOHC models	21 to 28	15 to 21
Thermostat housing bolts:		
SOHC/DOHC models	17 to 20	13 to 15
CVH models	8 to 11	6 to 8
CVH (R6A type) models	8 to 12	6 to 9
Cooling fan shroud-to-radiator nuts/bolts	8 to 11	6 to 8
Coolant pump pulley bolts:		
SOHC models	21 to 28	15 to 21
DOHC models	20 to 25	15 to 18
Coolant pump/alternator drivebelt tensioner bolt:		
CVH models	23 to 30	17 to 22
DOHC models	70 to 97	52 to 72
Cooling fan blades-to-fan hub bolts (SOHC models)	8 to 10	6 to 7
Air conditioning compressor-to-bracket bolts	65 to 75	48 to 55
Air conditioning compressor bracket-to-engine bolts:		
M10	85 to 92	63 to 68
M12	110 to 120	81 to 89
Air conditioning condenser fan assembly-to-condenser bolts:		
Models up to 1987	2 to 3	1 to 2
Models from 1987	8 to 11	6 to 8
Air conditioning condenser securing bolts (models from 1987)	27 to 33	20 to 24

1 General information and precautions

General information

The cooling system is of pressurised type, and consists of a front mounted radiator, coolant pump, cooling fan, wax type thermostat, and an expansion tank.

The radiator matrix is manufactured from honeycombed metal, and the end tanks are made of plastic. On automatic transmission models, the right-hand end tank incorporates the transmission fluid cooler.

The coolant pump is located on the front face of the engine block, and is belt-driven. The pump is of the impeller type.

The cooling fan draws cold air over the radiator matrix to assist the cooling process when the forward speed of the vehicle is too low to provide sufficient cooling airflow, or the ambient temperature is unusually high. SOHC models have a thermo-viscous fan, whereas CVH and DOHC models have an electrically-operated fan.

The thermo-viscous fan is controlled by the temperature of the air behind the radiator. When the air temperature reaches a predetermined level, a bi-metallic coil commences to open a valve within the unit, and silicon fluid is fed through a system of vanes. Half the vanes are driven directly by the coolant pump, and the remaining half are connected to the fan blades. The vanes are arranged so that drive is transmitted to the fan blades in relation to the viscosity of the silicon fluid, and this in turn depends on ambient temperature and engine speed. The fan is therefore only operating when required, and compared with direct-drive type fans represents a considerable improvement in fuel economy, drivebelt wear and fan noise.

The electrically-operated fan is switched on by a temperature sensor mounted in the thermostat housing when the temperature reaches a predetermined level. The fan is therefore only operating when required, and like the thermo-viscous fan, offers a considerable advantage over direct-drive type fans.

A thermostat is fitted. Its purpose is to ensure rapid engine warm-up by restricting the flow of coolant to the engine when cold and also to assist in regulating the normal operating temperature of the engine.

The expansion tank incorporates a pressure cap which effectively pressurises the cooling system as the coolant temperature rises, thereby increasing the boiling point of the coolant. The tank also has a further degas function. Any accumulation of air bubbles in the coolant is returned to the tank and released in the air space, thus maintaining the efficiency of the coolant. The pressure cap also incorporates a vacuum relief valve which prevents a vacuum forming in the system as it cools.

The system functions as follows. Cold coolant in the bottom of the radiator circulates through the bottom hose to the coolant pump where the pump impeller pushes the coolant through the passages within the cylinder block, cylinder head and inlet manifold. After cooling the cylinder bores, combustion chambers and valve seats, the coolant reaches the underside of the thermostat which is initially closed. A small proportion of the coolant passes from the thermostat housing to the expansion tank, but the main circulation is through the inlet manifold, automatic choke (where applicable), and heater matrix, finally returning to the coolant pump. When the coolant reaches a predetermined temperature, the thermostat opens and hot water passes through the top hose to the top of the radiator. As the coolant circulates through the radiator, it is cooled by the flow of air to the vehicle's forward motion, supplemented by the action of the cooling fan where necessary. By the time it reaches the bottom of the radiator the coolant is cooled, and the cycle is repeated. Circulation of coolant continues through the expansion tank, inlet manifold, automatic choke (where applicable) and heater at all times, the heater temperature being controlled by an air flap.

An air conditioning system is available as an optional extra on certain models. In conjunction with the heater, the system enables any reasonable air temperature to be achieved inside the vehicle; it also reduces the humidity of the incoming air, aiding demisting even when cooling is not required.

The refrigeration side of the air conditioning system functions in a similar way to a domestic refrigerator. A compressor, belt-driven from the crankshaft pulley, draws refrigerant in its gaseous phase from an evaporator. The compressed refrigerant passes through a condenser where it loses heat and enters its liquid phase. After passing through the dehydrator, which acts as a reservoir and filter to extract moisture from the circuit, the refrigerant returns to the evaporator where it absorbs heat from the air passing over the evaporator fins on its way to the vehicle interior. The refrigerant becomes a gas again and the cycle is repeated.

Various subsidiary controls and sensors protect the system against excessive temperature and pressures. Additionally, engine idle speed is increased when the system is in use to compensate for the additional load imposed by the compressor.

Precautions

Air conditioning refrigerant

Although the refrigerant is not itself toxic, in the presence of a naked flame (or a lighted cigarette) it forms a highly toxic gas. Liquid refrigerant spilled on the skin will cause frostbite. If refrigerant enters the eyes, rinse them with a dilute solution of boric acid and seek medical advice immediately.

In view of the above points, and of the need for specialised equipment for evacuating and recharging the system, any work which requires the disconnection of a refrigerant line must be left to a specialist.

Do not allow refrigerant lines to be exposed to temperatures above 230°F (110°C) - eg during welding or paint drying operations and do not operate the air conditioning system if it is known to be short of refrigerant, or further damage may result.

Antifreeze mixture

Antifreeze mixture is poisonous. Keep it out of reach of children and pets. Wash splashes off skin and clothing with plenty of water. Wash splashes off vehicle paintwork to avoid discolouration.

Antifreeze/water mixture must be renewed at the specified intervals to preserve its anti-corrosive properties. In climates where antifreeze protection is unnecessary, a corrosion inhibitor may be used instead - consult a Ford dealer. Never run the engine for long periods with plain water as coolant. Only use the specified antifreeze as inferior brands may not contain the necessary corrosion inhibitors, or may break down at high temperatures. Antifreeze containing methanol is particularly to be avoided, as the methanol evaporates.

The specified mixture is 45 to 50% antifreeze and 50 to 55% clean soft water (by volume). Mix the required quantity in a clean container.

2 Cooling system - draining

Refer to Chapter 1, Section 46.

3 Cooling system - flushing

Refer to Chapter 1, Section 46.

4 Cooling system - filling

Refer to Chapter 1, Section 46.

5.9 Unscrew the fan shroud/radiator retaining nuts

5 Radiator - removal and refitting

Removal

1 Disconnect the battery negative lead.
2 Drain the cooling system.
3 If not already done, disconnect the bottom hose from the radiator.
4 Disconnect the top hose and the expansion tank hose from the radiator.
5 On automatic transmission models, place a suitable container beneath the fluid cooler pipe connections at the radiator. Unscrew the union and plug the upper pipe, then repeat the procedure on the lower pipe.
6 Apply the handbrake, jack up the front of the vehicle and support on axle stands (see "*Jacking and Vehicle Support*").
7 To improve access, remove the cooling fan shroud as follows, according to model.
8 On SOHC models, remove the four retaining clips and unscrew the two retaining screws, then withdraw the upper section of the fan shroud. Unclip and remove the lower section of the shroud.
9 On CVH and DOHC models, unclip the wiring connector from the fan motor(s) then unscrew the retaining nuts and washers, and withdraw the fan shroud(s) and cooling fan assembly(s) **(see illustration)**.
10 On early models, unscrew and remove the upper radiator mounting nuts and washers **(see illustration)**. Unscrew and remove the lower mounting bolts and washers and withdraw the radiator from under the vehicle **(see illustration)**.

5.10b Lower radiator mounting bolt

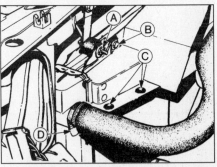

5.10a Radiator and cooling fan shroud upper mountings

  A *Radiator mounting nut*
  B *Shroud securing screw*
  C *Shroud securing clips*
  D *Radiator top hose clip*

11 On all later models, the radiator is secured to the engine compartment front panel using clips and locking pegs. To release the top of the radiator, work through the cut-outs in the engine compartment front panel and remove the two radiator upper locking pegs **(see illustration)**. Working under the front of the vehicle, remove the two radiator lower mounting bolts. Support the radiator from underneath. Squeeze the upper radiator locking pegs to release them from the engine compartment front panel and lower the radiator assembly from the vehicle.

Refitting

12 Refitting is a reversal of removal, bearing in mind the following points.
13 Refill the cooling system.
14 On automatic transmission models, check and if necessary top-up the transmission fluid level.

6 Radiator - inspection and cleaning

1 If the radiator has been removed because of suspected blockage, reverse-flush it.
2 Clean dirt and debris from the radiator fins using an air jet or water and a soft brush. Be careful not to damage the fins or cut your fingers.

5.11 Removing a radiator upper locking peg

3

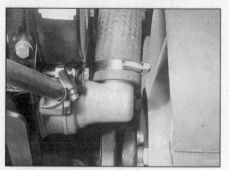

7.4a Radiator top hose connection at thermostat housing

7.4b Disconnect the expansion tank hose from the thermostat housing

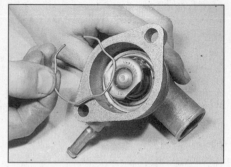

7.6a Prise out the retaining clip . . .

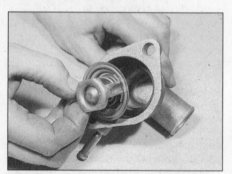

7.6b . . . and extract the thermostat . . .

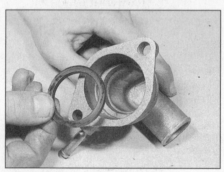

7.6c . . . and sealing ring

7.9 Thermostat flow direction markings (arrowed)

3 A radiator specialist can perform a "flow test" on the radiator to establish whether an internal blockage exists.

4 A leaking radiator must be referred to a specialist for permanent repair. Do not attempt to weld or solder a leaking radiator, as damage to the plastic parts may result.

5 In an emergency, minor leaks from the radiator can be cured by using a sealant.

7 Thermostat - removal and refitting

1 Disconnect the battery negative lead.
2 Drain the cooling system.
3 Proceed as follows according to model:

SOHC models

4 Disconnect the radiator top hose and expansion tank hose from the thermostat housing situated at the front of the cylinder head **(see illustrations)**.
5 Unscrew the two securing bolts and remove the housing and gasket.
6 Using a screwdriver, prise the retaining clip from the housing, and extract the thermostat and sealing ring **(see illustrations)**.
7 Refitting is a reversal of removal, bearing in mind the following points.
8 Clean the housing and the mating face of the cylinder head. Check the thermostat sealing ring for condition and renew it if necessary. Use a new gasket when refitting the housing.
9 The thermostat wax capsule must face into the cylinder head with the flow direction arrow facing forward **(see illustration)**.
10 Refill the cooling system.

CVH models

11 Disconnect the wiring plug from the cooling fan switch on the thermostat housing situated at the front of the inlet manifold.
12 Disconnect the automatic choke hose, radiator top hose and expansion tank hose from the thermostat housing. Where applicable, take care not to strain the wiring which is routed around the housing. If necessary, disconnect the wiring connector **(see illustrations)**.
13 Unscrew the three securing bolts and remove the housing and gasket **(see illustration)**.
14 Lift the thermostat from the housing, and carefully prise out the sealing ring.
15 Refitting is a reversal of removal, bearing in mind the following points.
16 Clean the housing and the mating face of the inlet manifold. Check the thermostat sealing ring for condition and renew it if necessary. Use a new gasket when refitting the housing.

7.12a Disconnect the automatic choke hose . . .

7.12b . . . the radiator top hose . . .

7.12c . . . and the expansion tank hose

7.13 Removing the thermostat housing and gasket

17 Note that the thermostat wax capsule must face into the inlet manifold, with the flow direction arrow pointing forward, in line with the pressure relief valve in the housing **(see illustration)**.
18 Refill the cooling system.

DOHC models

19 On fuel injection models, for access to the thermostat housing loosen the clips and remove the air inlet tube which connects the plenum chamber to the inlet manifold.
20 Disconnect the coolant hoses from the thermostat housing **(see illustrations)**.
21 Disconnect the wiring plug from the cooling fan switch mounted in the thermostat housing **(see illustration)**.
22 Unscrew the three securing bolts, and withdraw the thermostat housing **(see illustration)**.
23 Manipulate the thermostat from the inlet manifold, and recover the O-ring. If it is

7.20b . . . from the thermostat housing

7.22 Withdrawing the thermostat housing

7.17 Correct orientation of thermostat with flow direction arrow pointing towards pressure relief valve

necessary to prise the thermostat out, take care not to damage the surface of the housing in the inlet manifold.
24 Refitting is a reversal of removal, bearing in mind the following points.
25 Ensure that the O-ring seal is correctly fitted around the edge of the thermostat.
26 When fitting the thermostat to the inlet manifold, ensure that the relief valve is located in the 12 o'clock position **(see illustration)**.
27 Tighten the thermostat housing securing bolts to the specified torque.
28 Refill the cooling system.

8 Thermostat - testing

1 To test the thermostat, suspend it by a piece of string in a container of water **(see illustration)**.

7.21 Disconnect the cooling fan switch wiring plug

7.26 Thermostat relief valve (arrowed) should be in the 12 o'clock position

7.20a Disconnect the coolant hoses . . .

2 Gradually heat the water, and using a thermometer with a range of at least 100°C, note the temperature at which the thermostat starts to open.
3 Remove the thermostat from the water and check that it is fully closed when cold.
4 Renew the thermostat if the opening temperature is not as given in the Specifications, or if the unit does not fully close when cold.

9 Coolant pump - removal and refitting

1 Disconnect the battery negative lead.
2 Drain the cooling system.
3 Proceed as follows according to model:

SOHC models

4 Disconnect the heater and radiator bottom hoses from the coolant pump.
5 Remove the thermo-viscous fan (Section 12).
6 If not already done, remove the coolant pump drivebelt, then unscrew the four retaining bolts and remove the coolant pump pulley. If necessary, the pulley can be prevented from turning using a strap wrench.

> **HAYNES HINT** *Holding the pulley can be improvised using an old drivebelt, and a suitable socket and wrench.*

7 Unbolt and remove the timing belt cover.

8.1 Testing the thermostat opening temperature

3

9.8 Location of the alternator adjusting link under the right-hand retaining bolt

8 Unscrew the three retaining bolts and remove the coolant pump and gasket from the front of the cylinder block. Note that on certain models, the alternator adjusting link is secured by the right-hand retaining bolt **(see illustration)**.
9 If the coolant pump is faulty, it must be renewed, as it is not possible to obtain individual components.
10 Before refitting, clean the mating faces of the coolant pump and cylinder block.
11 Refitting is a reversal of removal, bearing in mind the following points.
12 Use a new gasket, and tighten the retaining bolts to the specified torque.
13 Before fitting the coolant pump pulley, ensure that the timing belt cover support bolt is located in its hole in the pump.

9.21 Withdraw the coolant pump

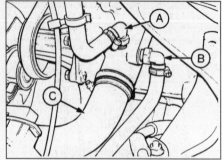

9.29 Coolant pump housing hose connections

A *Heater hose connection - up to May 1990*
B *Expansion tank hose connection - up to May 1990*
C *Bottom radiator hose*

9.15 Disconnect the coolant elbow from the coolant pump

14 Refill the cooling system.

CVH models

15 Unscrew the two securing nuts, and disconnect the coolant elbow from the left-hand side of the coolant pump **(see illustration)**.
16 Remove the timing belt.
17 Unscrew the camshaft sprocket bolt and withdraw the distributor drive sleeve.
18 Screw the camshaft sprocket bolt part way back into the end of the camshaft, and using a suitable puller, pull the sprocket from the camshaft.
19 Remove the plastic rear timing belt cover.
20 Unscrew the two retaining bolts, and remove the timing belt tensioner **(see illustration)**.
21 Unscrew the four securing bolts, and withdraw the coolant pump **(see illustration)**.
22 If the coolant pump is faulty it must be renewed, as it is not possible to obtain individual components.
23 Before refitting, clean the mating faces of the coolant pump and cylinder block.
24 Refitting is a reversal of removal, bearing in mind the following points.
25 Use a new gasket, and tighten the securing bolts to the specified torque.
26 Before refitting the camshaft sprocket bolt, the threads must be coated with sealer (Loctite 74 or 274, or Omnifit 30M blue), as the bolt acts as an oil seal for the hollow camshaft. Do not forget to fit the distributor drive sleeve.
27 Correctly tension the timing belt.
28 Refill the cooling system.

9.32 Withdrawing the coolant pump from the cylinder block (engine removed)

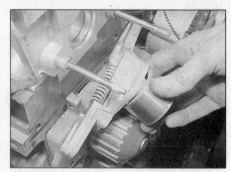

9.20 Remove the timing belt tensioner

DOHC models

Note: *Before proceeding, take note of the following modifications: On models up to May 1990, the coolant hoses were connected to the coolant pump housing as shown* **(see illustration)**. *On models from May 1990, the heater hose (A) and the expansion tank hose (B) connections were swapped over. If the hoses are disconnected on earlier models, they should be reconnected as on later models, ie connect the heater hose to connection "B", and connect the expansion tank hose to connection "A". This will prevent the possibility of noises from the heater matrix due to air in the system.*
29 On fuel injection models, for access to the coolant pump, remove the air inlet hose, plenum chamber, and air cleaner lid as an assembly.
30 Remove the coolant pump/alternator drivebelt.
31 If the pump pulley is to be removed, it is easiest to do this with the pump in position, as follows. Prevent the pulley from rotating using a strap wrench and unscrew the four pulley securing bolts. Withdraw the pulley.
32 Position a suitable container beneath the coolant pump, to catch the coolant which will be released as the pump is removed. Unscrew the five securing bolts, and withdraw the pump from the housing in the cylinder block **(see illustration)**. Recover the O-ring seal.
33 Before refitting, clean the mating faces of the coolant pump and the cylinder block.
34 Refitting is a reversal of removal, bearing in mind the following points.
35 Use a new O-ring seal **(see illustration)**.

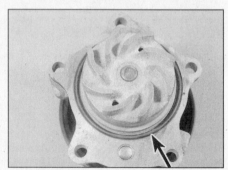

9.35 Coolant pump O-ring (arrowed)

36 Tighten the coolant pump securing bolts, and where applicable the pump pulley securing bolts, to the specified torque.
37 On completion, refill the cooling system.

10 Coolant pump/alternator drivebelt(s) - checking, renewal and tensioning

Refer to Chapter 1, Section 21.

11 Coolant pump/alternator drivebelt tensioner (DOHC models with power steering) - removal and refitting

Removal

1 Remove the alternator drivebelt.
2 Loosen the alternator lower mounting through-bolt, then remove the alternator upper mounting bolt and swing the alternator away from the engine.
3 Unscrew the central securing bolt, and withdraw the drivebelt tensioner assembly (see illustration).

Refitting

4 Commence refitting by positioning the tensioner on the cylinder block, ensuring that the lug on the rear of the tensioner bracket engages with the corresponding hole in the cylinder block. Tighten the securing bolt.
5 Swing the alternator into position, to align the upper mounting bolt hole with the corresponding hole in the drivebelt tensioner

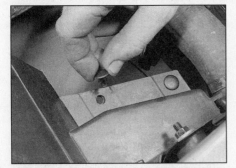

12.2a Remove the retaining clips followed by the screws . . .

12.2b . . . and withdraw the upper section of the fan shroud

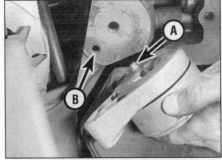

11.3 Withdrawing the coolant pump/alternator drivebelt tensioner assembly. Note lug (A) on tensioner which engages with hole (B) in mounting bracket

assembly. Refit the upper mounting bolt, and tighten the upper bolt and lower through-bolt.
6 Fit the drivebelt by reversing the removal procedure, and release the tensioner to tension the drivebelt.
7 Observe the tensioner indicator, which should be central in its slot (see illustration).

12 Thermo-viscous cooling fan (SOHC models) - removal and refitting

Removal

1 Disconnect the battery negative lead.
2 Remove the four retaining clips and unscrew the two retaining screws, then withdraw the upper section of the fan shroud (see illustrations).
3 The cooling fan hub nut must now be unscrewed from the coolant pump drive flange. A thin cranked 32.0 mm (1.25 in AF) spanner with a jaw thickness not exceeding 5.0 mm (0.2 in) will be required (see illustration). Alternatively, if two of the coolant pump pulley bolts are removed, a normal thickness spanner can be used. *Note that the fan hub nut has a left-hand thread*, (ie it is undone in a clockwise direction.) If the pulley turns as the nut is undone, remove the drivebelt, and clamp an old drivebelt round the pulley to restrain it, using self-locking pliers. Tap the spanner with a mallet if required to remove the nut.

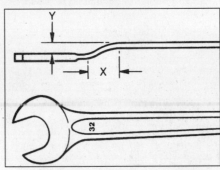

12.3 Modified spanner required for removing the thermo-viscous cooling fan

X = 25.0 mm (1.0 in)   Y = 12.0 mm (0.5 in)

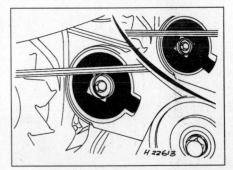

11.7 Alternator/coolant pump drivebelt tensioner indicator position
Inset shows tensioner at maximum adjustment

4 If required, the fan blades can be separated from the fan hub by unscrewing the four securing bolts.

Refitting

5 Refitting is a reversal of removal, but where applicable, take care not to overtighten the bolts securing the fan blades to the fan hub, as thread damage may require the whole unit to be renewed. Where applicable, refit and tension the drivebelt.

13 Electric cooling fan - removal and refitting

CVH models

1 Disconnect the battery negative lead. Unclip the wiring connector from the fan motor then unscrew the retaining nuts and washers. Withdraw the fan shroud and cooling fan assembly (see illustration).
2 To remove the fan blades, prise the securing clip from the end of the motor shaft (see illustration).
3 The motor can be separated from the fan shroud by unscrewing the three securing nuts and bolts.
4 Where two cooling fans are fitted, both fans are secured to the fan shroud in the same manner.
5 Refitting is a reversal of removal, but when refitting the fan blades, ensure that the direction of rotation arrow faces away from the motor, towards the radiator.

3

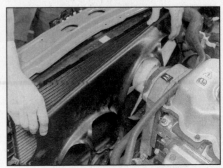

13.1 Withdrawing the fan shroud and cooling fan assembly

13.2 Fan blade securing clip and direction of rotation arrow

DOHC models

6 Disconnect the battery negative lead.

7 To provide additional clearance when removing the cooling fan shroud assembly (which is removed from below the vehicle), apply the handbrake, then jack up the front of the vehicle and support it securely on axle stands (see "*Jacking and Vehicle Support*").

8 Disconnect the wiring plug(s) from the motor(s), and where applicable, unclip the wiring from the fan shroud.

9 Unclip the expansion tank hose from the fan shroud.

10 Unscrew the two nuts securing the fan shroud to the top of the radiator, then tilt the top of the shroud away from the radiator, and lift the shroud to release the lower securing clips. Withdraw the assembly from below the vehicle.

11 To remove the fan blades, prise the securing clip from the end of the motor shaft.

12 The motor can be separated from the fan shroud by unscrewing the three securing nuts and bolts.

13 Where two cooling fans are fitted, both are secured to the shroud in the same manner.

14 Refitting is a reversal of removal, but when fitting the fan blades, ensure that the drive dog on the motor shaft engages with the slot in the rear of the fan blades.

14 Cooling fan switch - removal and refitting

On CVH models, the cooling fan switch is located on the right-hand side of the thermostat housing **(see illustration)**. On DOHC models, the switch is located in the end of the thermostat housing.

Removal and refitting of the switch is as described for the temperature gauge sender.

15 Expansion tank and coolant level sensor - removal and refitting

Removal

1 With the engine cold, slowly unscrew the expansion tank cap to release any remaining pressure from the cooling system. Remove the cap.

2 Place a suitable container beneath the expansion tank.

3 Disconnect and plug the upper hose.

4 Where applicable, disconnect the coolant level sensor wiring plug.

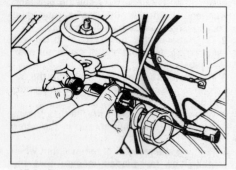

15.8a Removing the coolant level sensor from the expansion tank

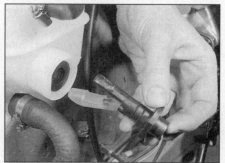

15.8b Fitting the coolant level sensor

14.1 Disconnecting the wiring plug from the cooling fan switch

5 Unscrew the expansion tank securing screws, and tilt the tank so that the coolant runs to the sealed end.

6 Disconnect and plug the lower hose.

7 Drain the expansion tank into the container and remove the tank.

8 Where applicable, the coolant level sensor can be removed from the tank by unscrewing the collar from the sensor, then withdrawing the spacer, sensor and seal **(see illustration)**. Renew the seal if necessary. Note that the sensor can only be fitted in one position **(see illustration)**.

Refitting

9 Refitting is a reversal of removal.

10 On completion, top-up the coolant level to the maximum mark, then refit the expansion tank cap and run the engine at a fast idling speed for several minutes. Check the expansion tank for leaks, then stop the engine and if necessary top-up the coolant level.

16 Temperature gauge sender - removal and refitting

Removal

1 On SOHC models, the temperature gauge sender is located on the front left-hand side of the cylinder head, just in front of the inlet manifold. On CVH models, the sender is located on the front face of the inlet manifold, next to the thermostat housing. On DOHC models, the sender is located at the front of the inlet manifold **(see illustration)**.

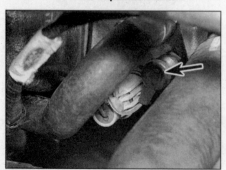

16.1 Temperature gauge sender location (arrowed)

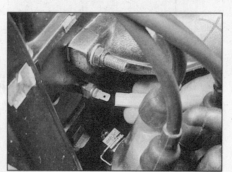

16.3a Disconnect the temperature gauge sender wiring - SOHC

16.3b Disconnect the temperature gauge sender wiring - CVH

2 With the engine cold, slowly unscrew the expansion tank cap to release any remaining pressure from the cooling system, then refit the cap.
3 Disconnect the wiring from the sender terminal (see illustrations).
4 Unscrew and remove the sender, and temporarily plug the aperture.

Refitting

5 Refitting is a reversal of removal, but smear a little sealing compound on the sender unit threads before fitting.
6 On completion, check and if necessary top-up the coolant level.

17 Heater controls - removal and refitting

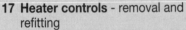

Removal

1 Disconnect the battery negative lead.
2 Remove the securing screws and unclip the lower and upper steering column shrouds.
3 Remove the four securing screws and withdraw the instrument panel surround. Note that the bottom right-hand screw is covered by a plastic panel which must be prised out.
4 Remove the passenger side lower facia panel.
5 Where necessary for improved access, detach the two vent hoses from the left-hand side of the heater, then detach the lower ends of the two control cables from the heater by removing the retaining screws (see illustration).
6 Unscrew the three securing screws, and remove the heater control panel by sliding it through the facia panel and withdrawing it downwards. Disconnect the wiring from the control panel illumination bulb.
7 If necessary, the bulb can be removed with its holder.

Refitting

8 Refitting is a reversal of removal, bearing in mind the following points.
9 When reconnecting the wiring to the control panel illumination bulb, wrap insulating tape

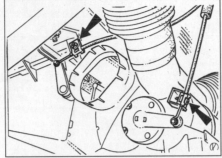

17.5 Heater control cable lower end fittings (arrowed)

around the wiring loom over a length of approximately 330.0 mm (13.0 in) starting from the bulbholder. Route the loom, ensuring that it is located in the two retaining clips, bend it over and secure it to the bulbholder with insulating tape as shown (see illustration). This procedure will prevent the wiring loom from chafing against the heater control levers.
10 When reconnecting the control cables to the heater, move the control levers on the control panel to the fully up position, then attach the cables to the clips on the heater. The cable ends should project from the clips by between 0 and 4.0 mm (0 and 0.16 in). The cables are adjusted automatically by moving the control levers fully downwards. It is possible that considerable resistance may have to be overcome when moving the control levers.

18 Heater unit - removal and refitting

Removal

1 Disconnect the battery negative lead.
2 If the coolant is still hot, release the pressure in the system by slowly unscrewing the expansion tank cap. Place a thick rag over the cap to prevent scalding as the pressure is released.
3 Note the location of the two heater hoses

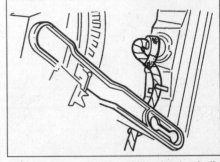

17.9 Heater control panel illumination bulb wiring loom correctly routed

on the engine compartment bulkhead, then disconnect and plug them (see illustration). Alternatively, the hoses can be secured high enough to prevent the coolant from draining.
4 To prevent unnecessary spillage of coolant when the heater unit is removed, blow into the upper heater pipe until all the coolant has been expelled through the lower pipe.
5 Remove the two securing screws and withdraw the heater pipe cover from the bulkhead (see illustration). Recover the gasket.
6 Working inside the vehicle, remove the passenger side lower facia panel.
7 Disconnect the ends of the two control cables from the heater by removing the two retaining screws.
8 Detach the five vent hoses from the heater.
9 Unscrew the two mounting bolts, and move the heater to the rear until the pipes are clear of the bulkhead, then withdraw the heater to the left. If necessary, remove the lower facia bracket (see illustration).

Refitting

10 Refitting is a reversal of removal, but adjust the control cables by moving the levers on the control panel to the top and then the bottom stops. Considerable resistance may be encountered when moving the levers towards the bottom stops, which should be overcome.
11 On completion, top-up the coolant level.

3

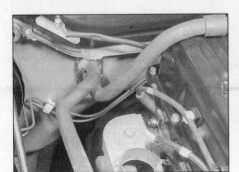

18.3 Location of heater hoses on engine compartment bulkhead

18.5 Heater pipe cover

18.9 Withdrawing the heater

19.1a Remove the securing screws . . .

19.1b . . . and withdraw the heater matrix

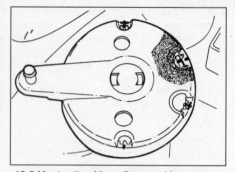

19.3 Heater "up/down" control lever must be aligned as shown before removal
Note that the cross marks are for right-hand drive vehicles

19 Heater unit - overhaul

1 With the heater unit removed from the vehicle, remove the two securing screws and withdraw the heater matrix from the casing (see illustrations).
2 Cut the heater casing gasket in line with the casing joint, then use two suitable screwdrivers to prise off the retaining clips and separate the casing halves. Withdraw the lower part of the casing to the side.
3 Remove the air flap valves, then press the control levers from the casing. Note that the "up/down" control lever can only be removed when the marks are aligned as shown (see illustration).
4 Clean all components and hose through the matrix to remove any debris. If necessary use

a chemical cleaner to clear the inner passage of the matrix. Renew the components as necessary.
5 Reassembly is a reversal of dismantling.

20 Heater motor - removal and refitting

Removal

1 Disconnect the battery negative lead.
2 Where necessary, unclip the brake servo vacuum hose for improved access.
3 On models from 1987, unclip the windscreen washer hoses and wiring from the motor cover, and secure them to the bodywork out of the way.
4 Unscrew the two securing bolts from the motor cover, pull off the rubber moulding, then withdraw the cover (see illustration).
5 Disconnect the wiring from the motor, and detach the earth lead from its bracket.

6 Unscrew the two motor securing nuts, and withdraw the motor assembly (see illustration).
7 Unclip the casing halves, then prise open the motor retaining strap using a screwdriver, or if necessary a drift.
8 Detach the wiring from the motor, then remove the motor and fan wheels from the casing.

Refitting

9 Refitting is a reversal of removal.

21 Air conditioning system - component renewal

1 Only those items which can be renewed without discharging the system are described here (see illustration). Other items must be dealt with by a Ford dealer or air conditioning specialist.

20.4 Unscrew the securing bolts and withdraw the heater motor cover

20.6 Heater motor and wiring

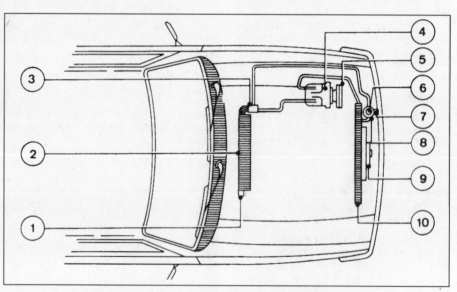

21.1 Layout of air conditioning system components

1 De-ice thermostat	6 Pressure switch	
2 Evaporator	7 Sight glass	
3 Expansion valve	8 Dehydrator/collector	
4 Compressor	9 Cooling fan	
5 Compressor clutch	10 Condenser	

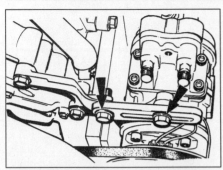

21.4 Typical air conditioning compressor mounting and pivot bolts (arrowed)

Compressor drivebelt

2 Disconnect the battery negative lead.

3 On SOHC models, remove the thermo-viscous cooling fan.

4 Slacken the compressor mounting and pivot bolts, move the compressor towards the engine and remove the old drivebelt **(see illustration)**.

5 Fit the new drivebelt, position the compressor to achieve the correct belt tension, then tighten the mounting and pivot bolts.

6 On SOHC models, refit the thermo-viscous cooling fan.

7 Reconnect the battery negative lead.

Condenser fan and motor

Models up to 1987

8 Disconnect the battery negative lead, and remove the radiator grille. On Ghia models, remove the front bumper.

9 Disconnect the fan wiring connector at the side of the condenser.

10 Remove the three securing bolts and withdraw the fan assembly. Turn the frame to position the fan wiring on the dehydrator side to avoid damaging the wiring. Take care also not to damage the condenser fins or tube.

11 To remove the fan blades from the motor, remove the retaining nut and circlip. The nut has a left-hand thread, ie, it is undone in a clockwise direction.

12 With the blades removed, the motor can be unscrewed from the frame.

13 Reassemble and refit in the reverse order of dismantling and removal.

Models from 1987

14 Disconnect the battery negative lead.

15 Remove the bonnet lock.

16 Unclip the guard from the fan frame.

17 Disconnect the fan wiring connector **(see illustration)**.

18 Apply the handbrake, jack up the front of the vehicle and support on axle stands (see "*Jacking and Vehicle Support*").

19 Unscrew the two lower condenser securing bolts and disengage the condenser from the top of the radiator by releasing the three clips.

20 Unscrew the four securing bolts and detach the fan assembly from the condenser. Withdraw the fan assembly from underneath the vehicle.

21 Proceed as described in paragraphs 11 to 13 inclusive.

De-ice thermostat

22 Disconnect and remove the battery.

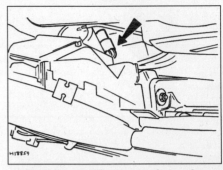

21.17 Air conditioning condenser fan wiring connector location (arrowed) - models from 1987

23 Disconnect any vacuum hoses, windscreen washer hoses and electrical wiring as necessary, then unscrew the four securing bolts and on models up to 1987 the single nut, and remove the right-hand plenum chamber cover plate from the bulkhead.

24 Disconnect the thermostat from the evaporator casing and withdraw it. Also withdraw the thermostat probe from the casing.

25 Refitting is a reversal of removal.

Heating/air conditioning controls

26 The procedure is similar to that described for the heater controls but additionally the vacuum hoses must be disconnected from the control unit vacuum valve during removal, and reconnected when refitting.

Notes

Chapter 4 Part A:
Fuel and exhaust systems - carburettor

Contents

Degrees of difficulty

Easy, suitable for novice with little experience	**Fairly easy,** suitable for beginner with some experience	**Fairly difficult,** suitable for competent DIY mechanic	**Difficult,** suitable for experienced DIY mechanic	**Very difficult,** suitable for expert DIY or professional

Specifications

General

Fuel tank capacity:	
All models except P100	60.0 litres (13.2 gals)
P100 models	66.0 litres (14.5 gals)
Fuel octane rating:	
Leaded	97 RON (4-star)
Unleaded	95 RON (Premium)

Air filter element

1.3 litre and 1.6 litre (Ford carburettor)	Champion W110
1.6 litre (Weber carburettor) and 1.8 litre (SOHC engine)	Champion W118
1.6 litre (1984-on) and 2.0 litre (SOHC engine)	Champion W152
1.8 litre CVH engine	Champion W219
2.0 litre DOHC engine	Champion W152

Carburettor type:

1.3 litre models	Ford VV
1.6 litre models (engine codes LCS and LCT)	Ford VV
1.6 litre models (engine codes LSD and LSE)	Weber 2V (28/30 DFTH)
1.8 litre models	Pierburg 2V (2E3)
2.0 litre SOHC models up to 1985	Weber 2V (32/36 DGAV)
2.0 litre SOHC models from 1985 (except P100)	Weber 2V (30/34 DFTH)
P100 models	Ford VV
2.0 litre DOHC models	Weber 2V (TLD)

Ford VV carburettor

Idle speed:	
1.3 and 1.6 litre models	800 ± 25 rpm
P100 models	800 ± 50 rpm
Idle mixture (CO content):	
1.3 and 1.6 litre models	1.5 ± 0.5%
P100 models	1.0 ± 0.5%

4A

Weber 2V (28/30 DFTH) carburettor

Idle speed	775 to 825 rpm	
Idle mixture (CO content)	0.75 to 1.25%	
Fast idle speed	1600 to 1800 rpm	
Float level (with gasket)	5.5 to 6.5 mm (0.22 to 0.26 in)	
Automatic choke vacuum pull-down	6.0 to 6.5 mm (0.24 to 0.26 in)	
	Primary	**Secondary**
Throttle barrel diameter	28.0 mm	30.0 mm
Venturi diameter	21.0 mm	23.0 mm
Idle jet	50	40 (70*)
Main jet	97 (95*)	110 (115*)
Air correction jet	185 (195*)	190 (170*)
Emulsion tube	F59	F22

*Re-jetting sizes for improved economy

Weber 2V (32/36 DGAV) carburettor

Idle speed	800 ± 25 rpm	
Idle mixture (CO content)	1.5 ± 0.2%	
Fast idle speed	2900 ± 100 rpm	
Float level (without gasket):		
Brass float	41.0 mm (1.61 in)	
Plastic float	35.3 mm (1.39 in)	
Automatic choke vacuum pull-down	6.5 ± 0.25 mm (0.26 ± 0.01 in)	
Automatic choke phasing dimension	1.5 ± 0.25 mm (0.06 ± 0.01 in)	
	Primary	**Secondary**
Throttle barrel diameter	32.0 mm	36.0 mm
Venturi diameter	26.0 mm	27.0 mm
Idle jet	45	45
Main jet:		
Manual gearbox	130	130
Automatic transmission	130	132
Air correction jet:		
Manual gearbox	165	120
Automatic transmission	170	120
Emulsion tube:		
Manual gearbox	F66	F66
Automatic transmission	F50	F66

Weber 2V (30/34 DFTH) carburettor (Part Nos 85HF 9510 CA and DA)

Idle speed	800 rpm (electronically controlled)	
Idle mixture (CO content)	0.75 to 1.25%	
Float level (with gasket)	7.5 to 8.5 mm (0.30 to 0.33 in)	
Automatic choke vacuum pull-down:		
Manual gearbox	9.0 mm (0.35 in)	
Automatic transmission	8.0 mm (0.32 in)	
Throttle barrel diameter	30.0 mm	34.0 mm
Venturi diameter	25.0 mm	27.0 mm
Idle jet	45	45
Main jet:		
Manual gearbox	112	135
Automatic transmission	110	135
Air correction jet:		
Manual gearbox	165	150
Automatic transmission	160	150
Emulsion tube	F22	F22

Weber 2V (30/34 DFTH) carburettor (Part Nos 85HF 9510 CB and DB)

Idle speed	875 rpm (electronically controlled)	
Idle mixture (CO content)	1.0 ± 0.25%	
Float level (with gasket)	8.0 ± 0.5 mm (0.32 ± 0.02 in)	
Automatic choke vacuum pull-down	6.0 mm (0.24 in)	
	Primary	**Secondary**
Throttle barrel diameter	30.0 mm	34.0 mm
Venturi diameter	25.0 mm	27.0 mm
Idle jet	42	45
Main jet	110	130
Air correction jet:		
Manual gearbox	160	160
Automatic transmission	170	160
Emulsion tube	F22	F22

Pierburg 2V (2E3) carburettor - SOHC models (Part No 85HF 9510 AB)

Idle speed	800 ± 20 rpm	
Idle mixture (CO content)	1.3%	
Fast idle speed	830 ± 30 rpm	
Automatic choke vacuum pull-down	3.0 mm (0.12 in)	
Idle fuel jet	45	
Idle air bleed	115	

	Primary	**Secondary**
Venturi diameter	23.0 mm	26.0 mm
Main jet	107.5	130

Pierburg 2V (2E3) carburettor - SOHC models (Part Nos 85HF 9510 JB and KC)

Idle speed:		
Manual gearbox	850 to 900 rpm	
Automatic transmission	775 to 825 rpm	
Idle mixture (CO content)	1.0 to 1.5%	
Fast idle speed	1850 to 1950 rpm	
Automatic choke vacuum pull-down:		
Manual gearbox	4.0 mm (0.16 in)	
Automatic transmission	3.7 mm (0.15 in)	
Idle fuel jet	45	
Idle air bleed:		
Manual gearbox	120	
Automatic transmission	115	

	Primary	**Secondary**
Venturi diameter	23.0 mm	26.0 mm
Main jet	102.5	130

Pierburg 2V (2E3) carburettor- CVH models

Idle speed:		
Manual gearbox	850 to 900 rpm	
Automatic transmission	775 to 825 rpm	
Idle mixture (CO content)	0.75 to 1.25%	
Fast idle speed	2000 rpm	
Automatic choke vacuum pull-down:		
Manual gearbox	2.3 mm (0.09 in)	
Automatic transmission	2.5 mm (0.10 in)	
Idle fuel jet	47.5	
Idle air bleed	135	

	Primary	**Secondary**
Venturi diameter	22.0 mm	23.0 mm
Main jet:		
Manual gearbox	100	105
Automatic transmission	97.5	105

Weber 2V (TLD) carburettor

Idle speed	850 ± 25 rpm	
Idle mixture (CO content)	1.0 ± 0.25%	
Fast idle speed	1800 ± 50 rpm	
Float level (with gasket)	29.0 ± 0.5 mm	
Automatic choke vacuum pull-down	5.0 ± 0.5 mm	
Throttle kicker speed (see text)	2000 ± 50 rpm	

	Primary	**Secondary**
Venturi diameter	23.0 mm	25.0 mm
Main jet	115	157
Air correction jet	175	145
Emulsion tube	F114	F3

Torque wrench settings

	Nm	lbf ft
All models except 2.0 litre DOHC		
Fuel pump bolts (mechanical pump)	14 to 18	10 to 13
Inlet manifold	16 to 20	12 to 15
Exhaust manifold	35 to 40	26 to 30
Exhaust manifold-to-downpipe nuts	35 to 40	26 to 30
Exhaust downpipe-to-main system nuts	35 to 40	26 to 30
Exhaust U-bolt clamp nuts	38 to 45	28 to 33

4A

2.0 litre DOHC models

Inlet manifold nuts and bolts	20 to 24	15 to 18
Exhaust manifold nuts	21 to 25	15 to 18
Carburettor bolts	8 to 10	6 to 7

1 General information and precautions

General information

The fuel system on carburettor models may comprise a fuel tank, a fuel pump, a fuel pressure regulator and/or vapour separator, a downdraught carburettor and a thermostatically-controlled air cleaner.

On Saloon, Hatchback and Estate models, the fuel tank is mounted under the rear of the vehicle, on the right-hand side. On P100 models, the fuel tank is mounted behind the cab, between the chassis frame and the load area. The tank is ventilated, and has a simple filler pipe and a fuel gauge sender unit.

The mechanical fuel pump is a diaphragm type, actuated by a pushrod bearing on an eccentric cam on the auxiliary shaft on SOHC models, or on the camshaft on CVH models. DOHC models and models with air conditioning have an electric fuel pump mounted under the rear of the vehicle, next to the fuel tank. DOHC models have a combined pump and fuel level sender unit.

The fuel pressure regulator and/or vapour separator is used to stabilise the fuel supply to the carburettor. The pressure regulator provides a constant fuel pressure, and hence maintains a constant float level in the carburettor which reduces exhaust emission levels. The vapour separator purges vapour from the carburettor fuel supply, thus improving hot starting qualities. All models up to 1985 are fitted with a fuel pressure regulator. All models from 1985 except 2.0 litre SOHC models and CVH models are fitted with a combined fuel pressure regulator/vapour separator. 2.0 litre models from 1985 and CVH models are fitted with a vapour separator only. DOHC models have no pressure regulator or vapour separator fitted.

The carburettor may be either a Ford variable venturi (VV) type, a Weber twin venturi (2V or 2V TLD) type, or a Pierburg twin venturi (2V) type, depending on model. Each type of carburettor is available in several versions to suit particular engine and equipment combinations.

The air cleaner has a vacuum or waxstat controlled air inlet supplying a blend of hot and cold air to suit the prevailing engine operating conditions.

Precautions

⚠ *Warning - Fuel - Many of the procedures given in this Chapter involve the disconnection of fuel pipes and system components which may result in some fuel spillage. Before carrying out any operation on the fuel system, refer to the precautions given in the "Safety first" Section at the beginning of this manual and follow them implicitly. Petrol Is a highly dangerous and volatile substance, and the precautions necessary when handling it cannot be over stressed.*

Tamperproof adjustment screws - caution

Certain adjustment points in the fuel system (and elsewhere) are protected by "tamperproof" caps, plugs or seals. The purpose of such tamperproofing is to discourage, and to detent, adjustment by unqualified operators.

In some EEC countries (though not yet in the UK) it is an offence to drive a vehicle with missing or broken tamperproof seals. Before disturbing a tamperproof seal, satisfy yourself that you will not be breaking local or national anti-pollution regulations by doing so. Fit a new seal when adjustment is complete when this is required by law.

Do not break tamperproof seals on a vehicle which is still under warranty.

Work proceedures

When working on fuel system components, scrupulous cleanliness must be observed, and care must be taken not to introduce any foreign matter into fuel lines or components. Carburettors in particular are delicate instruments, and care should be taken not to disturb any components unnecessarily. Before attempting work on a carburettor, ensure that the relevant spares are available. Full overhaul procedures for carburettors have not been given in this Chapter, as complete strip-down of a carburettor is unlikely to cure a fault which is not immediately obvious, without introducing new problems. If persistent problems are encountered, it is recommended that the advice of a Ford dealer or carburettor specialist is sought. Most dealers will be able to provide carburettor re-jetting and servicing facilities, and if necessary it should be possible to purchase a reconditioned carburettor of the relevant type.

2 Air cleaner element - renewal

Refer to Chapter 1, Section 38.

3 Air cleaner - removal and refitting

Removal

1 On CVH models, disconnect the battery negative lead.

2 Remove the screws from the top of the air cleaner cover (see illustration).

3 Disconnect the cold air inlet hose from the air cleaner spout or the inlet on the front body panel. The hose is secured by toggle clips (see illustration).

4 Disconnect the hot air inlet hose from the air cleaner spout or the hot air shroud on the exhaust manifold (see illustration).

5 Disconnect the vacuum hose from the inlet manifold (see illustration).

6 On DOHC models, disconnect the camshaft cover breather hose

7 Where applicable, on OHC models remove the screw securing the air cleaner body to the camshaft cover.

8 Withdraw the air cleaner, and on CVH models, disconnect the wiring plug from the

3.2 Air cleaner securing screws (arrowed)

3.3 Disconnecting the cold air intake hose from the air cleaner spout

3.4 Hot air intake hose on hot air shroud

air charge temperature sensor mounted in the base of the air cleaner body, and disconnect the breather hose from the camshaft cover.

Refitting

9 Refitting is a reversal of removal, ensuring that the disturbed hoses are securely connected.

4 Air cleaner inlet air temperature control - testing

Refer to Chapter 1, Section 36.

5 Fuel pressure regulator (models up to 1985) - removal and refitting

> **Caution: Refer to the precautions in Section 1 before proceeding.**

Removal

1 The fuel pressure regulator is located on the left-hand side of the engine compartment **(see illustration)**.

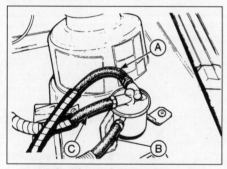

6.1a Fuel vapour separator location - 2.0 litre SOHC models from 1985

A Fuel return hose
B Fuel supply hose
C Carburettor fuel feed hose

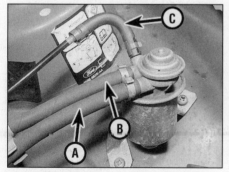

6.1b Fuel pressure regulator/vapour separator location - SOHC models from 1985

A Fuel supply hose
B Carburettor fuel feed hose
C Fuel return hose

3.5 Disconnecting the air cleaner vacuum hose from the inlet manifold

2 Disconnect the battery negative lead.
3 Identify the fuel hose locations, as an aid to refitting. Note that there are three hose connections on models without a fuel flow sensor unit, and two hose connections on models with a fuel flow sensor unit.
4 Disconnect and plug the fuel hoses.
5 Remove the two securing screws and withdraw the regulator.

Refitting

6 Refitting is a reversal of removal, ensuring that the fuel hoses are correctly connected. If the hoses were originally secured with crimped type clips, discard them and use new worm drive clips.

6 Fuel vapour separator (models from 1985) - removal and refitting

> **Caution: Refer to the precautions in Section 1 before proceeding.**

Removal

1 On SOHC models, the vapour separator is located on the left-hand side of the engine compartment. On CVH models, the vapour separator is located on the right-hand side of the engine compartment **(see illustrations)**.
2 Disconnect the battery negative lead.

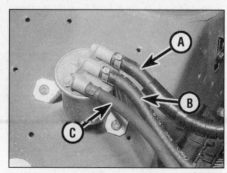

6.1c Fuel vapour separator location - CVH models

A Fuel supply hose
B Carburettor fuel feed hose
C Fuel return hose

5.1 Fuel pressure regulator location - models up to 1985

3 Identify the fuel hose locations as an aid to refitting, then disconnect and plug the hoses.
4 Remove the two securing screws and withdraw the vapour separator.

Refitting

5 Refitting is a reversal of removal, ensuring that the fuel hoses are correctly connected. If the hoses were originally secured with crimped type clips, discard them and use new worm drive clips.

7 Fuel pump - testing

> **Caution: Refer to the precautions in Section 1 before proceeding.**

Mechanical pump

1 On SOHC engines, the fuel pump is located on the left-hand side of the cylinder block, next to the oil filter. On CVH engines the fuel pump is located on the rear right-hand corner of the cylinder head.
2 To test the pump, disconnect the ignition coil LT "-/1" lead to prevent the engine from firing.
3 Disconnect the outlet hose from the pump, and place a wad of rag next to the pump outlet **(see illustration)**. Take appropriate fire precautions.
4 Have an assistant crank the engine on the starter motor, and check that well-defined spurts of petrol are ejected from the fuel pump outlet. If not, the pump is faulty. Dispose of the petrol-soaked rag safely.

7.3 Disconnecting outlet hose from fuel pump - SOHC model

4A

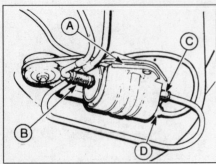

7.7 Electric fuel pump - SOHC and CVH models with air conditioning

A Clamping bracket   C Fuel outlet
B Fuel inlet   D Wiring plug

5 On some early pumps, the top cover can be removed for access to the filter. Removing the pump and cleaning the filter may cure the problem. On models with a sealed pump, or where cleaning the interior of the pump and filter does not solve the problem, the pump should be renewed, as no spares are available. Check that there is petrol in the fuel tank before condemning the pump!

6 On completion of the test, reconnect the outlet hose to the pump. If the hose was originally secured with a crimped type clip, discard this and use a new worm drive clip. Reconnect the coil LT lead.

Electric pump

SOHC and CVH models with air conditioning

7 The fuel pump is located under the rear of the vehicle, next to the fuel tank **(see illustration)**.

8 If the pump is functioning, it should be possible to hear it "buzzing" by listening under the rear of the vehicle when the ignition is switched on.

9 If the pump appears to have failed completely, check the fuse and relay.

10 To test the pump, disconnect the fuel supply hose from the pressure regulator or vapour separator (as applicable) in the engine compartment. Lead the hose into a measuring cylinder.

11 Take appropriate fire precautions, then switch on the ignition for 30 seconds (do not

start the engine), and measure the quantity of petrol delivered: it should be at least 400 ml (0.7 pint). If not, the pump is faulty and should be renewed, as no spares are available.

12 On completion of the test, reconnect the hose to the pressure regulator or vapour separator, as applicable, and if the hose was originally secured with a crimped type clip, discard this and fit a new worm drive clip.

2.0 litre DOHC models

13 If the fuel pump is functioning, it should be possible to hear it "buzzing" by listening under the rear of the vehicle when the ignition is switched on. Unless the engine is started, the fuel pump should switch off after approximately one second.

14 If the pump appears to have failed completely, check the appropriate fuse and relay, and where applicable check the state of the fuel pump inertia cut-off switch as follows.

15 The inertia cut-off switch is located in the spare wheel well. The switch incorporates a reset button, which should normally be in the depressed position. Check the position of the reset button before assuming that a fault exists in the fuel pump.

16 To test the fuel pump, special equipment is required, and it is recommended that any suspected faults are referred to a Ford dealer.

8 Fuel pump - removal and refitting

⚠️ *Caution:* **Refer to the precautions in Section 1 before proceeding.**

Mechanical pump

Note: *A new gasket must be used when refitting the pump.*

1 Disconnect the battery negative lead.

2 For improved access on CVH models, remove the air cleaner.

3 Identify the hose locations as an aid to refitting, then disconnect the hoses from the pump and plug them.

4 Remove the two securing bolts and withdraw the pump from the cylinder block or cylinder head, as applicable **(see illustration)**.

5 Recover the gasket, and if desired remove the operating pushrod **(see illustration)**.

6 Clean the exterior of the pump with paraffin and wipe dry. Clean all traces of gasket from the pump flange and the cylinder block or cylinder head, as applicable.

7 On early pumps with a removable top cover, remove the securing screw and withdraw the cover and the nylon mesh filter with seal **(see illustration)**. Clean the filter, the cover and the pump with petrol. Locate the filter in the cover and fit the cover to the pump, so that the indentations on the cover and pump are aligned. Tighten the cover securing screw.

8 Refitting is a reversal of removal, but fit a new gasket, and tighten the securing bolts to the specified torque. Ensure that the hoses are correctly connected, and if the hoses were originally secured with crimped type clips, discard these and use new worm drive clips.

Electric pump

SOHC and CVH models with air conditioning

9 Disconnect the battery negative lead.

10 Chock the front wheels, then jack up the rear of the vehicle and support on axle stands. (see "Jacking and Vehicle Support").

11 Clean the area around the pump mounting, and position a suitable container under the pump.

12 Using a hose clamping tool or self-locking pliers, clamp the fuel tank-to pump hose to prevent excessive petrol spillage, or alternatively make arrangements to collect the contents of the fuel tank which will otherwise be released. Disconnect the hose from the pump.

13 Disconnect the fuel outlet hose from the pump and plug the hose to prevent petrol spillage.

⚠️ *Caution: Petrol under pressure may spray out of the outlet as the hose is disconnected.*

14 Disconnect the wiring plug from the pump.

15 Slacken the clamping bolt, and slide the pump from the bracket assembly.

16 Refitting is a reversal of removal, but make sure that the rubber sleeve is correctly located around the pump body in the bracket, and ensure that the fuel hoses are securely

8.4 Withdrawing the fuel pump from the cylinder head - CVH model

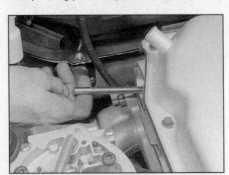

8.5 Withdrawing the fuel pump operating pushrod - CVH model

8.7 Removing the top cover from an early type fuel pump for access to the mesh filter

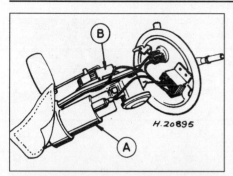

8.17 Combined fuel pump/fuel level sender unit - 1.6/1.8 litre (R6A) CVH models

A Fuel pump   *B Fuel level sender unit*

connected. If the hoses were originally secured with crimped type clips, discard these and use new worm drive clips.

2.0 litre DOHC models

17 On these models the fuel pump is mounted in the fuel tank, on the same mounting as the fuel level sender unit **(see illustration)**.

18 To remove the pump, first remove the fuel tank.

19 Unscrew the fuel pump/fuel level sender unit by engaging two crossed screwdrivers in the slots on either side of the unit mounting flange. Recover the seal.

20 Refitting is a reversal of removal. It is necessary to fit a new seal.

9 Fuel tank - removal and refitting

> ⚠ **Caution: Refer to the precautions in Section 1 before proceeding.**

1 Run the fuel level as low as possible before removing the tank.

2 Disconnect the battery negative lead.

3 Remove the tank filler cap, then syphon or pump out the tank contents (there is no drain plug). It may be necessary to disconnect the fuel tank-to-fuel pump hose in order to fully drain the tank. Store the petrol in a suitable sealed container.

Saloon, Hatchback and Estate models

4 Working in the fuel filler recess, remove the two screws on models up to 1987, or the single screw on models from 1987, securing the upper end of the fuel filler pipe to the body panel.

5 Chock the front wheels, then jack up the rear of the vehicle and support on axle stands (see "Jacking and Vehicle Support").

6 Unscrew the two securing bolts from the left-hand tank flange, and on models from 1987, the single bolt from the right-hand tank flange.

7 Support the tank, then remove the bolt from the securing strap. Unhook the remaining end of the strap from the underbody.

8 Lower the tank sufficiently to disconnect the two wiring plugs from the fuel level sender (pump) unit **(see illustration)**.

9 Identify the fuel hose locations for use when refitting, then disconnect the hoses from the sender unit and plug them.

10 Withdraw the fuel tank from under the vehicle.

11 The fuel filler and ventilation pipes can be removed from the tank by loosening the securing clips.

12 If the tank is contaminated with sediment or water, swill it out with clean petrol. If the tank has a leak, or is damaged, it should be repaired by a specialist, or alternatively renewed. Do not under any circumstances attempt to solder or weld a fuel tank.

13 Refitting is a reversal of removal, but ensure that the ventilation pipe is correctly positioned in its groove in the tank, and is not trapped between the tank and the vehicle underbody. Ensure that the fuel hoses and the fuel filler and ventilation pipes are correctly connected, and if the hoses or pipes were originally secured with crimped type clips, discard these and use new worm drive clips.

P100 models

14 Remove the cargo area (Chapter 12).

15 Disconnect the wiring plug from the fuel level sender unit, and release the wiring from the clip on the fuel tank flange.

16 Identify the fuel hose locations for use when refitting, then disconnect the hoses from the sender unit and plug them.

17 Detach the fuel pipes from their clips on the tank.

18 Remove the five tank securing bolts, and lift the tank from the chassis frame **(see illustration)**.

19 Proceed as described in paragraphs 11 and 12.

20 Commence refitting by loosening the bolts securing the front tank mounting brackets to the chassis frame.

21 Lower the tank into position and loosely refit the securing bolts. Tighten the three rear securing bolts.

22 Pull down on the front of the tank and tighten the bolts securing the front tank mounting brackets to the chassis frame when

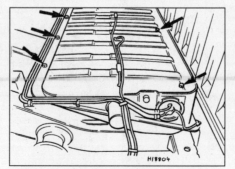

9.18 Fuel tank securing bolts (arrowed) - P100 models

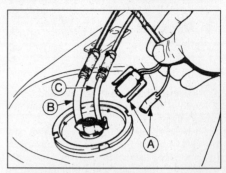

9.8 Fuel level sender unit connections - Saloon, Hatchback and Estate models

A Wiring plugs   *C Fuel inlet pipe*
B Fuel outlet pipe

the brackets contact the insulating pads, then tighten the front tank securing bolts.

23 Further refitting is a reversal of removal, but ensure that all hoses and pipes are correctly connected, and if the hoses or pipes were originally secured with crimped type clips, discard these and use new worm drive clips. Refit the cargo area.

10 Fuel level sender unit - removal and refitting

> ⚠ **Caution: Refer to the precautions in Section 1 before proceeding. A new seal must be used when refitting the sender unit.**

Saloon, Hatchback and Estate models

All models except 2.0 litre DOHC

1 Remove the fuel tank.

2 Unscrew the sender unit from the tank by engaging two crossed screwdrivers in the slots on either side of the sender unit mounting flange. Recover the seal. Check the condition of the gauze filter on the fuel pick-up pipe, and renew it if there is any sign of deterioration.

3 Refitting is a reversal of removal, but fit a new seal.

2.0 litre DOHC models

4 On these models the sender unit is combined with the fuel pump. See Section 8 for unit removal and refitting.

P100 models

5 Remove the cargo area (Chapter 12).

6 Disconnect the wiring plug from the sender unit.

7 Identify the fuel hose locations, as an aid to refitting, then disconnect the hoses from the sender unit and plug them.

8 Proceed as described in paragraph 2.

9 Refitting is a reversal of removal, but fit a new seal, and ensure that the fuel hoses are correctly connected. If the hoses were originally secured with crimped type clips, discard these and use new worm drive clips. Refit the cargo area.

4A

11 Throttle pedal - removal and refitting

Removal

1 Disconnect the battery negative lead.
2 Remove the lower facia panel from the driver's side.
3 Prise off the securing clip and disconnect the end of the throttle cable from the top of the pedal (see illustration).
4 Remove the two securing nuts, one accessible from the driver's footwell, the other from the engine compartment, and withdraw the pedal and bracket assembly (see illustration).

Refitting

5 Refitting is a reversal of removal, but on completion check the throttle cable adjustment.

12 Throttle cable - removal, refitting and adjustment

Removal

1 Disconnect the battery negative lead.
2 Working inside the vehicle, remove the lower facia panel from the driver's side.
3 Prise off the securing clip and disconnect the end of the throttle cable from the top of the pedal.
4 Working in the engine compartment, free the cable sheath from the bulkhead, and pull the cable through into the engine compartment. It will probably be necessary to pull the cable grommet from the bulkhead in order to free the cable sheath.
5 For improved access, remove the air cleaner.
6 Disconnect the cable end from the throttle linkage. The cable end may be attached to the linkage with a balljoint and spring clip, a spring clip only, or the cable end may simply

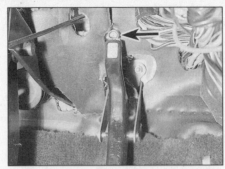

11.3 Throttle pedal assembly - cable connection arrowed

locate in a slot in the throttle lever (see illustration).
7 Prise off the spring clip securing the cable sheath to the cable bracket at the carburettor inlet manifold. Depress the four lugs on the plastic cable retainer simultaneously so that the retainer can be slid from the bracket, or remove the retainer securing clip, as applicable (see illustration). Take care not to damage the cable sheath.

Refitting

8 Refitting is a reversal of removal, but before refitting the air cleaner, adjust the cable as follows.

Adjustment

9 Have an assistant fully depress the throttle pedal and hold it in this position. On models with automatic transmission, where applicable ensure that the kickdown cable does not restrict the pedal movement. Turn the adjusting sleeve at the carburettor inlet manifold cable bracket until the throttle is just fully open. Have the assistant release and then fully depress the throttle pedal, and check that the throttle is again fully open. Adjust if necessary, then refit the air cleaner. On models with automatic transmission, where applicable check the operation of the kickdown cable, and adjust if necessary.

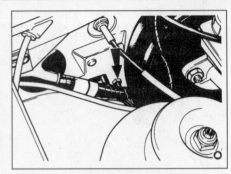

11.4 Throttle pedal securing nut (arrowed) in engine compartment

13 Carburettors (all types) - dismantling and reassembly

1 A complete strip-down of a carburettor is unlikely to cure a fault which is not immediately obvious without introducing new problems. If persistent carburation problems are encountered, it is recommended that the advice of a Ford dealer or carburettor specialist is sought.
2 If it is decided to go ahead and service a carburettor, check the cost and availability of spare parts before commencement. Obtain a carburettor repair kit, which will contain the necessary gaskets, diaphragms and other renewable items.
3 When working on carburettors, scrupulous cleanliness must be observed and care must be taken not to introduce any foreign matter into components. Carburettors are delicate instruments and care should be taken not to disturb any components unnecessarily.
4 Referring to the relevent exploded view of the carburettor (see illustrations), remove each component part whilst making a note of its fitted position. Make alignment marks on linkages etc.
5 Reassemble the carburettor in the reverse order to dismantling, using new gaskets, O-rings etc. Be careful not to kink any diaphragms.

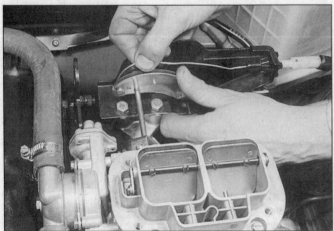

12.6 Disconnecting the throttle cable end from the throttle lever - Weber 2V carburettor

12.7 Removing the throttle cable sheath retainer securing clip - CVH model

13.4a Exploded view of Ford VV carburettor

A Throttle spindle
B Mixture screw
C By-pass leak adjuster
D Float
E Needle valve
F Main jet body
G Metering rod
H Air valve
J Automatic choke unit
K Bi-metal coil
L Carburettor control diaphragm
M Accelerator pump diaphragm

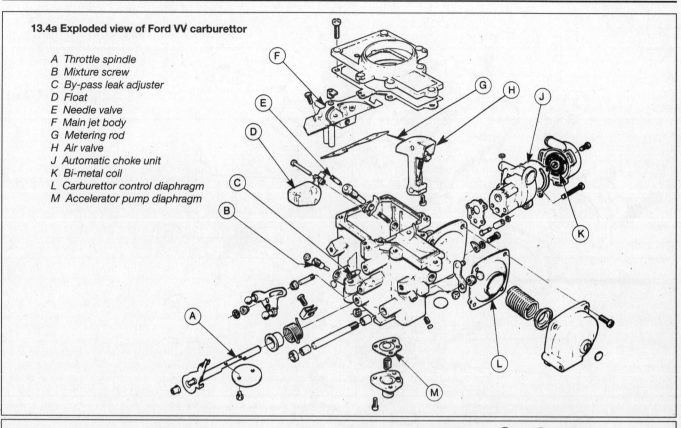

13.4b Exploded view of Weber 2V carburettor - 1.6 models

A Top cover assembly
B Automatic choke assembly
C Automatic choke bi-metal housing assembly
D Secondary idle jet
E Secondary throttle valve vacuum unit
F Idle speed screw
G Idle mixture screw
H Accelerator pump assembly
J Power valve diaphragm
K Float
L Primary emulsion tube
M Primary idle jet
N Needle valve
P Fuel filter
Q Secondary emulsion tube

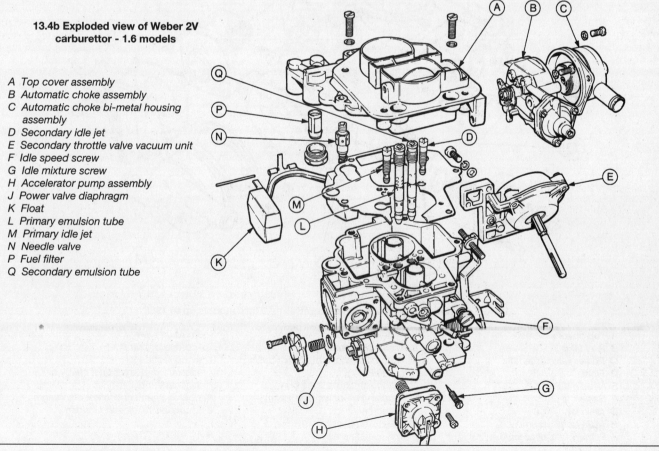

4A

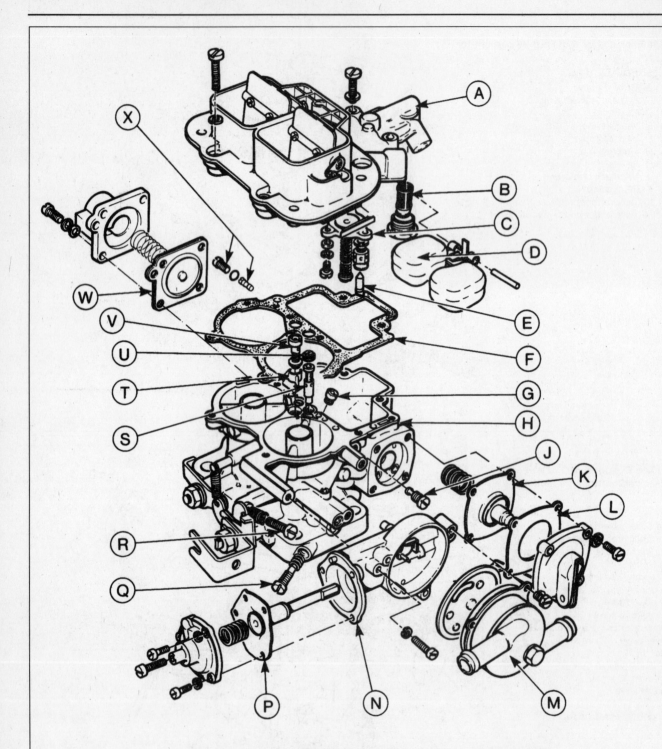

13.4c Exploded view of Weber 2V carburettor - 2.0 litre models up to 1985

A Top cover assembly	K Accelerator pump diaphragm	S Emulsion tube
B Fuel filter	L Accelerator pump gasket	T Accelerator pump jet
C Power valve assembly	M Automatic choke bi-metal housing	U Air correction jet
D Float	assembly	V Accelerator pump outlet check ball
E Needle Valve	N Automatic choke assembly	valve assembly
F Gasket	P Vacuum pull-down diaphragm	W Low vacuum enrichment diaphragm
G Main jet	assembly	X Secondary idle jet and holder
H Main body assembly	Q Idle mixture screw	
J Primary idle jet assembly	R Idle speed screw	

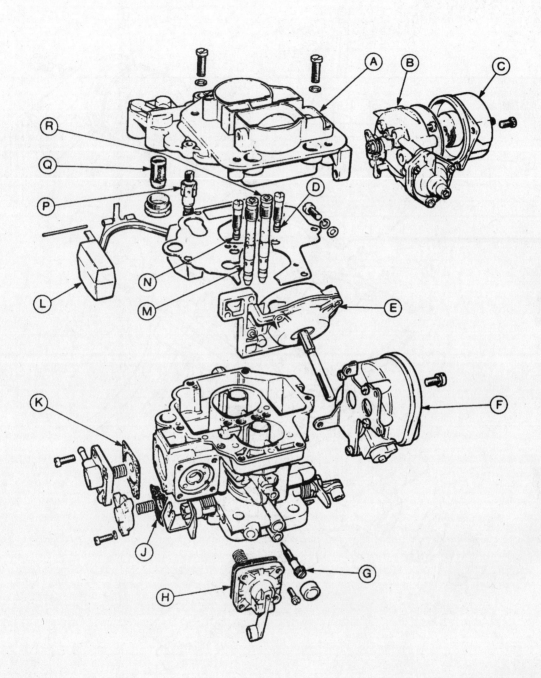

13.4d Exploded view of Weber 2V carburettor - 2.0 litre models from 1985

A Top cover assembly
B Automatic choke assembly
C Automatic choke bi-metal housing
D Secondary idle jet
E Secondary throttle valve vacuum unit
F Stepper motor

G Idle mixture screw
H Accelerator pump assembly
J Power valve diaphragm
K Low vacuum enrichment diaphragm
L Float

M Primary emulsion tube
N Primary idle jet
P Needle valve
Q Fuel filter
R Secondary emulsion tube

4A

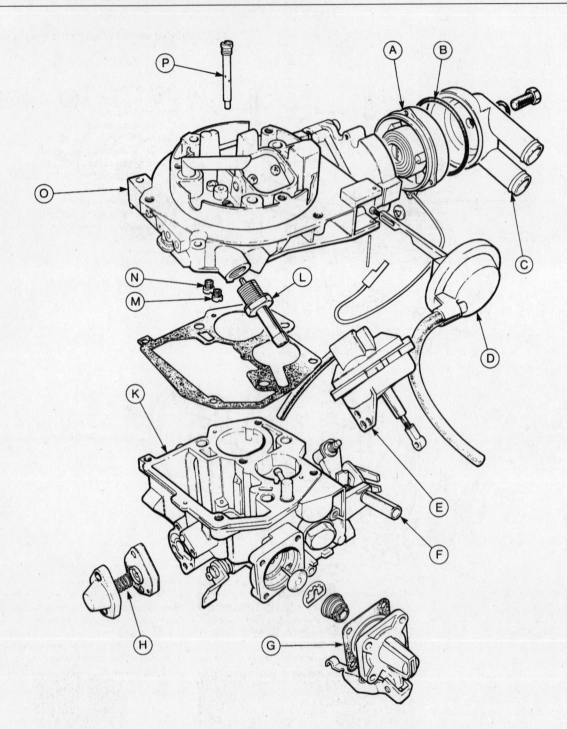

13.4e Exploded view of Pierburg 2V carburettor

A Automatic choke bi-metal housing
B O-ring
C Automatic choke coolant housing
D Automatic choke vacuum pull-down
   unit
E Secondary throttle valve vacuum unit
F Idle speed screw
G Accelerator pump diaphragm
H Power valve assembly
K Carburettor body
L Fuel inlet pipe and filter
M Primary main jet
N Secondary main jet
O Top cover assembly
P Idle jet

13.4f Exploded view of Weber 2V TLD carburettor

A Anti-dieselling valve
B Emulsion tubes
C Air correction jets
D Choke pull-down diaphragm assembly
E Choke linkage
F Needle valve
G Float
H Fast idle adjustment screw
J Idle speed adjustment screw
K Idle mixture adjustment screw
L Throttle valves
M Power valve assembly
N Accelerator pump assembly
P Low vacuum enrichment device
Q Throttle kicker
R Gasket
S Main jets

H.22616

4A

14 Carburettor (Ford VV type) - removal and refitting

Caution: Refer to the precautions in Section 1 before proceeding.

Note: *A new gasket must be used when refitting the carburettor. A tachometer and an exhaust gas analyser will be required to check the idle speed and mixture on completion.*

Removal

1 Disconnect the battery negative lead.
2 Remove the air cleaner.
3 Relieve the pressure in the cooling system by unscrewing the expansion tank cap. If the engine is warm, place a thick rag over the cap and unscrew the cap slowly as a precaution against scalding. Refit the cap after relieving the pressure.

4 Identify the automatic choke coolant hose locations, as an aid to refitting, then disconnect the hoses (being prepared for coolant spillage.) Either plug the hoses or secure them with their ends facing upwards to prevent loss of coolant.
5 Disconnect the wiring from the anti-dieselling (anti-run-on) valve.
6 Disconnect the fuel hose and vacuum pipe **(see illustration)**. Plug the end of the fuel hose to minimise petrol spillage.
7 Disconnect the throttle cable from the carburettor throttle lever **(see illustration)**.
8 Remove the two securing nuts and

14.6 Disconnecting the fuel hose - Ford VV carburettor

14.7 Disconnecting the throttle cable from the throttle lever - Ford VV carburettor

washers, and lift the carburettor from the inlet manifold studs **(see illustrations)**. Recover the gasket.

Refitting

9 Refitting is a reversal of removal, bearing in mind the following points.

10 Ensure that the mating faces of the inlet manifold and carburettor are clean, and use a new gasket.

11 Ensure that the coolant hoses, fuel hose, and vacuum pipe are correctly routed and free from restrictions. If any of the hoses were originally secured with crimped type clips, discard these and use new worm drive clips on refitting.

12 On completion, check and if necessary top-up the coolant level. Check and if necessary adjust the idle speed and mixture.

15 Carburettor (Ford VV type) - idle speed and mixture adjustment

Refer to Chapter 1, Sections 15 and 16.

16 Carburettor (Weber 2V type) - removal and refitting

1 Proceed as described for the Ford VV carburettor but note the following.

2 On models with an electrically-heated automatic choke, ignore all references to the cooling system and coolant hoses.

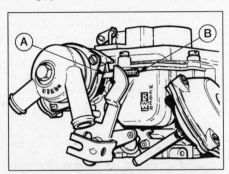

18.5a Fast idle speed adjustment - Weber 2V carburettor (1.6 litre models)

A Screw on third (middle) step of cam
B Fast idle screw

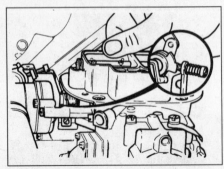

18.5b Fast idle speed adjustment - Weber 2V carburettor (2.0 litre models)

14.8a Remove the securing nuts and washers . . .

3 Not all Weber carburettors are fitted with an anti-dieselling valve.

4 Disconnect all relevant wiring plugs and vacuum pipes, if necessary noting their locations for use when refitting.

5 Disconnect the link arm from the throttle linkage instead of disconnecting the throttle cable.

6 The carburettor is secured to the inlet manifold by four nuts and washers.

17 Carburettor (Weber 2V type) - idle speed and mixture adjustment

Refer to Chapter 1, Sections 15 and 16.

18 Carburettor (Weber 2V type) - fast idle speed adjustment

1 This procedure does not apply to models fitted with a carburettor stepper motor, for which no adjustment is possible.

2 Check the idle speed and mixture. The idle speed must be correct before attempting to check or adjust the fast idle speed.

3 With the engine at normal operating temperature, and a tachometer connected in accordance with the manufacturer's instructions, proceed as follows.

4 Remove the air cleaner.

5 Partially open the throttle, hold the choke plate(s) fully closed, then release the throttle so that on 1.6 litre models the fast idle adjustment screw rests on the third (middle) step of the fast idle cam **(see illustration)** and on 2.0 litre models the fast idle adjustment screw rests on the highest step of the fast idle cam **(see illustration)**.

6 Release the choke plate(s), checking that it/they remain(s) fully open; if not, the automatic choke mechanism is faulty, or the engine is not at normal operating temperature.

7 Without touching the throttle pedal, start the engine and check that the fast idle speed is as specified. If adjustment is necessary, turn the fast idle adjustment screw until the correct speed is obtained.

8 On completion of adjustment, stop the engine and disconnect the tachometer, then refit the air cleaner.

14.8b . . . and lift the carburettor from the inlet manifold - Ford VV carburettor

19 Carburettor (Pierburg 2V type) - removal and refitting

1 Proceed as described for the Ford VV carburettor but note the following.

2 The Pierburg carburettor is not fitted with an anti-dieselling valve.

3 Disconnect all relevant wiring plugs and vacuum pipes, if necessary noting their locations as an aid to refitting.

4 Disconnect the throttle arm from the throttle lever by removing the retaining clip instead of disconnecting the cable **(see illustration)**.

5 The carburettor is secured to the inlet manifold by three Torx type screws **(see illustration)**.

6 On CVH models an insulator block is fitted between the carburettor and the inlet manifold in place of a gasket. There is no need to renew the insulator block on refitting.

19.4 Throttle arm retaining clip (arrowed) - Pierburg 2V carburettor

19.5 Removing the carburettor securing screws (arrowed) - Pierburg 2V carburettor

20 Carburettor (Pierburg 2V type) - idle speed and mixture adjustment

Refer to Chapter 1, Sections 15 and 16.

21 Carburettor (Pierburg 2V type) - fast idle speed adjustment

1 Check the idle speed and mixture adjustment. The idle speed **must** be correct before attempting to check or adjust the fast idle speed.
2 With the engine at normal operating temperature, and a tachometer connected in accordance with the manufacturer's instructions proceed as follows.
3 Remove the air cleaner.
4 Position the fast idle speed adjustment screw on the lowest (6th) step of the fast idle cam **(see illustration)**.
5 Check that the fast idle speed is as specified. If adjustment is required, stop the engine and proceed as follows.
6 Remove the tamperproof cap from the fast idle speed adjustment screw.
7 Ensure that the adjustment screw is still resting on the lowest step of the fast idle cam, then open the throttle so that a small screwdriver can be used to adjust the screw from below the carburettor.
8 Start the engine and recheck the fast idle speed.
9 If necessary, repeat the procedure given in paragraphs 7 and 8 until the correct fast idle speed is obtained.
10 On completion of adjustment, stop the engine and disconnect the tachometer, then refit the tamperproof cap to the adjustment screw, and refit the air cleaner.

22 Carburettor (Weber 2V TLD) - removal and refitting

 Caution: Refer to the precautions in Section 1 before proceeding.

Note: *A new gasket must be used when refitting the carburettor. A tachometer and an exhaust gas analyser will be required to check the idle speed and mixture on completion.*

Removal

1 Disconnect the battery negative lead.
2 Remove the air cleaner.
3 Disconnect the wiring from the anti-dieselling (anti-run-on) valve.
4 Disconnect the wiring from the automatic choke heater.
5 Disconnect the fuel supply and return hoses, noting their locations to aid refitting. Plug the ends of the hoses to minimise petrol spillage.
6 Disconnect the link arm from the throttle linkage.
7 Disconnect the vacuum pipe.
8 Release the coolant hose from the bracket under the automatic choke housing.
9 Unscrew the four Torx screws, and lift the carburettor from the inlet manifold. Recover the gasket.

Refitting

11 Refitting is a reversal of removal, bearing in mind the following points.
12 Ensure that the mating faces of the inlet manifold and the carburettor are clean, and use a new gasket.
13 Ensure that all hoses, pipes and wiring are correctly routed, and free from restrictions. If any of the hoses were originally secured with crimped-type clips, discard these, and use new worm-drive clips on refitting.
14 Make sure that the coolant hose is correctly positioned in the bracket under the automatic choke housing.
15 On completion, check and if necessary adjust the idle speed and mixture.

23 Carburettor (Weber 2V TLD) - idle speed and mixture adjustment

Refer to Chapter 1, Sections 15 and 16.

24 Carburettor (Weber 2V TLD) - fast idle speed adjustment

1 Proceed as described for the Weber 2V carburettor, noting the following.
2 The fast idle adjustment screw should be positioned on the third (middle) step of the fast idle cam **(see illustration)**.
3 Refer to the Specifications at the beginning of this Chapter for the correct fast idle speed.

25 Inlet manifold - removal and refitting

SOHC models

Removal

1 Disconnect the battery negative lead.
2 Partially drain the cooling system.
3 Remove the air cleaner.
4 Disconnect the coolant hoses from the automatic choke (where applicable), and the inlet manifold. Identify the hose locations for use when refitting.
5 Disconnect the fuel supply hose at the carburettor and plug the end to minimise petrol spillage.
6 Disconnect all relevant wiring and vacuum pipes from the carburettor, if necessary noting the locations for use when refitting.
7 Disconnect the throttle cable from the throttle linkage.
8 Disconnect the crankcase ventilation and brake servo vacuum hoses from the inlet manifold. The brake servo vacuum hose is secured with a union nut **(see illustrations)**.
9 Disconnect any remaining wiring and vacuum pipes from the inlet manifold, if necessary noting the locations as an aid to refitting.
10 Where necessary, unbolt the throttle cable bracket from the top of the inlet manifold for improved access, and unbolt the dipstick tube bracket.
11 Unscrew the two nuts and four bolts securing the manifold to the cylinder head, noting the location of the rear engine lifting

4A

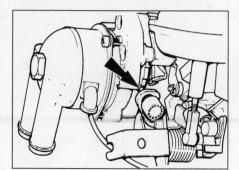
21.4 Fast idle speed adjustment - Pierburg 2V carburettor
Screw (arrowed) should rest on lowest (6th) step of cam

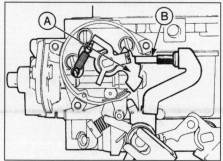
24.2 Fast idle speed adjustment - Weber 2V TLD carburettor
A Fast idle cam
B Adjustment screw on middle step of cam

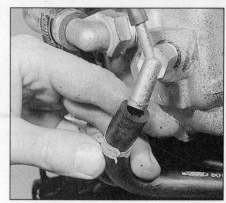
25.8a Disconnecting the crankcase ventilation . . .

25.8b . . . and brake servo vacuum hoses from the inlet manifold - SOHC models

25.11 Rear engine lifting bracket location - SOHC models

25.12 Lifting the inlet manifold from the cylinder head - SOHC models

bracket **(see illustration)**.

12 Lift the inlet manifold from the cylinder head, and recover the gasket **(see illustration)**.

13 If desired, the carburettor can be removed from the inlet manifold by unscrewing the securing nuts or screws. Refer to the relevant Section describing carburettor removal and refitting. Recover the gasket.

Refitting

14 Refitting is a reversal of removal bearing in mind the following points.

15 Ensure that all mating faces are clean.

16 Renew the gasket(s), and apply a bead of sealant at least 5.0 mm (0.2 in) wide around the central coolant aperture on both sides of the manifold-to-cylinder head gasket.

17 Tighten the manifold securing nuts and bolts progressively to the specified torque, ensuring that the engine lifting bracket is in place.

18 Make sure that all hoses, pipes and wires are correctly reconnected, and if the fuel supply hose was originally secured with a crimped type clip, discard this and use a new worm drive clip on refitting.

19 On completion, refill the cooling system, adjust the throttle cable and check and if necessary adjust the idle speed and mixture.

DOHC models

Removal

20 Disconnect the battery negative lead.

21 Partially drain the cooling system.

22 Remove the air cleaner.

23 Disconnect the coolant hoses from the thermostat housing and the inlet manifold, noting their locations to assist with refitting.

24 Disconnect the fuel supply and return hoses from the carburettor. Plug their ends to minimise petrol spillage.

25 Release the coolant hose from the bracket under the automatic choke housing.

26 Disconnect the HT leads from the spark plugs, and move them to one side.

27 Disconnect all relevant wiring and vacuum pipes from the carburettor, thermostat housing and inlet manifold, noting the locations as an aid to refitting.

28 Disconnect the crankcase breather hose from the inlet manifold.

29 Disconnect the throttle cable from the throttle linkage.

30 Make a final check to ensure that all relevant wires, pipes and hoses have been disconnected to facilitate removal of the manifold.

31 Unscrew the ten bolts and two nuts securing the manifold to the cylinder head.

32 Lift the manifold clear of the cylinder head. Recover the gasket.

33 Recover the two plastic spark plug spacers from the recesses in the cylinder head.

34 If desired, the carburettor can be removed from the manifold by unscrewing the securing screws. Refer to the carburettor removal and refitting Sections as necessary.

Refitting

35 Refitting is a reversal of removal, bearing in mind the following points.

36 Ensure that all mating faces are clean.

37 Ensure that the spark plug spacers are in position in the cylinder head recesses before refitting the manifold.

38 Renew all gaskets.

39 Tighten all manifold securing nuts and bolts progressively to the specified torque.

40 Make sure that all hoses, pipes and wires are securely reconnected in their original positions.

41 On completion, refill the cooling system. Check the adjustment of the throttle cable. Check, and if necessary adjust, the idle speed and mixture.

CVH models

Removal

42 Proceed as described in paragraphs 1 to 3 inclusive.

43 Disconnect the coolant hoses from the automatic choke, thermostat housing and inlet manifold, noting their locations for use when refitting.

44 Disconnect the fuel supply hose at the carburettor and plug the end to minimise petrol spillage.

45 Disconnect all relevant wiring and vacuum pipes from the carburettor, thermostat housing and inlet manifold, noting the locations as an aid to refitting.

46 Disconnect the throttle cable from the throttle linkage.

47 Unbolt the dipstick tube from the inlet manifold and withdraw the dipstick and dipstick tube from the cylinder block.

48 Unscrew the seven nuts securing the manifold to the cylinder head, then lift the manifold from the cylinder head, and recover the gasket.

49 If desired, the carburettor can be removed from the manifold by removing the securing screws. Recover the insulator block **(see illustrations)**.

50 The carburettor intermediate plate can be removed from the manifold by unscrewing the three securing screws. Recover the gasket.

51 If necessary, the thermostat and housing can be removed from the manifold.

25.49a Removing the carburettor . . .

25.49b . . . and the insulator block from the inlet manifold - CVH models

Refitting

52 Refitting is a reversal of removal, bearing in mind the following points.

53 Ensure that all mating faces are clean and renew the gasket(s).

54 Tighten the manifold securing nuts progressively to the specified torque.

55 Make sure that all hoses, pipes and wires are correctly reconnected, and if the fuel supply hose was originally secured with a crimped type clip, discard this and use a new worm drive clip on refitting.

56 On completion, refill the cooling system, adjust the throttle cable and check and if necessary adjust the idle speed and mixture.

26 Exhaust manifold - removal and refitting

Removal

1 Disconnect the battery negative lead.

2 Remove the air cleaner and pull the hot air pick-up pipe from the exhaust manifold hot air shroud.

3 Remove the securing screws (1 screw on DOHC models, 2 screws on SOHC models, 3 screws on CVH models) and lift the hot air shroud from the manifold. Note the position of the coolant hose bracket which is secured by the front hot air shroud securing screw on SOHC models **(see illustration)**.

4 Unscrew the securing nuts, and disconnect the exhaust downpipe from the manifold **(see illustration)**. Recover the gasket. Support the exhaust downpipe from underneath the

vehicle, with an axle stand for example, to avoid placing unnecessary strain on the exhaust system.

5 Disconnect the HT leads from the spark plugs, if necessary identifying them for locations, and place them to one side out of the way.

6 Unscrew the eight securing nuts, noting the location of the front engine lifting bracket secured by the front two nuts on SOHC models, and lift the manifold from the cylinder head. Recover the gasket(s) where applicable **(see illustrations)**.

Refitting

7 Refitting is a reversal of removal, bearing in mind the following.

8 Ensure that all mating faces are clean, and renew all gaskets. Note that on CVH models, no gasket is fitted between the manifold and

cylinder head in production, but a gasket must be used when refitting. Where applicable, remove the plastic spacer from the rear manifold stud before fitting the gasket **(see illustrations)**.

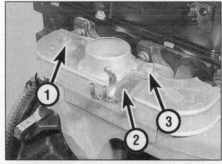

26.3 Exhaust manifold hot air shroud showing securing screws (1 and 3) and coolant hose clip (2) - SOHC models

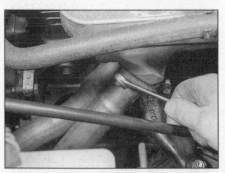

26.4 Unscrewing an exhaust downpipe securing nut

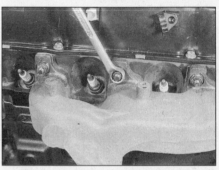

26.6a Unscrew the exhaust manifold securing nuts . . .

26.6b . . . noting the location of the front engine bracket . . .

26.6c . . . and lift off the exhaust manifold - SOHC models

26.6d SOHC models have separate manifold gaskets for each exhaust port

26.8a Exhaust manifold gaskets in position on cylinder head - DOHC models

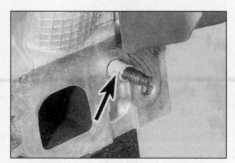

26.8b Remove the plastic spacer (arrowed) before fitting exhaust manifold gasket - CVH models

26.8c Fitting the exhaust manifold - DOHC models

4A

27.4a Exhaust downpipe-to-manifold flanged joint viewed from underneath vehicle

27.4b Exhaust downpipe-to-main system flanged joint

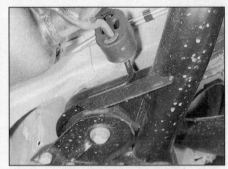

27.5a Rear exhaust section mounting - Hatchback model

9 Tighten the manifold securing nuts progressively to the specified torque, and similarly tighten the exhaust downpipe securing nuts. Do not forget to fit the engine lifting bracket on SOHC models.

10 Ensure that the HT leads are reconnected to their correct cylinders.

27 Exhaust system - inspection, removal and refitting

Inspection

1 The exhaust system should be examined for leaks, damage, and security at regular intervals. To do this, apply the handbrake, then start the engine and allow it to idle. Lie down on each side of the vehicle in turn and check the full length of the exhaust system for leaks, while an assistant temporarily places a wad of cloth over the tailpipe. If a leak is evident, stop the engine and use a proprietary repair kit to seal it. If an excessive leak or damage is evident, renew the relevant section of the exhaust system. Check the rubber mountings for deterioration and renew if necessary.

Removal

2 To remove the exhaust system, jack up the front and rear of the vehicle and support on axle stands (see "*Jacking and Vehicle Support*").

3 If desired, the exhaust downpipe can be removed independently of the remainder of the system, and similarly the main part of the system can be removed, leaving the downpipe in place.

4 To remove the downpipe, unscrew the securing nuts and disconnect the downpipe from the manifold. Recover the gasket. Unscrew the two nuts and bolts, and separate the downpipe flanged joint from the remainder of the system. Withdraw the downpipe **(see illustrations)**.

5 To remove the main section of the exhaust system leaving the downpipe in place, unscrew the two securing nuts and bolts and separate the flanged joint from the downpipe. Unhook the rubber mountings and withdraw the system from underneath the vehicle. The number and type of rubber mountings varies

27.5b Rear exhaust mounting - P100 model

according to model **(see illustrations)**. If necessary to avoid confusion, note how the mountings are fitted to enable correct refitting. Note that on P100 models the system must be manipulated to pass over the rear axle.

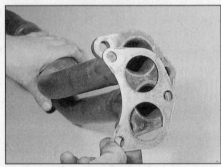

27.6 Fit a new downpipe-to-manifold gasket

Refitting

6 Refitting is a reversal of removal, but ensure that all mating faces are clean, and fit a new gasket between the downpipe and manifold **(see illustration)**. Do not fully tighten the joint

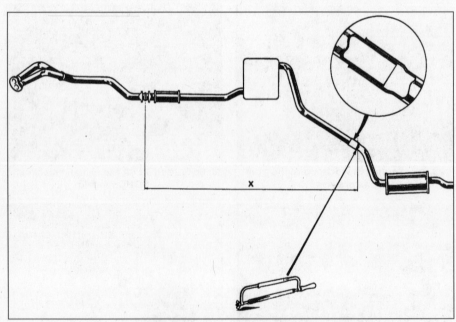

27.9a Cutting point when fitting a service replacement exhaust system section - Saloon, Hatchback and Estate models

X = 1639 mm for all models up to 1987 except 1.3 and 1.6 litre Hatchback
X = 1681 mm for 1.3 and 1.6 litre Hatchback models up to 1987
X = 2063 mm for all models from 1987

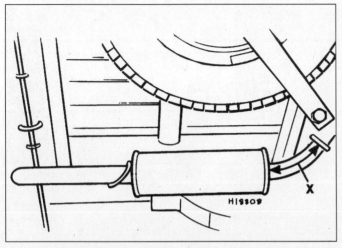
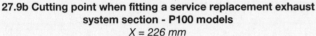

27.9b Cutting point when fitting a service replacement exhaust system section - P100 models
X = 226 mm

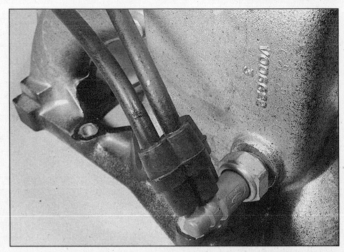

28.1 Low vacuum enrichment ported vacuum switch location in inlet manifold - model with Weber 2V carburettor

fittings until the system is in position and correctly aligned in its mountings under the vehicle. Ensure that no part of the exhaust system is closer than 25.0 mm (1.0 in) to the underbody.

7 Service replacement exhaust systems are available in three sections; downpipe, centre section and rear section. The service replacement sections fit together using socket joints, therefore the centre section of a production exhaust system cannot be renewed without also renewing the rear section.

8 To renew the centre and/or rear section(s) of the exhaust system, first remove the main system as described in paragraph 5.

9 To fit a service replacement rear section to a production system, use a hacksaw to cut through the pipe at the applicable point shown **(see illustrations)**. Apply exhaust sealant to the mating surfaces of the two sections, then push the two sections together and fit a U-bolt clamp to the centre of the joint. Do not fully tighten the U-bolt clamp nuts until the system is in position and correctly aligned in its mountings under the vehicle.

10 To renew a service replacement section, unscrew the nuts and remove the U-bolt clamp from the joint. Tap around the joint to break the seal, and separate the centre and

rear sections. Ensure that the joint mating surfaces are clean, then apply exhaust sealant, push the new section onto the remaining section, and fit the U-bolt clamp to the centre of the joint. Do not fully tighten the U-bolt clamp nuts until the system is in position and correctly aligned in its mountings under the vehicle.

28 Vacuum valves, ported vacuum switches and fuel traps - removal and refitting

Refer to Chapter 5, Section 22 **(see illustration)**.

4A

Notes

Chapter 4 Part B:
Fuel and exhaust systems - fuel injection

Contents

Degrees of difficulty

Easy, suitable for novice with little experience		Fairly easy, suitable for beginner with some experience		Fairly difficult, suitable for competent DIY mechanic		Difficult, suitable for experienced DIY mechanic		Very difficult, suitable for expert DIY or professional	

4B

Specifications

General

Fuel tank capacity (all models)	60.0 litres (13.1 gallons)
Fuel octane rating:	
Leaded	97 RON (4-star)
Unleaded	95 RON (Premium)

*Models fitted with a catalytic converter must be operated on unleaded fuel at all times. **Do not** use leaded fuel in such models, as the catalyst will be destroyed:*

System control pressure	2.5 bar

System type:

2.0 litre SOHC models	Bosch L-Jetronic
2.0 litre DOHC models	Multi-point fuel injection system, controlled by EEC IV engine management system
1.6 and 1.8 litre (R6A type) CVH models	Central fuel injection (CFI) controlled by EEC IV engine management system

Idle adjustments

All models except 2.0 litre DOHC

Idle speed (dependent on idle speed adjustment wire):	
Manual gearbox	875 rpm
Automatic transmission	800 rpm
Idle mixture (CO content)	0.5 to 1.0%

2.0 litre DOHC

Idle speed (not adjustable)	875 + 50 rpm
Idle mixture (CO content) - models without catalytic converter	1.0 to 1.5%

Torque wrench settings

	Nm	lbf ft
2.0 litre SOHC models		
Refer to Chapter 4, Part A Specifications for items not listed here		
Fuel pressure regulator fuel feed union nut	15 to 20	11 to 15
Fuel pressure regulator securing nut	20 to 25	15 to 18
Fuel rail securing bolts	8 to 10	6 to 7
Idle speed control valve nuts	8 to 10	6 to 7
2.0 litre DOHC models		
Inlet manifold nuts and bolts	20 to 24	15 to 18
Exhaust manifold nuts	21 to 25	15 to 18
Exhaust gas oxygen sensor	50 to 70	37 to 52
Throttle body bolts	9 to 11	7 to 8
Fuel rail bolts	21 to 26	15 to 19
Idle speed control valve bolts	9 to 11	7 to 8
Fuel pressure regulator bolts	9 to 12	7 to 9
Fuel filter unions	14 to 20	10 to 15
1.6 and 1.8 litre (R6A type) CVH models		
Inlet manifold nuts and bolts	16 to 20	12 to 15
Exhaust manifold nuts:		
1.6 litre	14 to 17	10 to 13
1.8 litre	21 to 27	15 to 20
Exhaust downpipe-to-manifold nuts	35 to 40	26 to 30
CFI unit bolts	9 to 11	7 to 8
Exhaust gas oxygen sensor	50 to 70	37 to 52
EGR valve	20 to 30	15 to 22
Fuel filter unions	14 to 20	10 to 15
Pulse-air tube unions	29 to 35	21 to 26

1 General information and precautions

General information

2.0 litre SOHC models

The fuel injection system fitted to these models is of the Bosch L-Jetronic type. The system is under the overall control of an EEC IV engine management system which also controls the ignition timing.

Fuel is supplied from the rear-mounted fuel tank by an electric fuel pump mounted next to the tank, via a pressure regulator, to the fuel rail. The fuel rail acts as a reservoir for the four fuel injectors, which inject fuel into the cylinder inlet tracts, upstream of the inlet valves. The fuel injectors receive an electrical pulse once per crankshaft revolution, which operates all four injectors simultaneously. The duration of the electrical pulse determines the quantity of fuel injected, and pulse duration is computed by the EEC IV module on the basis of information received from the various sensors.

Inducted air passes from the air cleaner through a vane type airflow meter before passing to the cylinder inlet tracts via the throttle valve. A flap in the vane airflow meter is deflected in proportion to the airflow; this deflection is converted into an electrical signal and passed to the EEC IV module. An adjustable air bypass channel provides the means of idle mixture adjustment.

A throttle position sensor enables the EEC IV module to compute not only throttle position, but also its rate of change. Extra fuel can thus be provided for acceleration when the throttle is opened suddenly. Information from the throttle position sensor is also used to cut off fuel on the overrun, thus improving fuel economy and reducing exhaust gas emissions.

Idle speed is controlled by a variable orifice solenoid valve which regulates the amount of air bypassing the throttle valve. The valve is controlled by the EEC IV module; there is no provision for adjustment of the idle speed.

Additional sensors inform the EEC IV module of engine coolant and air temperature. On models fitted with automatic transmission, a sensor registers the change from "P" or "N" to a drive position, and causes the idle speed to be adjusted accordingly to compensate for the additional load. Similarly on models fitted with air conditioning, a sensor registers when the compressor clutch is in operation.

A "limited operation strategy" (LOS) means that the vehicle is still driveable, albeit at reduced power and efficiency, in the event of a failure in the EEC IV module or its sensors.

A fuel filter is incorporated in the fuel supply line to ensure that the fuel supplied to the injectors is clean.

On models produced from mid-1986 onwards, a fuel pump inertia cut-off switch is fitted. This switch breaks the electrical circuit to the fuel pump in the event of an accident or similar impact, cutting off the fuel supply to the engine.

2.0 litre DOHC models

The fuel injection system fitted to these models is under the overall control of an EEC IV engine management system which also controls the ignition timing.

Fuel is supplied from the rear-mounted fuel tank by an electric fuel pump, which is integral with the fuel level sender unit mounted inside the fuel tank. Fuel passes via a fuel filter and a pressure regulator to the fuel rail. The fuel rail acts as a reservoir for the four fuel injectors, which inject fuel into the cylinder inlet tracts, upstream of the inlet valves. The fuel injectors are operated in pairs by electrical pulses supplied by the EEC IV module, and fuel is injected by one pair of injectors every half-revolution of the crankshaft. The duration of each electrical pulse determines the quantity of fuel injected, and pulse duration is computed by the EEC IV module on the basis of information received from the various sensors.

Inducted air passes through the air cleaner, and through a plenum chamber, before passing on to the cylinder inlet tracts via the throttle valve and inlet manifold. The volume of air entering the engine is calculated by the EEC IV module from information supplied by various sensors. These sensors include an air charge temperature sensor mounted in the inlet manifold, which measures the temperature of the air entering the engine; a manifold absolute pressure (MAP) sensor, which measures the pressure of the air entering the engine; a throttle position sensor; and a crankshaft speed/position sensor, which supplies information on engine speed and provides a timing reference.

Additional sensors inform the EEC IV module of fuel temperature, engine coolant temperature, and vehicle speed (from a gearbox-mounted sensor).

Idle speed is controlled by a variable-orifice solenoid valve, which regulates the amount of air bypassing the throttle valve. The valve is controlled by the EEC IV module; there is no provision for direct adjustment of the idle speed.

On models without a catalytic converter, idle mixture adjustment is by means of a potentiometer connected directly to the EEC IV module. On models with a catalytic converter, an exhaust gas oxygen (HEGO) sensor enables the EEC IV module to control the fuel/air mixture to suit the operating parameters of the catalytic converter; no manual mixture adjustment is possible.

On models with a catalytic converter, an evaporative emission control (EVAP) system is fitted. This prevents the release of fuel vapour into the atmosphere. With the ignition switched off, vapours from the fuel tank are fed to a carbon canister, where they are absorbed. When the engine is started, the EEC IV module opens a purge solenoid valve, and the fuel vapours are fed into the inlet manifold and mixed with fresh air. This cleans the carbon filter. A blow-back valve prevents inlet air being forced back into the fuel tank.

A fuel pump inertia switch is fitted. This switch breaks the electrical circuit to the fuel pump in the event of an accident or similar impact, cutting off the fuel supply to the engine.

A "limited operation strategy" (LOS) means that the vehicle will still be driveable, albeit at reduced power and efficiency, in the event of a failure in the EEC IV module or its sensors.

1.6 and 1.8 litre (R6A type) CVH models

The fuel injection system fitted to these models is under the overall control of an EEC IV engine management system which also controls the ignition timing.

Fuel is supplied from the rear-mounted fuel tank by an electric fuel pump which is integral with the fuel level sender unit mounted inside the fuel tank. Fuel passes via a fuel filter to the Central Fuel Injection (CFI) unit. A fuel pressure regulator, mounted on the CFI unit, maintains a constant fuel pressure to the fuel injector. Excess fuel is returned from the regulator to the tank.

The CFI unit, resembling a carburettor, houses the throttle valve, throttle valve control motor, throttle position sensor, air charge temperature sensor, fuel injector, and pressure regulator.

The duration of the electrical pulse supplied to the fuel injector determines the quantity of fuel injected, and pulse duration is computed by the EEC IV module on the basis of information received from the various sensors. The fuel injector receives a pulse twice per crankshaft revolution under normal operating conditions, and once per crankshaft revolution under engine idle conditions. A ballast resistor is used in the fuel injector control circuit on 1.6 litre engines.

Inlet air passes through the air cleaner into the CFI unit. The volume of air entering the engine is calculated by the EEC IV module from information supplied by various sensors. These sensors include the air charge temperature sensor and throttle position sensor, mounted in the CFI unit; a crankshaft speed/position sensor which supplies information on engine speed; and a manifold absolute pressure (MAP) sensor which measures the pressure of the air entering the engine.

Additional sensors inform the EEC IV module of engine coolant temperature, and vehicle speed (from a gearbox-mounted sensor).

An exhaust gas oxygen (HEGO) sensor enables the EEC IV module to control the fuel/air mixture to suit the operating parameters of the catalytic converter. No manual mixture adjustment is possible.

Idle speed is controlled by a throttle valve control motor, which controls the position of the throttle valve under conditions of idling, deceleration/part-throttle, and engine start-up and shut-down.

On 1.6 litre engines, a pulse-air system is fitted to reduce the exhaust gas emissions during engine warm-up. The system is controlled by a vacuum-operated valve, which is operated by the EEC IV module via a solenoid. The system introduces air into the exhaust manifold to increase the exhaust gas temperature, which oxidises more of the pollutants, and brings the catalyst up to working temperature more quickly. The system operates until the catalyst reaches operating temperature, when the control solenoid shuts off the system.

On 1.8 litre engines, an exhaust gas recirculation (EGR) system is used to recirculate a small amount of exhaust gas into the inlet manifold. This process lowers the combustion temperature, resulting in a reduction of NOx (oxides of nitrogen) emissions. The EGR system is controlled by the EEC IV module in conjunction with an Electronic Pressure Transducer (EPT) and an Electronic Vacuum Regulator (EVR).

On certain models, an evaporative emission control system may be fitted. This prevents the release of fuel vapour into the atmosphere. With the ignition switched off, vapours from the fuel tank are fed to a carbon canister, where they are absorbed. When the engine is started the EEC IV module opens a purge solenoid valve, and the fuel vapours are fed into the inlet manifold and mixed with fresh air. This cleans the carbon filter. A blow-back valve prevents inlet air being forced back into the fuel tank.

A fuel pump inertia switch is fitted. This switch breaks the electrical circuit to the fuel pump in the event of an accident or similar impact cutting off the fuel supply to the engine.

A "limited operation strategy" (LOS) means that the vehicle will still be driveable, albeit at reduced power and efficiency, in the event of a failure in the EEC IV module or its sensors.

Precautions

Many of the procedures in this Chapter require the removal of fuel lines and connections which may result in some fuel spillage. Before carrying out any operation on the fuel system refer to the precautions given in "Safety first!" at the beginning of this Manual and follow them implicitly. Petrol is a highly dangerous and volatile liquid and the precautions necessary when handling it cannot be overstressed.

Residual pressure will remain in the fuel lines long after the vehicle was last used, therefore extra care must be taken when disconnecting a fuel line hose. Loosen any fuel hose slowly to avoid a sudden release of pressure which may cause fuel spray. As an added precaution place a rag over each union as it is disconnected to catch any fuel which is forcibly expelled.

Certain adjustment points in the fuel system (and elsewhere) are protected by "tamperproof" caps, plugs or seals. The purpose of such tamperproofing is to discourage, and to detent, adjustment by unqualified operators.

In some EEC countries (though not yet in the UK) it is an offence to drive a vehicle with missing or broken tamperproof seals. Before disturbing a tamperproof seal, satisfy yourself that you will not be breaking local or national anti-pollution regulations by doing so. Fit a new seal when adjustment is complete when this is required by law.

Do not break tamperproof seals on a vehicle which is still under warranty.

Catalytic converter - precautions

The catalytic converter is a reliable and simple device which needs no maintenance in itself, but there are some facts of which an owner should be aware if the converter is to function properly for the full service life.

a) *DO NOT use leaded petrol in a car equipped with a catalytic converter the lead will coat the precious metals, reducing their converting efficiency and will eventually destroy the converter.*

b) *Always keep the ignition and fuel systems well-maintained in accordance with the manufacturers schedule, ensure that the air cleaner filter element, the fuel filter (where fitted) and the spark plugs are renewed at the correct interval if the inlet air/fuel mixture is allowed to become too rich due to neglect, the unburned surplus will enter and burn in thecatalytic converter, overheating the element and eventually destroying the converter.*

c) *If the engine develops a misfire, do not drive the car at all (or at least as little as possible) until the fault is cured - the misfire will allow unburned fuel to enter the converter, which will result in overheating, as noted above.*

d) *DO NOT push- or tow-start the car - this will soak the catalytic converter in unburned fuel, causing it to overheat when the engine does start - see b) above.*

e) *DO NOT switch off the ignition at high engine speeds - if the ignition is switched off at anything above idle speed, unburned fuel will enter the (very hot) catalytic converter, with the possible risk of igniting on the element and damaging the converter.*

f) *DO NOT use fuel or engine oil additives - these may contain substances harmful to the catalytic converter.*

g) *DO NOT continue to use the car if the engine burns oil to the extent of leaving a visible trail of blue smoke - the unburned carbon deposits will clog the converter passages and reduce the efficiency; in severe cases the element will overheat.*

h) *Remember that the catalytic converter operates at very high temperatures - hence the heat shields on the car's underbody and the casing will become hot enough to ignite combustible materials which brush against it - DO NOT, therefore, park the car in dry undergrowth, over long grass or piles of dead leaves.*

i) *Remember that the catalytic converter is FRAGILE, do not strike it with tools during servicing work, take great care when* working on the exhaust system, ensure that the converter is well clear of any jacks or other lifting gear used to raise the car and do not drive the car over rough ground, road humps, etc., in such a way as to "ground" the exhaust system.

j) In some cases, particularly when the car is new and/or is used for stop/start driving, a sulphurous smell (like that of rotten eggs) may be noticed from the exhaust. This is common to many catalytic converter-equipped cars and seems to be due to the small amount of sulphur found in some petrols reacting with hydrogen in the exhaust to produce hydrogen sulphide (H_2S) gas; while this gas is toxic, it is not produced in sufficient amounts to be a problem. Once the car has covered a few thousand miles the problem should disappear - in the meanwhile a change of driving style or of the brand of petrol used may effect a solution.

k) The catalytic converter, used on a well-maintained and well-driven car, should last for between 50 000 and 100 000 miles - from this point on, careful checks should be made at all specified service intervals of the CO level to ensure that the converter is still operating efficiently - if the converter is no longer effective it must be renewed.

EEC IV module - warning

Following disconnection of the battery, the information stored in the EEC IV module memory will be erased. After reconnecting the battery, the engine should be allowed to idle for three minutes. Once the engine has reached normal operating temperature, the idle speed should be increased to 1200 rpm and maintained for approximately 2 minutes, which will allow the module to "re-learn" the optimum idle values. It may be necessary to drive the vehicle in order for the module to "re-learn" the values under load. The module should complete its learning process after approximately 5 miles (8 kilometres) of varied driving.

2 Air cleaner element - renewal

Refer to Chapter 1, Section 38.

3 Air cleaner - removal and refitting

2.0 litre SOHC models

1 Disconnect the battery negative lead.
2 Depress the locking clip on the airflow meter wiring plug and disconnect the plug. Pull on the plug, not the wiring.
3 Loosen the securing clip and disconnect the air inlet hose from the airflow meter.
4 Release the four securing clips and lift off the air cleaner lid with the airflow meter.
5 Remove the left-hand front wheel arch liner.
6 Working under the wheel arch, unscrew the three air cleaner securing nuts and washers.
7 Disconnect the air inlet tube, and withdraw

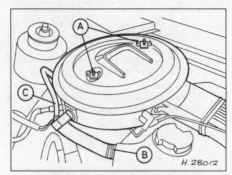

3.26a Air cleaner cover and hose attachments - 1.8 litre (R6A) CVH

A Cover retaining nuts
B Engine breather hose
C Oil separator hose

the air cleaner from the engine compartment.
8 Refitting is a reversal of removal.

2.0 litre DOHC models

9 Disconnect the battery negative lead.
10 Disconnect the wiring plug from the idle speed control valve at the front of the plenum chamber.
11 Loosen the clamp, and detach the air inlet hose from the air inlet tubing.
12 Unscrew the securing nut, and release the air inlet tube from the bracket on the engine compartment front panel.
13 Release the air cleaner lid securing clips, then lift away the air inlet tube, plenum chamber and air cleaner lid as an assembly, disconnecting the breather hose from the air inlet tube.
14 Lift out the air cleaner element then wipe the inside of the air cleaner lid and casing clean.
15 Remove the left-hand front wheel arch liner.
16 Working under the wheel arch, unscrew the three air cleaner securing nuts and washers.
17 Disconnect the air inlet tube, and withdraw the air cleaner from the engine compartment.
18 Refitting is a reversal of removal.

1.6 and 1.8 litre (R6A type) CVH models

1.6 litre

19 Remove the screws from the top of the air cleaner cover.
20 Disconnect the cold air inlet hose from the air cleaner spout or the inlet on the front body panel. The hose is secured by toggle clips.
21 Disconnect the hot air inlet hose from the air cleaner spout or the hot air shroud on the exhaust manifold.
22 Where applicable, remove the screw securing the air cleaner body to the camshaft cover.
23 Withdraw the air cleaner and disconnect the breather hose from the camshaft cover.
24 Refitting is a reversal of removal, ensure the disturbed hoses are securely connected.

1.8 litre

25 Undo the two nuts, lift off the air cleaner cover, and remove the element.

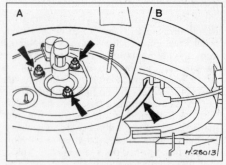

3.26b Air cleaner casing attachments - 1.8 litre (R6A) CVH

A Casing retaining nuts (arrowed)
B Vacuum hose (arrowed)

26 Disconnect the engine breather hose and the oil separator hose, then undo the three nuts and lift up the air cleaner casing **(see illustrations)**.
27 Disconnect the yellow striped vacuum hose from the underside of the casing, detach the air inlet hose, and remove the air cleaner assembly.
28 Refitting is a reversal of removal, ensuring all hoses are correctly attached.

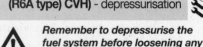

4 Fuel system (1.6 and 1.8 litre (R6A type) CVH) - depressurisation

⚠ **Remember to depressurise the fuel system before loosening any connections.**
Refer to the precautions in Section 1 before proceeding. The fuel system will remain pressurised after the engine is switched off.

1 Disconnect the battery negative lead.
2 Remove the air cleaner assembly.
3 Position a suitable container (or a sufficient quantity of absorbent cloth) beneath the fuel inlet connection on the CFI unit.
4 Use an open-ended spanner on the flats of the inlet union screwed into the CFI unit, to prevent it from turning while the inlet pipe union is loosened **(see illustration)**. Allow all pressure/fuel seepage to dissipate before fully unscrewing the union if it is to be disconnected, or tightened if another part of the system is to be worked on.

4.4 CFI unit fuel inlet union (arrowed)

5 The system will remain depressurised until the fuel pump is primed prior to starting the engine. Remove the container or cloth, as applicable, on completion.

5 Fuel filter - renewal

Refer to Chapter 1, Section 41.

6 Fuel pressure regulator - removal and refitting

⚠ Caution: Refer to the precautions in Section 1 before proceeding.

2.0 litre SOHC models

1 Disconnect the battery negative lead.
2 Slowly loosen the fuel feed union to relieve the pressure in the fuel lines.
3 Disconnect the fuel feed and return lines. Be prepared for petrol spillage.
4 Disconnect the vacuum pipe from the top of the pressure regulator.
5 Unscrew the securing nut from the base of the pressure regulator and withdraw the unit **(see illustration)**.
6 Refitting is a reversal of removal, but if the fuel return line was originally secured with a crimped type clip, discard this and use a new worm drive clip.
7 On completion check the fuel line connections for leaks. Pressurise the system by switching the ignition on and off several times.

2.0 litre DOHC models

Note: A new pressure regulator seal will be required on refitting.
8 Disconnect the battery negative lead.
9 Slowly loosen the fuel rail fuel feed union to relieve the pressure in the system **(see illustration)**. Be prepared for fuel spillage, and take adequate fire precautions.
10 Disconnect the fuel return hose from the pressure regulator **(see illustration)**. Again, be prepared for fuel spillage.
11 Disconnect the vacuum pipe from the top of the pressure regulator.
12 Unscrew the two securing bolts, and withdraw the regulator from the fuel rail. Recover the seal.

6.10 Disconnecting the fuel return hose (arrowed) from the pressure regulator

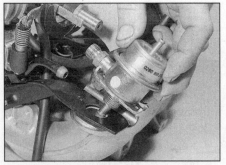

6.5 Withdrawing the fuel pressure regulator

13 Fit a new seal to the regulator, and lubricate with clean engine oil.
14 Fit both the securing bolts to the regulator, then position the regulator on the fuel rail, and tighten the securing bolts.
15 Further refitting is a reversal of removal. If the fuel return line was originally secured with a crimped-type clip, discard this, and use a new worm-drive clip.
16 On completion, pressurise the system by switching the ignition on and off several times, and check the fuel line connections for leaks.

1.6 and 1.8 litre (R6A type) CVH models

Note: On completion of refitting, the fuel system pressure should be checked by a Ford dealer at the earliest opportunity.

6.9 Fuel rail fuel feed union (arrowed)

1.6 litre

17 Remove the CFI unit.
18 Remove the four screws securing the regulator housing to the CFI unit, then carefully lift off the housing and recover the ball, cup, large spring, diaphragm, valve, and small spring, noting the position and orientation of all components **(see illustration)**. Do not attempt to prise the plug from the regulator housing, or adjust the Allen screw (if no plug is fitted); this will alter the fuel system pressure.
19 Check all components, and renew any faulty items as necessary.
20 Commence reassembly by supporting the CFI unit on its side, so that the regulator components can be fitted from above.

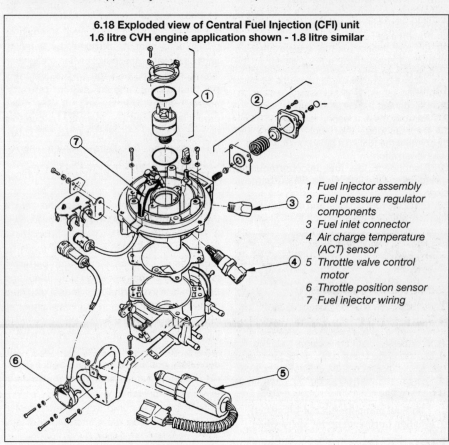

6.18 Exploded view of Central Fuel Injection (CFI) unit
1.6 litre CVH engine application shown - 1.8 litre similar

1 Fuel injector assembly
2 Fuel pressure regulator components
3 Fuel inlet connector
4 Air charge temperature (ACT) sensor
5 Throttle valve control motor
6 Throttle position sensor
7 Fuel injector wiring

4B

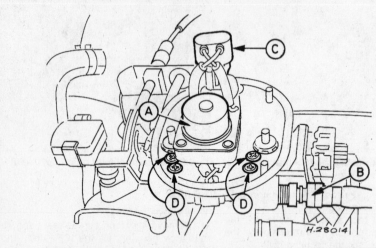

6.28 Fuel injector/pressure regulator attachments - 1.8 litre (R6A) CVH

A Pressure regulator assembly
B Fuel inlet pipe
C Injector/regulator wiring plug
D Injector/regulator screws

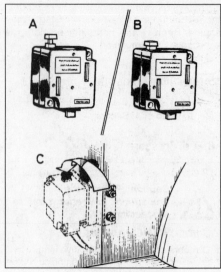

7.3a Fuel pump inertia cut-off switch - pre-1987 SOHC Hatchback and Estate models

A Activated mode (fuel cut-off)
B Normal mode (fuel flowing)
C Trim panel access hole

21 Fit the small spring, valve, diaphragm (ensuring that it locates correctly), large spring, and the spring cup.
22 Carefully place the ball into position on the spring cup, and ensure that it locates correctly.
23 Refit the regulator housing, taking great care to avoid disturbing the ball, and once correctly in position, tighten the screws evenly to avoid distorting the diaphragm.
24 Refit the CFI unit.
25 On completion, the fuel system pressure should be checked by a Ford dealer at the earliest opportunity.

1.8 litre

26 Disconnect the battery negative lead.
27 Remove the air cleaner assembly.
28 Depressurise the fuel system and disconnect the fuel inlet pipe from the CFI unit **(see illustration)**.
29 Disconnect the fuel injector/regulator wiring plug, and move the wiring harness clear.
30 Undo the four screws, and carefully lift the injector/regulator assembly off the CFI unit.

7.3b Fuel pump inertia cut-off switch location (arrowed) under spare wheel

31 Refitting is a reversal of removal. On completion, the fuel system pressure should be checked by a Ford dealer at the earliest opportunity.

7 Fuel pump - testing

1 If the fuel pump is functioning, it should be possible to hear it "buzzing" by listening under the rear of the vehicle when the ignition is switched on. Unless the engine is started, the fuel pump should switch off after approximately one second. If the noise produced is excessive, this may be due to a faulty fuel flow damper (not fitted to 2.0 litre DOHC models). The damper can be renewed by unscrewing it from the pump outlet union.
2 If the pump appears to have failed completely, check the appropriate fuse and relay, and where applicable check the state of the fuel pump inertia cut-off switch as follows.
3 The inertia cut-off switch is fitted to all models from mid-1986 onwards, and can be found behind the passenger compartment left-hand side trim panel on Hatchback and Estate models up to the 1987 model year **(see illustration)**. The location of the switch for all other models is in the spare wheel well **(see illustration)**. The switch incorporates a reset button, which should normally be in the depressed position. Check the position of the reset button before assuming that a fault exists in the fuel pump.
4 To test the fuel pump, special equipment is required, and it is recommended that any suspected faults are referred to a Ford dealer.

8 Fuel pump (2.0 litre SOHC) - removal and refitting

⚠️ **Caution: Refer to the precautions in Section 1 before proceeding.**

Removal

1 The fuel pump is located under the rear of the vehicle next to the fuel tank **(see illustration)**.
2 Disconnect the battery negative lead.
3 Chock the front wheels, then jack up the rear of the vehicle and support on axle stands (see "*Jacking and Vehicle Support*").
4 Clean the area around the pump mounting, and position a suitable container under the pump.
5 Using a hose clamping tool or self-locking pliers, clamp the fuel tank-to-pump hose to prevent excessive petrol spillage, or

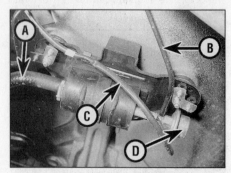

8.1 Fuel pump location

A Inlet hose
B Outlet hose
C Electrical feed
D Flow damper

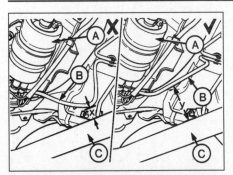

8.9 Correct and incorrect routing of fuel pump outlet pipe

A Fuel pump   X = 30.0 mm (1.2 in)
B Outlet pipe   Y = 100.0 mm (3.9 in)
C Exhaust pipe

alternatively make arrangements to collect the contents of the fuel tank which will otherwise be released. Disconnect the hose from the pump.

6 Slowly loosen the fuel flow damper fitted to the pump outlet union, to relieve the pressure in the fuel line, then remove the damper and disconnect the outlet pipe from the pump. Plug the end of the pipe to prevent excessive petrol spillage.

7 Disconnect the wiring plug(s), then slacken the clamp bolt and slide the pump from the bracket assembly.

Refitting

8 Refitting is a reversal of removal, noting the following.

9 When refitting the flow damper to the pump ensure that the pump outlet pipe is correctly routed (see illustration). It is possible to inadvertently rotate the banjo union through 180°, which routes the outlet pipe too close to the exhaust.

10 After refitting and securing the pump, but before lowering the vehicle, reconnect the battery and switch the ignition on and off several times to pressurise the fuel system. Check for leaks around the pump; if all is satisfactory, switch off the ignition and lower the vehicle.

9 Fuel pump/fuel level sender unit (2.0 litre DOHC/1.6 & 1.8 litre (R6A type) CVH) - removal and refitting

⚠️ **Caution: Refer to the precautions in Section 1 before proceeding.**

1 Remove the fuel tank.
2 Unscrew the fuel pump/fuel level sender unit by engaging two crossed screwdrivers in the slots on either side of the unit mounting flange. Recover the seal.
3 Refitting is a reversal of removal but fit a new seal.

10 Fuel tank - removal and refitting

Refer to Chapter 4 Part A, Section 9.

11 Fuel level sender unit (2.0 litre SOHC) - removal and refitting

Refer to Chapter 4 Part A, Section 10.

12 Idle speed and mixture - adjustment

Refer to Chapter 1, Sections 15 and 16.

13 Idle speed control valve - removal and refitting

Note: A new gasket must be used when refitting the valve.

2.0 litre SOHC models

1 Disconnect the battery negative lead.
2 Disconnect the idle speed control valve wiring plug by releasing the retaining clip and pulling on the plug, not the wiring (see illustration).
3 Unscrew the two retaining nuts and withdraw the valve from the inlet manifold (see illustration). Recover the gasket.

4 Clean the valve and manifold mating faces before refitting, taking care not to allow dirt to enter the manifold.
5 Refitting is a reversal of removal, using a new gasket.
6 On completion, start the engine and check that the idle speed is stable if not, check for air leaks around the valve. Switch on all available electrical loads and check that the idle speed is maintained - if not, suspect a faulty valve.

2.0 litre DOHC models

7 Disconnect the battery negative lead.
8 Loosen the securing clip, and disconnect the air inlet hose from the throttle body.
9 Unscrew the securing nut, and release the air inlet tube from the bracket on the engine compartment front panel.
10 Disconnect the wiring plug from the idle speed control valve.
11 Release the air cleaner lid securing clips then remove the air inlet tube, plenum chamber, and air cleaner lid as an assembly, disconnecting the breather hose from the air inlet tube.
12 Unscrew the two securing bolts, and withdraw the valve from the air inlet tube. Recover the gasket (see illustration).
13 Clean the valve and air inlet tube mating faces before refitting, taking care not to allow dirt to enter the air inlet tube.
14 Refitting is a reversal of removal, using a new gasket.
15 On completion, start the engine and check that the idle speed is stable if not, check for air leaks around the valve. Switch on all available electrical loads, and check that the idle speed is maintained - if not, suspect a faulty valve.

14 Mixture adjustment potentiometer (2.0 litre DOHC) - removal and refitting

1 The potentiometer is located at the rear right-hand side of the engine compartment, behind the MAP sensor.
2 Disconnect the battery negative lead.
3 Remove the screw, then withdraw the potentiometer and disconnect the wiring plug.
4 Refitting is a reversal of removal.

13.2 Disconnecting the idle speed control valve wiring plug

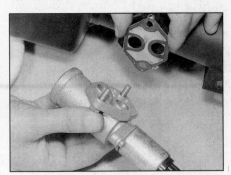

13.3 Unscrewing an idle speed control valve retaining nut

13.12 Withdrawing the idle speed control valve and gasket

4B

15.5 Airflow meter-to-air cleaner lid bolts (arrowed)

15 Airflow meter - removal and refitting

Note: *A tachometer and an exhaust gas analyser will be required to check the idle mixture on completion.*

1 Disconnect the battery negative lead.
2 Depress the locking clip on the airflow meter wiring plug and disconnect the plug. Pull on the plug, not the wiring.
3 Loosen the securing clip and disconnect the air inlet hose from the airflow meter.
4 Release the four securing clips and lift off the air cleaner lid with the airflow meter.
5 Remove the four securing bolts and separate the airflow meter from the air cleaner lid **(see illustration)**. Recover the seal.
6 Refitting is a reversal of removal, ensuring that the seal is correctly located on the air cleaner lid, and that the air inlet hose clip is correctly aligned **(see illustration)**.

7 On completion, check and if necessary adjust the idle mixture.

16 Fuel injector (1.6 and 1.8 litre (R6A type) CVH) - removal and refitting

⚠ **Caution:** *Refer to the precautions in Section 1 before proceeding.*

1.6 litre

Note: *New fuel injector seals must be used on refitting.*
1 Disconnect the battery negative lead.
2 Remove the air cleaner.
3 Depressurise the fuel system.
4 Release the securing lugs, and disconnect the fuel injector wiring plug **(see illustration)**.
5 Bend back the injector retaining collar securing bolt locktabs, then unscrew the bolts. Remove the injector retaining collar **(see illustrations)**.
6 Withdraw the injector from the CFI unit **(see illustration)**, noting its orientation, then withdraw the injector seals.
7 Remove the seal from the injector retaining collar **(see illustration)**.
8 Refitting is a reversal of removal, noting the following points.
9 Use new injector seals, and lubricate them with clean engine oil before fitting.
10 Ensure that the locating peg on the injector is correctly positioned **(see illustration)**.

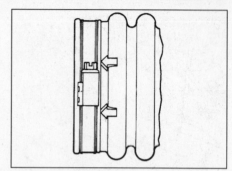

15.6 Air intake hose clip correctly aligned

1.8 litre

11 On these engines, the fuel pressure regulator and injector are one assembly. Proceed as described for the fuel pressure regulator.

17 Fuel injector ballast resistor (1.6 litre CVH) - removal and refitting

1 The ballast resistor is located on the right-hand side of the engine compartment, and is only fitted to 1.6 litre engines **(see illustration)**.
2 Disconnect the battery negative lead.
3 Disconnect the ballast resistor wiring connector, then remove the securing screw, and withdraw the ballast resistor from the body panel.
4 Refitting is a reversal of removal.

16.4 Disconnecting the fuel injector wiring plug

16.5a Removing an injector retaining collar securing bolt and locktab

16.5b Removing the injector retaining collar

16.6 Withdrawing the fuel injector

16.7 Removing the seal from the injector retaining collar

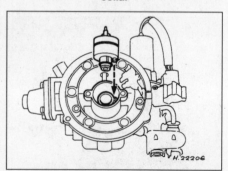

16.10 Align locating peg on injector with slot in CFI unit on refitting - 1.6 litre CVH

17.1 Fuel injector ballast resistor location (arrowed)

18.9a Fuel rail front securing bolt (arrowed) . . .

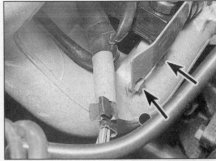

18.9b . . . and rear securing bolts

18 Fuel injectors - removal and refitting

Caution: Refer to the precautions in Section 1 before proceeding.

Note: *A tachometer and an exhaust gas analyser will be required to check the idle mixture on completion. New seals and retaining clips must be used when refitting the injectors, and special grease will be required - see relevant paragraph. If the injectors are thought to be faulty, it may be worth trying the effect of a fuel injector cleaning agent before removing them.*

2.0 litre SOHC models

1 Disconnect the battery negative lead.
2 Disconnect the crankcase ventilation hose from the air inlet hose, then disconnect the air inlet hose from the inlet manifold and the airflow meter.
3 Disconnect the HT lead from the coil, then remove the distributor cap and position the cap and HT leads clear of the fuel rail assembly.
4 Disconnect the wiring plugs from the idle speed control valve, the throttle position sensor and the engine coolant temperature sensor.
5 Remove the fuel pressure regulator.
6 Unscrew the securing bolt and remove the throttle return spring bracket. Disconnect the throttle return spring.

7 Disconnect the fuel supply hose from the fuel rail. Be prepared for petrol spillage.
8 Disconnect the wiring plugs from the fuel injectors, noting their locations for use when refitting.
9 Remove the three securing bolts and withdraw the fuel rail and fuel injectors from the inlet manifold as an assembly **(see illustrations)**.
10 To remove a fuel injector from the fuel rail, remove the retaining clip and withdraw the injector **(see illustration)**.
11 Overhaul of the fuel injectors is not possible, as no spares are available. If faulty, an injector must be renewed.
12 Commence refitting by fitting new seals to both ends of each fuel injector. Even if only one injector has been removed, new seals must be fitted to all four injectors **(see illustration)**. Coat the seals with silicone grease to Ford specification ESEM - ICI71 A. Similarly, renew all four fuel injector retaining clips.
13 Further refitting is a reversal of removal, ensuring that all hoses, wiring plugs and leads are correctly connected. When reconnecting the air inlet hose, make sure that the hose clips are correctly aligned - see illustration, Section 15.
14 On completion, check and if necessary adjust the idle mixture.

2.0 litre DOHC models

15 Disconnect the battery negative lead.
16 If desired, to improve access, disconnect

the wiring from the inlet air temperature sensor in the inlet manifold. Similarly, the throttle cable can be moved to one side by disconnecting the cable from the throttle linkage. The spark plug HT leads can be disconnected and moved to one side, noting their locations and routing to aid refitting.
17 Slowly loosen the fuel rail fuel feed union to relieve the pressure in the system. Be prepared for fuel spillage, and take adequate fire precautions.
18 Disconnect the fuel feed hose from the fuel rail **(see illustration)**.
19 Disconnect the fuel return hose from the fuel pressure regulator. Again, be prepared for fuel spillage.
20 Disconnect the vacuum pipe from the top of the fuel pressure regulator.
21 Disconnect the wiring plugs from the fuel temperature sensor and the fuel injectors, noting their locations to assist with refitting.
22 Unscrew the two securing bolts, and withdraw the fuel rail.
23 Lift the fuel injectors from their locations in the cylinder head **(see illustration)**.
24 Overhaul of the fuel injectors is not possible, as no spares are available. If faulty, an injector must be renewed (refer to the note at the start of this procedure before condemning an injector).
25 Commence refitting by fitting new seals to both ends of each fuel injector. It is advisable to fit new seals to all the injectors, even if only one has been removed. Lubricate the seals with clean engine oil.

4B

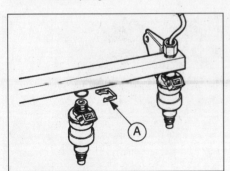

18.10 Fuel injector retaining clip (A)

18.12 Fuel injector with seals removed

18.18 Disconnecting the fuel feed hose from the fuel rail

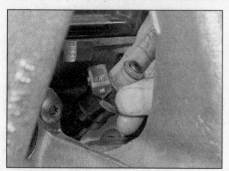

18.23 Lifting a fuel injector from the cylinder head

19.9 CFI unit securing bolts (arrowed) - 1.6 litre CVH

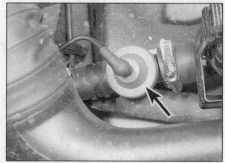

21.1 Pulse air system vacuum-operated air valve (arrowed)

26 Further refitting is a reversal of removal, ensuring that all hoses, pipes and wiring plugs are correctly connected.

27 On completion, where applicable, check and if necessary adjust the idle mixture.

19 CFI unit (1.6 and 1.8 litre (R6A type) CVH) - removal and refitting

 Caution: Refer to the precautions in Section 1 before proceeding. A new gasket must be used on refitting.

Removal

1 Disconnect the battery negative lead.

2 Remove the air cleaner assembly.

3 Depressurise the fuel system and disconnect the fuel inlet pipe from the CFI unit.

4 Disconnect the fuel return pipe from the CFI unit. Be prepared for fuel spillage.

5 Disconnect the throttle cable from the linkage on the CFI unit.

6 On 1.6 litre models, either partially drain the cooling system or clamp the coolant hoses as close as possible to the CFI unit to minimise coolant loss, then disconnect the hoses from the unit.

7 Disconnect the wiring plugs for the throttle position sensor, throttle valve control motor, fuel injector and, on 1.6 litre models, the air charge temperature sensor.

8 Disconnect the vacuum pipe from the CFI unit.

9 Unscrew the four (1.6 litre), or three (1.8 litre) securing bolts, and lift the CFI unit from the inlet manifold **(see illustration)**. Recover the gasket.

Refitting

10 Refitting is a reversal of removal, bearing in mind the following points.

11 Ensure that all mating faces are clean, and use a new gasket.

12 Top-up the cooling system.

13 On completion, turn the ignition on and off five times to pressurise the system, and check for fuel leaks.

20 Pulse-air filter element (1.6 litre CVH) - renewal

Refer to Chapter 1, Section 37.

21 Pulse-air system vacuum-operated air valve (1.6 litre CVH) - removal and refitting

1 The valve is mounted at the end of the pulse-air filter housing **(see illustration)**.

2 Disconnect the vacuum hose from the top of the valve, then loosen the hose clips at either end of the valve, and remove the valve. Note the orientation of the arrow on the valve body, which denotes the direction of flow.

3 Refitting is a reversal of removal, ensuring that the arrow on the valve body is orientated as noted before removal.

22 Pulse-air delivery tubing (1.6 litre CVH) - removal and refitting

1 Remove the air cleaner assembly.

2 Loosen the hose clips, and disconnect the air hoses from the check valves next to the exhaust manifold **(see illustration)**.

3 Remove the two bolts securing the check valve bracket to the exhaust manifold.

4 Unscrew the unions securing the air tubes to the manifold, then carefully withdraw the tubing assembly, taking care not to distort the tubes **(see illustration)**.

5 Refitting is a reversal of removal.

23 Pulse-air control solenoid (1.6 litre CVH) - removal and refitting

1 The solenoid is located at the right-hand side of the engine compartment.

2 Disconnect the battery negative lead.

3 Disconnect the vacuum pipe connector from the pulse-air control solenoid **(see illustration)**.

4 Disconnect the solenoid wiring plug, pulling on the plug, not the wiring.

5 Unscrew the securing screw, and withdraw the solenoid from the body panel.

6 Refitting is a reversal of removal, ensuring that the locating lug is correctly positioned, and noting that the vacuum pipes will only fit in one position.

22.2 Pulse-air delivery check valves (arrowed)

22.4 Unscrewing a pulse-air delivery tube union

23.3 Disconnect the vacuum pipe connector from the solenoid

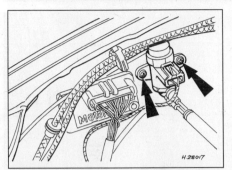

24.4 Electronic vacuum regulator retaining screws (arrowed) - 1.8 litre (R6A) CVH

24 Electronic vacuum regulator (1.8 litre (R6A type) CVH) - removal and refitting

1 The EVR unit is located on the right-hand side of the engine compartment, near the front of the car.
2 Disconnect the battery negative lead.
3 Disconnect the EVR wiring plug, and detach the two vacuum hoses, noting their correct location for refitting.
4 Undo the retaining screws, and remove the EVR unit from the car **(see illustration)**.
5 Refitting is a reversal of removal.

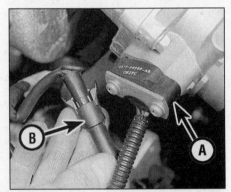

27.6 Throttle position sensor (A) and wiring plug (B)

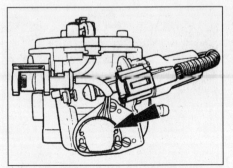

27.11a Throttle position sensor location (arrowed) on CFI unit - 1.6 litre CVH

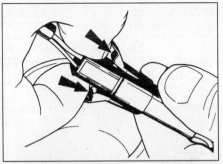

27.2 Releasing locktabs to disconnect throttle position sensor wiring plug halves

25 Throttle pedal - removal and refitting

Refer to Chapter 4 Part A, Section 11.

26 Throttle cable - removal, refitting and adjustment

Refer to Chapter 4 Part A, Section 12.

27 Throttle position sensor - removal and refitting

Note: *During this procedure ensure that the sensor wiper is not rotated beyond its normal operating arc.*

2.0 litre SOHC models

1 Disconnect the battery negative lead.
2 Free the throttle position sensor wiring plug from the retaining clip located on the underside of the throttle body. Disconnect the wiring plug halves by releasing the locktabs and pulling on the plug halves **(see illustration)**.
3 Bend back the locktabs and unscrew the two sensor retaining bolts **(see illustration)**. Withdraw the locking plate and sensor from the throttle shaft.
4 Refitting is a reverse of removal, ensuring that the moulded side of the sensor faces towards the inlet manifold. The flat on the sensor wiper engages with the flat on the throttle shaft.

2.0 litre DOHC models

5 Disconnect the battery negative lead.

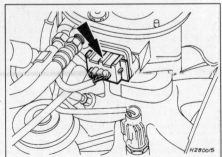

27.11b Throttle position sensor location (arrowed) on CFI unit - 1.8 litre (R6A) CVH

27.3 Unscrewing the throttle position sensor retaining bolts

6 Free the throttle position sensor wiring plug from the retaining clip located on the underside of the throttle body. Disconnect the wiring plug halves by releasing the locktabs and pulling on the plug halves **(see illustration)**.
7 Unscrew the two sensor securing screws, and withdraw the sensor from the throttle shaft.
8 Refitting is a reversal of removal, noting that the sensor fits with the wiring at the bottom. Ensure that the sensor actuating arm engages correctly with the throttle spindle.

1.6 and 1.8 litre (R6A type) CVH models

9 Disconnect the battery negative lead.
10 Remove the air cleaner.
11 Unclip and disconnect the sensor wiring connector, pulling on the plug, not on the wiring **(see illustrations)**.
12 Remove the two screws, and withdraw the sensor from the throttle valve shaft.
13 Refitting is a reversal of removal, but ensure that the sensor actuating arm locates correctly on the throttle valve spindle.

28 Throttle valve control motor (1.6 and 1.8 litre (R6A type) CVH) - removal and refitting

1.6 litre

1 Disconnect the battery negative lead.
2 Remove the air cleaner.
3 Disconnect the wiring connectors from the throttle valve control motor, and the throttle position sensor, pulling on the plugs, not on the wiring **(see illustration)**.

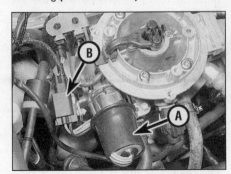

28.3 Throttle valve control motor (A) and wiring plug (B)

4B

4 Remove the three screws securing the motor and the throttle position sensor assembly mounting bracket to the CFI unit, and withdraw the assembly.

5 Remove the three motor securing screws, and withdraw the motor from the bracket.

6 Refitting is a reversal of removal, bearing in mind the following points.

7 Ensure that the throttle position sensor actuating arm locates correctly on the throttle valve spindle, and that the mounting bracket aligns with its locating pegs.

8 On completion, the idle speed should be checked by a Ford dealer at the earliest opportunity.

1.8 litre

9 Disconnect the battery negative lead.

10 Remove the air cleaner assembly.

11 Disconnect the wiring connector from the throttle valve control motor.

12 Remove the three screws securing the motor and the mounting bracket to the CFI unit, and withdraw the assembly.

13 Remove the three motor securing screws, and withdraw the motor from the bracket.

14 Refitting is a reversal of removal, ensuring that the motor is located on the throttle linkage, and that the bracket and locating pegs are aligned.

29 Throttle body - removal and refitting

Note: *A tachometer and an exhaust gas analyser will be required to check the idle mixture on completion. A new gasket must be used when refitting the throttle body.*

2.0 litre SOHC models

1 Disconnect the battery negative lead.

2 Free the throttle position sensor wiring plug from the retaining clip on the underside of the throttle body. Disconnect the wiring plug halves by releasing the locktabs and pulling on the plug halves, not the wiring.

3 Disconnect the throttle cable from the lever.

4 Disconnect the crankcase ventilation hose from the air inlet hose, then disconnect the air inlet hose from the throttle body and the airflow meter.

5 Remove the four securing bolts and withdraw the throttle body from the inlet manifold. Recover the gasket.

6 Refitting is a reversal of removal, bearing in mind the following points.

7 Ensure that all mating faces are clean, and fit a new gasket.

8 When reconnecting the air inlet hose, make sure that the hose clips are correctly aligned, see illustration, Section 15.

9 On completion, adjust the throttle cable and check and if necessary adjust the idle mixture.

2.0 litre DOHC models

10 Disconnect the battery negative lead.

11 Free the throttle position sensor wiring plug from the retaining clip located on the underside of the throttle body. Disconnect the

30.5 Unscrew the securing bolts and remove the throttle cable bracket

wiring plug halves by releasing the locktabs and pulling on the plug halves, not the wiring.

12 Disconnect the throttle cable from the linkage.

13 Loosen the securing clip, and disconnect the air inlet hose from the throttle body.

14 Unscrew the four securing bolts, and withdraw the throttle body from the inlet manifold. Recover the gasket.

15 Refitting is a reversal of removal, bearing in mind the following points.

16 Ensure that the mating faces of the throttle body and the inlet manifold are clean, and fit a new gasket.

17 On completion, adjust the throttle cable. Where applicable, check and if necessary adjust the idle mixture.

30 Inlet manifold - removal and refitting

 Caution: Refer to the precautions in Section 1 before proceeding.

Note: *A tachometer and an exhaust gas analyser will be required to check the idle mixture on completion. A new gasket must be used when refitting the manifold.*

2.0 litre SOHC models

1 Disconnect the battery negative lead.

2 Partially drain the cooling system.

3 Disconnect the crankcase ventilation hose from the air inlet hose. Disconnect the air inlet

30.11 Unscrew the two securing nuts (arrowed) and remove the inlet manifold bracing strut

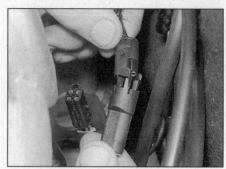

30.6 Disconnecting a fuel injection harness wiring plug

hose from the inlet manifold and the airflow meter.

4 Disconnect the HT lead from the coil, then remove the distributor cap and position the cap and HT leads clear of the inlet manifold assembly.

5 Unscrew the two securing bolts and remove the throttle cable bracket **(see illustration)**. Disconnect the cable end from the throttle lever, and move the bracket to one side.

6 Disconnect the fuel injection harness wiring plugs at the bulkhead end of the manifold **(see illustration)**.

7 Disconnect the oil pressure warning lamp switch wire from below the manifold.

8 Disconnect the fuel supply hose from the fuel rail. Loosen the union nut slowly to relieve the pressure in the fuel system, and be prepared for petrol spillage.

9 Disconnect the fuel return hose from the fuel pressure regulator. Be prepared for fuel spillage.

10 Disconnect the coolant hose and the brake servo vacuum hose from the inlet manifold.

11 Unscrew the two securing nuts and remove the bracing strut which runs from the manifold to the right-hand side of the cylinder head **(see illustration)**.

12 Unscrew the two bolts securing the lower manifold bracket to the left-hand side of the cylinder block **(see illustration)**.

13 Remove the four bolts and two nuts securing the inlet manifold to the cylinder head, and carefully withdraw the manifold. If the distributor obstructs removal, extract the front manifold stud by locking two nuts

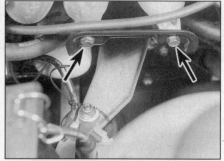

30.12 Lower inlet manifold bracket (arrowed)

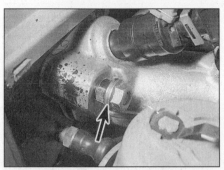

30.13 Where necessary use two nuts locked together (arrowed) to remove the front inlet manifold stud

together and using them to unscrew the stud **(see illustration)**. Alternatively, the distributor can be removed, although this is not recommended unless absolutely essential. Recover the gasket. Note that an earth strap may be located on one of the manifold securing bolts or studs; where applicable, note its location as an aid to refitting.

14 With the manifold removed, the various fuel injection system components can be separated from the manifold with reference to the relevant Sections of this Chapter.

15 Refitting is a reversal of removal, bearing in mind the following points.

16 Renew the gasket, and apply a bead of sealant at least 5.0 mm (0.2 in) wide around the central coolant aperture on both sides of the gasket. Ensure that all mating faces are clean.

30.25a Disconnect the throttle cable from the securing bracket . . .

30.25b . . . and the throttle linkage

17 Tighten the manifold securing nuts and bolts progressively to the specified torque, where applicable ensuring that the earth strap is in position.

18 Make sure that all hoses, cables, wires and leads are correctly reconnected. When reconnecting the air inlet hose, make sure that the hose clips are correctly aligned, see illustration, Section 15.

19 On completion, refill the cooling system, adjust the throttle cable and check and if necessary adjust the idle mixture.

2.0 litre DOHC models

Note: New fuel injector seals must be used on refitting.

20 Disconnect the battery negative lead.

21 Partially drain the cooling system.

22 Disconnect the coolant hoses from the thermostat housing and the inlet manifold.

23 Disconnect the air inlet hose from the front of the inlet manifold.

24 Disconnect the breather hoses and the vacuum hoses from the inlet manifold noting their locations when disconnecting the brake servo vacuum hose.

25 Disconnect the throttle cable from the throttle linkage **(see illustrations)**.

26 Disconnect the HT leads from the spark plugs, noting their locations to aid refitting, and move them to one side.

27 Disconnect the wiring from the cooling fan switch, the engine coolant temperature sensor, and the temperature gauge sender.

28 Release the throttle position sensor wiring connector from the clip under the throttle body, and separate the two halves of the connector.

29 Remove the fuel injectors.

30 Check that all relevant wiring, hoses and pipes have been disconnected, to facilitate removal of the manifold.

31 Unscrew the ten bolts and two nuts securing the inlet manifold to the cylinder head, and carefully withdraw the manifold. Recover the gasket.

32 Recover the two plastic spark plug spacers from the recesses in the cylinder head **(see illustration)**.

33 If desired, the manifold can be dismantled with reference to the relevant paragraphs of this Chapter.

34 Refitting is a reversal of removal, bearing in mind the following points.

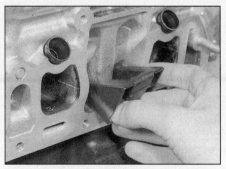

30.32 Removing a spark plug spacer from the cylinder head recess

35 Ensure that the spark plug spacers are in position in the cylinder head recesses before refitting the manifold.

36 Renew all gaskets.

37 Tighten all manifold securing nuts and bolts progressively to the specified torque.

38 Make sure that all hoses, pipes and wires are securely reconnected in their original positions.

39 On completion, refill the cooling system. Check the adjustment of the throttle cable and if necessary adjust the idle speed and mixture (as applicable).

1.6 and 1.8 litre (R6A type) CVH models

40 Disconnect the battery negative lead.

41 Remove the air cleaner assembly.

42 Depressurise the fuel system and disconnect the fuel inlet pipe from the CFI unit.

43 Disconnect the fuel return pipe from the CFI unit. Be prepared for fuel spillage.

44 Disconnect the throttle cable from the linkage on the CFI unit.

45 Partially drain the cooling system.

46 Disconnect the coolant hoses from the thermostat housing and, where applicable, the CFI unit.

47 Disconnect the vacuum and breather hoses from the inlet manifold and the CFI unit, noting their locations.

48 Disconnect the wiring from the following components, according to engine type.

Air charge temperature sensor.
Throttle position sensor.
Fuel pressure regulator/injector.
Throttle valve control motor.
Engine coolant temperature sensor.
Cooling fan switch.
Temperature gauge sender.

49 Unbolt the dipstick tube from the inlet manifold, and withdraw the dipstick and dipstick tube from the cylinder block.

50 Make a final check to ensure that all relevant wires, hoses and pipes have been disconnected to facilitate removal of the manifold.

51 Unscrew the seven nuts, or six securing nuts and the single bolt, securing the inlet manifold to the cylinder head, then lift the manifold from the cylinder head. Recover the gasket.

52 If desired, the CFI unit can be removed from the inlet manifold.

53 If necessary, the thermostat and housing can be removed from the manifold.

54 Refitting is a reversal of removal, noting the following points.

55 Ensure that all mating faces are clean, and renew all gaskets.

56 Tighten the manifold nuts (and bolt, where applicable) progressively to the specified torque.

57 Make sure that all wires, hoses and pipes are reconnected as noted before removal.

58 Top-up the cooling system.

59 On completion, turn the ignition on and off five times to pressurise the system, and check for fuel leaks.

4B

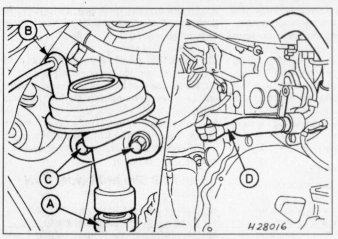

31.3 Exhaust gas recirculation valve attachments -
1.8 litre (R6A) CVH

A Metal tube-to-EGR valve
   retaining nut
B Vacuum hose

C EGR valve retaining bolts
D EGR valve metal tube location

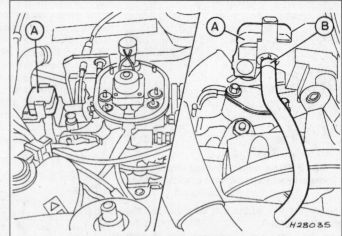

32.1 Exhaust pressure transducer attachments -
1.8 litre (R6A) CVH

A Exhaust pressure transducer   B Vacuum hose

31 Exhaust gas recirculation valve (1.8 litre (R6A type) CVH) - removal and refitting

1 The EGR valve is located on the right-hand side of the engine, below the CFI unit.
2 Disconnect the battery negative lead.
3 Disconnect the vacuum hose connecting the EGR valve to the electronic vacuum regulator (see illustration).
4 Undo the nut securing the metal tube to the underside of the valve. Undo the two bolts, and remove the valve from the engine.
5 Refitting is a reversal of removal, but loosely fit the metal tube securing nut to the EGR valve before fitting the valve in position. Tighten the nut securely on completion.

32 Exhaust pressure transducer (1.8 litre (R6A type) CVH) - removal and refitting

1 The EPT unit is located on the right-hand side of the engine, behind the CFI unit (see illustration).
2 Disconnect the battery negative lead.
3 Remove the air cleaner assembly.
4 Disconnect the EPT wiring plug, and slip the unit out of its mounting bracket.
5 Detach the vacuum hose, and remove the unit from the car.
6 Refitting is a reversal of removal.

33 Carbon canister (models with catalytic converter) - removal and refitting

2.0 litre DOHC models

1 Where fitted, the carbon canister is located on the right-hand side of the engine compartment, underneath the coolant expansion tank.
2 Disconnect the battery negative lead.
3 Pull the plastic pipe from the canister (the connector is a push-fit in the canister) (see illustration).
4 Unscrew the securing bolt, and lift the canister from its location.
5 Refitting is a reversal of removal.

1.6 and 1.8 litre (R6A type) CVH models

6 The carbon canister (where fitted) is located on the right-hand side of the engine compartment.
7 Proceed as detailed in paragraphs 2 to 5 inclusive.

34 Carbon canister-purge solenoid (models with catalytic converter) - removal and refitting

2.0 litre DOHC models

1 The purge solenoid is located next to the carbon canister, on the right-hand side of the engine compartment.
2 Disconnect the battery negative lead.
3 Disconnect the solenoid wiring plug halves by releasing the locktabs and pulling on the plug halves, not the wiring.

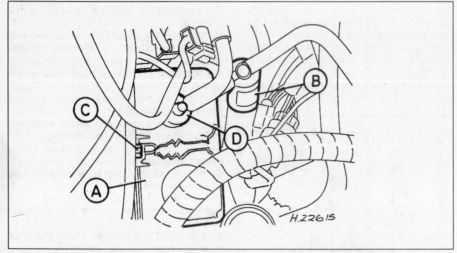

33.3 Carbon canister and purge solenoid locations - DOHC

A Carbon canister
B Purge solenoid

C Canister retaining bolt
D Pipe

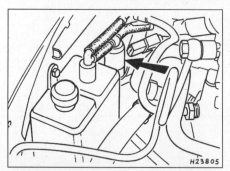

34.7 Carbon canister-purge solenoid location (arrowed) - 1.6/1.8 litre (R6A) CVH

4 Note the locations of the two solenoid pipes, and the orientation of the solenoid, to assist with refitting.
5 Disconnect the two pipes from the solenoid, and withdraw the solenoid from its location.
6 Refitting is a reversal of removal. Ensure that the solenoid pipes are correctly reconnected, and that the solenoid is correctly orientated, as noted before removal.

1.6 and 1.8 litre (R6A type) CVH models

7 On 1.6 litre engines, the purge solenoid is located to the rear of the carbon canister, on the right-hand side of the engine compartment. On 1.8 litre engines, the location varies according to model and equipment, but can be traced by following the solenoid pipes back from the carbon canister **(see illustration).**
8 Proceed as detailed in paragraphs 2 to 6 inclusive.

35 Exhaust gas oxygen (HEGO) sensor (2.0 litre DOHC/1.6 & 1.8 litre (R6A type) CVH) - removal and refitting

Note: *Do not touch the tip of the HEGO sensor as this will drastically shorten its service life.*
Note: *A new sealing ring should be used on refitting.*

Removal

1 Ensure that the engine and the exhaust system are cold.
2 Disconnect the battery negative lead.
3 Apply the handbrake, then jack up the front of the vehicle, and support it securely on axle stands (see "*Jacking and Vehicle Support*").
4 Disconnect the sensor wiring plug halves by releasing the locktabs and pulling on the plug halves, not the wiring.
5 Where fitted, slide the heat shield from the sensor **(see illustration).**
6 Unscrew the sensor from the exhaust downpipe, and recover the sealing ring. Do not touch the tip of the sensor if it is to be refitted.

Refitting

7 Commence refitting by ensuring that the sensor threads and the corresponding threads in the downpipe are clean.
8 Refit the sensor using a new sealing ring, and tighten it to the specified torque.
9 Further refitting is a reversal of removal, but on completion start the engine, and check for leaks around the sensor sealing ring.

36 Exhaust manifold - removal and refitting

2.0 litre SOHC models

1 Refer to Chapter 4 Part A, Section 26, but note the following points.
2 Ignore the references to removal and refitting of the air cleaner and hot air pick-up pipe, and note that a heat shield is fitted in place of the hot air shroud.
3 Note the location of the inlet manifold bracing strut which is secured to one of the manifold studs by an extra nut.

2.0 litre DOHC models

Note: *A new manifold gasket must be used on refitting.*
4 Disconnect the battery negative lead.
5 Disconnect the wiring plug from the idle speed control valve at the front of the plenum chamber.
6 Loosen the clamp, and detach the air inlet hose from the air inlet tubing.
7 Unscrew the securing nut, and release the air inlet tube from the bracket on the engine compartment front panel.
8 Release the air cleaner lid securing clips, then lift away the air inlet tube, plenum chamber and air cleaner lid as an assembly disconnecting the breather hose from the air inlet tube.
9 On models with a catalytic converter, disconnect the exhaust gas oxygen sensor wiring plug.
10 Unscrew the securing nuts, and disconnect the exhaust downpipe from the manifold. Recover the gasket. Support the exhaust downpipe from underneath the vehicle (eg with an axle stand) to avoid placing unnecessary strain on the exhaust system.
11 Unscrew the six securing nuts, and lift the manifold from the cylinder head. Recover the gasket.
12 Refitting is a reversal of removal, bearing in mind the following points.
13 Ensure that all mating faces are clean, and use a new gasket.
14 Tighten the manifold securing nuts and the downpipe securing nuts progressively to the specified torque (where given).

1.6 and 1.8 litre (R6A type) CVH models

Note. *A new manifold gasket and downpipe gaskets must be used on refitting.*
15 Disconnect the battery negative lead.

35.5 Sliding the heat shield from the exhaust gas oxygen sensor

16 Remove the air cleaner and, where fitted, pull the hot-air pick-up pipe from the exhaust manifold hot-air shroud.
17 On 1.6 litre engines, remove the pulse-air delivery tubing.
18 Remove the securing bolts, and withdraw the hot-air shroud from the manifold.
19 Disconnect the exhaust gas oxygen sensor wiring plug. Unscrew the securing nuts, and disconnect the exhaust downpipe from the manifold. Recover the gasket. Support the exhaust downpipe from underneath the vehicle (eg with an axle stand) to avoid placing unnecessary strain on the exhaust system.
20 Unscrew the securing nuts, and lift the manifold from the cylinder head. Recover the gasket.
21 Refitting is a reversal of removal, bearing in mind the following points.
22 Ensure that all mating faces are clean, and renew all gaskets.
23 Tighten the manifold securing nuts progressively to the specified torque, and similarly tighten the exhaust downpipe securing nuts.

37 Exhaust system - inspection, removal and refitting

1 Refer to Chapter 4 Part A, Section 27.
2 On all models except 2.0 litre SOHC, flanged joints incorporating gaskets may be used to join exhaust sections on certain models. Where applicable, renew the gaskets on refitting.
3 On models fitted with a catalytic converter, disconnect the battery negative lead and disconnect the exhaust gas oxygen (HEGO) sensor wiring plug before removing the downpipe.

4B

Notes

Chapter 5
Engine electrical systems

Contents

Degrees of difficulty

Easy, suitable for novice with little experience	Fairly easy, suitable for beginner with some experience	Fairly difficult, suitable for competent DIY mechanic	Difficult, suitable for experienced DIY mechanic	Very difficult, suitable for expert DIY or professional

Specifications

System type

1.3 litre models	Bosch inductive discharge system
1.6 litre models (except Economy)	Bosch inductive discharge system
1.6 litre Economy models	ESC system with Lucas "Hall effect" distributor
1.6 litre CVH (R6A type)	Distributorless controlled by EEC IV system
1.8 litre SOHC models	ESC II system with Bosch "Hall effect" distributor
1.8 litre CVH models	ESC Hybrid system
1.8 litre CVH (R6A type)	Distributorless controlled by EEC IV system
2.0 litre SOHC carburettor models up to 1985	Bosch inductive discharge system
2.0 litre SOHC carburettor models from 1985 (except P100)	ESC II system with Bosch "Hall effect" distributor
2.0 litre DOHC carburettor models	ESC II system
P100 models	Bosch inductive discharge system
2.0 litre SOHC fuel injection models up to 1987	EEC IV system with Motorcraft "Hall effect" distributor
2.0 litre SOHC fuel injection models from 1987	EEC IV system with Bosch "Hall effect" distributor
2.0 litre DOHC fuel injection models	EEC IV system

Coil

All models except CVH (R6A type) and 2.0 litre DOHC

Output (minimum)	25.0 kilovolts
Primary winding resistance	0.72 to 0.88 ohm
Secondary winding resistance	4500 to 7000 ohms

1.6 and 1.8 litre CVH (R6A type)

Output (minimum)	37.0 kilovolts
Primary winding resistance	0.50 ± 0.05 ohms

2.0 litre DOHC carburettor model

Output (minimum)	25.0 kilovolts
Primary winding resistance	0.72 to 0.88 ohms
Secondary winding resistance	4500 to 8600 ohms

2.0 litre DOHC fuel injection model

Output (minimum)	30.0 kilovolts
Primary winding resistance	0.72 to 0.88 ohms
Secondary resistance	4500 to 8600 ohms

Distributor

Direction of rotor arm rotation	Clockwise
Firing order	1- 3 - 4 - 2 (No 1 cylinder nearest timing cover)
Dwell angle	Automatically controlled by electronic module (not adjustable)

Ignition timing

(at idle with vacuum pipe disconnected)	Leaded petrol (4-star, 97 RON)	Unleaded petrol (Premium, 95 RON)
Early "Economy" models (800 rpm - vacuum pipe connected)	16° BTDC	12° BTDC
1.3 litre models	12° BTDC	8° BTDC*
1.6 litre models with VV carburettor	12° BTDC	8° BTDC*
1.6 litre models with 2V carburettor	10° BTDC	6° BTDC†
1.8 litre SOHC models	10° BTDC	6° BTDC†
1.8 litre CVH models	ESC Hybrid controlled, no adjustment possible	
2.0 litre carburettor models up to 1985	8° BTDC	4° BTDC*
2.0 litre carburettor models from 1985 (except P100)	10° BTDC	6° BTDC†
P100 models	6° BTDC	2° BTDC†
2.0 litre fuel injection models	12° BTDC	8° BTDC†

*Fill with leaded petrol (4-star, 97 RON) every 4th tankful
†Not all vehicles are suitable for continuous operation on unleaded petrol.

Spark plugs

Make and type:

All models except 1.8 CVH, CVH (R6A), 2.0 DOHC and P100	Champion RF7YCC or RF7YC
1.8 CVH engine	Champion RC7YCC or RC7YC
P100 model	Champion RF7YC or F7YC
1.6 and 1.8 CVH (R6A type) and 2.0 DOHC	Champion RC7YCC

Electrode gap:

Champion F7YCC or RC7YCC	0.8 mm (0.032 in)
Champion RF7YC, F7YC or RC7YC	0.7 mm (0.028 in)

Note: *The electrode gap above is the figure quoted by Champion for use with their recommended spark plugs. If plugs of any other type are fitted, refer to their manufacturer's gap recommendations.*

HT leads

All SOHC models	Champion LS-09 or LS-10 boxed set
1.8 CVH	Champion LS-10 boxed set
1.6 and 1.8 CVH (R6A type)	Champion LS-30 boxed set
2.0 DOHC	Champion LS-29 boxed set
Maximum resistance per lead	30 000 ohms

Alternator

Type	Bosch, Lucas, Motorola, or Mitsubishi
Regulated output voltage at 4000 rpm (3 to 7 amp load)	13.7 to 14.6 volts
Minimum brush length:	
All alternator types except Motorola	5.0 mm (0.20 in)
Motorola type alternators	4.0 mm (0.16 in)

Starter motor

Type	Pre-engaged; Bosch, Cajavec, Lucas, or Nippondenso
Minimum brush length:	
All except Bosch long frame 1.1 kW and JF, and Nippondenso	8.0 mm (0.32 in)
Bosch long frame 1.1 kW and JF, Nippondenso starter motors	10.0 mm (0.40 in)

Battery charge condition:

Poor	12.5 volts
Normal	12.6 volts
Good	12.7 volts

Torque wrench settings

	Nm	lbf ft
Spark plugs:		
SOHC models	20 to 28	15 to 21
CVH models	18 to 33	13 to 24
DOHC models	15 to 21	11 to 15
Crankshaft speed/position sensor clamp bolt (ESC Hybrid system) ...	4 to 7	3 to 5
Crankshaft speed/position sensor screw (DOHC)	3 to 5	2 to 4
Camshaft sprocket bolt (CVH models)	95 to 115	70 to 85
Air charge temperature sensor (CVH-R6A and DOHC)	20 to 25	15 to 18
Engine coolant temperature sensor (CVH-R6A and DOHC)	20 to 25	15 to 18
Fuel temperature sensor (DOHC injection)	8 to 11	6 to 8
Alternator adjustment bolt	21 to 28	15 to 20
Alternator mounting bolts:		
With coloured patch on threads	41 to 51	30 to 38
Without coloured patch	20 to 25	15 to 18

1 General information and precautions

General information

The electrical system is of the 12 volt negative earth type, and consists of a 12 volt battery, alternator with integral voltage regulator, starter motor and related electrical accessories, components and wiring. The battery is of the low maintenance or maintenance-free "sealed for life" type and is charged by an alternator which is belt-driven from the crankshaft pulley. The starter motor is of the pre-engaged type, incorporating an integral solenoid. On starting the solenoid moves the drive pinion into engagement with the flywheel ring gear before the starter motor is energised. Once the engine has started, a one-way clutch prevents the motor armature being driven by the engine until the pinion disengages from the flywheel.

The ignition system is responsible for igniting the air/fuel mixture in each cylinder at the correct moment in relation to engine speed and load. A number of different ignition systems are fitted to models within the Sierra/P100 range, ranging from a basic breakerless electronic system to a fully integrated engine management system controlling ignition and fuel injection systems.

The ignition system is based on feeding low tension voltage from the battery to the coil where it is converted to high tension voltage. The high tension voltage is powerful enough to jump the spark plug gap in the cylinders many times a second under high compression pressures, providing that the system is in good condition. The low tension (or primary) circuit consists of the battery, the lead to the ignition switch, the lead from the ignition switch to the low tension coil windings (terminal + /15) and also to the supply terminal on the electronic module, and the lead from the low tension coil windings (terminal - /1) to the control terminal on the electronic module. The high tension (or secondary) circuit consists of the high tension coil windings, the HT (high tension) lead from the coil to the distributor cap, the rotor arm, the HT leads to the spark plugs, and the spark plugs.

The system functions in the following manner. Current flowing through the low tension coil windings produces a magnetic field around the high tension windings. As the engine rotates, a sensor produces an electrical impulse which is amplified in the electronic module and used to switch off the low tension circuit.

The subsequent collapse of the magnetic field over the high tension windings produces high tension voltage which is then fed to the relevant spark plug via the distributor cap and rotor arm. The low tension circuit is automatically switched on again by the electronic module, to allow the magnetic field to build up again before the firing of the next spark plug. The ignition is advanced and retarded automatically to ensure that the spark occurs at the correct instant in relation to the engine speed and load.

To improve driveability during warm-up conditions and to reduce exhaust emission levels, a vacuum-operated, temperature-sensitive spark control system is fitted to certain vehicles.

Inductive discharge system

This is the least sophisticated system fitted to the Sierra/P100 range, and comprises a breakerless distributor and an electronic switching/amplifier module in addition to the coil and spark plugs.

The electrical impulse which is required to switch off the low tension circuit is generated by a magnetic trigger coil in the distributor. A trigger wheel rotates within a magnetic stator, the magnetic field being provided by a permanent magnet. The magnetic field across the two poles (stator arm and trigger wheel) is dependent on the air gap between the two poles. When the air gap is at its minimum, the trigger wheel arm is directly opposite the stator arm, and this is the trigger point. As the magnetic flux between the stator arm and trigger wheel varies, a voltage is induced in the trigger coil mounted below the trigger wheel, and this voltage is sensed and then amplified by the electronic module and used to switch off the low tension circuit. There is one trigger wheel arm and one stator arm for each cylinder (4).

The ignition advance is a function of the distributor and is controlled both mechanically and by a vacuum operated system. The mechanical governor mechanism consists of two weights which move out from the distributor shaft as the engine speed rises due to centrifugal force. As they move outwards, they rotate the trigger wheel relative to the distributor shaft and so advance the spark. The weights are held in position by two light springs and it is the tension of the springs which is largely responsible for correct spark advancement.

The vacuum control consists of a diaphragm, one side of which is connected via a small bore hose to the carburettor or inlet manifold and the other side to the distributor. Depression in the inlet manifold and/or carburettor, which varies with engine speed and throttle position, causes the diaphragm to move, so moving the baseplate and advancing or retarding the spark. A fine degree of control is achieved by a spring in the diaphragm assembly.

ESC (Electronic Spark Control) system

This system is only fitted to early "Economy" models, and comprises a "Hall effect" distributor, and an ESC module, in addition to the coil and spark plugs.

The electrical impulse which is required to switch off the low tension circuit is generated by a sensor in the distributor. A trigger vane rotates in the gap between a permanent magnet and the sensor. The trigger vane has four cut-outs, one for each cylinder. When one of the trigger vane cut-outs is in line with the sensor, magnetic flux can pass between the magnet and the sensor. When a trigger vane segment is in line with the sensor, the magnetic flux is diverted through the trigger vane away from the sensor. The sensor senses the change in magnetic flux and sends an impulse to the ESC module, which switches off the low tension circuit.

The ignition advance is a function of the ESC module and is controlled by vacuum. The module is connected to the inlet manifold by a vacuum pipe, and a transducer in the module translates the vacuum signal into electrical voltage. From the vacuum signal, the ESC module determines engine load, and engine speed is determined from the interval between impulses supplied by the distributor sensor. The module has a range of spark advance settings stored in its memory, and a suitable setting is selected for the relevant engine speed and load. The degree of advance can thus be constantly varied to suit the prevailing engine speed and load conditions.

ESC II (Electronic Spark Control II) system

1.8 and 2.0 litre SOHC carburettor models

This system is a development of the ESC system described previously in this Section, but it enables more accurate control of engine operation due to the inclusion of additional monitoring features and control outputs.

Vehicles fitted with the ESC II system have an electric inlet manifold heater which warms the air/fuel mixture when the engine is cold, thus reducing the amount of fuel enrichment required, lowering fuel consumption and improving driveability when the engine is cold. The heater is operated by the ESC II module receiving information on the engine temperature from an engine coolant temperature sensor mounted in the inlet manifold.

On 2.0 litre SOHC models, the ESC II module operates a carburettor stepper motor to control the engine idle speed. Using information on engine speed, load, temperature and throttle position (supplied by a switch on the carburettor), the module operates the stepper motor to maintain a constant idle speed. On models equipped with automatic transmission and/or air conditioning, additional inputs are supplied to the module to allow it to operate the stepper motor to compensate for the additional engine load imposed by the automatic transmission/air conditioning. The ESC II module also operates a "power hold" relay which allows the stepper motor to function briefly after the ignition has been switched off in order to perform an anti-run-on and manifold ventilation cycle.

2.0 litre DOHC carburettor models

A development of the ESC II system is used to control the operation of the engine. The module receives information from a crankshaft speed/position sensor (similar to that described for the ESC Hybrid system), except that the sensor is activated by a toothed disc on the rear of the crankshaft, inside the cylinder block), and an engine coolant temperature sensor.

5

The ignition advance is a function of the ESC II module, and is controlled by vacuum. The module is connected to the carburettor by a vacuum pipe, and a transducer in the module translates the vacuum signal into an electrical voltage. From the vacuum signal, the module determines engine load; engine speed and temperature are determined from the crankshaft speed/position sensor and the engine coolant temperature sensor. The module has a range of spark advance settings stored in its memory, and a suitable setting is selected for the relevant engine speed, load and temperature. The degree of advance can thus be constantly varied to suit the prevailing engine speed and load conditions.

ESC Hybrid (Electronic Spark Control Hybrid) system

This system is fitted to 1.8 CVH models, and comprises various sensors and an ESC Hybrid module, in addition to the coil and spark plugs. The distributor serves purely to distribute the HT voltage to the spark plugs and consists simply of a rotor arm mounted directly on the end of the camshaft, and a distributor cap.

The electrical impulse which is required to switch off the low tension circuit is generated by a crankshaft speed/position sensor which is activated by a toothed wheel on the crankshaft. The toothed wheel has 35 equally spaced teeth with a gap in the 36th position. The gap is used by the sensor to determine the crankshaft position relative to TDC (top dead centre) of No 1 piston.

Engine load information is supplied to the ESC Hybrid module by a vacuum transducer within the module which is connected to the inlet manifold by a vacuum pipe. Additional inputs are supplied by an inlet manifold-mounted engine coolant temperature sensor, and an air charge temperature sensor mounted in the base of the air cleaner. The module selects the optimum ignition advance setting based on the information received from the various sensors. The degree of advance can thus be constantly varied to suit the prevailing engine conditions.

In addition to the ignition circuit, the module also controls an electric choke heater, and a solenoid valve which in turn controls a throttle damper on the carburettor. The electric choke heater is operated by the module using information supplied by the engine coolant temperature sensor. The heater is used to slow down the rate at which the choke comes off, thereby improving driveability and overall fuel consumption when the engine is cold. The solenoid valve controls the vacuum supply to the carburettor throttle damper. The throttle damper prevents sudden closing of the throttle during deceleration, thus maintaining combustion of the air/fuel mixture which reduces harmful exhaust gas emissions.

Note that there is no provision for adjustment of ignition timing with the ESC Hybrid system.

EEC IV (Electronic Engine Control IV) system

2.0 litre SOHC fuel injection models

This system controls both the ignition and fuel injection systems. The EEC IV module receives information from a "Hall effect" distributor sensor (similar to that described previously in this Section for the ESC system), an engine coolant temperature sensor mounted in the inlet manifold, a throttle position sensor, and an air flow meter.

Additionally, on models equipped with automatic transmission and/or air conditioning, additional inputs are supplied to the module to allow it to raise the idle speed to compensate for the additional engine load imposed by the automatic transmission/air conditioning. The module provides outputs to control the fuel pump, fuel injectors, idle speed, and ignition circuit. Using the inputs from the various sensors, the EEC IV module computes the optimum ignition advance, and fuel injector pulse duration to suit the prevailing engine conditions. This system gives very accurate control of the engine under all conditions, improving fuel consumption and driveability, and reducing exhaust gas emissions. A "limited operation strategy" (LOS) means that the vehicle is still driveable, albeit at reduced power and efficiency, in the event of a failure in the module or its sensors.

2.0 litre DOHC fuel injection models

A development of the EEC IV system is used to control both the ignition and fuel injection systems. The module receives information from a crankshaft speed/position sensor (similar to that described for the ESC Hybrid system), except that the sensor is activated by a toothed disc on the rear of the crankshaft, inside the cylinder block), a throttle position sensor, an engine coolant temperature sensor, a fuel temperature sensor, an air charge temperature sensor, a manifold absolute pressure (MAP) sensor, and a vehicle speed sensor (mounted on the gearbox). Additionally, on models with a catalytic converter, an additional input is supplied to the EEC IV module from an exhaust gas oxygen (HEGO) sensor. On models with automatic transmission, additional sensors are fitted to the transmission, to inform the EEC IV module when the transmission is in neutral, and when the kickdown is being operated.

The module provides outputs to control the fuel pump, fuel injectors, idle speed, ignition system and automatic transmission. Additionally, on models with air conditioning, the EEC IV module disengages the air conditioning compressor clutch when starting the engine, and when the engine is suddenly accelerated. On models fitted with a catalytic converter, the EEC IV module also controls the carbon canister-purge solenoid valve.

Using the inputs from the various sensors, the EEC IV module computes the optimum ignition advance, and fuel injector pulse duration to suit the prevailing engine conditions. A "limited operation strategy" (LOS)

means that the vehicle is still driveable, albeit at reduced power and efficiency, in the event of a failure in the module or one of its sensors.

1.6 litre and 1.8 litre (R6A type) CVH models

A development of the EEC IV system is used to control both the ignition and fuel injection systems. A fully electronic Distributorless Ignition System (DIS) is fitted, replacing the mechanical distribution of high tension voltage (by a rotating distributor) with "static" solid-state electronic components.

The system selects the most appropriate ignition advance setting for the prevailing engine operating conditions from a three-dimensional map of values stored in the EEC IV control module memory. The module selects the appropriate advance value according to information supplied on engine load, speed, and operating temperature from various sensors.

The EEC IV module receives information from a crankshaft speed/position sensor (similar to that described for the ESC Hybrid system), except that on 1.6 litre engines, the sensor is activated by a toothed disc on the flywheel), a throttle position sensor, an engine coolant temperature sensor, an air charge temperature sensor, a manifold absolute pressure (MAP) sensor, a vehicle speed sensor (mounted on the gearbox), and an exhaust gas oxygen sensor.

The module provides outputs to control the fuel pump, fuel injector, throttle valve control motor, pulse-air control solenoid, carbon canister purge solenoid (where applicable), and the ignition system.

Using the inputs from the various sensors, the EEC IV module computes the optimum ignition advance and fuel injector pulse duration to suit the prevailing engine conditions. A "limited operation strategy" (LOS) means that the vehicle will still be driveable, albeit at reduced power and efficiency, in the event of a failure in the module or one of its sensors.

Precautions

General

It is necessary to take extra care when working on the electrical system to avoid damage to semi-conductor devices (diodes and transistors), and to avoid the risk of personal injury. In addition to the precautions given in the "Safety first!" Section at the beginning of this manual, take note of the following points when working on the system.

Always remove rings, watches, etc before working on the electrical system. Even with the battery disconnected, capacitive discharge could occur if a component live terminal is earthed through a metal object. This could cause a shock or nasty burn.

Do not reverse the battery connections. Components such as the alternator or any other having semi-conductor circuitry could be irreparably damaged.

If the engine is being started using jump leads and a slave battery, connect the batteries positive to positive and negative to negative. This also applies when connecting a battery charger.

Never disconnect the battery terminals, or alternator multi-plug connector, when the engine is running.

The battery leads and alternator multi-plug must be disconnected before carrying out any electric welding on the car.

Never use an ohmmeter of the type incorporating a hand cranked generator for circuit or continuity testing.

Ignition and engine management systems

 Warning: The HT voltage generated by an electronic ignition system is extremely high, and in certain circumstances could prove fatal. Take care to avoid receiving electric shocks from the HT side of the ignition system. Do not handle HT leads, or touch the distributor or coil when the engine is running. If tracing faults in the HT circuit, use well insulated tools to manipulate live leads.

Engine management modules are very sensitive components, and certain precautions must be taken to avoid damage to the module when working on a vehicle equipped with an engine management system as follows.

When carrying out welding operations on the vehicle using electric welding equipment, the battery and alternator should be disconnected.

Although underbonnet-mounted modules (all except EEC IV) will tolerate normal underbonnet conditions, they can be adversely affected by excess heat or moisture. If using welding equipment or pressure washing equipment in the vicinity of the module, take care not to direct heat, or jets of water or steam at the module. If this cannot be avoided, remove the module from the vehicle, and protect its wiring plug with a plastic bag.

Before disconnecting any wiring, or removing components, always ensure that the ignition is switched off.

On models with underbonnet-mounted modules, do not run the engine with the module detached from the body panel, as the body acts as an effective heat sink, and the module may be damaged due to internal overheating.

Do not attempt to improvise fault diagnosis procedures using a test lamp or multimeter, as irreparable damage could be caused to the module.

After working on ignition/engine management system components, ensure that all wiring is correctly reconnected before reconnecting the battery or switching on the ignition.

On some early Bosch distributors it is possible that with the distributor cap removed, if the engine is cranked, the cap securing clips may fall inward and jam the trigger wheel/vane, knocking it out of alignment. If this happens, the distributor will have to be renewed as the trigger wheel/vane cannot be repositioned. Care should therefore be taken not to crank the engine with the distributor cap removed. Later distributors have redesigned clips which eliminate the problem.

2 Battery - removal and refitting

Removal

1 The battery is located in the engine compartment on the left-hand side of the bulkhead.

2 Disconnect the leads at the negative (earth) terminal by unscrewing the retaining nut and removing the bulb. Pull off the plastic cover, and disconnect the positive terminal leads in the same way.

3 Unscrew the clamp bolt sufficiently to enable the battery to be lifted from its location **(see illustration)**. Keep the battery in an upright position to avoid spilling electrolyte on the bodywork.

Refitting

4 Refitting is a reversal of removal, but smear petroleum jelly on the terminals when reconnecting the leads, and always connect the positive lead first and the negative lead last.

3 Battery - testing and charging

Testing

Standard and low maintenance battery

1 If the vehicle covers a small annual mileage it is worthwhile checking the specific gravity of the electrolyte every three months to determine the state of charge of the battery. Use a hydrometer to make the check and compare the results with the following table.

Ambient temperature:

	above 25°C	below 25°C
Fully charged	1.21 to 1.23	1.27 to 1.29
70% charged	1.17 to 1.19	1.23 to 1.25
Fully discharged	1.05 to 1.07	1.11 to 1.13

Note that the specific gravity readings assume an electrolyte temperature of 15°C (60°F); for every 10°C (50°F) below 15°C (60°F) subtract 0.007. For every 10°C(50°F) above 15°C(60°F) add 0.007.

2 If the battery condition is suspect first check the specific gravity of electrolyte in each cell. A variation of 0.040 or more between any cells indicates loss of electrolyte or deterioration of the internal plates.

3 If the specific gravity variation is 0.040 or more, the battery should be renewed. If the cell variation is satisfactory but the battery is discharged, it should be charged as described later in this Section.

Maintenance-free battery

4 In cases where a "sealed-for-life" maintenance-free battery is fitted, topping-up and testing of the electrolyte in each cell is not possible. The condition of the battery can therefore only be tested using a battery condition indicator or a voltmeter.

5 If testing the battery using a voltmeter, connect the voltmeter across the battery and compare the result with those given in the

Specifications under "charge condition". The test is only accurate if the battery has not been subject to any kind of charge for the previous six hours. If this is not the case, switch on the headlights for 30 seconds, then wait four to five minutes before testing the battery after switching off the headlights. All other electrical components must be switched off, so check that the doors and tailgate are fully shut when making the test.

6 If the voltage reading is less than 12.2 volts, then the battery is discharged, whilst a reading of 12.2 to 12.4 volts indicates a partially discharged condition.

7 If the battery is to be charged, first remove it from the vehicle.

Charging

Standard and low maintenance battery

8 Charge the battery at a rate of 3.5 to 4 amps and continue to charge the battery at this rate until no further rise in specific gravity is noted over a four hour period.

9 Alternatively, a trickle charger charging at the rate of 1.5 amps can be safely used overnight.

10 Specially rapid "boost" charges which are claimed to restore the power of the battery in 1 to 2 hours are not recommended as they can cause serious damage to the battery plates through overheating.

11 While charging the battery, note that the temperature of the electrolyte should never exceed 37.8°C (100°F).

Maintenance-free battery

12 This battery type takes considerably longer to fully recharge than the standard type, the time taken being dependent on the extent of discharge, but it can take anything up to three days.

13 A constant voltage type charger is required, to be set, when connected, to 13.9 to 14.9 volts with a charger current below 25 amps. Using this method the battery should be useable within three hours, giving a voltage reading of 12.5 volts, but this is for a partially discharged battery and, as mentioned, full charging can take considerably longer.

14 If the battery is to be charged from a fully discharged state (condition reading less than 12.2 volts) have it recharged by your Ford dealer or local automotive electrician as the charge rate is higher and constant supervision during charging is necessary.

2.3 Battery securing clamp and bolt

4.2a Disconnecting the multi-plug from a Bosch alternator

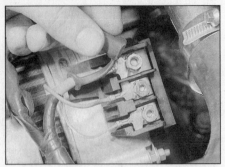

4.2b Removing the insulating cap from the main wiring terminal on a Lucas A127 alternator (CVH model)

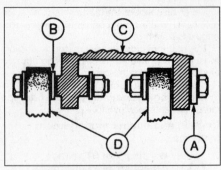

4.7 Alternator mounting bracket arrangement
A Large flat washer
B Small flat washer (models up to 1985 only)
C Mounting bracket (engine)
D Mounting lugs (alternator)

4 Alternator - removal and refitting

Removal

1 Disconnect the battery leads.
2 Disconnect the multi-plug, or disconnect the wires from their terminals on the rear of the alternator, noting their locations (as applicable), then slacken the mounting and adjustment bolts and tilt the alternator towards the engine **(see illustrations)**.
3 Remove the drivebelt(s) from the alternator pulley(s).
4 Remove the mounting and adjustment nuts and bolts, and withdraw the alternator from the engine.

Refitting

5 Refitting is a reversal of removal, noting the following points.
6 To avoid breakage of the alternator mounting bracket lugs, it is important that the following procedure is adhered to when refitting the mounting bolts.
7 Always refit the large flat washer (A) **(see illustration)**.
8 Earlier models (before 1985) also have a small washer (B) which must be fitted between the sliding bush and the mounting bracket.
9 Ensure that the bushes and bolts are assembled as shown - except on 2.0 litre DOHC models where a through-bolt is used, then tension the drivebelt(s) and tighten the mounting and adjustment bolts as shown in the relevant illustration in Chapter 3.

5 Alternator drivebelt(s) - checking, renewal and tensioning

Refer to Chapter 1, Section 21.

6 Alternator - testing

Note: *To carry out the complete test procedure use only the following test equipment - a 0 to 20 volt moving coil voltmeter, a 0 to 100 amp moving coil ammeter, and a rheostat rated at 30 amps.*
1 Check that the battery is at least 70% charged by using a hydrometer.
2 Check the drivebelt tension.
3 Check the security of the battery leads, alternator multi-plug, and interconnecting wire.

Cable continuity check

4 Pull the multi-plug from the alternator and switch on the ignition, being careful not to crank the engine. Connect the voltmeter between a good earth and each of the terminals in the multi-plug in turn. If battery voltage is not indicated, there is an open circuit in the wiring which may be due to a blown ignition warning light bulb if on the small terminal.

Alternator output check

5 Connect the voltmeter, ammeter and rheostat as shown **(see illustration)**. Run the engine at 3000 rpm and switch on the headlamps, heater blower and, where fitted, the heated rear window. Vary the resistance

to increase the current and check that the alternator rated output is reached without the voltage dropping below 13 volts.

Charging circuit positive side check

6 Connect the voltmeter as shown **(see illustration)**. Start the engine and switch on the headlamps. Run the engine at 3000 rpm and check that the indicated voltage drop does not exceed 0.5 volt. A higher reading indicates a high resistance such as a dirty connection on the positive side of the charging circuit.

Charging circuit negative side check

7 Connect the voltmeter as shown **(see illustration)**. Start the engine and switch on the headlamps. Run the engine at 3000 rpm and check that the indicated voltage drop does not exceed 0.25 volt. A higher reading indicates a high resistance such as a dirty connection on the negative side of the charging circuit.

Voltage regulator check

8 Connect the voltmeter and ammeter as shown **(see illustration)**. Run the engine at 3000 rpm and when the ammeter records a current of 3 to 5 amps check that the voltmeter records 13.7 to 14.15 volts. If the result is outside the limits the regulator is faulty.

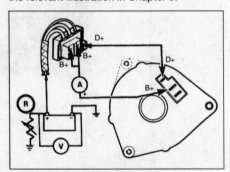

6.5 Alternator output test circuit

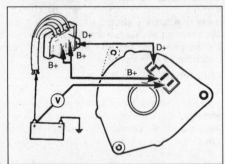

6.6 Alternator positive check circuit

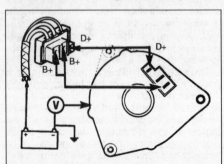

6.7 Alternator negative check circuit

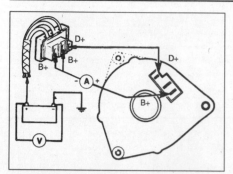

6.8 Alternator voltage regulator test circuit

7 Alternator brushes - removal, inspection and refitting

1 Remove the alternator.

Bosch type

2 Remove the two securing screws and withdraw the regulator/brush box assembly from the rear of the alternator (see illustration).

3 If the length of either brush is less than the minimum given in the Specifications, unsolder the wiring and remove the brushes and the springs (see illustration).

4 Wipe the slip rings clean with a fuel-moistened cloth. If the rings are very dirty use fine glasspaper to clean them, then wipe with the cloth (see illustration).

7.4 Inspect the condition of the slip rings (arrowed) - Bosch alternator

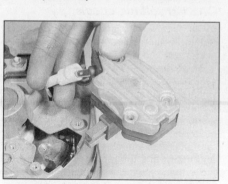

7.14 Disconnect the wiring plug and withdraw the regulator/brushbox - Lucas A127 alternator

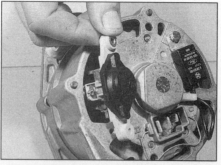

7.2 Withdrawing the regulator/brush box from a Bosch alternator

5 Refitting is a reversal of removal, but make sure that the brushes move freely in their holders.

Lucas A 115 and A 133 type

6 Disconnect the wiring plug, then remove the securing screw and withdraw the interference suppression capacitor from the rear cover.

7 Extract the two securing screws and remove the alternator rear cover.

8 Make a careful note of the fitted positions of the regulator wires, then disconnect the wires from the diode pack and the brush box.

9 Remove the regulator securing screws and withdraw the regulator. Note that the regulator securing screw also holds one of the brush mounting plates in position.

10 Remove the two securing screws and withdraw the brush box. Remove the securing

7.13 Removing the terminal cover from a Lucas A127 alternator.

7.15 Compare the brush length with the figure given in the Specifications - Lucas A127 alternator

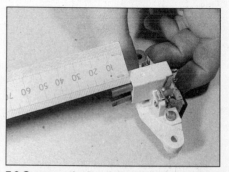

7.3 Compare the brush length with the figure in the Specifications - Bosch alternator

screws and lift the brushes from the brush box.

11 If the length of either brush is less than the minimum given in the Specifications, renew both brushes.

12 Proceed as shown in paragraphs 4 and 5.

Lucas A 127 type

13 Where applicable, for improved access remove the terminal cover from the rear of the alternator, then remove the three screws securing the regulator/brush box assembly to the rear of the alternator (see illustration).

14 Tip the outside edge of the assembly upwards, and withdraw it from its location. Disconnect the wiring plug and withdraw the assembly from the alternator (see illustration).

15 If the length of either brush is less than the minimum given in the Specifications, the complete regulator/brush box assembly must be renewed (see illustration).

16 Proceed as described in paragraphs 4 and 5 (see illustration).

Motorola type

17 Remove the two securing screws and withdraw the regulator. Disconnect the regulator wires after noting their locations.

18 Remove the single securing screw (35 and 45 amp types) or two securing screws (55 and 70 amp types) and carefully withdraw the brush box.

19 If the length of either brush is less than the minimum given in the Specifications, the brush box must be renewed.

20 Proceed as shown in paragraphs 4 and 5.

5

7.16 Inspect the condition of the slip rings (arrowed) - Lucas A127 alternator

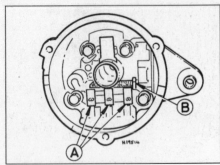

7.28 Stator-to-diode pack connections (A) and brushbox-to-diode pack terminal (B) - Mitsubishi alternator

8.3 Solenoid wiring connections on Lucas M79 starter motor- CVH engine

8.5 Unscrew the starter motor mounting bolts

Mitsubishi type

21 Unscrew the pulley nut. To prevent the shaft rotating, insert an Allen key in the end of the shaft.

22 Remove the spring washer, pulley, fan, spacer and dust shield.

23 Scribe an alignment mark along the length of the alternator to facilitate reassembly of the drive end housing, stator and rear housing.

24 Unscrew the through-bolts and withdraw the drive end housing from the rotor shaft.

25 Remove the seal and spacer from the rotor shaft.

26 Remove the rotor from the rear housing and the stator. This may require the application of local heat to the rear housing using a large soldering iron. Do not use a heat gun, as this may result in damage to the diodes.

27 Unscrew the four securing bolts and withdraw the diode pack stator assembly from the rear housing.

28 Unsolder the stator leads from the diode pack terminals. Use a pair of pliers when unsoldering to act as a heat sink, otherwise damage to the diodes may occur **(see illustration)**.

29 If the length of either brush is less than the minimum given in the Specifications, the brush box must be renewed.

30 To renew the brush box, unsolder the connection to the diode pack, and solder the

connection to the new brush box. Use a pair of pliers as a heat sink to avoid damage to the diodes.

31 Examine the surfaces of the slip rings. Clean them with a fuel moistened cloth, or if necessary fine glasspaper and then the cloth.

32 Solder the stator leads to the diode pack terminals, again using a pair of pliers as a heat sink.

33 Refit the diode pack/stator assembly to the rear housing and tighten the securing bolts.

34 Insert a thin rod (an Allen key is ideal) through the hole in the rear housing to hold the brushes in the retracted position.

35 Fit the rotor to the rear housing and then remove the temporary rod to release the brushes.

36 Reassemble the remaining components by reversing the dismantling operations. Make sure that the scribed marks are in alignment.

8 Starter motor - removal and refitting

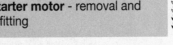

Removal

1 Apply the handbrake, jack up the front of the vehicle and support on axle stands (see "*Jacking and Vehicle Support*").

2 Disconnect the battery negative lead.

3 Working underneath the vehicle, unscrew

the nut and disconnect the main cable from the starter solenoid **(see illustration)**.

4 Disconnect the ignition switch wire from the solenoid.

5 Unscrew the three mounting bolts and withdraw the starter motor from the gearbox bellhousing **(see illustration)**.

Refitting

6 Refitting is a reversal of removal.

9 Starter motor - testing in the vehicle

1 If the starter motor fails to operate first check the condition of the battery.

2 Check the security and condition of all relevant wiring.

Solenoid check

3 Disconnect the battery negative lead and all leads from the solenoid.

4 Connect a 3 watt test lamp and a 12 volt battery between the starter terminal on the solenoid and the solenoid body as shown **(see illustration)**. The testlamp should light. If not, there is an open circuit in the solenoid windings.

5 Now connect an 18 watt testlamp between both solenoid terminals **(see illustration)**, then energise the solenoid with a further lead to the spade terminal. The solenoid should be heard to operate and the testlamp should light. Reconnect the solenoid wires.

On load voltage check

6 Connect a voltmeter across the battery terminals, then disconnect the low tension lead from the coil positive terminal and operate the starter by turning the ignition switch. Note the reading on the voltmeter which should not be less than 10.5 volts.

7 Now connect the voltmeter between the starter motor terminal on the solenoid and the starter motor body. With the coil low tension lead still disconnected operate the starter and check that the recorded voltage is not more than 1 volt lower than that noted in paragraph 6. If the voltage drop is more than 1 volt a fault exists in the wiring from the battery to the starter.

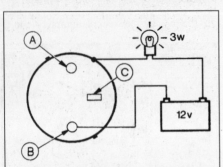

9.4 Starter motor solenoid winding test circuit

A Battery terminal
B Motor terminal
C Spade terminal

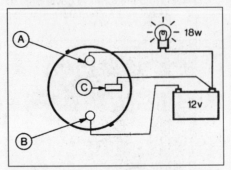

9.5 Starter motor solenoid continuity test circuit

A Battery terminal
B Motor terminal
C Spade terminal

8 Connect the voltmeter between the battery positive terminal and the terminal on the starter motor. With the coil low tension lead disconnected operate the starter for two or three seconds. Battery voltage should be indicated initially, then dropping to less than 1 volt. If the reading is more than 1 volt, there is a high resistance in the wiring from the battery to the starter and the check in paragraph 9 should be made. If the reading is less than 1 volt proceed to paragraph 10.

9 Connect the voltmeter between the two main solenoid terminals and operate the starter for two or three seconds. Battery voltage should be indicated initially, then dropping to less than 0.5 volt. If the reading is more than 0.5 volt, the ignition switch and connections may be faulty.

10 Connect the voltmeter between the battery negative terminal and the starter motor body, and operate the starter for two or three seconds. A reading of less than 0.5 volt should be recorded. If the reading is more than 0.5 volt, there is a fault in the earth circuit, and the earth connections to the battery and body should be checked.

10 Starter motor - brush renewal

Bosch long frame and JF, and Cajavec types

1 With the starter motor removed from the vehicle and cleaned, grip the unit in a vice fitted with soft jaw protectors.
2 Remove the two screws securing the commutator end housing cap, then remove the cap and rubber seal **(see illustration)**.
3 Wipe any grease from the armature shaft, and remove the C-clip, or E-clip, as applicable, and shims from the end of the shaft **(see illustrations)**.
4 Unscrew the two nuts and remove the washers, or remove the securing screws (as applicable), then lift off the commutator end housing **(see illustrations)**.
5 Carefully prise the thrust retaining springs from their locations, then slide the brushes from the brush plate.
6 If the brushes have worn to less than the specified minimum, renew them as a set. To

10.2 Remove the commutator end housing cap securing screws - Bosch long frame starter motor

renew the brushes, cut the leads at their midpoint and make a good soldered joint when connecting the new brushes.
7 The commutator face should be clean and free from burnt spots. Where necessary burnish with fine glass paper (not emery) and wipe with a fuel-moistened cloth.
8 On starter motors where the commutator end housing is secured by nuts and washers, position the brush plate over the end of the armature, with the cut-outs in the brush plate aligned with the end housing securing studs.
9 On starter motors where the commutator end housing is secured by screws, position the brush plate over the end of the armature with the cut-outs in the brush plate aligned with the loops in the field windings **(see illustration)**. The brush plate will be positively located when the commutator end housing screws are fitted.
10 Position the brushes in their respective locations in the brush plate, and fit the brush retaining springs.
11 Guide the commutator end housing into position, at the same time sliding the rubber insulator into the cut-out in the housing. Secure the commutator end housing with the nuts and washers or screws, as applicable.
12 Fit sufficient shims to the end of the armature shaft to eliminate endfloat when the C-clip or E-clip, as applicable is fitted, then fit the clip.
13 Fit the armature shaft bearing seal to the commutator end housing, then apply a little lithium-based grease to the end of the armature shaft and refit the end housing cap, securing with the two screws.

10.3a Remove the C-clip . . .

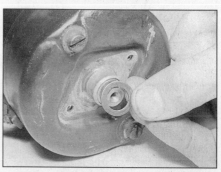

10.3b . . . and shims from the end of the armature shaft - Bosch long frame starter motor

Bosch short frame, EV and EF types

14 To remove and refit the brush assembly, proceed as for the Bosch long frame except for the following **(see illustration):**
15 Release the brush holders complete with brushes by pushing the brush holders towards the commutator and unclipping them from the brush plate. Withdraw the brush plate.
16 To renew the brushes, the leads must be unsoldered from the terminals on the brush plate, and the leads of the new brushes must be soldered to the terminals.
17 To refit the brush assembly, position the brush plate over the end of the armature shaft, then assemble the brush holders, brushes and springs, ensuring that the brush holder clips are securely located. The brush plate will be

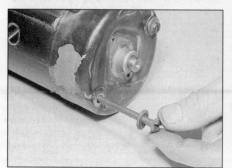

10.4a Remove the commutator end housing securing screws - Bosch long frame starter motor

10.4b Commutator end housing removed to expose brush plate - Bosch long frame starter motor

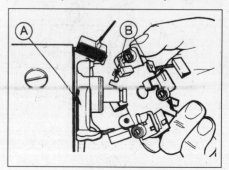

10.9 Align the cut-outs in the brush plate (B) with the loops in the field windings (A) - Bosch long frame starter motor

5

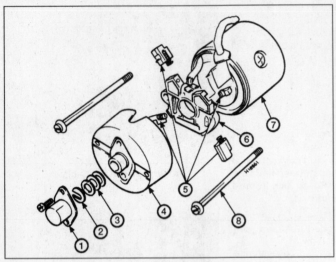

10.14 Bosch EV starter motor brush assembly

1 Commutator end housing cap
2 C-clip
3 Shims
4 Commutator end housing
5 Brushes
6 Brush plate
7 Yoke
8 Commutator end housing screw

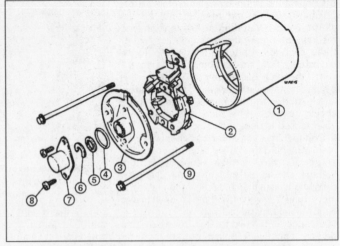

10.18a Bosch DM starter motor brush assembly

1 Yoke
2 Brush plate
3 Commutator end housing
4 Seal
5 Shim
6 C-clip
7 Commutator end housing cap
8 Securing screw
9 Commutator end housing securing screw

positively located when the commutator end housing screws are fitted.

Bosch DM and DW types

18 The procedure is basically as described previously for the Bosch short frame and EF type starter motors, except that a commutator end plate is fitted in place of the end housing **(see illustrations).**

Lucas 5M90 type

Note: *New star clips must be obtained for the armature shaft on reassembly*

19 With the starter motor removed from the vehicle and cleaned, grip the unit in a vice fitted with soft jaw protectors.
20 Remove the plastic cap from the end of the armature shaft, then remove the star clip from the end of the shaft, using a chisel at an angle of 45° to the shaft to distort the prongs

of the clip until it can be removed **(see illustrations).**
21 Unscrew the two securing nuts and remove the connector cable from the main feed terminal **(see illustration).**
22 Extract the two commutator end plate securing screws, and carefully tap the end plate to free it. Lift the end plate clear to allow access to the two field brushes. Disconnect the two field brushes from the brush box to allow complete removal of the commutator end plate. Take care not to damage the gasket as the end plate is removed.
23 Remove the nut, washer and insulator from the main terminal stud on the commutator end plate, then push the stud and the second insulator through the end plate and unhook the brushes.
24 To remove the brush box, drill out the rivets securing the brush box to the end plate, then remove the brush box and gasket.

25 If the brushes have worn to less than the specified minimum, renew them as a set. To renew the brushes, cut the leads at their midpoint and make a good soldered joint when connecting the new brushes.
26 The commutator face should be clean and free from burnt spots. Where necessary burnish with fine glass paper (not emery) and wipe with a fuel-moistened cloth.
27 Commence reassembly by positioning the brush box gasket on the commutator end plate, then position the brush box on the gasket and rivet the brush box to the end plate. Use a new gasket if necessary.
28 Fit the main terminal stud and insulator to the commutator end plate, then secure the stud with the remaining insulator, washer and nut. Fit the two brushes which are attached to the terminal stud into their respective locations in the brush box.

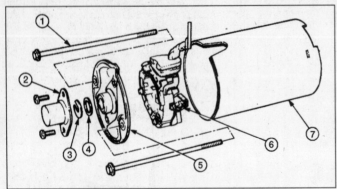

10.18b Bosch DW starter motor brush assembly

1 Commutator end plate securing screw
2 Commutator end plate cap
3 C-clip
4 Shim
5 Commutator end plate
6 Brush plate
7 Yoke

10.20a Remove the plastic cap from the end of the armature shaft . . .

10.20b . . . followed by the star clip - Lucas 5M90 starter motor

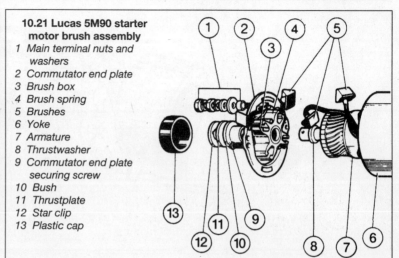

10.21 Lucas 5M90 starter motor brush assembly
1 Main terminal nuts and washers
2 Commutator end plate
3 Brush box
4 Brush spring
5 Brushes
6 Yoke
7 Armature
8 Thrustwasher
9 Commutator end plate securing screw
10 Bush
11 Thrustplate
12 Star clip
13 Plastic cap

10.30 Use a soft faced hammer and socket to fit a new star clip to the end of the armature shaft - Lucas 5M90 starter motor

29 Fit the two field brushes into their locations in the brush box, then position the commutator end plate on the yoke and fit the two securing screws.

30 Fit a new star clip to the end of the armature shaft, ensuring that the clip is pressed home firmly to eliminate any endfloat in the armature **(see illustration)**. Fit the plastic cap over the end of the armature shaft.

Lucas 8M90 type

31 The procedure is basically as described previously for the 5M90 type starter motor with the following difference **(see illustration)**:
32 The commutator end plate is secured by two screws. The end plate and brush box are serviced as an assembly and should be renewed.

Lucas M79 type

33 With the starter motor removed from the vehicle and cleaned, grip the unit in a vice

fitted with soft jaw protectors.
34 Unscrew the securing nut and washer and disconnect the wiring from the solenoid terminal.
35 Remove the two screws securing the commutator end housing cap. Remove the cap.
36 Remove the C-clip and spacers from the end of the armature shaft.
37 Remove the two commutator end housing securing screws and withdraw the end housing.
38 Separate the brush components **(see illustration)**.
39 If the brushes have worn to less than the specified minimum, renew them as a set. To renew the brushes, cut the leads at their midpoint and make a good soldered joint when connecting the new brushes.
40 The commutator face should be clean and free from burnt spots. Where necessary burnish with fine glass paper (not emery) and wipe with a fuel-moistened cloth.

5

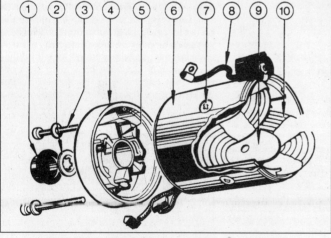

10.31 Lucas 8M90 starter motor brush assembly

1 Plastic cap
2 Star clip
3 Commutator end plate screw
4 Commutator end plate
5 Brush box
6 Yoke
7 Pole securing screw
8 Solenoid connector link
9 Pole shoe
10 Field coils

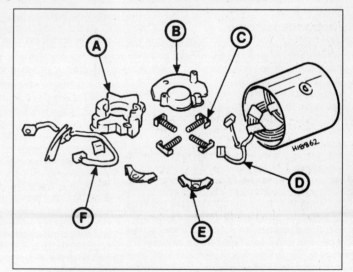

10.38 Lucas M79 starter motor brush plate components

A Brush plate
B Brush plate insulator
C Brush holders and springs
D Brushs
E Insulators
F Brush link

10.47 Nippondenso starter motor brush assembly

1 Yoke
2 Solenoid connecting link
3 Pole shoe
4 Rubber grommet
5 Brush
6 Brush spring
7 Brush plate
8 Commutator end housing
9 Bush
10 Spring
11 C-clip
12 Commutator end housing cap
13 Commutator end housing securing bolt

41 Locate the brush box over the commutator, position the brushes, then fit the nylon cover over the brushes. Route the brush wiring into the locating channel, then secure the brushes in the channels with the locking clips and springs.
42 Refit the commutator end housing, locating the rubber block in the cut-out in the housing, then secure with the two screws.
43 Refit the spacers and C-clip to the end of the armature shaft, then fit the commutator end housing cap and secure with the two screws.
44 Reconnect the wiring to the solenoid terminal and fit the washer and securing nut.

Nippondenso type

45 With the starter motor removed from the vehicle and cleaned, grip the unit in a vice fitted with soft jaw protectors.
46 Unscrew the retaining nut and washer and disconnect the wiring from the terminal on the solenoid.
47 Remove the two screws securing the commutator end housing cap and remove the cap **(see illustration)**.
48 Remove the C-clip from the groove in the armature shaft, and remove the spring.
49 Unscrew the two bolts and washers, and withdraw the commutator end housing.
50 Withdraw the two field brushes from the brush plate, then remove the brush plate.
51 If the brushes have worn to less than the specified minimum, renew them as a set. To renew the brushes, cut the leads at their midpoint and make a good soldered joint when connecting the new brushes.
52 The commutator face should be clean and free from burnt spots. Where necessary burnish with fine glass paper (not emery) and wipe with a fuel-moistened cloth.

53 Position the brush plate over the end of the armature, aligning the cut-outs in the brush plate with the loops in the field windings. The brush plate will be positively located when the commutator end housing bolts are fitted.
54 Fit the brushes to their locations in the brush plate, and retain with the springs.
55 Fit the commutator end housing and secure with the two bolts and washers.
56 Fit the spring and the C-clip to the end of the armature shaft, then smear the end of the shaft with a little lithium-based grease, and refit the commutator end housing cap, securing with the two screws.
57 Reconnect the wiring to the solenoid terminal and fit the washer and retaining nut.

11 Spark plugs and HT leads - removal, inspection and refitting

Note: *The correct functioning of the spark plugs is vital for the correct running and efficiency of the engine. It is essential that the plugs fitted are appropriate for the engine, and the suitable type is specified at the beginning of this Chapter. If this type is used and the engine is in good condition, the spark plugs should not need attention between scheduled replacement intervals. Spark plug cleaning is rarely necessary and should not be attempted unless specialised equipment is available as damage can easily be caused to the firing ends.*

Removal

1 Where necessary, for improved access remove the air cleaner and/or the inlet hose.
2 If necessary, identify each HT lead for position, so that the leads can be refitted to their correct cylinders, then disconnect the leads from the plugs by pulling on the connectors, not the leads. Note that the position of No 1 cylinder HT lead in the distributor cap is marked with either a pip, or a number "1".
3 On 2.0 litre DOHC carburettor models, the location of the spark plugs and the close proximity of the carburettor makes spark plug access difficult, particularly when removing the plugs from cylinders 2 and 3. It is suggested that a 3/8 inch ratchet drive spark plug socket with rubber insert and long extension bar is used, possibly in conjunction with a universal joint adapter. It is also advisable to disconnect No 3 cylinder HT lead from the distributor first, to allow some slack for disconnection at the spark plug.
4 Clean the area around each spark plug using a small brush, then using a plug spanner (preferably with a rubber insert), unscrew and remove the plugs. Cover the spark plug holes with a clean rag to prevent the ingress of any foreign matter.

Inspection

5 The condition of the spark plugs will tell much about the overall condition of the engine.
6 If the insulator nose of the spark plug is clean and white, with no deposits, this is indicative of a weak air/fuel mixture, or too hot a plug. (A hot plug transfers heat away from the electrode slowly - a cold plug transfers it away quickly).
7 If the tip and insulator nose is covered with hard black-looking deposits, then this is indicative that the mixture is too rich. Should the plug be black and oily, then it is likely that the engine is fairly worn, as well as the mixture being too rich.
8 If the insulator nose is covered with light tan to greyish brown deposits, then the mixture is correct and it is likely that the engine is in good condition.
9 The spark plug gap is of considerable importance, as, if it is too large or too small, the size of the spark and its efficiency will be seriously impaired. The spark plug gap should be set to the figure given in the Specifications at the beginning of this Chapter. To set it, measure the gap with a feeler blade, and then bend open, or close the *outer* plug electrode until the correct gap is achieved **(see illustrations)**. The centre electrode should *never* be bent as this may crack the insulation and cause plug failure, if nothing worse.

11.9a Measuring a spark plug gap using a feeler blade

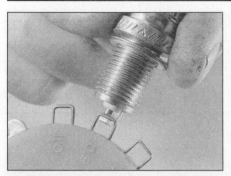

11.9b Measuring a spark plug gap using a wire gauge

11.9c Adjusting a spark plug gap using a special tool

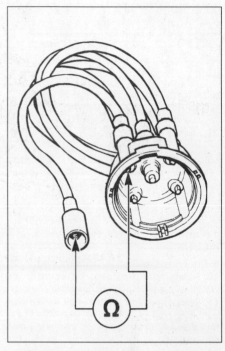

11.10 Method of testing an HT lead with an ohmmeter

10 The distributor cap (except on 1.6 and 1.8 litre CVH (R6A type) engines) and the HT leads should be cleaned and checked at the specified intervals. To test the HT leads, remove them together with the distributor cap, then connect an ohmmeter to the end of each lead and its appropriate terminal within the cap in turn **(see illustration)**. If the resistance of any lead is greater than the maximum given in the Specifications, check that the lead connection in the cap is good before renewing the lead.

Refitting

11 Before fitting the spark plugs, check that the threaded connector sleeves are tight and that the plug exterior surfaces are clean. As the plugs incorporate taper seats also make sure that the threads and seats are clean.
12 On DOHC models before refitting the

spark plugs, coat their threads with suitable antiseize compound, taking care not to contaminate the electrodes.
13 Screw in the spark plugs by hand, then tighten them to the specified torque. *Do not exceed the torque figure.*
14 Push the HT leads firmly onto the spark plugs, and where applicable refit the air cleaner and/or inlet hose.

12 Coil - testing, removal and refitting

Testing

All models except 1.6 and 1.8 litre CVH (R6A type)

1 The coil is located on the left-hand side of the engine compartment and is retained by a metal strap **(see illustration)**. It is of high output type and the HT tower should be kept clean at all times to prevent possible arcing. Bosch and Femsa coils are fitted with protective plastic covers and Polmot coils are fitted with an internal fusible link.
2 To ensure that the correct HT polarity at the spark plugs, the LT coil leads must always be connected correctly. The black lead must always be connected to the terminal marked + 115, and the green lead to the terminal marked /1. Incorrect connections can cause poor starting, misfiring, and short spark plug life.
3 To test the coil first disconnect the LT and HT leads. Connect an ohmmeter between

both LT terminals and check that the primary winding resistance is as given in the Specifications. Connect the ohmmeter between the HT terminal and either LT terminal and check that the secondary winding resistance is as given in the Specifications. If either winding resistance is not as specified, the coil should be renewed. Reconnect the LT and HT leads on completion.

1.6 and 1.8 litre (R6A type) CVH models

4 The coil fitted to these models is located towards the front right-hand side of the cylinder block **(see illustration)**.
5 Testing of the coil should be entrusted to a Ford dealer or a suitable specialist.

Removal

All models except 1.6 and 1.8 litre CVH (R6A type)

6 Disconnect the battery negative lead,
7 Disconnect the LT and HT leads from the coil **(see illustration)**.
8 Remove the securing screw(s) and detach the coil and strap assembly from the body panel. Note that on models with the ESC system, the coil strap is secured by the top ESC module securing screw. On certain models with the ESC II or EEC IV systems, an "octane adjustment" service lead may be connected to one of the coil securing screws. On 2.0 litre DOHC fuel-injected models, the coil/ignition module heat shield must be removed for access to the coil securing bolts. The heat shield is secured by two screws. Note that on certain models, an earthing lead

12.1 Ignition coil - CVH model. Plastic cover arrowed

12.4 Ignition coil (A) and suppressor (B) viewed from under vehicle (shroud removed)

12.7 Disconnecting the HT lead from the coil

5

12.8a Ignition coil viewed with heat shield removed

12.8b Suppressor secured by one of the coil securing bolts

12.11a Disconnecting the coil wiring plug . . .

and/or a suppressor may be secured by one of the coil securing bolts **(see illustrations)**.

1.6 and 1.8 litre (R6A type) CVH models

9 Disconnect the battery negative lead.
10 Remove the two securing screws, and withdraw the plastic ignition module shroud.
11 Disconnect the ignition coil wiring plug and, where fitted, the suppressor wiring plug, pulling on the plugs, not on the wiring **(see illustrations)**.
12 Release the securing lugs, and disconnect the HT leads from the coil, noting their locations to aid refitting.
13 Remove the four Torx screws, and withdraw the coil from the cylinder block.

Refitting

14 Refitting is a reversal of removal, but ensure that all leads are securely connected.

13.2 Unclipping the distributor screening can - Motorcraft distributor

13.3 HT lead holder on camshaft cover

13 Distributor cap and rotor arm (OHC models) - removal and refitting

SOHC models

1 Disconnect the battery negative lead.
2 Where applicable, unclip the screening can from the top of the distributor and disconnect the earth strap **(see illustration)**.
3 If necessary, identify each HT lead for position, so that the leads can be refitted to their correct cylinders, then disconnect the leads from the spark plugs by pulling on the connectors, not the leads. Similarly, disconnect the HT lead from the coil. Where applicable, slide the HT lead holder from the clip on the camshaft cover **(see illustration)**.

Lucas distributors

4 Remove the two securing screws and lift off the distributor cap.
5 The rotor arm is a push-fit on the end of the distributor shaft.
6 Refitting is a reversal of removal, noting that the rotor arm can only be fitted in one position. Ensure that the HT leads are correctly connected.

Bosch distributors

7 Prise away the spring clips with a screwdriver and lift off the distributor cap **(see illustration)**. On fuel injection models, disconnect the crankcase ventilation hose from the air inlet hose, then disconnect the air inlet hose from the inlet manifold and the airflow meter for improved access.

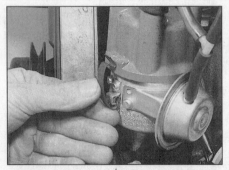

13.7 Securing distributor cap with spring clip - Bosch distributor

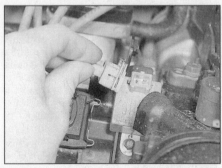

12.11b . . . and the suppressor wiring plug

8 Refitting is a reversal of removal, noting that the rotor arm can only be fitted in one position. Ensure that the HT leads are correctly connected, and on fuel injection models ensure that the air inlet hose clips are correctly aligned (refer to illustration, Section 15, Chapter 4, Part B).

Motorcraft distributors

9 For improved access, disconnect the crankcase ventilation hose from the air inlet hose, then disconnect the air inlet hose from the inlet manifold and the airflow meter for improved access.
10 Remove the two securing screws and lift off the distributor cap **(see illustration)**.
11 Remove the two securing screws and withdraw the rotor arm (disc) **(see illustration)**. Note that on some vehicles, the rotor arm tip may be coated with silicone grease to assist radio interference suppression. Do not attempt to clean the grease off if it is present. If radio interference

13.10 Removing a distributor cap securing screw - Motorcraft distributor

13.11 Removing a rotor arm (disc) securing screw - Motorcraft distributor

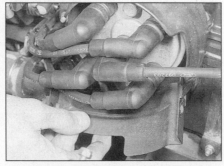

13.14a Unclipping the lower section . . .

13.14b . . . and the upper section of the distributor shield

problems are experienced, consult a Ford dealer or an in-car entertainment specialist.

12 Proceed as described in paragraph 6, but additionally ensure that the air inlet hose clips are correctly aligned (refer to illustration, Section 15, Chapter 4, **Part B**).

DOHC models

13 Disconnect the battery negative lead.

14 Unclip the lower section of the distributor shield from the upper section, then unscrew the two securing nuts, and withdraw the upper section of the shield from the studs on the upper timing chain cover **(see illustrations)**.

15 If necessary, identify each HT lead for position, so that the leads can be refitted to their correct cylinders, then disconnect the leads from the spark plugs by pulling on the

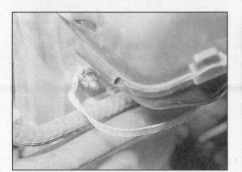

13.17 Removing the distributor cap and rotor arm

connectors, not the leads. Similarly, disconnect the HT lead from the coil, and release it from the clip on the timing chain cover.

16 Using a suitable Torx key or socket, unscrew the two distributor cap securing screws, then lift off the cap.

17 The rotor arm is a push-fit on the end of the rotor shaft **(see illustration)**.

18 If desired, the rotor housing can be pulled from the timing chain cover.

19 Refitting is a reversal of removal, ensuring that the rotor arm is pushed fully home on the rotor shaft. Make sure that the HT leads are fitted to their correct cylinders. Note that the rotor arm will only fit in one position.

14 Distributor components (CVH models) - removal and refitting

1 The distributor fitted to the CVH engine is unlike any conventional distributor, in that it has no main body and no adjustments are possible. The distributor is used purely to distribute HT voltage to the spark plugs. To remove the distributor components, proceed as follows.

2 Disconnect the battery negative lead.

Distributor cap

3 Pull the two halves of the distributor cap shroud apart and remove the shroud. Disconnect the earth strap from the tag on the timing cover **(see illustration)**.

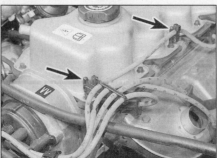

14.4 HT lead holders (arrowed) on camshaft cover

4 If necessary, identify each HT lead for position, so that the leads can be refitted to their correct cylinders, then disconnect the leads from the spark plugs by pulling on the connectors, not the leads. Unclip the HT lead holders from their studs on the camshaft cover **(see illustration)**.

5 Depress the two securing screws and turn them anti-clockwise through 90°, then lift off the distributor cap.

6 Disconnect the HT lead from the coil by pulling on the connector not the lead, and remove the distributor cap.

7 Refitting is a reversal of removal, but ensure that the HT leads are fitted to their correct cylinders.

Rotor arm and housing

8 With the distributor cap removed as described previously, compress the two lugs on the rotor shaft and withdraw the rotor arm **(see illustration)**.

9 The rotor housing can now be removed by pulling it from the timing cover **(see illustration)**.

10 Refitting is a reversal of removal, but note that the rotor arm can only be fitted in one position.

Rotor shaft

11 The rotor shaft is retained by the camshaft sprocket bolt.

12 To remove and refit the rotor shaft, first remove the timing cover and the camshaft

5

14.8 Removing the rotor arm

14.3 Distributor cap shroud earth strap connection

sprocket bolt. Note that there is no need to remove the timing belt or the sprockets.

15 Distributor (OHC models) - removal and refitting

Note: *During production the engine ignition timing is accurately set using a microwave process, and sealant is applied to the distributor clamp bolt. Removal of the distributor should be avoided except where excessive bearing wear has occurred due to high mileage or during major engine overhaul. A timing light will be required to check the ignition timing after refitting the distributor.*

All models except early "Economy"

Removal

1 Disconnect the battery negative lead.
2 If necessary, identify each HT lead for position, so that the leads can be refitted to their correct cylinders, then disconnect the leads from the spark plugs by pulling on the connectors, not the leads.
3 Where applicable, unclip the screening can from the top of the distributor and disconnect the earth strap. On fuel injection models, disconnect the crankcase ventilation hose from the air inlet hose, then disconnect the air inlet hose from the inlet manifold and the airflow meter for improved access.

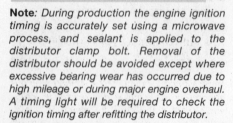

15.6 Disconnecting vacuum pipe from vacuum advance unit - Bosch distributor

14.9 Removing the rotor housing

4 Prise away the spring clips with a screwdriver, or remove the two securing screws, as applicable, and lift off the distributor cap.
5 Disconnect the HT lead from the coil by pulling on the connector, not the lead, then slide the HT lead holder from the clip on the camshaft cover, and withdraw the distributor cap.
6 Where applicable, disconnect the vacuum pipe from the vacuum advance unit on the side of the distributor **(see illustration)**.
7 Using a suitable socket or spanner on the crankshaft pulley bolt, turn the crankshaft to bring No 1 cylinder to the firing point. If the distributor cap is secured by clips, make sure that the clips stay clear of the distributor

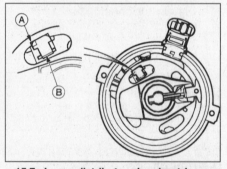

15.7a Lucas distributor showing trigger vane position No 1 cylinder at firing point

A Trigger vane cut   B Sensor
-out

moving parts. No 1 cylinder is at the firing point when:
a) *The relevant timing marks are in alignment.*
b) *The tip of the rotor arm is pointing to the position occupied by the No 1 cylinder HT lead terminal in the distributor cap. Note that the position of No 1 HT lead terminal is identified by a pip or a number "1"*
c) *On Lucas distributors, the cut-out in the trigger vane is aligned with the sensor **(see illustration)***
d) *On Bosch distributors, the tip of the rotor arm is aligned with the scribed line on the distributor body (where applicable, remove rotor arm and dust cover, then refit rotor arm to check alignment with scribed line) **(see illustration)***
e) *On Motorcraft distributors, the tip of the rotor arm is aligned with a notch in the distributor body. Mark the relevant notch (there may be several) for reference when refitting. Also, the leading edge of one of the trigger vane segments is aligned with the rib on the sensor (remove the two securing screws and lift off the rotor arm to view the trigger vane and sensor) **(see illustration)**.*

8 Disconnect the distributor wiring plug, where applicable depressing the locking tab(s). Pull on the plug, not the wiring **(see illustration)**.
9 Make alignment marks between the distributor body and the cylinder block.
10 Scrape the sealant from the distributor clamp bolt, then unscrew and remove the bolt and clamp **(see illustration)**.
11 Withdraw the distributor from the cylinder block. As the distributor is removed, the rotor arm will turn clockwise due to the skew gear drive. Note the new position of the rotor arm relative to the distributor body, if necessary making an alignment mark (some distributors already have an alignment mark).
12 Check the distributor spindle for excessive side-to-side movement. If evident, the distributor must be renewed, as the only spares available are the cap, rotor arm, module (where applicable), and driveshaft O-ring **(see illustration)**.

15.7b Rotor arm tip aligned with scribed line on distributor body - Bosch distributor

15.7c Trigger vane segment leading edge aligned with sensor rib - Motorcraft distributor

15.8 Disconnecting distributor wiring plug - Bosch distributor

15.10 Unscrewing distributor clamp bolt - Bosch distributor

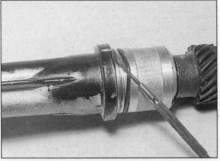

15.12 Removing distributor driveshaft O-ring - Motorcraft distributor

Refitting

13 Commence refitting by checking that No 1 cylinder is still at the firing point. The relevant timing marks should be aligned. If the engine has been turned whilst the distributor has been removed, check that No 1 cylinder is on its firing stroke by removing the No 1 cylinder spark plug and placing a finger over the plug hole. Turn the crankshaft until compression can be felt, which indicates that No 1 piston is rising on its firing stroke. Continue turning the crankshaft until the relevant timing marks are in alignment.

14 Turn the rotor arm to the position noted in paragraph 11. If a new distributor is being fitted, and no alignment marks are present, transfer the marks from the old distributor to the new distributor.

15 Hold the distributor directly over the aperture in the cylinder block with the previously made marks on the distributor body and cylinder block aligned, then lower the distributor into position. Again, if a new distributor is being fitted, transfer the alignment mark from the old distributor body to the new distributor body. As the skew gear drive meshes, the rotor arm will turn anti-clockwise.

16 With the distributor fitted and the marks on the distributor body and cylinder block aligned, check that the rotor arm is positioned as described in paragraph 7 - if not, withdraw the distributor, re-position the driveshaft and try again.

17 Refit the clamp, then insert and tighten the bolt. Do not fully tighten the bolt at this stage.

18 Refit the distributor wiring plug, and where applicable reconnect the vacuum pipe, and refit the dust cover and/or rotor arm.

19 Refit the distributor cap, and reconnect the HT leads to the spark plugs and coil. Ensure that the leads are refitted to their correct cylinders.

20 Where applicable, refit the screening can to the top of the distributor and reconnect the earth strap. On fuel injection models, reconnect the air inlet hose, ensuring that the clips are correctly aligned (refer to illustration, Section 15, Chapter 4, Part B).

21 Reconnect the battery negative lead.
22 Check and if necessary adjust the ignition timing.

Early "Economy" models

Removal

23 Removal of the distributor fitted to these models is a similar process to that described above.

Refitting

24 Turn the crankshaft to bring No 1 cylinder to the firing point, with the 16° BTDC mark on the crankshaft pulley aligned with the pointer on the crankshaft front oil seal housing, as described above.

25 Fit the new distributor to the engine as described above, then proceed as follows.

26 Cut the original distributor wiring plug from the wiring loom. Make the cut close to the connector.

27 Strip back 10 mm of insulation from each of the wires on the wiring loom, and on the adapter loom supplied with the new distributor.

28 Solder the adapter loom wires to the corresponding identically coloured wires in the main loom.

29 Carefully insulate each individual soldered joint using insulating tape, then apply tape to cover the join between the looms.

30 Fit a new distributor cap (and screening can, where applicable), and connect the HT leads.

16.2a Highlighted timing marks - SOHC engine with cast crankshaft pulley

31 Connect the adapter loom to the distributor.

32 Start the engine, and adjust the ignition timing to the value given in the Specifications at the beginning of this Chapter. Work as described above whilst noting that the vacuum pipe must be left connected.

16 Ignition timing (OHC models) - adjustment

Note: *During production the ignition timing is accurately set using a microwave process, and sealant is applied to the distributor clamp bolt. Because the electronic components require no maintenance, checking the ignition timing does not constitute part of the routine maintenance schedule, and the procedure is therefore only necessary after removal and refitting of the distributor. A timing light will be required for this procedure. For details of ignition timing adjustment in order to operate vehicles on unleaded petrol refer to the appropriate Section of this Chapter.*

All models except 2.0 litre DOHC

1 Before checking the ignition timing, the following conditions must be met:

a) *The engine must be at normal operating temperature*

b) *Where applicable, the vacuum pipe to the distributor vacuum unit or electronic module (as applicable) must be disconnected from the vacuum unit or electronic module and plugged*

c) *The idle speed must be below 900 rpm (isolate "idle speed adjustment" wire if necessary)*

d) *Any earthed "octane adjustment" wires must be temporarily isolated*

2 Wipe clean the crankshaft pulley timing marks and the pointer on the crankshaft front oil seal housing. Note that two alternative types of pulley may be fitted **(see illustration)**. The desired timing values are given in the Specifications. If necessary, use white paint or chalk to highlight the relevant timing mark(s) **(see illustration)**.

3 Connect a stroboscope timing light to the No 1 cylinder HT lead, following the manufacturer's instructions.

4 With the engine idling at normal operating temperature, point the timing light at the marks on the crankshaft pulley, and check that the appropriate timing mark appears stationary in line with the timing cover pointer. Take care not to get the timing light leads, clothing etc tangled in the cooling fan blades or other moving parts of the engine.

5 If adjustment is necessary, stop the engine, slacken the distributor clamp bolt, and turn the distributor body slightly. Turn the distributor body clockwise to retard the ignition timing (move the timing closer to TDC) and anti-clockwise to advance the timing.

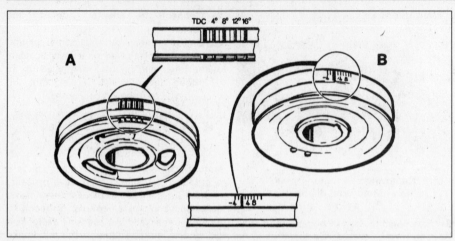

16.2b Crankshaft pulley timing marks - SOHC engine

A Cast pulley

B Pressed steel pulley

Note that the required distributor body movement will be half of the required crankshaft movement (ie an adjustment of 5° in ignition timing will require the distributor body to be turned 2°. Tighten the clamp bolt and re-check the timing.

6 On models with inductive discharge ignition systems, the mechanical and vacuum advance mechanisms can be checked as follows. On all other models, proceed to paragraph 10.

7 With the engine idling, timing light connected, and vacuum pipe disconnected as described in the preceding paragraphs, increase the engine speed to approximately 2000 rpm (if desired, connect a tachometer to the engine in accordance with the manufacturer"s instructions). Note the approximate distance which the relevant pulley mark moves out of alignment with the pointer.

8 Reconnect the vacuum pipe to the distributor or electronic module, as applicable, and repeat the procedure given in the previous paragraph, when for the same increase in engine speed, the alignment differential between the pulley mark and pointer should be greater than previously observed.

9 If the pulley mark does not appear to move during the first part of the check, a fault in the distributor mechanical advance mechanism is indicated. No increased movement of the mark during the second part of the check indicates a punctured diaphragm in the distributor vacuum unit, or a leak in the vacuum line.

10 On completion of the adjustments and checks, stop the engine and disconnect the timing light. Where applicable, reconnect the vacuum pipe, if not already done, and reconnect any "octane adjustment" and "idle speed adjustment" wires. Make a final check to ensure that the distributor clamp bolt is tight.

11 Finally, the idle speed and mixture should be checked and adjusted.

2.0 litre DOHC carburettor model

12 The ignition timing is controlled by the ESC II module, and no adjustment is possible.

2.0 litre DOHC fuel injection model

13 The ignition timing is controlled by the EEC IV module, and no adjustment is possible.

17 Ignition timing - adjustment for use with unleaded petrol

Note: *Refer to the Specifications Section at the beginning of this Chapter for ignition timing values for use with unleaded petrol.*

1 To run an engine on unleaded petrol, certain criteria must be met, and it may be helpful to first describe the various terms used for the different types of petrol:

Normal leaded petrol (4-star, 97 RON): Petrol which has a low amount of lead added during manufacture (0.15 g/litre), in addition to the natural lead found in crude oil.

Unleaded petrol (Premium, 95 RON): Has no lead added during manufacture, but still has the natural lead content of crude oil.

Lead free petrol: Contains no lead. It has no lead added during manufacture, and the natural lead content is refined out. This type of petrol is not currently available for general use in the UK and should not be confused with unleaded petrol.

2 To run an engine continuously on unleaded petrol, suitable hardened valve seat inserts must be fitted to the cylinder head.

3 The OHC engines fitted to the Sierra/P100 range which have suitable valve seat inserts fitted at manufacture can be identified by letters stamped on the cylinder head next to No 4 spark plug as follows:

1.6 litre engines   M, MM, N, or NN
1.6 litre engines   S or SS
2.0 litre engines   L, P, PP, R, or RR

4 All CVH engines have suitable valve seat inserts fitted.

5 Vehicles which have no identification letter stamped on the cylinder head, and are not fitted with suitable valve seat inserts, may still be run on unleaded petrol (although continuous use is not recommended), provided that every fourth tank filling is of normal leaded petrol, ie: three tanks of unleaded petrol followed by one tank of normal leaded petrol.

6 When running an OHC engine on unleaded petrol (Premium, 95 RON), the ignition timing **must** be retarded as described in the following sub-Sections. There is no requirement for ignition timing adjustment when running CVH engines on unleaded petrol.

Inductive discharge ignition system and ESC system

7 On vehicles fitted with an inductive discharge ignition system, or the ESC system, the ignition timing should be retarded as specified.

ESC II and EEC IV systems

8 On vehicles fitted with the ESC II or EEC IV systems, there is a facility for retarding the ignition timing without physically disturbing the distributor.

9 Adjustment is made by earthing one or two wires ("octane adjustment" wires) which terminate in a wiring plug next to the ignition coil. Ideally a service adjustment lead, available from a Ford dealer should be used **(see illustration)**. One end of the lead plugs into the "octane adjustment" wiring plug, and the other end should be earthed by fixing to one of the ignition coil securing screws.

10 Cut and insulate the wires in the service lead which are not to be earthed.

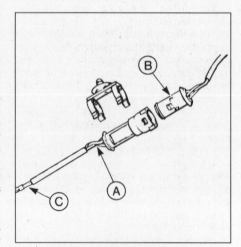

17.9 Service adjustment lead and plug - ESC II and EEC IV systems

A Red, blue and yellow wires
B Plug
C Wire cutting point

System	Degrees of retardation		
	Blue wire	Red wire	Blue and red wires
ESC II (except 1.8 litre) models from February1987	2	4	6
ESC II (1.8 litre models from February 1987)	4	2	6
EEC IV	4	2	6

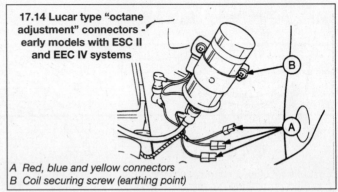

17.14 Lucar type "octane adjustment" connectors - early models with ESC II and EEC IV systems

A Red, blue and yellow connectors
B Coil securing screw (earthing point)

11 The amount of ignition retardation provided by earthing the wire(s) is as shown in the table above.

12 Once the ignition timing has been retarded, the vehicle can be operated on either leaded or unleaded petrol.

13 On 2.0 litre models, if the yellow wire ("idle speed adjustment" wire) in the service lead is earthed, the idle speed will be raised by 75 rpm. If the vehicle already has a single yellow fly lead connected prior to connecting the service lead, ensure that the yellow wire in the service lead is earthed.

14 Note that some early models have coloured "Lucar" connectors fitted in place of the "octane adjustment" wiring plug (see illustration). The principle for ignition timing adjustment on these vehicles is as described previously for vehicles with the "octane adjustment" wiring plug.

15 On completion of ignition timing adjustment, the idle speed and mixture should be checked and adjusted as necessary.

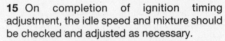

18 Electronic modules - removal and refitting

Note: Refer to Section 1 for precautions to be observed when working with electronic modules.

1 Disconnect the battery negative lead.

All ESC modules except ESC (early "Economy" models)

2 All modules except the ESC Hybrid module are mounted on the left-hand side of the engine compartment (see illustration). The ESC Hybrid module is mounted on the right-hand side of the engine compartment.

3 Disconnect the module wiring plug by pulling on the plug, not the wiring. On ESC II

modules, except those fitted to 1.8 litre models from February 1987, a locking tab at the lower end of the wiring plug must be depressed before unhooking the upper end of the plug from the module. On ESC II modules fitted to 1.8 litre models from February 1987 (see illustration) and ESC Hybrid modules, the wiring plug is secured by a screw which is integral with the plug (see illustrations).

4 Where applicable, disconnect the vacuum pipe from the module (see illustration).

5 Remove the two or three securing screws, as applicable, and withdraw the module from the engine compartment. Note that the top securing screw of the ESC module also secures the ignition coil strap.

6 Refitting is a reversal of removal, but ensure that the underside of the module and the corresponding area of the body panel are clean.

ESC module (early "Economy" models)

7 Remove the module complete with its securing bracket, as described above.

8 Fit the new module, slightly behind the old module position, on the flat vertical surface of the body panel, and secure with the two screws supplied. Note that the module must be mounted against the flat area of the body panel to prevent distortion of the module, and to ensure good heat transfer from the module to the body.

9 Reconnect the module vacuum pipe.

10 Connect the adapter loom supplied with the new module between the module and the old module's wiring plug.

11 Where applicable, refit the coil to its original location.

5

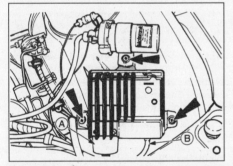

18.2 ESC module securing screws (arrowed)
A Wiring plug B Vacuum pipe

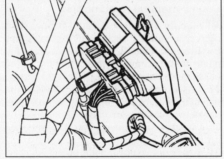

18.3a ESC II module - 1.8 litre models from February 1987

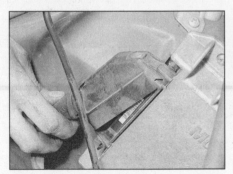

18.3b Disconnecting ESC II module wiring plug

18.3c Disconnecting ESC Hybrid module wiring plug

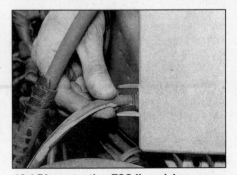

18.4 Disconnecting ESC II module vacuum pipe

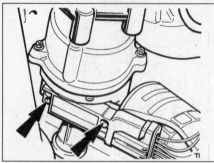

18.14 EEC IV ignition module securing screws (arrowed) - models up to 1987

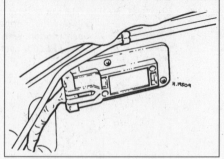

18.16 EEC IV ignition module - models from 1987

18.22 Disconnecting the ignition module wiring plug

EEC IV modules

Ignition module

Models up to 1987

Note: *When refitting, the rear face of the module must be coated with heat sink compound. Refer to a Ford dealer for advice if necessary.*

12 The module is mounted on the distributor body.

13 Disconnect the distributor wiring plug by depressing the locking tabs. Pull on the plug, not the wiring.

14 Remove the two securing screws from the module, then slide the module downwards and withdraw it **(see illustration)**.

15 Refitting is a reversal of removal, but the rear face of the module must be coated with heat sink compound. Do not force the module into position, as damage to the electrical contacts may result.

Models from 1987

16 The module is mounted on the left-hand side of the engine compartment **(see illustration)**.

17 Disconnect the module wiring plug by depressing the locking tabs. Pull on the plug, not the wiring.

18 Remove the two securing screws and withdraw the module from the engine compartment.

19 Refitting is a reversal of removal, but ensure that the underside of the module and the corresponding area of the body panel are clean.

1.6 and 1.8 litre (R6A type) CVH models

20 The ignition module is located at the front right-hand side of the engine compartment.

21 Disconnect the battery negative lead.

22 Release the securing lug, and pull the wiring plug from the module. Pull on the plug, not on the wiring **(see illustration)**.

23 Remove the two securing screws, and withdraw the module from the body panel.

24 Refitting is a reversal of removal.

2.0 litre DOHC fuel injection models

25 The ignition module is located on the left-hand side of the engine compartment, beneath the coil **(see illustration)**.

26 Disconnect the battery negative lead.

27 Remove the two securing screws, and withdraw the coil/ignition module heat shield.

28 Release the locking lug and disconnect the ignition module wiring plug. Pull on the plug, not on the wiring.

29 Remove the two securing screws, and withdraw the module from the body panel.

30 Refitting is a reversal of removal, ensuring that the underside of the module and the corresponding area of the body panel are clean.

Engine management module

All models except 1.6 and 1.8 litre CVH (R6A type) and 2.0 litre DOHC fuel injection

31 The module is located inside the passenger compartment behind the passenger side facia.

32 Unclip the trim panel from below the glovebox on models up to 1987, or from above the glovebox on models from 1987.

33 Unclip the module retainer and withdraw the module.

34 The wiring plug is secured by a screw which is integral with the plug. Disconnect the wiring plug and remove the module.

35 Refitting is a reversal of removal, noting that the wiring plug will only fit in one position.

1.6 and 1.8 litre (R6A type) CVH models

36 The module is located in the passenger compartment, behind the glovebox.

37 Disconnect the battery negative lead.

38 Open the glovebox, and carefully pull it from its retaining clips.

39 Unclip and withdraw the module from its retaining bracket **(see illustration)**.

40 The wiring plug is secured by a screw which is integral with the plug. Disconnect the wiring plug, and withdraw the module.

41 Refitting is a reversal of removal, noting that the wiring plug will only fit in one position.

2.0 litre DOHC fuel injection models

42 For models up to 1990 refer to the first 5 paragraphs of this sub Section.

43 For models from 1990 refer to the procedure given for 1.6 and 1.8 litre CVH (R6A type) engines.

19 ESC II system components - removal and refitting

Note: *Procedures for removal and refitting of the ignition system components and electronic module are given elsewhere in the relevant Sections of this Chapter.*

1 Disconnect the battery negative lead.

Engine coolant temperature sensor

All models except 2.0 litre DOHC

2 The sensor is located in the underside of the inlet manifold.

18.25 Ignition module location (arrowed)

18.39 Engine management module withdrawn from its mounting bracket

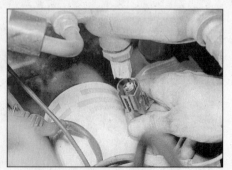

19.4 Disconnect engine temperature sensor wiring plug - ESC II system

19.11 Removing inlet manifold heater - ESC II system

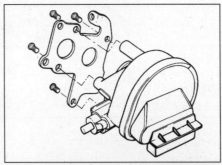

19.16 Carburettor stepper motor adjustment - 2.0 litre models with ESC II system

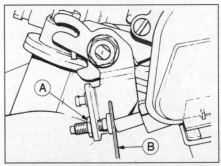

19.25 Carburettor stepper motor adjustment - 2.0 litre models with ESC II system

A Locknut   B Feeler blade

3 Partially drain the cooling system. There is no need to remove the cylinder block drain plug.
4 Disconnect the sensor wiring plug by pulling on the plug, not the wiring (**see illustration**).
5 Unscrew the sensor from the inlet manifold and remove it.
6 Refitting is a reversal of removal. Fill the cooling system.

2.0 litre DOHC models
7 The sensor is located in the side of the inlet manifold. The removal and refitting procedures are as described for the 1.6 and 1.8 litre CVH (R6A type) engines in the relevent Section of this Chapter.

Inlet manifold heater

Note: *When refitting the heater, a new gasket and O-ring must be used.*
8 Do not attempt to remove the heater while it is hot.
9 For improved access, remove the air cleaner.
10 Disconnect the wiring from the heater.
11 Unscrew the three securing bolts and remove the heater. Recover the gasket and O-ring (**see illustration**).
12 Refitting is a reversal of removal, using a new gasket and O-ring, but be careful to tighten the securing bolts evenly, otherwise the heater may tilt and jam in its recess.

Carburettor stepper motor (2.0 litre models)

Note: *Irregular idle is not necessarily caused by a faulty or badly adjusted stepper motor. Good electrical contact between the stepper motor plunger and the adjusting screw (which from the throttle position switch) is essential. Before attempting adjustment or renewal of the motor, try the effect of cleaning the plunger and adjusting screw contact faces with abrasive paper followed by switch cleaning fluid. Switch cleaning fluid is available from electronic component shops. Refer to the precautions in Chapter 3 before proceeding.*
13 Remove the air cleaner.
14 Depress the locking tab and disconnect the stepper motor wiring plug. Pull on the plug, not the wiring.
15 Remove the four securing screws and withdraw the stepper motor and bracket from the carburettor.
16 If desired, the stepper motor can be separated from the bracket by removing the

four securing screws (**see illustration**).
17 Commence refitting by securing the stepper motor to the bracket, where applicable.
18 Refit the stepper motor and bracket to the carburettor and secure with the four screws.
19 Reconnect the wiring plug.
20 Reconnect the air cleaner vacuum hose to the inlet manifold, and position the air cleaner to one side to allow access to the carburettor and stepper motor.
21 Reconnect the battery negative lead.
22 Connect a tachometer to the engine in accordance with the manufacturer's instructions.
23 Start the engine, then check and if necessary adjust the idle mixture.
24 Ensure that all electrical loads are switched off (headlamps, heater blower etc). If the "idle speed adjustment" wire is earthed, temporarily isolate it. Where applicable, ensure that the automatic transmission gear selector lever is in the "N" or "P" position.
25 Accelerate the engine to a speed greater than 2500 rpm, allow it to return to idle, then repeat. Insert a feeler blade of 1.0 mm (0.04 in) thickness between the stepper motor plunger and the adjusting screw (**see illustration**). With the feeler blade in place the engine speed should be 875 ± 25 rpm.
26 If adjustment is necessary, remove the tamperproof cap from the adjusting screw locknut. Slacken the locknut, then turn the adjusting screw to achieve the correct engine

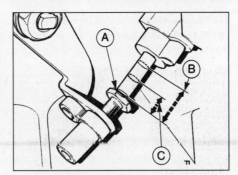

19.30 Carburettor stepper motor plunger positions - 2.0 litre models with ESC II system

A Vent manifold/start
B Anti-dieselling
C Normal idle

speed and tighten the locknut.
27 Repeat the procedure given in paragraph 24 and check that the engine speed is still correct. Readjust if necessary.
28 Stop the engine, remove the feeler blade, and disconnect the tachometer.
29 Refit the air cleaner, ensuring that the vacuum hose is securely connected. If the "idle speed adjustment" wire was previously earthed, reconnect it.
30 Re-start and then stop the engine, observing the movement of the stepper motor plunger. Immediately after stopping the engine, the plunger should move to the "anti-dieselling" position, and after a few seconds it should extend to the "vent manifold/start" position (**see illustration**).
31 Re-check and adjust the idle mixture.
32 If necessary, refit the tamperproof caps to the mixture adjustment screw and the stepper motor adjustment screw locknut.

Crankshaft speed/position sensor (2.0 litre DOHC models)

33 The sensor is located at the right-hand rear of the cylinder block behind the oil filter.
34 Disconnect the battery negative lead.
35 Access is most easily obtained from underneath the vehicle. To improve access, apply the handbrake, then jack up the front of the vehicle and support it securely on axle stands (see "*Jacking and Vehicle Support*").
36 Disconnect the wiring plug from the sensor.
37 Remove the securing screw, and withdraw the sensor from its location in the cylinder block (**see illustration**).

5

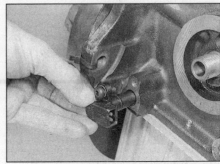

19.37 Removing the crankshaft speed/position sensor (engine removed)

38 Before refitting the sensor, examine the O-ring, and renew it if damaged or worn.
39 Refitting is a reversal of removal, noting the torque setting for the sensor screw.

20 ESC Hybrid system components - removal and refitting

Note: *Procedures for removal and refitting of the ignition system components and electronic module are given elsewhere in the relevant Sections of this Chapter.*
1 Disconnect the battery negative lead.

Crankshaft speed/position sensor

2 The sensor is mounted in a bracket on the timing cover.
3 Disconnect the sensor wiring plug by pulling on the plug, not the wiring (see illustration).
4 Slacken the sensor clamping screw and slide the sensor from its bracket.
5 Refitting is a reversal of removal, but the clearance between the sensor and the toothed wheel on the crankshaft must be set at 1.0 mm (0.04 in). This can be achieved by inserting a suitable length of wire or rod with a diameter of 1.0 mm (0.04 in) between the sensor and the toothed wheel (see illustration). Do not overtighten the clamping screw, as damage to the sensor may result.

Engine coolant temperature sensor

6 The sensor is located in the side of the inlet manifold (see illustration).
7 Partially drain the cooling system.
8 Disconnect the sensor wiring plug by pulling on the plug, not the wiring.
9 Unscrew the sensor from the inlet manifold and remove it.
10 Refitting is a reversal of removal. Fill the cooling system.

Air charge temperature sensor

11 The sensor is located in the base of the air cleaner.
12 Remove the air cleaner.
13 Disconnect the sensor wiring plug by pulling on the plug, not the wiring (see illustration).

20.17 Electric choke heater relay location (arrowed) in main fusebox - ESC Hybrid system

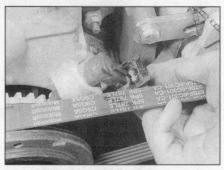

20.3 Disconnecting crankshaft speed/position sensor wiring plug - ESC Hybrid system

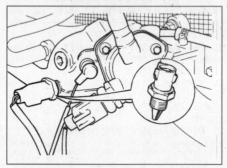

20.6 Engine coolant temperature sensor location - ESC Hybrid system

14 Unscrew the sensor from the air cleaner using a suitable spanner.
15 Refitting is a reversal of removal. Refit the air cleaner. Ensure that the vacuum hose is securely connected.

Electric choke heater

16 The electric choke heater is an integral part of the automatic choke housing on the carburettor. Removal and refitting of the choke housing is covered in Chapter 4.
17 The operation of the electric choke heater relay can be checked by starting the engine from cold, and placing a finger on the relay (see illustration). It should be possible to feel the relay switching on and off. If this is not the case, renew the relay.

Throttle damper control solenoid

18 The solenoid is on the right-hand side of the engine compartment (see illustration).

20.18 Throttle damper control solenoid - ESC Hybrid system

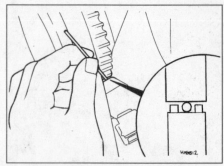

20.5 Setting the gap between the crankshaft speed/position sensor and the crankshaft toothed wheel - ESC Hybrid system

20.13 Disconnecting air charge temperature sensor wiring plug - ESC Hybrid system

19 Disconnect the solenoid wiring plug by pulling on the plug, not the wiring.
20 Disconnect the two vacuum pipes from the solenoid, noting their locations for use when refitting.
21 Remove the securing screw and withdraw the solenoid from the body panel.
22 Refitting is a reversal of removal, but note that the locating lug on the solenoid bracket should engage with the body panel, and make sure that the vacuum pipes are correctly connected.

Throttle damper

23 Remove the air cleaner.
24 Disconnect the vacuum pipe from the throttle damper.

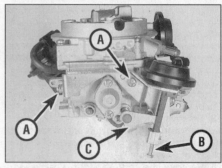

20.25 Throttle damper assembly - ESC Hybrid system

A Securing screws   C Throttle lever
B Adjusting screw

20.32 Service adjustment lead location (arrowed) - ESC Hybrid system

25 Remove the two securing screws and detach the throttle damper and bracket assembly from the carburettor **(see illustration)**.
26 Commence refitting by securing the throttle damper and bracket assembly to the carburettor with the two screws. Ensure that the throttle lever is correctly positioned in the slot in the throttle damper actuating arm.
27 Reconnect the vacuum pipe to the throttle damper.
28 Reconnect the air cleaner vacuum hose to the inlet manifold, and reconnect the air change temperature sensor wiring plug, then place the air cleaner to one side to allow access to the throttle damper.
29 Reconnect the battery negative lead.
30 Connect a tachometer to the engine in accordance with the manufacturer's instructions.
31 Start the engine, then check and if necessary adjust the idle speed and mixture.
32 Earth the "service adjustment" lead, located in the battery negative wiring loom **(see illustration)**, for a minimum of 10 seconds. The throttle damper actuating arm should move to the fully retracted position, raising the engine speed.
33 The engine speed should stabilise at 1700 ± 100 rpm. If adjustment is necessary, turn the adjusting screw on the end of the throttle damper actuating arm to give the correct speed. Turn the screw clockwise to increase the engine speed, or anti-clockwise to reduce the engine speed.

21.9 Crankshaft speed/position sensor (arrowed) viewed from front of engine with shroud removed

34 On completion of adjustment, stop the engine and disconnect the tachometer.
35 Where necessary, ensure that any tamperproof seals are refitted, then refit the air cleaner, ensuring that the vacuum hose is securely connected. Isolate the "service adjustment" lead.
36 Start the engine and check that normal idle speed is resumed, then stop the engine.

21 EEC IV system components - removal and refitting

Note: *Procedures for removal and refitting of the ignition system components and electronic module are given elsewhere in the relevant Sections of this Chapter.*

Engine coolant temperature sensor

2.0 litre SOHC fuel injection models
1 For details of engine coolant temperature sensor removal and refitting, refer to the Section appertaining to the ESC II system.
1.6 and 1.8 litre (R6A type) CVH models
2 The sensor is located in the side of the inlet manifold.
3 Disconnect the battery negative lead.
4 Partially drain the cooling system.
5 Disconnect the sensor wiring plug by pulling on the plug, not the wiring **(see illustration)**.
6 Unscrew the sensor from the inlet manifold and remove it.
7 Refitting is a reversal of removal. Refill the cooling system.
2.0 litre DOHC fuel injection models
8 The sensor is located in the side of the inlet manifold, behind the throttle body. The removal and refitting procedure is as described for the 1.6 and 1.8 litre (R6A type) CVH models above.

Crankshaft speed/position sensor

1.6 and 1.8 litre (R6A type) CVH models
1.6 litre
9 The sensor is located at the left-hand rear of the cylinder block, above the starter motor **(see illustration)**.

21.17 Air charge temperature sensor location on 1.6 litre engines (arrowed)

21.5 Disconnecting the engine coolant temperature sensor wiring plug

10 Disconnect the battery negative lead.
11 Remove the securing screw, and withdraw the sensor shroud.
12 Disconnect the sensor wiring plug.
13 Remove the Torx securing screw, and withdraw the sensor.
14 Refitting is a reversal of removal.
1.8 litre
15 Proceed as described for the ESC Hybrid module. If a new sensor (not the original unit) is being fitted, position it in the mounting bracket so that it is in actual contact with one of the teeth of the toothed wheel on the crankshaft. Hold the sensor in this position, and tighten the clamping screw. New sensors have projections on their base, which will wear away when the engine is cranking, and automatically set the specified clearance.
2.0 litre DOHC fuel injection models
16 This procedure is as described for the 2.0 litre DOHC carburettor models (ESC II module).

Air charge temperature sensor

1.6 and 1.8 litre (R6A type) CVH models
17 The sensor is located in the side of the CFI unit on 1.6 litre engines **(see illustration)**, and on the inlet manifold on 1.8 litre engines.
18 Disconnect the battery negative lead.
19 Disconnect the sensor wiring plug by pulling on the plug, not the wiring.
20 Unscrew the sensor from its location, and remove it.
21 Refitting is a reversal of removal, but coat the threads of the sensor with suitable sealant before fitting.
2.0 litre DOHC fuel injection models
22 The sensor is located in the upper section of the inlet manifold.
23 Disconnect the battery negative lead.
24 Disconnect the sensor wiring plug by pulling on the plug, not the wiring **(see illustration)**.
25 Unscrew the sensor from the inlet manifold, and remove it.
26 Refitting is a reversal of removal, noting the torque setting for the sensor.

5

21.24 Disconnecting the air charge temperature sensor wiring plug

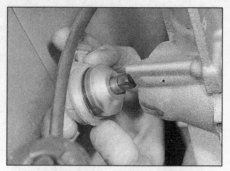

21.32 Withdrawing the vehicle speed sensor from the gearbox casing

21.35 Manifold absolute pressure (MAP) sensor location

Vehicle speed sensor

1.6 and 1.8 litre CVH (R6A type) and 2.0 litre DOHC fuel injection models

27 The sensor is located in the left-hand side of the gearbox/transmission.

28 Disconnect the battery negative lead.

29 Jack up the vehicle and support it securely on axle stands (see "Jacking and Vehicle Support").

30 Detach the sensor wiring connector from its bracket, and separate the two halves of the connector.

31 Unscrew the securing bolt, and withdraw the wiring connector bracket, noting its orientation.

32 Withdraw the sensor from the gearbox/transmission casing **(see illustration)**.

33 Before refitting the sensor, examine the O-ring, and renew if damaged or worn.

34 Refitting is a reversal of removal, ensuring that the wiring connector bracket is correctly located.

Manifold absolute pressure (MAP) sensor

1.6 and 1.8 litre CVH (R6A type) and 2.0 litre DOHC fuel injection models

35 The sensor is located at the rear right-hand side of the engine compartment **(see illustration)**.

36 Disconnect the battery negative lead.

37 Remove the two screws securing the sensor to the body panel, and carefully withdraw the sensor, taking care not to strain

21.42 Disconnecting the fuel temperature sensor wiring plug

the wiring.

38 Disconnect the wiring plug from the sensor, pulling on the plug, not the wiring, then disconnect the vacuum hose and remove the sensor.

39 Refitting is a reversal of removal.

Fuel temperature sensor - removal and refitting

2.0 litre DOHC fuel injection models

40 The sensor is located in the top of the fuel rail.

41 Disconnect the battery negative lead, and to improve access, disconnect the wiring plug from the air charge temperature sensor (in the inlet manifold). Disconnect the sensor wiring plug by pulling on the plug, not the wiring.

42 Disconnect the fuel temperature sensor wiring plug, again pulling on the plug **(see illustration)**.

43 Unscrew the sensor from the fuel rail, and remove it.

44 Refitting is a reversal of removal, noting the torque setting for the sensor.

22 Spark control system components (carburettor models) - removal and refitting

Spark delay and sustain valves

1 Disconnect the vacuum pipes at the valve and withdraw the valve.

2 When refitting a spark delay valve, the valve must be positioned with the black end (marked "CARB") towards the carburettor and the coloured end (marked "DIST") towards the distributor or electronic module (as applicable).

3 When refitting a spark sustain valve, the valve must be positioned with the end marked "VAC" towards the carburettor and the side marked "DIST" towards the distributor or electronic module (as applicable).

Ported vacuum switch

4 Where fitted, the switch(es) may be located in the inlet manifold and/or in an adapter fitted in one of the coolant hoses.

5 To remove a switch, partially drain the cooling system. Note that there is no need to remove the cylinder block drain plug.

6 Mark the vacuum pipes for location so that they can be refitted in their correct positions, then disconnect the pipes from the switch.

7 Unscrew the valve from its location.

8 Refitting is a reversal of removal, ensuring that the vacuum pipes are correctly connected. Refill the cooling system.

Fuel trap

9 Disconnect the vacuum pipes at the fuel trap and withdraw the fuel trap.

10 When refitting, the fuel trap must be positioned with the black end (marked "CARB") towards the carburettor, and the white side (marked "DIST") towards the distributor, electronic module, or ported vacuum switch (as applicable) **(see illustration)**.

Spark control system additional components

11 According to model, engine and equipment, additional components such as one-way valves or solenoids may also be fitted as part of the spark control system.

12 The removal and refitting procedures for these components are basically as described previously, and provided that all attachments are marked for position prior to removal, no problems should be encountered.

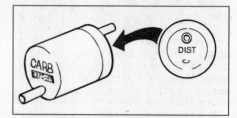

22.10 Fuel trap vacuum connection markings

Chapter 6
Clutch

Contents

Degrees of difficulty

Easy, suitable for novice with little experience		Fairly easy, suitable for beginner with some experience		Fairly difficult, suitable for competent DIY mechanic		Difficult, suitable for experienced DIY mechanic		Very difficult, suitable for expert DIY or professional	

Specifications

Clutch type	Single dry plate operated by self-adjusting cable	

Friction disc diameter

1.3 models	190.0 mm (7.5 in)	
1.6 litre models:		
Early models	190.0 mm (7.5 in)	
Later models	215.0 mm (8.5 in)	
1.8 and 2.0 litre models	215.0 mm (8.5 in)	

Torque wrench setting	Nm	lbf ft
Clutch cover to flywheel	20 to 25	15 to 18

6

1 General information

The clutch is of single dry plate type, and consists of five main components: friction disc, pressure plate, diaphragm spring, cover and release bearing.

The friction disc is free to slide along the splines of the gearbox input shaft, and is held in position between the flywheel and the pressure plate due to the pressure exerted on the pressure plate by the diaphragm spring. Friction lining material is riveted to both sides of the friction disc, and spring cushioning between the friction linings and the hub absorbs transmission shocks and helps to ensure a smooth take up of power as the clutch is engaged.

The diaphragm spring is mounted on pins and is held in place in the cover by annular fulcrum rings.

The release bearing is located on a guide sleeve at the front of the gearbox, and the bearing is free to slide on the sleeve under the action of the release arm which pivots inside the clutch bellhousing.

The release arm is operated by the clutch pedal via a cable. A self-adjusting mechanism on the clutch pedal automatically adjusts the cable free play to compensate for wear in the clutch components. The self-adjusting mechanism consists of a pawl, toothed quadrant and tension spring. When the pedal is released the tension spring pulls the quadrant through the teeth of the pawl until all free play of the clutch cable is taken up. When the pedal is depressed the pawl teeth engage with the quadrant teeth thus locking the quadrant.

Depressing the clutch pedal actuates the release arm by means of the cable. The release arm pushes the release bearing forwards to bear against the centre of the diaphragm spring, thus pushing the centre of the diaphragm spring inwards. The diaphragm spring is sandwiched between two fulcrum rings in the cover, and so as the centre of the spring is pushed in, the outside of the spring is pushed out, so allowing the pressure plate to move backwards away from the friction disc.

When the clutch pedal is released, the diaphragm spring forces the pressure plate into contact with the friction linings on the friction disc, and simultaneously pushes the friction disc forwards on its splines, forcing it against the flywheel. The friction disc is now firmly sandwiched between the pressure plate and the flywheel, and drive is taken up.

Note: *Modified clutch components are available to reduce the pedal pressure required to operate the clutch. Some later models may have been fitted with these components in production. Overhaul procedures are unaffected, but "Low-lift" components are not interchangeable with standard clutch components. The clutch driven plate and pressure plate are stamped "Low-lift" for identification.*

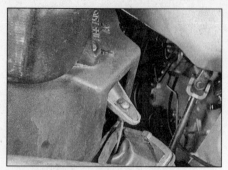

2.3 Rubber boot removed to expose release arm and cable end

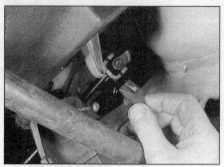

2.4a Removing the cable retainer to release the cable end

2.4b Alternative type of cable-to-release arm fitting

2 Clutch cable - removal and refitting

Removal

1 Apply the handbrake, jack up the front of the vehicle and support on axle stands (see "*Jacking and Vehicle Support*").
2 Place a wooden block under the clutch pedal to raise it fully against its stop which will hold the automatic adjuster pawl clear of the toothed quadrant.
3 Working beneath the vehicle, remove the rubber boot from the clutch release arm on the bellhousing **(see illustration)**. On some models the boot is secured with a clip.
4 To disconnect the end of the inner cable from the release arm, pull the cable end towards the rear of the vehicle and either slide the cable so that it passes through the larger hole in the release arm, or remove the cable retainer as applicable **(see illustrations)**.
5 Remove the rubber boot from the cable.
6 Working inside the vehicle, remove the lower facia panel from the driver's side.
7 Unhook and remove the inner cable from the toothed quadrant on the pedal.
8 Withdraw the cable through the bulkhead into the engine compartment, taking careful note of its routing.
9 Pull the clutch end of the cable through the hole in the bellhousing and remove the rubber bush from the cable where applicable.

Refitting

10 Refitting is a reversal of removal, bearing in mind the following points.
11 Ensure that the cable is routed as noted during removal.
12 Ensure that the clutch pedal is held firmly against its stop, (paragraph 2), until the inner cable is secured to the release arm.
13 On completion, release the clutch pedal and operate the clutch normally to ensure that the adjuster pawl is engaged with the toothed quadrant.

14 Check the operation of the clutch mechanism. The pedal should move by hand 10 to 15 mm (0.39 to 0.59 in) from its rest position upwards to the pedal stop position and should return the same distance when released.

3 Clutch pedal - removal, overhaul and refitting

Removal

1 Apply the handbrake, jack up the front of the vehicle and support on axle stands (see "*Jacking and Vehicle Support*") Disconnect the battery negative lead.
2 Proceed as described in Section 2, paragraphs 2 to 4 inclusive.
3 Working inside the vehicle, remove the lower facia panel from the driver's side.
4 Unhook and remove the inner cable from the toothed quadrant on the clutch pedal and disconnect the leads from the brake lamp switch **(see illustrations)**.
5 Remove the clip from the brake servo/ABS hydraulic unit pushrod on the brake pedal.
6 Unscrew the two nuts and single bolt which hold the pedal bracket to the bulkhead. Note that the two nuts are screwed onto the brake servo/ABS hydraulic unit studs **(see illustrations)**.
7 Carefully withdraw the pedal bracket from around the steering column.

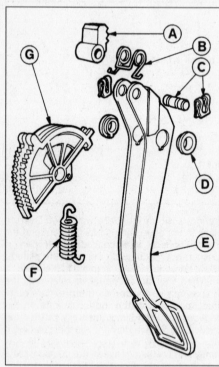

3.4a Clutch pedal and automatic adjuster components

  A *Adjuster pawl*
  B *Spring*
  C *Pawl pivot shaft and clip*
  D *Nylon bush*
  E *Pedal*
  F *Toothed quadrant tension spring*
  G *Adjuster toothed quadrant*

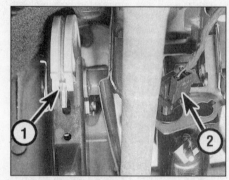

3.4b Unhook the cable from the toothed quadrant (1) and disconnect the brake light switch (2)

3.6a Pedal bracket/brake servo right-hand securing nut (arrowed)

3.6b Unscrewing the pedal bracket top securing bolt

3.8 Pivot shaft outboard circlip

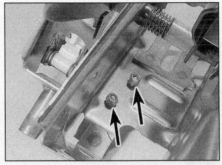

3.9a Cable bracket self-locking nuts (arrowed)

Overhaul

8 With the pedal assembly on the bench, extract the outboard circlip from the clutch pedal end of the pivot shaft **(see illustration)**.

9 Unscrew the two small self-locking nuts, and remove the clutch cable bracket **(see illustrations)**.

10 The clutch pedal can now be slid from the pivot shaft, noting the position of any washers, spacers and springs which may be fitted.

11 To dismantle the clutch pedal and adjuster mechanism, proceed as follows.

12 Prise the nylon bushes from each side of the pedal and remove the toothed quadrant. Unhook the spring.

13 Prise one of the clips from the adjuster pawl pivot shaft, withdraw the shaft and remove the pawl and spring.

14 Clean all the components and examine them for wear and damage, renewing as necessary.

15 Lubricate the bores of the adjuster pawl and toothed quadrant with graphite grease.

16 Assemble the adjuster pawl, spring and pivot shaft to the pedal, and refit the clip removed when dismantling.

17 Attach the spring to the toothed quadrant, then insert the quadrant into the pedal and press in the two nylon bushes.

18 Lift the adjuster pawl and turn the toothed quadrant so that the pawl rests on the smooth curved surface at the end of the teeth **(see illustration)**.

3.9b Removing the cable bracket

19 Attach the toothed quadrant spring to the pedal.

20 Lubricate the pedal pivot shaft with a molybdenum disulphide based grease, then refit the pedal assembly to the shaft. Refit any washers, spacers and springs in their original positions.

21 Refit the clutch cable bracket, and tighten the two self-locking nuts.

22 Refit the circlip to the clutch pedal end of the pivot shaft.

Refitting

23 Refitting of the pedal assembly is a reversal of removal, but refer to Section 2, paragraphs 11 to 14 inclusive when reconnecting the clutch cable.

3.18 Adjuster pawl and toothed segment at initial setting

4 Clutch assembly - removal, inspection and refitting

Removal

1 In order to remove the clutch it will be necessary to remove either the engine or the gearbox. Unless the engine requires a major overhaul, it is easier and quicker to remove the gearbox.

2 If the original clutch is to be refitted, mark the clutch cover and flywheel for alignment which will ensure identical positioning on refitting. This is not necessary if a new clutch is to be fitted.

3 Progressively unscrew, in a diagonal sequence, the six bolts and spring washers which secure the clutch cover to the flywheel. This will prevent distortion of the cover and will also prevent the cover from suddenly flying off due to binding on the dowels.

4 With all the bolts removed, lift off the clutch assembly, pulling it from the dowels if necessary. Be prepared to catch the friction disc as the cover assembly is lifted from the flywheel, and note which way round the friction disc is fitted. The side nearest the flywheel is normally marked "FLYWHEEL SIDE" or "SHWUNGRADSEITE".

Inspection

5 With the clutch assembly removed **(see illustration)**, clean off all traces of dust using a dry cloth. Although most friction discs now have asbestos-free linings, some do not, and it

4.5 Clutch components

1 Friction disc
2 Pressure plate / diaphragm spring / cover assembly
3 Cable
4 Release bearing
5 Release arm

AH18814

6

4.10a Fitting friction disc and cover assembly. Note orientation of friction disc

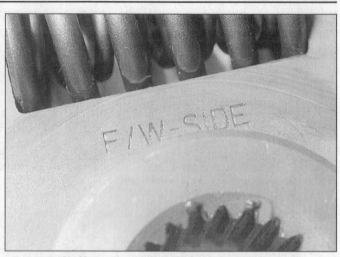

4.10b Alternative friction disc orientation marking

is wise to take suitable precautions; *asbestos dust is harmful and must not be inhaled.*

6 Examine the linings of the friction disc for wear and loose rivets, distortion, cracks, broken torsion springs and worn splines. The surface of the friction linings may be highly glazed, but, as long as the friction material pattern can be clearly seen, this is satisfactory. If there is any sign of oil contamination, indicated by a continuous, or patchy, shiny black discolouration, the plate must be renewed and the source of the contamination traced and rectified. This will be either a leaking crankshaft oil seal or gearbox input shaft oil seal or both. The friction disc must also be renewed if the lining thickness has worn down to, or just above, the level of the rivet heads.

7 Check the machined faces of the flywheel and pressure plate. If either is grooved, or heavily scored, renewal is necessary. The pressure plate must also be renewed if any cracks are apparent, or if the diaphragm spring is damaged or its pressure suspect.

8 With the gearbox removed it is advisable to check the condition of the release bearing.

Refitting

9 It is important to ensure that no oil or grease gets on the friction disc linings, or the pressure plate and flywheel faces. It is advisable to refit the clutch assembly with clean hands, and to wipe down the pressure plate and flywheel faces with a clean rag before assembly begins.

10 Place the friction disc against the flywheel, ensuring that it is fitted the correct way round. The projecting torsion spring hub should be farthest from the flywheel, and the "FLYWHEEL SIDE" or "SHWUNGRADSEITE" mark should face towards the flywheel **(see illustrations)**.

11 Fit the clutch cover assembly, fitting it over the locating dowels, and aligning the previously made marks on the clutch cover and flywheel. Insert the six bolts and spring washers and tighten them finger-tight so that the friction disc is gripped, but can still be moved.

12 The friction disc must now be centralised so that when the engine and gearbox are mated, the gearbox input shaft splines will pass through the splines in the centre of the friction disc.

13 Centralisation can be carried out by inserting a round bar or a long screwdriver through the hole in the centre of the friction disc, so that the end of the bar rests in the spigot bearing in the centre of the crankshaft. Where possible use a blunt instrument, and if a screwdriver is used, wrap tape around the blade to prevent damage to the bearing surface. Moving the bar sideways or up and down will move the friction disc in whichever direction is necessary to achieve centralisation. With the bar removed, view the friction disc hub in relation to the hole in the end of the crankshaft and the circle created by the ends of the diaphragm spring fingers. When the hub appears exactly in the centre, all is correct. Alternatively, if a clutch aligning tool can be obtained, this will eliminate all the guesswork obviating the need for visual alignment **(see illustration)**.

4.13 Centralising the friction disc using a clutch aligning tool

4.14 Clutch fitted to flywheel ready for fitting of the gearbox

5.3a Withdrawing the release bearing from the guide sleeve

5.3b Release bearing retaining clip with tag arrowed

14 Tighten the cover retaining bolts gradually, in a diagonal sequence, to the specified torque wrench setting **(see illustration)**.
15 Refit the gearbox or engine, as applicable.

5 Clutch release bearing and arm - removal, inspection and refitting

Note: *Where the release bearing is secured to the release arm with spring clips. If the bearing is to be removed but not renewed, check to ensure that new spring clips can be obtained, as the old clips cannot be re-used. New clips will be supplied with a new bearing. On models fitted with an MT75 type gearbox, the clutch release bearing may be secured to the arm using a circlip instead of spring clips.*

Removal

1 With the gearbox and engine separated to provide access to the clutch, attention can be given to the release bearing located in the clutch bellhousing over the gearbox input shaft.
2 If not already done, remove the rubber boot from the release arm and disconnect the clutch cable.
3 The release bearing must now be freed from the release arm. The bearing is secured by spring clips which can only be freed by reaching behind the release arm. Access is extremely limited, and a small angled tool such as an Allen key will be required to depress the tags at top and bottom of the bearing. It is likely that the clips will be broken during the removal process, and in any case they should be renewed when the bearing is refitted. When the bearing is free, withdraw it from the guide sleeve **(see illustrations)**.
4 Pull the release arm from the fulcrum pin, then withdraw the arm over the input shaft, guiding the end through the bellhousing aperture **(see illustration)**.

Inspection

5 Spin the release bearing and check it for roughness. Hold the outer race and attempt to move it laterally against the inner race. If any excessive movement or roughness is evident, renew the bearing. If a new clutch has been fitted, it is wise to renew the release bearing as a matter of course.

Refitting

6 Refitting is a reversal of removal, but use new bearing retaining clips, and reconnect the cable to the release arm with reference to Section 2.

6

5.4 Release arm and fulcrum pin (arrowed)

Notes

Chapter 7 Part A:
Manual gearbox

Contents

Degrees of difficulty

Easy, suitable for novice with little experience		Fairly easy, suitable for beginner with some experience		Fairly difficult, suitable for competent DIY mechanic		Difficult, suitable for experienced DIY mechanic		Very difficult, suitable for expert DIY or professional	

Specifications

General

Type . . . . Four forward speeds (A, B and C type gearboxes) or five forward speeds (N and MT75 type gearboxes) and reverse. Synchromesh on all forward speeds

Application

1.3 litre models	A1 and C types
1.6 litre models with Ford VV carburettor	A2, B, C and N types
1.6 litre models with Weber 2V carburettor	B, C and N types
1.8 litre models	B and N types
2.0 litre SOHC models	B and N types
2.0 litre DOHC models	MT75 type

Capacities . . . . Refer to Chapter 1 Specifications

Torque wrench settings	Nm	lbf ft
A,B,C and N types		
Clutch housing-to-gearbox casing bolts	70 to 90	52 to 66
Clutch housing-to-engine bolts	40 to 50	30 to 37
Clutch release bearing guide sleeve bolts:		
All except C type	9 to 11	7 to 8
C-type	21 to 25	15 to 18
Extension housing-to-gearbox casing bolts	45 to 49	33 to 36
Top cover bolts:		
All except C type	10 to 13	7 to 10
C type	21 to 25	15 to 18
Gearbox crossmember-to-underbody bolts	20 to 25	14 to 18
Gearbox crossmember-to-gearbox bolt	50 to 57	37 to 42
Reversing light switch	1 to 2	0.8 to 1.5
Oil filler/level plug	33 to 41	24 to 30
Gear lever-to-extension housing screws	21 to 26	15 to 19
MT75 type		
Gearbox crossmember-to-underbody bolts	30 to 40	22 to 30
Gearbox crossmember-to-gearbox bolt	52 to 71	38 to 52
Gear linkage support bracket-to-gearbox bolts	21 to 29	15 to 21
Engine-to-gearbox bolts	29 to 41	21 to 30
Oil filler/level plug	29 to 41	21 to 30
Oil drain plug	29 to 41	21 to 30

1 General information

The manual gearbox may be of four or five-speed type, depending on model. Three different types of four-speed gearbox have been fitted to Sierra models, these being the A, B and C types. The A and B type gearboxes are similar but all A type gearboxes have an integral clutch housing, whereas B type gearboxes may have either an integral or bolt-on clutch housing. The C type gearbox is substantially different to the A and B types, and procedures differ in detail.

A five-speed N type gearbox is also available, with the fifth gear installed in the tailshaft housing of the gearbox on an extended gear cluster.

The MT75 type gearbox is of a five-speed type and is completely new, owing nothing to the previous types used in the Sierra range. The gearbox is lighter, more compact, and more reliable than its predecessors. Its casing consists of front and rear housings manufactured from aluminium alloy, and as the 5th gear components are accommodated in the main casing, there is no need for an extension housing.

2 Removal and refitting (engine in vehicle)

A,B,C and N types

Removal

1 Removal of the engine and manual gearbox as an assembly is described in Chapter 2.
2 Disconnect the battery negative lead.
3 Working in the engine compartment, unscrew and remove the four upper engine-to-gearbox bolts, noting the location of the earth lead.
4 Working inside the vehicle, unscrew the gear lever knob and remove the centre console. Where a full length console is fitted, it is only necessary to remove the front tray.
5 Detach the outer gaiter from the retaining frame and withdraw it over the gear lever.
6 Undo the securing screws on early models, or release the clips on later models, and

2.6a With the outer gaiter removed, remove the gaiter retaining frame . . .

2.6b . . . and the inner gaiter

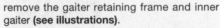

2.7a Remove the gear lever securing screws . . .

2.7b . . . and withdraw the gear lever

remove the gaiter retaining frame and inner gaiter **(see illustrations)**.
7 Using a suitable Torx key, remove the screws securing the gear lever to the gearbox extension housing, and withdraw the gear lever. Note how the base of the gear lever locates over the selector shaft **(see illustrations)**.
8 Jack up the vehicle and support on axle stands (see "*Jacking and Vehicle Support*"). Ensure that there is sufficient working room beneath the vehicle.
9 To improve access, disconnect the exhaust downpipe from the manifold and remove the exhaust system.
10 Remove the propeller shaft.
11 Where applicable, bend back the locktabs, then unscrew the two bolts securing each of the two anti-roll bar U-clamps to the vehicle underbody. Lower the anti-roll bar as far as possible.

12 Disconnect the wiring from the starter motor and remove the starter motor.
13 Disconnect the wiring from the reversing lamp switch **(see illustration)**.
14 Remove the retaining circlip, and withdraw the speedometer cable from the gearbox extension housing **(see illustration)**.
15 Disconnect the clutch cable from the release arm.
16 Support the gearbox with a trolley jack, and an interposed block of wood to spread the load.
17 Unscrew the four bolts securing the gearbox crossmember to the vehicle underbody. Unscrew the central bolt securing the crossmember to the gearbox and remove the crossmember. Note the position of the earth strap, where applicable. Recover the mounting cup and where applicable the exhaust mounting bracket and heat shield **(see illustrations)**.
18 Unscrew and remove the remaining engine-to-gearbox bolts, noting the location of the engine/gearbox brace on the right-hand side of the gearbox on SOHC models **(see illustration)**.
19 With the help of an assistant, lift the gearbox from the engine, using the trolley jack to take the weight. Do not allow the weight of the gearbox to hang on the input shaft. It may be necessary to rock the transmission a little to release it from the engine.
20 With the gearbox removed, temporarily reconnect the anti-roll bar to the underbody if the vehicle is to be moved.

2.13 Disconnect the wiring from the reversing lamp switch

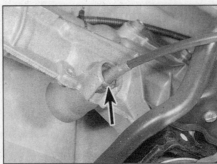

2.14 Remove the circlip (arrowed) and withdraw the speedometer cable

2.17a Unscrew the gearbox crossmember securing bolts (arrowed) . . .

2.17b . . . and recover the mounting cup

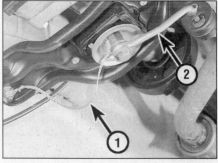

2.17c Gearbox crossmember earth strap (1) and exhaust mounting bracket (2) - 1.8 litre (R2A) CVH

Refitting

21 Refitting is a reversal of removal, taking note of the following points.

22 Before attempting to refit the gearbox, check that the clutch friction disc is centralised. This is necessary to ensure that the gearbox input shaft splines will pass through the splines in the centre of the friction disc.

23 Check that the clutch release arm and bearing are correctly fitted, and lightly grease the input shaft splines.

24 Check that the engine adapter plate is correctly positioned on its locating dowels.

25 Refit the propeller shaft.

26 Refit the exhaust system.

27 Connect the clutch cable to the release arm.

28 On completion, check and if necessary top-up the gearbox oil level.

MT75 type

Removal

29 Removal of the engine and gearbox as an assembly is described in Chapter 2

30 Disconnect the battery negative lead.

31 Unscrew and remove the top engine-to-gearbox bolts which are accessible from the engine compartment. Note the location of the bolts, and note the positions of the earth strap, and of any wiring clips attached to the bolts.

32 Jack up the vehicle and support it on axle stands (see *"Jacking and Vehicle Support"*).

33 To improve access, disconnect the exhaust downpipe from the manifold and remove the exhaust system.

34 On models with a catalytic converter, release the securing clips and withdraw the

exhaust heat shield from under the vehicle for access to the propeller shaft.

35 Remove the propeller shaft.

36 Where applicable, bend back the locktabs, then unscrew the two bolts securing each of the two anti-roll bar U-clamps to the vehicle underbody. Lower the anti-roll bar as far as possible.

37 Disconnect the wiring from the starter motor, and remove the starter motor.

38 Support the gearbox with a trolley jack, using an interposed block of wood to spread the load.

39 Unscrew the four nuts securing the gearbox crossmember to the vehicle underbody.

40 Unscrew the central bolt securing the crossmember to the gearbox, and remove the crossmember. Note the position of the earth strap, where applicable. Recover the mounting cup, and where applicable the exhaust mounting bracket and heat shield **(see illustration)**.

41 Lower the gearbox slightly on the jack, then remove the securing circlip and disconnect the speedometer drive cable from the gearbox **(see illustration)**.

42 Disconnect the wiring from the reversing lamp switch. On models with fuel injection, disconnect the wiring from the vehicle speed sensor mounted in the side of the gearbox **(see illustration)**.

43 Unscrew the two securing bolts, and disconnect the gear linkage support bracket from the gearbox **(see illustration)**.

7A

2.18 Unscrew the engine/gearbox brace

2.40 Gearbox crossmember and earth strap

2.41 Speedometer drive cable connection at gearbox

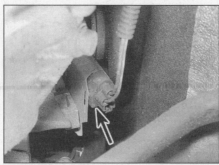

2.42 Vehicle speed sensor wiring plug and bracket (arrowed) - fuel injection models

2.43 Gear linkage support bracket securing bolt (arrowed)

44 Using a suitable pin punch, drive out the roll-pin securing the gearchange rod to the gear linkage.

45 Place a suitable rod across the vehicle underbody, to support the gear linkage support bracket whilst the gearbox is removed.

46 Working inside the vehicle, place a wooden block under the clutch pedal to raise it fully against its stop, so holding the automatic adjuster pawl clear of the toothed quadrant.

47 Disconnect the clutch cable from the clutch release arm, and pass the cable through the bellhousing. Take note of the routing of the cable, to aid refitting.

48 Unscrew and remove the remaining engine-to-gearbox bolts, and remove the bolt from the engine adapter plate. Recover any shims fitted between the sump and the gearbox when removing the lower engine-to-gearbox bolts.

49 With the aid of an assistant, lift the gearbox from the engine, using the trolley jack to take the weight. Do not allow the weight of the gearbox to hang on the input shaft. It may be necessary to rock the gearbox a little to release it from the engine.

50 With the gearbox removed, temporarily reconnect the anti-roll bar to the underbody if the vehicle is to be moved.

Refitting

51 Refitting is a reversal of removal, taking note of the following points.

52 Before attempting to refit the gearbox, check that the clutch friction disc is centralised.

53 Check that the clutch release arm and bearing are correctly fitted, and lightly grease the input shaft splines.

54 Check that the engine adapter plate is correctly positioned on its dowels. If necessary, a cable-tie can be used to temporarily secure the adapter plate in position on the cylinder block, using one of the engine-to-gearbox bolt holes.

55 If shims were fitted between the sump and the gearbox, refit them in their original locations when mating the engine to the gearbox. If the engine has been overhauled, fit the relevant shims as calculated during engine reassembly .

56 Reconnect the clutch cable to the release arm, ensuring that it is routed as noted during removal.

57 Refit the propeller shaft.

58 Refit the exhaust system.

59 Tighten all fixings to the specified torque, where applicable.

60 On completion, check the gearbox oil level, and top-up if necessary.

3 Gear linkage (MT75 type) - removal and refitting

Removal

1 Working inside the vehicle, unclip the knob from the gear lever by pressing it sideways. Do not turn the gear lever knob.

2 Where applicable, detach the tray from the centre console.

3 Release the gear lever outer gaiter from the centre console/tray, then turn it inside-out and pull it up the gear lever **(see illustration)**.

4 Detach the gear lever inner gaiter, together with the retaining frame, from the centre console.

5 Proceed as described in paragraphs 32 to 47 of Section 2, ignoring paragraph 45.

6 Manipulate the rubber gaiter from the gear linkage support bracket for access to the base of the gear lever.

7 Remove the circlip and the pivot pin, then disconnect the gear shift rod from the base of the gear lever. Withdraw the gear shift rod.

8 Remove the circlip securing the base of the gear lever to the gear linkage support bracket, and withdraw the gear lever assembly through the floor from inside the vehicle, and the gear linkage support bracket from under the vehicle.

9 The gear lever assembly cannot be dismantled, and must be renewed as a unit if faulty.

Refitting

10 Refitting is a reversal of removal, bearing in mind the following points.

11 Reconnect the clutch cable to the release arm, ensuring that it is routed as noted during removal.

12 Tighten all fixings to the specified torque, where applicable.

4 Overhaul - general information

Overhauling a gearbox is a difficult and involved job for the DIY home mechanic. In addition to dismantling and reassembling many small parts, clearances must be precisely measured and, if necessary, changed by selecting shims and spacers.Gearbox internal components are also often difficult to obtain and in many instances extremely expensive. Because of this, if the gearbox develops a fault or becomes noisy, the best course of action is to have the unit overhauled by a specialist or to obtain an exchange reconditioned unit.

Nevertheless, it is not impossible for the more experienced mechanic to overhaul a gearbox provided that the special tools are available and the job is done in a deliberate step-by-step manner so that nothing is overlooked.

The tools necessary for overhaul include internal and external circlip pliers, bearing pullers, a slide-hammer, a set of pin punches, a dial test indicator and possibly an hydraulic press. In addition, a large sturdy workbench and a vice will be required.

All work should be done in conditions of extreme cleanliness. When dismantling, make careful notes of how each component is fitted. This will facilitate accurate and straightfoward reassembly.

Before dismantling the gearbox, it will help to have some idea of which component is malfunctioning. Certain problems can be related to specific areas in the gearbox which can in turn make component examination and replacement more straightfoward. Refer to the Fault Diagnosis Section at the beginning of this Manual for more information.

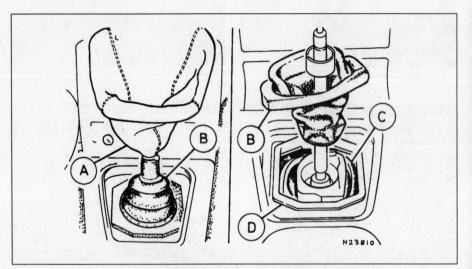

3.3 Gear lever gaiters - MT75 gearbox

A Outer gaiter *B Inner gaiter* *C Noise damping pad* *D Retaining frame*

Chapter 7 Part B:
Automatic transmission

Contents

Degrees of difficulty

Easy, suitable for novice with little experience		Fairly easy, suitable for beginner with some experience		Fairly difficult, suitable for competent DIY mechanic		Difficult, suitable for experienced DIY mechanic		Very difficult, suitable for expert DIY or professional	

Specifications

Type

Models up to 1985	Ford C3 type with three forward speeds and one reverse, epicyclic gear train with hydraulic control and torque converter
Models from 1985	Ford A4LD type with four forward speeds and one reverse, epicyclic gear train with hydraulic control and torque converter. Torque converter lock-up in third and fourth gears
Late model 2.0 litre DOHC	Ford A4LD type with partial electronic control

Capacities . . . . Refer to Chapter 1 Specifications

Torque wrench settings

	Nm	lbf ft
Engine-to-transmission bolts	30 to 37	22 to 27
Transmission crossmember-to-underbody bolts	20 to 25	15 to 19
Transmission crossmember-to-transmission bolt	50 to 57	37 to 42
Fluid cooler pipe connector to transmission housing	24 to 30	18 to 22
Fluid cooler pipe to connector	22 to 24	16 to 18
Torque converter-to-driveplate nuts:		
C3 transmission	30 to 40	22 to 30
A4LD transmission	32 to 38	24 to 28
Torque converter fluid drain plug	27 to 40	20 to 29
Kickdown solenoid mounting bracket bolts (A4LD type transmission) .	29 to 41	21 to 30
Brake band adjuster screw	13	10
Brake band adjuster screw locknut	50 to 58	37 to 43
Vacuum diaphragm unit bracket bolt	1 to 2	0.7 to 1.5
Starter inhibitor/reversing light switch	10 to 14	7 to 10
Sump bolts:		
C3 type transmission	13 to 20	10 to 15
A4LD type transmission:		
Plastic gasket	8 to 11	6 to 8
Cork gasket	15 to 18	11 to 13

7B

1 General information

The automatic transmission takes the place of the clutch and manual gearbox. Early models were fitted with a C3 type 3-speed transmission whilst later models use the more advanced A4LD type 4-speed unit.

The transmission consists of two main components. A hydraulic torque converter, capable of torque multiplication, transmits power from the engine to a hydraulically-operated epicyclic gearbox.

In the case of the C3 type transmission, the gearbox comprises two planetary gearsets providing three forward ratios and one reverse ratio. The A4LD type transmission comprises three planetary gearsets providing four forward ratios and one reverse ratio, and the torque converter locks up in 3rd and 4th gears, so avoiding power losses due to converter slip. 4th gear on the A4LD type transmission is an overdrive, maximum speed being obtained in 3rd.

The planetary geartrains provide the desired gear ratio according to which of their components are held stationary or allowed to turn. The geartrain components are held or released by friction clutches and brake bands which are actuated by hydraulic valves. The C3 type transmission has three friction clutches and two brake bands, whereas the A4LD type transmission has three friction clutches, three brake bands, and additionally two one-way clutches. An oil pump within the transmission provides the necessary hydraulic pressure to operate the various clutches and brakes.

Driver control of the transmission is by a selector lever which allows fully automatic operation with a hold facility on 1st and 2nd gear in the case of the C3 type transmission, and 1st, 2nd and 3rd gears in the case of the A4LD type transmission. The transmission will change automatically through all forward gears according to speed, load and throttle position. If gears are selected manually, the transmission will not change down until speed has reduced sufficiently to avoid damage.

A "kickdown" facility causes the transmission to change down a gear (subject to speed) if the accelerator pedal is depressed fully and held down. This is useful when rapid acceleration is required, for example when overtaking. Kickdown is controlled by a cable linked to the transmission and the throttle cable, or on later models with the A4LD type transmission, by a throttle-operated switch and a solenoid actuator on the transmission.

An A4LD type transmission with partial electronic control is fitted to later 2.0 litre DOHC models, earlier models being fitted with the conventionally-controlled transmission described above. A transmission with partial electronic control can be identified by looking at the lock-up clutch solenoid wiring plug, which has three wires instead of the previous two. This transmission behaves in exactly the same way as the earlier type for gearchanges up and down between the first three gears. Changes up from 3rd to 4th, and down from 4th to 3rd, and the torque converter lock-up clutch, are controlled by an EEC IV engine management module which provides more accurate control of the transmission according to the prevailing engine operating conditions.

Due to the complexity of the automatic transmission, any repair or overhaul work must be referred to a Ford dealer or automatic transmission specialist with the necessary equipment for fault diagnosis and repair. The contents of this Chapter are therefore confined to supplying any service information and instructions which can be used by the home mechanic.

2 Removal and refitting (engine in vehicle)

Note: *Any suspected faults must be referred to a Ford dealer or automatic transmission specialist before removal of the unit, as the specialist fault diagnosis equipment is designed to operate with the transmission in the vehicle.*

All except 2.0 DOHC

Removal

1 Removal of the engine and transmission as an assembly is described in Chapter 2.
2 Disconnect the battery negative lead.
3 Working in the engine compartment, unscrew and remove the four upper engine-to-transmission bolts, noting the location of the earth lead, vacuum pipe bracket, and the transmission dipstick tube bracket.
4 Jack up the vehicle and support on axle stands (see *"Jacking and Vehicle Support"*). Ensure that there is sufficient working room beneath the vehicle.
5 To improve access, disconnect the exhaust downpipe from the manifold and remove the exhaust system.
6 Remove the propeller shaft.
7 If applicable bend back the locktabs, then unscrew the two bolts securing each of the two anti-roll bar U-clamps to the vehicle underbody. Lower the anti-roll bar as far as possible.
8 Withdraw the dipstick and remove the dipstick tube from the right-hand side of the transmission **(see illustration)**. Plug the opening

2.8 Transmission fluid dipstick tube (arrowed)

in the transmission to prevent dirt ingress.
9 Disconnect the wiring from the starter motor and remove the starter motor.
10 Where applicable, pull the blanking plug from the engine adapter plate.
11 Unscrew the unions and disconnect the fluid cooler pipes from the transmission **(see illustration)**. Plug the open ends of the pipes and the transmission to prevent dirt ingress and fluid leakage. If necessary, remove the fluid cooler pipe bracket from the engine mounting and place it to one side.
12 Remove the two clips securing the selector rod, and detach the selector rod from the manual selector lever, and the selector lever on the transmission.
13 Disconnect the kickdown cable from the lever on the transmission, and where applicable, detach the cable from the bracket on the transmission housing. On C3 type transmissions it will be necessary to unscrew the locknut in order to remove the cable from the bracket.
14 Disconnect the wiring from the starter inhibitor/reversing lamp switch and where applicable, on A4LD type transmissions, the kickdown solenoid and the lock-up clutch.
15 Remove the securing screw, and disconnect the speedometer cable from the transmission extension housing. Plug the opening in the transmission to prevent dirt ingress.
16 Disconnect the vacuum pipe from the vacuum diaphragm unit **(see illustration)** and unclip the pipe from its securing bracket on the transmission housing where applicable.

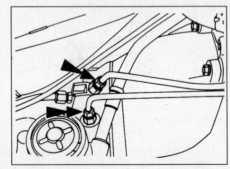

2.11 Transmission fluid cooler pipes (arrowed)

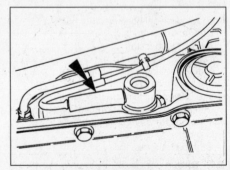

2.16 Vacuum diaphragm unit pipe (arrowed)

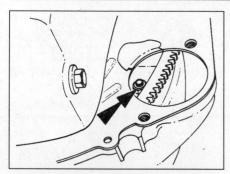

2.17 Torque converter-to-driveplate nut (arrowed) positioned in starter motor aperture

17 Working through the starter motor aperture, unscrew the four torque converter-to-driveplate nuts. It will be necessary to turn the crankshaft using a suitable spanner on the crankshaft pulley bolt in order to gain access to each nut in turn through the aperture (see illustration).
18 Support the transmission with a trolley jack, using an interposed block of wood to spread the load.
19 Unscrew the four bolts securing the transmission crossmember to the vehicle underbody. Note the position of the earth strap where applicable. Unscrew the central bolt securing the crossmember to the transmission and remove the crossmember. Recover the mounting cup and where applicable the exhaust mounting bracket (see illustration).
20 Unscrew and remove the remaining engine-to-transmission bolts, noting the location of the engine/transmission brace on the right-hand side of the transmission on SOHC models.
21 With the help of an assistant, lift the transmission from the engine, using the trolley jack to take the weight. Ensure that the torque converter is held firmly in place in the transmission housing during removal, otherwise it could fall out resulting in fluid spillage and possible damage. It may be necessary to rock the transmission a little to release it from the engine.
22 With the transmission removed, temporarily reconnect the anti-roll bar to the

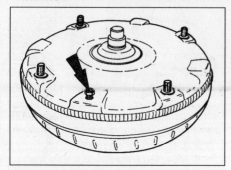

2.25 Torque converter drain plug (arrowed) must line up with opening in driveplate - C3 transmission

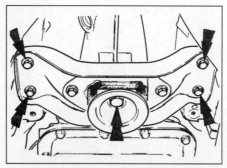

2.19 Transmission crossmember securing bolts (arrowed)

underbody if the vehicle is to be moved.

Refitting

23 Refitting is a reversal of removal, taking note of the following points.
24 As the torque converter is only loosely engaged in the transmission, the transmission must be kept inclined during installation to prevent the torque converter from falling out forwards. When the torque converter hub is fully engaged with the fluid pump drivegear in the transmission, distance "A" (see illustration) must be as specified. Incorrect installation of the torque converter will result in damage to the transmission.
25 As the transmission is installed, guide the torque converter studs through the holes in the driveplate, noting that on the C3 type transmission, the torque converter fluid drain plug must line up with the opening in the driveplate (see illustration). When the transmission housing is positioned flush with the engine adapter plate and the engine block, check that the torque converter is free to move axially a small amount before refitting and tightening the engine-to-transmission bolts.
26 Do not tighten the torque converter-to-driveplate nuts until the lower engine-to-transmission bolts and the transmission crossmember have been fitted and tightened.

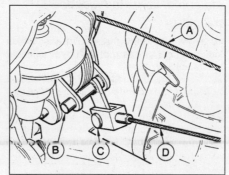

3.1 Kickdown cable linkage at carburetter - C3 transmission

A Throttle cable
B Lever
C Pin and spring clip
D Kickdown cable

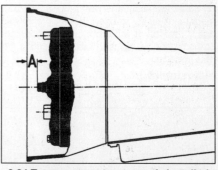

2.24 Torque converter correctly installed

A = 10.0 mm (0.39 in) minimum for C3 transmission
A = 9.0 mm (0.35 in) minimum for A4LD transmission

27 Where applicable, reconnect and adjust the kickdown cable.
28 Reconnect and adjust the selector rod.
29 Refit the propeller shaft.
30 Refit the exhaust system.
31 On completion, with the vehicle standing on level ground, check and if necessary top-up the hydraulic fluid level.

2.0 DOHC

32 To remove and refit the transmission fitted to this model, proceed as described above but ignore any reference to the kickdown cable, and on models fitted with a transmission having partial electronic control, ignore any reference to the vacuum pipe.

3 Kickdown cable - removal, refitting and adjustment

C3 type transmission

Removal

1 Disconnect the cable from the lever on the carburettor/inlet manifold by removing the pin and spring clip (see illustration).
2 Unscrew the locknut, and release the cable from the bracket on the carburettor/inlet manifold by sliding the cable through the slotted opening in the bracket.
3 To improve access, apply the handbrake, jack up the front of the vehicle and support on axle stands (see "Jacking and Vehicle Support").
4 Repeat the procedure given in paragraph 2 at the cable bracket on the transmission.
5 Unhook the cable from the kickdown lever on the transmission, and withdraw the cable from the vehicle (see illustration).

Refitting

6 Refitting is a reversal of removal, but on completion check the cable adjustment as follows.
7 Before adjusting the cable, check that the carburettor throttle valve(s) is/are fully open when the throttle pedal is fully depressed.

7B

8 Have an assistant depress the throttle pedal sufficiently to open the throttle valve(s) fully, then pivot the kickdown lever on the transmission as far as the stop, and lock it in this position.

Adjustment

9 Adjust the cable by means of the locknuts until the gap "A" **(see illustration)** between the throttle quadrant and the kickdown lever is as specified. Tighten the locknuts.
10 Re-check the adjustment on completion by releasing then fully depressing the throttle pedal, and re-adjust the cable if necessary.

A4LD type transmission (mechanically-operated kickdown)

Removal and refitting

11 Cable removal and refitting is as described in paragraphs 1 to 6.

Adjustment

12 Cable adjustment should be carried out as follows: Make up a sheet metal setting gauge to the dimensions shown **(see illustration)**.
13 Slacken the adjuster nut "A" and the locknut "B" **(see illustration)** and unscrew the nuts to the ends of the thread on the cable sheath.

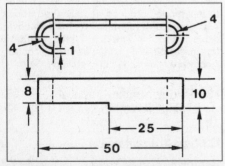

3.12 Kickdown cable setting gauge - A4LD transmission (mechanically-operated kickdown)

All dimensions in mm

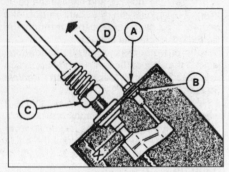

3.13 Kickdown cable adjustment - A4LD transmission (mechanically-operated kickdown)

A Kickdown cable adjuster nut
B Locknut
C Throttle cable adjuster nut
D Kickdown cable
X See text

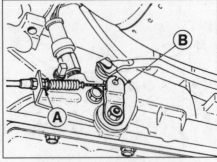

3.5 Kickdown cable linkage at transmission - C3 transmission

A Locknut   B Kickdown lever

14 Have an assistant depress the throttle pedal to its stop and hold it in this position. Ensure that the pedal travel is not restricted by mats or carpets.
15 Working in the engine compartment, turn the throttle cable adjuster nut "C" to achieve a dimension "X" (see illustration, paragraph 13) of 10.0 mm (0.39 in). Use the appropriate end of the setting gauge to check the gap. Ensure that the spring and spring cup at the end of the cable sheath do not turn as the adjuster nut is turned, as this may result in the dimension "X" altering when the vehicle is in use.
16 Remove the setting gauge and re-insert it with the 8.0 mm (0.32 in) end in gap "X". Have the assistant release the throttle pedal, which will clamp the gauge in position.
17 Pull the kickdown cable sheath in the direction of the arrow (see previous illustration, paragraph 13) as far as the stop. Hold the sheath in this position, ensuring that the locknut "B" is not touching the cable bracket, and secure the sheath by tightening adjuster nut "A" and locknut "B". When tightening locknut "B" ensure that the cable sheath and adjuster nut "A" do not turn. Adjustment is now complete.
18 On completion, check that the kickdown mechanism operates correctly.

A4LD type transmission (solenoid-operated kickdown)

Removal

19 From mid-1986, the A4LD transmission kickdown cable was replaced by a solenoid unit **(see illustration)**.
20 The solenoid is bolted to the transmission housing and is connected to the kickdown lever by a cable.
21 To remove the solenoid and cable, for improved access, apply the handbrake, then jack up the front of the vehicle and support on axle stands (see *"Jacking and Vehicle Support"*).
22 Prise the cable end from the ball-stud on the kickdown lever.
23 Pull the wiring connector from its bracket, and separate the two halves of the connector.
24 Loosen the solenoid mounting bracket bolts, and withdraw the solenoid from the bracket.

3.9 Kickdown cable adjustment dimension
A = 0.8 to 1.0 mm (0.03 to 0.04 in)

Refitting

25 Refitting is a reversal of removal, but before tightening the mounting bracket bolts, adjust the cable as follows.

Adjustment

26 Have an assistant switch on the ignition, with the selector lever in any position. **Under no circumstances start the engine.**
27 Have the assistant depress the throttle pedal to its stop, actuating the kickdown, and hold the pedal in this position.
28 Turn the kickdown lever on the transmission anti-clockwise against its stop, then slide the solenoid towards the front of the vehicle to put the cable under slight tension.
29 Tighten the lower solenoid mounting bracket bolt, then the upper bolt to the specified torque.
30 Have the assistant release the throttle pedal, when the kickdown cable should return to its normal position, then depress and release the pedal several times. Check that with the throttle pedal fully depressed, there is a clearance of between 0.3 and 0.8 mm (0.01 to 0.03 in) between the kickdown lever and its stop. This clearance must exist, as if the cable is over-tensioned the kickdown lever may return to its normal position inadvertently during operation.

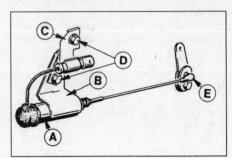

3.19 Kickdown solenoid assembly - A4LD transmission (solenoid operated kickdown)

A Solenoid
B Mounting bracket
C Wiring connector bracket
D Bolts
E Cable end ball-stud

31 Note: On models from late 1989, a modified kickdown solenoid with a shorter operating cable is fitted. The removal, refitting and adjustment procedures are as described above, but note that the clearance between the kickdown lever and its stop should be between 0.5 and 1.0 mm (0.02 to 0.04 in).
32 Switch off the ignition and lower the vehicle.

4 Brake band(s) - adjustment

Refer to Chapter 1, Section 40.

5 Selector rod - removal, refitting and adjustment

Note: *The vehicle must be standing on its wheels when adjusting the selector rod.*

Removal

1 Remove the securing clips from each end of the selector rod, and withdraw the rod (see illustration). Check the condition of the guide bushes at each end of the rod and renew as necessary.

Refitting

2 Engage the manual selector lever in the following position according to transmission type (see illustration):
C3 type transmission - "D"
A4LD type transmission up to 1987 - "DE"
A4LD type transmission from 1987 - "D"
3 Move the selector lever on the transmission housing to the corresponding position.
4 Fit the selector rod to the selector lever on the transmission housing, and secure it with the clip.
5 Offer the remaining end of the selector rod to the manual selector lever. If it will fit without strain, and without disturbing the selector lever on the transmission, or the manual selector lever, adjustment is correct.

Adjustment

6 If adjustment is necessary, slacken the selector rod locknut, then rotate the rod end-piece to lengthen or shorten the rod until it is a comfortable fit on the manual selector lever. Tighten the locknut when adjustment is complete.

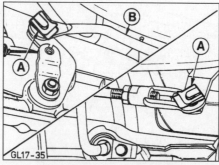

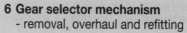

5.1 Selector rod end fittings

A Securing clips　　　*B Selector rod*

7 Check that the manual selector lever accurately engages each function, and check the operation of the starter inhibitor/reversing light switch. It should only be possible to start the engine with the manual selector lever in positions "N" or "P", and the reversing lights should operate with the selector lever in position "R" when the ignition is switched on. Also check that the parking pawl engages correctly with the selector lever in position "P" the selector lever must be pressed down before it can be moved from position "P" to another position, and also before it can be moved from position "N" to "R". Re-adjust the selector rod if necessary.

6 Gear selector mechanism - removal, overhaul and refitting

Removal

1 Remove the securing clip and disconnect the selector rod from the manual selector lever underneath the vehicle.
2 Working inside the vehicle, unscrew the selector lever handle from the threaded end of the lever, then remove the three retaining screws and withdraw the centre console front upper panel.
3 Pull the selector gate cover and the bulbholder from the selector housing.
4 Unscrew the four securing bolts and withdraw the selector housing and selector gate from the floorpan (see illustration).

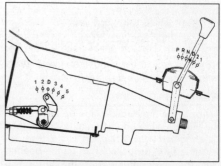

5.2 Manual selector lever and transmission selector lever in "D" position - C3 transmission

Overhaul

5 To dismantle the gear selector mechanism, proceed as follows.
6 Detach the manual selector lever from the lower selector shaft, by removing the clip from the end of the link pin, and withdrawing the pin (see illustration). Recover the two bushes and the spring.
7 Remove the clip from the end of the lower selector shaft (see illustration) and withdraw the selector lever arm and the shaft from the selector housing. Lift out the complete upper selector lever assembly.
8 Withdraw the upper selector lever and spring from the selector lever guide.
9 Examine all components for wear and damage, and renew as necessary.

Refitting

10 Reassembly and refitting is a reversal of dismantling and removal, but on completion, check selector rod adjustment (Section 5).

7 Transmission extension housing oil seal - renewal

1 Remove the propeller shaft.
2 Using a suitable thin-bladed tool, prise the oil seal from the end of the extension housing. Be prepared for fluid spillage.
3 Fit the new oil seal carefully using a suitable tube drift.
4 Refit the propeller shaft.
5 Check and if necessary top-up the transmission fluid level.

7B

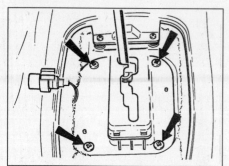

6.4 Selector housing and selector gate securing bolts (arrowed)

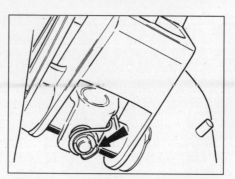

6.6 Selector shaft link pin clip (arrowed)

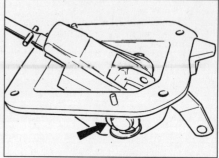

6.7 Lower selector shaft end clip (arrowed)

8 Vacuum diaphragm unit - removal and refitting

Note: *A new O-ring must be used when refitting the vacuum diaphragm unit.*

Removal

1 Apply the handbrake, jack up the front of the vehicle and support on axle stands (see *"Jacking and Vehicle Support"*).

2 Detach the propeller shaft centre bearing from the underbody by unscrewing the two securing bolts. Note the position and number of the slotted shims between the centre bearing bracket and the underbody.

3 Support the weight of the transmission with a trolley jack.

4 Where applicable, unhook the exhaust mounting from the bracket on the transmission crossmember, then unbolt the crossmember from the underbody and the transmission.

5 Carefully lower the transmission.

6 Disconnect the vacuum hose from the diaphragm unit, on the right-hand side of the transmission housing.

7 Unscrew the diaphragm unit bracket bolt **(see illustration)** and detach the bracket.

8 Remove the diaphragm unit and actuating pin. Be prepared for fluid spillage.

Refitting

9 Before refitting the diaphragm unit, check that the throttle valve moves freely.

10 Refitting is a reversal of removal, bearing in mind the following points.

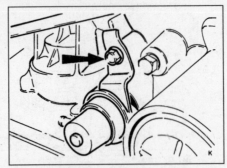

8.7 Vacuum diaphragm unit bracket bolt (arrowed) - C3 transmission

11 Use a new O-ring when refitting the diaphragm unit to the transmission.

12 Refit the slotted shims between the propeller shaft centre bearing bracket and the underbody in their original noted positions.

13 On completion, check and if necessary top-up the transmission fluid level.

9 Starter inhibitor/reversing lamp switch - removal and refitting

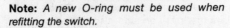

Note: *A new O-ring must be used when refitting the switch.*

Removal

1 For improved access, apply the handbrake, jack up the front of the vehicle and support on axle stands (see *"Jacking and Vehicle Support"*).

2 Disconnect the battery negative lead.

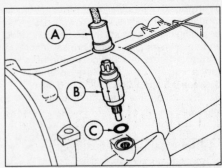

9.3 Starter inhibitor/reversing light switch - C3 transmission

   A *Wiring plug*
   B *Switch*
   C *O-ring*

3 Disconnect the wiring plug from the switch on the left-hand side of the transmission housing **(see illustration)**.

4 Unscrew the switch and remove the O-ring.

Refitting

5 Refitting is a reversal of removal, but use a new O-ring.

6 On completion, check the operation of the switch. It should only be possible to start the engine with the manual selector lever in positions "N" or "P", and the reversing lamps should operate with the selector lever in position "R" when the ignition is switched on.

Chapter 8
Propeller shaft

Contents

Degrees of difficulty

| Easy, suitable for novice with little experience | | Fairly easy, suitable for beginner with some experience | | Fairly difficult, suitable for competent DIY mechanic | | Difficult, suitable for experienced DIY mechanic | | Very difficult, suitable for expert DIY or professional | |

Specifications

Type	. . . .	Two-piece tubular steel with rubber mounted centre bearing. Hardy-Spicer universal joints with front rubber coupling on most models

Torque wrench settings	Nm	lbf ft
All gearbox types except MT75		
Propeller shaft-to-final drive unit bolts	57 to 67	42 to 49
Centre bearing bracket to underbody	18 to 23	13 to 17
MT75 gearbox		
Gearbox output flange studs:		
Models with GAF 30 rubber coupling	70 to 90	52 to 66
Models with GAF 41 rubber coupling	100 to 120	74 to 89
Front rubber coupling-to-vibration damper nuts	67 to 83	49 to 61

8

1 General information

Drive is transmitted from the gearbox/automatic transmission at the front of the vehicle to the final drive unit at the rear of the vehicle by means of a two-piece propeller shaft **(see illustration)**.

To allow for relative movement of the gearbox/automatic transmission and final drive unit, the propeller shaft has a flexible joint at each end, and the two sections of the shaft are joined by a central flexible joint. Standard universal joints are used at the rear and centre of the shaft, and on some models at the front. On later models, a rubber coupling is used at the front of the shaft which reduces noise and vibration levels. Some models have a vibration damper fitted to the forward end of the coupling. A propeller shaft with a front rubber coupling may be fitted to early models in place of the universal joint

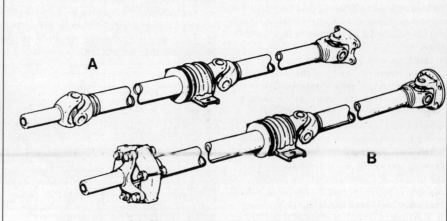

1.1 Alternative types of propeller shaft

A Early type with front universal joint

B Later type with front rubber coupling

type if desired. The front end of the propeller shaft is splined, allowing it to slide in the gearbox/automatic transmission in order to take up fore and aft movement of the gearbox/automatic transmission relative to the final drive unit.

The propeller shaft is supported at its centre, forward of the central universal joint, by a bearing secured to the vehicle underbody.

On Saloon, Hatchback and Estate models, the position of the final drive unit ensures that the working angles of the joints do not exceed one degree, and therefore wear in the joints is likely to be minimal unless very high mileages have been covered. The universal joints cannot be serviced, although it is possible to renew the centre bearing and the front rubber coupling where applicable.

A modified propeller shaft is used in conjunction with the MT75 type gearbox. Instead of the splined spigot on the end of the propeller shaft which fits into the gearbox on earlier models, a vibration damper is fitted between the front end of the propeller shaft and the output flange on the gearbox.

2 Shaft - removal and refitting

Note: *New spring washers must be fitted to the propeller shaft-to-final drive unit bolts on refitting.*

All gearbox types except MT75

Removal

1 Jack up the vehicle and support on axle stands (see *"Jacking and Vehicle Support"*). It is only strictly necessary to jack up the rear of the vehicle, but this provides only limited access.

2 For improved access the rear section of the exhaust system (ie. from the joint) can be removed but this is not essential.

3 Mark the rear universal joint flange and final drive flange in relation to each other if the original propeller shaft is to be refitted. This is not necessary if a new propeller shaft is to be fitted.

4 Unscrew and remove the four bolts and spring washers securing the propeller shaft to the final drive unit (see illustration). In order to hold the shaft stationary as the bolts are unscrewed, apply the handbrake, or alternatively, insert a suitable bar or screwdriver through the universal joint yoke.

5 Unscrew the two bolts securing the centre bearing bracket to the underbody, and lower the bracket and shaft, noting the location and number of slotted shims between the bracket and underbody (see illustration).

6 The front of the propeller shaft must now be disconnected from the gearbox/transmission by pulling the shaft rearwards. To prevent any loss of oil/fluid from the gearbox/automatic transmission, a suitable plug should be

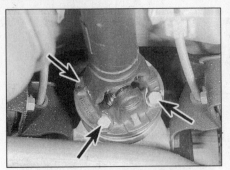

2.4 Three of the propeller shaft-to-final drive securing bolts (arrowed)

inserted into the oil seal. Alternatively a plastic bag can be positioned over the opening and retained with an elastic band.

7 Withdraw the propeller shaft from under the vehicle.

8 Remove the plug or plastic bag, as applicable, from the gearbox automatic transmission and wipe clean the oil seal and the propeller shaft splined spigot. If there is evidence that the oil seal has been leaking, or if it is damaged, now is an opportune time to renew it. To renew the oil seal, prise out the old seal using a suitable screwdriver, and drive in the new seal carefully, using a suitable tube drift.

Refitting

9 Insert the propeller shaft splined spigot into the gearbox/automatic transmission, taking care to avoid damage to the oil seal.

10 Locate the rear of the propeller shaft on the final drive unit, aligning any previously made marks. Fit new spring washers and tighten the securing bolts to the specified torque. Hold the shaft stationary as during the removal procedure.

11 Loosely attach the axle bearing bracket to the underbody with the two bolts.

12 Insert the slotted shims between the centre bearing bracket and the underbody in their original noted locations. Hand-tighten the two securing bolts.

13 On Saloon, Hatchback and Estate models, using a straight edge of suitable length, check that the two sections of the propeller shaft are accurately aligned. The

2.16 Exhaust heat shield fixings (arrowed) - DOHC engine with catalytic converter

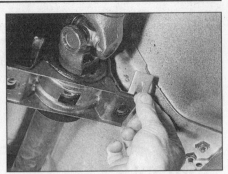

2.5 Removing a slotted shim from the centre bearing bracket

joint angles should not exceed one degree, although this is impossible to measure in practice, and it is sufficient to ensure that the shaft runs straight in the horizontal plane from front to rear. If necessary adjust the shim thickness to give accurate alignment. Tighten the centre bearing bracket bolts to the specified torque on completion.

14 Refit the rear section of the exhaust system, if removed, then lower the vehicle to the ground.

15 With the vehicle level, check and if necessary top-up the oil/fluid level in the gearbox/automatic transmission.

MT75 gearbox

Note: *New nuts must be used to secure the propeller shaft to the gearbox on refitting.*

16 The removal and refitting procedures for this gearbox are as described above. Note that on models with a catalytic converter, the exhaust heat shield must be removed from the underbody for access to the propeller shaft (see illustration). Also note that, instead of pulling the propeller shaft from the rear of the gearbox, the shaft is removed as follows.

17 Counterhold the gearbox output flange studs using a suitable socket, ensuring that the studs cannot turn in the output flange, and unscrew the three nuts securing the propeller shaft rubber coupling to the vibration damper.

18 The propeller shaft can now be disconnected from the gearbox.

19 Two types of rubber coupling may be fitted to the propeller shaft, and both carry identifying marks - either "GAF 30" or "GAF 41".

20 When reconnecting the propeller shaft to the gearbox, proceed as detailed in Section 4, according to the type of rubber coupling used.

3 Centre bearing - renewal

Note: *A suitable bearing puller will be required to pull the centre bearing from the propeller shaft.*

1 Remove the propeller shaft.

2 Mark the front and rear sections of the propeller shaft in relation to each other, and also mark the exact position of the U-shaped

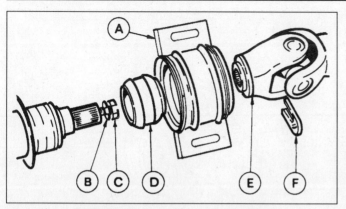

3.2 Exploded view of the centre bearing

A Mounting bracket with rubber
   insulator
B Lock washer
C Bolt

D Bearing and dust caps
E Splined universal joint yoke
F U-shaped washer

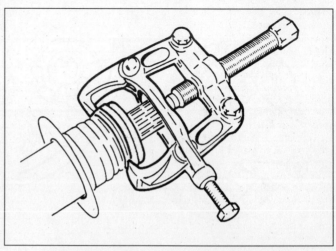

3.6 Using a puller to remove the centre bearing

washer located beneath the bolt head in the central universal joint **(see illustration)**.

3 Bend back the tab on the lock washer and loosen the bolt in the central universal joint so that the U-shaped washer can be removed.

4 With the U-shaped washer removed, slide the rear section of the propeller shaft from the front section.

5 Pull the mounting bracket and insulator rubber from the centre bearing.

6 Remove the outer protective dust cap, then using a suitable puller, pull the centre bearing and inner dust cap from the front section of the propeller shaft **(see illustration)**.

7 Wipe clean the centre bearing components, and fit the inner dust cap to the new bearing. Pack the cavity between the cap and the bearing with molybdenum disulphide based grease.

8 Push the centre bearing and inner dust cap onto the front section of the propeller shaft, using a metal tube of suitable diameter on the bearing inner race. Note that the red seal end of the bearing must face towards the splined end of the shaft.

9 Fit the outer dust cap, and pack the cavity between the cap and bearing with molybdenum disulphide grease.

10 If necessary a new insulator rubber can be fitted to the bearing bracket by bending back

the retaining tongues on the bracket. Make sure that the flange of the new insulator is located on its seat before bending the retaining tongues back.

11 Ease the bearing bracket together with the insulator rubber over the centre bearing.

12 Slide the rear section of the propeller shaft onto the front section, ensuring that the previously made marks are aligned.

13 Refit the U-shaped washer in its previously noted position, with the peg facing towards the bearing bracket **(see illustration)**.

14 Tighten the bolt and bend over the tab on the lock washer to secure.

15 Refit the propeller shaft.

4 Front rubber coupling - renewal

All gearbox types except MT75

1 Remove the propeller shaft.

2 Fit a compressor around the circumference of the rubber coupling and tighten it until it just begins to compress the coupling. If a compressor is not available, two large worm drive hose clips joined end to end will serve the same purpose.

3 Mark the relative positions of the propeller shaft sections on either side of the coupling, and then progressively slacken and remove the six nuts, spring washers and bolts. Note which way round each bolt is fitted **(see illustration)**.

4 Remove the coupling from the propeller shaft. If the original coupling is to be refitted, leave the compressor in position. A new coupling is normally supplied with a compressor already fitted, but if this is not the case, fit the compressor to the new coupling.

5 Refitting is a reversal of removal, ensuring that the previously made marks on the shaft sections are aligned, and that the bolts are fitted as noted during removal.

6 Remove the compressor on completion and refit the propeller shaft.

MT75 gearbox

Note: *The rubber coupling cannot be renewed on models fitted with an MT75 gearbox, as it is balanced as an assembly with the propeller shaft at the factory. The coupling is not available as a spare part, and if worn or damaged, the complete propeller shaft must be renewed. If the propeller shaft is renewed, always fit the latest GAF 41 type as a replacement.*

GAF 30 coupling

7 Check that the studs are seated securely in the gearbox output flange by applying a torque of 80 Nm (59 lbf ft) to the stud heads using a torque wrench. If a stud turns, it must be removed and refitted as follows.

8 Clean the stud threads at the gearbox flange end.

9 Apply two drops of thread-locking fluid to the threads at 180° to one another.

10 Insert the stud, and tighten it to a torque of 80 Nm (59 lbf ft). The stud must be fitted and tightened within 5 minutes of applying the thread-locking fluid.

11 Allow the thread-locking fluid to harden for 30 minutes, then reconnect the propeller shaft to the gearbox.

8

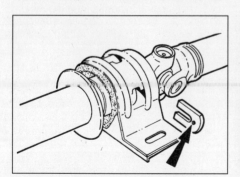

3.13 Correct position of peg (arrowed) when fitting U-shaped washer

4.3 Note the fitted direction of the rubber coupling bolts

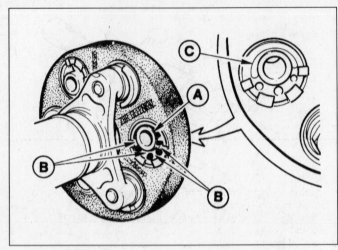

4.13 GAF 30 type propeller shaft rubber coupling

A Metal bush
B Rubber "spokes"
C Rubber skin (front side only)

4.16 GAF 41 type propeller shaft rubber coupling

A Coupling-to-vibration damper nuts
B GAF 41 type coupling
C Vibration damper
D Propeller shaft-to-coupling nuts

12 Before reconnecting the propeller shaft to the gearbox, the washers on both sides of the coupling must be greased, and the condition of the rubber coupling must be checked as follows.

13 Examine the rubber "spokes" for cracks **(see illustration)**. If cracks are visible, the complete propeller shaft and coupling assembly must be renewed with one of the later GAF 41 type. The propeller shaft is balanced with the rubber coupling as an assembly, and therefore the coupling must not be removed from the propeller shaft. Cracks in the rubber skin (area "C") are insignificant.

14 Secure the propeller shaft rubber coupling to the vibration damper using new nuts.

15 Further refitting is a reversal of removal.

GAF 41 coupling

16 Check that the studs are seated securely in the gearbox output flange by applying a torque of 110 Nm (81 lbf ft) to the stud heads using a torque wrench. If a stud turns, it must be renewed, and the new stud must be tightened to a torque of 110 Nm (81 lbf ft). Note that only studs with hexagonal collars must be used (Torx type studs must not be used) **(see illustration)**.

17 Secure the propeller shaft rubber coupling to the vibration damper using new nuts.

18 Further refitting is a reversal of removal.

5 Vibration damper (MT75 gearbox) - removal and refitting

Note: *New nuts must be used to secure the propeller shaft to the gearbox on refitting, and on models fitted with a GAF 41 type rubber coupling, new studs must be used to secure the vibration damper to the gearbox output flange.*

Removal

1 The propeller shaft vibration damper is attached to the gearbox output flange **(see illustration)**.

2 Two alternative types of vibration damper may be used, depending on whether a GAF 30 or GAF 41 type rubber coupling is used.

3 To remove the vibration damper, detach the propeller shaft rubber coupling from the damper then unscrew and remove the studs securing the damper to the gearbox output flange.

Refitting

4 For models fitted with a GAF 30 type rubber coupling, proceed as described in Section 4.

5 On models fitted with a GAF 41 type rubber coupling, new studs must be used to secure the vibration damper to the gearbox output flange, and new nuts must be used to secure the rubber coupling to the vibration damper. Further refitting is a reversal of removal, ensuring that all fixings are tightened to the specified torque.

5.1 Vibration damper fitted to front rubber coupling on some models

Chapter 9
Final drive and driveshafts

Contents

Degrees of difficulty

Easy, suitable for novice with little experience	Fairly easy, suitable for beginner with some experience	Fairly difficult, suitable for competent DIY mechanic 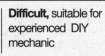	Difficult, suitable for experienced DIY mechanic	Very difficult, suitable for expert DIY or professional

Specifications

Final drive type
Saloon, Hatchback and Estate models . . . .   Light alloy housing, bolted to rear suspension crossmember and underbody.

P100 models . . . .   Cast iron housing. Live beam axle, bolted to rear leaf springs.

Driveshaft type
Saloon, Hatchback and Estate models:
 Rear drum brakes . . . .   Open, fully floating with double tripode joints. Splined fit in final drive unit and rear hubs

 Rear disc brakes . . . .   Open, fully floating with double Lobro joints. Bolted to final drive unit and rear hubs

P100 models . . . .   Enclosed, one-piece shafts running in rear axle housing. Splined fit in differential and bolted to rear hubs

Capacities . . . .   Refer to Chapter 1 Specifications

Torque wrench settings

	Nm	lbf ft
Saloon, Hatchback and Estate models		
Final drive unit rear cover bolts	45 to 60	33 to 44
Oil filler plug	35 to 45	26 to 33
Final drive pinion drive flange nut	100 to 120	74 to 89
Final drive unit-to-suspension crossmember bolts	70 to 90	52 to 66
Final drive unit-to-underbody bolts (gold coloured)	60	44
Rear hub nut	250 to 290	185 to 214
Lobro type driveshaft-to-final drive bolts	38 to 43	28 to 32
Lobro type driveshaft-to-rear hub bolts	38 to 43	28 to 32
Rear hub carrier/brake backplate-to-lower suspension arm bolts:		
Type X	52 to 64	38 to 47
Type Y	80 to 100	60 to 74
P100 models		
Brake backplate-to-axle nuts	45 to 54	33 to 40
Driveshaft-to-hub bolts	60 to 78	44 to 58
Rear hub nut	280 to 300	207 to 221
Axle-to-leaf spring U-bolt nuts	39 to 58	29 to 43

1 General information

On Saloon, Hatchback and Estate models, the final drive unit is bolted directly to the rear underbody and the rear suspension crossmember. The final drive housing is made from light alloy. Oil seals are fitted to the final drive housing to retain oil at the drive pinion and the two differential side bearings.

A conventional crownwheel and pinion arrangement is used, with both the differential and the drive pinion housing in taper roller bearings. Drive from the differential is taken to the roadwheels by two open driveshafts with a constant velocity joint at each end. Two types of driveshaft are used depending on model. Models with rear drum brakes use tripode joint type driveshafts which are splined at both ends. The inner ends fit into the differential, and the outer ends fit into the rear hubs and are retained by the rear hub nuts. Models with rear disc brakes use Lobro joint type driveshafts which are simply bolted by flanges to the final drive unit and the rear hubs.

On P100 models, the rear axle assembly is bolted rigidly to the rear suspension leaf springs. The rear axle casing is made from cast iron. A conventional crownwheel and pinion arrangement is used, with both the differential and the drive pinion running in taper roller bearings. Drive from the differential is taken to the roadwheels by two rigid driveshafts enclosed in the rear axle casing. The inner ends of the driveshafts are splined and fit into the differential, and the outer ends are bolted to the rear hubs.

2 Final drive unit (Saloon, Hatchback and Estate models) - removal and refitting

Note: *From May 1986, revised final drive unit rear mounting bolts have been used in production. Whenever the earlier type of bolts are removed, they should be discarded and the later type fitted. The earlier bolts are coloured blue, and the later type bolts are coloured gold.*

Removal

1 Loosen the rear roadwheel nuts, jack up the vehicle and support on axle stands (see "*Jacking and Vehicle Support*"). It is only strictly necessary to jack up the rear of the vehicle, but this provides only limited access.
2 Remove the rear roadwheels.
3 If required for improved access, the rear section of the exhaust system (ie from the joint) can be removed but this is not essential. The same applies to the rear anti-roll bar where applicable.
4 Remove the propeller shaft.
5 On models fitted with rear drum brakes, disconnect the driveshafts at their outboard ends and withdraw the inboard ends of the

2.8 Final drive unit rear mounting

driveshafts from the final drive unit. Once withdrawn from the final drive unit, the driveshafts can be left in place, but support the centre and inboard sections of the shafts so that the deflection of each tripode joint does not exceed 13°.
6 On models fitted with rear disc brakes, unbolt the inboard ends of the driveshafts from the final drive unit. The driveshafts can be left in place, but they should be supported to avoid straining the joints.
7 Support the final drive unit with a trolley jack, using an interposed block of wood between the jack and the final drive to spread the load.
8 Unscrew the four bolts from the final drive unit rear mounting on the underbody **(see illustration)**. Note the location and number of any shims which may be fitted.
9 Remove the final drive unit vent pipe from the hole in the underbody **(see illustration)**.
10 Unscrew the single front bolt on each side securing the final drive unit to the rear suspension crossmember **(see illustration)**.
11 Lower the final drive unit slightly, and unscrew the two throughbolts and nuts securing the final drive unit to the rear suspension crossmember. Note the location and number of any shims which may be fitted to the top through-bolt between the final drive unit and the crossmember mating flanges. Be prepared to catch these shims as the through-bolt is removed.
12 Lower the final drive unit and remove it from under the vehicle.

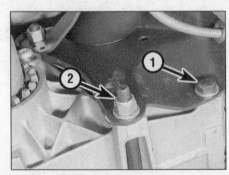

2.10 Final drive unit-to-rear crossmember front securing bolt (1) and through-bolts (2)

2.9 Removing the final drive unit vent pipe

Refitting

13 When refitting the final drive unit, the following procedure must be observed.
14 Refit the final drive unit to the rear suspension crossmember, and loosely fit the securing bolts. Insert the top through-bolt with any shims noted during removal.
15 Refit the final drive unit rear mounting to the vehicle underbody, with reference to the note at the beginning of this Section. Position any shims noted during removal in their original positions and tighten the securing bolts to the specified torque.
16 Tighten the single front bolt on each side, and the bottom throughbolt securing the final drive unit to the rear suspension crossmember, to the specified torque. A spanner will be required to hold the nut on the through-bolt as the bolt is tightened.
17 If shims were not fitted to the top through-bolt during removal, they should have been located in their original positions, and the through-bolt can be tightened to the specified torque, holding the nut with a spanner. If no shims were fitted, proceed as follows.
18 Using feeler blades, measure the gap "A" **(see illustration)** on each side between the final drive unit and the rear suspension crossmember mating flanges.
19 Select and insert appropriate shims at each end of the through-bolt so that with the

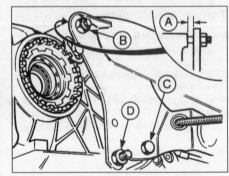

2.18 Final drive unit mounting details

A Gap to be shimmed
B Top through-bolt
C Front bolt
D Bottom through-bolt

3.3 Loosening the pinion drive flange nut

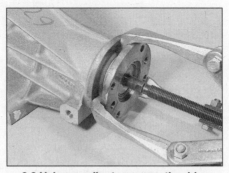

3.6 Using a puller to remove the drive flange (nut removed)

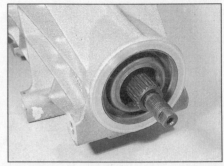

3.7 Pinion oil seal location in final drive unit

shims in position they just contact both the final drive unit and the rear suspension crossmember. If no gap was measured, then no shims will be required. Shims are available from a Ford dealer in thicknesses of 0.5, 1.0 and 1.5 mm (0.03, 0.04 and 0.05 in).

20 With the appropriate shims located where necessary, tighten the through-bolt to the specified torque, holding the nut with a spanner.

21 The remainder of refitting is a reversal of removal, bearing in mind the following.

22 On models with rear drum brakes, reconnect the driveshafts.

23 Refit the propeller shaft.

24 Where applicable, refit the rear section of the exhaust system and/or the rear anti-roll bar.

25 On completion, check and if necessary top-up the final drive unit oil level.

3 Final drive unit pinion oil seal (Saloon, Hatchback and Estate models) - renewal

Note: *A suitable puller will be required to remove the final drive flange from the pinion.*

1 The pinion oil seal can be renewed without removing the final drive unit, as follows.

2 Remove the propeller shaft.

3 Hold the final drive flange stationary by applying the handbrake. Alternatively bolt a long bar to the flange, or screw two bolts into adjacent holes and insert a long bar between them **(see illustration)**.

4 Unscrew the self-locking drive flange nut.

5 Place a suitable container beneath the final drive unit to catch any oil which may be lost as the drive flange is removed.

6 Using a suitable puller, pull the drive flange from the pinion **(see illustration)**.

7 Using a screwdriver, lever the oil seal from the final drive unit **(see illustration)**.

8 Clean the area of the final drive housing where the oil seal seats, and clean the drive flange and the end of the pinion.

9 The new oil seal will be supplied ready packed with grease, and the grease must be left in place when the seal is fitted. Drive the new seal squarely into the final drive housing until flush using a tube drift **(see illustration)**.

10 Slide the drive flange onto the pinion splines, taking care not to damage the oil seal.

11 Fit the self-locking nut and tighten it to the specified torque while holding the drive flange stationary using one of the methods described in paragraph 3. Ideally a new self-locking nut should be used, but if the old nut is re-used, it should not be unscrewed and tightened more than three times otherwise it will lose its self-locking characteristic.

12 Refit the propeller shaft.

13 Check and if necessary top-up the final drive unit oil level.

4 Final drive unit differential bearing oil seal (Saloon, Hatchback and Estate models) - renewal

Models with rear drum brakes

1 The differential bearing oil seals can be renewed without removing the final drive unit, as follows.

2 Remove the relevant driveshaft.

3 Using a depth gauge, or a narrow steel rule, measure the fitted depth of the oil seal. This should be approximately 11.0 mm (0.4 in) measured from the outer face of the bearing retaining ring **(see illustration)**.

4 Using a screwdriver, lever the oil seal from the differential bearing housing.

5 Clean the oil seal seating area in the bearing housing.

6 Smear the lips of the new oil seal with a little molybdenum disulphide grease, then using a suitable tube drift, press the seal squarely into the bearing housing to the previously noted depth.

7 Refit the driveshaft.

Models with rear disc brakes

8 Remove the final drive unit.

9 Remove the final drive unit rear cover. Place a container under the final drive unit, as the oil will drain out when the rear cover is removed. The cover is secured by nine Torx bolts.

10 Clean the old sealant from the cover and final drive unit mating faces, taking care to keep it out of the interior of the unit.

11 Remove the circlip securing the relevant output flange inside the final drive unit. If both oil seals are being renewed, do not get the circlips mixed up, as their thickness is selected and may differ from side to side.

12 Withdraw the output flange, and clean the seal seating area.

13 Proceed as described in paragraphs 3 to 6 inclusive.

14 Refit the output flange, being careful not to damage the oil seal. Refit the original securing clip.

15 Apply liquid sealant (to Ford spec SQM-46 9523-A) to the mating faces of the rear cover and final drive unit.

16 Fit the rear cover, and tighten the securing bolts in a diagonal sequence to the specified torque.

17 Refit the final drive unit.

3.9 Installing the final drive unit pinion oil seal

4.3 Differential bearing oil seal location in final drive unit (arrowed)

9

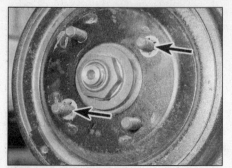

6.4a Brake drum retaining spire washers (arrowed)

6.4b Removing the brake drum

6.5 Removing the plastic shield from the brake backplate

5 Final drive unit (Saloon, Hatchback and Estate models) - overhaul

Overhaul of the final drive unit is a complex task, and requires the use of several special tools and fixtures not normally available to the home mechanic. The pinion and differential bearing oil seals can be renewed as described in Sections 3 and 4 respectively, but it is recommended that any further overhaul work is referred to a Ford dealer.

6 Driveshaft (Saloon, Hatchback and Estate models) - removal and refitting

Models with rear drum brakes

Removal

1 If a driveshaft is being removed for dismantling or renewal, loosen the relevant rear hub nut with the vehicle resting on its wheels. If the driveshaft is being removed for access, this is not necessary. On early models, relieve the staking before loosening the nut. Later models use self-locking nuts, and it is important to note that where this type of nut is fitted, the left-hand nut has a left-hand thread, ie. it is undone in a clockwise direction. Before loosening the nut, ensure that the handbrake is applied, and check the relevant rear wheel. A suitable extension bar will be required, as the nut is extremely tight.

2 Loosen the rear roadwheel nuts on the side concerned, chock the front wheels, and jack up the rear of the vehicle and support on axle stands (see "Jacking and Vehicle Support").
3 Remove the rear roadwheel.
4 Remove the brake drum retaining spire washer(s) from the wheel stud(s) and remove the brake drum (see illustrations). Ensure that the handbrake is released before removing the brake drum, otherwise the drum will be held in place by the clamping action of the brake shoes.
5 Remove the two nylon fasteners, and remove the plastic shield from the rear of the brake backplate (see illustration).
6 Using a socket inserted through one of the holes in the drive flange, unscrew the four bolts securing the hub carrier and brake backplate to the lower suspension arm (see illustration). The drive flange can be rotated to gain access to all four bolts.
7 Place a suitable container beneath the final drive unit to catch any oil which may be released as the driveshaft is withdrawn.
8 The complete driveshaft and hub assembly can now be withdrawn, passing it through the hole in the brake backplate (see illustration). Note that the driveshaft joints should not be allowed to deflect through an angle exceeding 13°.
9 When the driveshaft and hub assembly has been withdrawn, refit the brake backplate with the four securing bolts to avoid straining the brake pipe.
10 If the driveshaft has been removed for dismantling or renewal, proceed as described in Section 7.

Refitting

11 Refitting is a reversal of removal, bearing in mind the following.
12 When refitting the bolts securing the hub carrier and brake backplate to the lower suspension arm, note that there are two types of bolts used to secure the rear hub carrier to the lower arm. The two types of bolt must not be mixed on a vehicle, but can be changed in complete sets for the alternative type. A complete set is eight bolts, four each side. Note that the two types of bolt have different torque wrench settings. When renewing the wheel bearings a suitable puller will be required to remove the drive flange, and a new rear hub nut must be used on reassembly.
13 Where applicable, tighten the rear hub nut to the specified torque with the vehicle resting on its roadwheels. Apply the handbrake and chock the relevant rear wheel. If a staked type nut is used, lock the nut by staking its outer ring into the groove in the driveshaft.
14 On completion, check and if necessary top-up the final drive unit oil level.

Models with rear disc brakes

Removal

15 Chock the front wheels, jack up the rear of the vehicle and support on axle stands (see "Jacking and Vehicle Support").
16 Apply the handbrake to prevent the driveshaft from turning, then unscrew the six Torx bolts securing the inboard end of the driveshaft to the final drive unit (see illustration). Recover the lockwashers. Support the driveshaft.

6.6 Unscrewing a hub/brake backplate-to-lower suspension arm securing bolt

6.8 Withdrawing the driveshaft and hub assembly

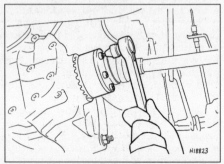

6.16 Unscrewing the driveshaft-to-final drive unit bolts - models with rear disc brakes

7.3 Removing the hub from the stub shaft

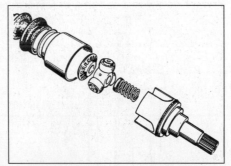

7.4 Exploded view of driveshaft joint - models with rear drum brakes

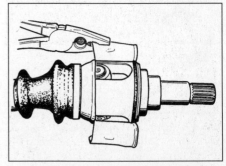

7.6 Removing a driveshaft joint cover - models with rear drum brakes

17 Similarly remove the six bolts which secure the outboard end of the driveshaft to the rear hub. Remove the driveshaft.

18 At all times, avoid bending the driveshaft joints to excessive angles, and do not allow the shaft to hang down from one end.

Refitting

19 Refitting is a reversal of removal. Tighten the securing bolts to the specified torque.

7 Driveshaft (Saloon, Hatchback and Estate models) - overhaul

Models with rear drum brakes

Note: *Before contemplating overhaul of a driveshaft, check to ensure that suitable replacement parts can be obtained. Suitable pullers will be required to remove the drive flange and joint spiders, and to refit the joint cover. A new rear hub nut of the correct type must be used on reassembly.*

1 With the driveshaft removed, unscrew and discard the rear hub nut.

2 Using a suitable puller, pull the drive flange from the end of the stub shaft.

3 The hub carrier complete with bearings can now be removed by sliding it from the end of the stub shaft **(see illustration)**.

4 If the complete driveshaft is being renewed, refit the hub carrier and drive flange to the new driveshaft as described in paragraph 25 onwards. If the driveshaft is to be dismantled for overhaul, proceed as follows, bearing in mind the note at the beginning of this Section **(see illustration)**.

5 Remove the clips from the rubber gaiter on the outboard joint.

6 Using a hacksaw, cut the metal joint cover around part of its circumference, then cut the cover along the driveshaft axis, and using a pair of pliers, peel back the cover from the joint until the swaged end is released **(see illustration)**. As the cover is removed, the end stub shaft will be pushed from the driveshaft under the action of the spring in the joint. The spring will drop out as the stub shaft is removed.

7 Mark the joint spider in relation to the driveshaft centre section, then extract the retaining circlip.

8 Push the rubber gaiter and the remains of the joint cover along the driveshaft away from the joint.

9 Using a suitable puller, pull the joint spider from the splined end of the driveshaft **(see illustration)**.

10 Remove the plastic washer, the remains of the joint cover and the rubber gaiter from the driveshaft.

11 Remove the rubber O-ring from the groove in the stub shaft.

12 Wash all the components in paraffin and wipe them dry, then examine them for wear and damage. Check the joint spider roller bearings for rough operation and excessive wear. Renew the components as necessary, and obtain a new joint cover gaiter, and rubber O-ring.

13 Locate the rubber gaiter followed by the joint cover and plastic washer (convex side first) onto the driveshaft centre section.

14 Locate the joint spider on the driveshaft splines, aligning the previously made marks, and drive it onto the shaft using a suitable tube drift.

15 Fit the joint spider retaining circlip to the end of the driveshaft.

16 Fit the rubber O-ring into the groove in the stub shaft, and locate the spring in the hole inside the stub shaft.

17 Mount the driveshaft centre section in a vice, and fit the stub shaft over the joint spider. Pack the joint with approximately 15 grammes of the specified grease at point "A" **(see illustration)** and smear a little grease on the rubber O-ring.

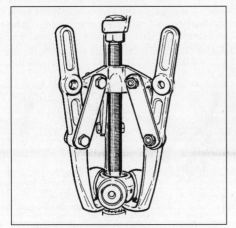

7.9 Removing a driveshaft joint spider using a three-legged puller - models with rear drum brakes

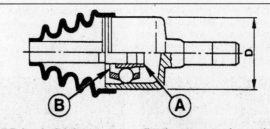

7.17 Driveshaft joint grease application areas and quantities

Model with rear drum brakes		
Gaiter type	**Grease at A**	**Grease at B**
Gaiter with 2 beads	*15g*	*65 to 70g*
Gaiter with 3 beads	*15g*	*85g*
Models with rear disc brakes		
Diameter D	**Grease at A**	**Grease at B**
100 mm	*60g*	*10g*
108 mm	*80g*	*15g*

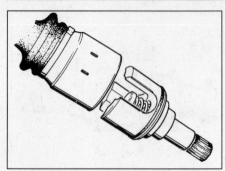

7.18a The six notches in the joint cover must engage with the cut-outs in the stub shaft - models with rear drum brakes

18 Push the stub shaft onto the driveshaft centre section so that the internal spring is compressed, then using a suitable puller, pull the joint cover over the stub shaft, making sure that the six notches in the cover engage with the cut-outs in the stub shaft. Take care not to damage the O-ring **(see illustrations)**.

19 Swage the joint cover onto the stub shaft at three equally spaced points, then remove the puller.

20 Swage the remainder of the joint cover around its complete circumference.

21 From the inner end of the joint cover, pack the joint at point "B" - refer to illustration, paragraph 17, with the specified type and quantity of grease.

22 Locate the rubber gaiter on the joint cover and driveshaft, ensuring that it is not twisted or stretched, then fit and tighten the retaining clips.

23 Repeat the procedure given in paragraphs 5 to 22 on the inboard joint.

24 When overhaul of the driveshaft assembly

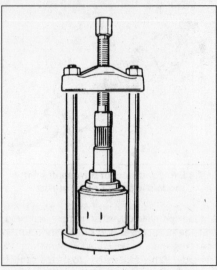

7.18b Using a puller to fit the joint cover - models with rear drum brakes

is complete, the hub carrier and drive flange can be refitted as follows.

25 Fit the drive flange to the hub carrier in order to centralise the bearings, then using a soft-faced mallet, drive the drive flange/hub carrier assembly onto the stub shaft **(see illustration)**.

26 Fit a new rear hub nut of the correct type but leave tightening the nut until the driveshaft has been refitted and the vehicle is resting on its wheels.

Models with rear disc brakes

27 The driveshafts cannot be dismantled for overhaul, but the joints and rubber gaiters can be renewed as follows.

7.25 Driving the drive flange/hub assembly onto the driveshaft

28 With the driveshaft removed, undo or cut the clips which secure the relevant gaiter to the driveshaft. Pull the gaiter back from the joint.

29 Remove the outer circlip which secures the joint to the driveshaft.

30 Pull the joint from the driveshaft and remove the dished washer (where fitted) and the inner circlip from the shaft.

31 The gaiter can now be removed from the driveshaft.

32 Renew the components as necessary, the gaiter clips must be renewed in any case.

33 Pack the joint with the specified type and quantity of grease - refer to illustration, paragraph 17.

34 Fit the gaiter and the joint inner cover to the driveshaft, then fit the inner circlip and the dished washer (where applicable).

35 Apply sealant (to Ford specification ESK-M46275-A available from a Ford dealer) to the joint inner cover face where it mates with the joint (inset) **(see illustration)**. Clean any grease from the corresponding face of the joint.

36 Fit the joint, grooves outermost, and secure with the outer circlip **(see illustration)**.

37 Secure the gaiter with new clips.

38 Repeat the procedure for the remaining joint as necessary.

39 Refit the driveshaft.

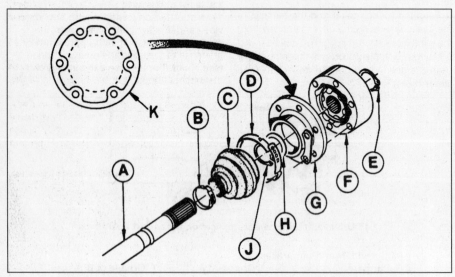

7.35 Exploded view of driveshaft joint - models with rear disc brakes

A Shaft
B Gaiter securing clip
C Gaiter
D Gaiter securing clip
E Outer circlip

F Joint
G Joint inner cover
H Dished washer (if fitted)
J Inner circlip
K Sealant application area

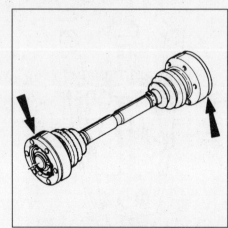

7.36 Correct fitting of joints to driveshaft with grooves (arrowed) outermost - models with rear disc brakes

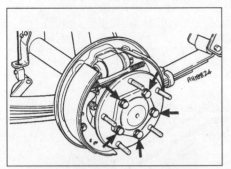

8.4 Brake drum removed showing driveshaft retaining bolts (arrowed)

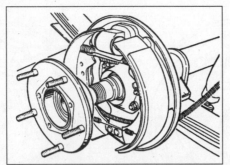

8.6 Removing a rear hub

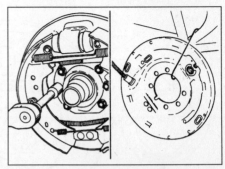

8.8 Unscrewing the brake backplate and oil baffle retaining bolts

8 Rear axle (P100 models) - removal and refitting

Note: *When refitting the rear axle, new rear hub nuts and driveshaft O-rings must be used, and all self-locking nuts and spring washers must be renewed.*

Removal

1 Loosen the rear roadwheel nuts, chock the front wheels, and jack up the rear of the vehicle and support on axle stands placed under the side members. Note that a loaded vehicle must not be jacked under the differential casing.

2 Mark the position of one of the roadwheels

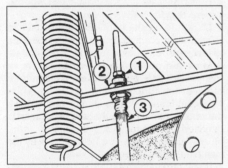

8.10 Brake pipe connection on chassis crossmember

1 Union nut   3 Brake hose
2 U-shaped clip

in relation to the brake drum, then remove the roadwheel.

3 Mark the position of the brake drum in relation to one of the wheel studs, then remove the brake drum retaining spire washer(s) from the wheel stud(s) and remove the brake drum. Ensure that the handbrake is released before removing the brake drum, otherwise the drum will be held in place by the clamping action of the brake shoes.

4 Mark the position of the driveshaft flange in relation to the hub, unscrew the five retaining bolts, and remove the driveshaft from the axle tube **(see illustration)**. Be prepared for oil spillage. Note the gasket fitted between the driveshaft flange and the hub.

5 Relieve the staking on the rear hub nut, and using a 50 mm socket and a suitable extension bar, unscrew the nut. Note that the nut is extremely tight.

6 Pull off the hub, and remove the O-ring and spacer sleeve from the recess in the hub **(see illustration)**.

7 Unscrew the brake pipe from the wheel cylinder on the brake backplate. Plug the end of the pipe and the wheel cylinder to prevent leakage and dirt ingress.

8 Unscrew the six retaining nuts, and remove the brake backplate and the oil baffle. Tie the backplate to the vehicle underbody, away from the axle tube **(see illustration)**.

9 Repeat the operations described in paragraphs 2 to 8 inclusive on the remaining side of the vehicle.

10 Unscrew the brake pipe from the brake hose on the right-hand side of the chassis crossmember. Plug the ends of the pipe and

hose to prevent leakage and dirt ingress, then detach the hose from the crossmember by removing the U-shaped retaining clip **(see illustration)**.

11 Unscrew the two bolts securing the brake load apportioning valve spring bracket to the right-hand axle tube, and allow the bracket to hang freely from the spring **(see illustration)**.

12 Unscrew the bolt securing the brake pipe junction to the right-hand axle tube.

13 Unclip the brake pipe from the axle, and place to one side to avoid damage **(see illustration)**.

14 Disconnect the propeller shaft from the final drive unit. Support the propeller shaft by suspending it from one of the chassis crossmembers with string.

15 Unscrew the nuts, and remove the two U-bolts on each side of the vehicle which secure the axle to the leaf springs. Note that there is no need to disconnect the shock absorbers from the U-bolt counterplates **(see illustration)**.

16 The axle can now be removed from the vehicle with the aid of an assistant, by sliding it to one side until it can be withdrawn under the leaf spring on the opposite side.

Refitting

17 To refit the axle proceed as follows, with reference to the note at the beginning of this Section.

18 Slide the axle under the vehicle, and with the aid of an assistant, lift one end and slide it over the leaf spring. Slide the axle fully to one side, so that the remaining end can be slid over its leaf spring.

9

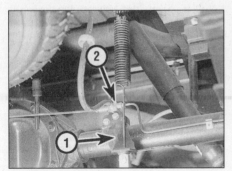

8.11 View of right-hand axle tube showing brake load apportioning valve spring bracket (1) and brake pipe junction (2)

8.13 Brake pipe securing clips (arrowed) on rear axle

8.15 Rear axle-to-leaf spring U-bolts and counterplate

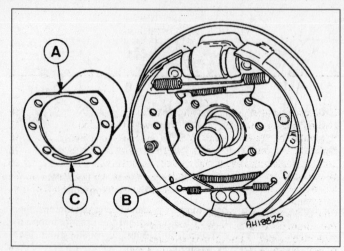

8.27 Fitting the oil baffle to the brake backplate

A Oil baffle   C Sealant application area
B Drain hole

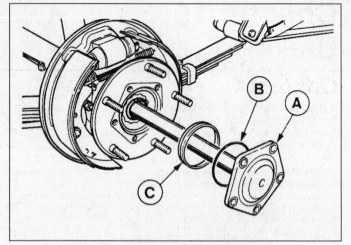

10.4 Withdrawing a driveshaft

A Driveshaft flange   C Spacer sleeve
B O-ring

19 Align the axle on the left springs so that the locating pins on the springs engage with the corresponding holes in the axle.
20 Fit the U-bolts over the axle tubes and into the U-bolt counterplates (with shock absorbers still attached). Screw on the nuts and tighten them to the specified torque. Note that the U-bolt counterplates must be engaged with the locating pins on the leaf springs.
21 Reconnect the propeller shaft to the final drive unit but note that the propeller shaft centre bearing may have to be unbolted from the underbody and refitted after the propeller shaft has been connected to the final drive unit, in order to ensure that the propeller shaft is fitted without any undue stress.
22 Refit the brake pipe to its clips on the axle.
23 Refit the brake pipe junction to the right-hand axle tube and tighten its securing bolt.
24 Refit the brake load apportioning valve spring bracket to the right-hand axle tube and tighten its two retaining bolts.
25 Refit the brake hose to the pipe on the chassis crossmember. Refit the retaining clip and tighten the union.
26 The brake, hub and driveshaft assemblies can now be refitted to each side of the axle as follows.
27 Coat the area of the oil baffle shown **(see illustration)** with sealant (to Ford spec SPM-46-911 2-F), then refit the baffle and the backplate to the axle, tightening the six securing nuts to the specified torque. Ensure that the drain hole in the brake backplate is free from blockage.
28 Refit the brake pipe to the cylinder on the brake backplate, and tighten the union.
29 Lightly grease the hub oil seal, and fit the wheel seal.
30 Screw on a new rear hub nut, and tighten

to the specified torque. Stake the nut into the groove in the axle tube after tightening.
31 Refit the spacer sleeve to the recess in the hub, bevelled side facing outwards, and fit a new O-ring.
32 Slide the driveshaft into the axle tube, with a new gasket, and tighten the five retaining bolts to the specified torque. Ensure that the previously made marks on the driveshaft flange and the hub are aligned.
33 Refit the brake drum and retaining spire washer(s), ensuring that the previously made marks on the drum and wheel stud are aligned.
34 Repeat the procedure given in paragraphs 27 to 33 inclusive on the remaining side of the vehicle.
35 Bleed the rear brake circuit.
36 Check the handbrake operation and adjust if necessary.
37 Check the axle oil level and top-up if necessary. Note that the vehicle must be level.
38 Refit the roadwheels, ensuring that the previously made marks on wheels and brake drums are aligned, then lower the vehicle to the ground.
39 Tighten the roadwheel nuts with the vehicle resting on its wheels.
40 Check the brake load apportioning adjustment.

9 Rear axle (P100 models) - overhaul

Overhaul of the rear axle is a complex task and requires the use of several special tools and fixtures not normally available to the home mechanic. The driveshafts and their O-rings can be renewed as described in Section 10 but it is recommended that any further overhaul work is referred to a Ford dealer.

10 Driveshaft and driveshaft O-ring (P100 models) - renewal

1 Loosen the rear roadwheel nuts on the relevant side of the vehicle, chock the front wheels, and jack up the rear of the vehicle and support on axle stands (see "Jacking and Vehicle Support").
2 Mark the position of the roadwheel in relation to the brake drum, then remove the roadwheel.
3 Mark the position of the brake drum in relation to one of the wheel studs, then remove the brake drum retaining spire washer(s) from the wheel stud(s) and remove the brake drum. Ensure that the handbrake is released before removing the brake drum, otherwise the drum will be held in place by the clamping action of the brake shoes.
4 If the original driveshaft is to be refitted, mark the position of the driveshaft flange in relation to the hub. If a new driveshaft is to be fitted, this is not necessary. Unscrew the five retaining bolts and remove the driveshaft from the axle tube. Be prepared for oil spillage. Note the gasket fitted between the driveshaft flange and the hub **(see illustration)**.
5 The O-ring can now be prised from the spacer sleeve in the hub recess.
6 Refitting is a reversal of removal, bearing in mind the following points.
7 Always renew the O-ring when a driveshaft is removed, and use a new gasket between the driveshaft flange and the hub.
8 If the original driveshaft is being refitted, align the previously made marks on the driveshaft flange and hub. Align the marks on the brake drum and wheel stud, and on the roadwheel and brake drum.
9 On completion, check and if necessary top-up the axle oil level.

Chapter 10
Braking system

Contents

Degrees of difficulty

Easy, suitable for novice with little experience	Fairly easy, suitable for beginner with some experience	Fairly difficult, suitable for competent DIY mechanic	Difficult, suitable for experienced DIY mechanic	Very difficult, suitable for expert DIY or professional

Specifications

System type

Conventional braking system (except P100 models)	Front discs and rear drums with vacuum servo assistance, dual hydraulic circuit split front/rear, deceleration sensitive pressure relief valve in rear hydraulic circuit. Cable-operated handbrake on rear wheels.
ABS	Front and rear discs operated via electrically-driven hydraulic pump, dual hydraulic circuit split front/rear, pressure regulating valve in rear hydraulic circuit. Cable-operated handbrake on rear wheels
P100 models	Front discs and rear drums with vacuum servo assistance, dual hydraulic circuit split front/rear, load apportioning valve in rear hydraulic circuit. Cable-operated handbrake on rear wheels

Front discs

Type:
1.3 and 1.6 litre models	Solid
1.8 and 2.0 litre models	Ventilated
Diameter	240.0 mm (9.46 in)
Maximum disc run-out	0.15 mm (0.006 in)
Minimum pad friction material thickness	1.5 mm (0.06 in)

Rear discs

Type	Solid
Diameter	252.7 mm (9.96 in)
Maximum disc run-out	0.15 mm (0.006 in)
Minimum pad friction material thickness	1.5 mm (0.06 in)

Rear drums

Internal diameter:
1.3 and 1.6 litre Saloon and Hatchback models	203.2 mm (8.0 in)
1.8 and 2.0 litre Saloon and Hatchback models and all Estate models .	228.6 mm (9.0 in)
P100 models	256.0 mm (10.1 in)
Minimum shoe friction material thickness	1.0 mm (0.04 in)

Torque wrench settings

	Nm	lbf ft
Caliper carrier bracket-to-hub carrier bolts	51 to 61	38 to 45
Front caliper guide bolts	20 to 25	15 to 18
Rear caliper guide bolts	31 to 35	23 to 26
Rear brake backplate nuts - P100 models	45 to 54	33 to 40
Servo-to-bulkhead nuts (conventional braking system)	35 to 45	26 to 33
Master cylinder-to-servo nuts	20 to 25	15 to 18
Hydraulic unit-to-bulkhead nuts (ABS)	41 to 51	30 to 38
Hydraulic unit accumulator (ABS)	34 to 46	25 to 34
Pump mounting bolt (ABS)	7 to 9	5 to 7
High pressure hose-to-pump union (ABS)	7 to 12	5 to 9
Wheel sensor mounting bolts (ABS)	8 to 11	6 to 8

1 General information and precautions

General information

The braking system is of the dual circuit hydraulic type. The front and rear circuits are operated independently from a tandem master cylinder, so that in the event of a hydraulic failure in one circuit, full braking force will still be available to two wheels through the remaining circuit.

A deceleration sensitive valve on Saloon, Hatchback and Estate models not fitted with an Anti-lock Braking System (ABS), and a load apportioning valve on P100 models, is incorporated in the rear brake hydraulic circuit. The valve regulates the pressure applied to the rear brakes and reduces the possibility of the rear wheels locking under heavy braking.

All models are fitted with front disc brakes, with solid or ventilated discs depending on model. The calipers are of single piston sliding type, which ensures that equal pressure is applied to each disc pad.

Non-ABS models are fitted with rear disc brakes or rear drum brakes, incorporating leading and trailing shoes operated by double-acting wheel cylinders. A self-adjuster mechanism is fitted which consists of a toothed quadrant which is kept in contact with a toothed pin attached to the shoe strut by means of a spring. The quadrant incorporates an arm which locates in a slot in the leading shoe. As the shoe linings wear the quadrant is pulled from the pin when the footbrake is operated, and automatically repositioned to effectively lengthen the shoe strut.

ABS is available as an option for all models except the P100. The system comprises an electronic control unit, roadwheel sensors, hydraulic actuator with electrically-driven hydraulic pump, and the necessary valves and switches. Disc brakes are fitted to all four wheels. The front disc brakes are similar to those fitted to non-ABS models, but the rear brakes incorporate a self-adjusting mechanism, and a mechanical handbrake mechanism. The purpose of the system is to prevent wheel(s) locking during heavy brake applications. This is achieved by automatic release of the brake on the locked wheel,

followed by reapplication of the brake. This procedure is carried out four times per second by the control valves in the valve block. The valves are controlled by the electronic control unit which itself receives signals from the wheel sensors, which monitor the locked or unlocked state of the wheels. A pressure regulating valve is incorporated in the rear hydraulic circuit to maintain the desired pressure ratio between the front and rear circuits.

Precautions

Note: *Hydraulic fluid is poisonous; wash off immediately and thoroughly in the case of skin contact and seek immediate medical advice if any fluid is swallowed or gets into the eyes. Certain types of hydraulic fluid are inflammable and may ignite when allowed into contact with hot components; when servicing any hydraulic system it is safest to assume that the fluid is inflammable and to take precautions against the risk of fire as though it is petrol that is being handled. Hydraulic fluid is also an effective paint stripper and will attack plastics; if any is spilt, it should be washed off immediately using copious quantities of fresh water. Finally, it is hygroscopic (it absorbs moisture from the air) old fluid may be contaminated and unfit for further use. When topping-up or renewing the fluid, always use the recommended type and ensure that it comes from a freshly-opened sealed container*

Note: *When working on the brake components, take care not to disperse brake dust into the air, or to inhale it, since it may contain asbestos which is injurious to health.*

2.5 Removing the dust cap from a wheel cylinder bleed screw

2 Brake hydraulic system (conventional braking system) - bleeding

⚠️ **Caution: Refer to the precautions in Section 1.**

General

1 If any of the hydraulic components in the braking system have been removed or disconnected, or if the fluid level in the reservoir has been allowed to fall appreciably, it is inevitable that air will have been introduced into the system. The removal of all this air from the hydraulic system is essential if the brakes are to function correctly, and the process of removing it is known as bleeding.

2 Where an operation has only affected one circuit (front or rear) of the hydraulic system, then it will only be necessary to bleed the relevant circuit. If the master cylinder has been disconnected and reconnected, or the fluid level has been allowed to fall appreciably, then the complete system must be bled.

3 One of three methods can be used to bleed the system.

Bleeding

Two-man method

4 Gather together a clean jar and a length of rubber or plastic bleed tubing which will fit the bleed screws tightly. The help of an assistant will be required.

5 Remove the dust cap where fitted, and clean around the bleed screw on the relevant caliper or wheel cylinder, then attach the bleed tube to the screw **(see illustration)**. If the complete system is being bled, start at the front left-hand caliper.

6 Check that the fluid reservoir is topped up and then destroy the vacuum in the brake servo by giving several applications of the brake pedal.

7 Immerse the open end of the bleed tube in the jar which should contain two or three inches of hydraulic fluid. The jar should be positioned about 300 mm (12.0 in) above the bleedscrew to prevent any possibility of air entering the system down the threads of the bleed screw when it is slackened.

8 Open the bleed screw half a turn and have your assistant depress the brake pedal slowly to the floor and then, after the bleed screw is retightened, quickly remove his foot to allow the pedal to return unimpeded. Repeat the procedure.

9 Observe the submerged end of the tube in the jar. When air bubbles cease to appear, tighten the bleed screw when the pedal is being held fully down by your assistant.

10 Top-up the fluid reservoir. It must be kept topped up throughout the bleeding operations. If the connecting holes to the master cylinder are exposed at any time due to low fluid level, then air will be drawn into the system and work will have to start all over again.

11 Assuming that the complete system is being bled, the procedure described in the preceding paragraphs should be repeated on the front right-hand caliper followed by the rear right-hand and left-hand wheel cylinders.

12 On completion, remove the bleed tube, and discard the fluid which has been bled from the system unless it is required for bleed jar purposes. Never re-use old fluid.

13 On completion of bleeding, top-up the fluid level in the reservoir. Check the action of the brake pedal, which should be firm and free from any "sponginess" which would indicate that air is still present in the system.

With one-way valve

14 There are a number of one-man brake bleeding kits currently available from motor accessory shops. It is recommended that one of these kits should be used whenever possible, as they greatly simplify the bleeding operation and also reduce the risk of expelled air or fluid being drawn back into the system.

15 Proceed as described in paragraphs 5 and 6.

16 Open the bleed screw half a turn then depress the brake pedal to the floor and slowly release it. The one-way valve in the bleeder device will prevent expelled air from returning to the system at the completion of each stroke. Repeat this operation until clear hydraulic fluid, free from air bubbles, can be seen coming through the tube. Tighten the bleed screw.

17 Proceed as shown in paragraphs 11 to 13.

With pressure bleeding kit

18 These too are available from motor accessory shops and are usually operated by air pressure from the spare tyre.

19 By connecting a pressurised container to the master cylinder fluid reservoir, bleeding is then carried out by simply opening each bleed screw in turn and allowing the fluid to run out, rather like turning on a tap, until no air bubbles are visible in the fluid being expelled.

20 Using this system, the large reserve of fluid provides a safeguard against air being drawn into the master cylinder during the bleeding operations.

21 This method is particularly effective when bleeding "difficult" systems or when bleeding the entire system at time of routine fluid renewal.

22 Begin bleeding with reference to paragraphs 5 and 6 and proceed as described in paragraphs 11 to 13.

3 Brake hydraulic system (ABS) - bleeding

> ⚠ **Caution: The rear brake hydraulic circuit may be under considerable pressure, take care not to allow hydraulic fluid to spray into the face or eyes. Refer to the precautions in Section 1.**

1 Keep the fluid reservoir replenished throughout the bleeding operations.

2 Remove the dust cap where fitted, and clean around the bleed screw on the left-hand front caliper. Fit a bleed tube to the screw and immerse the open end in a jar containing clean hydraulic fluid.

3 Open the bleed valve one full turn and have an assistant depress the brake pedal fully and hold it down.

4 Close the bleed valve and release the brake pedal. Repeat the procedure until fluid ejected from the end of the tube is free from air bubbles.

5 Repeat the operations on the right-hand front caliper.

6 Fit the bleed tube to the left-hand rear caliper and open the bleed valve one full turn.

7 Have an assistant depress the brake pedal fully and hold it down.

8 Switch on the ignition to position II.

9 Allow the fluid to bleed from the tube for at least 15 seconds, when the fluid should be free from air bubbles.

10 Close the bleed valve.

11 Release the brake pedal and wait for the hydraulic pump to stop.

12 Fit the bleed tube to the right-hand rear caliper and open the bleed valve one full turn.

13 Have your assistant depress the brake pedal through half its travel and hold it there. Allow the fluid to bleed from the tube for at least 15 seconds, when the fluid should be free from air bubbles.

14 Close the bleed valve.

15 Release the brake pedal and wait for the hydraulic pump to stop then switch off the ignition.

16 Top-up the reservoir with clean fluid.

17 When the hydraulic system is being bled for the purpose of renewing the fluid at the specified interval, as each caliper is bled, operate the brake pedal continuously until clean fluid is seen to enter the jar.

18 When the hydraulic pump is running its note will be heard to change once fluid has purged through it. Do not allow the pump to run continuously for more than two minutes. If it does run for a longer period, switch off the ignition and allow the motor to cool for ten minutes.

19 On completion, discard the fluid which has been bled from the system unless it is required for bleed jar purposes. Never re-use old fluid.

20 Check the action of the brake pedal, which should be firm and free from any "sponginess", which would indicate that air is still present in the system.

4 Disc pads - inspection and renewal

> ⚠ **Caution: Refer to the precautions in Section 1.**

Front disc pads

1 The disc pad friction material can be inspected for wear without removing the roadwheels. Working beneath the vehicle, insert a mirror between the caliper and the roadwheel and check that the friction material thickness is not less than the minimum given in the Specifications.

2 If any one of the pads has worn below the specified limit, the front pads must be renewed as an axle set (4 pads).

3 To renew the pads, slacken the front roadwheel nuts, apply the handbrake, then jack up the front of the vehicle and support on axle stands (see "Jacking and Vehicle Support"). Remove the roadwheels. On P100 models, mark the position of the roadwheels in relation to the wheel studs before removal.

4 Proceed as follows according to model:

Girling caliper (1.3 and early 1.6 litre models)

5 Where applicable, disconnect the wiring to the disc pad wear sensor.

6 Unscrew and remove the bolt from the upper caliper guide pin while holding the pin stationary with a spanner **(see illustration)**.

7 Swing the caliper downwards and lift out the disc pads. If the outboard pad is stuck to

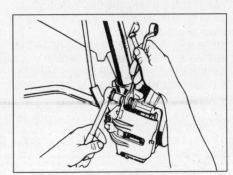

4.6 Unscrewing the bolt from the upper caliper guide pin - Girling caliper

10

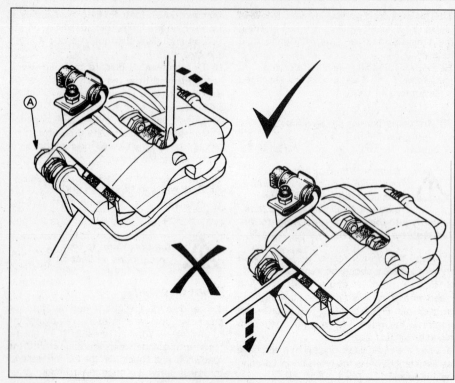

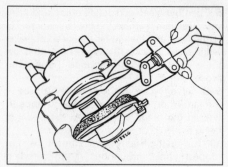

4.9 Using a spreader tool to depress the caliper piston into its bore

4.17 Disconnect the pad wear sensor wiring plug - Teves caliper

4.7 Correct and incorrect methods of freeing stuck outboard disc pad. Guide pin bolt (A) must be in position - Girling caliper

the caliper, free it using a screwdriver with the guide pin bolt fitted, as shown (see illustration). Do not use a screwdriver to free the inboard pad, as this may damage the piston dust seal. The inboard pad can be freed by hand after lowering the caliper.

8 Brush all dust and dirt from the caliper, pads and disc, but do not inhale it as it may be injurious to health. Scrape any corrosion from the disc.

9 As the new pads will be thicker than the old ones, the piston must be pushed squarely into its bore to accommodate the new thicker pads. Depressing the piston will cause the fluid level in the reservoir to rise so to avoid spillage, syphon out some fluid using an old hydrometer or a teat pipette. Do not lever between the piston and disc to depress the piston ideally a spreader tool, applying equal force to both sides of the caliper, should be used (see illustration).

10 Further refitting is a reversal of removal bearing in mind the following points.

11 If disc pads with wear sensors are fitted, the pad with the sensor wire should be fitted inboard.

12 Ensure that the anti-rattle clips are correctly located on the caliper.

13 Repeat the procedure on the opposite front brake.

14 On completion, apply the footbrake hard several times to settle the pads, then check and if necessary top-up the fluid level in the reservoir.

15 Avoid heavy braking, if possible, for the first hundred miles or so after fitting new pads. This will allow the pads to bed in and reach full efficiency.

Teves caliper (Later 1.6, 1.8 and 2.0 litre models)

16 Prise the retaining clip from the caliper. Hold it with a pair of pliers to avoid it causing personal injury.

17 Unclip the pad wear sensor from the caliper, and disconnect the wiring plug (see illustration).

18 Using a 7 mm Allen key, unscrew and remove the two guide bolts securing the caliper to the carrier bracket, and withdraw the caliper (see illustration). Support caliper on an axle stand to avoid straining the hydraulic hose.

19 Withdraw the disc pads from the caliper (see illustration). It may be necessary to prise the outboard pad with a screwdriver to release it from the caliper. Do not use a screwdriver to free the inboard pad, as this may damage the piston dust seal.

20 Proceed as described in paragraphs 8 to 15 inclusive, but in addition ensure that the clip on the back of the inboard pad fits into the piston recess (see illustration), refit the caliper retaining clip, and ignore the reference to the anti-rattle clips (see illustration). On P100 models align the previously made marks on the roadwheels and wheel studs.

Late model modification

21 On some later models, slightly revised front brake components are used. A new type of retaining clip is used to secure the pads in

4.18 Withdrawing a caliper from its carrier bracket - Teves caliper

4.19 Withdraw the disc pads from the caliper - Teves caliper

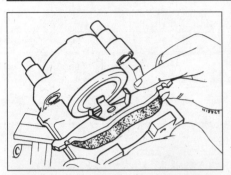

4.20a The clip on the back of the inboard disc pad fits into the piston recess - Teves caliper

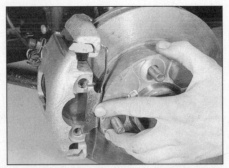

4.20b Refitting the caliper retaining clip - Teves caliper

4.21a Later type front disc pad retaining clip

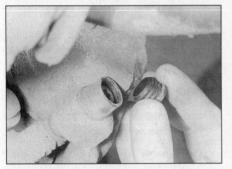

4.21b Removing a caliper guide bolt cover - later type

the caliper, and the caliper body is modified accordingly. Also, plastic covers are fitted to the caliper guide bolts (see illustrations).

22 Procedures are unchanged from those given above.

Rear disc pads

23 Slacken the rear roadwheel nuts, chock the front wheels, then jack up the rear of the vehicle and support on axle stands. (see *"Jacking and Vehicle Support"*). Remove the roadwheel.

24 The disc pads can be inspected through the top of the caliper after removal of the blanking spring clip. Check that the friction material thickness is not less than the minimum given in the Specifications.

25 If any one of the pads has worn below the specified limit, the rear pads must be renewed

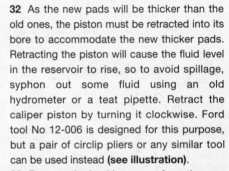

4.28 Rear disc pad wear sensor wiring clip (arrowed)

as an axle set (4 pads).

26 To renew the pads, proceed as follows.

27 Release the handbrake, and free the handbrake cable from the suspension lower arm by bending back the tangs.

28 Where applicable, disconnect the wiring to the disc pad wear sensor (see illustration).

29 Unscrew and remove the bolt from the forward caliper guide pin, while holding the pin stationary with a spanner (see illustration).

30 Swing the caliper rearwards and lift out the disc pads (see illustration). Do not depress the brake pedal with the caliper removed.

31 Brush all dirt and dust from the caliper, pads and disc, but do not inhale it as it may be injurious to health. Scrape any corrosion from the disc.

32 As the new pads will be thicker than the old ones, the piston must be retracted into its bore to accommodate the new thicker pads. Retracting the piston will cause the fluid level in the reservoir to rise, so to avoid spillage, syphon out some fluid using an old hydrometer or a teat pipette. Retract the caliper piston by turning it clockwise. Ford tool No 12-006 is designed for this purpose, but a pair of circlip pliers or any similar tool can be used instead (see illustration).

33 Remove the backing paper from the new pads, and fit them to the caliper.

34 Further refitting is a reversal of removal, bearing in mind the following points.

35 If disc pads with wear sensors are fitted, the pad with the sensor wire should be fitted inboard.

36 Repeat the procedure on the opposite rear brake.

37 On completion, switch on the ignition and apply the footbrake hard several times to settle the pads. Switch off the ignition, then check and if necessary top-up the fluid level in the reservoir. Check the operation of the handbrake.

38 Avoid heavy braking, if possible, for the first hundred miles or so after fitting new pads. This will allow the pads to bed in and reach full efficiency.

10

4.29 Unscrewing the forward caliper guide pin bolt

4.30 Lift out the disc pads

4.32 Retracting the piston using circlip pliers

5.5a Brake drum retaining spire washer (arrowed)

5.5b Releasing the automatic adjuster using a screwdriver

5.5c Drum removed showing screwdriver pressing on adjuster ratchet

5 Rear drum brake shoes - inspection and renewal

Caution: Refer to the precautions in Section 1

1 The shoe friction material can be inspected for wear without removing the roadwheels. Working beneath the vehicle, prise the plug from the brake backplate, and using an inspection lamp or torch, check that the friction material thickness is not less than minimum given in the Specifications.

2 If any one of the shoes has worn below the specified limit, the shoes must be renewed as an axle set (4 shoes).

3 To renew the shoes, slacken the rear roadwheel nuts, chock the front wheels, then jack up the rear of the vehicle and support on axle stands (see "Jacking and Vehicle Support"). Remove the rear roadwheels, and release the handbrake. On P100 models, mark the position of the roadwheels in relation to the brake drums before removal.

4 Proceed as follows according to model:

1.3 and 1.6 litre models

5 Remove the brake drum retaining spire washer(s) from the wheel stud(s) and remove the brake drum. If the drum will not pass over the shoes, it is possible to release the automatic adjuster mechanism by inserting a screwdriver through the small hole in the drum and pressing down on the ratchet (see illustrations).

6 Using a wire hook or a pair of long-nosed pliers, remove the top and bottom shoe return springs. Note the fitted positions of the springs for reference when refitting (see illustrations).

7 Remove the hold-down cup, spring and pin from each shoe by depressing the cup and turning it through 90° (see illustration).

8 Pull the bottom of the leading (front) shoe towards the front of the vehicle so that the self-adjuster ratchets separate, then disengage the shoe from the strut by twisting it. Remove the shoe and adjuster mechanism.

9 Pull the trailing (rear) shoe away from the backplate far enough to gain access to the handbrake cable. Disconnect the handbrake cable from the lever and remove the shoe with strut and lever (see illustration).

10 Clean and inspect all components, and lubricate the shoe contact points on the backplate (see illustration). Take care not to inhale any dust, as it may be injurious to health.

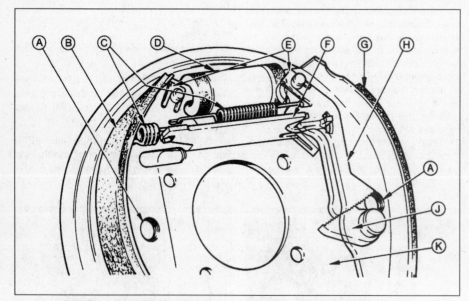

5.5d Rear drum brake self-adjuster assembly - 1.3 and 1.6 litre models

A Shoe hold-down points
B Trailing brake shoe
C Self-adjuster strut and top return springs
D Wheel cylinder
E Spring clips
F Self-adjuster strut
G Leading brake shoe
H Large ratchet segment
J Small ratchet segment
K Brake backplate

5.6a Top shoe return spring (arrowed)

5.6b Bottom shoe return spring

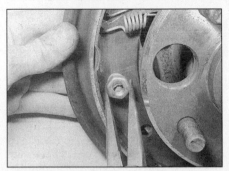

5.7 Using pliers to remove a shoe hold-down cup

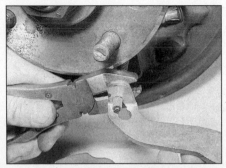

5.9 Disconnecting the handbrake cable from the trailing shoe lever

5.10 Lubrication points on brake backplate

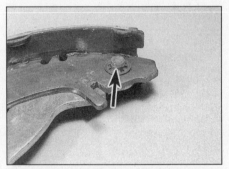

5.11 Handbrake lever-to-trailing shoe securing clip (arrowed)

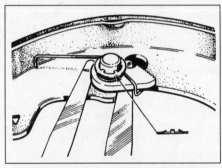

5.12 Using feeler blades to set clearance between smaller ratchet segment and brake shoe web. Spring clip arrowed

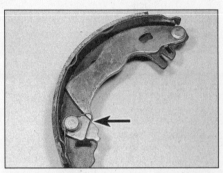

5.13 Fully retract the self-adjuster ratchet (arrowed) before refitting the trailing shoe

11 Remove the strut from the trailing shoe by unhooking it from its spring. If a handbrake lever is not attached to the new shoe, remove the old lever by prising off the clip and driving out the pin. Use a new clip on reassembly **(see illustration)**.

12 Similarly transfer the self-adjuster components to the new leading shoe. Note that a small clearance (0.2 mm/0.008 in) must exist between the underside of the smaller ratchet segment and the brake shoe web. Insert feeler blades of the correct thickness beneath the ratchet when fitting the spring clip, then withdraw the blades **(see illustration)**. The larger segment should be fitted without any clearance.

13 Commence reassembly by engaging the self-adjuster ratchet teeth as shown **(see illustration)**.

14 Offer the trailing shoe to the backplate, fitting the handbrake cable to the handbrake lever and (if not already done) the strut and spring to the top of the shoe **(see illustration)**.

15 Fit the leading shoe and adjuster mechanism, engaging the hole in the adjuster with the hook on the strut **(see illustration)**.

16 Fit the top and bottom return springs: this is most easily done by allowing the ends of the shoe to pass in front of the wheel cylinder and the bottom pivot point, then engaging the shoes in their correct positions after the springs have been fitted. Be careful not to damage the wheel cylinder rubber boots.

17 Fit and secure the hold-down pins, springs and cups.

18 Back off the self-adjuster mechanism, by depressing the lower (small) ratchet segment, to enable the brake drum to pass over the shoes. Centre the shoes relative to the backplate.

19 Refit the drum, making sure that the small hole is in line with one of the two large holes in the drive flange. Secure the drum by pushing the spire washer(s) over the wheel stud(s).

20 Have an assistant operate the footbrake several times: a series of clicks should be heard from the drum as the self-adjuster mechanism operates. When the clicking no longer occurs, adjustment is complete.

21 Renew the brake shoes on the other side of the vehicle, then check the handbrake adjustment.

22 Refit the roadwheels, lower the car and tighten the wheel nuts.

23 Avoid harsh braking if possible for the first hundred miles or so until the new linings have bedded in.

1.8 and 2.0 litre models

24 Proceed as described in paragraph 5, but on P100 models mark the position of the brake drum in relation to one of the wheel studs **(see illustration)**.

25 Remove the hold-down cup, spring and pin from the leading (front) shoe by depressing the cup and turning it through 90° **(see illustration)**.

26 Note the fitted positions of the shoe return springs for reference when refitting, then release the leading shoes from the wheel cylinder and the anchor bracket using a screwdriver as a lever.

5.14 Strut and spring fitted to top of trailing shoe

5.15 Engage the hole in the adjuster with the hook on the strut (arrowed)

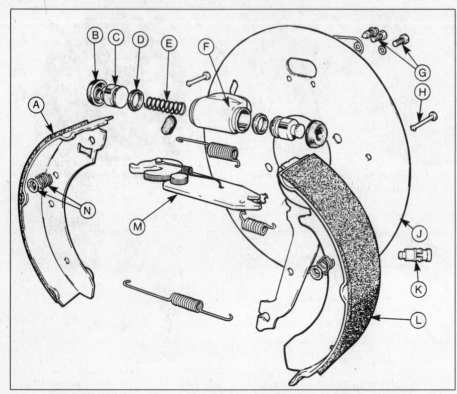

5.24 Exploded view of rear drum brake assembly - 1.8 and 2.0 litre models

A Leading brake shoe
B Dust-excluding seal
C Piston
D Piston seal
E Spring

F Wheel cylinder housing
G Bolts
H Hold-down pin
J Brake backplate
K Adjuster plunger

L Trailing brake shoe
M Self-adjuster strut
N Hold-down spring and
cup

27 Unhook the return springs and remove the leading shoe. Note the direction of wheel rotation arrows on the shoes.
28 Remove the hold-down cup, spring and pin from the trailing (rear) shoe by depressing the cup and turning it through 90º.
29 Withdraw the trailing shoe and disconnect the handbrake cable from the lever **(see illustration)**.

30 Unhook the springs from the trailing shoe and remove the self-adjuster strut.
31 Clean and inspect all components and lubricate the shoe contact points on the backplate - refer to illustration, paragraph 10. Take care not to inhale any dust, as it may be injurious to health.

32 Commence reassembly by fitting the springs to the trailing shoe and attaching the self-adjuster strut.
33 Attach the handbrake cable to the lever and position the trailing shoe on the wheel cylinder and anchor bracket. Ensure that the upper return spring is located on the self-adjuster strut.
34 Refit the hold-down pin, spring and cup to the trailing shoe.
35 Connect the return springs to the leading shoe, then locate the lower end in the anchor bracket and lever the upper end onto the toothed quadrant lever and wheel cylinder. Be careful not to damage the wheel cylinder rubber boot.
36 Refit the hold-down pin, spring and cup to the leading shoe.
37 Using a screwdriver, push the self-adjuster toothed quadrant fully towards the backplate to its initial setting.
38 Proceed as described in paragraphs 19 to 23 inclusive, but on P100 models, align the previously made marks on the brake drums and wheel studs, and on the roadwheels and brake drums.

6 Front disc caliper - removal, overhaul and refitting

⚠️ **Caution: Refer to the precautions in Section 1.**

Removal

1 Apply the handbrake, loosen the relevant roadwheel nuts, then jack up the front of the vehicle and support on axle stands. (see "Jacking and Vehicle Support"). Remove the roadwheel. On P100 models, mark the position of the roadwheel in relation to one of the wheel studs before removal.
2 Remove the brake fluid reservoir cap and secure a piece of polythene over the filler

5.25 Leading shoe hold-down cup (arrowed)

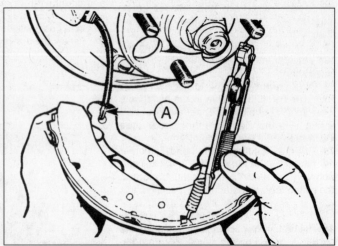

5.29 Removing the trailing brake shoe
A Handbrake cable and slot

neck with a rubber band, or by refitting the cap. This will reduce the loss of fluid during the following procedure.

3 Disconnect the flexible fluid hose from the rigid brake pipe under the wing of the vehicle, or alternatively unscrew the flexible hose from the union on the caliper. Take care not to twist the hose, and plug the open ends to prevent fluid loss and dirt ingress.

4 Remove the disc pads.

5 On models fitted with Girling calipers (1.3 and early 1.6 litre models) **(see illustration)**, unscrew and remove the bolt from the lower caliper guide pin, while holding the pin stationary with a spanner, then remove the caliper.

6 On models fitted with Teves calipers (later 1.6, 1.8 and 2.0 litre models) **(see illustration)**, remove the caliper from the vehicle.

7 If required, the caliper carrier bracket can be unbolted and removed from the hub carrier.

Overhaul

8 Brush away all external dirt and dust, but take care not to inhale any dust as it may be injurious to health.

9 Pull the dust-excluding rubber seal from the end of the piston.

10 Apply air pressure to the fluid inlet union, and eject the piston. Only low air pressure is required for this, such as is produced by a foot-operated tyre pump. Position a thin piece of wood between the piston and caliper body to prevent damage to the end face of the piston in the event of its being ejected suddenly.

11 Using a suitable pointed instrument, prise the piston seal from the groove in the cylinder bore. Take care not to scratch the surface of the bore.

12 Clean the piston and caliper body with methylated spirit and allow to dry. Examine the surfaces of the piston and cylinder bore for wear, damage and corrosion. If the piston surface alone is unserviceable, a new piston must be obtained, along with seals. If the cylinder bore is unserviceable, the complete caliper must be renewed. The seals must be renewed regardless of the condition of the other components.

13 Coat the piston and seals with clean brake fluid, then manipulate the piston seal into the groove in the cylinder bore.

14 Push the piston squarely into its bore.

15 Fit the dust-excluding rubber seal between the piston and caliper, then depress the piston fully.

Refitting

16 Refit the caliper and where applicable the carrier bracket by reversing the removal operations. Tighten the mounting bolts to the specified torque.

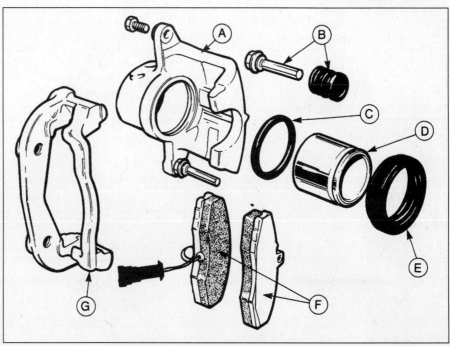

6.5 Exploded view of Girling front disc caliper

A Caliper
B Guide pin and dust boot
C Piston seal
D Piston
E Dust-excluding seal
F Disc pads
G Caliper carrier bracket

17 On P100 models, when refitting the roadwheel align the previously made marks on the roadwheel and wheel stud.

18 On completion, bleed the front brake circuit.

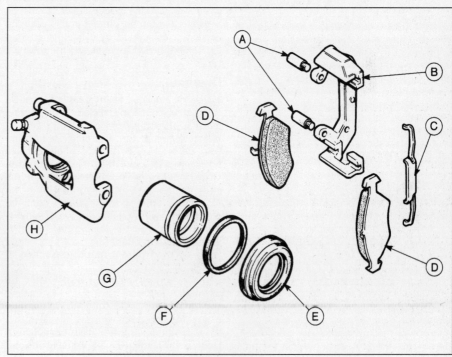

6.6 Exploded view of Teves front disc caliper

A Guide bolts
B Caliper carrier bracket
C Caliper retaining clip
D Disc pads
E Dust-excluding seal
F Piston seal
G Piston
H Caliper

10

7.10a Remove the circlip from the rear caliper piston . . .

7.10b . . . followed by the thrustwasher . . .

7.10c . . . a wave washer and (not shown) another thrustwasher . . .

7.10d . . . then the thrust bearing . . .

7.10e . . . and finally the adjuster nut itself. Note the seal (arrowed) on the nut

7.13 Using the piston adjuster nut to compress the adjuster spring

7 Rear disc caliper - removal, overhaul and refitting

Note: *Complete dismantling of the rear caliper should not be attempted unless Ford spring compressor (tool No 12-007) is available, or unless the problems likely to arise in the absence of the tool are understood. Renewal of the piston seal dust-excluding seal and piston adjuster nut seal requires no special tools.*

⚠️ **Caution: Refer to the precautions in Section 1.**

Removal

1 With the ignition switched off, pump the brake pedal at least 20 times, or until it becomes hard, to depressurise the system.
2 Chock the front wheels, slacken the relevant roadwheel nuts, then jack up the rear of the vehicle and support on axle stands (see *"Jacking and Vehicle Support"*). Remove the roadwheel and release the handbrake.
3 Where applicable, disconnect the wiring to the disc pad wear sensor.
4 Proceed as described in Section 6, paragraphs 2 and 3, but note that the rigid brake pipe is clipped to the suspension lower arm.
5 Unscrew and remove the two guide bolts securing the caliper to the carrier bracket, while holding the pins with a spanner. Unhook

the handbrake cable from the lever, and withdraw the caliper. Alternatively, the two carrier bracket-to-hub carrier bolts can be unscrewed, and the caliper and carrier can be separated on the bench, but in this case the handbrake cable must be disconnected from the carrier bracket by removing the retaining circlip.

Overhaul

6 Clean the caliper, taking care not to inhale any dust which may be injurious to health, and mount it in a soft-jawed vice.
7 Rotate the piston anti-clockwise, using Ford tool No 12-006, or a pair of circlip pliers or similar tool, until it protrudes from the caliper bore by approximately 20.0 mm (0.8 in). Free the dust-excluding seal from the groove in the piston, then continue unscrewing the piston and remove it. Remove and discard the dust-excluding seal.
8 The piston and bore may now be cleaned and examined as described in Section 6, paragraph 12.
9 The piston adjuster nut seal should be renewed as follows.
10 Remove the circlip from the piston, then extract the thrustwashers, wave washer and thrust bearing. Note the fitted sequence of these components. Finally remove the nut **(see illustrations)**.
11 Remove the seal from the nut, noting which way round it is fitted. Clean the nut with methylated spirit. Lubricate the new seal with clean hydraulic fluid and fit it to the nut.

12 If no further dismantling is required, proceed to paragraph 20.
13 For further dismantling it is virtually essential to have Ford tool 12-007 in order to compress the adjuster spring. This tool appears to be a cut-down adjuster nut with a handle for turning it. In the workshop it was found that the actual piston adjuster nut could be used to compress the spring if it were turned with circlip pliers **(see illustration)**. This works well enough for dismantling, but reassembly proved extremely difficult because of the limited clearance between the skirt of the nut and the caliper bore.
14 Having compressed the adjuster spring just enough to take the load off the circlip, release the circlip inside the caliper bore. Remove the spring compressor, then extract the circlip, spring cover, spring and washer **(see illustrations)**.

7.14a Extract the circlip from the caliper bore . . .

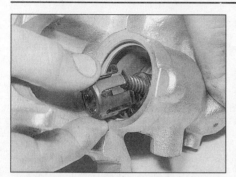

7.14b . . . then the spring cover . . .

7.14c . . . the spring itself . . .

7.14d . . . and the washer

7.15 Remove the circlip (ends arrowed) to release the pushrod and key plate

15 A long thin pair of circlip pliers will now be required to release the key plate retaining circlip from the caliper bore **(see illustration)**. With the circlip removed, the pushrod and key plate can be pulled out.
16 Remove the handbrake strut from the caliper bore.
17 Remove the handbrake lever return spring and stop bolt. Pull the lever and shaft nut out of the caliper. Prise out the shaft seal **(see illustration)**.
18 Clean the handbrake shaft using wire wool; renew the shaft if it is badly corroded. The shaft bush in the caliper can also be renewed if necessary. Pull out the old bush with an internal puller or slide hammer, and press in the new bush to 7.5 mm (0.30 in) below the shaft seal lip **(see illustration)**. The slot in the side of the bush must line up with the pushrod bore in the caliper.

19 Having renewed components as necessary, commence reassembly by smearing a little brake grease or anti-seize compound on the handbrake shaft and bush.
20 Fit a new handbrake shaft seal to the caliper. Pass the shaft through the seal and into the caliper, taking care not to damage the seal lips.
21 Refit the handbrake lever stop bolt and return spring.
22 Refit the handbrake strut, lubricating it with brake grease.
23 Fit a new O-ring to the base of the pushrod. Refit the pushrod and the key plate, engaging the pip on the key plate with the recess in the caliper. Secure the key plate with the circlip.
24 Refit the washer, spring and spring cover. Compress the spring and refit the circlip, then release the spring compressor.
25 Lubricate the caliper bore with clean hydraulic fluid and fit a new piston seal.
26 Reassemble the piston components. Lubricate the contact face of the adjuster nut with a little brake grease, then fit the adjuster nut (with new seal), thrust bearing, thrustwasher, wave washer and the second thrustwasher. Secure with the circlip.
27 Fit a new dust-excluding seal to the grooves in the piston and caliper bore as the piston is refitted **(see illustration)**. Screw the piston into the caliper bore with the tool used during removal.
28 Renew the guide pin gaiters and apply a little brake grease or anti-seize compound to the guide pins when refitting the caliper to its carrier bracket.

Refitting

29 Refitting is a reversal of removal, but on completion bleed the rear brake circuit and check the operation of the handbrake.

8 Brake disc - examination, removal and refitting

Note: *From 1987, thicker brake discs were fitted. If the later discs are fitted to earlier models, longer wheel studs must be fitted to accommodate the increased thickness. Consult a dealer for further advice.*

 Caution: Refer to the precautions in Section 1.

Front disc

1 Apply the handbrake, loosen the relevant roadwheel nuts, then jack up the front of the vehicle and support on axle stands (see *"Jacking and Vehicle Support"*). Remove the roadwheel.
2 Remove the disc caliper and carrier bracket but do not disconnect the flexible hose. Support the caliper on an axle stand to avoid straining the flexible hose.
3 Rotate the disc and examine it for deep scoring or grooving. Light scoring is normal, but if excessive, the disc should be removed and either renewed or reground by a suitable specialist. Scrape any corrosion from the disc.
4 Using a dial gauge or a flat metal block and feeler blades, check that the disc run-out does not exceed the limit given in the

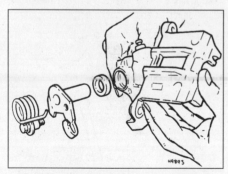

7.17 Handbrake shaft and associated components

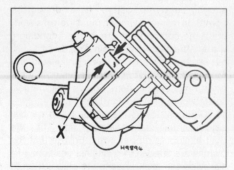

7.18 Handbrake shaft bush correctly fitted
X = 7.5 mm (0.30 in)

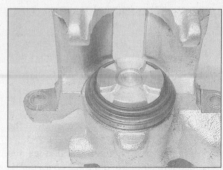

7.27 Dust-excluding seal fitted to piston and caliper bore

10

Specifications. To do this, fix the measuring equipment, and rotate the disc, noting the variation in measurement as the disc is rotated. The difference between the minimum and maximum measurements recorded is known as disc run-out.

5 Mark the position of the brake disc in relation to the drive flange and on Saloon, Hatchback and Estate models, remove the retaining screw or spire washer(s), as applicable, and remove the disc. On P100 models, also mark the position of the wheel adapter plate in relation to the disc and drive flange, then unscrew the five retaining nuts and remove the wheel adapter plate and disc.

6 Refitting is a reversal of removal, but when refitting ensure that the mating faces of the disc, drive flange and on P100 models the wheel adapter plate, are clean. Align the marks made on the disc, drive flange, and where applicable the wheel adapter plate, during removal. Refit the disc caliper and carrier bracket.

Rear disc

7 Chock the front wheels, loosen the relevant roadwheel nuts, then jack up the rear of the vehicle and support on axle stands.(see "Jacking and Vehicle Support"). Remove the roadwheel and release the handbrake.

8 Detach the handbrake cable from the retaining clip on the lower arm.

9 Unscrew the two caliper carrier bracket-to-hub carrier bolts and remove the caliper assembly. Support the caliper on an axle stand to avoid straining the flexible hose.

10 Proceed as described in paragraphs 3 and 4.

11 Mark the position of the brake disc in relation to the drive flange, remove the retaining spire washer(s), and withdraw the disc.

12 Refitting is a reversal of removal, but ensure that the mating faces of the disc and drive flanges are clean, and align the marks made on the disc and drive flange during removal.

9 Brake drum - inspection and renewal

1 Whenever a brake drum is removed, brush out the dust, taking care not to inhale any, as it may be injurious to health.

2 Examine the internal friction surface of the drum. If deeply scored, or so worn that the drum has become ridged to the width of the shoes, then both drums must be renewed.

3 Regrinding is not recommended as the internal diameter of the drum will no longer be compatible with the shoe friction material contact diameter.

10 Rear wheel cylinder (drum brakes) - removal, overhaul and refitting

⚠ **Caution: Refer to the precautions in Section 1.**

Saloon, Hatchback and Estate models

1 Chock the front wheels, loosen the relevant roadwheel nuts, then jack up the rear of the vehicle and support on axle stands (see "Jacking and Vehicle Support"). Remove the roadwheel and release the handbrake.

2 Remove the retaining spire washer(s) from the wheel stud(s) and pull off the brake drum. If the drum will not pass over the shoes, it is possible to release the automatic adjuster mechanism by inserting a screwdriver through the small hole in the drum and pressing down on the ratchet.

3 Remove the brake fluid reservoir cap and secure a piece of polythene over the filler neck with a rubber band, or by refitting the cap. This will reduce the loss of fluid during the following procedure.

4 Unscrew the union nut and disconnect the fluid pipe from the wheel cylinder (see illustration). Plug the open ends of the pipe and wheel cylinder to prevent fluid loss and dirt ingress.

5 Pull the tops of the brake shoes apart so that the self-adjuster mechanism holds them clear of the wheel cylinder.

6 Unscrew the two retaining bolts from the rear of the brake backplate, and withdraw the wheel cylinder and sealing ring.

7 The wheel cylinder can now be dismantled as follows.

8 Prise the dust-excluding rubber seals from the ends of the wheel cylinder, and withdraw the pistons and central spring, identifying the pistons so that they can be refitted in their original positions.

9 Prise the seals from the pistons.

10 Clean all the components in methylated spirit and allow to dry. Examine the surfaces of the pistons and cylinder bore for wear, scoring and corrosion. If evident, the complete wheel cylinder must be renewed, but if the components are in good condition, discard the seals and obtain a repair kit.

11 Dip the new seals in clean brake fluid and fit them to the piston grooves, using fingers only to manipulate them. Ensure that the seal lips face into the wheel cylinder.

12 Carefully insert the pistons and central spring into the cylinder, and fit the dust-excluding rubber seals. Ensure that the pistons are fitted in their original positions.

13 Wipe the brake backplate clean, then fit the wheel cylinder together with a new sealing ring, and tighten the securing bolts.

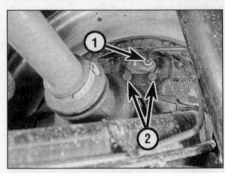

10.4 Fluid pipe union (1) and wheel cylinder retaining bolts (2)

14 Reconnect the fluid pipe to the wheel cylinder and tighten the union nut.

15 Using a screwdriver, push the self-adjuster toothed quadrant fully towards the backplate to its initial setting.

16 Further refitting is a reversal of removal, but on completion apply the footbrake several times in order to set the brake shoes in their normal positions, and bleed the rear brake circuit.

P100 models

17 The procedure is as described in paragraphs 1 to 16 inclusive, but with the following differences.

18 Before removing the roadwheel, mark its position in relation to the brake drum. Similarly, mark the position of the brake drum in relation to one of the wheel studs. Align the marks when refitting.

19 The wheel cylinder is secured to the brake backplate by a circlip instead of the two bolts used on other models (see illustration).

11 Rear brake backplate (drum brakes) - removal and refitting

⚠ **Caution: Refer to the precautions in Section 1.**

Saloon, Hatchback and Estate models

1 Remove the rear brake shoes.

2 Disconnect the handbrake cable from the backplate by extracting the U-clip.

10.19 Wheel cylinder securing circlip (arrowed)

3 Remove the wheel cylinder.

4 Remove the driveshaft but do not refit the securing bolts to the backplate.

5 Remove the backplate.

6 If required, prise out the handbrake stop button.

7 Refitting is a reversal of removal.

P 100 models

Note: *When refitting the backplate, a new rear hub nut and driveshaft O-ring must be used.*

8 Proceed as described in paragraphs 1 to 3 inclusive.

9 Remove the driveshaft.

10 Relieve the staking on the rear hub nut, and using a 50 mm socket and a suitable extension bar, unscrew the nut. Note that the nut is extremely tight.

11 Pull off the hub.

12 Unscrew the six retaining nuts and remove the backplate and the oil baffle **(see illustration)**.

13 If required, prise out the handbrake stop button.

14 Refitting is a reversal of removal, bearing in mind the following points.

15 When refitting the backplate and the oil baffle, coat the area of the oil baffle shown (see illustration - Chapter 9) with sealant to Ford spec SPM-4G-9112-F, then refit the baffle and the backplate to the axle, tightening the six securing nuts to the specified torque.

16 Use a new rear hub nut, and tighten to the specified torque. Stake the nut into the groove in the axle tube after tightening.

17 Refit the driveshaft, using a new O-ring.

12 Rear disc splash shield - removal and refitting

Note: *A suitable puller will be required to remove the drive flange, and a new rear hub nut must be used on reassembly.*

Caution: Refer to the precautions in Section 1.

Removal

1 Loosen the rear hub nut with the vehicle resting on its wheels. Note that the left-hand nut has a left-hand thread, ie it is undone in a clockwise direction. Before loosening the nut, ensure that the handbrake is applied, and chock the relevant rear wheel. A suitable extension bar will be required, as the nut is extremely tight.

2 Loosen the relevant rear roadwheel nuts, chock the front wheels, then jack up the rear of the vehicle and support on axle stands (see *"Jacking and Vehicle Support"*). Remove the roadwheel and release the handbrake.

3 Free the handbrake cable from its clip on the suspension lower arm.

4 Unscrew the two caliper carrier bracket-to-hub carrier bolts, and remove the caliper, supporting it on an axle stand to avoid straining the flexible hose.

5 Mark the position of the brake disc in relation to the drive flange, remove the retaining spire washer(s), and remove the disc.

6 Unscrew and remove the rear hub nut, and using a suitable puller, pull off the drive flange.

7 Unscrew the four bolts securing the hub carrier and splash shield to the lower arm. Remove the hub carrier and splash shield, whilst supporting the driveshaft. Support the driveshaft by placing axle stands underneath it, or by securing with string to the underbody. Avoid bending the driveshaft joints to excessive angles, and do not allow the shaft to hang down from one end.

Refitting

8 Refitting is a reversal of removal, bearing in mind the following points.

9 When reassembling the drive flange and the hub carrier, fit the drive flange to the hub carrier in order to centralise the bearings, then using a soft-faced mallet, drive the drive flange/hub carrier assembly onto the end of the stub axle.

10 Refit the hub carrier/splash shield-to-lower arm securing bolts. Note that there are two types of bolts used to secure the rear hub carrier to the lower arm. The two types of bolt must not be mixed on a vehicle but can be changed in complete sets for the alternative type. A complete set is eight bolts, four each side. Note that the two types of bolt have different torque wrench settings. When renewing the wheel bearings a suitable puller will be required to remove the drive flange, and a new rear hub nut must be used on reassembly.

11 When refitting the brake disc, align the previously made marks on disc and drive flange.

12 Fit a new rear hub nut of the correct type, and tighten it with the vehicle resting on its roadwheels. Apply the handbrake and chock the relevant rear wheel when finally tightening the hub nut.

13 Master cylinder (conventional braking system) - removal, overhaul and refitting

Note: *Before commencing overhaul obtain a repair kit containing new pistons and seals.*

Caution: Refer to the precautions in Section 1.

Removal

1 Depress the brake pedal several times to dissipate the vacuum in the servo.

2 Disconnect the wiring plug from the low fluid level switch on the fluid reservoir cap **(see illustration)**.

3 Place a suitable container beneath the master cylinder, then unscrew the union nuts and disconnect the two fluid pipes. Plug the ends of the pipes to prevent dirt ingress.

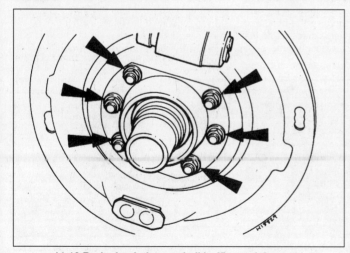

11.12 Brake backplate and oil baffle retaining nuts

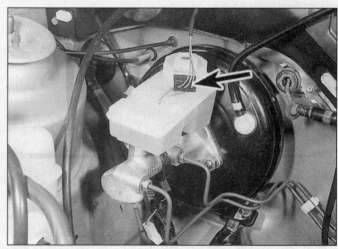

13.2 Disconnect the wiring plug from the low fluid level switch (arrowed)

10

4 Unscrew the two mounting nuts and spring washers, and withdraw the master cylinder from the servo. Cover the master cylinder with rag or a plastic bag to prevent spillage of hydraulic fluid on the vehicle paintwork. If fluid is accidentally spilt on the paintwork, wash off immediately with cold water.

Overhaul

5 Drain the remaining fluid from the master cylinder, and clean the exterior surfaces with methylated spirit.

6 Pull the fluid reservoir from the top of the master cylinder and prise out the sealing rubbers **(see illustration)**.

7 Mount the master cylinder in a vice, then depress the primary piston slightly and extract the circlip and washer. Withdraw the primary piston assembly.

8 Depress the secondary piston and remove the stop pin from the fluid aperture.

9 Remove the master cylinder from the vice and tap it on the bench to remove the secondary piston assembly.

10 Prise the seals from the secondary piston. Do not attempt to dismantle the primary piston.

11 Clean all the components in methylated spirit and examine them for wear and damage. In particular check the surfaces of the pistons and cylinder bore for scoring and corrosion. If the cylinder bore is worn, renew the complete master cylinder, otherwise obtain a repair kit including pistons and seals.

12 Check that the fluid inlet and outlet ports are free and unobstructed. Dip the new pistons and seals in clean brake fluid.

13 Fit the seals to the secondary piston using the fingers only to manipulate them into the grooves. Note that the sealing lips must face away from each other.

14 Insert the secondary piston and spring into the cylinder. Turn the piston slowly as the first seal enters to avoid trapping the sealing lip. Similarly insert the primary piston and spring, then fit the washer and circlip.

15 Depress the primary and secondary pistons and refit the secondary piston stop pin.

16 Fit the fluid reservoir sealing rubbers and

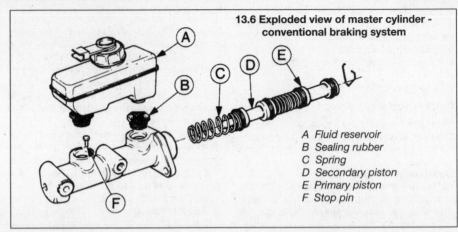

13.6 Exploded view of master cylinder - conventional braking system

A *Fluid reservoir*
B *Sealing rubber*
C *Spring*
D *Secondary piston*
E *Primary piston*
F *Stop pin*

press the reservoir into them. If the rubbers are worn or perished, or if leakage has been evident, fit the new rubbers.

Refitting

17 Refitting is a reversal of removal but tighten the mounting nuts and pipe union nuts to the specified torque and finally bleed the hydraulic system.

14 Vacuum servo (conventional braking system) - removal and refitting

 Caution: Refer to the precautions in Section 1.

Removal

1 To remove the servo, first remove the master cylinder.

2 Disconnect the vacuum hose from the servo **(see illustration)**.

3 Working inside the vehicle, remove the lower facia panel from the driver's side.

4 Remove the clip from the servo pushrod on the brake pedal **(see illustration)**.

5 Unscrew the two mounting nuts and washers securing the servo to the bulkhead, and lift the servo from the bulkhead. Note that the two mounting nuts also secure the pedal bracket to the bulkhead.

6 If required, the vacuum hose can be disconnected from the inlet manifold, and the non-return valve can be checked for correct operation by ensuring that it is only possible to blow through it in one direction.

7 No overhaul of the servo is possible, and if faulty, it must be renewed as a complete unit.

Refitting

8 Refitting is a reversal of removal, but when refitting the servo to the bulkhead, ensure that the pushrod is correctly located in the pedal and that the clip is secure.

Vacuum hose - modification

9 From mid-1989, a new type of brake servo vacuum hose-to-inlet manifold connector has been used in production. The connector comprises three parts; a collet which locks the hose in position, an O-ring, and a brass insert which is pressed into the inlet manifold.

10 To disconnect the hose from the inlet manifold, apply light even pressure, push and hold the flange of the collet against the manifold. While holding the collet forward, gently pull the hose from the collet **(see illustration)**. Take care not to pull at an angle or use excessive force, as this can cause the collet to snatch and lock the hose.

11 To reconnect the hose, push the hose into the collet until the swage on the hose is hard against the collet flange. Pull gently on the hose to check that it is locked by the collet.

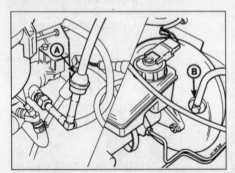

14.2 Servo vacuum hose non-return valve (A) and servo connection (B) - conventional braking system

14.4 Remove the clip (arrowed) from the servo pushrod

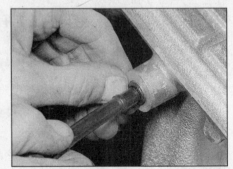

14.10 Disconnecting a later-type brake servo vacuum hose

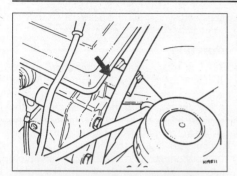
15.4 Reservoir securing clip (arrowed) also supports clutch cable - ABS

15.5a Remove the securing spring clip . . .

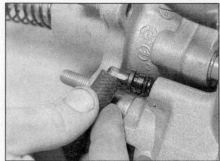
15.5b . . . and disconnect the low pressure fluid hose - ABS

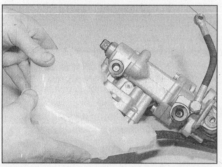
15.6 Removing the fluid reservoir from the hydraulic unit - ABS

15.7 Removing the spigot locating bush from the rear hydraulic unit inlet - ABS

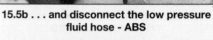**16 Hydraulic unit (ABS)**
- removal and refitting

Note: *A new gasket must be used between the hydraulic unit and the bulkhead on refitting.*

⚠ **Caution: Refer to the precautions in Section 1.**

15 Fluid reservoir (ABS)
- removal and refitting

Note: *New seals must be used between the reservoir and the hydraulic unit on reassembly.*

⚠ **Caution: Refer to the precautions in Section 1.**

Removal

1 Disconnect the battery negative lead.
2 Depressurise the hydraulic system by pumping the brake pedal at least 20 times, or until it becomes hard.
3 Disconnect the wiring multi-plugs from the reservoir cap and remove the cap.
4 Unscrew the reservoir securing screw, and remove the securing clip, noting that the clip also supports the clutch cable **(see illustration)**.

5 Prepare a suitable container to collect the fluid as the hydraulic unit is drained, then remove the securing spring clip and disconnect the low pressure fluid hose from the pump **(see illustrations)**. Allow the fluid to drain out of the hose into the container. If fluid is accidentally spilt on the paintwork, wash off immediately with cold water.
6 Pull the reservoir out of the seals on the hydraulic unit and remove it **(see illustration)**.
7 Note the spigot locating bush on the rear hydraulic unit inlet, which may stay in the hydraulic unit or may come out with the reservoir **(see illustration)**.

Refitting

8 Refitting is a reversal of removal, but use new seals between the reservoir and the hydraulic unit.
9 On completion, bleed the complete hydraulic system and check for leaks around all disturbed components.

Removal

1 Disconnect the battery negative lead.
2 Depressurise the hydraulic system by pumping the brake pedal at least 20 times, or until it becomes hard.
3 Disconnect the six multi-plugs from the hydraulic unit. They are all different, so there is no need to label them. When a plug has a spring clip retainer, lift the clip before pulling out the plug. To release the pump plug, pull back the rubber boot and the plug sleeve **(see illustrations)**.
4 Unbolt the earth strap from the unit.
5 Prepare a suitable container to catch spilt fluid. Mark the hydraulic pipes so that they can be refitted in their original positions, then disconnect them from the base of the unit. Plug the open ends of the pipes and hydraulic unit to prevent fluid leakage and dirt ingress. If fluid is accidentally spilt on the paintwork, wash off immediately with cold water.
6 Working inside the vehicle, remove the lower facia panel from the driver's side.

16.3a Disconnecting the low fluid level switch multi-plug . . .

16.3b . . . the main valve multi-plug . . .

16.3c . . . and the pressure switch multi-plug - ABS

10

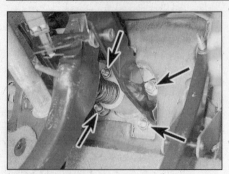

16.8 Hydraulic unit-to-bulkhead securing nuts (arrowed) - ABS

7 Remove the clip from the hydraulic unit pushrod on the brake pedal.

8 With an assistant supporting the hydraulic unit, unscrew the four nuts which secure the unit to the bulkhead **(see illustration)**. Withdraw the unit from under the bonnet.

9 Recover the gasket fitted between the unit and the bulkhead.

10 Drain the fluid from the reservoir. Do not actuate the pushrod with the unit removed.

11 Dismantling of the hydraulic unit should be limited to the operations described in the following Sections **(see illustration)**.

Refitting

12 Refitting is a reversal of removal, bearing in mind the following points.

13 Do not refill the fluid reservoir until reassembly and refitting is complete.

14 Use a new gasket between the hydraulic unit and the bulkhead.

15 Ensure that the hydraulic pipes are reconnected to the correct unions.

16 On completion, bleed the complete hydraulic system and check for leaks around all disturbed components.

17 Hydraulic unit accumulator (ABS) - removal and refitting

Note: *A new O-ring must be used between the accumulator and the hydraulic unit on refitting.*

⚠️ **Caution: Refer to the precautions in Section 1.**

Removal

1 Disconnect the battery negative lead.

2 Depressurise the hydraulic system by pumping the brake pedal at least 20 times, or until it becomes hard.

3 Wrap a clean rag round the base of the accumulator to catch any spilt fluid.

4 Unscrew the accumulator using a hexagon key. Remove the accumulator, noting the sealing ring and being prepared for fluid spillage **(see illustration)**. If fluid is

accidentally spilt on the paintwork, wash off immediately with cold water.

Refitting

5 Fit a new O-ring to the base of the accumulator, fit the accumulator and tighten it.

6 Reconnect the battery. Switch on the ignition and check that the hydraulic unit pump stops within 60 seconds; if not, the accumulator is likely to be faulty.

7 On completion, bleed the complete hydraulic system and check for leaks around all disturbed components.

18 Hydraulic unit pump and motor (ABS) - removal and refitting

Note: *New sealing washers must be used on the high pressure fluid hose banjo union, and a new O-ring must be used between the accumulator and the hydraulic unit on refitting.*

⚠️ **Caution: Refer to the precautions in Section 1.**

Removal

1 Remove the accumulator.

2 Prepare a suitable container to catch spilt fluid, and disconnect the high pressure fluid hose from the pump.

3 Remove the securing spring clip and disconnect the low pressure fluid hose from the pump. Allow the fluid to drain out of the hose into the container. If fluid is accidentally spilt on the paintwork, wash off immediately with cold water.

4 Disconnect the multi-plugs from the pressure switch and the pump motor.

5 Remove the pump mounting bolt **(see illustration)**.

6 Pull the pump and motor assembly off the mounting spigot and remove it.

7 Recover the mounting bushes and renew them if necessary.

8 If a new pump is to be fitted, transfer the pressure switch to it, using a new O-ring.

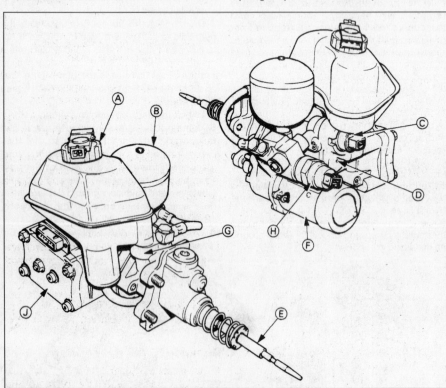

16.11 Hydraulic unit components - ABS

A Fluid reservoir	D Master cylinder	G Booster
B Accumulator	E Pushrod	H Pressure switch
C Main valve	F Pump and motor	J Valve block

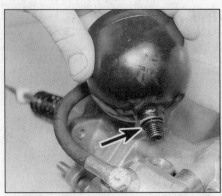

17.4 Unscrew the accumulator and remove it, noting the O-ring (arrowed)

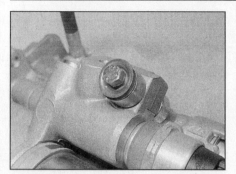

18.5 Hydraulic unit pump mounting bolt - ABS

Refitting

9 Commence refitting by offering the pump to the mounting spigot, then reconnecting the low pressure fluid hose.
10 Refit and tighten the pump mounting bolt.
11 Reconnect the high pressure fluid hose, using new sealing washers on the banjo union.
12 Refit the accumulator, using a new O-ring.
13 Reconnect the multi-plugs and the battery.
14 Refill the fluid reservoir, then switch on the ignition and allow the pump to prime itself. Allow the pump to run for a maximum of two minutes at a time then leave it for ten minutes to cool down.
15 On completion, bleed the complete hydraulic system and check for leaks around all disturbed components.

19 Hydraulic unit pressure switch (ABS) - removal and refitting

Note: To remove the pressure switch from the hydraulic unit in situ, Ford tool No 12-008 or a locally made equivalent will be required. The switch may be removed without special tools after removing the hydraulic unit complete or the pump above. A new O-ring must be used when refitting the switch.

 Caution: Refer to the precautions in Section 1.

Removal

1 Disconnect the battery negative lead.
2 Depressurise the hydraulic system by pumping the brake pedal at least 20 times, or until it becomes hard.
3 Disconnect the multi-plug from the switch, then unscrew and remove the switch.

Refitting

4 Refit the switch using a new O-ring. Position the plastic sleeve so that the drain hole faces the pump motor, then tighten the switch **(see illustration).**
5 Reconnect the multi-plug and the battery.
6 On completion, bleed the complete hydraulic system and check for leaks around all disturbed components.

19.4 Refit the pressure switch with the drain hole (arrowed) in the plastic sleeve facing the pump motor - ABS

20 Valve block (ABS) - removal and refitting

 Caution: Refer to the precautions in Section 1.

Removal

1 Disconnect the battery negative lead.
2 Depressurise the hydraulic system by pumping the brake pedal at least 20 times, or until it becomes hard.
3 Apply the handbrake, and slacken the left-hand front wheel nuts. Jack up the front of the vehicle and support on axle stands (see "Jacking and Vehicle Support").Remove the left-hand front wheel.
4 Remove the plastic liner from under the wheel arch.
5 Prepare a suitable container to catch spilt fluid, clean around the unions on the valve block, then unscrew and disconnect the fluid pipes **(see illustration)**. Plug the open ends of the pipes and valve block to prevent fluid leakage and dirt ingress. If fluid is accidentally spilt on the paintwork, wash off immediately with cold water.
6 Disconnect the multi-plug and the earth strap from the valve block.
7 Working through the wheel arch, unscrew the three nuts which secure the valve block mounting bracket **(see illustration).**

20.7 Unscrewing the valve block mounting bracket nuts (arrowed) - ABS

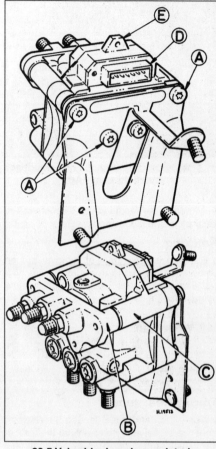

20.5 Valve block and associated components - ABS

A Bracket screws
B Adapter plate
C valve block
D Multi-plug
E Earth strap anchor point

8 Remove the valve block and mounting bracket, taking care not to spill brake fluid on the paintwork.
9 No further dismantling of the valve block is possible, but the pressure regulating valve in the rear brake pipe union can be renewed if desired.

Refitting

10 Refitting is a reversal of removal.
11 On completion, bleed the complete hydraulic system and check for leaks around all disturbed components.

21 Computer module (ABS) - removal and refitting

Removal

1 Disconnect the battery.
2 Working inside the vehicle, prise out the facia trim panel from the passenger's side. Remove the insulation.
3 To remove the now exposed module, push it as necessary to release the retaining catch.

10

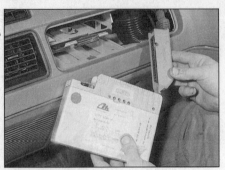

21.4 Withdraw the module and disconnect the multi-plug - ABS

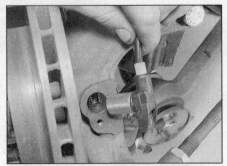

22.3 Unscrew the mounting bolt and withdraw the front wheel sensor - ABS

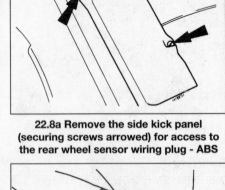

22.8a Remove the side kick panel (securing screws arrowed) for access to the rear wheel sensor wiring plug - ABS

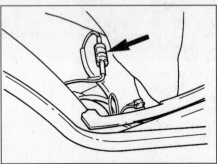

22.8b Rear wheel sensor wiring plug (arrowed) - ABS

4 Withdraw the module, and disconnect the multi-plug (see illustration).

Refitting

5 Refitting is a reversal of removal but on completion check the operation of the ABS warning lamp as described in the manufacturer's handbook.

22 Wheel sensor (ABS) - removal and refitting

Note: *A new O-ring must be used when refitting a sensor.*

Front wheel sensor

1 Apply the handbrake, loosen the relevant front roadwheel nuts, then jack up the front of the vehicle and support on axle stands (see *"Jacking and Vehicle Support")*. Remove the roadwheel.
2 Working under the bonnet, unclip the ABS wiring loom from the chassis side member, and disconnect the wheel sensor wiring plug.
3 Unscrew the mounting bolt and withdraw the sensor (see illustration).
4 Refitting is a reversal of removal, bearing in mind the following points.
5 Clean the bore in the hub carrier, and smear the bore and the sensor with lithium based grease.
6 Use a new O-ring seal when refitting the sensor.

Rear wheel sensor

7 Chock the front wheels, loosen the relevant rear roadwheel nuts, then jack up the rear of the vehicle and support on axle stands. Release the handbrake and remove the roadwheel.
8 Working inside the vehicle, lift up the rear seat cushion, then remove the side kick panel and fold the carpet forwards to gain access to the wheel sensor wiring plug (see illustrations).
9 Remove the wiring plug from its clip, and disconnect it.
10 Prise out the floor panel grommet, then feed the sensor wiring through the floor panel.
11 Free the handbrake cable from its clip on the suspension lower arm.

12 Where applicable, disconnect the wiring to the disc pad wear sensor.
13 Unscrew and remove the bolt from the forward caliper guide pin, while holding the pin stationary with a spanner.
14 Swing the caliper rearwards to gain access to the wheel sensor.
15 Unscrew the bolt securing the sensor to its mounting bracket.
16 Refitting is a reversal of removal, bearing in mind the following points.
17 Clean the bore in the sensor mounting bracket, and smear the bore and the sensor with lithium based grease.
18 Use a new O-ring seal when refitting the sensor.

23 Deceleration sensitive valve (all models with conventional braking system) - removal and refitting

 Caution: Refer to the precautions in Section 1.

Removal

1 The deceleration sensitive valve is located on the left-hand side of the engine compartment (see illustrations).
2 Place a suitable container beneath the valve to catch spilt fluid, then unscrew the union nuts and disconnect the fluid pipes.

Plug the open ends of the pipes and valve to prevent fluid leakage and dirt ingress. If fluid is accidentally spilt on the paintwork, wash off immediately with cold water.
3 On early models, the valve is secured to the mounting bracket on the inner wing by a single bolt. Unscrew the bolt and remove the valve.
4 On later models, the valve is secured to the mounting bracket by a clip. Remove the clip and slide out the valve.

Refitting

5 Refitting is a reversal of removal, but note that the early type of valve must be fitted with the cover bolts facing forwards, and the later type of valve must be fitted with the smaller diameter stepped end facing forwards.
6 On completion, bleed the rear hydraulic circuit.

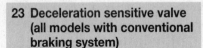

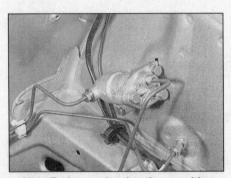

23.1a Early type deceleration sensitive valve

23.1b Later type deceleration sensitive valve

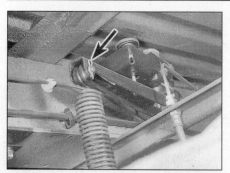

24.3 Remove the spring clip (arrowed) and clevis pin from the valve operating lever

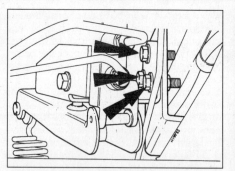

24.5 Load apportioning valve securing bolts (arrowed)

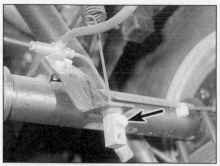

25.3 Loosen the locknut (arrowed) on the abutment block

24 Load apportioning valve (P100 models) - removal and refitting

Caution: Refer to the precautions in Section 1.

Removal

1 Chock the front wheels, jack up the rear of the vehicle and support on axle stands (see "*Jacking and Vehicle Support*").
2 The load apportioning valve is located on the right-hand side of the vehicle underbody above the axle.
3 Remove the spring clip and clevis pin, and detach the spring from the valve operating lever **(see illustration)**.
4 Place a suitable container beneath the valve to catch spilt fluid, then unscrew the union nuts and disconnect the fluid pipes. Plug the open ends of the pipes and valve to prevent fluid leakage and dirt ingress.
5 Unscrew the three securing nuts and bolts from the valve mounting bracket, and remove the valve assembly **(see illustration)**.

Refitting

6 Refitting is a reversal of removal, but note that the fluid inlet pipe from the master cylinder

must be connected to the lower valve port, and the fluid outlet pipe to the rear brakes must be connected to the upper valve port.
7 On completion, bleed the rear hydraulic circuit and check the valve adjustment.

25 Load apportioning valve (P100 models) - adjustment

Models before mid-April 1989

1 The vehicle must be unladen, at normal kerb weight (a full tank of petrol, but no driver or load).
2 With the vehicle standing on its roadwheels, remove the spring clip and clevis pin, and detach the spring from the valve operating lever.
3 Loosen the locknut on the abutment block at the bottom of the spring **(see illustration)**.
4 Slide the spring through the grommet in the bracket on the axle, until the correct "X" dimension is obtained between the centre of the spring eye and the centre of the valve operating lever eye **(see illustration)**.
5 Hold the spring in position, slide the abutment block against the underside of the grommet, and tighten the locknut.
6 Attach the free end of the spring to the valve operating lever, and refit the clevis pin and spring clip.

Models from mid-April 1989

7 The procedure is as described above, but note that the dimension "X" has been revised to 92.0 mm (3.6 in) with the vehicle unladen at normal kerb weight.

26 Brake fluid pipes and hoses - removal and refitting

Caution: Refer to the precautions in Section 1.

Removal

1 To remove a flexible hose, always free it from any mounting bracket(s) first by prising out the U-shaped retaining clip, and then using two close-fitting spanners to disconnect the hose-to-rigid pipe union **(see illustration)**.
2 Once disconnected from the rigid pipe, the flexible hose may be unscrewed from the caliper or wheel cylinder union, as applicable.

Refitting

3 When reconnecting pipe or hose fittings, note that the seal is made at the swaged end of the pipe, so do not continue to tighten a union if it is tight, yet still stands proud of the surface into which it is screwed.

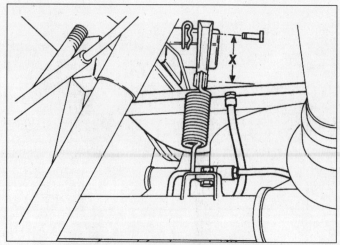

25.4 Load apportioning valve adjustment
X = 77.0 mm (3.0 in) with vehicle unladen at normal kerb weight

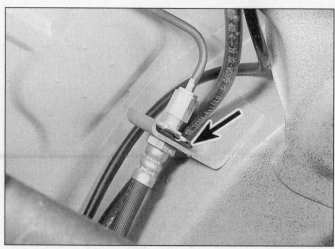

26.1 Flexible hose-to-rigid pipe union. U-shaped retaining clip arrowed

10

4 A flexible hose must never be installed twisted, but a slight "set" is permissible to give it clearance from adjacent components. This can be achieved by turning the hose slightly before fitting the U-shaped retaining clip to the mounting bracket.

5 Rigid pipelines can be made to pattern by motor factors supplying brake components.

27 Handbrake cable - removal and refitting

Removal

1 Chock the front wheels, loosen the rear roadwheel nuts, then jack up the rear of the vehicle and support on axle stands. Release the handbrake and remove the roadwheels.

2 Slacken the handbrake cable adjuster.

3 Extract the securing circlip and pivot pin, and detach the handbrake equaliser from the linkage on the underbody **(see illustration)**.

4 On models with a conventional braking system, remove the brake shoes and disconnect the handbrake cables from the operating levers, then disconnect the cables from the brake backplates by extracting the U-clips.

5 On models with ABS, unhook the handbrake cables from the operating levers on the calipers, then disconnect the cables from the caliper carrier brackets by removing the retaining circlips **(see illustrations)**.

6 On Saloon, Hatchback and Estate models bend back the tangs and release the cables from the lower suspension arms, then feed the cables through the holes in the suspension crossmember and release them from the brackets on the underbody, noting that the right-hand cable is retained by a circlip **(see illustration)**. Withdraw the cable assembly from the vehicle.

7 On P100 models, release the cables from the brackets on the chassis crossmember, noting that the left-hand cable is retained by a circlip, then unhook the cable support springs

27.3 Handbrake equaliser securing circlip (arrowed) and pivot pin

and withdraw the cable assembly from the vehicle **(see illustration)**.

Refitting

8 Refitting is a reversal of removal. On models with a conventional braking system refit the brake shoes.

9 On completion, adjust the cable.

27.5a Handbrake cable-to-operating lever attachment - ABS

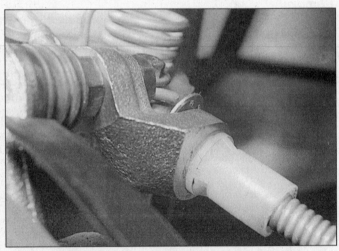

27.5b Handbrake cable-to-caliper carrier bracket attachment - ABS

27.6 Handbrake cable-to-lower suspension arm attachment

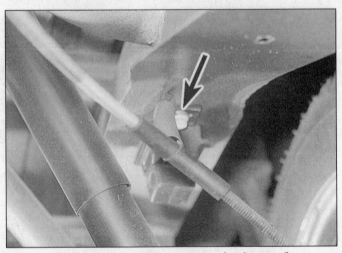

27.7 Handbrake cable support spring (arrowed)

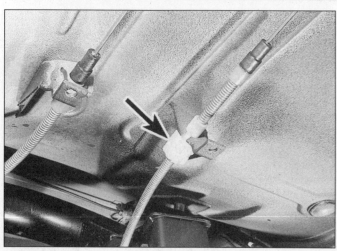

28.3 Handbrake cable adjuster on left-hand underbody bracket (arrowed)

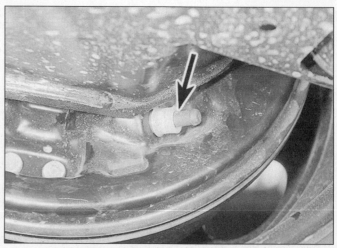

28.5 Plastic plunger (arrowed) in brake backplate

28 Handbrake cable - adjustment

Note: *Where fitted, the adjuster locking pin must be renewed on completion of adjustment.*

Conventional braking system (except P100 models)

1 The handbrake cable is normally self-adjusting in use, however adjustment may be required to compensate for cable stretch over a long period, and is also necessary after fitting a new cable.

2 Chock the front wheels, jack up the rear of the vehicle and support on axle stands (see "*Jacking and Vehicle Support*"). Release the handbrake.

3 Unscrew the locknut from the adjuster located on the left-hand underbody bracket **(see illustration)**. On later models, a locking pin is fitted to the bracket to lock the adjuster nuts in position. Where applicable, remove the locking pin before unscrewing the locknut.

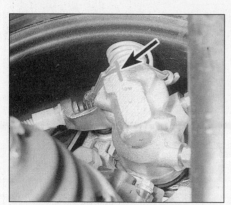

28.11 Make alignment marks between each handbrake operating lever and caliper body (arrowed) - ABS

4 Apply the footbrake vigorously several times to set the self-adjuster mechanism.

5 Turn the adjuster until the plastic plungers located in the brake lockplates are free to turn, and the total movement of both plungers added together is between 0.5 and 1.0 mm (0.02 and 0.04 in) **(see illustration)**.

6 Tighten the adjuster locknut against the adjuster nut by hand (two clicks), then tighten further by a minimum of two and a maximum of four clicks, using a suitable spanner or pliers.

7 Where applicable, fit a new adjuster locking pin. The old pin should not be re-used.

8 Check that with the handbrake released, the rear wheels are free to rotate and no brake "bind" is evident. The handbrake lever travel should be between two and four clicks of the ratchet. If brake "bind" or excessive lever travel is evident, check the handbrake cable routing, and check the self-adjuster mechanism for wear or damage.

ABS

9 Proceed as described in paragraphs 1 to 3 inclusive.

10 Bend back the tangs and release the cables from the lower suspension arms.

11 Ensure that both handbrake operating levers are returned to their stops on the calipers, then make alignment marks between the levers and the caliper bodies **(see illustration)**.

12 Turn the adjuster until either lever just starts to move, as indicated by the alignment marks.

13 Apply the handbrake and release it several times to equalise the cable runs.

14 With the handbrake released, proceed as described in paragraphs 6 and 7.

15 Refit the cables to the lower suspension arms, and secure by bending over the tangs.

16 Check that with the handbrake released, the rear wheels are free to rotate and no brake

"bind" is evident. The handbrake lever travel should be between two and four clicks of the ratchet. If brake "bind" or excessive lever travel is evident, check the handbrake cable routing, and check the caliper mechanism for wear or damage.

P100 models

17 Proceed as described in paragraphs 1 to 4 inclusive, but note that the adjuster is located on the right-hand side of the chassis crossmember **(see illustration)**.

18 Apply the handbrake, pulling the lever upwards three clicks.

19 Turn the adjuster until both rear wheels are locked and cannot be turned by hand.

20 Proceed as described in paragraphs 6 and 7.

21 Check that with the handbrake released, the rear wheels are free to rotate and no brake "bind" is evident. The handbrake lever travel should be between three and five clicks of the ratchet. If brake "bind" or excessive lever travel is evident, check the handbrake cable routing, and check the self-adjuster mechanism for wear or damage.

28.17 Handbrake cable adjuster on right-hand side of chassis crossmember

29.3 Handbrake equaliser and linkage on underbody

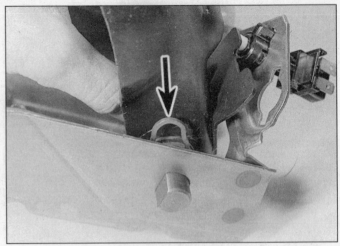

30.2 Extract the inboard circlip (arrowed) to remove the pedal pivot shaft

29 Handbrake lever - removal and refitting

Removal

1 Chock the rear wheels, jack up the front of the vehicle and support on axle stands. Release the handbrake. Disconnect the battery negative lead.
2 Slacken the handbrake cable adjuster.
3 Extract the securing circlip and pivot pin, and detach the handbrake equaliser from the linkage on the underbody (see illustration).
4 Working inside the vehicle, remove the handbrake lever rubber gaiter and/or the centre console, as necessary.
5 Disconnect the wiring connector from the handbrake "on" warning switch.

6 Unscrew the two handbrake lever mounting bolts, and carefully lift the lever through the underfloor gaiter.
7 If required, the handbrake "on" warning switch can be removed.

Refitting

8 Refitting is a reversal of removal, but on completion, adjust the handbrake cable.

30 Brake pedal - removal and refitting

Removal

1 Remove the clutch pedal as described in Chapter 6.
2 Extract the inboard circlip from the brake pedal end of the pivot shaft (see illustration).

3 The brake pedal can now be removed from the pedal bracket by sliding out the pivot shaft, noting the position of any washers and spacers which may be fitted.
4 If desired, the nylon bushes can be prised from each side of the pedal for renewal, and the brake lamp switch removed.

Refitting

5 Refitting is a reversal of removal, fitting any washers and spacers in their original positions. Refit the clutch pedal.

Chapter 11
Suspension and steering

Contents

Degrees of difficulty

Easy, suitable for novice with little experience	**Fairly easy,** suitable for beginner with some experience	**Fairly difficult,** suitable for competent DIY mechanic	**Difficult,** suitable for experienced DIY mechanic	**Very difficult,** suitable for expert DIY or professional

Specifications

Front suspension
Type . . . . Independent by MacPherson struts with coil springs and integral telescopic shock absorbers. Anti-roll bar fitted to all models

Rear suspension
Type:
Saloon, Hatchback and Estate models . . . . Independent by semi-trailing arms and coil springs with telescopic shock absorbers mounted behind coil springs on Saloon and Hatchback models but concentric with coil springs on Estate models. Self-levelling rear shock absorbers on certain Estate models. Anti-roll bar fitted to certain models

P100 models . . . . Live beam axle with leaf springs and telescopic shock absorbers

Steering

11

Type . . . . Rack-and-pinion steering gear linked to collapsible steering column by flexible coupling and universal joint. Power steering available on certain models

Front wheel alignment*
Production toe-setting:
Saloon, Hatchback and Estate models . . . . 2.0 mm (0.08 in) ± 1.0 mm (0.04 in) toe-in
P100 models . . . . 2.0 mm (0.08 in) ± 2.0 mm (0.08 in) toe-in
Service tolerance before adjustment is required . . . . 0.5 mm (0.02 in) toe-out to 4.5 mm (0.18 in) toe-in
*Toe-setting figures are quoted for vehicle at kerb weight with 3.0 litres (0.66 gallons) of fuel in tank

Wheels

Type . . . . Pressed steel or alloy
Size:
  Saloon, Hatchback and Estate models:
    Steel . . . . 13 x 4.50 in, 13 x 5.50 in, or 14 x 5.50 in
    Alloy . . . . 14 x 5.50 in
  P100 models . . . . 14 x 5.50 in

Tyre sizes

Note: *Manufacturers often modify tyre sizes and pressure recommendations. The following is intended as a guide only. Refer to your vehicle handbook or a Ford dealer for the latest recommendations*

Saloon and Hatchback models . . . . 165 R 13H, 165 R 135, 165 R 13T, 185/70 R 13H, 185/70 R 135,
185/70 R13T, 195/60 R 14H, 195/60 VR 14 or 195/65 R 14T

Estate models . . . . 175 R 13H, 175 R 135,175 R 13T, 195/70 R 13H, 195/65 R 14T,
195/60 R 14H or 195/60 VR 14 P100 models 185R 14 8PR

Tyre pressures (cold): lbf/in^2 (bar):	Front	Rear
All Saloon, Hatchback and Estate models with normal load*	26 (1.8)	26 (1.8)
All Saloon and Hatchback models with full load	29 (2.0)	36 (2.5)
Estate models with full load:		
175 R 13H, 175 R 135,175 R 13T, 195/70 R 13H and 195/65 R14T .	29 (2.0)	48 (2.8)
195/60 R 14H and 195/60 VR 14	29 (2.0)	36 (2.5)
P100 models with light load	26 (1.8)	36 (2.5)
P100 models with full load	50 (3.5)	65 (4.5)

Normal load is defined as up to three passengers (or equivalent). For sustained high speeds add 1.5 lbf/in^2 (0.1 bar) for every 6 mph (10 km/h) over 100 mph (160 km/h)

†A light load is defined as one passenger plus up to 100 kg (220 lb) payload

Torque wrench settings

	Nm	lbf ft
Roadwheel nuts		
Wheelnuts:		
Saloon, Hatchback and Estate models (steel and alloy wheels)	70 to 100	52 to 74
P100 models	85 to 90	63 to 66
Hub nuts:		
Saloon, Hatchback and Estate models	310 to 350	229 to 258
P100 models	390 to 450	288 to 332
Front suspension		
Strut upper mounting nut	40 to 52	30 to 38
Hub carrier-to-strut pinch-bolt	77 to 92	57 to 68
Crossmember-to-underbody bolts	70 to 90	52 to 66
Engine mounting-to-crossmember nut:		
Saloon, Hatchback and Estate models	50 to 70	37 to 52
P100 models	41 to 58	30 to 43
Anti-roll bar-to-lower arm nut	70 to 110	52 to 81
Anti-roll bar U-clamp-to-underbody bolts	55 to 70	41 to 52
Lower arm-to-hub carrier balljoint nut	65 to 85	48 to 63
Lower arm inner pivot bolt:		
Stage 1 ("clamping"torque)	45	33
Loosen fully, then Stage 2 ("snug" torque)	15	11
Stage 3	Tighten through a further 90°	
Rear suspension		
Saloon, Hatchback and Estate models:		
Lower arm-to-crossmember pivot bolts	80 to 95	59 to 70
Front guide plate-to-underbody bolts	41 to 51	30 to 38
Front guide plate-to-crossmember bolt	100	74
Suspension/final drive unit rear mounting-to-underbody bolts (gold coloured)	60	44
Suspension/final drive unit rear mounting-to-final drive unit rear cover bolts	40 to 50	30 to 37
Anti-roll bar-to-underbody bracket bolts	20 to 25	15 to 18
Hub carrier/brake backplate-to-lower arm bolts*:		
Type X	52 to 64	38 to 47
Type Y	80 to 100	59 to 74
Hub nut	250 to 290	185 to 214

*See Section 15

Torque wrench settings (continued)

	Nm	lbf ft
P100 models:		
Shock absorber-to-chassis crossmember bolt	60 to 70	44 to 52
Leaf spring-to-front bracket bolt	157 to 196	116 to 145
Leaf spring-to-spring shackle bolt	157 to 196	116 to 145
Spring shackle-to-underbody bolt	80 to 85	59 to 63
Axle-to-leaf spring U-bolt nuts	39 to 58	29 to 43
Manual steering		
Steering gear-to-crossmember bolts:		
Stage 1 ("clamping" torque)	45	33
Loosen fully, then Stage 2 ("snug" torque)	15	11
Stage 3	Tighten through a further 90°	
Steering column adjuster through-bolt	6 to 8	4 to 6
Tie-rod end locknut	57 to 68	42 to 50
Tie-rod end-to-hub carrier nut*	20 to 32	15 to 24
Tie-rod-to-steering rack balljoint	72 to 88	53 to 65
Steering wheel nut	45 to 55	33 to 41
Intermediate shaft-to-inner column clamp bolt	20 to 25	15 to 18
Flexible coupling-to-steering gear clamp nut	24 to 26	17 to 19
Column mounting pinch-bolt	45 to 55	33 to 41
Pinion retaining nut	70 to 100	52 to 74
Slipper plug†	4 to 5	3 to 4

Tighten nut to specified torque and then tighten to next available split pin hole
†Tighten nut to specified torque and then loosen off 60° to 70°

Power steering (where different to manual steering)

	Nm	lbf ft
Tie-rod to steering rack balljoint	70 to 77	52 to 57
Flexible coupling-to-steering gear clamp bolt	16 to 20	12 to 15
Intermediate shaft-to-inner column clamp bolt	16 to 20	12 to 15
Pinion locknut	37 to 47	27 to 35
Slipper plug	3 to 4	2 to 3
Pump rear support bar nut and bolt	41 to 51	30 to 38
Pump mounting bracket-to-engine bolts	52 to 64	38 to 47
Pump pulley bolt	10 to 12	7 to 9
Fluid hose-to-pinion housing bolt	21 to 26	15 to 19
Fluid pressure hose-to-pump union	26 to 31	19 to 23
Fluid return hose-to-pump union	16 to 20	12 to 15

1 General information

The front suspension is of independent MacPherson strut type incorporating coil springs and integral telescopic shock absorbers. The lower end of each strut is attached to a hub carrier, which carries the wheel hub and bearings, and the brake assembly. The lower end of each hub carrier is attached to a suspension lower arm by a sealed balljoint. The inboard ends of the lower arms are attached to the front suspension crossmember and the lower arms thus provide lateral location for the strut assemblies. The upper end of each strut is bolted to a suspension turret on the vehicle body. An anti-roll bar is mounted to the rear of the lower arms, and resists the roll tendency of the front suspension.

On Saloon, Hatchback and Estate models, the rear suspension is also of independent type, incorporating semi-trailing arms, coil springs and telescopic shock absorbers. The semi-trailing arms are attached to the suspension crossmember at their forward ends, and to the hub carriers at the rear. The coil springs are located between the semi-trailing arms and the vehicle underbody. On Saloon and Hatchback models, the shock absorbers are mounted behind the coil springs, but on Estate models they are concentric with the coil springs. On some Estate models the shock absorbers are of the self-levelling type. The suspension crossmember is attached to the vehicle underbody, and to the final drive unit. Certain models are fitted with an anti-roll bar which is mounted to the rear of the final drive unit, and is attached to the semi-trailing arms by connecting links.

The rear suspension on P100 models consists of a beam axle located and supported by a leaf spring on each side, and utilizing telescopic shock absorbers to control vertical movement. The hub and brake assemblies are attached directly to each side of the axle. The axle is bolted to the leaf springs using U-bolts and counterplates, and the shock absorbers are attached to the counterplates at their lower ends and the vehicle underbody at their upper ends.

The steering gear is of the conventional rack and pinion type located ahead of the front wheels. Movement of the steering wheel is transmitted to the steering gear by means of a shaft containing a universal joint. The front hub carriers are connected to the steering gear by tie-rods, each having an inner and outer balljoint. Power-assisted steering is available on some models, assistance being provided hydraulically by an engine-driven pump.

2 Front suspension crossmember - removal and refitting

Removal

1 Remove the steering gear.
2 Support the engine with a jack and interposed block of wood under the sump.
3 Unscrew and remove the engine mounting nuts from the top of the mountings in the engine bay **(see illustration)**.
4 Raise the engine slightly with the jack, and ensure that it is safely supported, and just clear of the engine mounting rubbers.
5 Unscrew and remove the nuts, washers and pivot bolts securing the lower arms to the crossmember, and pull the arms from the crossmember. Note that the pivot bolt heads face to the rear of the vehicle.

11

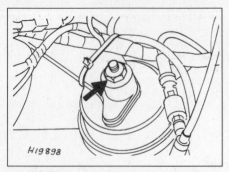

2.3 Engine mounting nut (arrowed)

6 Where applicable, remove the brake pipes from the clips on the crossmember, taking care not to strain them, and detach any cables or electrical leads which may be secured with clips or cable-ties, noting their positions.

7 Support the crossmember with a jack, then unscrew and remove the four mounting bolts **(see illustration)**.

8 Lower the crossmember and withdraw it from under the vehicle.

9 If desired, the engine mountings can now be unbolted from the crossmember.

Refitting

10 Refitting is a reversal of removal, but bear in mind the following points.

11 Do not tighten the lower arm pivot bolts until the weight of the vehicle is resting on its wheels. This is to prevent "wind up" of the rubber bushes which will occur when the vehicle is lowered if the bolts have been tightened with no load on the suspension. The following procedure must be used when tightening the pivot bolts. Tighten the bolt to the specified "clamping" torque, then loosen the bolt fully. Re-tighten to the specified "snug" torque and then further tighten the bolt through the specified angle.

12 Refit any cables or electrical leads in their original positions, where applicable.

13 When lowering the engine onto its mountings, ensure that the locating pegs on the mountings engage with the holes in the mounting brackets.

3 Front suspension lower arm - removal, overhaul and refitting

Note: A balljoint separator tool will be required for this operation.

Removal

1 To improve access, raise the front of the vehicle on ramps. Do not jack the vehicle up at this stage. Apply the handbrake.

2 Unscrew and remove the nut, washer and pivot bolt securing the relevant lower arm to the crossmember **(see illustration)**.

3 Remove the anti-roll bar-to-lower arm securing nut and recover the dished washer and plastic cover (where applicable) **(see illustration)**.

2.7 Front suspension crossmember mounting bolts (arrowed)

4 Ensure that the handbrake is applied, jack up the front of the vehicle and support on axle stands (see *"Jacking and Vehicle Support"*).

5 Remove the split pin and unscrew the castellated nut from the lower arm balljoint. Using a balljoint separator tool, disconnect the lower arm from the hub carrier. The lower arm can now be withdrawn from the vehicle. Recover the remaining dished washer and plastic cover (where applicable) from the end of the anti-roll bar.

Overhaul

6 If the lower arm has been removed due to a worn balljoint, the complete arm must be renewed.

7 The anti-roll bar compliance bushes can be renewed as described in Section 8, but note that the bushes on both sides of the vehicle must be renewed at the same time. The lower arm inner pivot bush can be renewed as described in Section 9.

Refitting

8 To refit the lower arm, proceed as follows.

9 Fit the shallow dished washer (colour coded black or green) and the plastic cover (where applicable) to the end of the anti-roll bar, then refit the lower arm to the anti-roll bar. Fit the remaining plastic cover (where applicable) and the deep dished washer (colour coded yellow or black) and refit the securing nut. Do not tighten the nut at this stage. Note that the convex faces of the dished washers must face the lower arm.

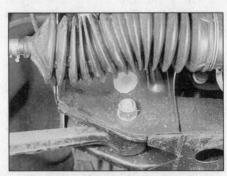

3.2 Front suspension lower arm-to-crossmember pivot bolt and nut

10 Reconnect the balljoint to the hub carrier, refit the castellated nut and tighten to the specified torque. Fit a new split pin.

11 Locate the end of the lower arm in the crossmember and refit the pivot bolt, washer and nut. If necessary, push the outer rim of the roadwheel in order to line up the holes in the lower arm bush and the crossmember. Note that the pivot bolt head should face to the rear of the vehicle. Do not tighten the bolt at this stage.

12 Lower the vehicle so that its weight is resting on the roadwheels, and bounce the vehicle to settle the suspension.

13 Tighten the lower arm pivot bolt, following the procedure given in Section 2.

14 Tighten the anti-roll bar-to-lower arm securing nut to the specified torque.

15 Lower the vehicle from the ramps, if not already done.

4 Front suspension strut - removal, overhaul and refitting

Note: A *spring compressor tool will be required if the strut is to be dismantled.*

Removal

1 Loosen the relevant front roadwheel nuts, apply the handbrake, jack up the front of the vehicle and support on axle stands (see *"Jacking and Vehicle Support"*).

2 Remove the roadwheel. On P100 models mark the position of the roadwheel in relation to one of the wheel studs before removal.

3 Remove the front brake caliper but do not disconnect the hydraulic hose. Support the caliper on an axle stand to avoid straining the hose.

4 Where applicable, unbolt the ABS wheel sensor from the hub carrier and detach the wire from the clip on the strut. Unplug the connector and place the sensor to one side.

5 Unscrew and remove the pinch-bolt which secures the hub carrier to the strut. Using a suitable lever, such as a cold chisel, lever the hub carrier clamp legs and wedge them apart.

6 Lever the suspension lower arm downwards to separate the hub carrier from the bottom of the strut.

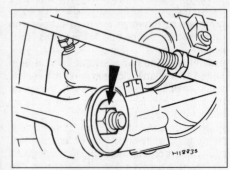

3.3 Front anti-roll bar-to-lower arm securing nut (arrowed)

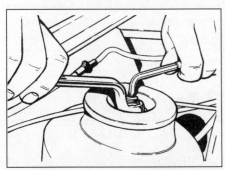

4.7 Hold the strut piston rod with a 6 mm Allen key when unscrewing the upper mounting nut

7 Working in the engine compartment, unscrew the strut upper mounting nut, at the same time supporting the strut from below. Use a 6 mm Allen key inserted in the end of the strut piston rod to prevent the rod from turning as the upper mounting nut is unscrewed (see illustration). On some models, the upper mounting nut may be fitted with a plastic cover. Note the upper mounting cup under the nut.

8 Withdraw the strut from under the wing of the vehicle.

Overhaul

9 To dismantle the strut, proceed as follows.

10 Using spring compressors, compress the coil spring. Do not attempt to compress the spring without using purpose-made spring compressors, as the spring is under considerable tension, and personal injury may occur if it is suddenly released (see illustration).

11 Hold the piston rod as described in paragraph 7, unscrew the nut from the piston

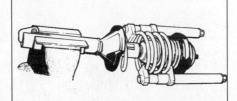

4.10 Suspension strut fitted with spring compressors

rod and remove the lower cup, bearing, spring seat, gaiter, coil spring and bump stop (see illustration).

12 Working in the engine compartment, remove the upper cup and nylon spacer, and if required prise out the rubber insulator.

13 Clean all the components and examine them for wear and damage. Check the action of the shock absorber by mounting it vertically in a vice and operating the piston rod several times through its full stroke. If any uneven resistance is evident, the shock absorber must be renewed. Renew any worn or damaged components as applicable.

Refitting

14 Reassembly and refitting is a reversal of dismantling and removal, bearing in mind the following points.

15 When reassembling, ensure that the gaiter is fitted over the bump stop, and that the ends of the coil spring are correctly located on the spring seats. Also ensure that the bearing is correctly located on the upper spring seat.

16 Fit the nylon spacer over the piston rod before fitting the strut to the top mounting.

17 Tighten all fixings to the specified torque.

18 On P100 models align the previously made marks on the roadwheel and wheel stud.

5 Front hub carrier - removal and refitting

Note: A balljoint separator tool will be required for this operation.

Removal

1 Loosen the relevant front roadwheel nuts, apply the handbrake, jack up the front of the vehicle and support on axle stands (see "Jacking and Vehicle Support").

2 Remove the roadwheel. On P100 models mark the position of the roadwheel in relation to one of the wheel studs before removal.

3 Remove the front brake caliper but do not disconnect the hydraulic hose. Support the caliper on an axle stand, or suspend it with wire from the coil spring to avoid straining the hose.

4 Mark the position of the brake disc in relation to the drive flange, and on Saloon, Hatchback and Estate models, remove the retaining screw or spire washer(s), as applicable, and remove the disc. On P100 models, unscrew the five retaining nuts and remove the wheel adapter plate and disc.

5 Where applicable, unbolt the ABS wheel sensor from the hub carrier and unplug the wiring connector. Place the sensor to one side.

6 Remove the split pin and unscrew the castellated nut securing the tie-rod end to the hub carrier. Using a balljoint separator tool, disconnect the tie-rod end from the hub carrier.

7 Repeat the procedure given in the previous paragraph for the lower arm-to-hub carrier balljoint.

8 Unscrew and remove the pinch-bolt which secures the hub carrier to the strut (see illustration). Using a suitable lever, such as a cold chisel, lever the hub carrier clamp legs and wedge them apart. Withdraw the hub carrier from the strut.

Refitting

9 Refitting is a reversal of removal, but use new split pins on the castellated nuts, and align the previously made marks on the brake disc and hub. Tighten all fixings to the specified torque.

10 On P100 models align the previously made marks on the roadwheel and wheel stud.

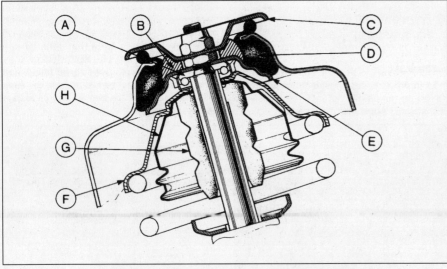

4.11 Cross-section of the front strut upper mounting

A Bearing
B Nylon spacer
C Upper cup
D Rubber insulator
E Lower cup
F Spring seat
G Bump stop
H Gaiter

5.8 Unscrewing the hub carrier-to-strut pinch-bolt

11

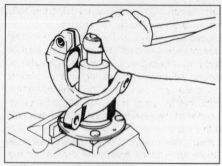

6.2 Front hub carrier mounted in vice to unscrew hub nut

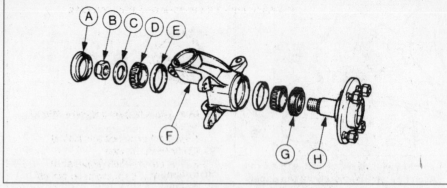

6.4 Front hub components

A Dust cap	C Splined washer	E Bearing outer race	G Oil seal
B Hub nut	D Taper roller bearing	F Hub carrier	H Drive flange

6 Front wheel bearings - renewal

1 Remove the hub carrier.
2 Reverse the roadwheel nuts and screw them fully onto the studs to protect the threads, then mount the hub carrier assembly in a vice as shown (see illustration).
3 Prise the dust cap from the rear of the hub carrier, and unscrew the hub nut with a suitable socket. Note that on all models manufactured before late December 1982, both left and right-hand nuts have a right-hand thread, but as from this date, left-hand thread assemblies were progressively fitted to the right-hand hub carrier. The modified right-hand hub can be identified by the letter "R" stamped on its outer face, or by the colour of the hub nut nylon insert, blue indicates a normal right-hand thread, and yellow indicates a left-hand thread.
4 Remove the splined washer, and tap the hub carrier from the drive flange. Recover the bearing inner race and rollers from the inner end of the hub carrier (see illustration).
5 Prise the oil seal from the outer end of the hub carrier and remove the remaining bearing inner race and rollers.
6 Using a soft metal drift, drive the bearing outer races from the hub carrier, taking care not to damage the inner surface of the carrier.
7 Clean the hub carrier and drive flange with paraffin, wipe dry and examine for damage and wear. Note that the components are machined to very close tolerances, and the bearings are supplied in matched pairs, therefore scrupulous cleanliness must be observed.
8 Using a metal tube of suitable diameter, drive the new bearing outer races fully into the hub carrier. Ensure that the races are seated correctly.
9 Pack the inner bearing races and rollers with high-melting-point lithium-based grease, and locate the outer bearing assembly in the hub camber.
10 Fill the cavities between the sealing lips of the oil seal with grease, then drive it fully into the hub carrier using a block of wood or a metal tube of suitable diameter. Note that on

early models the oil seal has a rubber casing, and this early type of seal should be replaced with the later type which has a metal casing. The oil seal should be renewed regardless of type, and a new seal of the correct type is normally supplied with the new wheel bearings.
11 With the drive flange mounted in a vice, as during dismantling, tap the hub carrier onto the drive flange.
12 Fit the inner bearing assembly, tapping it into place with a metal tube of suitable diameter if necessary, and fit the splined washer. Note that the bearings are self-setting on assembly, and no subsequent adjustment is required.
13 Refit the hub nut and tighten it to the specified torque.
14 Tap the dust cap into position in the hub carrier.
15 Remove the assembly from the vice, remove the roadwheel nuts, and refit the hub carrier.

7 Front anti-roll bar - removal and refitting

Removal

1 To improve access, raise the front of the vehicle on ramps. Do not jack the vehicle up at this stage. Apply the handbrake.

7.2a Bend back the locktabs (arrowed) . . .

2 Where applicable bend back the locktabs, then unscrew the two bolts securing each of the two anti-roll bar U-clamps to the vehicle underbody (see illustrations).
3 Ensure that the handbrake is applied, jack up the front of the vehicle and support on axle stands (see "Jacking and Vehicle Support").
4 Remove the anti-roll bar-to-lower arm securing nuts and recover the dished washers and plastic covers, where applicable (see illustration).
5 Unscrew and remove the nut, washer and pivot bolt securing one of the lower arms to the crossmember, and pull the end of the lower arm from the crossmember.
6 Pull the anti-roll bar from the bush in the "free" lower arm then slide the anti-roll bar from the remaining fixed lower arm. Recover the remaining dished washers and plastic covers (where applicable) from the ends of the anti-roll bar.
7 If necessary, the anti-roll bar compliance bushes can be renewed as described in Section 8, and the anti-roll bar U-clamp bushes can be renewed by sliding them off the ends of the bar. Note that although the U-clamp bushes are of a split design, they should not be levered open to aid fitting, and the new bushes must be slid on from the ends of the anti-roll bar. The bushes should always be renewed in pairs.

7.2b . . . unscrew the bolts and remove the anti-roll bar U-clamps

7.4 Front anti-roll bar-to-lower arm mounting

A Rear (black or green) shallow dished washer
B Plastic cover (where applicable)
C Compliance bushes
D Plastic cover (where applicable)
E Front (yellow or black) deep dished washer

Refitting

8 To refit the anti-roll bar, proceed as follows.
9 Fit the shallow dished washers (colour coded black or green) and the plastic covers (where applicable) to the ends of the anti-roll bar, then push the anti-roll bar through the bushes in the lower arms. Fit the remaining plastic covers (where applicable) and the deep dished washers (colour coded yellow or black) and loosely fit the securing nuts. Note that the convex faces of the dished washers must face the lower arm. Do not tighten the nuts fully at this stage.
10 Locate the "free" lower arm inner pivot bush in the crossmember, and refit the pivot bolt, washer and nut. If necessary, push the outer rim of the roadwheel in order to line up the holes in the lower arm bush and the crossmember. Note that the pivot bolt head should face to the rear of the vehicle. Do not tighten the bolt at this stage.
11 Lower the vehicle so that its weight is resting on the roadwheels.
12 Refit the anti-roll bar U-clamps to the vehicle underbody. Note that various different types of clamping components have been used during production, and if any of the components are to be renewed, it is important to retain the old components for identification when ordering new parts. The same type of clamp assembly must be used on both sides of the vehicle. Tighten the bolts evenly on each clamp to the specified torque. Where applicable, secure the bolts with the locktabs.
13 Bounce the vehicle to settle the suspension, then tighten the lower arm pivot bolt, following the procedure given in Section 2.
14 Tighten the anti-roll bar-to-lower arm securing nuts to the specified torque.
15 Lower the vehicle from the ramps, if not already done.

8 Front anti-roll bar-to-lower arm compliance bushes - renewal

Note: The compliance bushes must be renewed in vehicle sets, therefore the bushes on both sides of the vehicle must be renewed at the same time. If plastic covers were not originally fitted between the dished washers and the bushes, suitable covers should be obtained for fitting during reassembly.

1 Remove the anti-roll bar.
2 Using a thin-bladed chisel or screwdriver, carefully prise out the compliance bushes from the lower arms.
3 Tap the new bushes into place using a suitable socket or tube drift **(see illustration)**.
4 Some vehicles may have small rubber spacer washers fitted to the ends of the anti-roll bar, and these should be discarded on reassembly.
5 Refit the anti-roll bar.

9 Front suspension lower arm inner pivot bush - renewal

1 To improve access, raise the front of the vehicle on ramps. Apply the handbrake.
2 Unscrew and remove the nut, washer and pivot bolt securing the relevant lower arm to the crossmember.
3 Remove the anti-roll bar-to-lower arm securing nut and recover the dished washer and plastic cover (where applicable).
4 Ensure that the handbrake is applied, jack up the front of the vehicle and support on axle stands (see "Jacking and Vehicle Support").
5 Pull the inner end of the lower arm from the crossmember.
6 The pivot bush can now be removed from the lower arm using a long bolt with nut, washers and a suitable metal tube.
7 Lubricate the new bush with soapy water, and fit with a single continuous action to avoid

deformation of the bush, again using the bolt, nut, washers and tube.
8 Locate the end of the lower arm in the crossmember, and refit the pivot bolt, washer and nut. If necessary, push the outer rim of the roadwheel in order to line up the holes in the lower arm bush and the crossmember. Note that the pivot bolt head should face to the rear of the vehicle. Do not tighten the bolt at this stage.
9 Refit the plastic cover, dished washer (where applicable), and nut to the end of the anti-roll bar. Do not tighten the nut at this stage.
10 Lower the vehicle so that its weight is resting on the roadwheels, and bounce the vehicle to settle the suspension.
11 Tighten the lower arm pivot bolt, following the procedure given in Section 2.
12 Tighten the anti-roll bar-to-lower arm securing nut to the specified torque.
13 Lower the vehicle from the ramps, if not already done.

10 Rear suspension and final drive unit assembly (Saloon, Hatchback and Estate models) - removal and refitting

Note: From May 1986, revised final drive unit rear mounting bolts have been used in production. Whenever the earlier type of bolts are removed, they should be discarded and the later type fitted. The earlier bolts are coloured blue, and the later type bolts are coloured gold.

Removal

1 Jack up the vehicle and support on axle stands (see "Jacking and Vehicle Support"). It is only strictly necessary to jack up the rear of the vehicle, but this provides only limited access. Note that the axle stands should be positioned under the side members.
2 Remove the rear section of the exhaust system - ie. from the joint.
3 Remove the propeller shaft.
4 Disconnect the handbrake equaliser from the operating rod by removing the circlip and

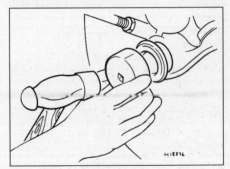

8.3 Tapping a front anti-roll bar-to-lower arm compliance bush into position

11

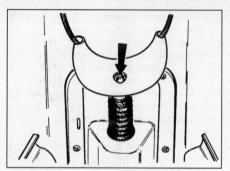

10.4 Handbrake equaliser-to-operating rod circlip and pivot pin (arrowed)

10.6 Rear underbody brake pipe bracket - U-shaped hose retaining clip arrowed

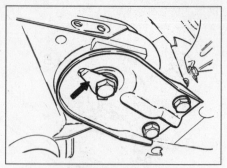

10.11 Rear suspension front guide plate - lockwasher arrowed

pivot pin. Take care not to lose the components **(see illustration)**.

5 Remove the brake cable sheaths from their brackets on the vehicle underbody.

6 Unscrew the brake pipes from the brake hoses at the brackets on the vehicle underbody. Plug the ends of the pipes and hoses to prevent leakage and dirt ingress, then detach the hoses from the brackets by removing the U-shaped retaining clips **(see illustration)**.

7 Where applicable, disconnect the ABS sensors, and detach the leads from the clips on the lower arms.

8 Place suitable blocks beneath the rear wheels, then lower the vehicle so that the rear coil springs are lightly loaded. Reposition the axle stands under the side members.

9 Support the final drive unit with a jack, using an interposed block of wood to spread the load.

10 Where applicable, unscrew and remove the two anti-roll bar mountings from the underbody.

11 Unscrew and remove the three bolts securing each of the front guide plates to the underbody and the suspension crossmember **(see illustration)**. Where applicable, bend back the lockwasher tabs on the larger bolts.

12 Unscrew and remove the four bolts securing the final drive unit rear mounting to the underbody. Note the location and number of any shims which may be fitted **(see illustration)**.

13 Working inside the rear of the vehicle, disconnect the shock absorber upper mountings. On Saloon and Hatchback

models, access is gained by removing the trim covers behind the side cushions. Each cover is secured by two self-tapping screws, and the shock absorber is secured by a bolt and nut. On Estate models, fold down the rear seat backrest, fold back the floor covering and remove the front section of the luggage compartment floor, which is secured with 12 self-tapping screws. Remove the nut and washer from the shock absorber.

14 Using a jack and a wooden beam positioned beneath the longitudinal underbody side members, raise the rear of the vehicle until the rear suspension and final drive unit assembly can be withdrawn from under the vehicle.

15 If desired, the assembly can be dismantled with reference to the relevant Sections of this Chapter and Chapter 9.

Refitting

16 Refitting is a reversal of removal, bearing in mind the following points.

17 Where applicable, secure the larger front guide plate bolts by bending up the lockwasher tabs.

18 Ensure that the coil springs are located correctly on their seats on the vehicle underbody.

19 When refitting the final drive rear mounting to the underbody, refit any shims in their original noted positions, and fit the bolts with reference to the note at the beginning of this Section.

20 Tighten all fixings to the specified torque.

21 On completion, bleed the brakes and adjust the handbrake. With the vehicle level, check the final drive unit oil level.

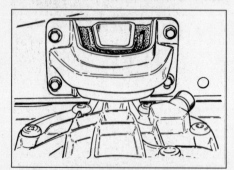

10.12 Final drive unit-to-underbody rear mounting

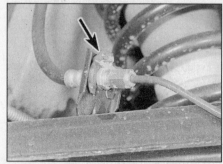

11.4 Brake pipe bracket on lower arm. U-shaped retaining clip arrowed

11 Rear suspension lower arm (Saloon, Hatchback and Estate models) - removal and refitting

Models with rear drum brakes

Removal

1 Chock the front wheels, jack up the rear of the vehicle and support on axle stands placed under the side members.

2 Remove the relevant driveshaft.

3 Remove the handbrake cable from the clip on the lower arm.

4 Unscrew the brake pipe from the brake hose at the bracket on the lower arm. Plug the ends of the pipe and hose to prevent leakage and dirt ingress, then detach the hose from the bracket by removing the U-shaped retaining clip **(see illustration)**.

5 Unscrew the brake pipe from the wheel cylinder on the brake backplate and plug the end of the pipe and the cylinder to prevent leakage and dirt ingress.

6 Unscrew the bolts securing the brake backplate to the lower arm and tie the backplate to one side.

7 Where applicable, prise the anti-roll bar connecting strap from the lower arm.

8 Support the lower arm on a jack, and raise it slightly to place the coil spring under load.

9 Remove the shock absorber.

10 Unscrew and remove the three bolts securing the front guide plate to the underbody and the suspension crossmember **(see illustration)**. Where applicable, bend back the lockwasher tab(s) on the larger bolt.

11 Lower the lower arm, and remove the coil spring and rubber cup.

12 Note the orientation of the two lower arm-to-crossmember pivot bolts and nuts, then unscrew and remove them and withdraw the lower arm from under the vehicle **(see illustration)**.

13 If the lower arm is to be renewed, unclip the brake pipe, and refit to the new arm.

14 If required, the pivot bushes may be renewed using a long bolt, nut, washers and a suitable metal tube. Lubricate the new bushes with soapy water before fitting.

11.10 Rear suspension front guide plate

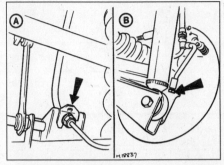

11.12 Lower arm-to-crossmember inner pivot

11.23 Rear suspension lower arm brake pipe brackets (arrowed)

A Left-hand bracket   B Right-hand bracket

Refitting

15 Refitting is a reversal of removal, bearing in mind the following points.

16 Where applicable, secure the larger front guide plate bolt by bending up the lockwasher tab(s).

17 Before tightening the lower arm-to-crossmember pivot bolts and nuts, lower the vehicle so that its weight is resting on the roadwheels, and bounce the vehicle to settle the suspension. Ensure that the bolts are orientated as noted during removal.

18 On completion, bleed the brakes and adjust the handbrake.

Models with rear disc brakes

Note: *A suitable puller will be required to remove the drive flange, and a new rear hub nut must be used on reassembly.*

Removal

19 With the vehicle resting on its wheels, loosen the rear hub nut. A suitable extension bar will be required, as the nut is extremely tight. Note that the left-hand nut has a left-hand thread, ie it is undone in a clockwise direction. Before loosening the nut, ensure that the handbrake is applied, and chock the relevant rear wheel.

20 Loosen the rear roadwheel nuts on the side concerned, chock the front wheels, jack up the rear of the car and support on axle stands placed under the side members.

21 Remove the rear roadwheel.

22 Remove the rear section of the exhaust system - ie from the joint.

23 Unscrew the brake pipe from the brake hose at the bracket on the lower arm **(see illustration)**. Plug the ends of the pipe and hose to prevent leakage and dirt ingress, then detach the hose from the bracket by removing the U-shaped retaining clip.

24 Remove the handbrake cable from the clip on the lower arm.

25 Unbolt the brake caliper and tie it to one side, taking care not to strain the brake hose.

26 Mark the position of the brake disc in relation to the hub, remove the retaining spire washer(s), and remove the disc.

27 Disconnect the driveshaft from the hub assembly by unscrewing the six securing bolts. Support the driveshaft to avoid straining the joints, or alternatively, unbolt it from the final drive unit at the inboard end and remove the driveshaft from the vehicle. At all times, avoid bending the driveshaft joints to excessive angles, and do not allow the shaft to hang down from one end.

28 Unscrew and remove the rear hub nut, and using a puller pull off the drive flange.

29 Unscrew the four bolts securing the hub carrier and splash shield to the lower arm. Remove the hub carrier and splash shield. Note that the stub axle is retained in the hub carrier.

30 Disconnect the ABS sensor, and detach the lead from the clip on the lower arm.

31 Remove the propeller shaft.

32 Proceed as shown in paragraphs 7 to 14 inclusive.

Refitting

33 Refitting is a reversal of removal, bearing in mind the following points.

34 Where applicable, secure the larger front guide plate bolt by bending up the lockwasher tabs.

35 When refitting the hub carrier to the lower arm note that there are two types of bolts used . The two types of bolt must not be mixed on a vehicle, but can be changed in complete sets for the alternative type. A complete set is eight bolts, four each side. Note that the two types of bolt have different torque wrench settings. When renewing the wheel bearings a suitable puller will be required to remove the drive flange, and a new rear hub nut must be used on reassembly.

36 When refitting the drive flange to the hub assembly, use a new hub nut, and leave tightening until the vehicle is resting on its wheels. Apply the handbrake and chock the relevant rear wheel when tightening the nut.

37 When refitting the brake disc, align the previously made marks on disc and hub.

38 Before tightening the lower arm-to-crossmember pivot bolts and nuts, lower the vehicle so that its weight is resting on the roadwheels, and bounce the vehicle to settle the suspension. Ensure that the bolts are orientated as noted during removal.

39 On completion, bleed the brakes and adjust the handbrake.

12 Rear shock absorber - removal and refitting

Saloon and Hatchback models

1 With the weight of the vehicle resting on the roadwheels, work under the vehicle to unscrew and remove the shock absorber lower mounting bolt and nut from the relevant lower arm **(see illustration)**. If desired, the rear of the vehicle can be raised on ramps to improve access.

2 Working inside the rear of the vehicle, remove the trim cover behind the side cushion. The cover is secured by two self-tapping screws **(see illustrations)**.

12.1 Rear shock absorber lower mounting - Saloon and Hatchback models

12.2a Remove the trim cover . . .

12.2b . . . for access to the rear shock absorber upper mounting

3 With an assistant supporting the shock absorber from below, unscrew and remove the upper mounting bolt and nut. Withdraw the shock absorber from under the vehicle.

4 Refitting is a reversal of removal. Tighten the mounting bolts securely.

Estate models

Note: *On models fitted with heavy duty Nivomat shock absorbers, follow the procedure given in Section 13, as the shock absorber and coil spring are an integrated unit.*

5 With the weight of the vehicle resting on the roadwheels, work under the vehicle to unscrew and remove the two shock absorber lower mounting bolts from the relevant lower arm **(see illustration)**. If desired, the rear of the vehicle can be raised on ramps to improve access.

6 Working inside the rear of the vehicle, fold down the rear seat backrest, fold back the floor covering and remove the front section of the luggage compartment floor, which is secured with 12 self-tapping screws.

7 With an assistant supporting the shock absorber from below, unscrew and remove the upper mounting nut and washer **(see illustration)**. Withdraw the shock absorber from under the vehicle.

8 Refitting is a reversal of removal. Tighten the mounting bolts and nut securely.

P100 models

9 With the weight of the vehicle resting on the roadwheels, work under the vehicle to unscrew and remove the shock absorber lower mounting nut, washer, and rubber insulator. If desired, the rear of the vehicle can be raised on ramps to improve access.

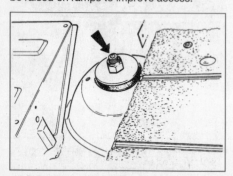

12.7 Rear shock absorber upper mounting (arrowed) - Estate models

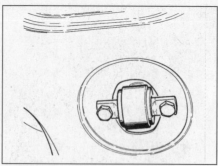

12.5 Rear shock absorber lower mounting bolts - Estate models

10 Unscrew and remove the top mounting bolt, nut and washer from the chassis crossmember. Withdraw the shock absorber upwards.

11 Refitting is a reversal of removal. Tighten the mounting bolt and nut securely.

13 Rear coil spring (Saloon, Hatchback and Estate models) - removal and refitting

Models with rear drum brakes

1 Remove the relevant driveshaft.

2 Unscrew the brake pipe from the brake hose at the bracket on the vehicle underbody. Plug the ends of the pipe and hose to prevent leakage and dirt ingress.

3 Where applicable, prise the anti-roll bar connecting strap from the lower arm.

4 Support the lower arm on a jack, and raise it slightly to place the coil spring under load.

5 On Saloon and Hatchback models, unscrew and remove the shock absorber lower mounting bolt and nut from the lower arm.

6 On Estate models fitted with standard shock absorbers, remove the shock absorber as described in Section 12. On Estate models fitted with heavy duty Nivomat shock absorbers, disconnect the upper and lower mountings.

7 Unscrew and remove the three bolts securing the front guide plate to the underbody and the suspension crossmember. Where applicable, bend back the lockwasher tab(s) on the larger bolt.

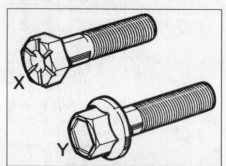

14.1a Alternative types of rear hub carrier-to-lower arm securing bolts

8 Lower the lower arm, and remove the coil spring, or coil spring/heavy duty shock absorber as applicable, and the rubber cup.

9 Refitting is a reversal of removal, bearing in mind the following points.

10 Where applicable, secure the larger front guide plate bolt by bending up the lockwasher tab(s).

11 Refit the driveshaft.

12 On completion, bleed the brakes.

Models with rear disc brakes

13 Chock the front wheels, jack up the rear of the vehicle and support on axle stands placed under the side members.

14 Disconnect the driveshaft from the hub assembly by unscrewing the six securing bolts. Support the driveshaft to avoid straining the joints, or alternatively, unbolt it from the final drive unit at the inboard end and remove the driveshaft from the vehicle. At all times, avoid bending the driveshaft joints to excessive angles, and do not allow the shaft to hang down from one end.

15 Proceed as shown in paragraphs 2 to 8 inclusive.

16 Refitting is a reversal of removal. Where applicable, secure the larger front guide plate bolt by bending up the lockwasher tab(s), and on completion, bleed the brakes.

14 Rear wheel bearings - renewal

Saloon, Hatchback and Estate models

With rear drum brakes

Note: *There are two types of bolts used to secure the rear hub carrier to the lower arm (see illustration). The two types of bolt must not be mixed on a vehicle, but can be changed in complete sets for the alternative type. A complete set is eight bolts, four each side. Note that the two types of bolt have different torque wrench settings. When renewing the wheel bearings a suitable puller will be required to remove the drive flange, and a new rear hub nut must be used on reassembly.*

1 Loosen the rear hub nut with the vehicle resting on its wheels. On early models, relieve the staking before loosening the nut **(see illustration)**. Later models use self-locking

14.1b On early models relieve the staking (arrowed) on the rear hub nut

nuts, and it is important to note that where this type of nut is fitted, the left-hand nut has a left-hand thread, ie. it is undone in a clockwise direction. Before loosening the nut, ensure that the handbrake is applied, and chock the relevant rear wheel. A suitable extension bar will be required, as the nut is extremely tight.

2 Loosen the rear roadwheel nuts on the side concerned, chock the front wheels, and jack up the rear of the vehicle and support on axle stands (see *"Jacking and Vehicle Support"*). Remove the rear roadwheel.

3 Remove the brake drum retaining spire washer(s) from the wheel stud(s) and remove the brake drum. Ensure that the handbrake is released before removing the brake drum, otherwise the drum will be held in place by the clamping action of the brake shoes.

4 Remove the two nylon fasteners, and remove the plastic shield from the rear of the brake backplate **(see illustration)**.

5 Unscrew and remove the rear hub nut.

6 Using a suitable puller, pull the drive flange from the end of the driveshaft **(see illustration)**.

7 Unscrew and remove the four bolts securing the hub carrier and brake backplate to the lower arm **(see illustration)**. Remove the hub carrier, whilst supporting the driveshaft. Support the driveshaft by placing axle stands underneath it, or by securing with string to the underbody. Note that the driveshaft joints should not be allowed to deflect through an angle exceeding 13°.

8 Refit the brake backplate with the four securing bolts to avoid straining the brake pipe.

9 With the hub carrier removed, the bearings can be renewed as follows **(see illustration)**.

10 Prise the inner and outer oil seals from the hub carrier using a suitable screwdriver, and withdraw the taper roller bearings.

11 Using a soft metal drift, drive the bearing outer races from the hub carrier, taking care not to damage the inner surface of the carrier.

14.4 Remove the nylon fasteners (arrowed) to free the plastic shield from the brake backplate

12 Clean the hub carrier and drive flange with paraffin, wipe dry and examine for damage and wear. Note that the components are machined to very close tolerances, and the bearings are supplied in matched pairs, therefore scrupulous cleanliness must be observed.

13 Using a metal tube of suitable diameter, drive the new bearing outer races fully into the hub carrier. Ensure that the races are seated correctly.

14 Pack the inner bearing races and rollers with high-melting-point lithium-based grease, and locate the outer bearing assembly in the hub carrier.

15 Fill the cavities between the sealing lips of the oil seal with grease, then drive it fully into the hub carrier using a block of wood or a metal tube of suitable diameter. Note than on early models the oil seal has a rubber casing, and this type of seal should be replaced with the later type which has a metal casing. The oil seal should be renewed regardless of type, and a new oil seal of the correct type is normally supplied with the new wheel bearings.

16 Repeat the procedure shown in paragraphs 14 and 15 for the outer bearing and oil seal.

14.6 Pull the drive flange from the end of the driveshaft

17 Fit the drive flange to the hub carrier in order to centralise the bearings, then remove the securing bolts from the brake backplate, and using a soft-faced mallet, drive the drive flange/hub carrier assembly onto the end of the driveshaft.

18 Further refitting is a reversal of removal, bearing in mind the following points.

19 Refit the hub carrier/brake backplate-to-lower arm securing bolts with reference to the note at the beginning of this sub-Section.

20 Fit a new rear hub nut of the correct type, and tighten it with the vehicle resting on its roadwheels. Apply the handbrake and chock the relevant rear wheel. If a staked type nut is used, lock the nut by staking its outer ring into the groove in the driveshaft.

With rear disc brakes

Note: See note at the beginning of this Section

21 Loosen the rear hub nut with the vehicle resting on its wheels. Note that the left-hand nut has a left-hand thread, ie. it is undone in a clockwise direction. Before loosening the nut, ensure that the handbrake is applied, and chock the relevant rear wheel. A suitable extension bar will be required, as the nut is extremely tight.

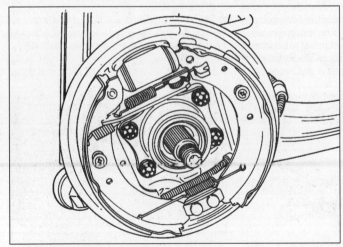

14.7 Rear hub carrier/brake backplate-to-lower arm securing bolts

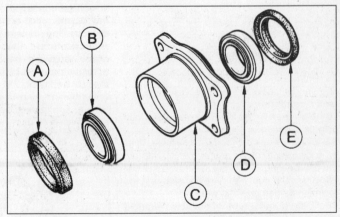

14.9 Rear hub carrier components - Saloon, Hatchback and Estate models

A Outer oil seal   C Hub carrier   E Inner oil seal
B Outer bearing   D Inner bearing

11

22 Loosen the rear roadwheel nuts on the side concerned, chock the front wheels, and jack up the rear of the vehicle and support on axle stands. Remove the roadwheel and release the handbrake.

23 Unbolt the brake caliper carrier bracket and support the caliper on an axle stand, taking care not to strain the flexible hose.

24 Mark the position of the brake disc in relation to the drive flange, remove the retaining spire washer(s), and remove the disc.

25 Unscrew and remove the rear hub nut, and using a puller, pull off the drive flange.

26 Unscrew the four bolts securing the hub carrier and splash shield to the lower arm. Remove the hub carrier and splash shield, whilst supporting the driveshaft. Support the driveshaft by placing axle stands underneath it, or by securing with string to the underbody. Avoid bending the driveshaft joints to excessive angles, and do not allow the shaft to hang down from one end.

27 With the hub carrier removed, the bearings can be renewed as described in paragraphs 10 to 16 of this Section.

28 Fit the drive flange to the hub carrier in order to centralise the bearings, then using a soft-faced mallet, drive the drive flange/hub carrier assembly onto the end of the stub axle. Do not forget to fit the splash shield.

29 Further refitting is a reversal of removal, bearing in mind the following points.

30 Refit the hub carrier/splash shield-to-lower arm securing bolts with reference to the note at the beginning of this sub-Section.

31 When refitting the brake disc, align the previously made marks on disc and drive flange.

32 Fit a new rear hub nut of the correct type, and tighten it with the vehicle resting on its roadwheels. Apply the handbrake and chock the relevant rear wheel.

P100 models

Note: *A new rear hub nut must be used on reassembly.*

33 Remove the relevant driveshaft.

34 Relieve the staking on the rear hub nut, and using a 50 mm socket and an extension bar, unscrew the nut. Note that the nut is extremely tight.

35 Pull off the hub, and remove the O-ring and spacer sleeve from the recess in the hub **(see illustration)**.

36 Prise the oil seal from the rear of the hub using a screwdriver.

37 Using a block of wood, or a suitable metal tube inserted from the rear of the hub, tap out the ball-bearing.

38 Clean the hub with paraffin, wipe dry and examine for damage and wear.

39 Using a metal tube of suitable diameter, resting on the bearing outer race only, tap the new bearing into the hub. Ensure that the bearing is correctly seated.

40 Carefully fit a new oil seal to the rear of the hub, using a suitable metal tube.

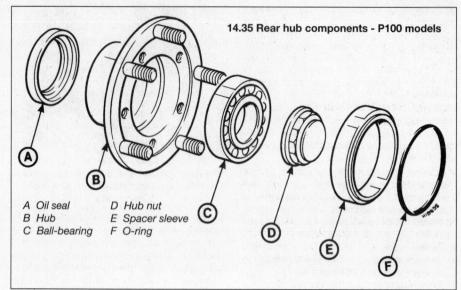

14.35 Rear hub components - P100 models

A Oil seal
B Hub
C Ball-bearing
D Hub nut
E Spacer sleeve
F O-ring

41 Refitting is a reversal of removal, bearing in mind the following points.

42 Fit a new rear hub nut, and stake in position after tightening to the specified torque.

15 Rear suspension front mounting (Saloon, Hatchback and Estate models) - renewal

1 Chock the front wheels, jack up the rear of the vehicle and support on axle stands placed under the side members.

2 Unscrew and remove the three bolts securing the relevant front guide plate to the underbody and the suspension crossmember. Where applicable, bend back the lockwasher tab(s) on the larger bolt.

3 Using a length of wood, lever the suspension crossmember downwards a few inches from the underbody, and insert the wood as a wedge.

4 Using a tool similar to the Ford special tool shown **(see illustration)**, or a long bolt with nut, washers and a suitable metal tube, pull the mounting rubber from the crossmember.

5 Lubricate the new mounting rubber with soapy water, and use the tool described in the previous paragraph to press the rubber into the crossmember.

6 Further refitting is a reversal of removal. Where applicable, secure the larger front guide plate bolt by bending up the lockwasher tab(s).

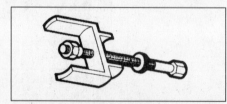

15.4 Ford special tool 15-014 for removing rear suspension front mounting rubber

16 Rear suspension/final drive unit rear mounting (Saloon, Hatchback and Estate models) - renewal

Note: *From May 1986, revised rear suspension/final drive unit rear mounting bolts have been used in production. Whenever the earlier type of bolts are removed, they should be discarded and the later type fitted. The earlier bolts are coloured blue, and the later type bolts are coloured gold.*

1 Chock the front wheels, jack up the rear of the vehicle and support on axle stands placed under the side members.

2 Support the final drive unit with a jack, using an interposed block of wood to spread the load.

3 Unscrew and remove the four bolts securing the mounting to the underbody. Note the location and number of any shims which may be fitted.

4 Lower the final drive unit sufficiently to enable the mounting to be unbolted from the final drive unit rear cover **(see illustration)**.

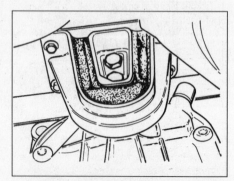

16.4 Rear suspension/final drive unit rear mounting-to-final drive unit rear cover bolts

5 Refitting is a reversal of removal, with reference to the note at the beginning of this Section. Refit any shims in their original noted positions, and tighten all bolts to the specified torque.

17 Rear anti-roll bar (Saloon, Hatchback and Estate models) - removal and refitting

Removal

1 Loosen the rear roadwheel nuts, chock the front wheels, jack up the rear of the vehicle and support on axle stands placed under the side members.
2 Prise off the straps which connect the anti-roll bar to the suspension lower arms (see illustration).
3 Unbolt the two securing brackets from the underbody, and remove the anti-roll bar (see illustration).
4 The connecting straps can be prised from the ends of the anti-roll bar, and the underbody mounting brackets and rubbers, which are of a split design, can be pulled off.
5 When fitting new mounting components, lubricate the rubber parts with soapy water to ease assembly.

Refitting

6 Refitting is a reversal of removal. Tighten the anti-roll bar-to-underbody securing bolts to the specified torque.

18 Rear suspension and axle assembly (P100 models) - removal and refitting

Note: All self-locking nuts and spring washers must be renewed on reassembly.

Removal

1 Chock the front wheels, jack up the rear of the vehicle and support on axle stands placed under the side members. Note that a loaded vehicle must not be jacked under the differential casing.

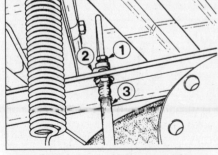

18.6 Brake pipe-to-hose connection on right-hand side of chassis crossmember - P100 models

1 Brake pipe   3 Brake hose
2 U-shaped clip

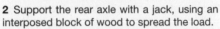

17.2 Anti-roll bar-to-lower arm connecting strap

2 Support the rear axle with a jack, using an interposed block of wood to spread the load.
3 Remove the propeller shaft.
4 Remove the securing circlip and the pivot pin, and detach the handbrake equaliser from the linkage on the underbody.
5 Remove the handbrake cables from the clips on the underbody, and from the brackets on the crossmember. To remove the cables from the crossmember, remove the U-shaped retaining clips. Note that the cable adjuster is secured to the right-hand crossmember bracket. Ensure that the handbrake is released before attempting to disconnect any part of the mechanism.
6 Unscrew the brake pipe from the brake hose on the right-hand side of the chassis crossmember. Plug the ends of the pipe and hose to prevent leakage and dirt ingress, then detach the hose from the crossmember by removing the U-shaped retaining clip (see illustration).
7 Remove the spring clip and clevis pin and disconnect the spring from the brake load apportioning valve lever on the right-hand side of the underbody (see illustration).
8 Detach the exhaust system from the two rear mountings.
9 Unbolt the shock absorbers from the chassis crossmember.
10 Unbolt the leaf springs from the front brackets on the underbody, (Section 19).
11 Lower the rear axle.
12 Loosen the spring shackle-to-underbody bolts, then unbolt the leaf springs from the spring shackles, and remove the rear suspension and axle assembly from under the

18.7 Remove the split pin (arrowed) from the brake load apportioning valve lever

17.3 Anti-roll bar-to-underbody securing bracket

vehicle, guiding the handbrake cables over the exhaust system.

Refitting

13 Refitting is a reversal of removal, bearing in mind the following points.
14 Do not fully tighten the leaf spring mounting bolts or the spring shackle-to-underbody bolts until the weight of the vehicle is resting on the roadwheels.
15 Renew all self-locking nuts and spring washers.
16 On completion, check the brake load apportioning valve adjustment and the handbrake adjustment. Bleed the rear brake circuit and check the axle oil level.

19 Rear suspension leaf spring (P100 models) - removal and refitting

Note: All self-locking nuts and spring washers must be renewed on reassembly.

Removal

1 Chock the front wheels, jack up the rear of the vehicle and support on axle stands placed under the side members. Note that a loaded vehicle must not be jacked under the differential casing.
2 Support the relevant side of the rear axle with a jack, using an interposed block of wood under the axle tube to spread the load.
3 Unscrew the nuts, and remove the two U-bolts on each side of the vehicle which secure the axle to the leaf springs (see illustration). Note that there is no need to

19.3 Unscrew the nuts (arrowed) from the rear axle-to-leaf spring U-bolts

11

19.4 Leaf spring front bracket

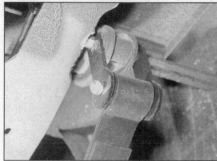

19.5 Leaf spring shackle

disconnect the shock absorber from the U-bolt counterplate.

4 Unbolt the leaf spring from the front bracket on the underbody (see illustration).

5 Loosen the spring shackle-to-underbody bolt, then unbolt the leaf spring from the spring shackle and remove the spring (see illustration).

Refitting

6 Refitting is a reversal of removal, bearing in mind the following points.

7 Do not fully tighten the leaf spring mounting bolts or the spring shackle-to-underbody bolt until the weight of the vehicle is resting on its roadwheels.

8 Renew all self-locking nuts and spring washers.

9 Align the axle on the leaf spring so that the locating pin on the spring engages with the corresponding hole in the axle. Similarly ensure that the U-bolt counterplate engages with the locating pin on the leaf spring.

20 Rear suspension leaf spring shackle (P100 models) - removal and refitting

Note: All self-locking nuts and spring washers must be renewed on reassembly.

Removal

1 Chock the front wheels, jack up the rear of the vehicle and support on axle stands placed under the side members. Note that a loaded vehicle must not be jacked under the differential casing.

2 Support the relevant side of the rear axle with a jack, using an interposed block of wood under the axle tube to spread the load.

3 Unscrew and remove the spring shackle-to-underbody bolt and the leaf spring-to-spring shackle bolt, and remove the shackle components.

4 Examine the components for wear and damage and renew as necessary.

Refitting

5 Refitting is a reversal of removal, but renew all self-locking nuts and spring washers, and do not fully tighten the bolts until the weight of the vehicle is resting on its roadwheels.

21 Rear suspension leaf spring bush (P100 models) - renewal

Note: All self-locking nuts and spring washers must be renewed on reassembly.

1 Proceed as described in Section 19, paragraphs 1 to 3 inclusive.

2 Unbolt the relevant end of the leaf spring, and lower it to gain access to the bush. Note that if the shackle end of the spring is unbolted, the shackle-to-underbody bolt should be loosened in order to aid refitting.

3 The bush can be removed using a long bolt with nut, washers and a suitable metal tube.

4 Lubricate the new bush with soapy water and fit using the bolt, nut, washers and tube.

5 Proceed as described in Section 19, paragraphs 6 to 9 inclusive.

22 Steering wheel - removal and refitting

Removal

1 Set the front wheels in the straight-ahead position.

2 Prise the trim insert from the centre of the steering wheel, and where applicable, disconnect the horn electrical lead(s) (see illustration).

3 Insert the ignition key and check that the steering lock is disengaged.

4 Unscrew the retaining nut and withdraw the steering wheel from the hexagon shaped inner column (see illustration). If the wheel is tight on the inner column, sit in the driver's seat and tap the wheel from behind with the palms of the hands (but screw the nut back on two or three turns for safety).

Refitting

5 Refitting is a reversal of removal, but check that the lug on the direction indicator cam is aligned with the cut-out in the steering wheel, and make sure that the direction indicator switch is in the neutral position. Tighten the retaining nut to the specified torque.

23 Steering wheel - centralising

1 This operation is for correcting small errors in steering wheel centralisation - up to 60°. For larger errors, remove the steering wheel and make a rough correction by repositioning the wheel on refitting.

2 Drive the vehicle in a straight line on a level surface. Note the angle by which the steering wheel deviates from the desired straight-ahead position.

3 Raise the front of the vehicle by driving it onto ramps, or with a jack and axle stands.

4 Slacken both tie-rod end locknuts. Also slacken the steering rack bellows outer clips.

5 Make alignment marks between each tie-rod end and its rod, so that the amount of rotation applied can be accurately determined (see illustration).

22.2 Prise off the steering wheel trim insert and disconnect the horn electrical lead

22.4 Removing the steering wheel retaining nut

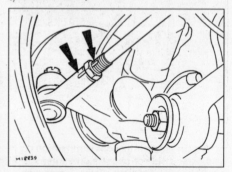

23.5 Make alignment marks (arrowed) between each tie-rod end and its rod when centralising the steering wheel

24.4a Remove the steering column upper shroud . . .

24.4b . . . and lower shroud

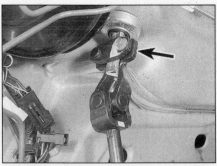

24.7 Intermediate shaft-to-inner column universal joint and clamp plate (arrowed)

6 Turn both tie-rods in the same direction to correct the steering wheel position. As a rough guide, 19° of tie-rod rotation will change the steering wheel position by 1°. To correct a clockwise error at the steering wheel, rotate both tie-rods anti-clockwise (when viewed from the left-hand side of the vehicle), and the reverse to correct an anti-clockwise error. Both tie-rods must be rotated by the same amount.

7 Tighten the bellows clips and the tie-rod end locknuts when adjustment is correct. Lower the vehicle.

24 Steering column - removal and refitting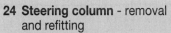

Removal

1 Set the front wheels in the straight-ahead position.

2 Disconnect the battery negative lead.

3 Remove the driver's side lower facia trim panels.

4 Remove the screws and withdraw the steering column upper and lower shrouds **(see illustrations)**.

5 Unscrew the two crosshead screws and withdraw the two combination switches from the column.

6 Remove the screw from the bonnet release lever and remove the lever.

7 Working in the engine compartment, unscrew the bolt securing the intermediate shaft to the inner column, swivel the clamp plate to one side, and disconnect the intermediate shaft **(see illustration)**.

8 Unscrew the nuts securing the outer column to the facia.

9 Disconnect the multi-plugs and withdraw the column assembly upwards **(see illustration)**.

Refitting

10 Refit the column assembly in the car and tighten the upper mounting nuts lightly. Loosen the mounting pinch-bolt.

11 Temporarily fit the upper column shroud and adjust the position of the steering column until there is a gap of 5.0 mm (0.2 in) between the shroud and the facia **(see illustration)**.

12 Tighten the pinch-bolt and the mounting nuts and remove the upper column shroud.

13 With the steering wheel in the straight-ahead position, reconnect the intermediate shaft and tighten the clamp plate bolt to the specified torque.

14 Refit the bonnet release lever and combination switches and reconnect the multi-plugs.

15 Refit the steering column shrouds and trim panels.

16 Reconnect the battery negative lead.

25 Steering column adjuster - dismantling and reassembly

Note: *A new adjuster locknut and washer must be used on reassembly.*

Dismantling

1 To dismantle the adjuster assembly, proceed as follows.

2 Remove the locknut and washer securing the adjuster through-bolt **(see illustration)**.

3 Remove the through-bolt, adjuster handle, locking plates, sliders and washers, then unclip the spring assembly.

Reassembly

4 Reassemble the components as follows.

5 Refit the spring to the adjuster assembly bracket.

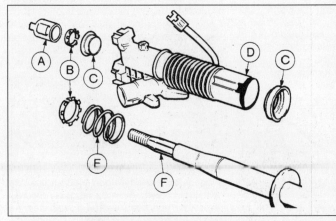

24.9 Steering column components

A *Direction indicator cam*
B *Thrustwashers*
C *Bearings*
D *Outer column*
E *Spring*
F *Inner column*

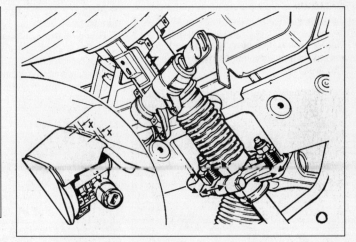

24.11 Upper column shroud-to-facia gap adjustment

X = 5.0 mm (0.2 in)

11

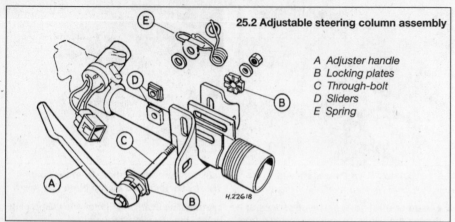

25.2 Adjustable steering column assembly

A Adjuster handle
B Locking plates
C Through-bolt
D Sliders
E Spring

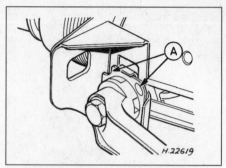

25.6 Cut-out and Ford logo (A) must be positioned as shown when reassembling adjustable steering column

6 Align the washers, sliders and locking plates, ensuring that the handle locking plate is fitted so that the cut-out and Ford logo are positioned as shown **(see illustration)**.

7 Coat the through-bolt threads with a suitable thread-locking compound, then refit the through-bolt and the adjuster handle, ensuring that all components are engaged.

8 Position the handle in the locked position, and secure the through-bolt with a new locknut and washer.

26 Steering intermediate shaft and flexible coupling - removal and refitting

Removal

1 Apply the handbrake, jack up the front of the vehicle and support on axle stands.

2 Working in the engine compartment, unscrew the bolt securing the intermediate shaft to the inner column, swivel the clamp plate to one side, and disconnect the intermediate shaft.

3 Unscrew and remove the clamp bolt securing the flexible coupling to the steering gear **(see illustration)**.

4 Mark the coupling in relation to the pinion, then pull off the intermediate shaft and remove it from the vehicle. The pinion has a master spline, but making alignment marks will aid refitting **(see illustration)**.

26.3 Intermediate shaft-to-steering gear flexible coupling

Refitting

5 Refitting is a reversal of removal, but align the marks on the coupling and pinion, and tighten all bolts to the specified torque.

27 Manual steering gear - removal and refitting

Note: A balljoint separator tool will be required for this operation.

Removal

1 Set the front wheels in the straight-ahead position. Ensure that the steering lock is engaged and remove the ignition key.

2 Apply the handbrake. Loosen the front roadwheel nuts, jack up the front of the vehicle and support on axle stands.

3 Remove the roadwheels. On P100 models, mark the position of the roadwheels in relation to the wheel studs.

4 Unscrew and remove the clamp bolts securing the intermediate shaft flexible coupling to the steering gear.

5 If the original steering gear is to be refitted, mark the coupling in relation to the pinion. The pinion has a master spline, but making alignment marks will aid refitting.

6 Slacken the tie-rod end locknuts **(see illustration)**.

7 Remove the split pins and unscrew the castellated nuts from the tie-rod end-to-hub carrier balljoints.

8 Using a balljoint separator tool, disconnect the tie-rod ends from the hub carriers.

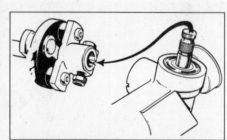

26.4 Master spline location on the steering gear pinion and intermediate shaft coupling

9 Unscrew the two steering gear-to-front suspension crossmember securing bolts, and withdraw the steering gear from under the vehicle.

10 If required, remove the tie-rod ends.

Refitting

11 Refitting is a reversal of removal, bearing in mind the following points.

12 If new steering gear is being fitted, the central pinion position can be ascertained by halving the number of turns required to move the rack from lock to lock.

13 Where applicable, align the marks made on the coupling and pinion.

14 When tightening the steering gear-to-front suspension crossmember bolts, the following procedure should be used. Tighten the bolts to the specified "clamping" torque, then loosen the bolts fully. Re-tighten to the specified "snug" torque and then further tighten the bolts through the specified angle.

15 Tighten all fixings to the specified torque, and use new split pins on the balljoint castellated nuts.

16 On P100 models, align the previously made marks on the roadwheels and wheel studs.

17 On completion, check the front wheel alignment.

28 Power steering gear - removal and refitting

Note: New power steering fluid hose O-rings will be required when refitting.

Removal

1 The procedure is as described for manual steering gear with the following differences **(see illustration)**.

2 Before removing the steering gear from the suspension crossmember, place a suitable container beneath the steering gear. Unscrew the single bolt securing the power steering fluid hoses to the pinion housing. Unscrew the hose unions and drain the power steering fluid. Plug the ends of the hoses and the steering gear apertures, or cover them with masking tape to prevent dirt ingress.

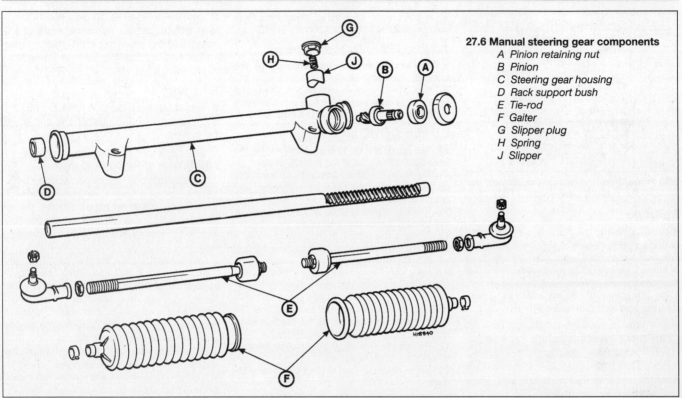

27.6 Manual steering gear components
A Pinion retaining nut
B Pinion
C Steering gear housing
D Rack support bush
E Tie-rod
F Gaiter
G Slipper plug
H Spring
J Slipper

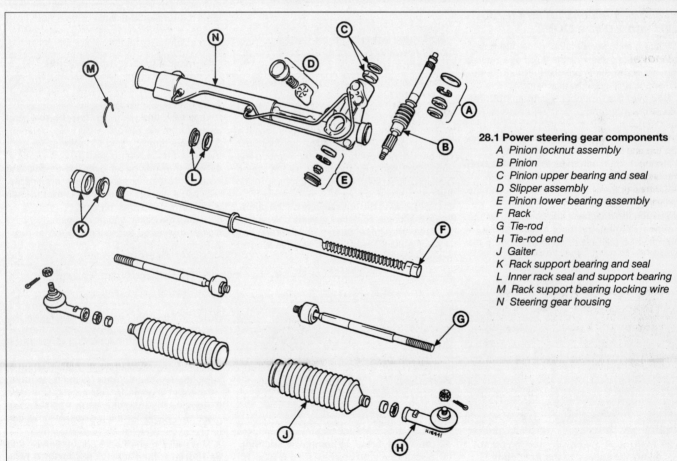

28.1 Power steering gear components
A Pinion locknut assembly
B Pinion
C Pinion upper bearing and seal
D Slipper assembly
E Pinion lower bearing assembly
F Rack
G Tie-rod
H Tie-rod end
J Gaiter
K Rack support bearing and seal
L Inner rack seal and support bearing
M Rack support bearing locking wire
N Steering gear housing

11

29.3 Power steering pump rear support bar bolts (arrowed)

Refitting

3 When refitting the fluid hoses, use new O-rings, and take care not to overtighten the unions. Note that with the unions fully tightened it is still possible to rotate and move the hoses.

4 On completion of refitting, bleed the power steering fluid circuit (Section 34).

29 Power steering pump - removal and refitting

Note: *New power steering fluid hose O-rings will be required when refitting.*

All engines except 1.8 litre (R6A) CVH and 2.0 litre DOHC

1 Place a suitable container under the power steering pump, unscrew the fluid hose unions, and drain the fluid. Ensure that fluid is not allowed to spill onto the alternator.

2 Remove the drivebelts and unbolt the power steering pump pulley if necessary to ease removal.

3 Unbolt the rear support bar from the pump and the engine block **(see illustration)**.

4 Unbolt the pump from its mounting bracket, and withdraw the pump from the engine.

5 Refitting is a reversal of removal, noting the following points.

6 Tension the drivebelts correctly.

7 When refitting the fluid hoses, use new O-rings, and take care not to overtighten the unions.

8 On completion of refitting, bleed the power steering fluid circuit.

1.8 litre (R6A) CVH engine

9 The removal and refitting procedures are basically the same as described below for the 2.0 litre DOHC engine, except that the pump is mounted on a bracket above the alternator on the front left-hand side of the engine.

2.0 litre DOHC engine

10 The pump is mounted on a bracket on the front right-hand side of the cylinder block.

11 Place a suitable container under the pump, unscrew the fluid pipe unions, and drain the fluid.

12 Remove the drivebelt which also drives the coolant pump and alternator.

13 Prevent the pulley from rotating using a strap wrench (which can be improvised using an old drivebelt and a large socket and wrench), and unscrew the three pulley securing bolts. Withdraw the pulley.

14 Unscrew the three pump securing bolts from the front of the pump bracket, and the single bolt from the rear of the bracket, and withdraw the pump **(see illustrations)**.

15 Refitting is a reversal of removal, bearing in mind the following points.

16 Reconnect the fluid unions using new O-rings.

17 On completion, bleed the power steering fluid circuit.

30 Power steering fluid hoses - removal and refitting

Note: *New fluid hose O-rings will be required when refitting.*

Removal

1 Clean around the hose unions on the steering gear. Place a suitable container beneath the steering gear, then remove the single bolt securing the hoses to the pinion housing, unscrew the hose unions and drain the power steering fluid.

2 Clean around the hose unions on the pump. Place a suitable container beneath the pump, unscrew the hose unions, and drain any remaining fluid. Ensure that no fluid is allowed to spill onto the alternator.

3 If the hoses are to be left disconnected for a long period of time, plug the ends of the hoses and the apertures in the steering gear and pump, or cover them with masking tape to prevent dirt ingress.

Refitting

4 Refit in reverse order using new O-rings.

5 On completion top-up the fluid and bleed the system.

31 Power steering fluid circuit - bleeding

1 Unscrew the filler cap from the power steering pump reservoir and top-up the fluid level to the maximum mark using the specified fluid.

2 Disconnect the low tension negative lead from the ignition coil and crank the engine several times for two second periods while slowly turning the steering wheel from lock-to-lock. Top-up the fluid level if necessary and continue cranking the engine until the fluid is free of air bubbles.

3 Reconnect the coil lead and start the engine. Check the system for leaks.

4 Switch off the engine and refit the filler cap.

5 Drive the vehicle for a few miles to warm up the fluid and expel any remaining air, then stop the engine and make a final fluid level check.

32 Steering gear rubber gaiter - renewal

1 Remove the tie-rod end.

2 Unscrew and remove the tie-rod end locknut from the tie-rod.

3 Remove the clips and slide the gaiter from the tie-rod and steering gear.

4 Slide the new gaiter over the tie-rod and onto the steering gear. Where applicable, make sure that the gaiter seats in the cut-outs in the tie-rod and steering gear.

5 Secure the gaiter with new clips.

6 Refit the tie-rod end locknut to the tie-rod.

7 Refit the tie-rod end.

33 Tie-rod end - removal and refitting

Note: *A balljoint separator tool will be required for this operation.*

Removal

1 Loosen the relevant front roadwheel nuts, apply the handbrake, jack up the front of the vehicle and support on axle stands.

2 Remove the roadwheel. On P100 models mark the position of the roadwheel in relation to one of the wheel studs before removal.

3 Make alignment marks on the tie-rod and tie-rod end, then loosen the locknut by a quarter of a turn.

29.14a Unbolt the power steering pump pulley for access to the front pump securing bolts (arrowed)

29.14b Power steering pump rear securing bolt

33.4 Extracting the split pin from the tie-rod balljoint castellated nut

33.5 Using a balljoint separator tool to release the tie-rod end from the hub carrier

4 Extract the split pin and unscrew the castellated nut **(see illustration)**.
5 Using a balljoint separator tool, release the tie-rod end from the hub carrier **(see illustration)**.
6 Unscrew the tie-rod end from the tie-rod, noting the number of turns necessary to remove it.

Refitting

7 Refitting is a reversal of removal, bearing in mind the following points.
8 Screw the tie-rod end onto the tie-rod the number of turns noted during removal.
9 Tighten the nuts to the specified torque, and fit a new split pin to the castellated nut.
10 On P100 models, align the previously made marks on the roadwheel and wheel stud.
11 On completion, check and if necessary adjust the front wheel alignment.

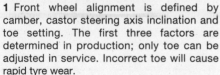

34 Front wheel alignment
- checking and adjusting

1 Front wheel alignment is defined by camber, castor steering axis inclination and toe setting. The first three factors are determined in production; only toe can be adjusted in service. Incorrect toe will cause rapid tyre wear.
2 Toe is defined as the amount by which the distance between the front wheels, measured at hub height, differs from the front edges to

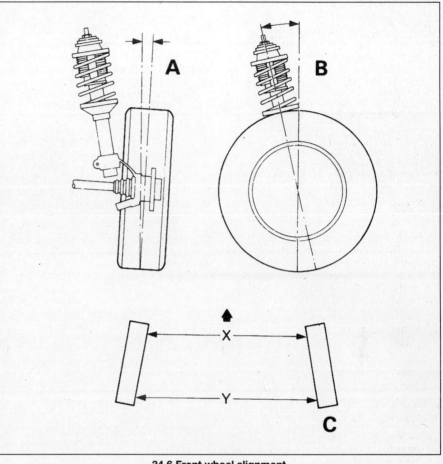

34.6 Front wheel alignment

A Camber	B Castor	C Toe setting

For X and Y, see text

the rear edges. If the distance between the front edges is less than that at the rear, the wheels are said to toe-in; the opposite case is known as toe-out.
3 To measure toe, it will be necessary to obtain or make a tracking gauge. These are available in motor accessory shops, or one can be made from a length of rigid pipe or bar with some kind of threaded adjustment facility at one end. Many tyre specialists will also check toe free, or for a nominal sum.
4 Before measuring toe, check that all steering and suspension components are undamaged and that tyre pressures are correct. The vehicle must be at approximately kerb weight, with the spare wheel and jack in their normal positions and any abnormal loads removed.
5 Park the vehicle on level ground and bounce it a few times to settle the suspension.
6 Use the tracking gauge to measure the distance between the inside faces of the front wheel rims, at hub height, at the rear of the front wheels. Record this distance; call it measurement "Y" **(see illustration)**.

7 Push the vehicle forwards or backwards so that the wheels rotate exactly 180° (half a turn). Measure the distance between the front wheel rims again, this time at the front of the wheels. Record this distance; call it measurement "X".
8 Subtract measurement "X" from measurement "Y". If the answer is positive it is the amount of toe-in; if negative it is the amount of toe-out. Permissible values are given in the Specifications.
9 If adjustment is necessary loosen the tie-rod end locknuts and the outer bellows clips, then rotate each tie-rod by equal amounts until the setting is correct. Hold the tie-rod ends in their horizontal position with a spanner while making the adjustment.
10 Tighten the locknuts and outer bellows clips.
11 Provided the tie-rods have been adjusted by equal amounts the steering wheel should be central when moving straight-ahead. The amount of visible thread on each tie-rod should also be equal. If necessary refer to Section 23.

11

Chapter 12
Bodywork and fittings

Contents

Degrees of difficulty

Easy, suitable for novice with little experience	Fairly easy, suitable for beginner with some experience	Fairly difficult, suitable for competent DIY mechanic	Difficult, suitable for experienced DIY mechanic	Very difficult, suitable for expert DIY or professional

Specifications

Torque wrench settings

	Nm	lbf ft
Front seat belt stalk-to-seat bolts	24 to 28	18 to 22
Seat belt anchor bolts	29 to 41	22 to 30
Seat belt inertia reel securing bolts	29 to 41	22 to 30
Seat mounting bolts	25 to 32	18 to 24
Cab safety grille securing bolts (P100 models)	20 to 27	15 to 20
Rear bump stop securing nuts (P100 models)	8 to 11	6 to 8
Cargo area-to-chassis bolts (P100 models)	40 to 50	29 to 37
Tailboard hinge securing screws (P100 models)	20 to 25	15 to 18

12

1 General information

The model range includes 4-door Saloon, 3 and 5-door Hatchback, 5-door Estate, and 2-door Pick-up body styles.

Each body is of all-steel welded energy-absorbing monocoque construction, with a separate load-bearing rear chassis frame on P100 Pick-up models. Corrosion protection is applied to all new vehicles, and includes zinc phosphate dipping of the body panels, and wax injection of box sections and doors.

All models have flush direct-glazed fixed glass panels, and integrated polycarbonate bumpers.

All body panels are welded, including the front wings, so it is recommended that major body damage repairs are entrusted to a dealer.

A wide range of interior equipment and trim options are available depending on model. The procedures given in this Chapter apply to original equipment fitments, and do not cover after-market products.

2 Maintenance - bodywork, underside and fittings

The general condition of a vehicle's bodywork is the one thing that significantly affects its value. Maintenance is easy but needs to be regular. Neglect, particularly after minor damage, can lead quickly to further deterioration and costly repair bills. It is important also to keep watch on those parts of the vehicle not immediately visible, for instance the underside, inside all the wheel arches and the lower part of the engine compartment.

The basic maintenance routine for the bodywork is washing - preferably with a lot of water, from a hose. This will remove all the loose solids which may have stuck to the vehicle. It is important to flush these off in such a way as to prevent grit from scratching the finish. The wheel arches and underframe need washing in the same way to remove any accumulated mud which will retain moisture and tend to encourage rust. Oddly enough, the best time to clean the underframe and wheel arches is in wet weather when the mud is thoroughly wet and soft. In very wet weather the underframe is usually cleaned of large accumulations automatically and this is a good time for inspection.

Periodically, except on vehicles with a wax-based underbody protective coating, it is a good idea to have the whole of the underframe of the vehicle steam cleaned, engine compartment included, so that a thorough inspection can be carried out to see what minor repairs and renovations are necessary. Steam cleaning is available at many garages and is necessary for removal of the accumulation of oily grime which sometimes is allowed to become thick in certain areas. If steam cleaning facilities are not available, there are one or two excellent grease solvents available, which can be brush applied. The dirt can then be simply hosed off. Note that these methods should not be used on vehicles with wax-based underbody protective coating or the coating will be removed. Such vehicles should be inspected annually, preferably just prior to winter, when the underbody should be washed down and any damage to the wax coating repaired using a proprietry brand undershield. Ideally, a completely fresh coat should be applied. It would also be worth considering the use of such wax-based protection for injection into door panels, sills, box sections, etc, as an additional safeguard against rust damage where such protection is not provided by the vehicle manufacturer.

After washing paintwork, wipe off with a chamois leather to give an unspotted clear finish. A coat of clear protective wax polish, will give added protection against chemical pollutants in the air. If the paintwork sheen has dulled or oxidised, use a cleaner/polisher combination to restore the brilliance of the shine. This requires a little effort, but such dulling is usually caused because regular washing has been neglected. Care needs to be taken with metallic paintwork, as special non-abrasive cleaner/polisher is required to avoid damage to the finish. Always check that the door and ventilator opening drain holes and pipes are completely clear so that water can be drained out. Bright work should be treated in the same way as paint work. Windscreens and windows can be kept clear of the smeary film which often appears by the use of a proprietary glass cleaner. Never use any form of wax or other body or chromium polish on glass.

At the specified intervals, check the operation of the door locks and check straps and lubricate the hinges with a little oil. Also lubricate the hinges of the bonnet and boot lid or tailgate, as applicable, and the bonnet release mechanism.

3 Maintenance - upholstery and carpets

Mats and carpets should be brushed or vacuum cleaned regularly to keep them free of grit. If they are badly stained remove them from the vehicle for scrubbing or sponging and make quite sure they are dry before refitting. Seats and interior trim panels can be kept clean by wiping with a damp cloth and a proprietry wax polish. If they do become stained (which can be more apparent on light coloured upholstery) use a little liquid detergent and a soft nail brush to scour the grime out of the grain of the material. Do not forget to keep the headlining clean in the same way as the upholstery. When using liquid cleaners inside the vehicle do not over-wet the surfaces being cleaned. Excessive damp could get into the seams and padded interior causing stains, offensive odours or even rot. If the inside of the vehicle gets wet accidentally it is worthwhile taking some trouble to dry it out properly, particularly where carpets are involved. Do not leave oil or electric heaters inside the vehicle for this purpose.

4 Minor body damage - repair

Repair of minor scratches in bodywork

If the scratch is very superficial, and does not penetrate to the metal of the bodywork, repair is very simple. Lightly rub the area of the scratch with a paintwork renovator, or a very fine cutting paste, to remove loose paint from the scratch and to clear the surrounding bodywork of wax polish. Rinse the area with clean water.

Apply touch-up paint to the scratch using a fine paint brush; continue to apply fine layers of paint until the surface of the paint in the scratch is level with the surrounding paintwork. Allow the new paint at least two weeks to harden: then blend it into the surrounding paintwork by rubbing the scratch area with a paintwork renovator or a very fine cutting paste. Finally, apply a good wax polish.

Where the scratch has penetrated right through to the metal of the bodywork, causing the metal to rust, a different repair technique is required. Remove any loose rust from the bottom of the scratch with a penknife, then apply rust inhibiting paint, to prevent the formation of rust in the future. Using a rubber or nylon applicator fill the scratch with bodystopper paste. If required, this paste can be mixed with cellulose thinners to provide a very thin paste which is ideal for filling narrow scratches. Before the stopper-paste in the scratch hardens, wrap a piece of smooth cotton rag around the top of a finger. Dip the finger in cellulose thinners; and then quickly sweep it across the surface of the stopper-paste in the scratch; this will ensure that the surface of the stopper-paste is slightly hollowed. The scratch can now be painted over as described earlier in this Section.

Repair of dents in bodywork

When deep denting of the vehicle's bodywork has taken place, the first task is to pull the dent out, until the affected bodywork almost attains its original shape. There is little point in trying to restore the original shape completely, as the metal in the damaged area will have stretched on impact and cannot be reshaped fully to its original contour. It is better to bring the level of the dent up to a point which is about 1/8 in (3 mm) below the level of the surrounding bodywork. In cases where the dent is very shallow anyway, it is not worth trying to pull it out at all. If the underside of the dent is accessible, it can be hammered out gently from behind, using a mallet with a wooden or plastic head. Whilst doing this, hold a suitable block of wood firmly against the outside of the panel to absorb the impact from the hammer blows and thus prevent a large area of the bodywork from being "belled-out".

Should the dent be in a section of the bodywork which has a double skin or some other factor making it inaccessible from behind, a different technique is called for. Drill several small holes through the metal inside the area particularly in the deeper section.

Then screw long self-tapping screws into the holes just sufficiently for them to gain a good purchase in the metal. Now the dent can be pulled out by pulling on the protruding heads of the screws with a pair of pliers.

The next stage of the repair is the removal of the paint from the damaged area, and from an inch or so of the surrounding "sound" bodywork. This is accomplished most easily by using a wire brush or abrasive pad on a power drill, although it can be done just as effectively by hand using sheets of abrasive paper. To complete the preparation for filling, score the surface of the bare metal with a screwdriver or the tang of a file, or alternatively, drill small holes in the affected area. This will provide a really good "key" for the filler paste.

To complete the repair see the Section on filling and re-spraying.

Repair of rust holes or gashes in bodywork

Remove all paint from the affected area and from an inch or so of the surrounding "sound" bodywork, using an abrasive pad or a wire brush on a power drill. If these are not available a few sheets of abrasive paper will do the job just as effectively. With the paint removed you will be able to gauge the severity of the corrosion and therefore decide whether to renew the whole panel (if this is possible) or to repair the affected area. New body panels are not as expensive as most people think and it is often quicker and more satisfactory to fit a new panel than to attempt to repair large areas of corrosion.

Remove all fittings from the affected area except those which will act as a guide to the original shape of the damaged bodywork (eg headlamp shells etc). Then, using tin snips or a hacksaw blade, remove all loose metal and any other metal badly affected by corrosion. Hammer the edges of the hole inwards in order to create a slight depression for the filler paste.

Wire brush the affected area to remove the powdery rust from the surface of the remaining metal. Paint the affected area with rust inhibiting paint; if the back of the rusted area is accessible treat this also.

Before filling can take place it will be necessary to block the hole in some way. This can be achieved by the use of aluminium or plastic mesh, or aluminium tape.

Aluminium or plastic mesh or glass fibre matting is probably the best material to use for a large hole. Cut a piece to the approximate size and shape of the hole to be filled, then position it in the hole so that its edges are below the level of the surrounding bodywork. It can be retained in position by several blobs of filler paste around its periphery.

Aluminium tape should be used for small or very narrow holes. Pull a piece off the roll and trim it to the approximate size and shape required, then pull off the backing paper (if used) and stick the tape over the hole; it can be overlapped if the thickness of one piece is insufficient. Burnish down the edges of the tape with the handle of a screwdriver or similar, to ensure that the tape is securely attached to the metal underneath.

Bodywork repairs - filling and re-spraying

Before using this Section, see the Sections on dent, deep scratch, rust holes and gash repairs.

Many types of bodyfiller are available, but generally speaking those proprietary kits which contain a tin of filler paste and a tube of resin hardener are best for this type of repair. A wide, flexible plastic or nylon applicator will be found invaluable for imparting a smooth and well contoured finish to the surface of the filler.

Mix up a little filler on a clean piece of card or board measure the hardener carefully (follow the maker's instructions on the pack) otherwise the filler will set too rapidly or too slowly. Alternatively, a no-mix filler can be used straight from the tube without mixing, but daylight is required to cure it. Using the applicator apply the filler paste to the prepared area; draw the applicator across the surface of the filler to achieve the correct contour and to level the filler surface. As soon as a contour that approximates to the correct one is achieved, stop working the paste - if you carry on too long the paste will become sticky and begin to "pick up" on the applicator. Continue to add thin layers of filler paste at twenty-minute intervals until the level of the filler is just proud of the surrounding bodywork.

Once the filler has hardened, excess can be removed using a metal plane or file. From then on, progressively finer grades of abrasive paper should be used, starting with a 40 grade production paper and finishing with 400 grade wet-and-dry paper. Always wrap the abrasive paper around a flat rubber, cork, or wooden block - otherwise the surface of the filler will not be completely flat. During the smoothing of the filler surface the wet-and-dry paper should be periodically rinsed in water. This will ensure that a very smooth finish is imparted to the filler at the final stage.

At this stage the "dent" should be surrounded by a ring of bare metal, which in turn should be encircled by the finely "feathered" edge of the good paintwork. Rinse the repair area with clean water, until all of the dust produced by the rubbing-down operation has gone.

Spray the whole repair area with a light coat of primer, this will show up any imperfections in the surface of the filler. Repair these imperfections with fresh filler paste or bodystopper, and once more smooth the surface with abrasive paper. If bodystopper is used, it can be mixed with cellulose thinners to form a really thin paste which is ideal for filling small holes.

Repeat this spray and repair procedure until you are satisfied that the surface of the filler, and the feathered edge of the paintwork are perfect. Clean the repair area with clean water and allow to dry fully.

The repair area is now ready for final spraying. Paint spraying must be carried out in a warm, dry, windless and dust free atmosphere. This condition can be created artificially if you have access to a large indoor working area, but if you are forced to work in the open, you will have to pick your day very

carefully. If you are working indoors, dousing the floor in the work area with water will help to settle the dust which would otherwise be in the atmosphere. If the repair area is confined to one body panel, mask off the surrounding panels; this will help to minimise the effects of a slight mis-match in paint colours. Bodywork fittings (eg chrome strips, door handles etc) will also need to be masked off. Use genuine masking tape and several thicknesses of newspaper for the masking operations.

Before commencing to spray, agitate the aerosol can thoroughly, then spray a test area (an old tin, or similar) until the technique is mastered. Cover the repair area with a thick coat of primer; the thickness should be built up using several thin layers of paint rather than one thick one. Using 400 grade wet-and-dry paper, rub down the surface of the primer until it is really smooth. While doing this, the work area should be thoroughly doused with water, and the wet-and-dry paper periodically rinsed in water. Allow to dry before spraying on more paint.

Spray on the top coat, again building up the thickness by using several thin layers of paint. Start spraying in the centre of the repair area and then work outwards, with a side-to-side motion, until the whole repair area and about 2 inches of the surrounding original paintwork is covered. Remove all masking material 10 to 15 minutes after spraying on the final coat of paint.

Allow the new paint at least two weeks to harden, then, using a paintwork renovator or a very fine cutting paste, blend the edges of the paint into the existing paintwork. Finally, apply wax polish.

Plastic components

With the use of more and more plastic body components by the vehicle manufacturers (eg bumpers, spoilers, and in some cases major body panels), rectification of more serious damage to such items has become a matter of either entrusting repair work to a specialist in this field, or renewing complete components. Repair of such damage by the DIY owner is not really feasible owing to the cost of the equipment and materials required for effecting such repairs. The basic technique involves making a groove along the line of the crack in the plastic using a rotary burr in a power drill. The damaged part is then welded back together by using a hot air gun to heat up and fuse a plastic filler rod into the groove. Any excess plastic is then removed and the area rubbed down to a smooth finish. It is important that a filler rod of the correct plastic is used, as body components can be made of a variety of different types (eg polycarbonate, ABS, polypropylene).

Damage of a less serious nature (abrasions, minor cracks etc) can be repaired by the DIY owner using a two-part epoxy filler repair material. Once mixed in equal proportions, this is used in similar fashion to the bodywork filler on metal panels. The filler is usually cured in twenty to thirty minutes, ready for sanding and painting.

If the owner is renewing a complete component himself, or if he has repaired it with epoxy filler, he will be left with the problem of finding a suitable paint for finishing which is

12

compatible with the type of plastic used. At one time the use of a universal paint was not possible owing to the complex range of plastics encountered in body component applications. Standard paints, generally speaking, will not bond to plastic or rubber satisfactorily. However, it is now possible to obtain a plastic body parts finishing kit which consists of a pre-primer treatment, a primer and coloured top coat. Full instructions are normally supplied with a kit, but basically the method of use is to first apply the pre-primer to the component concerned and allow it to dry for up to 30 minutes. Then the primer is applied and left to dry for about an hour before finally applying the special coloured top coat. The result is a correctly coloured component where the paint will flex with the plastic or rubber, a property that standard paint does not normally possess.

5 Major body damage - repair

Where serious damage has occurred or large areas need renewal due to neglect, it means certainly that completely new sections or panels will need welding in and this is best left to professionals. If the damage is due to impact, it will also be necessary to completely check the alignment of the bodyshell structure. Due to the principle of construction, the strength and shape of the whole car can be affected by damage to one part. In such instances the services of a Ford agent with specialist checking jigs are essential. If a body is left misaligned, it is first of all dangerous as the car will not handle properly, and secondly uneven stresses will be imposed on the steering, engine and transmission, causing abnormal wear or complete failure. Tyre wear may also be excessive.

6 Bonnet - removal and refitting

Removal

1 Support the bonnet in its open position, and place protective covers (old rags or cardboard) beneath the corners of the bonnet, and over the front wings to prevent damage to the paintwork.
2 Remove the screw and disconnect the earth strap from the rear left-hand edge of the bonnet (see illustration). Where applicable, disconnect the wiring from the underbonnet lamp.
3 Mark the location of the hinges on the sides of the bonnet with a soft pencil or masking tape, then loosen the four hinge bolts.
4 With the help of an assistant, remove the bolts and lift the bonnet from the vehicle (see illustration).
5 If required, the underbonnet insulation can be removed by prising out the two-piece plastic securing clips.

Refitting

6 Refitting is a reversal of removal, bearing in mind the following points.

6.2 Remove the screw and disconnect the bonnet earth cable

7 Adjust the hinges to their original marked positions before tightening the bolts.
8 On completion, check that the bonnet is central within its aperture and aligned with the surrounding bodywork. Re-adjust the hinges to give satisfactory alignment if necessary.
9 Check that the bonnet lock striker engages fully in the lock, and if necessary adjust the position of the lock striker and/or the height of the bonnet rubber bump stops (see illustration).

7 Bonnet lock release cable - removal and refitting

Removal

1 Working inside the vehicle, remove the three retaining screws, and withdraw the lower steering column shroud.
2 Remove the retaining screw, and withdraw the release cable bracket from the steering column.
3 Working in the engine compartment, pull the cable sheath end fitting from its bracket, and release the cable end fitting from the lock lever (see illustration).
4 Release the cable from the clips in the engine compartment.
5 Pull the cable through the bulkhead into the passenger compartment, taking care not to lose the bulkhead grommet.

Refitting

6 Refitting is a reversal of removal, but ensure that the grommet is correctly located in the

7.3 Bonnet lock release cable end fittings - models up to 1987

6.4 Lifting the bonnet from the vehicle

6.9 Adjustable bonnet rubber bump stop

bulkhead, and that the cable is free from sharp bends and kinks. There should be a small amount of free play at the lock end of the cable if necessary re-route the cable to achieve this condition.
7 Note that should the release cable snap while the bonnet is shut, the bonnet may be opened as follows.
8 Apply the handbrake, jack up the front of the vehicle and support on axle stands (see "Jacking and Vehicle Support").
9 Using an inspection lamp or torch, look up between the radiator and the radiator grille panel and locate the circular hole below the bonnet lock (see illustration).
10 Insert a screwdriver through the hole so that it passes to the right of the lock striker. Twist or lever the lock sliding plate to the right until the striker is released. The bonnet can now be opened.

7.9 Access hole (arrowed) below bonnet lock

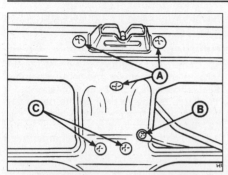

10.3 Boot lid lock - Saloon models

A *Lock retaining*   C *Reinforcing plate*
  screws   *screws*
B *Earth lead*

8 Bonnet lock - removal and refitting

Models up to 1987

1 Working in the engine compartment, disconnect the cable from the bonnet lock by pulling the cable sheath end fitting from its bracket, then releasing the end fitting from the lock lever.
2 Remove the three securing screws and withdraw the lock from the front panel.
3 Refitting is a reversal of removal.

Models from 1987

4 Remove the radiator grille panel.
5 Disconnect the cable from the bonnet lock by pulling the cable sheath end fitting from its bracket, then releasing the end fitting from the lock lever.
6 Detach the bracing strut from the lock by removing the screw, then remove the two securing screws and withdraw the lock from the front panel.
7 Refitting is a reversal of removal.

9 Boot lid (Saloon models) - removal and refitting

Removal

1 Open the boot lid, and place protective covers (old rags or cardboard) beneath the corners of the lid, and over the rear wings to prevent damage to the paintwork.
2 Where applicable, disconnect the wiring from the lock solenoid and "boot lid ajar" sensor, after disconnecting the battery negative lead.
3 Release the wiring loom grommets, taking care not to lose them, then tie string to the wiring loom(s), and pull the loom(s) through the boot lid. Leave the string(s) in position in the boot lid to aid refitting of the loom(s).
4 Mark the location of the hinges on the underside of the lid using a soft pencil or masking type, then loosen the four hinge bolts.

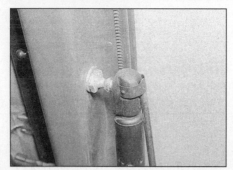

11.5 Prising out a tailgate strut retaining clip

5 With the help of an assistant, remove the bolts and lift the boot lid from the vehicle.

Refitting

6 Refitting is a reversal of removal, bearing in mind the following points.
7 Adjust the hinges to their original marked positions before tightening the bolts.
8 On completion, check that the boot lid is central within its aperture and aligned with the surrounding bodywork. Re-adjust the hinges to give satisfactory alignment if necessary.
9 Check that the lock striker engages fully in the lock, and if necessary adjust the position of the lock striker.

10 Boot lid lock (Saloon models) - removal and refitting

Removal

1 With the boot lid raised, remove the lock barrel retaining clip.
2 Where applicable, disconnect the operating lever from the central locking solenoid/motor, then withdraw the lock barrel.
3 Remove the three retaining screws from the lock assembly, if necessary loosening the reinforcing plate **(see illustration)**.
4 Where applicable, disconnect the battery negative lead, the earth lead from the bootlid and the "boot lid ajar" sensor wiring plug. Unclip the luggage compartment light switch from the lock assembly, where applicable.
5 Withdraw the lock assembly from the boot lid.

Refitting

6 Commence refitting by inserting the lock assembly and loosely refitting the retaining screws.
7 Insert the lock barrel, where applicable reconnecting the operating lever to the solenoid, and refit the retaining clip.
8 Tighten the lock assembly retaining screws, and where applicable reconnect the earth lead and "boot lid ajar" sensor wiring plug, and the battery negative lead.
9 If the reinforcing plate was loosened during removal, tighten the retaining screws.

11 Tailgate (Hatchback and Estate models) - removal and refitting

Note: On Hatchback models made before 1990 with an integral heated rear window/radio aerial, note that the radio aerial lead is routed through different openings to that of other models in the rear bodywork and the tailgate. If a new, later-specification tailgate is to be fitted to an earlier vehicle, a new opening must be made in the bodywork for the aerial lead. Ideally, this work should be carried out by a Ford dealer, who will have the necessary template available to ensure that the opening is positioned accurately.

Removal

1 Disconnect the battery negative lead.
2 Open the tailgate and prise out the trim panel using a wide-bladed screwdriver.
3 Disconnect the wiring from the heated rear window, rear wash/wipe, interior light, lock solenoid and "tailgate ajar" sensor, as applicable. Disconnect the washer fluid hose where applicable; be prepared for fluid spillage.
4 Release the wiring loom/hose grommet(s) taking care not to lose it/them, then tie string to the wiring loom(s)/hose, and pull the loom(s)/hose through the tailgate. Leave the string(s) in position in the tailgate to aid refitting of the loom(s)/hose.
5 Have an assistant support the tailgate, then disconnect the support struts by prising out the retaining clips. Do not remove the clips completely, just raise them by a maximum of 4.0 mm (0.16 in) and pull the struts off their mountings **(see illustration)**.
6 Prise out the hinge fixing covers from the headlining, unscrew the hinge nuts and washers, and with the aid of the assistant, withdraw the tailgate from the vehicle **(see illustration)**.

Refitting

7 Refitting is a reversal of removal, but do not fully tighten the hinge nuts until the tailgate is positioned centrally in its aperture. If necessary, adjust the position of the lock striker so that it engages fully in the lock.

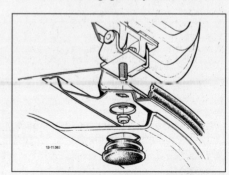

11.6 Tailgate hinge assembly - Hatchback and Estate models

12

12 Tailgate lock (Hatchback and Estate models) - removal and refitting

Removal

1 Open the tailgate and prise out the trim panel using a wide-bladed screwdriver (see illustration).
2 Remove the lock barrel retaining clip, and where applicable disconnect the operating lever from the central locking solenoid/motor, then withdraw the lock barrel (see illustration). Central locking solenoid/motor removal and refitting is covered in Chapter 13.
3 Remove the two securing screws and detach the lock barrel support bracket from the tailgate.
4 Where applicable, disconnect the battery negative lead, the earth lead from the tailgate and the "tailgate ajar" sensor wiring plug. Unclip the luggage compartment light switch from the lock assembly, where applicable.
5 Remove the securing screws and withdraw the lock assembly.

Refitting

6 Refitting is a reversal of removal, but do not tighten the lock barrel support bracket screws until the lock barrel has been fitted.

13 Tailgate strut (Hatchback and Estate models) - removal and refitting

Removal

1 Support the tailgate in the open position using a prop, or with the aid of an assistant.
2 Disconnect the strut from the tailgate by prising out the retaining clip. Do not remove the clip completely, just raise it by a maximum of 4.0 mm (0.16 in) and then pull the strut off its mounting.
3 Pull the strut from the pivot stud on the body.

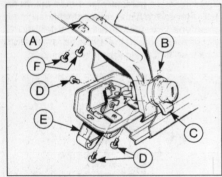

12.2 Tailgate lock assembly - Hatchback and Estate models

A Lock barrel support bracket
B Lock barrel retaining clip
C Lock barrel
D Torx screw
E Lock assembly
F Screws

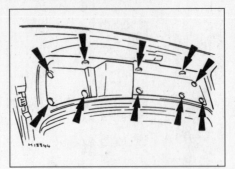

12.1 Tailgate trim panel fixings - Hatchback and Estate models

Refitting

4 Refitting is a reversal of removal.

14 Tailgate/boot lid/fuel filler flap release cable - removal and refitting

Removal

1 Operate the control lever to open the tailgate/boot lid and the fuel filler flap (see illustration).
2 Remove the driver's side centre pillar lower trim panel and the sill trim panel.
3 Withdraw the cover from the control lever.
4 Unscrew the two securing bolts, and detach the control lever assembly from the body panel. Detach the cable from the control assembly.
5 Fold the rear seat cushion forwards or remove it, as applicable, and remove the rear seat side cushion for access to the wheel arch trim panel.
6 Detach the trim panel from the wheel arch by removing the two securing screws from the parcel shelf bracket. Free the cable up to the wheel arch.
7 Working inside the luggage compartment, remove the trim panels for access to the petrol flap lock and tailgate/boot lid lock.
8 Disengage the petrol flap catch from the housing by twisting and pulling out (see illustration). Carefully pull the cable through into the luggage compartment, noting its routing.
9 Remove the securing screws, and withdraw the tailgate/boot lid lock striker from the body panel. Withdraw the striker and cable assembly.

Refitting

10 Commence refitting by installing the tailgate/boot lid striker and cable assembly. Secure the cable to the body with tape.
11 Route the cable back to the petrol flap housing, and refit the petrol flap catch.
12 Route the cable into the interior of the vehicle, and refit the luggage compartment trim panels.
13 Route the cable to the control lever, securing the cable with tape to the body, then refit the wheel arch trim panel, and refit the seat cushions.
14 Reconnect the cable to the control lever assembly, then refit the assembly.
15 Refit the control lever cover and the trim panels.

15 Tailgate/boot lid spoiler - removal and refitting

Models up to 1990

1 Open the tailgate/boot lid.
2 Prise the four screw covers from the spoiler, then remove the screws, and withdraw the spoiler.
3 Refitting is a reversal of removal.

Models from 1990

4 Open the tailgate/boot lid.
5 Remove the inner tailgate/boot lid trim panel for access to the spoiler securing nuts.
6 Unscrew the central spoiler securing nut, then unscrew the four outer securing nuts (two on each side), and withdraw the spoiler.
7 Refitting is a reversal of removal.

16 Door - removal and refitting

Front door

1 On models with electric mirrors, electric windows, central-locking, door-mounted speakers, or "door ajar" sensors, remove the trim panel and disconnect the wiring inside the door. Withdraw the wiring loom(s) through the grommet(s) in the front edge of the door.

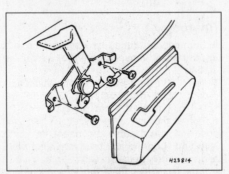

14.1 Tailgate/boot lid/fuel filler flap control lever assembly

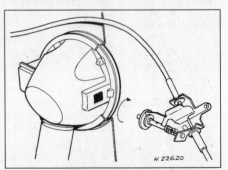

14.8 Disengaging the petrol flap catch from the housing

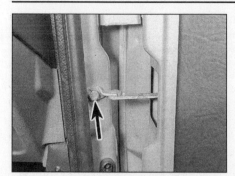

16.2 Remove the door check arm-to-body pillar bolt (arrowed)

2 Unscrew and remove the bolt securing the check arm to the body pillar (see illustration).
3 Remove the two securing screws, and withdraw the side trim panel from the footwell.
4 If working on the driver's side, remove the lower facia panels and disconnect the face level vent hose.
5 If working on the passenger side, remove the face level vent cover.
6 Support the door on blocks of wood.
7 Working through the body pillar aperture, unscrew the two securing nuts and remove the reinforcing plate from the lower hinge. Repeat the procedure for the upper hinge (see illustration).
8 Withdraw the door from the vehicle.
9 Refitting is a reversal of removal, but do not fully tighten the hinge bolts until the door is positioned centrally in the body aperture and aligned with the surrounding bodywork. If necessary, remove the lock striker from the body centre pillar before adjusting the door, then refit it and adjust its position so that the lock operates correctly.

Rear door

10 On models equipped with electric windows, central-locking, or "door ajar" sensors, remove the trim panel and disconnect the wiring inside the door. Withdraw the wiring loom(s) through the grommet(s) in the front edge of the door.

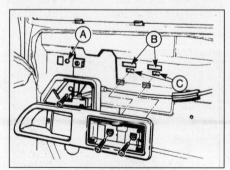

16.16 Later-type rear door - Estate models

A Internal handle mounting hole
B Early-type ashtray/handle mounting holes
C Revised mounting holes

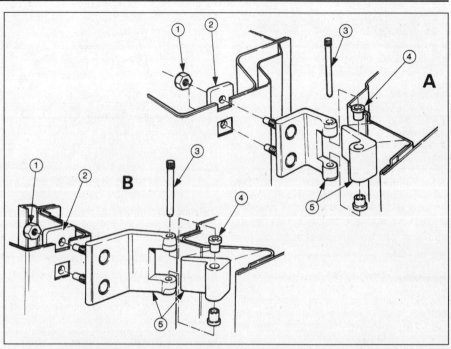

16.7 Exploded view of the front door hinge (A) and rear door hinge (B)

1 Nut   3 Hinge pin   5 Hinge assembly
2 Reinforcing plate   4 Bush

11 Unscrew and remove the bolt securing the check arm to the body centre pillar.
12 Remove the centre pillar trim panel.
13 Proceed as described in paragraphs 6 to 9 inclusive.

Rear door (late model Estate)

14 The door internal components have been modified on later Estate models. If a new, later-specification rear door is to be fitted to an earlier vehicle, the door panels must be modified as follows to enable refitting of the original components.
15 Remove all the serviceable components and fasteners from the original door.
16 Working on the new door, use a small round file to elongate the door interior handle mounting hole "A" (see illustration) vertically downwards so that it will align with the mounting hole in the handle/ashtray bezel. Refit the original retaining clip.

17 The earlier type of trim fasteners (located at "B") are no longer used, and must be replaced with the latest type of fasteners, available from a Ford dealer.

17 Door inner trim panel - removal and refitting

Front door

Models up to 1987

1 On models with manually-operated windows, prise the cover from the window regulator handle, note the position of the handle with the window fully shut, then remove the securing screw and withdraw the handle and bezel (see illustrations).
2 Remove the securing screw and withdraw the trim panel from behind the door grip (see illustration).

17.1a Prise the cover from the window handle, remove the securing screw ...

17.1b ... then withdraw the window handle and bezel (arrowed)

12

17.2 Withdraw the trim panel from behind the door grip

17.3a Remove the securing screw . . .

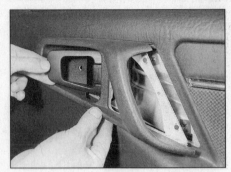

17.3b . . . and withdraw the handle surround and door grip

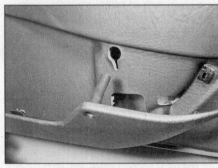

17.4 Withdraw the door pocket

3 Remove the securing screw from the interior door handle surround, lift the handle, and withdraw the surround and grip **(see illustrations)**.

4 Remove the two securing screws and withdraw the door pocket **(see illustration)**.

5 If working on the driver's side of models fitted with electric mirrors, first disconnect the battery negative lead, then prise the mirror switch assembly from the door trim panel and disconnect the wiring plug.

6 The trim panel can now be prised from the door. To prevent damage to the panel, only prise under the retaining clips **(see illustration)**. It is advisable to use a forked tool similar to that shown **(see illustration)** to prise around the retaining clips, but failing this, use a wide-bladed screwdriver. If a clip will not release, sever it with a chisel or sharp knife, taking care not to damage the trim panel, and renew the clip on reassembly.

7 Refitting is a reversal of removal, but ensure that all the retaining clips are correctly aligned before pressing them into the door, and make sure that the upper lip of the trim panel locates under the mirror trim panel.

Models from 1987

8 Proceed as described in paragraph 1.

9 Remove the securing screw from the interior door handle surround, lift the handle, and withdraw the surround **(see illustration)**.

10 Prise out the armrest trim panel, remove the three securing screws, and withdraw the armrest **(see illustrations)**.

11 On models with manually-operated mirrors, unscrew the bezel from the adjuster knob, then prise off the mirror trim panel.

12 When working on the driver's side of models with electric mirrors, prise the securing screw cover from the mirror control panel, then remove the screw and withdraw the control panel. Disconnect the wiring plug after disconnecting the battery negative lead **(see illustrations)**.

13 When working on the passenger side of models with electric mirrors, the mirror trim panel can simply be prised off.

14 Remove the now exposed door trim panel securing screw.

15 Remove the two trim panel securing screws from each side of the door, and the four securing screws from the door pocket,

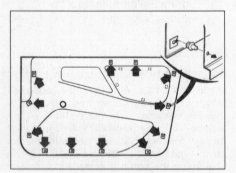

17.6a Door inner trim panel retaining clip locations (arrowed)

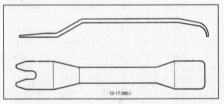

17.6b Trim panel retaining clip removal tool

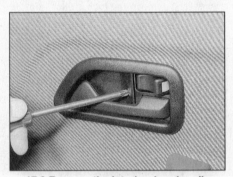

17.9 Remove the interior door handle surround securing screws

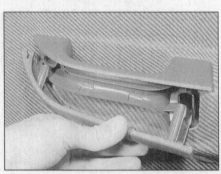

17.10a Prise out the armrest trim panel . . .

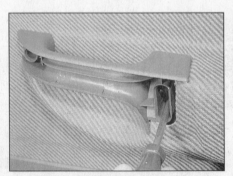

17.10b . . . and remove the armrest securing screws

17.12a Prise the securing screw cover from the mirror control panel . . .

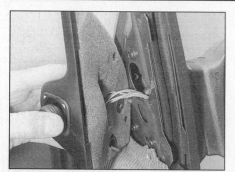

17.12b . . . and withdraw the mirror control panel

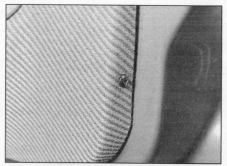

17.15a Trim panel securing screw at bottom rear edge of door

17.15b Trim panel securing screw at top edge of door pocket

then lift the trim panel to disengage it from the top retaining clips, and withdraw the panel from the door **(see illustrations)**.

16 Refitting is a reversal of removal.

Rear door

Models up to 1987

17 Proceed as shown in paragraphs 1 to 3.

18 On models fitted with electric windows, disconnect the battery negative lead, then prise the switch from the armrest and disconnect the wiring plug.

19 Proceed as described in paragraph 6.

20 Refitting is a reversal of removal, but ensure that all the retaining clips are correctly aligned before pressing them into the door.

Models from 1987

21 Proceed as described in paragraph 1.

22 Remove the securing screw from the interior door handle, then pull out the ashtray, and remove the two now exposed screws.

18.3a Remove the securing screws . . .

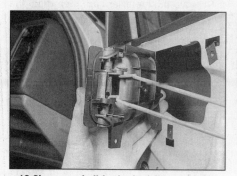

18.3b . . . and slide the handle assembly from the door aperture

23 Lift the interior door handle, and withdraw the handle/ashtray surround.

24 Prise out the armrest trim panel, remove the three securing screws and withdraw the armrest.

25 Remove the two trim panel securing screws from each side of the door, then lift the trim panel to disengage it from the top retaining clips, and withdraw the panel from the door.

26 Refitting is a reversal of removal.

18 Door interior handle - removal and refitting

Removal

1 Remove the door inner trim panel.

2 Where necessary for improved access, peel back the waterproof plastic sheet from the door.

3 Remove the two securing screws in the case of models up to 1987, or the single securing screw on models from 1987, and slide the handle assembly from the door aperture, if necessary unclipping the remote control rods from their guides **(see illustrations)**.

4 Disconnect the remote control rods from the handle assembly, and withdraw the handle assembly.

Refitting

5 Refitting is a reversal of removal, but check that the remote control rods are correctly located in their guides **(see illustration)**.

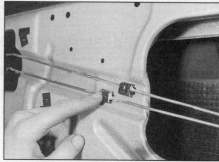

18.5 Remote control rods correctly located in their guides

19 Door exterior handle - removal and refitting

Removal

1 Remove the door inner trim panel.

2 Where necessary for improved access, peel back the waterproof plastic sheet from the door.

3 If working on a front door, remove the window channel extension screw from the bottom rear corner of the door, and withdraw the channel through the lower door aperture **(see illustration)**.

4 Disconnect the handle operating rod at the lock.

5 Remove the two handle securing screws and withdraw the handle and operating rod from the door.

Refitting

6 Refitting is a reversal of removal, but if working on a front door, ensure that the window channel extension is correctly located.

20 Door lock barrel - removal and refitting

Removal

1 Remove the door inner trim panel.

2 Where necessary for access, peel back the waterproof plastic sheet from the door.

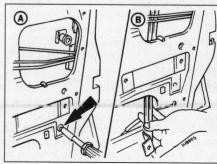

19.3 Front door window channel extension

A Remove the retaining screw (arrowed)
B Withdraw the channel through the lower door aperture

12

20.4 Door lock barrel location. Retaining clip arrowed

3 Remove the window channel extension screw from the bottom rear corner of the door, and withdraw the channel through the lower door aperture.

4 Working inside the door aperture, pull out the lock barrel retaining clip using pliers, then unhook the lock operating rod from the barrel, and withdraw the barrel from outside the door **(see illustration)**.

Refitting

5 Refitting is a reversal of removal.

21 Door lock - removal and refitting

Models up to 1990

1 Remove the door inner trim panel.
2 Where necessary for improved access, peel back the waterproof plastic sheet from the door.
3 Withdraw the window channel extension through the lower rear door aperture after removing the single securing screw if working on a front door or the two securing screws if working on a rear door.
4 Remove the three securing screws from the rear edge of the door, then reach inside the door and turn the lock to disconnect it from the control rods.
5 Where applicable, disconnect the "door ajar" sensor wiring plug and the central locking component wiring plug(s). Central locking component removal and refitting is covered in Chapter 13.
6 Withdraw the lock from inside the door.
7 Refitting is a reversal of removal, but ensure that the window channel extension is correctly located.

Models from 1990

8 From 1990, cable-operated door locks have been fitted to all Sierra models. To remove the later type of lock, proceed as follows. *Do not bend or stretch the cable during removal and refitting, as the operation of the lock will be impaired.*
9 Remove the door inner trim panel.
10 Where necessary for improved access, peel back the waterproof plastic sheet from the door.

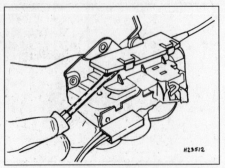

21.17 Prising the cover plate from a cable-operated door lock

11 Remove the securing screw, and withdraw the window channel extension through the door's lower aperture.
12 Disconnect the door outer handle and the lock barrel (front doors) operating rods at the lock assembly.
13 Disconnect the battery negative lead, and disconnect the door lock motor and the alarm system wiring plugs (where applicable).
14 Remove the screw securing the door interior handle to the door panel.
15 Remove the three lock securing screws from the rear edge of the door, then withdraw the lock assembly complete with the operating cable and the door interior handle.
16 To disconnect the cable from the lock, proceed as follows.
17 Carefully prise the cover plate from the lock, using a screwdriver **(see illustration)**.
18 Using a suitable pair of pliers, carefully remove the outer cable from the groove in the lock assembly casing.
19 Extend the inner cable until the flats on the plastic end piece align with the guide, then withdraw the cable **(see illustration)**.
20 Commence reassembly and refitting as follows.
21 Align the flats on the inner cable end piece with the cable guide, and refit the inner cable.
22 Using a suitable pair of pliers, carefully refit the outer cable to the groove in the lock assembly casing.
23 Refit the lock cover plate.
24 Insert the lock, cable and interior handle into the door, and refit the three lock securing screws.

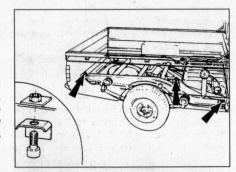

23.6 Cargo area-to-chassis Torx bolt locations (arrowed) - one side shown for clarity

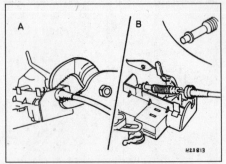

21.19 Disconnecting the operating cable from a cable-operated door lock

A Removing outer cable
B Disconnecting inner cable

25 Push the interior handle assembly towards the lock to adjust the cable, and when adjustment is correct, refit and tighten the interior handle securing screw.
26 Further refitting is a reversal of removal, ensuring that the window channel extension is correctly located.

22 Door check arm - removal and refitting

Removal

1 Remove the door inner trim panel.
2 Unscrew and remove the bolt securing the check arm to the body pillar.
3 Unscrew and remove the two bolts securing the check arm to the door, and withdraw the check arm from inside the door. Peel back the waterproof plastic sheet where necessary for improved access.

Refitting

4 Refitting is a reversal of removal.

23 Cargo area (P100 models) - removal and refitting

Note: *A suitable lifting crane and tackle will be required for this operation.*

Removal

1 Disconnect the battery negative lead.
2 Remove the fuel filler cap, then drain the fuel tank.
3 Remove the two securing screws and detach the fuel filler pipe from the cargo area.
4 Disconnect the number plate lamp and the rear lamp wiring plugs, and release the wiring from the cargo area.
5 Disconnect the earth lead from the right-hand front cargo area mounting bracket underneath the vehicle.
6 Working underneath the vehicle, remove the three Torx bolts on each side securing the cargo area to the chassis **(see illustration)**.
7 Make up a cradle to lift the cargo area from the chassis, using suitable ropes or chains attached to the tonneau tie-down points.

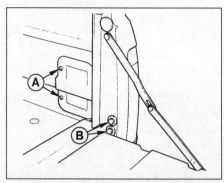

24.2 Rear lamp wiring cover screws (A)
and tailboard hinge screws (B)

8 Position the crane with the lifting arm diagonally over the centre of the cargo area, and attach the cradle. Carefully lift the cargo area from the chassis. Note that the lip of the cargo area rear panel fits over the rear chassis crossmember, therefore the cargo area must be pulled rearwards as it is removed to disengage it from the crossmember.

Refitting

9 Refitting is a reversal of removal, but ensure that the insulators are in place between the cargo area and the chassis. Before finally tightening the securing bolts, adjust the position of the cargo area to give an equal clearance on both sides of the vehicle between the cab rear panel and the cargo area front panel.

24 Tailboard (P100 models) - removal and refitting

Removal

1 Lower the tailboard to the open position.
2 Detach the rear lamp wiring cover on one side of the vehicle by removing the two securing screws (see illustration).
3 Remove the four rear lamp securing nuts, and withdraw the rear lamp assembly. Disconnect the wiring plug.
4 Raise the tailboard by approximately 20°, lift the centre pivot of one of the support arms, and when the bolt head on the tailboard is aligned with the slot in the support arm, pull the support arm clear. Repeat this procedure for the remaining support arm, and lower the tailboard to the vertical position.
5 On the side of the vehicle from which the rear lamp has been removed, remove the two screws securing the tailboard hinge to the cargo area.
6 Close the tailboard and lever out the hinge.
7 Pull the free end of the tailboard away from the cargo area, and carefully prise the remaining end from its hinge. Withdraw the tailboard from the vehicle.
8 If required, the pivot bushes can be removed from the tailboard for renewal.

Refitting

9 Refitting is a reversal of removal.

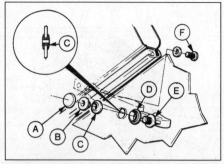

26.2 Opening the rear quarter window catch

A Cap   D Spacer
B Retainer E Catch
C Grommet F Screw (one of two)

25 Windscreen, rear window and fixed rear quarter windows - removal and refitting

Removal

1 With the exception of the cab rear window on P100 models, all fixed glass panels are direct glazed to the body using a special adhesive. Special tools are required to remove the old glass and to fit the new glass, therefore the work is best entrusted to a dealer or replacement glass specialist.
2 The cab rear window on P100 models can be removed as follows, although it is advisable to entrust the work to a specialist.
3 Remove the six Torx bolts and nut/washer assemblies, and withdraw the safety grille from the rear of the cab.
4 Prise out one end of the trim insert from the window rubber, then pull out the remainder of the trim.
5 With the aid of an assistant, carefully push the glass and rubber into the passenger compartment.
6 Remove all traces of old sealer from the glass, rubber and cab aperture.

Refitting

7 Commence refitting by pushing the window rubber into the aperture, ensuring that the trim panel and body panel engage in their respective grooves in the rubber.
8 Working from outside the cab, enter the bottom edge of the glass into the rubber, and hold the glass against the rubber while an assistant working from inside the passenger compartment pushes the rubber over the glass.
9 The trim insert must now be refitted to the rubber, preferably using a suitable windscreen trim insert tool. If no special tool is available, the trim can be refitted by prising open the rubber lips and pressing the trim into its groove, although this is likely to prove difficult and time consuming.
10 Refit the safety grille to the rear of the cab on completion.

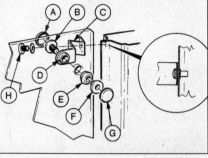

26.3 Opening the rear quarter window hinge

A Cap   E Grommet
B Screw   F Retainer
C Hinge   G Cap
D Spacer   H Screw

26 Opening rear quarter window - removal and refitting

Removal

1 Remove the rear pillar interior trim panel.
2 Remove the two screws securing the window catch to the body (see illustration).
3 Prise the two screw covers from the hinges. Support the glass, and remove the two hinge screws, then lift out the glass (see illustration).
4 If a new window is to be fitted, transfer the catch to it.

Refitting

5 Refitting is a reversal of removal.

27 Door window - removal and refitting

Front door

1 Remove the door inner trim panel.
2 Where necessary for access, peel back the waterproof plastic sheet from the door.
3 Remove the door mirror.
4 Remove the window channel extension screw from the bottom rear corner of the door, and withdraw the channel through the lower door aperture.
5 Lower the window until the lower support channel is visible through the lower door aperture. Prise the regulator arms from the sockets in the support channel, then lower the window to the bottom of the door.
6 Carefully prise the weatherstrip from the rear edge of the window aperture, then tilt the window forwards and lift it outwards through the aperture.
7 Refitting is a reversal of removal, but position the rear window channel extension screw to allow approximately 5.0 mm (0.2 in) fore and aft movement of the window. Check to ensure that the window does not tip as it is raised, and that the regulator effort is acceptable (check that the motor is not being

12

28.3 Front door window lower support channel and regulator arms

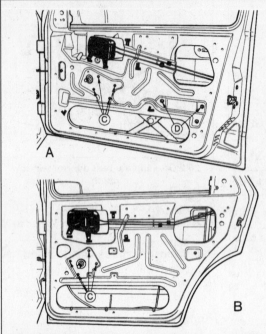

28.4 Door window regulator fixings

A *Front door*
B *Rear door*
C *Regulator assembly securing rivets*
D *Regulator guide rivets*

overloaded on models with electric windows). Adjust the channel extension screw if necessary.

Rear door

8 Proceed as shown in paragraphs 1 and 2.
9 On Saloon and Hatchback models, prise the interior quarter trim panel from the rear of the door, then remove the now exposed screw and withdraw the exterior trim panel.
10 Remove the three window channel extension screws from the rear of the door, and withdraw the channel through the lower door aperture.
11 Lower the window until the lower support channel is visible through the lower door aperture. Prise the regulator arms from the sockets in the support channel, then lower the window to the bottom of the door.
12 Carefully prise the weatherstrip from the front edge of the window aperture, then tilt the window rearwards and lift it outwards through the aperture.
13 Refitting is as described in paragraph 7.

28 Door window regulator - removal and refitting

Removal

1 Remove the door inner trim panel.
2 Where necessary for improved access, peel back the waterproof plastic sheet from the door.
3 Lower the window until the lower support channel is visible through the lower door aperture. Prise the regulator arms from the sockets in the support channel, then lower the window to the bottom of the door **(see illustration)**.
4 Drill out the four rivets securing the regulator assembly to the inner door skin, and if working on a front door, drill out the two rivets securing the regulator guide **(see illustration)**.
5 On models with electric windows, disconnect the motor wiring plug after disconnecting the battery negative lead. Removal and refitting of the motor is described in Chapter 13.
6 Withdraw the regulator assembly through the lower door aperture.

Refitting

7 Refitting is a reversal of removal, but fit new rivets, using a hand riveter.

29 Door mirror - removal and refitting

Manually-operated mirror

1 On remote-control type mirrors, unscrew the bezel from the adjuster knob **(see illustration)**.
2 Prise the mirror trim panel from the door **(see illustration)**.
3 Remove the three mirror securing screws, and withdraw the mirror by tilting its rear edge outwards and disengaging its front edge from under the window surround. Where applicable, withdraw the mirror control cable through the door.
4 To remove the mirror glass, proceed as follows according to model.

5 On "high specification" models with fixed (ie not remote control) mirrors, lever the glass assembly outwards to disengage it from the balljoint on the mirror glass mounting.
6 On "low specification" models with fixed (ie not remote control) mirrors, unclip the cover, then remove the securing screw and withdraw the glass assembly **(see illustration)**.

29.1 Unscrew the bezel from the adjuster knob . . .

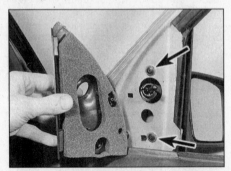

29.2 . . . and prise the mirror trim panel from the door to reveal the 3 mirror securing screws (2 arrowed)

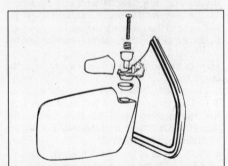

29.6 Fixed door mirror assembly

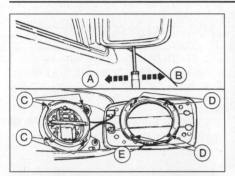

29.7 Manual remote control and electric door mirror glass removal

A *Locking operation*
B *Unlocking operation*
C *Locating pegs*
D *Locking slots*
E *Locking ring*

7 On models with remote control mirrors, insert a thin screwdriver through the hole in the bottom of the mirror assembly, and whilst supporting the glass, release the locking ring (see illustration).

8 Refitting is a reversal of removal, but ensure that the front edge of the mirror is correctly located under the window surround.

Electric mirror

9 Disconnect the battery negative lead.

10 If working on the driver's side of models up to 1987, prise the mirror switch assembly from the door trim panel and disconnect the wiring plug.

11 If working on the driver's side of models from 1987, prise the securing screw cover from the mirror control panel, then remove the screw and withdraw the control panel. Disconnect the wiring plug.

12 On models up to 1987, and when working on the passenger side of models from 1987, prise out the mirror trim panel.

13 Remove the three mirror securing screws, and withdraw the mirror by tilting its rear edge outwards and disengaging its front edge from under the window surround. Withdraw the wiring through the door.

14 To remove the mirror glass proceed as described in paragraph 7.

15 Refitting is a reversal of removal, but ensure that the front edge of the mirror is correctly located under the window surround.

30.15 Rear bumper plastic fastener

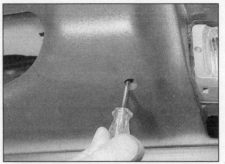

30.12a Adjusting the height of a front bumper - models from 1987

30 Bumper - removal and refitting

Front bumper

Models up to 1987

1 Remove the radiator grille panel.

2 Disconnect the battery negative lead, then disconnect the wiring plugs from the indicators, and where applicable the foglamps.

3 Working under the front wing, release the single bumper fastener from each side of the vehicle by turning the plastic clip through 90° (quarter of a turn).

4 On Ghia models, unclip the support strap between each front wing and the bumper.

5 Unscrew the single bolt securing each bumper fixing bracket to the body front panel, then pull the bumper forwards away from the body, disengaging the retaining pegs from the clips in each wing.

6 Refitting is a reversal of removal; ensure that all fixings are correctly located and secure.

Models from 1987

7 If foglamps are fitted, disconnect the battery negative lead, then disconnect the wiring plugs from the foglamps.

8 Working under the front wings, unscrew the single bolt from each side of the bumper.

9 Release the plastic retaining screws and pull the wheel arch liners away from the ends of the bumper.

10 Pull the bumper forwards away from the body, releasing the front mounting spigots from their sockets.

30.18 Adjusting the height of a rear bumper

30.12b Front bumper height adjusting screw - models from 1987

11 Refitting is a reversal of removal, but ensure that the reinforcing plate and O-ring are located on the right-hand mounting spigot.

12 The bumper height can be adjusted by turning the adjusters located on the front mounting spigots using a suitable Torx screwdriver with a length of at least 150.0 mm (6.0 in) (see illustrations).

Rear bumper - Saloon, Hatchback and Estate models

13 Disconnect the battery negative lead, then prise the number plate lamps from the bumper, and disconnect the wiring plugs. Withdraw the wiring through the bumper assembly.

14 Working inside the luggage compartment, unscrew the two bumper securing bolts.

15 Working under the rear wings, release the single bumper fastener from each side of the vehicle by turning the plastic clip through 90° (quarter of a turn) (see illustration).

16 Pull the bumper rearwards away from the body, disengaging the retaining pegs from the clips in each wing.

17 Refitting is a reversal of removal, but ensure that all fixings are correctly located and secure.

18 On some later models, the bumper height can be adjusted by means of the adjusters located on the mounting brackets - see paragraph 12 (see illustration).

Rear bump stop - P100 models

19 Working underneath the vehicle, unscrew the two securing nuts and washers from the bump stop studs, and withdraw the bump stop (see illustration).

20 Refitting is a reversal of removal.

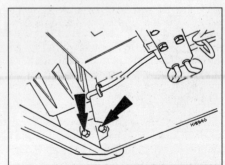

30.19 Rear bump stop securing nut locations (arrowed) - P100 models

32.5a Radiator grille panel upper retaining clip - models from 1987

32.5b Radiator grille panel lower retaining clip - models from 1987

31 Bumper trim moulding - renewal

New bumpers are supplied without the trim moulding fitted. Special primer and adhesive tape are specified by the manufacturer to retain the moulding: it is suggested that a Ford dealer is consulted for further details.

A damaged moulding can be removed by prising it from the bumper using a screwdriver.

32 Radiator grille panel - removal and refitting

Models up to 1987

1 With the bonnet raised, remove the four grille panel securing screws from the top of the front panel.
2 Lift the grille panel from its lower mounting bushes, and withdraw it from the vehicle.
3 Refitting is a reversal of removal, but ensure that the lower mounting lugs are correctly located in their bushes.

Models from 1987

4 With the bonnet raised, remove the two grille panel securing screws from the front face of the panel.
5 Release the upper and lower grille retaining clips, and withdraw the grille panel from the vehicle **(see illustrations)**.
6 Refitting is a reversal of removal, but align the grille panel carefully before tightening the securing screws.

32.8 Removing the later type front grille panel

Models from 1990

7 With the bonnet raised, remove the two securing screws from the top of the grille panel.
8 Slide the panel towards the driver's side of the vehicle, then pull the panel forwards to release the retaining clips **(see illustration)**.
9 Refitting is a reversal of removal.

33 Windscreen cowl panel - removal and refitting

Removal

1 Open the bonnet and disconnect the windscreen washer hose at the T-piece connector.
2 Remove both windscreen wiper arm assemblies.
3 Remove the single securing screw from each end of the cowl panel.
4 On models up to 1987, prise out the screw covers and remove the eight plastic screws securing the cowl panel to the body. Withdraw the panel.
5 On models from 1987, prise out the screw covers and remove the plastic securing screws. Pull the front edge of the cowl panel upwards to disengage the front fixing clips, then move the panel to the left and then to the right to disengage the hooks on the panel underside. Withdraw the panel.

Refitting

6 Refitting is a reversal of removal.

34.2 Exterior rear pillar trim panel securing nut locations (arrowed) - Saloon models

A Heated rear window wiring plug

34 Exterior rear pillar trim panel (Saloon models) - renewal

1 Remove the interior rear pillar trim panel.
2 Unscrew the three now exposed securing nuts and withdraw the exterior trim panel **(see illustration)**.
3 Refitting is a reversal of removal, but do not overtighten the securing nuts, as this may result in damage to the rubber seals.

35 Cab air vent panel (P100 models) - renewal

1 Remove the cab interior side trim panel.
2 Working inside the cab, remove the two rubber grommets from the rear pillar, then unscrew the two now exposed nuts, and withdraw the air vent panel.
3 Refitting is a reversal of removal.

36 Wheel arch liners - renewal

1 Where fitted, the wheel arch liners may be retained by self-tapping screws, plastic clips, or a combination of both.
2 To remove a liner, simply unscrew the retaining screws, or where plastic clips are fitted, release them by turning with a screwdriver **(see illustration)**.
3 Refitting is a reversal of removal.

37 Fuel filler flap - removal and refitting

Removal

1 Open the filler flap and the tailgate or boot lid, as applicable.
2 Remove the fuel filler cap and then remove the screw securing the filler housing to the fuel tank neck **(see illustration)**.
3 Working inside the luggage compartment, depress the filler housing retaining tangs, and push the assembly out through the body panel. Recover the gasket.

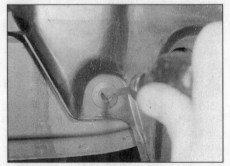

36.2 Releasing a wheel arch liner plastic clip

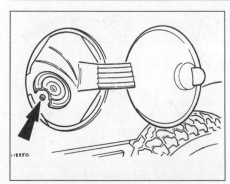

37.2 Fuel filler housing securing screw (arrowed)

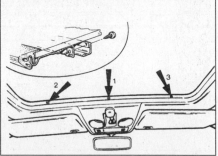

39.1 Sunroof lower frame-to-glass panel securing screws and clips (arrowed) *Tighten screws in the order shown when refitting*

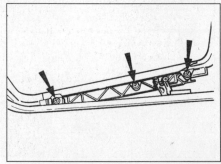

39.2 Sunroof glass panel-to-sliding gear securing screws (one side shown for clarity)

4 Immerse the housing assembly in a container of hot water for approximately ten minutes, then prise the hinge cover from the housing, and using a screwdriver, prise the filler flap hinge legs out of the sockets in the housing.

Refitting

5 Commence refitting by warming the filler flap and housing, as during removal, then push the flap hinge legs into the housing.
6 Further refitting is a reversal of removal, ensuring that the housing gasket and retaining tangs are correctly located.

38 Inner gutter weatherstrip (Saloon, Hatchback and Estate models) - removal and refitting

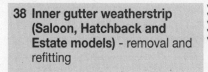

Removal

1 Open both the front and rear doors to expose the relevant weatherstrip.
2 Carefully pull the weatherstrip from the base of the front pillar, taking care to release the flap which is stuck to the pillar with adhesive.
3 Pull the remainder of the weatherstrip from its flange.
4 Carefully clean the old adhesive from the base of the front pillar using methylated spirits.

Refitting

5 Commence refitting by pushing the weatherstrip onto its flange at the top corner of the rear pillar, running it for approximately 200 mm (8.0 in) along the horizontal flange.
6 Align the flap on the front pillar, and apply a thin bead of rubber-based adhesive to the flap. Refit the flap to the front pillar, ensuring that it lies naturally. Should the flap not lie naturally, or start to lift, temporarily secure it in position with adhesive tape.
7 Refit the remainder of the weatherstrip, starting at the front pillar and working rearwards, then close the doors and allow the adhesive to dry for at least an hour.

39 Sunroof - removal, refitting and adjustment

Glass panel - removal and refitting

1 Open the sunblind and remove the three screws and clips shown **(see illustration)** then slide the lower frame rearwards into the roof.
2 Remove the six screws securing the glass panel to the sliding gear **(see illustration)** then push the glass panel upwards and remove it from outside of the vehicle, taking care not to damage the paintwork.
3 Commence refitting by securing the glass panel to the sliding gear with the six screws.
4 Adjust the sunroof as described in paragraphs 10 and 12 to 14 inclusive, but note that there is no need to open and close the roof before checking adjustment.
5 Refit the three clips to the glass panel, then pull the lower frame forwards and secure it to the glass panel with the three screws. Tighten the screws in the order shown.

Complete assembly - removal and refitting

6 Fully open the sliding roof panel, then remove the screw securing the roof operating handle and detach the handle.
7 Remove the four screws on each side and the two screws at the front securing the sliding roof assembly to the roof tray.
8 Lift the front rail and carefully withdraw the assembly forwards from the roof tray, taking care not to damage the paintwork.
9 Refitting is a reversal of removal, but on completion, adjust the sunroof as described in paragraph 10 onwards, and if necessary adjust the position of the roof operating handle so that with the roof in its closed position, the handle can fold into its recess.

Adjustment

10 Fully open and close the sliding roof, then check that the front edge of the glass panel is flush with, or a maximum of 2.0 mm (0.08 in) *below* the adjacent roof panel. The rear edge of the glass panel should be flush with, or a

maximum of 2.0 mm (0.08 in) *above* the adjacent roof panel.
11 If adjustment is necessary, remove the three screws securing the glass panel to the lower frame, then slide the lower frame rearwards into the roof.
12 To adjust the front edge of the glass panel, loosen the front and centre screws securing the glass panel to the sliding gear.
13 To adjust the rear edge of the glass panel, loosen the rear and centre screws securing the glass panel to the sliding gear (see illustration 39.1).
14 On completion of adjustment, tighten the glass panel-to-sliding gear securing screws.
15 Pull the lower frame forwards and secure it to the glass panel with the three screws. Tighten the screws in the order shown.

40 Interior trim panels - general information

1 The method of removal and refitting for most interior trim panels is self-explanatory. The panels are fixed in place either by screws, which may be concealed by plastic blanking plugs in some cases, or by clips on the rear of the panel.
2 When removing a panel secured by clips, prise the panel as close as possible to each clip, using a forked tool similar to that shown (see illustration, 17.6b) or a wide-bladed screwdriver to prevent damage to the panel.
3 Refer to the relevant Sections of this Chapter for removal and refitting details of the major trim panels.

41 Interior pillar trim panels - removal and refitting

Front pillar

1 Remove the two trim panel securing screws and withdraw the panel (see illustration)..
2 Refitting is a reversal of removal.

Centre pillar

3 Where applicable, lever the seat belt height adjuster button downwards and detach the button by removing the two securing screws.

12

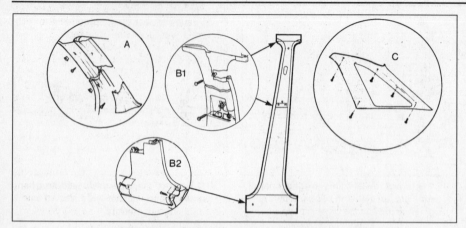

41.1 Interior pillar trim panel fixings - Hatchback models

A   Front pillar trim panel   B2 Centre pillar lower trim panel
B1 Centre pillar upper trim panel   C   Rear pillar trim panel

4 Unscrew the upper seat belt anchor nut, noting the fitted positions of any washers and spacers so that they can be refitted in their original positions.
5 Remove the two securing screws, and withdraw the upper trim panel.
6 Remove the two or three securing screws as applicable, and withdraw the lower trim panel, passing the seat belt webbing through the panel as it is removed.
7 Refitting is a reversal of removal.

Rear pillar

Saloon models

8 Remove the rear seat cushion.
9 Unbolt the lower seat belt anchor.
10 On models with fixed rear seats, remove the backrest.
11 On models with folding rear seats, remove the side cushion.
12 Remove the two securing screws from the base of the pillar trim panel, then pull the trim panel from the pillar, passing the seat belt webbing through the panel as it is removed.
13 Refitting is a reversal of removal.

Hatchback models

14 Remove the rear seat side cushion.
15 Remove the rear parcel shelf, and where applicable unbolt the rear seat belt upper anchor and spacer.
16 On "high specification" models, lift the seat catch release lever, push out the pin securing the link rod to the lever and disconnect the link rod.
17 Remove the securing screws from the rear parcel shelf support (nine screws on models up to 1987, eight screws from 1987 onwards) and on "high specification" models remove the two bolts securing the rear seat catch assembly to the wheel arch, then withdraw the catch assembly. Remove the rear parcel shelf support.
18 Remove the five securing screws and detach the rear pillar trim panel.
19 Refitting is a reversal of removal, but where applicable check the operation of the rear seat catch on completion.

P100 models

20 Remove the cover from the seat belt upper anchor, then unscrew the anchor, noting the fitted positions of any washers and spacers so that they can be refitted in their original positions.
21 Remove the three securing screws from the upper trim panel, and withdraw the panel **(see illustration)**.
22 Remove the three securing screws from the lower trim panel, then pull the panel away from the pillar and pass the seat belt webbing through the slot.
23 Withdraw the trim panel by disengaging it from the seat belt inertia reel mounting bracket.
24 Refitting is a reversal of removal.

42 Cab interior trim panels (P100 models) - removal and refitting

Side trim panel

1 Remove the rear pillar trim panel.
2 Remove the side trim panel by prising out the four expander pins from the clips, then pulling out the clips and withdrawing the panel.
3 Refitting is a reversal of removal.

Upper rear trim panel

4 Remove the side trim panels from both sides of the cab as previously described in this Section.
5 Remove the cab rear window.
6 Prise out the four expander pins from the trim panel clips beneath the rear window aperture, then pull out the clips **(see illustration)**.
7 Remove the blanking covers, then remove the three securing screws from the rear of the headlining.
8 Lower the rear of the headlining and remove the trim panel.
9 Refitting is a reversal of removal.

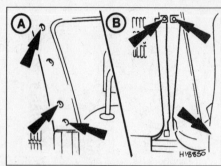

41.21 Interior rear pillar trim panel fixings (arrowed) - P100 models

A Upper trim panel   B Lower trim panel

Lower rear trim panel

10 Remove the side trim panels from both sides of the cab as previously described in this Section.
11 Prise out the four expander pins from the trim panel clips beneath the rear window aperture, then pull out the clips.
12 Pull the jack handle from its two retaining clips, then remove the clips.
13 Prise out the two expander pins from the trim panel lower clips, then pull out the clips.
14 Pull the bottom edge of the trim panel away from the rear of the cab, and slide the panel out from under the upper trim panel.
15 Refitting is a reversal of removal.

43 Facia panels - removal and refitting

Models up to 1992

1 Note the locations of the facia panel securing screws **(see illustration)**. Disconnect the battery negative lead.

Driver's side lower facia panel

2 Remove the two securing screws and withdraw the side trim panel from the right-hand side of the footwell **(see illustration)**.
3 Remove the securing screws and unclip the lower and upper steering column shrouds.

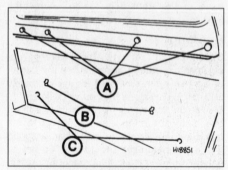

42.6 Cab interior rear panel fixings - P100 models

A Upper and lower trim panel fixings
B Jack handle retaining clips
C Lower trim panel fixings

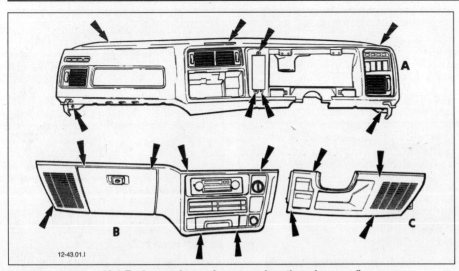

43.1 Facia panel securing screw locations (arrowed)

A Upper facia panel
B Passenger side lower facia panel
C Driver's side lower facia panel

4 Unclip the trim panel from the lower edge of the lower facia panel.

5 Remove the four securing screws and withdraw the lower facia panel. Where applicable, disconnect the loudspeaker wiring.

6 Refitting is a reversal of removal.

Passenger side lower facia panel

7 Remove the two securing screws and withdraw the side trim panel from the left-hand side of the footwell.

8 Remove the centre console to gain access to the lower facia panel securing screws.

9 Unclip the trim panel from the lower edge of the lower facia panel.

10 Unscrew the seven securing screws and withdraw the lower facia panel. Disconnect the wiring from the loudspeaker, glovebox lamp, ashtray lamp, heater switch, cigarette lighter, radio/cassette player, and loudspeaker balance control, as applicable. It is advisable to label the wiring plugs to assist refitting in the correct positions.

11 Refitting is a reversal of removal.

Upper facia panel

12 Remove the lower facia panels as described previously in this Section.

43.2 Withdraw the side trim panel from the footwell

13 Remove the instrument panel (Chapter 13).

14 Where applicable, remove the trip computer and "door ajar" monitor.

15 Remove the heater control panel.

16 Prise out the front and rear foglamp, heated rear window and heated windscreen switches and the instrument light and intermittent wiper rheostats, as applicable, from the upper facia panel, and disconnect their wiring plugs. It is advisable to label the wiring plugs to assist refitting in the correct positions.

17 Remove the five securing screws and withdraw the upper facia panel through the passenger door aperture. Disconnect the heater vent hoses, and ensure that any remaining wiring is disconnected and where applicable unclipped from the facia panel.

18 Refitting is a reversal of removal.

Models from 1992

19 A restyled facia is fitted from 1992. The procedures for removal and refitting of the various panels are essentially as described above, noting the following points (**see illustration**).

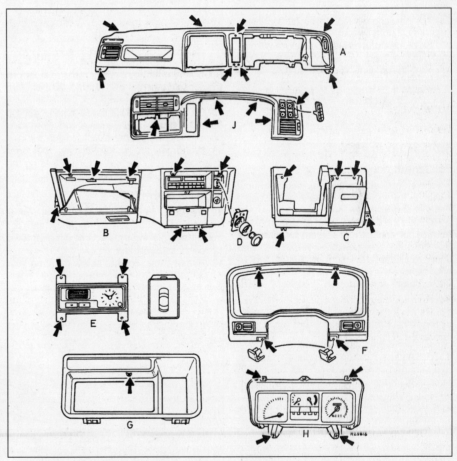

43.19 Facia components and securing screw locations (arrowed) - models from 1992

A Upper facia panel
B Passenger's side lower facia panel
C Driver's side lower facia panel
D Heater fan control cover and bezel
E Clock/auxiliary warning system display
F Instrument panel surround and screw covers
G Clock/auxiliary warning system display surround
H Instrument cluster
J Instrument cluster surround

12

44.3a Removing a rear upper console panel front retaining screw - "high specification" model

20 On models with an adjustable steering column, fully extend and lower the steering column before attempting to remove any of the panels on the driver's side.
21 The steering column shrouds are secured by six screws - five through the lower shroud, and one through the upper shroud.
22 If necessary, remove the centre console.
23 The driver's side lower facia panel is secured by five screws.
24 The passenger's side lower facia panel is secured by eight screws.
25 On models with an alarm, the alarm warning light must be disconnected and removed before removing the upper facia panel.

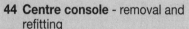

44 Centre console - removal and refitting

Models up to 1990

Full length console

1 Where applicable, prise the electric window switches from the front upper console panel and disconnect the wiring.
2 Remove the three securing screws from the front upper console panel, then withdraw the panel over the gear selector lever, at the same time releasing the rubber gaiter where applicable.
3 On "high specification" models, where applicable prise the electric window switches from the rear upper console panel and disconnect the wiring. Remove the five securing screws and withdraw the rear upper console panel **(see illustrations)**.
4 On "low specification" models, remove the two securing screws and release the single rear clip, then withdraw the rear upper console panel.
5 Where applicable, remove the two screws securing the lower console centre bracket to the transmission tunnel, and remove the bracket.
6 Remove the six screws securing the lower console panel, and withdraw the panel **(see illustrations)**.
7 Refitting is a reversal of removal.

Short console

8 Prise out the blanking plug, and remove the rear console securing screw.

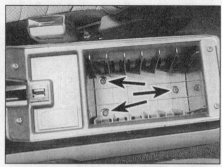

44.3b Rear upper console panel rear retaining screws (arrowed)

44.6b . . . centre securing screw . . .

9 On automatic transmission models, lift out the console tray mat and remove the front two console securing screws.
10 On manual gearbox models, prise out the blanking plugs and remove the front two console securing screws.
11 Withdraw the console over the gear selector lever, at the same time releasing the rubber gaiter where applicable.

Models from 1990

12 Remove the switch assembly (after disconnecting the battery negative lead), or remove the blanking plate from the gear lever surround, as applicable.
13 Remove the securing screw from the gear

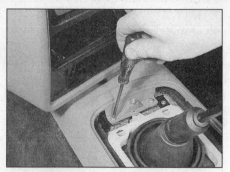

44.6a Removing a lower console panel front securing screw . . .

44.6c . . . and rear securing screw

lever surround, and withdraw the gear lever surround from the console by releasing the two securing clips.
14 Remove the seven console securing screws **(see illustration)**.
15 Chock the rear wheels, then release the handbrake lever.
16 Jack up the vehicle and support it on axle stands (see "*Jacking and Vehicle Support*"). Disconnect the handbrake equaliser from the linkage on the underbody.
17 Raise the handbrake lever fully, and lift the console over the handbrake lever.
18 Refitting is a reversal of removal, but on completion, check the handbrake/cable adjustment.

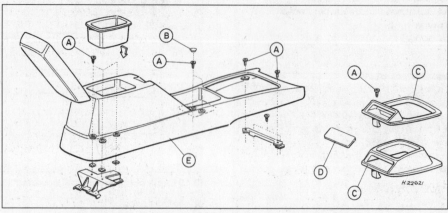

44.14 Centre console components - models from 1990

A Screw
B Screw cover
C Gear lever surround
D Blanking plate
E Centre console

45 Overhead console - removal and refitting

Removal

1 Disconnect the battery negative lead.
2 Open the sunroof.
3 On models with a manually-operated sunroof, remove the sunroof handle securing screw, then withdraw the handle and trim plate.
4 On models with an electric sunroof, remove the operating switch.
5 Remove the courtesy lamp, if necessary, then remove the two screws from the front of the console (see illustration).
6 Remove the two screws securing the rear of the console to the sunroof flange, and withdraw the console.

Refitting

7 Refitting is a reversal of removal.

46 Headling - removal and refitting

Saloon, Hatchback and Estate models

1 On Saloons, remove the rear seat back.
2 Loosen the upper screws of all the pillar trim panels touching the headlining.
3 Prise off the covers and remove the screws from the passenger grab handles. Withdraw the grab handles. Similarly, prise off the blanking covers and remove the headlining securing screws from the driver's position.
4 Disconnect the battery negative lead, then prise the courtesy light(s) from the headlining or overhead console. Disconnect the wiring and remove the courtesy light(s).
5 Where applicable, remove the two securing screws and withdraw the overhead console.
6 Remove the sunroof (where fitted). The headlining is folded around the sunroof aperture flange and is held in place with adhesive tape and a moulding which must be removed.
7 Support the headlining, then remove the screws and withdraw the sun visors and clips. Where applicable, disconnect the wiring from the vanity mirror lamp.
8 On Estate models, remove the two plastic fasteners from the headlining between the rear door and tailgate pillars.
9 Remove the two plastic fasteners from the rear of the headlining, and withdraw the headlining through the luggage compartment.
10 Refitting is a reversal of removal.

P100 models

11 Loosen the front pillar trim panel upper securing screws.
12 Prise off the covers and remove the screws from the passenger grab handle. Withdraw the grab handle.

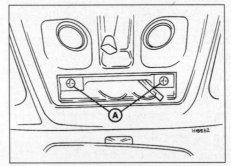

45.5 Overhead console securing screws (A)

13 Prise off the blanking cover and remove the headlining securing screw from the driver's side.
14 Disconnect the battery negative lead, then prise the courtesy light from the headlining. Disconnect the wiring and remove the courtesy light.
15 Support the headlining, then remove the screws and withdraw the sun visors and clips.
16 Remove the blanking covers, and the three securing screws from the rear of the headlining, then withdraw the headlining through one of the door apertures.
17 Refitting is a reversal of removal.

47 Seats - removal and refitting

Front seat

1 Slide the seat fully forwards, and on seats with height adjustment unhook the tension spring from the rear crosstube. Where applicable, disconnect the wiring from the seat heating pad(s).
2 Unscrew and remove the two bolts from the inner rear seat mounting bracket and the single bolt from the outer rear seat mounting bracket (see illustration).
3 Slide the seat fully rearwards, then unscrew and remove the single bolt from each front seat mounting bracket. Withdraw the seat from the vehicle.
4 Refitting is a reversal of removal, but when fitting the front and rear mounting bolts,

47.2 Front seat inner rear mounting

tighten the inner bolts first in each case. Where applicable locate the height adjustment tension spring between the weld pips on the crosstube.

Rear seat cushion

5 Remove the single screw from each side, securing the cushion to the heel kick panel.
6 Pull the cushion forwards and remove it from the vehicle.
7 Refitting is a reversal of removal.

Rear seat backrest

Fixed rear seats

8 Remove the seat cushion as described in paragraphs 5 to 7.
9 Remove the three now exposed Torx screws from the base of the backrest.
10 Working inside the luggage compartment, remove the three nuts securing the backrest to the body.
11 Pull the backrest forwards into the passenger compartment and remove it from the vehicle. Where applicable, feed the rear seat belt straps and buckles around the edges of the backrest.
12 Refitting is a reversal of removal.

Folding rear seats

13 Release the catch and fold the seat backrest forwards.
14 Remove the two Torx screws from each backrest hinge.
15 Pull the backrest forwards into the passenger compartment and remove it from the vehicle. Where applicable, feed the rear seat belt straps and buckles around the edges of the backrest.
16 Refitting is a reversal of removal, but where necessary adjust the position of the seat catch striker to achieve correct operation of the catch.

Rear seat side cushion

Saloon models

17 Working in the luggage compartment, remove the nut from the side cushion stud.
18 Working in the passenger compartment, remove the rear seat cushion as described in paragraphs 5 and 6.
19 Expose the seat backrest hinge bolt by removing the cover, then remove the bolt.
20 Pull the top of the side cushion forwards to disengage the stud from the body.
21 Straighten the metal retaining tangs at the base of the side cushion, then withdraw the cushion.
22 Refitting is a reversal of removal.

Hatchback and Estate models

23 Fold down the rear seat backrest.
24 Carefully bend back the side cushion lower retaining tangs, then unhook the cushion from the upper fixing on the rear parcel shelf support (see illustration).
25 Refitting is a reversal of removal.

12

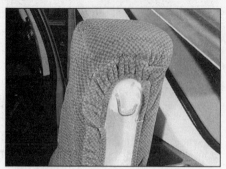

47.24 Rear seat side cushion removed exposing upper fixing hook

Rear seat armrest

26 Fold the rear seat backrest forwards, and remove the three armrest securing screws.
27 Remove the armrest by prising out the trim clips securing the cover material to the seat backrest.
28 Refitting is a reversal of removal.

48 Rear seat catch - removal and refitting

Saloon models

1 Working in the luggage compartment, release the seat catch by pulling the release knob, or if the cable is broken, use a screwdriver to release the catch itself.
2 Fold the backrest forwards into the passenger compartment and remove the two screws shown (see illustration).
3 Detach the cover and then remove the catch from the body.
4 Disconnect the release cable and sheath from the catch.
5 Refitting is a reversal of removal, but on completion check the catch for correct operation, and if necessary adjust the position of the striker on the seat backrest to achieve satisfactory engagement with the catch.

Hatchback and Estate models

Low specification

6 Release the seat catch by pulling the release knob, and fold the backrest forwards into the passenger compartment.

48.13 Rear seat catch assembly - "high specification" Hatchback model

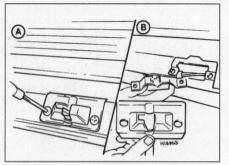

48.2 Rear seat catch fixings - Saloon models
A Remove the securing screws
B Withdraw the cover and catch

7 Unscrew the release knob from the top of the seat backrest.
8 Carefully pull the edge of the seat cover from the flange on the seat backrest, then pull the backrest cushion away from the seat panel to gain access to the catch (see illustration).
9 Remove the catch assembly by unscrewing the two securing bolts.
10 Refitting is a reversal of removal, but on completion check the catch for correct operation, and if necessary adjust the position of the striker to achieve satisfactory engagement with the catch.

High specification

11 Release the seat catch and fold the backrest forwards into the passenger compartment.
12 Remove the rear parcel shelf for improved access, then remove the screws and withdraw the cover for access to the catch.
13 Unscrew the two bolts securing the catch to the bracket on the rear wheel arch (see illustration).
14 Using a small screwdriver, push out the pin securing the link rod to the catch, then withdraw the catch.
15 If required, lift the release lever, push out the securing pin and remove the link rod. The lever can be removed by drilling out the two securing rivets from the parcel shelf support.
16 Refitting is a reversal of removal, but where applicable fit new rivets using a hand riveter to secure the release lever. On

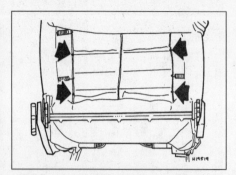

49.3 Front seat air cushion securing rings (arrowed)

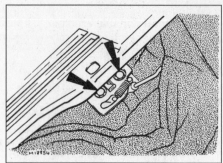

48.8 Pull back the seat cover to expose the rear seat catch securing bolts - "low spec." Hatchback and Estate models

completion check the operation of the catch and if necessary adjust the position of the striker to achieve satisfactory engagement with the catch.

49 Front seat air cushion assembly - removal and refitting

Complete assembly - removal and refitting

1 Remove the seat.
2 Straighten the seat back cover retaining tangs, and pull the cover upwards to expose the air cushion.
3 Cut through the four securing rings (see illustration) and remove the two screws securing the metal air tube to the side of the seat, then withdraw the assembly from the seat frame.
4 Refitting is a reversal of removal, using new cushion securing rings.

Air inflator ball - renewal

5 Remove the seat.
6 Remove the two screws securing the metal air tube to the side of the seat (see illustration), then cut through the plastic hose as close to the end of the metal tube as possible. Discard the old tube and the inflator ball.

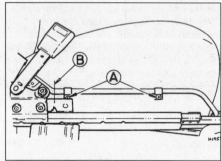

49.6 Front seat air cushion tube and inflator ball

A Air tube securing screws
B Hose cutting point

50.4 Front seat belt upper anchor fixings

A Adjuster securing screws
B Anchor nut

7 Fit a new hose clamp over the plastic hose, and warm the end of the hose in hot water until it is pliable. Push the metal tube into the plastic hose, ensuring an overlap of at least 20.0 mm (0.8 in).
8 Crimp the new clamp onto the hose to ensure an airtight seal.
9 Refit the two screws securing the tube to the side of the seat.
10 Refit the seat.

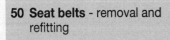

50 Seat belts - removal and refitting

Front seat belt stalk

1 Remove the front seat.
2 Detach the seat belt stalk from the seat by removing the two Torx screws.
3 Refitting is a reversal of removal.

Front seat belt assembly

4 Where applicable, prise out the cover from the height adjuster using a small coin or similar implement, and detach the adjuster by removing the two screws **(see illustration)**.
5 Unscrew the seat belt upper anchor nut, noting the fitted positions of any washers and spacers so that they can be refitted in their original positions.
6 Remove the centre pillar trim panels.
7 On 3-door models, remove the waist-level seat belt webbing guide, and remove the bolt securing the belt slider bar to the body. Disengage the slider bar from the heel kick panel, and slide off the belt webbing loop.
8 Unscrew the bolt securing the inertia reel unit to the centre pillar, noting the fitted positions of any washers and spacers so that they can be refitted in their original positions.

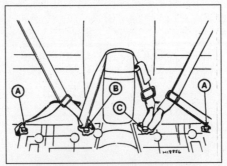

50.11 Rear seat belt lower anchors

A Inertia reel belt lower anchors
B Static belt and buckle
C Twin buckle assembly

9 Refitting is a reversal of removal, taking care to install the belt without twists in the webbing, and refitting any washers and spacers in their original positions.

Rear seat belt assembly

Saloon models

10 Remove the rear seat cushion.
11 Unbolt the relevant belt anchor(s) from the floor **(see illustration)**, noting the fitted positions of any washers and spacers so that they can be refitted in their original positions. The central lap strap and buckle assemblies can be withdrawn after unbolting the anchors.
12 To remove a side belt and inertia reel assembly, proceed as follows.
13 Remove the rear pillar trim panel.
14 Unscrew the upper belt anchor **(see illustration)**, noting the fitted positions of any washers and spacers so that they can be refitted in their original positions.
15 Unscrew the bolt securing the inertia reel unit to the rear pillar, again noting the positions of any washers and spacers.
16 Refitting is a reversal of removal, taking care to install the belt(s) without twists in the webbing, and refitting any washers and spacers in their original positions.

Hatchback and Estate models

17 Remove the rear seat cushion.
18 Unbolt the relevant belt anchor(s) from the floor **(see illustration)**, noting the fitted positions of any washers and spacers so that they can be refitted in their original positions.
19 To remove the central lapstrap and buckle assemblies, disconnect the buckle(s) from the elasticated straps by withdrawing the retaining dowel(s). To prevent the strap(s) from moving into the interior of the seat, insert

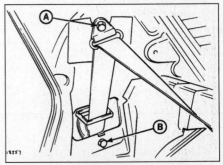

50.14 Rear seat belt upper anchor (A) and inertia reel securing bolt (B) - Saloon models

a length of wire through the strap loop(s).
20 To remove a side belt and inertia reel assembly, proceed as follows.
21 Unbolt the upper left anchor, noting the position of any washers and spacers, and allow the webbing to pass into the inertia reel unit.
22 On Hatchback models, pull back the inertia reel cover in the luggage compartment, and unbolt the inertia reel from the body, noting the position of any washers and spacers. Prise out the belt guide from the rear parcel shelf support, and push the guide, upper and lower anchors, and buckle plate through the aperture.
23 On Estate models, remove the luggage compartment side trim panel then unbolt the inertia reel unit, noting the position of any washers and spacers, and withdraw the belt assembly.
24 Refitting is a reversal of removal, taking care to install the belt(s) without twists in the webbing, and refitting any washers and spacers in their original positions. Ensure that the cut-outs in the lower anchor brackets are correctly located around the raised dimples in the floor.

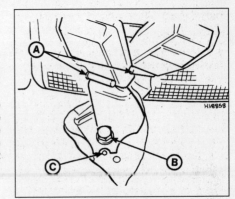

50.18 Rear seat belt twin buckle assembly lower anchor bracket - Hatchback and Estate models

A Elasticated strap retaining dowels
B Anchor belt
C Floor dimple

12

Chapter 13
Body electrical system

Contents

Degrees of difficulty

Easy, suitable for novice with little experience		Fairly easy, suitable for beginner with some experience		Fairly difficult, suitable for competent DIY mechanic	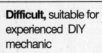	Difficult, suitable for experienced DIY mechanic		Very difficult, suitable for expert DIY or professional	

Specifications

System type .... 12 volt, negative earth

Bulbs

	Fittings	Wattage
Halogen headlamps	H4	60/55
Auxiliary driving lamps	H3	55
Front foglamps	H3	55
Side lamps	Glass base	5
Direction indicator lamps	Bayonet	21
Brake/tail lamps	Bayonet	21/4
Reversing lamp(s)	Bayonet	21
Rear foglamp(s)	Bayonet	21
Rear number plate lamps	Glass base	5
Luggage compartment lamp	Bayonet	10
Underbonnet lamp	Bayonet	10
Courtesy lamp(s)	Bayonet	10
Map reading lamps	Glass base	5
Vanity mirror illumination lamp	Festoon	3
Glove compartment lamp	Glass base	3
Ashtray lamp	Glass base	1.2
Warning lamps	Glass base	1.2 or 2.5
Instrument illumination lamps	Glass base	1.2 or 2.5
Heater control illumination lamp	Glass base	1
Automatic transmission gear selector lamp	Bayonet	1.2
Clock illumination lamp	Bayonet	1.4
Cigarette lighter lamp	Glass base	1.2

Torque wrench settings

	Nm	lbf ft
Trip computer fuel flow sensor unit fuel pipe unions	14 to 17	10 to 13

1 General information and precautions

General information

The electrical system is of the 12 volt. negative earth type. Electricity is generated by an alternator, belt-driven from the crankshaft pulley. A lead-acid storage battery provides a reserve of power for starting and when the demands of the system temporarily exceed the alternator output.

The battery negative terminal is connected to "earth" - vehicle metal - and most electrical system components are wired so that they only receive a positive feed, the current returning via vehicle metal. This means that the component mounting forms part of the circuit. Loose or corroded mountings can therefore cause apparent electrical faults.

Many semiconductor devices are used in the electrical system, both in the "black boxes" which control vehicle functions and in other components. Semiconductors are very sensitive to excessive (or wrong polarity) voltage, and to extremes of heat. Observe the appropriate precautions to avoid damage.

Precautions

It is necessary to take extra care when working on the electrical system to avoid damage to semi-conductor devices (diodes and transistors), and to avoid the risk of personal injury. In addition to the precautions given in the "Safety first!" Section at the beginning of this manual, take note of the following points when working on the system.

Always remove rings, watches, etc before working on the electrical system. Even with the battery disconnected, capacitive discharge could occur if a component live terminal is earthed through a metal object. This could cause a shock or nasty burn.

Do not reverse the battery connections. Components such as the alternator or any other having semi-conductor circuitry could be irreparably damaged.

If the engine is being started using jump leads and a slave battery, connect the batteries *positive to positive* and *negative to negative.* This also applies when connecting a battery charger.

Never disconnect the battery terminals, or alternator multi-plug connector, when the engine is running.

The battery leads and alternator multi-plug must be disconnected before carrying out any electric welding on the car.

Never use an ohmmeter of the type incorporating a hand cranked generator for circuit or continuity testing.

2 Electrical fault-finding - general information

Note: *Refer to the precautions given in "Safety first!" and in Section 1 of this Chapter before starting work. The following tests relate to testing of the main electrical circuits, and should not be used to test delicate electronic circuits (such as anti-lock braking systems), particularly where an electronic control unit (ECU) is involved.*

General

1 A typical electrical circuit consists of an electrical component, any switches, relays, motors, fuses, fusible links or circuit breakers related to that component, and the wiring and connectors which link the component to both the battery and the chassis. To help to pinpoint a problem in an electrical circuit, wiring diagrams are included at the end of this Chapter.

2 Before attempting to diagnose an electrical fault, first study the appropriate wiring diagram, to obtain a more complete understanding of the components included in the particular circuit concerned. The possible sources of a fault can be narrowed down by noting whether other components related to the circuit are operating properly. If several components or circuits fail at one time, the problem is likely to be related to a shared fuse or earth connection.

3 Electrical problems usually stem from simple causes, such as loose or corroded connections, a faulty earth connection, a blown fuse, a melted fusible link, or a faulty relay. Visually inspect the condition of all fuses, wires and connections in a problem circuit before testing the components. Use the wiring diagrams to determine which terminal connections will need to be checked, in order to pinpoint the trouble-spot.

4 The basic tools required for electrical fault-finding include: a circuit tester or voltmeter (a 12-volt bulb with a set of test leads can also be used for certain tests), a self-powered test light (sometimes known as a continuity tester), an ohmmeter (to measure resistance), a battery and set of test leads, and a jumper wire, preferably with a circuit breaker or fuse incorporated, which can be used to bypass suspect wires or electrical components. Before attempting to locate a problem with test instruments, use the wiring diagram to determine where to make the connections.

5 To find the source of an intermittent wiring fault (usually due to a poor or dirty connection, or damaged wiring insulation), an integrity test can be performed on the wiring, which involves moving the wiring by hand, to see if the fault occurs as the wiring is moved. It should be possible to narrow down the source of the fault to a particular section of wiring. This method of testing can be used in conjunction with any of the tests described in the following sub-Sections.

6 Apart from problems due to poor connections, two basic types of fault can occur in an electrical circuit - open-circuit, or short-circuit.

7 Open-circuit faults are caused by a break somewhere in the circuit, which prevents current from flowing. An open-circuit fault will prevent a component from working, but will not cause the relevant circuit fuse to blow.

8 Short-circuit faults are caused by a "short" somewhere in the circuit, which allows the current flowing in the circuit to "escape" along an alternative route, usually to earth. Short-circuit faults are normally caused by a breakdown in wiring insulation, which allows a feed wire to touch either another wire, or an earthed component such as the bodyshell. A short-circuit fault will normally cause the relevant circuit fuse to blow.

Note: *A short-circuit that occurs in the wiring between a circuit's battery supply and its fuse will not cause the fuse in that particular circuit to blow. This part of the circuit is unprotected - bear this in mind when fault-finding on the vehicle's electrical system.*

Finding an open-circuit

9 To check for an open-circuit, connect one lead of a circuit tester or voltmeter to either the negative battery terminal or a known good earth.

10 Connect the other lead to a connector in the circuit being tested, preferably nearest to the battery or fuse.

11 Switch on the circuit, bearing in mind that some circuits are live only when the ignition switch is moved to a particular position.

12 If voltage is present (indicated either by the tester bulb lighting or a voltmeter reading, as applicable), this means that the section of the circuit between the relevant connector and the battery is problem-free.

13 Continue to check the remainder of the circuit in the same fashion.

14 When a point is reached at which no voltage is present, the problem must lie between that point and the previous test point with voltage. Most problems can be traced to a broken, corroded or loose connection.

Finding a short-circuit

15 To check for a short-circuit, first disconnect the load(s) from the circuit (loads are the components which draw current from a circuit, such as bulbs, motors, heating elements, etc).

16 Remove the relevant fuse from the circuit, and connect a circuit tester or voltmeter to the fuse connections.

17 Switch on the circuit, bearing in mind that some circuits are live only when the ignition switch is moved to a particular position.

18 If voltage is present (indicated either by the tester bulb lighting or a voltmeter reading, as applicable), this means that there is a short-circuit.

19 If no voltage is present, but the fuse still blows with the load(s) connected, this indicates an internal fault in the load(s).

Finding an earth fault

20 The battery negative terminal is connected to "earth" - the metal of the engine/transmission and the car body - and most systems are wired so that they only receive a positive feed, the current returning via the metal of the car body. This means that the component mounting and the body form part of that circuit. Loose or corroded mountings can therefore cause a range of electrical faults, ranging from total failure of a circuit, to a puzzling partial fault. In particular, lights may shine dimly (especially when another circuit sharing the same earth point is in operation), motors (eg wiper motors or the radiator cooling fan motor) may run slowly, and the operation of one circuit may have an apparently-unrelated effect on another. Note that on many vehicles, earth straps are used between certain components, such as the engine/transmission and the body, usually where there is no metal-to-metal contact between components, due to flexible rubber mountings, etc.

21 To check whether a component is properly earthed, disconnect the battery, and connect one lead of an ohmmeter to a known good earth point. Connect the other lead to the wire or earth connection being tested. The resistance reading should be zero; if not, check the connection as follows.

22 If an earth connection is thought to be faulty, dismantle the connection, and clean back to bare metal both the bodyshell and the wire terminal, or the component's earth connection mating surface. Be careful to remove all traces of dirt and corrosion, then use a knife to trim away any paint, so that a clean metal-to-metal joint is made. On reassembly, tighten the joint fasteners securely; if a wire terminal is being refitted, use serrated washers between the terminal and the bodyshell, to ensure a clean and secure connection. When the connection is remade, prevent the onset of corrosion in the future by applying a coat of petroleum jelly or silicone-based grease, or by spraying on (at regular intervals) a proprietary ignition sealer.

3 Fuses and relays - location and renewal

Location

1 The main fuses and relays are located in a box in the engine compartment on the right-hand side of the bulkhead. The circuits protected are identified by symbols on the underside of the fusebox cover. On certain models, additional relays and fuses are located in various positions beneath the facia panels. If uncertain of the location of an auxiliary relay or fuse, it is suggested that a Ford dealer is consulted, as the relay and fuse locations vary substantially depending on model.

Renewal

2 Always renew a fuse with one of identical rating and never renew it more than once without finding the source of the trouble (usually a short circuit). Always switch off the ignition before renewing a fuse or relay, and when renewing the wiper motor fuse keep the hands clear of the wiper linkage as it may return to the parked position. Note that the fuses are colour-coded as follows:

10A	Red
15A	Blue
20A	Yellow
25A	Natural
10A	Green

3 Access to the fuses and relays in the fusebox is gained by removing the loose cover and spring clip (if fitted), pulling the plastic clip and removing the cover. All fuses and relays are a push fit **(see illustrations)**. The fuse/relay plate can be released from the fusebox for access to the wiring by carefully levering the plastic lugs around the perimeter of the plate.

4 For details of direction indicator/hazard warning flasher relay removal and refitting, refer to the relevant Section of this Chapter.

3.3a Remove the loose cover for access to the fusebox cover

3.3b Fusebox cover removed to expose fuses and relays (1.8 CVH model shown)

13

4 Ignition switch and lock barrel - removal and refitting

Removal

1 Disconnect the battery negative lead.
2 For improved access, remove the securing screws and unclip the lower and upper steering column shrouds.
3 Insert the ignition key and turn to position "I", then, working through the access hole, depress the spring clip using a suitable tool and pull the key to withdraw the lock barrel and cylinder from the ignition switch housing. The spring clip access hole is shown (see illustration). Note that, on certain models, the spring clip must be released by inserting the tool through a small circular hole at the top of the switch housing, above the rectangular slot shown. Slight movement of the key may be necessary to allow removal of the barrel and cylinder.
4 To remove the lock barrel from the cylinder insert the key fully into the barrel and remove the retaining circlip, taking care not to damage the circlip location, then withdraw the key approximately 5.0 mm (0.2 in) to retract the lock barrel securing lug, and withdraw the barrel from the cylinder.
5 To remove the ignition switch, disconnect the wiring plug, then remove the two grub screws and withdraw the switch.

Refitting

6 Refitting is a reversal of removal, bearing in mind the following points.
7 Note that the lock barrel can only be fitted to the cylinder in one position, and check with the key fully inserted that the barrel can be turned from position "O" to "III" satisfactorily.
8 The open jaws of the lock barrel retaining circlip must align with the keyway register on the cylinder, and the cylinder retaining circlip must locate in the slot in the ignition switch housing.
9 On completion, check the operation of the steering lock and ignition switch in all positions.

5 Direction indicator and hazard warning flasher switch assembly - renewal

1 Disconnect the battery negative lead.
2 Remove the securing screws and unclip the lower and upper steering column shrouds.
3 Remove the two securing screws and disconnect the two wiring plugs, then withdraw the switch from the steering column.
4 Refitting is a reversal of removal.

6 Direction indicator/hazard warning flasher relay - renewal

1 Disconnect the battery negative lead.

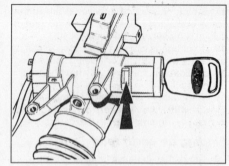

4.3 Ignition switch lock barrel spring clip location (arrowed)

2 The relay is located on a bracket above the steering column. Access is gained either by removing the driver's side lower facia panel or the instrument panel.
3 Unclip the relay from the bracket, and disconnect the wiring plug (see illustration).
4 Refitting is a reversal of removal. Check for correct operation before refitting the facia panel or instrument panel.

7 Lighting and wash/wipe switch assembly - renewal

The procedure is identical to that described for the direction indicator switch, except for the additional removal and refitting of an earth lead (see illustration).

8 Reversing lamp switch - renewal

1 For automatic transmission models, refer to Chapter 7, Part B. For manual gearbox models, proceed as follows:
2 Disconnect the battery negative lead.
3 Apply the handbrake, jack up the front of the vehicle and support on axle stands (see "Jacking and Vehicle Support").
4 Working underneath the vehicle, disconnect the wiring plug, then unscrew the switch from the gearbox extension housing.
5 Refitting is a reversal of removal, but make sure that the wiring is routed clear of the exhaust system.

7.1 Lighting and wash/wipe switch assembly earth lead securing screw (arrowed)

6.3 Direction indicator/hazard warning flasher relay location (arrowed)

9 Facia panel switches - removal and refitting

1 Disconnect the battery negative lead.

Rocker switches and push button switches

2 Using a thin-bladed screwdriver, carefully prise the switch from the facia panel.
3 Disconnect the wiring plug and withdraw the switch.
4 Refitting is a reversal of removal.

Instrument panel illumination and intermittent wipe rheostats

5 Proceed as described in paragraphs 2 to 4.

Heater blower switch

6 Carefully pull off the switch knob, using pliers with padded jaws if necessary.
7 Using a thin-bladed screwdriver, prise out the switch front plate from the facia panel.
8 Squeeze the switch retaining tabs, then withdraw the switch and disconnect the wiring plug (see illustration).
9 Refitting is a reversal of removal.

Loudspeaker balance joystick

10 Using a thin-bladed screwdriver, carefully prise the joystick front plate from the facia panel.
11 Twist the joystick assembly retaining ring anti-clockwise and remove the ring.
12 Working behind the facia panel, disconnect the wiring plug and slide out the joystick assembly.

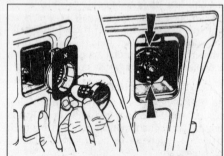

9.8 Heater blower switch removal. Switch retaining tabs arrowed

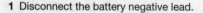

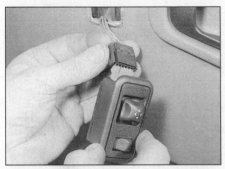

10.3 Disconnect the wiring plug from the door mirror switch - models up to 1987

13 Refitting is a reversal of removal, but note that the wiring plug can only be fitted in one position, and ensure that the joystick assembly locating lug engages in the corresponding hole in the facia panel.

10 Electric door mirror switch - removal and refitting

1 Disconnect the battery negative lead.

Models up to 1987

2 Using a thin-bladed screwdriver, carefully prise the switch from the door trim panel.
3 Disconnect the wiring plug and withdraw the switch (see illustration).
4 Refitting is a reversal of removal.

Models from 1987

5 Prise the securing screw cover from the

11.6 Prise the trim insert from the steering wheel, followed by the centre disc - models from 1987

11.14 Horn switch slip ring contact finger removal

mirror control panel, then remove the screw and withdraw the control panel.
6 Depress the switch retaining tang, then withdraw the switch from the control panel and disconnect the wiring plug.
7 Refitting is a reversal of removal.

11 Horn switch assembly - removal and refitting

1 Disconnect the battery negative lead.

Switch

Models up to 1987

2 Pull the trim insert from the centre of the steering wheel, and disconnect the lead from the horn push.
3 Disconnect the two leads from the horn slip ring, then remove the two securing screws and withdraw the switch assembly (see illustration).
4 Refitting is a reversal of removal, but check the operation of the switch on completion.

Models from 1987

5 Using a thin-bladed screwdriver, carefully prise the trim insert from the centre of the steering wheel. Disconnect the wire.
6 Prise the steering wheel centre disc from the steering wheel, and disconnect the wire (see illustration).
7 Refitting is a reversal of removal.

Slip ring

8 Remove the steering wheel.
9 On models up to 1987, remove the switch as described in paragraph 3.
10 Release the three slip ring retaining tangs and withdraw the slip ring from the steering wheel.
11 Refitting is a reversal of removal.

Slip ring contact finger

12 Remove the steering wheel.
13 Remove the securing screws and unclip the lower and upper steering column shrouds.
14 Disconnect the contact finger wiring plug, and pull the contact finger housing from its mounting (see illustration).
15 Refitting is a reversal of removal.

12.3 Withdrawing a courtesy lamp switch

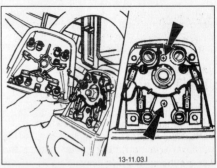

11.3 Horn switch removal - models up to 1987. Switch securing screws arrowed

12 Courtesy lamp switch - renewal

1 Disconnect the battery negative lead.
2 Open the door and remove the switch securing screw.
3 Withdraw the switch from the door pillar and pull the wiring out sufficiently to prevent it from springing back into the pillar (see illustration).
4 Disconnect the wiring and remove the switch.
5 Refitting is a reversal of removal.

13 Luggage compartment lamp switch - removal and refitting

1 Disconnect the battery negative lead.

Models up to 1987

2 A level-sensitive switch is fitted to the tailgate.
3 Unclip the tailgate trim panel.
4 Disconnect the wiring from the switch terminal, then remove the securing screw and withdraw the switch, noting its fitted position (see illustration).
5 Refitting is a reversal of removal, but ensure that the switch is refitted in its original position, as noted during removal, and test the operation of the switch on completion.

Models from 1987

6 Where applicable, unclip the tailgate/boot trim panel.

13.4 Luggage compartment lamp switch location - models up to 1987

7 Unclip the switch from the lock assembly, disconnect the wiring plug and remove the switch.

8 Refitting is a reversal of removal.

14 Handbrake "on" warning lamp switch - renewal

1 Disconnect the battery negative lead.

2 Working inside the vehicle, remove the handbrake lever rubber gaiter and/or the centre console, as necessary.

3 Disconnect the wiring connector from the switch, then remove the two securing screws and withdraw the switch from the handbrake lever **(see illustration)**.

4 Refitting is a reversal of removal.

15 Brake lamp switch - renewal

1 Disconnect the battery negative lead.

2 Unclip the trim panel from the lower edge of the driver's side lower facia trim panel. If required for improved access, remove the lower facia trim panel.

3 Disconnect the wiring from the terminal on the switch, then twist the switch anti-clockwise and remove it **(see illustration)**.

4 When refitting, insert the switch into its aperture in the pedal bracket, then push the switch inwards until the switch barrel touches the pedal. *Ensure that the pedal is not moved from its stop.* Twist the switch clockwise to lock it in position. No further adjustment is necessary.

5 Further refitting is a reversal of removal, but check the operation of the switch on completion.

16 Oil pressure warning lamp switch - renewal

1 Disconnect the battery negative lead.

2 The switch is located towards the left-hand rear of the cylinder block on SOHC models **(see illustration)**, towards the right-hand rear of the cylinder block on CVH models and on the right-hand side of the cylinder block, between the core plugs, on DOHC models.

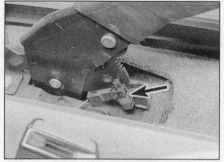

14.3 Handbrake "on" warning lamp switch location (arrowed)

3 Disconnect the wiring from the switch terminal, then unscrew and withdraw the switch. Be prepared for some oil spillage.

4 Clean the threads of the switch and its seat before refitting.

5 After refitting, run the engine and check for oil leaks around the switch, then stop the engine and check the oil level, topping-up if necessary.

17 Electric sunroof components - removal and refitting

Switch

1 Disconnect the battery negative lead.

2 Using a thin-bladed screwdriver, carefully prise the switch from the overhead console.

3 Disconnect the wiring plug and remove the switch.

4 Refitting is a reversal of removal.

Relay

5 Remove the overhead console.

6 Unclip the relay from the motor assembly and disconnect the wiring plug **(see illustration)**.

7 Refitting is a reversal of removal.

Motor

8 Remove the overhead console.

9 Disconnect the motor wiring plug.

10 Unscrew the three securing bolts, and withdraw the motor assembly from the roof.

11 Refitting is a reversal of removal, but ensure that the drive gear is aligned with the roof operating mechanism.

15.3 Brake lamp switch location (arrowed)

18 Cigarette lighter - renewal

1 Disconnect the battery negative lead.

2 Working behind the facia panel, disconnect the wiring, then push out the lighter assembly through the front of the facia panel.

3 If required, the illumination ring assembly can now be withdrawn after removing the bulbholder.

4 Refitting is a reversal of removal.

19 Clock - removal and refitting

1 Disconnect the battery negative lead.

Standard clock

2 Using a thin-bladed screwdriver, carefully prise the clock from the facia panel.

3 Disconnect the wiring plug and withdraw the clock.

4 Refitting is a reversal of removal.

Multi-function digital/analogue clock

5 Remove the single screw from the top edge of the facia panel in which the clock is housed, then withdraw the facia panel.

6 Remove the four now exposed securing screws, disconnect the wiring plug, and withdraw the clock **(see illustration)**.

7 Refitting is a reversal of removal.

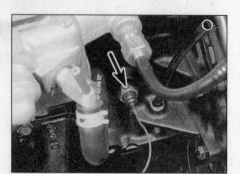

16.2 Oil pressure warning lamp switch location (arrowed) - SOHC engine

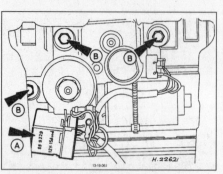

17.6 Electric sunroof relay (A) and motor securing bolts (B)

19.6 Multi-function digital/analogue clock securing screws (arrowed)

20.4a Unclip the cover . . .

20.4b . . . for access to the lower right-hand instrument panel surround securing screw

20.5 Removing an upper instrument panel surround securing screw

20 Instrument panel - removal and refitting

Models up to 1992

1 Disconnect the battery negative lead.
2 Remove the securing screws and unclip the lower and upper steering column shrouds.
3 Where applicable, remove the instrument panel illumination and intermittent wiper rheostats.
4 Unclip the cover for access to the lower right-hand instrument panel surround securing screw (see illustrations).
5 Remove the two upper and two lower securing screws, and withdraw the instrument panel surround (see illustration).
6 On models fitted with a trip computer, unscrew the knurled nut and disconnect the

20.8 Withdraw the instrument panel and disconnect the wiring plugs

speedometer cable from the speed sender unit on the engine compartment bulkhead.
7 Detach the speedometer cable grommet from the engine compartment bulkhead.
8 Remove the two upper and two lower securing screws, and withdraw the instrument panel sufficiently to disconnect the speedometer cable and the wiring plugs. The speedometer cable can be released by pushing the ribbed surface towards the centre of the cable to free the catch. Remove the instrument panel (see illustration).
9 Refitting is a reversal of removal but where applicable, ensure that the speedometer cable rubber sleeve is in place over the square Inner drive on the cable connector, and not in the speedometer head.
10 On completion, pull the speedometer cable from within the engine compartment to ensure that the cable is straight between the instrument panel and the bulkhead grommet.

Models from 1992

11 The procedure is as described above but note that both instrument panel surround lower securing screws are located beneath plastic covers (see illustration).
12 The steering column shrouds are secured by six screws - five through the lower shroud, and one through the upper shroud.

21 Instrument panel components - removal and refitting

1 Remove the instrument panel.

Panel illumination and warning lamp bulbs

2 Twist the relevant bulbholder anti-clockwise and withdraw it from the printed circuit board on the rear of the instrument panel.
3 The bulbs may be either a push-fit in the bulbholder, or integral with the bulbholder in which case the bulb and bulbholder must be renewed as a unit (see illustrations).
4 Refitting is a reversal of removal.

Panel lens

5 Remove the three upper and three lower securing screws and withdraw the lens from the instrument panel.
6 Refitting is a reversal of removal, but ensure that the two locating pegs on the upper corners of the instrument panel protrude through the lens, and locate the lugs on the lower edge of the lens in the cut-outs in the instrument panel.

Printed circuit board

7 Using a thin-bladed screwdriver, unclip and remove the wiring plug socket.
8 Remove all the illumination and warning lamp bulbs as described earlier in this Section.
9 Remove all the nuts and washers from the printed circuit board terminals.
10 Unclip the printed circuit board from the retainers at the back of the instrument panel, and carefully withdraw the board over the terminal pins on the gauges.
11 Refitting is a reversal of removal.

20.11 Removing an instrument panel surround lower securing screw (cover removed)

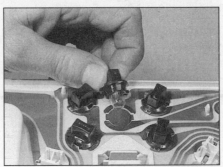

21.3a Removing an instrument panel warning lamp bulb - bulb is a push-fit in the bulbholder

21.3b Removing an instrument panel illumination bulb - bulb is integral with bulbholder

13

22.17 Trip computer fuel flow sensor unit location - carburettor models up to 1987. Bracket retaining screws arrowed

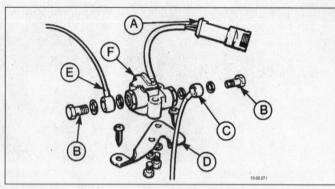

22.27 Trip computer fuel flow sensor unit - fuel injection models

A Wiring plug
B Hollow bolts
C Inlet port banjo connector
D Bracket
E Outlet port banjo connector
F Sensor unit

Speedometer

12 Remove the panel lens (paras. 5 and 6).
13 Remove the two screws securing the speedometer to the rear of the instrument panel, taking care not to lose the two brushes. Withdraw the speedometer through the front of the instrument panel.
14 Refitting is a reversal of removal.

Tachometer

Models up to 1990

15 Remove the four or five securing screws, as applicable, and separate the two halves of the instrument panel housing.
16 Remove the three securing nuts and washers from the rear of the instrument panel housing, and withdraw the tachometer.
17 Refitting is a reversal of removal, but ensure that the tachometer engages with the locating ribs in the housing around the dial edge.

Models from 1990

18 The procedure is as described above but before the tachometer can be withdrawn from the instrument panel housing, the printed circuit board must be carefully pulled from the tachometer terminals. Ensure that the printed circuit board is pushed fully home when refitting.

Fuel and temperature gauges

Models up to 1987

19 Remove the four securing screws and separate the two halves of the instrument panel housing.
20 Remove the four securing nuts and washers from the rear of the instrument panel housing, and withdraw the combined gauge assembly.
21 Refitting is a reversal of removal.

Models from 1987

22 Remove the five securing screws and separate the two halves of the instrument panel housing.
23 Remove the printed circuit board as described previously in this Section.
24 On "low specification" models, remove the two securing screws from the front of the gauge assembly, then withdraw the combined gauge assembly from the printed circuit board.

25 On "high specification" models, simply withdraw the combined gauge assembly from the printed circuit board.
26 Refitting is a reversal of removal, but on "high specification" models, ensure that the gauge assembly engages with the locating ribs in the housing around the gauge edge.

---

22 Trip computer components - removal and refitting

1 Disconnect the battery negative lead

Computer module

2 Remove the single screw from the top edge of the facia panel in which the module is housed, then withdraw the facia panel.
3 Remove the four now exposed securing screws, disconnect the wiring plug, and carefully withdraw the module. On later models a retaining lug must be depressed before the wiring plug can be disconnected.
4 Where applicable, the mounting brackets can be removed from the module by unscrewing the securing nuts.
5 If necessary, the illumination bulb can be removed from the module by twisting the bulbholder anti-clockwise using a pair of long-nosed pliers. The bulb is a push-fit in the holder.
6 Refitting is a reversal of removal.

Speed sender unit

Models up to 1987

7 The speed sender unit is located in the engine compartment on the right-hand side of the bulkhead.
8 Disconnect the plug from the sender unit.
9 Unscrew the two knurled nuts from the sender unit and disconnect the two speedometer cables.
10 Remove the three securing screws and remove the bracket and sender unit.
11 Unscrew and remove the securing nut and washer, and separate the sender unit from the bracket.
12 Refitting is a reversal of removal.

Models from 1987

13 Detach the wiring, hose retainers and

cover panel from the bulkhead to gain access to the sender unit.
14 Proceed as shown in paragraphs 7 to 9.
15 Remove the retaining nut and washer and withdraw the sender unit.
16 Refitting is a reversal of removal.

Fuel flow sensor unit

Carburettor models

17 The fuel flow sensor is located on the left-hand side of the engine compartment (see illustration).
18 Disconnect the wiring plug from the sensor unit.
19 Refer to the "Safety first!" Section at the front of the manual, and the precautions in Chapter 4, then disconnect the fuel pipes from the sensor unit. Note that on models up to 1987 there are three fuel pipe connections, and on models from 1987 there are two fuel pipe connections. Be prepared for fuel spillage.
20 Remove the three securing screws and withdraw the bracket and sender unit.
21 Unscrew the four nuts and separate the sender unit from the bracket.
22 Refitting is a reversal of removal, but ensure that the flow direction arrows on the fuel inlet and outlet ports are correctly orientated, and that the arrow on the rear of the unit points to the top.

Fuel injection models

23 The sensor is located on the left-hand side of the engine compartment.
24 Disconnect the wiring plug from the sensor unit.
25 Refer to the "Safety first!" Section at the front of the manual, and the precautions in Chapter 4, then unscrew the two union nuts and disconnect the fuel pipes from the sensor unit. Be prepared for fuel spillage.
26 Remove the two securing screws and withdraw the sensor unit.
27 Refitting is a reversal of removal, but ensure that the No 2 injector fuel pipe is fitted to the sensor unit outlet port marked with an arrow, and ensure that the union washers are in place (see illustration). Tighten the fuel pipe unions to the specified torque.

23.7 Remove the screw from the warning lamp facia panel

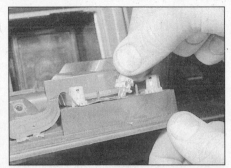

23.8 Removing an auxiliary warning lamp bulb

23.11a Removing the graphic display unit retaining screw

23 Auxiliary warning system components - location, testing, removal and refitting

Location

1 The AWS control unit, and (when fitted) the bulb failure monitor, are located behind the glovebox on models up to 1987.
2 On models from 1987, the control and bulb failure modules are located behind the driver's side footwell trim panel.

Testing

3 Thorough testing and fault finding should be left to a Ford dealer or other electrical specialist, having test equipment. Unskilled or uninformed testing may cause damage.
4 Investigation of malfunctions should begin by checking that all wiring is intact and securely connected. If checking wires or sensors for continuity, always disconnect the control unit and/or bulb failure monitor before so doing, otherwise damage may be caused.
5 Note that false oil level readings can result if the car is parked on a slope. False bulb failure warnings may occur if incorrect wattage bulbs are fitted.

Removal and refitting

6 Disconnect the battery negative lead.

Warning lamp bulbs

7 Remove the single screw from the top edge of the facia panel in which the warning lamps are housed, then withdraw the facia panel **(see illustration)**.
8 Twist the relevant bulbholder through 90° to remove it from the rear of the facia panel. The bulb is integral with the bulbholder and must be renewed as a unit **(see illustration)**.
9 Refitting is a reversal of removal.

Graphic display unit and bulbs

10 Remove the clock or trip computer.
11 Remove the display unit retaining screw and the retainer, then pull the unit forwards and disconnect the wiring plug using a thin-bladed screwdriver **(see illustrations)**.
12 To renew a bulb, remove the two securing screws and pull the circuit board from the back of the unit to reveal the bulbs. The bulbs are a push-fit.
13 Refitting is a reversal of removal.

Control unit and bulb failure monitor

14 Unclip the trim panel from the lower edge of the passenger side lower facia panel.
15 On models up to 1987, pull off the two clips to release the control unit/bulb failure monitor mounting bracket. Depress the retaining tab and disconnect the relevant wiring plug, then remove the two securing screws and withdraw the control unit/bulb failure monitor **(see illustration)**.
16 On models from 1987, release the retaining tang and carefully slide the control unit/bulb failure monitor downwards. Depress the retaining tab and disconnect the relevant wiring plug, then withdraw the control unit/bulb failure monitor.
17 Refitting is a reversal of removal. Note that when both a control unit and bulb failure monitor are fitted, the control unit wiring plug is coloured brown, and the bulb failure monitor wiring plug is coloured green.

Ice warning sender

18 This sender is located beneath the front panel on the right-hand side of the vehicle.
19 Where necessary, for improved access remove the horn.
20 Depress the two retaining tangs, disconnect the wiring plug and withdraw the sender unit from the slot in the front panel.
21 Refitting is a reversal of removal.

Door/tailgate/boot lid ajar switches

22 Remove the relevant lock.
23 Pull the switch from its location in the lock body, disconnect the wiring plug (if not already done) and withdraw the switch **(see illustration)**.

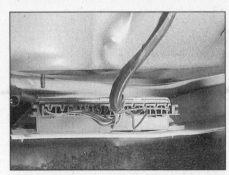

23.15 Auxiliary warning system control unit location

23.11b Disconnecting the wiring plug from the graphic display unit

24 Refitting is a reversal of removal.

Low coolant level sensor

25 Refer to Chapter 3.

Low washer fluid level switch

26 Syphon out the contents of the reservoir, then prise the switch from its grommet using a thin-bladed screwdriver. Disconnect the wiring plug.
27 Refitting is a reversal of removal, using a new grommet if necessary. Use a little liquid detergent as a lubricant.
28 On completion, refill the reservoir.

Low fuel level switch

29 The switch is integral with the fuel level sender unit. Details of fuel level sender unit removal and refitting are given in Chapter 4.

Low oil level switch

30 The switch is integral with the oil level dipstick. To remove, simply withdraw the

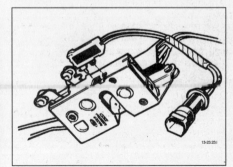

23.23 Door lock and door ajar switch

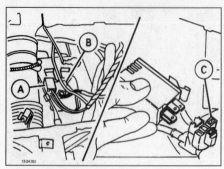

24.2 "Lights-on" warning module location

A "Lights-on" warning module
B Direction indicator relay
C "Lights-on" warning module wiring plug

25.2a Removing a courtesy lamp

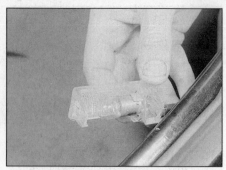

25.2b Removing a luggage compartment lamp

dipstick from its tube and disconnect the wiring plug.
31 Refitting is a reversal of removal.

24 "Lights-on" warning module - renewal

1 Remove the instrument panel.
2 Unclip the direction indicator relay from the steering column support bracket **(see illustration)**.
3 Unclip the "lights-on" warning module from the steering column support bracket, disconnect the wiring plug and remove the module.
4 Refitting is a reversal of removal.

25 Courtesy lamp and luggage compartment lamp - renewal

1 Disconnect the battery negative lead.
2 To remove a lamp, simply prise it from its location, using a thin-bladed screwdriver, and disconnect the wiring **(see illustrations)**. When working on an overhead console-mounted courtesy lamp, disconnect the wiring between the map reading lamps and the courtesy lamp before removing the courtesy lamp.
3 Refitting is a reversal of removal.

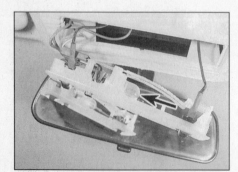

27.3 Overhead console-mounted courtesy lamp bulb (arrowed)

26 Map reading lamp - removal and refitting

1 Disconnect the battery negative lead.
2 Remove the courtesy lamp and disconnect the map reading lamp wires.
3 Push the map reading lamp out of its location by inserting a finger through the courtesy lamp aperture.
4 Refitting is a reversal of removal.

27 Interior lamp bulbs - renewal

1 Disconnect the battery negative lead.

Courtesy lamp

2 Remove the courtesy lamp.
3 Unclip the bulb from the lamp. On models fitted with an overhead console and map reading lamps, the courtesy lamp reflector must be unclipped for access to the bulb **(see illustration)**.
4 Refitting is a reversal of removal.

Map reading lamp

5 Remove the map reading lamp.
6 Pull the bulbholder from the rear of the lamp. The bulb is a push fit in the bulbholder **(see illustration)**.
7 Refitting is a reversal of removal.

Glove compartment lamp

8 Open the glove compartment and pull the bulb from its holder.
9 Refitting is a reversal of removal.

Ashtray lamp

10 Open the ashtray and remove the tray from its housing.
11 Pull the bulbholder from the housing. The bulb is a push fit in the bulbholder.
12 Refitting is a reversal of removal.

Heater blower switch illumination lamp

13 Carefully pull off the switch knob, using pliers with padded jaws if necessary. The bulb is a bayonet fit in the end of the switch shaft.
14 Refitting is a reversal of removal.

Heater control illumination lamp

15 Refer to Chapter 12.

Vanity mirror illumination lamp

16 Lower the sun visor and, using a thin-bladed screwdriver, prise out the mirror and diffuser assembly. Remove the festoon bulb(s) from its/their spring contacts.
17 Refitting is a reversal of removal.

Hazard flasher switch lamp

18 Remove the securing screws and unclip the upper steering column shroud.
19 Ensure that the switch is in the "on" position, then pull off the switch cap/bulb cover. Carefully pull the bulb from the switch using a pair of pliers with padded jaws.
20 Refitting is a reversal of removal.

Automatic transmission gear selector illumination lamp

21 Unscrew the selector lever handle from the threaded end of the lever, then remove the three securing screws and withdraw the centre console front upper panel.
22 Pull of the selector gate cover to expose the bulbholder. The bulb is a bayonet fit in the bulbholder.
23 Refitting is a reversal of removal.

Luggage compartment lamp

24 Remove the lamp by carefully prising it from its location using a thin-bladed screwdriver. Unclip and remove the bulb **(see illustration)**.
25 Refitting is a reversal of removal.

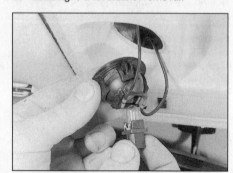

27.6 Removing a map reading lamp bulb

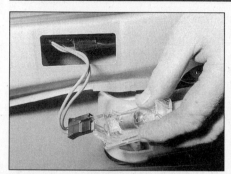

27.24 Removing a luggage compartment lamp bulb

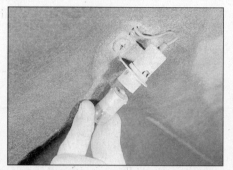

28.6 Removing an underbonnet lamp bulb

29.1 Horn location beneath front panel

Clock illumination lamp

26 Remove the clock.
27 The bulb is a bayonet fit in the rear of the clock.
28 Refitting is a reversal of removal.

28 Underbonnet lamp - removal, refitting and bulb renewal

1 Disconnect the battery negative lead.

Removal and refitting

2 Detach the wiring connector at the left-hand bonnet hinge, and attach a length of string to the end of the wire running from the lamp.
3 If necessary, remove the underbonnet insulation by prising out the two-piece plastic securing clips, then working at the lamp, pull the wiring and the string through the bonnet panel.
4 Detach the string from the end of the wire, and remove the screw securing the lamp to the bonnet. Withdraw the lamp.
5 Commence refitting by attaching the end of the wiring to the string, and pulling the string and wiring through the bonnet panel. Further refitting is a reversal of removal.

Bulb renewal

6 Simply press and twist the bulb to remove it from the bulbholder **(see illustration)**.
7 Refitting is a reversal of removal.

29 Horn - removal and refitting

Removal

1 The horn(s) is/are located in front of the radiator beneath the front panel **(see illustration)**. The horn(s) may be located on either side of the vehicle depending on model.
2 Disconnect the battery negative lead.
3 Disconnect the wiring from the horn, then unscrew the securing nut and washer and withdraw the horn and bracket assembly complete.
4 Repeat the operations for the remaining horn where applicable.

Refitting

5 Refitting is a reversal of removal.

30 Speedometer cable - removal and refitting

Removal

1 On models fitted with a trip computer, remove the speed sender unit.
2 Remove the instrument panel.
3 Pull the cable through the bulkhead into the engine compartment, and where applicable release it from the securing clips. On models fitted with a trip computer, the upper section of the cable can now be removed.
4 Apply the handbrake, jack up the front of the vehicle and support on axle stands (see "Jacking and Vehicle Support").
5 On vehicles with a manual gearbox, extract the circlip securing the cable end to the extension housing and withdraw the cable end **(see illustration)**.
6 On vehicles with automatic transmission, remove the securing screw and disconnect the cable end from the extension housing.
7 The cable can now be withdrawn from the vehicle, noting its routing so that it can be refitted in the same position.

Refitting

8 Refitting is a reversal of removal, but where applicable, ensure that the speedometer cable rubber sleeve is in place over the square inner drive on the cable connector, and not in the speedometer head. Position the cable so that the coloured bands on the cable sheath line up with the bulkhead grommet and the clips in the engine compartment. Route the cable as noted during removal.

9 On completion, pull the speedometer cable from within the engine compartment to ensure that the cable is straight between the instrument panel and the bulkhead grommet.

31 Wiper blades - renewal

1 The wiper blades should be renewed when they no longer clean the glass effectively.
2 Lift the wiper arm away from the glass.
3 With the blade at 90° to the arm, depress the spring clip and slide the blade clear of the hook, then slide the blade up off the arm.
4 If necessary extract the two metal inserts and unhook the wiper rubber.
5 Fit the new rubber and blade in reverse order, making sure where necessary that the cut-outs in the metal inserts face each other.

32 Wiper arms - removal and refitting

Windscreen and rear wipers

1 Lift the hinged covers and remove the nuts and washers securing the arms to the spindles.
2 Mark the arms and spindles in relation to each other then prise off the arms using a screwdriver. Take care not to damage the paintwork.
3 Refitting is a reversal of removal.

Headlamp wipers

4 The procedure is as described in paragraphs 1 to 3, but the washer hose must be disconnected from the nozzle on the wiper arm **(see illustration)**.

30.5 Speedometer cable end fitting in manual gearbox extension housing

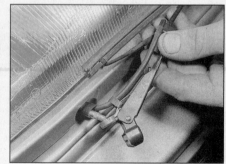

32.4 Removing a headlamp wiper arm

13

33 Washer nozzles - removal and refitting

Windscreen and rear window washers

1 To remove a nozzle, carefully prise it from its location using a thin-bladed screwdriver. Disconnect the washer hose and withdraw the nozzle.
2 To refit, reconnect the washer hose to the nozzle, and push the nozzle into its locating hole.
3 The nozzles can be adjusted by inserting a pin into the jet and swivelling to the required position.

Headlamp washers

Models up to 1987

4 Remove the radiator grille panel.
5 Disconnect the washer hose from the nozzle.
6 Separate the upper and lower halves of the nozzle by prising apart with a thin-bladed screwdriver, then withdraw the nozzle halves.
7 Refitting is a reversal of removal.
8 The nozzles can be adjusted as described in paragraph 3.

Models from 1987

9 Disconnect the washer hose from the nozzle on the end of the wiper arm.
10 Prise the combined wiper blade mounting and nozzle from the wiper arm using a thin-bladed screwdriver or a pair of pliers.
11 Refitting is a reversal of removal.
12 Note that the nozzles are not adjustable.

34 Windscreen wiper motor and linkage - removal and refitting

Removal

1 Disconnect the battery negative lead.
2 Remove the wiper arms.
3 Remove the windscreen cowl panel.
4 Disconnect the wiring plug from the motor.
5 Remove the seven securing screws, and withdraw the mounting bracket together with the linkage and motor **(see illustration)**.

6 Unscrew the nut securing the link arm to the motor shaft, then remove the three securing bolts, and withdraw the motor from the mounting bracket.

Refitting

7 Refitting is a reversal of removal.

35 Windscreen/headlamp washer pump - removal and refitting

Removal

1 Where headlamp washers are fitted, a separate pump is used. The pump(s) is/are a push-fit in the base of the washer fluid reservoir **(see illustration)**.
2 Disconnect the battery negative lead.
3 To remove a pump, syphon out the contents of the reservoir, then pull the pump from its grommet.
4 Disconnect the wiring plug and the washer hose.

Refitting

5 Refitting is a reversal of removal, using a new grommet if necessary. Use a little liquid detergent as a lubricant.
6 On completion, refill the reservoir and check for correct operation.

36 Windscreen/headlamp washer fluid reservoir - removal and refitting

1 Where headlamp washers are fitted, a combined windscreen/headlamp washer fluid reservoir is used. On models up to 1987, the reservoir is mounted on the right-hand side of the engine compartment. On models from 1987, the reservoir is mounted under the right-hand front wing, but has a filler within the engine compartment.
2 Disconnect the battery negative lead.

Models up to 1987

3 Syphon out the contents of the reservoir, and disconnect the wiring plug(s) and washer hose(s).
4 Remove the two or three reservoir retaining screws, as applicable, then withdraw the reservoir.

5 Refitting is a reversal of removal.

Models from 1987

6 Proceed as described in paragraph 3.
7 Working under the front wing, remove the three reservoir securing screws and pull the reservoir down slightly. On vehicles fitted with front foglamps, the bumper must be removed.
8 Withdraw the reservoir.
9 Refitting is a reversal of removal.

37 Rear window wiper motor - removal and refitting

Hatchback models

1 Disconnect the battery negative lead.
2 Remove the wiper arm.
3 Open the tailgate; remove the trim panel.
4 Unscrew the earth lead and disconnect the wiring plug from the motor.
5 Remove the three securing bolts and withdraw the mounting bracket and motor from the tailgate **(see illustration)**.
6 The motor can be separated from the mounting bracket by removing the three securing bolts.
7 Refitting is a reversal of removal.

Estate models

8 The procedure is as described for Hatchback models except that the washer hose must be disconnected from the motor assembly, and the mounting bracket is secured by four bolts.

38 Rear window washer pump - removal and refitting

The procedure is as described for the windscreen/headlamp washer pump.

39 Rear window washer fluid reservoir - removal and refitting

Removal

1 On models from 1987, the rear window washer circuit shares the same reservoir as the windscreen/headlamp washers.

34.5 Windscreen wiper motor bracket securing screws (arrowed)

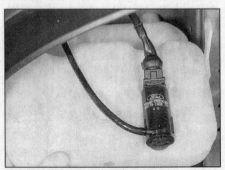

35.1 Windscreen washer pump - models from 1987

37.5 Rear window wiper motor location - mounting bracket securing bolts arrowed

39.2 Rear window washer fluid reservoir location - Hatchback models up to 1987. Securing screws arrowed

2 On models up to 1987, the reservoir is located behind the trim panel on the left-hand side of the luggage compartment **(see illustration)**. To remove the reservoir proceed as follows.
3 Disconnect the battery negative lead.
4 Remove the trim panel.
5 Operate the washers to reduce the fluid level in the reservoir.
6 Remove the reservoir filler cap, and disconnect the wiring plug and water hose.
7 Remove the two securing screws and withdraw the reservoir.

Refitting

8 Refitting is a reversal of removal.

40 Headlamp wiper motor - removal and refitting

Note: *On vehicles fitted with foglamps, the headlamp unit must be removed when the right-hand headlamp wiper motor is to be removed.*

Removal

1 Disconnect the battery negative lead.
2 Disconnect the washer hose from the nozzle on the end of the wiper arm, then remove the wiper arm.
3 Pull the washer hose and retainer from the end of the motor shaft.
4 Remove the radiator grille panel.
5 Where applicable, prise the trim strip from the bottom of the headlamp unit for access to the wiper motor mounting bolts **(see illustrations)**.

41.4b . . . the rear securing bolt . . .

40.5a Prise the trim strip from the bottom of the headlamp unit . . .

6 Remove the two mounting bolts, then working under the wheel arch, slide the wiper motor rearwards, disconnect the wiring plug and withdraw the motor.

Refitting

7 Refitting is a reversal of removal, but on completion adjust the free length of the washer hose between the nozzle and the retainer on the motor shaft.

41 Headlamp unit - removal and refitting

1 Disconnect the battery negative lead.
2 Remove the radiator grille panel.

Models up to 1987

3 Disconnect the headlamp wiring plug(s) **(see illustration)**.

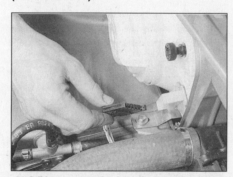

41.3 Disconnect the headlamp wiring plug - models up to 1987

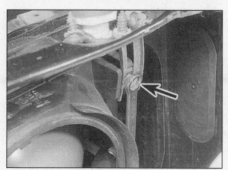

41.4c . . . and the lower sliding clamp bracket bolt . . .

40.5b . . . for access to the headlamp wiper motor mounting bolts

4 Remove the three or four headlamp securing bolts, as applicable, and the lower sliding clamp bracket bolt on the rear of the headlamp, then withdraw the headlamp **(see illustrations)**.
5 If required, the headlamp lens can be removed by releasing the spring clips around its edge.
6 Refitting is a reversal of removal, but the headlamp securing bolts should not be tightened until the headlamp is aligned with the front grille panel.
7 On completion, check the headlamp alignment.

Models from 1987

8 Disconnect the headlamp wiring plug(s) **(see illustration)**.
9 Where applicable, remove the headlamp wiper motor.

41.4a Remove the upper headlamp securing bolts (arrowed) . . .

41.4d . . . then withdraw the headlamp unit - models up to 1987

41.8 Disconnect the headlamp wiring plug - models from 1987

41.10a Remove the headlamp rear securing bolt . . .

41.10b . . . the upper securing nut . . .

10 Remove the headlamp securing bolt and the two nuts, then release the anchor spring and withdraw the direction indicator lamp unit **(see illustrations)**.
11 Pull the headlamp forwards, then swivel it and remove it sideways.
12 If required, the headlamp lens can be removed by releasing the spring clips around its edge.
13 Refitting is a reversal of removal.
14 On completion, check the headlamp alignment.

42 Headlamps - alignment

1 It is recommended that the headlamp alignment is carried out by a Ford dealer using specialist beam setting equipment. However, in an emergency the following procedure will provide an acceptable light pattern.
2 With the vehicle unladen, with a full tank of fuel, and with the tyres correctly inflated, position the vehicle approximately 10 metres

(33 feet) in front of, and at right-angles to, a wall or garage door.
3 Draw a vertical line on the wall corresponding to the centre line of the car. The position of the line can be ascertained by marking the centre of the front and rear screens with crayon then viewing the wall from the rear of the car.
4 Complete the lines shown **(see illustration)**.
5 Switch the headlamps on dipped beam and adjust them as necessary using the knobs located behind the headlamps **(see illustration)**. Cover the headlamp not being checked with cloth.

43 Rear lamp unit - removal and refitting

1 Disconnect the battery negative lead.

Saloon and Hatchback models

2 Working inside the luggage compartment, press the plastic retaining tab and remove the

41.10c . . . and the side securing nut - models from 1987

bulbholder assembly.
3 Disconnect the wiring plug from the bulbholder.
4 Unscrew the securing nuts, and withdraw the rear lamp unit from outside the vehicle. Recover the gasket.
5 Refitting is a reversal of removal.

Estate models

6 Working inside the luggage compartment, turn the retaining tabs a quarter-turn and remove the rear side trim panel cover.
7 Push out the retaining tabs and withdraw the bulbholder.
8 Disconnect the wiring plug from the bulbholder.
9 Unscrew the four securing nuts, and withdraw the rear lamp unit from outside the vehicle. Recover the gasket.
10 Refitting is a reversal of removal.

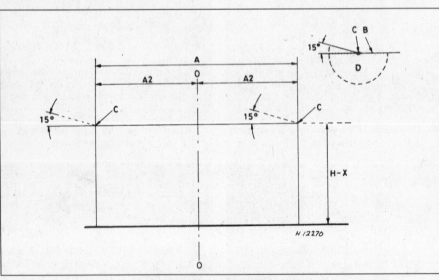

42.4 Headlamp alignment chart

A Distance between headlamp centres
B Light/dark boundary
C Centre of dipped beam
D Dipped beam pattern

H Height of headlamp centre from ground
X = 160.0 mm (6.3 in) for all models up to 1987
120.0 mm (4.7 in) for all models from 1987

42.5 Adjusting the headlamp alignment

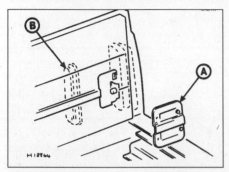

43.11 Rear lamp wiring cover (A) and rear lamp cover (B) - P100 models

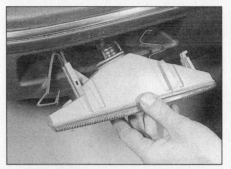

44.3 Withdrawing a front direction indicator lamp unit - "low specification" models up to 1987

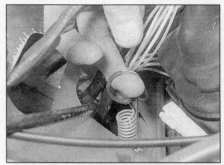

44.8a Unhook the front direction indicator lamp unit anchor spring . . .

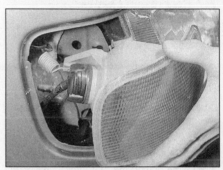

44.8b . . . and withdraw the lamp unit

P100 models

11 Remove the two securing screws and detach the rear lamp wiring cover from the side of the cargo area **(see illustration)**.

12 Working through the cargo area aperture, unscrew the two wing nuts and remove the rear lamp cover.

13 Disconnect the wiring plug from the back of the lamp unit.

14 Unscrew the four securing nuts and withdraw the lamp unit from outside the cargo area. Recover the gasket.

15 Refitting is a reversal of removal, but ensure that the plastic washer between the wiring plug and the lamp unit is seated correctly, and make sure that the wiring protective sheath is seated correctly in the opening in the lamp cover.

44 Front direction indicator lamp unit - removal and refitting

1 Disconnect the battery negative lead.

Models up to 1987

Low specification

2 Push the lamp unit rearwards into the bumper until the plastic retaining tang is heard to click in the locked position.

3 Withdraw the lamp unit from the front of the bumper and disconnect the wiring plug **(see illustration)**.

4 Commence refitting by reconnecting the wiring plug.

5 Release the retaining tang, then refit the lamp unit to the bumper, ensuring that the pivot on the lamp unit engages with the slot in the bumper. Reconnect the battery.

High specification

6 Press the release lever at the top of the lamp unit upwards, and withdraw the unit from the bumper. Disconnect the wiring plug.

7 To refit, reconnect the wiring plug, then push the lamp unit into the bumper until it locates securely. Reconnect the battery.

All models from 1987

8 Working in the engine compartment, unhook the lamp unit anchor spring from its

anchorage next to the headlamp, then withdraw the lamp unit sideways from its recess **(see illustrations)**. Disconnect the bulbholder by twisting it anti-clockwise.

9 Refitting is a reversal of removal, but ensure that the locating pins on the lamp unit engage with the corresponding holes in the headlamp mounting panel.

45 Front direction indicator side repeater lamp - removal and refitting

1 Disconnect the battery negative lead.

Models up to 1987

2 To improve access, turn the steering onto full lock.

3 Remove the relevant wheel arch liner.

4 Working under the wheel arch, depress the retaining tabs and withdraw the lamp through the outside of the wing **(see illustration)**. Disconnect the bulbholder by twisting it anti-clockwise.

5 Refitting is a reversal of removal.

Models from 1987

6 To improve access, turn the steering onto full lock.

7 Working in the engine compartment, disconnect the wiring plug.

8 Remove the relevant wheel arch liner.

9 Working under the wheel arch, twist the lamp clockwise and withdraw it through the

outside of the wing. Feed the wiring through the holes in the wing panels.

10 Refitting is a reversal of removal.

46 Front foglamps - removal and refitting

1 Disconnect the battery negative lead.

Models up to 1987

2 Remove the relevant front direction indicator lamp unit.

3 Release the retaining catch on the inside edge of the lamp, then withdraw the lamp from the bumper and disconnect the wiring plug **(see illustration)**.

4 Refitting is a reversal of removal.

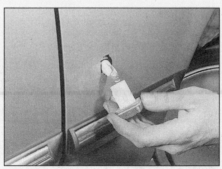

45.4 Withdrawing a front direction indicator side repeater lamp - models up to 1987

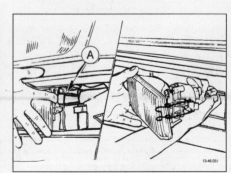

46.3 Front foglamp removal - models up to 1987
A Retaining catch

13

Models from 1987

5 Remove the two securing screws, then withdraw the lamp forwards and disconnect the two wiring plugs.

6 Refitting is a reversal of removal, but where necessary use a new gasket between the lamp and bumper.

7 On completion, the vertical alignment of the foglamp must be adjusted. For the foglamps, dimension "X" (see illustration, 42.4) should be taken as 220.0 mm (8.7 in). The adjuster screw is located on the inside edge of the lamp above the securing screw (see illustration).

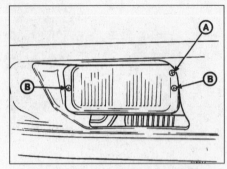

46.7 Front foglamp adjuster screw (A) and securing screws (B) - models from 1987

3 Pull the wiring plug from the base of the bulb, then release the spring clip, grasp the bulb by its contacts and carefully withdraw it (see illustrations). Do not touch the bulb glass.

4 Refitting is a reversal of removal, but on models up to 1987, refit the headlamp rear cover by aligning the arrow on the cover with the depression on the top of the headlamp unit and turning the cover clockwise until the arrow aligns with the lower depression. On models from 1987, the word "OBEN " or "TOP" on the rear cover should be exactly at the top after refitting.

Sidelamps

5 Working in the engine compartment, remove the headlamp rear cover by turning it anti-clockwise.

6 Pull the sidelamp bulbholder from its location in the headlamp reflector (see

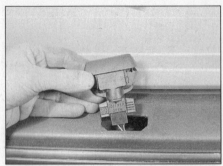

47.2 Removing a rear number plate lamp - Saloon, Hatchback and Estate models

illustration). On "high specification" models up to 1987 a retaining tab must be depressed before withdrawing the bulbholder. Note that the rubber sleeve should be left in position in the reflector.

7 Refitting is as described in paragraph 4.

Auxiliary driving lamps

Models up to 1987

8 Twist the cover on the top of the headlamp unit anti-clockwise and remove it to expose the bulb (see illustration).

9 Release the bulb from the two clips, then disconnect the wiring and remove the bulb. Do not touch the bulb glass (see illustration).

10 Refitting is a reversal of removal.

Models from 1987

11 Release the spring clip securing the cover to the rear of the headlamp unit, then remove the cover (see illustration).

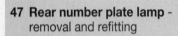

47 Rear number plate lamp - removal and refitting

1 Disconnect the battery negative lead.

Saloon, Hatchback and Estate models

2 To remove a lamp, simply prise it from the bumper using a thin-bladed screwdriver, and disconnect the wiring plug (see illustration).

3 Refitting is a reversal of removal.

P100 models

4 Working behind the rear crossmember, pull the wiring plug from its clip and disconnect it.

5 Pull the lamp cover from the rubber housing, then pull the rubber housing and the wiring from the crossmember.

6 Refitting is a reversal of removal.

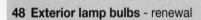

48 Exterior lamp bulbs - renewal

Note: *The glass envelopes of the headlamp, auxiliary driving lamp and front foglamp bulbs must not be touched with the fingers. If the glass is accidentally touched, it should be washed with methylated spirits and dried with a soft cloth. Failure to observe this procedure may result in premature bulb failure.*

1 Disconnect the battery negative lead.

Headlamps

2 Working in the engine compartment, remove the headlamp rear cover by turning it anti-clockwise (see illustration).

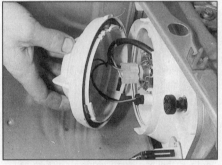

48.2 Remove the headlamp rear cover

48.3a Pull off the wiring plug . . .

48.3b Release the spring clip and withdraw the headlamp bulb

48.6 Removing a sidelamp bulbholder

48.8 Auxiliary drive lamp bulb cover (arrowed) - models up to 1987

48.9 Withdraw the auxiliary driving lamp bulb from the headlamp unit - models up to 1987

12 Disconnect the wiring from the bulb, then release the spring clip and withdraw the bulb. Do not touch the bulb glass.
13 Refitting is a reversal of removal.

Front direction indicator lamps

Models up to 1987

14 Remove the lamp unit.
15 Twist the bulbholder anti-clockwise and withdraw it from the rear of the lamp. The bulb is a bayonet fit in the bulbholder **(see illustration)**.
16 Refitting is a reversal of removal.

Models from 1987

17 Remove the lamp unit.
18 Release the bulbholder by pressing it and turning clockwise, then withdraw the bulb from the bulbholder **(see illustration)**.
19 Refitting is a reversal of removal.

Front direction indicator side repeater lamps

Models up to 1987

20 To improve access, turn the steering onto full lock.
21 Remove the relevant wheel arch liner.
22 Working under the wheel arch, twist the bulbholder anti-clockwise and withdraw it from the lamp. The bulb is a push-fit in the bulbholder.
23 Refitting is a reversal of removal.

Models from 1987

24 Remove the lamp unit.

48.29 Front foglamp bulb retaining spring clip - models from 1987

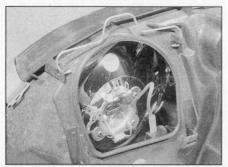

48.11 Auxiliary driving lamp bulb location - models from 1987

25 Twist the bulbholder anti-clockwise to remove it from the lamp. The bulb is a push-fit in the bulbholder.
26 Refitting is a reversal of removal.

Front foglamps

27 Remove the foglamp.
28 On models up to 1987, remove the bulb cover from the rear of the lamp, then release the two spring clips, disconnect the wiring and withdraw the bulb. Do not touch the bulb glass.
29 On models from 1987, release the spring clip and pull the bulb from the bulbholder. Do not touch the bulb glass **(see illustration)**.
30 Refitting is a reversal of removal.

Rear lamp unit

Saloon and Hatchback models

31 Working inside the luggage compartment, press the plastic retaining tab and remove the bulbholder assembly. The bulbs are a bayonet fit in the bulbholder **(see illustrations)**.
32 Refitting is a reversal of removal.

Estate models

33 Working inside the luggage compartment, turn the retaining tabs a quarter-turn and remove the rear side trim panel cover.
34 Push out the retaining tabs and withdraw the bulbholder. The bulbs are a bayonet fit in the bulbholder.
35 Refitting is a reversal of removal.

P100 models

36 Remove the two securing screws and detach the rear lamp wiring cover from the side of the cargo area.

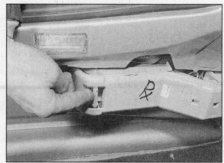

48.31a Press the plastic retaining tab to release the rear lamp bulbholder assembly - Saloon and Hatchback models

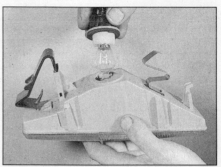

48.15 Removing a front direction indicator lamp bulb - models up to 1987

48.18 Removing a front direction indicator lamp bulb - models from 1987

37 Working through the cargo area aperture, unscrew the two wing nuts and remove the rear lamp cover.
38 Twist the relevant bulbholder anti-clockwise to remove it from the lamp. The bulb is a bayonet fit in the bulbholder.
39 Refitting is a reversal of removal, but ensure that the wiring protective sheath is seated correctly in the opening in the lamp cover.

Rear number plate lamp

Saloon, Hatchback and Estate models

40 Remove the lamp unit.
41 Twist the bulbholder anti-clockwise to remove it from the lamp. The bulb is a push-fit in the bulbholder **(see illustration)**.
42 Refitting is a reversal of removal.

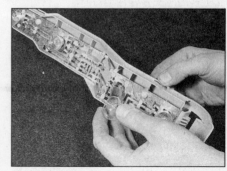

48.31b Removing a bulb from the rear lamp bulbholder - Saloon and Hatchback models

48.41 Removing a rear number plate lamp bulb - Saloon, Hatchback and Estate models

P100 models

43 Pull the lamp cover from the rubber housing to expose the bulb. The bulb is a bayonet fitting in the bulbholder.
44 Refitting is a reversal of removal.

49 Electric window components - removal and refitting

1 Disconnect the battery negative lead.

Switches

2 Prise the switch from its location using a thin-bladed screwdriver, and disconnect the wiring plug **(see illustration)**.
3 Refitting is a reversal of removal.

Operating motors

4 Remove the window regulator.
5 Remove the three securing bolts, and withdraw the motor from the regulator assembly **(see illustration)**.
6 Refitting is a reversal of removal, but ensure that the drive gear is correctly meshed with the regulator.

50 Central door locking components - operation, removal and refitting

Note: If a central locking solenoid or motor is to be renewed due to jamming or overheating, the central locking relay must be renewed at

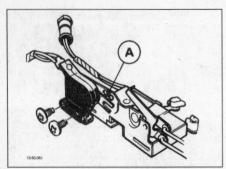

50.6 Driver's door central locking switch - models up to 1987

A Switch lever cut-out

49.2 Disconnecting the wiring plug from a centre console-mounted electric window switch - models from 1987

the same time even if it is believed to be working correctly. Before starting work on the central locking system, unlock all the doors and the tailgate/boot. Make sure that the keys are outside the vehicle before reconnecting the battery on completion of work.

Operation

Models up to 1987

1 The central locking system is activated by turning the key in the driver's door lock, and the locks are operated by solenoids.

Models from 1987

2 The system is activated by turning the key in either of the front door locks, and the locks are operated by electric motors.

Removal and refitting

3 Disconnect the battery negative lead.

Models up to 1987

Switch (driver's door lock)

4 Remove the door lock.
5 Remove the two securing screws, then withdraw the switch from the lock assembly and disconnect the wiring plug.
6 Refitting is a reversal of removal, but ensure that the cut-out in the switch lever engages with the lock lever **(see illustration)**.

Solenoids (passenger and rear door locks)

7 Remove the door lock **(see illustration)**.
8 Remove the two securing screws, then disconnect the solenoid operating rod and the

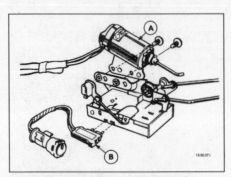

50.7 Central door locking assembly - models up to 1987

A Solenoid
B Door ajar switch (not fitted to all models)

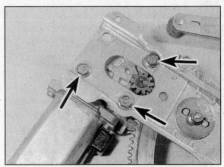

49.5 Electric window motor securing bolts (arrowed)

wiring plug and withdraw the solenoid from the lock assembly.
9 Refitting is a reversal of removal.

Solenoid (tailgate lock)
10 Open the tailgate and remove the trim panel.
11 Disconnect the solenoid wiring plug and earth lead, and the operating rod, then remove the two securing screws and withdraw the solenoid from the tailgate **(see illustration)**.
12 Refitting is a reversal of removal.

Models from 1987

Motors (door locks)
13 Remove the door inner trim panel.
14 Remove the retaining screws and disconnect the wiring plug and the motor operating rod, then withdraw the motor from the door.
15 Refitting is a reversal of removal.

Motor (tailgate and boot lid locks)
16 Open the tailgate/boot lid and where applicable remove the trim panel.
17 Remove the retaining screws and disconnect the wiring plug and the motor operating rod, then withdraw the motor from the tailgate/boot.
18 Refitting is a reversal of removal.

Models from 1990

Motors (door locking)
19 On models from 1990, the door locking motors are incorporated in the door lock units **(see illustrations)**.
20 To remove a motor, first remove the door lock.

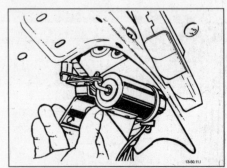

50.11 Removing a tailgate lock solenoid - Hatchback models up to 1987

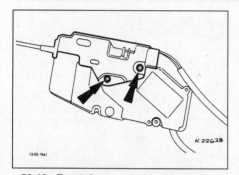

50.19a Front door central locking motor securing screws (arrowed) - models from 1990

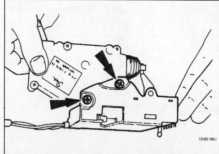

50.19b Rear door central locking motor securing screws (arrowed) - models from 1990

21 Remove the two securing screws, and detach the motor from the lock assembly.
22 Refitting is a reversal of removal, ensuring that the motor operating rod engages with the lock lever.

51 Anti-theft alarm - location, removal and refitting

Note: *The alarm system has a self-diagnosis function, which allows a Ford dealer to carry out fault diagnosis, using suitable specialist equipment. In the event of a problem with the alarm system, it is advisable not to tamper with the components until appropriate fault diagnosis has been carried out.*

Location

1 From 1990, certain models are fitted with an anti-theft alarm **(see illustration)**.
2 The alarm system consists of a control module mounted behind the driver's side facia; trip switches fitted to the doors, tailgate/boot lid, and bonnet; activating switches fitted to the front door locks; an additional horn mounted at the bulkhead next to the battery and an indicator light mounted on the top of the facia.

Module - removal and refitting

3 Disconnect the battery negative lead.
4 Release the carpet trim panel from under the driver's side facia.

5 Reach up behind the facia and locate the control module. Release the plastic retaining clips using a screwdriver, and lower the module.
6 Disconnect the wiring plug and withdraw the module.
7 Refitting is a reversal of removal.

52 Seat heating pad - removal and refitting

Removal

1 Disconnect the battery negative lead.
2 Remove the seat.
3 Remove the seat cushion trim or backrest trim as necessary.
4 Note which way round the pad is fitted, then remove the wire clips and adhesive tape which secure it to the seat. Retrieve the tie-rod and fit it to the new pad.

Refitting

5 Fit the new pad with the thermostat facing the cushion foam **(see illustration)**. Secure the pad with wire clips and tape, making sure that it is not too tight - it must be able to flex when sat on.
6 Refit the cushion or backrest trim, as applicable, being careful not to trap or kink the pad.
7 Refit the seat, reconnect the wiring and check the pads for correct operation.

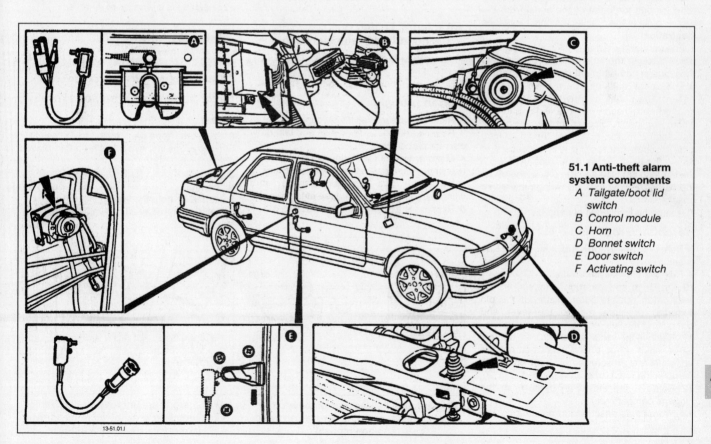

51.1 Anti-theft alarm system components

A Tailgate/boot lid switch
B Control module
C Horn
D Bonnet switch
E Door switch
F Activating switch

13

52.5 Seat heating pad

Thermostat (arrowed) must face foam

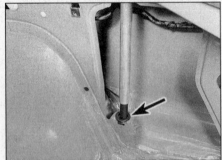

53.4 Pull the base of the aerial from the rubber bush (arrowed)

53.5 Removing an electric aerial - Saloon model

53 Radio aerial (exterior-mounted) - removal and refitting

1 On models fitted with an electric aerial, disconnect the battery negative lead.

Saloon and Estate models

2 Remove the right-hand side trim panel from the luggage compartment.
3 Working outside the vehicle, unscrew the nut and remove the spacer and seal from the base of the aerial.
4 Working inside the luggage compartment, either unscrew the aerial bracket securing screw and slide the bracket from the aerial tube, or pull the base of the aerial from the rubber bush in the bracket, as applicable **(see illustration)**.
5 Ensure that the aerial is fully retracted, then pull it through the hole in the bodywork into the luggage compartment **(see illustration)**.
6 The aerial lead may be a push-fit in the base of the aerial, or may be secured by a knurled nut. Disconnect the aerial lead and where applicable, disconnect the wiring from the electric motor. Note that the aerial lead runs through the roof. If it is necessary to renew the lead, it may prove easier to leave the old lead in place and run a new one under the carpet. Follow existing wiring runs where possible.
7 Refitting is a reversal of removal.

Hatchback models

8 Remove the right-hand rear seat side cushion.
9 Remove the rear parcel shelf.
10 On "high specification" models, lift the seat catch release lever, push out the pin securing the link rod to the lever and disconnect the link rod.
11 Remove the securing screws from the rear parcel shelf support (nine screws on models up to 1987, eight screws from 1987 onwards). Remove the rear parcel shelf support.
12 Remove the side trim panel from the luggage compartment.
13 Proceed as described in paragraphs 3 to 7 inclusive.

P100 models

14 Pull off the plastic trim cover and unscrew the aerial securing nut.
15 Withdraw the aerial assembly, and carefully prise the base seal from the roof panel.
16 The aerial lead runs across the roof panel under the headlining, and down the right-hand front pillar to the radio unit. Renewal is straightforward, but the front section of the headlining must be released for access and a length of string should be tied to the end of the aerial lead before removal to aid routing when refitting.
17 The aerial rod can be renewed by simply unscrewing it from the base.
18 Refitting is a reversal of removal.

54 Integral heated rear window/radio aerial amplifier - removal and refitting

1 Disconnect the battery negative lead.

Saloon models

2 Remove both rear seat side cushions.
3 Remove the securing screws and withdraw the rear parcel shelf.
4 Make a note of the wiring connections for use when refitting, then disconnect the wiring, remove the two securing screws, and withdraw the amplifier unit **(see illustration)**.
5 Refitting is a reversal of removal.

Hatchback models

6 Unclip the tailgate trim panel.
7 Remove the amplifier bracket securing screws, and withdraw the amplifier through the tailgate panel aperture **(see illustration)**.
8 Make a note of the wiring connections for use when refitting, then disconnect the wiring and remove the amplifier unit.
9 Refitting is a reversal of removal.

Estate models

10 Unclip the tailgate trim panel.
11 Make a note of the wiring connections for use when refitting, then disconnect the wiring, remove the four securing screws, and detach the loudspeaker/amplifier bracket assembly from the tailgate **(see illustration)**.
12 Refitting is a reversal of removal.

55 Loudspeakers - removal and refitting

1 Disconnect the battery earth lead.

Facia panel-mounted speakers

Upper

2 Prise the speaker grille from its four retaining clips in the facia using a thin-bladed screwdriver.
3 Remove the four securing screws, disconnect the wiring, and pull the loudspeaker from the facia panel.
4 Refitting is a reversal of removal.

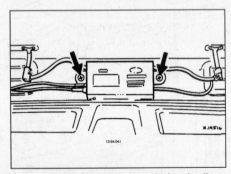

54.4 Integral heated rear window/radio aerial amplifier securing screws (arrowed) - Saloon models

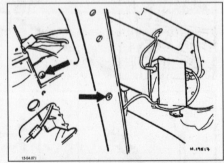

54.7 Integral heated rear window/radio aerial amplifier bracket securing screws (arrowed) - Hatchback models

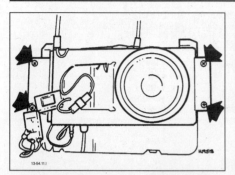

54.11 Loudspeaker/integral heated rear window/radio aerial amplifier bracket securing screws (arrowed) - Estate models

Lower

5 Remove the lower facia panel.
6 Remove the four securing screws, disconnect the wiring, and pull the loudspeaker from the facia panel.
7 Refitting is a reversal of removal.

Rear parcel shelf-mounted speakers

Saloon models

8 Working in the luggage compartment, remove the single securing screw, then lift the loudspeaker into the passenger compartment and disconnect the wiring. Withdraw the loudspeaker.
9 Note that it is important not to disturb the loudspeaker mounting gasket or retainer.
10 Refitting is a reversal of removal, but ensure that the wiring does not touch the retainer, shelf, or speaker, to prevent any audible rattles.

Hatchback models

11 Working under the parcel shelf, remove the four securing screws, disconnect the wiring, and withdraw the loudspeaker.
12 Refitting is a reversal of removal.

Door-mounted speakers

13 Remove the door inner trim panel.
14 Remove the four securing screws, then withdraw the loudspeaker from the door and disconnect the wiring. Remove the loudspeaker.
15 Do not remove the loudspeaker from the moulding, as the two are a sealed assembly.
16 Refitting is a reversal of removal.

Tailgate-mounted speakers - Estate models

17 Remove the tailgate trim panel.
18 Remove the four securing screws, disconnect the wiring and withdraw the loudspeaker. Note that on models with an integral heated rear window/radio aerial, the aerial amplifier unit is combined with one of the loudspeaker units.

57.4 Radio/cassette player securing tangs (arrowed) viewed from the rear of the unit - standard fixing

19 Refitting is a reversal of removal.

High frequency units

20 These units are used to reproduce high frequencies only, and incorporate an electronic filter network which must not be disconnected or bypassed. The units are located in the lower facia panels.
21 The removal and refitting procedure is as described for the lower facia panel-mounted loudspeakers earlier in this Section, but take care not to damage the extremely fragile speaker cones.

56 Radio/cassette player power amplifier - removal and refitting

Removal

1 Some "high specification" models are fitted with an audio power amplifier, which is mounted as a separate unit beneath the radio/cassette unit. To remove the unit proceed as follows.
2 Disconnect the battery negative lead.
3 Remove the two screws under the top edge of the power amplifier unit.
4 Slide the unit forwards from the facia panel, until the wiring plugs can be disconnected. Disconnect the wiring plugs and remove the unit.

Refitting

5 Refitting is a reversal of removal.

57 Radio/cassette player - removal and refitting

Standard fixing

1 Disconnect the battery negative lead.
2 Pull off the two control knob assemblies.
3 Release the trim panel by unscrewing the two securing nuts from the control spindles. Remove the trim panel.

57.10 Removing a radio/cassette player using special tools - DIN fixing

4 Using a hooked instrument, pull the mounting plate securing tangs towards the centre of the radio/cassette player, then slide the unit forwards from the facia panel **(see illustration)**.
5 Disconnect the wiring plugs and the aerial lead, then remove the unit.
6 Remove the plastic support bracket from the rear of the unit, and unscrew the nuts and washers from the control spindles to remove the mounting plate from the front of the unit.
7 Refitting is a reversal of removal.

DIN fixing

8 An increasing number of radio/cassette players have DIN standard fixings. Two special tools, obtainable from in-car entertainment specialists, are required for removal.
9 Disconnect the battery negative lead.
10 Insert the tools into the holes in the front of the radio/cassette player and push them until they snap into place. Pull the tools outwards to release the unit **(see illustration)**.
11 Pull the unit forwards and disconnect the wiring plugs and the aerial lead. Remove the unit from the facia panel.
12 To refit the radio/cassette player, reconnect the wiring and the aerial lead, then simply push the unit into its bracket until the retaining lugs snap into place.

58 Wiring diagrams - general information

Each wiring diagram covers a particular system of the appropriate vehicle; as indicated in each caption. Carefully read the Key to each diagram before commencing work.

13

NOTES:

1. All diagrams are divided into numbered circuits depending upon their function e.g Diagram 2 : Exterior lighting all models.
2. Some components may appear on more than one diagram so their positions are given in coded form in the key below e.g. 2/A1 denotes a component on diagram 2 grid location A1.
3. Feed wires are coloured red (black when switched) and originate from diagram 1. All other diagrams feed from fuse connections or common feeds.
4. Earth wires on all diagrams are coloured brown.
5. The tables below show where common feeds and common earths interconnect between diagrams.
6. Not all items are fitted to all models.
7. Brackets show how the circuit may be connected in more than one way.

FUSE	RATING	CIRCUIT
1	30A	Electric Windows
2	30A	Heated Rear Window, Heated Mirrors
3	10A	Wiper
4	30A	Heater Blower, Rear Wiper Motor, W/Screen Washer
5	30A	Headlamp Washer
6	15A	Horn - Steering Wheel Switch
7	15A	Driving Lamps
8	10A	Clock, Wiper Intermit., Warning Lamps
9	15A	Flasher, Stop Lamp, Reversing Lamp
10	15A	Front Fog Lamp
11	30A	Door Locking, Tailgate Release
12	25A	Interior Lights, Clock, Cigar Lighter
13	10A	Hazard, Horn - Multifunction Lever
14	10A	LH High Beam
15	10A	RH High Beam
16	10A	LH Low Beam, Rear Fog Lamp
17	10A	RH Low Beam
18	10A	LH Side, Licence, Engine Lamp
19	10A	RH Side, Glove Box, Switch Illumination
20		Free
21	1A	Fuel Computer
22	20A	Fuel Injection

COMMON EARTH POINT	DIAGRAM/ GRID REF.
G1004	2/C1
	4/B1
	4/B5
	4a/B1
G1005	1/A8
	2/C8
	4/B4
	4/B8
	4a/B8
G1007	1/K1
	2/E2
	2a/E2
	3/F2
	3a/F3
	4/K2
	4a/C2
G1009	1/F1
	3/E3
G1010	1/M5
	2/M6
	3a/M5
	4a/M6
G1014	3/L7
	3a/L6

Wire Colours

B	Blue	Rs	Pink
Bk	Black	S	Grey
Bn	Brown	V	Violet
Gn	Green	W	White
R	Red	Y	Yellow

COMMON FEED	DESCRIPTION	DIAGRAM/ GRID REF.
S1021	COMMON IGNITION FEED	1/L1
		2/H3
		3/J2
		4a/H2
S1022	COMMON BATTERY FEED	1/J2
		2/H2

ITEM	DESCRIPTION	DIAGRAM/ GRID REF.	ITEM	DESCRIPTION	DIAGRAM/ GRID REF.
1	Alternator	1/A3	14	Central Locking Actuator LH Front	3a/G8
2	Ashtray Illumination	2a/G5	15	Central Locking Actuator LH Rear	3a/L8
3	Auto. Trans. Inhibitor Switch	1/G4	16	Central Locking Actuator RH Rear	3a/L1
		2/E5	17	Central Locking Actuator Tailgate	3a/M5
4	Auto. Trans. Relay	1/H2	18	Central Locking Relay	3a/H6
5	Auto. Trans. Relay (Only 2.0 OHC With Elec. Aerial, From 1985)	1/H2	19	Central Locking Switch	3a/H1
			20	Cigar Lighter Front	2a/F5
6	Auto. Trans. Selector Illumination	2a/J4	21	Cigar Lighter Rear	2a/K5
7	Auxiliary Warning Module (Low Series)	4/J4	22	Clock	2a/F6
8	Auxiliary Warning Module (High Series)	4/H7	23	Coolant Temp. Sensor	1/B4
		4a/G5			1/B7
9	Battery	1/G7			1/F5
10	Brake Pad Sender LH	4/D4	24	Dip Beam Relay (From 1985)	2/C5
		4/D8	25	Distributor	1/D1
11	Brake Pad Sender RH	4/D1			1/D3
		4/D5			1/D5
12	Bulb Failure Module	4a/H6			1/E7
13	Carburettor Stepper Motor	1/C7			

Notes, tables, wire colours and key to wiring diagrams. Models up to 1987

ITEM	DESCRIPTION	DIAGRAM/ GRID REF.	ITEM	DESCRIPTION	DIAGRAM/ GRID REF.
26	Door Ajar Sender LH Front	4a/F8	81	Ignition Switch	1/M1
27	Door Ajar Sender LH Rear	4a/K8	82	Instrument Cluster	1/M3
28	Door Ajar Sender RH Front	4a/F1			2/F4
29	Door Ajar Sender RH Rear	4a/K1			2a/E3
30	Driving Lamp Relay	2/C4			4a/H3
31	Econolight Switch (Amber)	1/G8	83	Instrument Illumination Control	2a/F3
32	Econolight Switch (Red)	1/H8			4a/J4
33	Electric Choke	1/F4	84	Interior Lamp Delay Relay	2a/B3
34	Electric Door Mirror	3a/E1	85	Interior Lamp Door Switch LH Front	2a/E8
		3a/E8	86	Interior Lamp Door Switch LH Rear	2a/J8
35	Electric Mirror Control Switch	3a/F2	87	Interior Lamp Door Switch RH Front	2a/E1
36	Electric Window Control Switch Front	3a/H4	88	Interior Lamp Door Switch RH Rear	2a/J1
37	Electric Window Control Switch Rear	3a/K1	89	Interior Lamp/Switch Front	2a/H4
		3a/K8	90	Interior Lamp/Switch Rear	2a/K4
38	Electric Window Motor LH Front	3a/F8	91	Licence Plate Lamp	2/M3
39	Electric Window Motor LH Rear	3a/J8			2/M6
40	Electric Window Motor RH Front	3a/F1			4a/M3
41	Electric Window Motor RH Rear	3a/J1			4a/M6
42	Electronic Ignition Module	1/C1	92	Light Cluster LH Rear	2/M8
43	Engine Comp. Lamp/Switch	2a/D5			4a/M8
44	ESC 1 Ignition Module	1/C2	93	Light Cluster RH Rear	2/M1
45	ESC 2 Ignition Module	1/B5			4a/M1
		1/C8	94	Light/Wiper Switch	2/J3
46	Flasher Lamp LH	2/A8			3/J3
47	Flasher Lamp LH Side Marker	2/E8			4a/K3
48	Flasher Lamp RH	2/A1	95	Low Brake Fluid Sender	1/F2
49	Flasher Lamp RH Side Marker	2/E1	96	Low Coolant Sender	4/D2
50	Flasher Relay	2/H5			4/D6
51	Foglamp Front	2/A2	97	Low Oil Sender	4/E3
		2/A7			4/E7
52	Foglamp Relay	2/C5	98	Low Washer Fluid Sender	4/C2
53	Foglamp Switch Front	2/H2			4/C6
54	Foglamp Switch Rear	2/H3	99	Luggage Comp. Lamp/Switch	2a/M4
55	Footwell Illumination	2a/D2	100	Manifold Heater (1.8/2.0 OHC Only From 1985)	1/F5
		2a/D7			
56	Fuel Computer	4a/G5	101	Manifold Heater Relay (1.8/2.0 OHC Only From 1985)	1/J7
57	Fuel Flow Sensor	4a/C7			
58	Fuel Sender	1/M6	102	Multifunction Switch	2/J4
		4/L3			3/J5
		4/L7	103	Oil Pressure Switch	1/F7
		4a/L5	104	Power Hold Relay	1/J6
59	Fuel Shut Off Valve	1/F4	105	Reversing Lamp Switch	2/D5
60	Glove Box Lamp/Switch	2a/E7	106	Seat Belt Warning Relay	2a/B5
61	Graphic Display Module	4a/H5			4/E2
62	Handbrake Warning Switch	1/L6			4/E6
63	Headlamp Unit LH	2/A6	107	Spark Plugs	1/E1
		4a/A6			1/E3
64	Headlamp Unit RH	2/A3			1/E5
		4a/A3			1/F7
65	Headlamp Washer Pump	3/C3	108	Speed Sensor	4a/E2
66	Headlamp Washer Relay	3/D4	109	Starter Motor	1/G5
67	Heated Rear Window	3/L5	110	Stop Lamp Switch	2/F4
		3a/L5			4a/E4
68	Heated Rear Window Relay	3/C3	111	Tailgate Ajar Sender	4a/M4
69	Heated Rear Window Relay (Auto. Off)	3a/B3	112	Tailgate Release Actuator	3a/M4
70	Heated Rear Window Switch	3/H3	113	Tailgate Release Relay	1/J5
71	Heated Rear Window Switch (Auto. Off)	3a/H2			3a/C5
72	Heater Blower Illumination	2a/E5	114	Tailgate Release Switch	3a/K5
73	Heater Blower Motor	3/G6	115	Vanity Mirror Illumination	2a/G7
74	Heater Blower Switch	3/G5	116	Warning Lamp Cluster	4/K2
75	Horn	3/A7			4/K7
		3a/A7	117	Wash/Wipe Switch Rear	3/H3
76	Horn Relay	3a/C4	118	Washer Pump Front	3/B3
77	Horn Switch	3a/J3	119	Washer Pump Rear	3/L8
78	Ice Warning Sender	4a/H4	120	Wiper Intermittent Relay Front	3/B5
79	Ignition Coil	1/C1	121	Wiper Intermittent Relay Rear	3/C4
		1/C2	122	Wiper Intermittent Speed Control	3/H4
		1/C5	123	Wiper Motor Front	3/E3
		1/D7	124	Wiper Motor Rear	3/M6
80	Ignition Relay	1/G2			

Key to wiring diagrams (continued). Models up to 1987

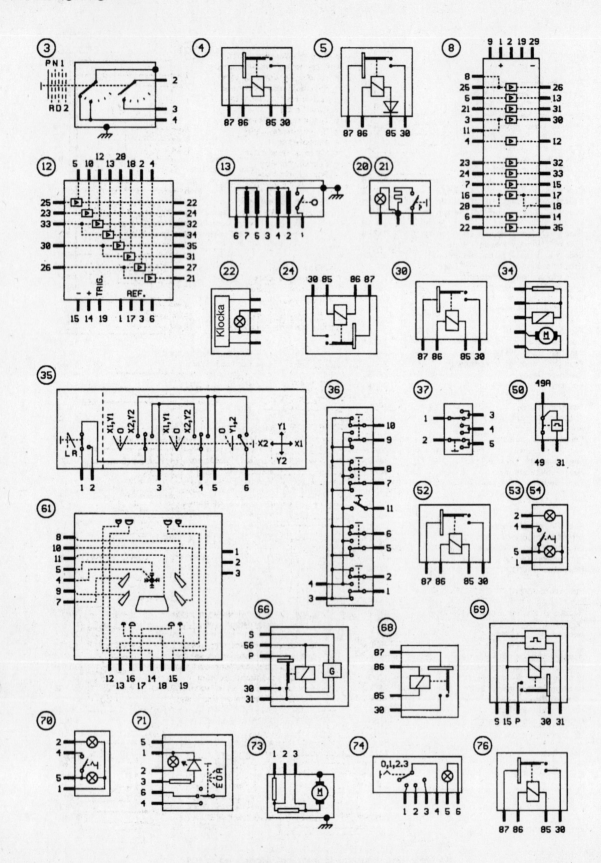

Internal connection details. Models up to 1987

H24035
T.M.MARKE

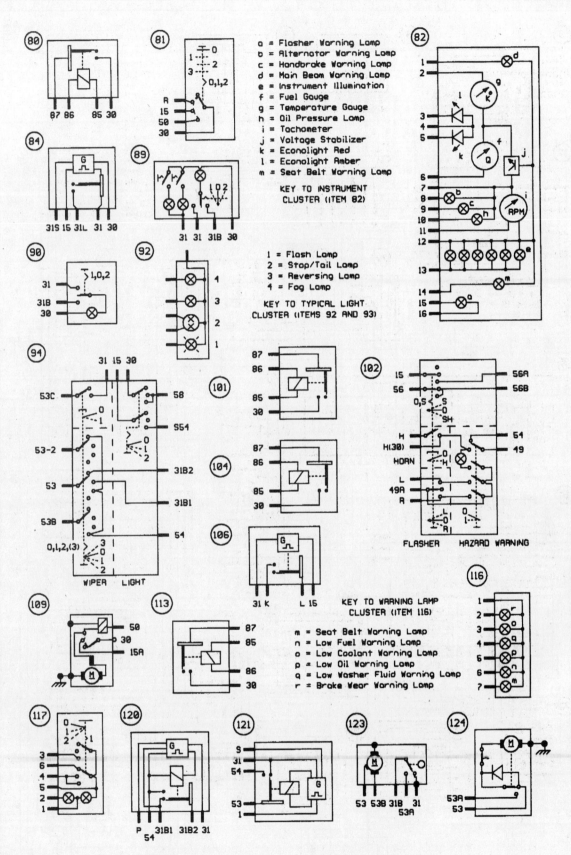

a = Flasher Warning Lamp
b = Alternator Warning Lamp
c = Handbrake Warning Lamp
d = Main Beam Warning Lamp
e = Instrument Illumination
f = Fuel Gauge
g = Temperature Gauge
h = Oil Pressure Lamp
i = Tachometer
j = Voltage Stabilizer
k = Econolight Red
l = Econolight Amber
m = Seat Belt Warning Lamp

KEY TO INSTRUMENT
CLUSTER (ITEM 82)

1 = Flash Lamp
2 = Stop/Tail Lamp
3 = Reversing Lamp
4 = Fog Lamp

KEY TO TYPICAL LIGHT
CLUSTER (ITEMS 92 AND 93)

KEY TO WARNING LAMP
CLUSTER (ITEM 116)

m = Seat Belt Warning Lamp
n = Low Fuel Warning Lamp
o = Low Coolant Warning Lamp
p = Low Oil Warning Lamp
q = Low Washer Fluid Warning Lamp
r = Brake Wear Warning Lamp

FLASHER   HAZARD WARNING

WIPER   LIGHT

Internal connection details (continued). Models up to 1987

H24036
T.M.MARKE

13

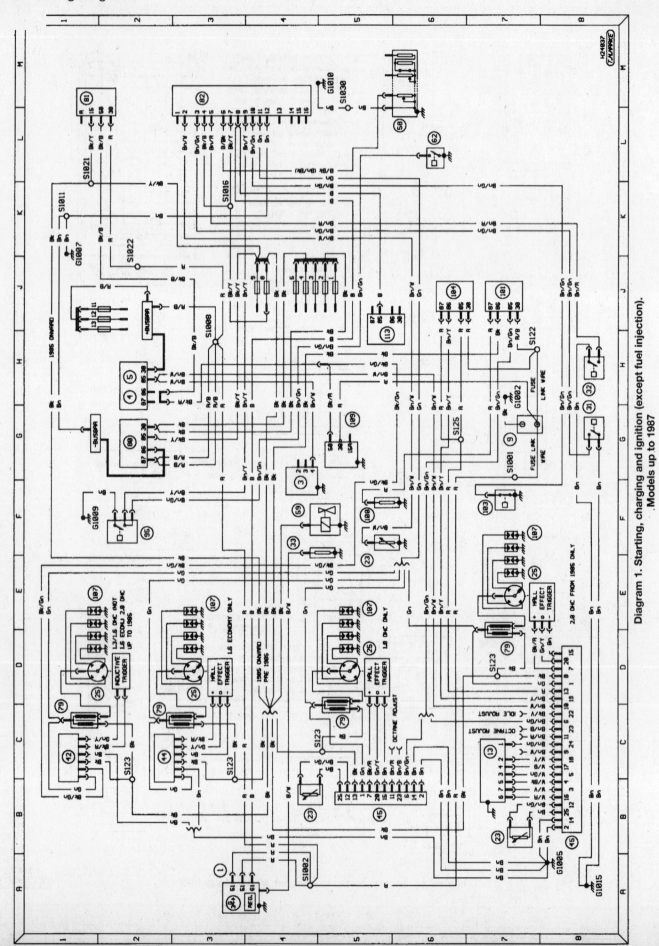

Diagram 1. Starting, charging and ignition (except fuel injection). Models up to 1987.

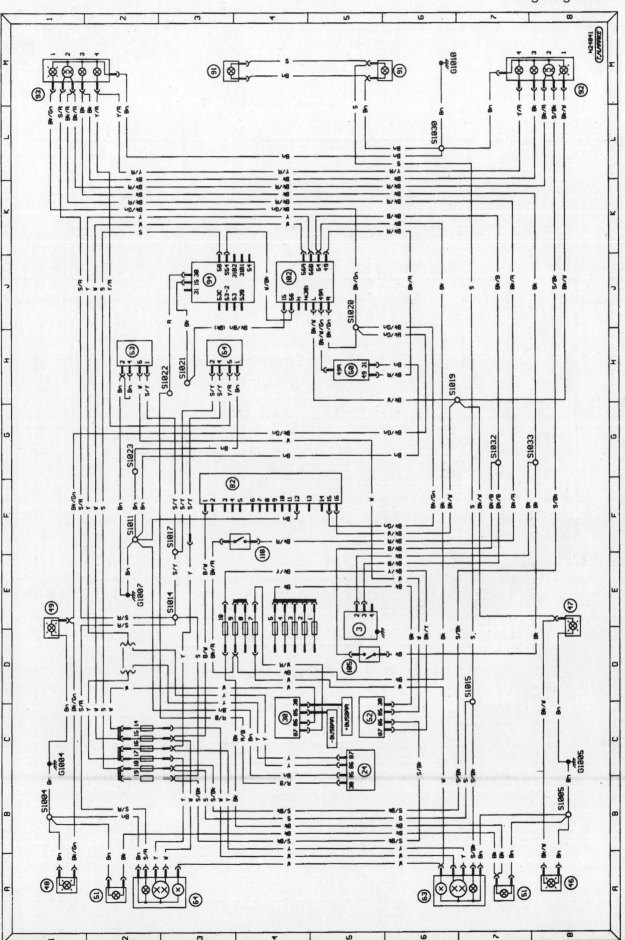

Diagram 2. Exterior lighting. Models up to 1987

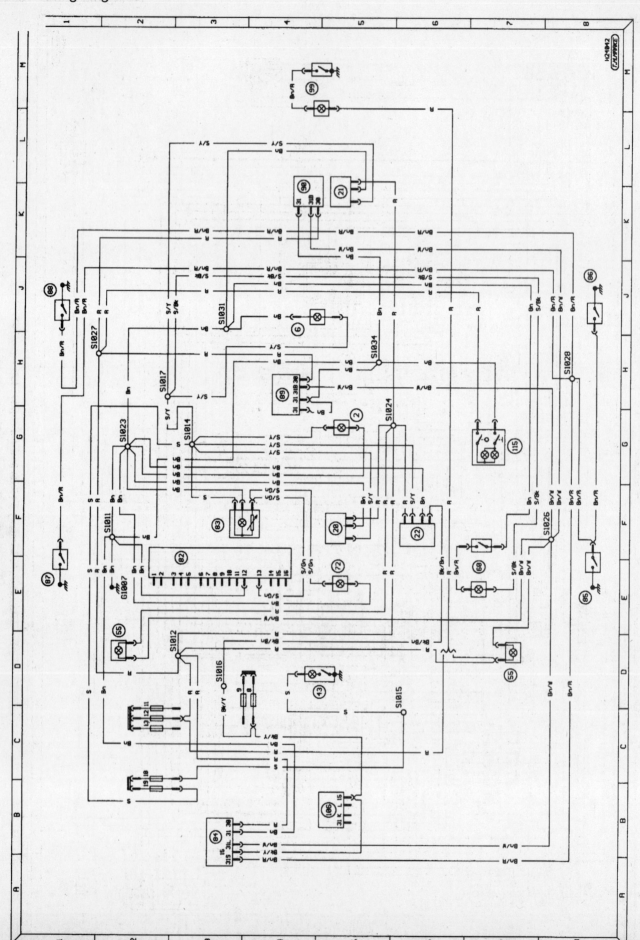

Diagram 2a. Interior lighting. Models up to 1987

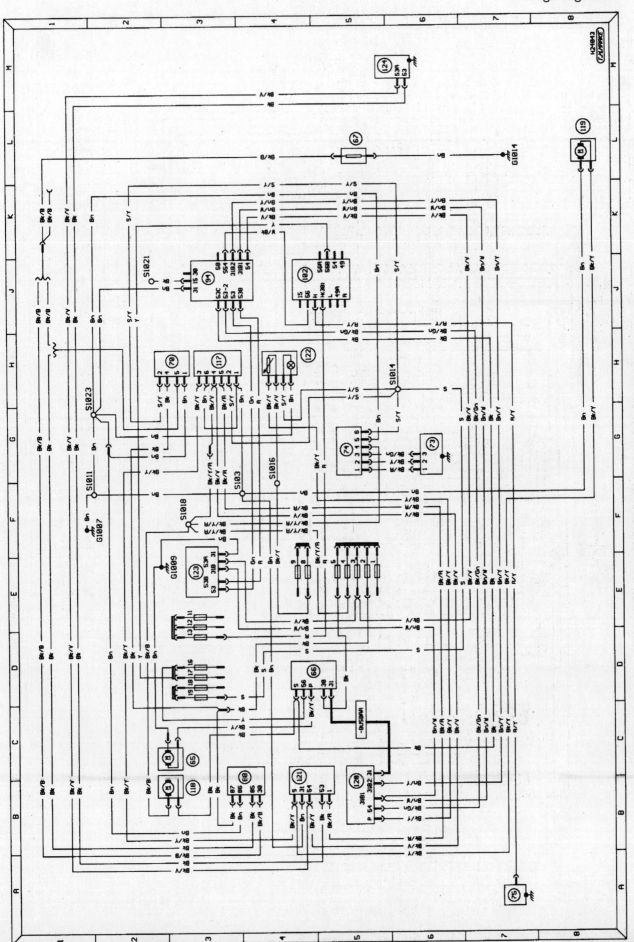

Diagram 3. Ancillary circuits (low series). Models up to 1987

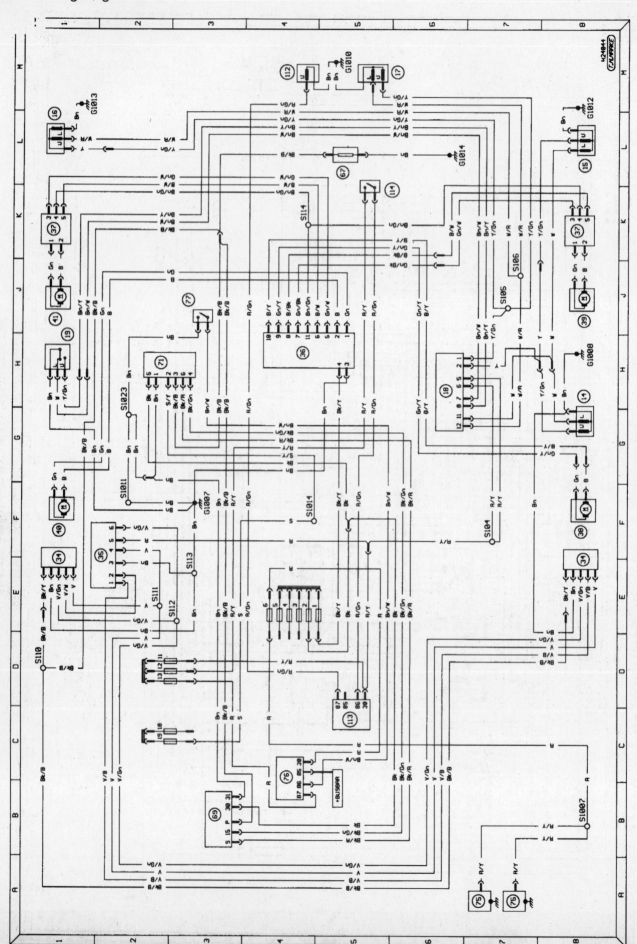

Diagram 3a. Additional ancillary circuits (high series only). Models up to 1987

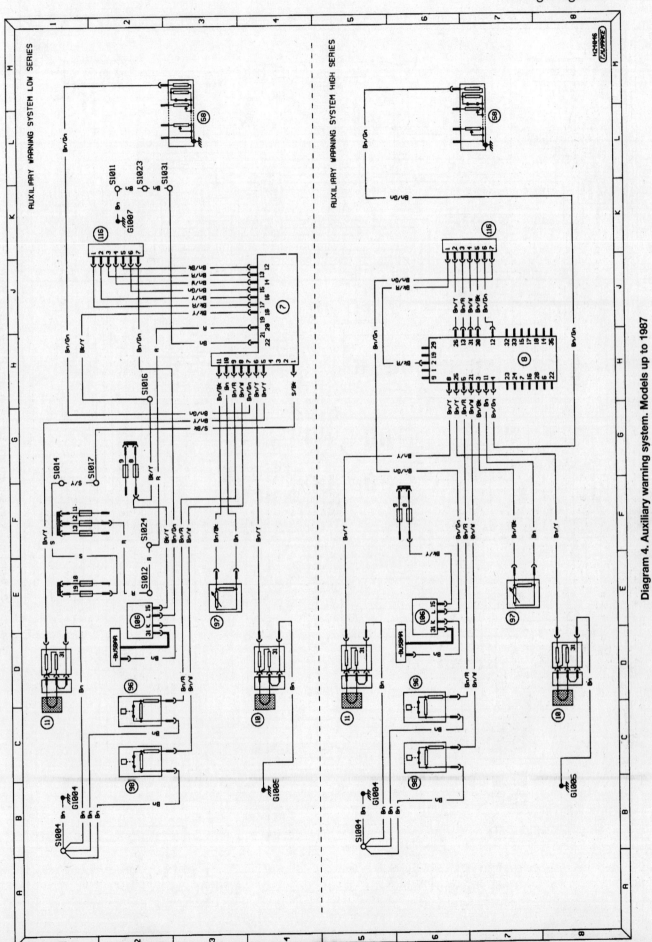

Diagram 4. Auxiliary warning system. Models up to 1987

13

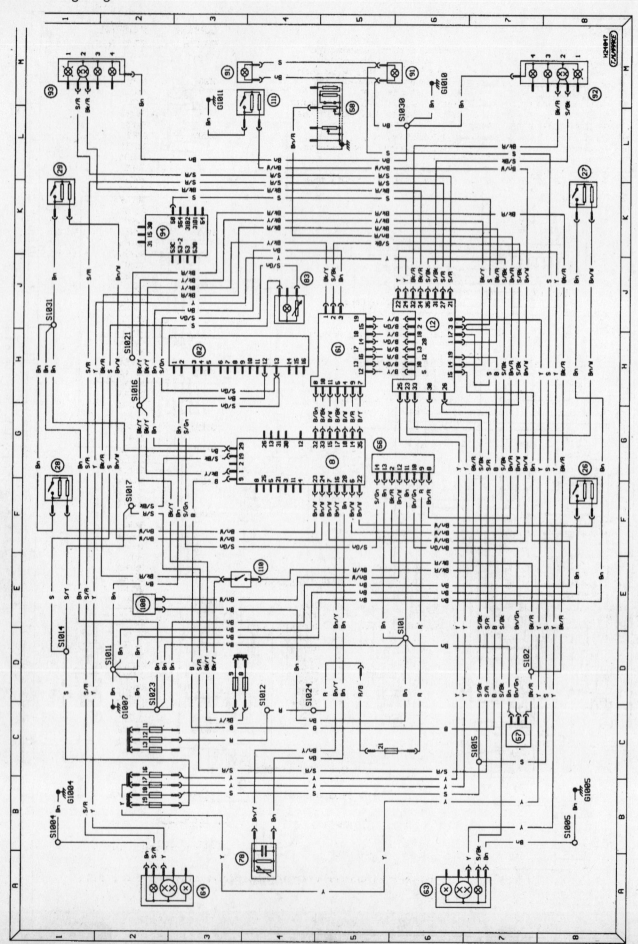

Diagram 4a. Graphic display system and fuel computer. Models up to 1987

NOTES:

1. All diagrams are divided into numbered circuits depending upon their function e.g Diagram 2 : Exterior lighting all models.
2. Some components may appear on more than one diagram so their positions are given in coded form in the key below e.g. 2/A1 denotes a component on diagram 2 grid location A1.
3. FEED WIRES ARE COLOURED RED (BLACK WHEN SWITCHED) AND ORIGINATE FROM DIAGRAM 1. ALL OTHER DIAGRAMS FEED FROM FUSE CONNECTIONS OR COMMON FEEDS (SEE BELOW).
4. Earth wires on all diagrams are coloured brown.
5. The tables below show where common feeds and common earths interconnect between diagrams.
6. Not all items are fitted to all models.
7. Brackets show how the circuit may be connected in more than one way.

FUSE	RATING	CIRCUIT
1	20A	LH Main Beam, LH Driving Lamp
2	20A	RH Main Beam, RH Driving Lamp
3	10A	LH Dip Beam
4	10A	RH Dip Beam
5	10A	LH Side Lamp
6	10A	RH Side Lamp
7	15A	Instrument Illum., Licence Plate Lamp
8	15A	Radio (From 1989 Only)
9	30A	Headlamp Wash
10	20A	Interior Lamps, Clock, Door Locking, Mirrors
11		Free
12	10A	Hazard Warning Lamps
13	30A	Cigar Lighter
14	30A	Horn
15	30A	Wiper Motors, Washer Pump
16	30A	Heated Rear Window, Heated Mirrors
17	20A	Front Fog Lamps, Dim/Dip
18	30A	Heater Blower
19		Free
20	15A	Flashers, Reversing Lamps
21	15A	Stop Lamps
22	10A	Control Circuits
23	30A	Fuel Pump
24	20A	Power Windows
30	20A	Anti-lock Brake
31	30A	Anti-lock Brake Pump
36	1A	Fuel Computer

COMMON FEED	DESCRIPTION	DIAGRAM/ GRID REF.
S1002	COMMON BATTERY FEED	1/F4, 2/H6, 3c/F6
S1004	COMMON BATTERY FEED	1/J2, 1a/K6, 2/J3, 2a/J3, 2b/H2, 3/K3, 3a/J3, 3c/K6, 3d/H2, 4/J2
S1012	COMMON IGNITION FEED	1/H2, 1a/C3, 1a/C4, 1a/F4, 1a/J2, 2/F4, 3b/H2, 4/E3
S1042	COMMON CRANKING FEED	1/J1, 1a/C1, 3b/H3

WIRE COLOURS

B	Blue
Bk	Black
Bn	Brown
Gn	Green
R	Red
Rs	Pink
S	Grey
V	Violet
W	White
Y	Yellow

KEY TO SYMBOLS

→● PLUG-IN CONNECTOR

⏚ EARTH

⊗ BULB

▷|— DIODE

(——▭——) FUSE

○S1012 SOLDERED JOINT

COMMON EARTH POINT	DIAGRAM/ GRID REF.
G1002	1/F8, 1a/L8, 3/D7, 3b/E8, 4/F8
G1003	1/B8, 1a/R3, 1a/D8, 2/B8, 2a/B8, 3a/B8, 3b/B8, 3c/B8, 4/B8
G1004	2/B1, 2a/B1, 3a/B1, 3c/B1, 3d/B1
G1005	1/E1, 2/E2, 2a/E2, 2b/E1, 3/F2, 3a/E2, 3c/E1, 3d/E1
G1006	1a/M7, 3/F8, 3a/F8, 3b/F8, 3d/E7
G1007	1a/F6, 4/B4
G1009	2/L7, 2a/L7, 3c/L7
G1010	2b/M3, 3/M3, 3d/M3
G1011	1/J1, 2/G1, 2a/G1, 2b/H1, 3/K1, 3a/G2, 3c/H1, 3d/G1
G1013	1/J8, 2/F7, 2a/F8, 3c/J7, 3d/K7, 4/H8
G1014	1/C1, 2/C2, 2a/C1, 2b/B1, 3c/D2, 3d/C2
G1016	3c/G8, 3d/F7, 4/F8

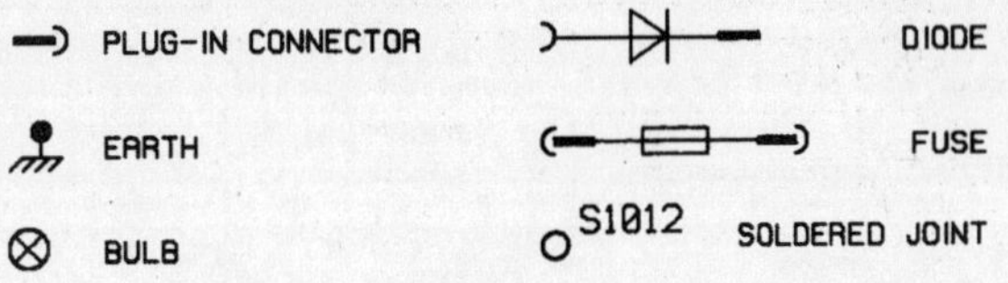

Notes, tables, wire colours and key to symbols on wiring diagrams. Models from 1987 to May 1989

13

ITEM	DESCRIPTION	DIAGRAM/GRID REF.
1	ABS Hydraulic Control Unit	3b/D2
2	ABS Hydraulic Motor Relay M6	3b/L6
3	ABS Main Relay M7	3b/K6
4	ABS Module	3b/J6
5	ABS Relay VII (PRE 1989)	3b/G3
6	ABS Warning Indicator	3b/L3
7	Air Flow Sensor	4/B6
8	Air Temp. Sensor	1a/B8
9	Alternator	1/A3, 1a/A4, 3/A3
10	Amplifier/Graphic Equalizer	5/C7, 5/J2
11	Antenna Module	3/L5, 5/E2, 5/E4, 5/F7, 5/L7, 5/M2, 5/M5
12	Ashtray Illumination	2b/H6
13	Auto. Gear Actuator	1/D7
14	Auto. Trans. Inhibitor Switch	1/D4, 2a/B5
15	Auto. Trans. Relay XII	1/G2
16	Auto. Trans. Selector Illumination	2b/J5
17	Auxiliary Warning Module	3c/H6, 3d/H6
18	Battery	1/E8, 1a/L8, 3/C8, 3b/D8, 4/E8
19	Bulb Failure Module	3c/H2, 3d/G2
20	Carburettor Stepper Motor	1a/G7
21	Cargo Space Lamp	2b/M5
22	Cargo Space Lamp Switch	2b/M3
23	Central Locking Motor LH Front	3a/G8
24	Central Locking Motor LH Rear	3a/M8
25	Central Locking Motor RH Front	3a/G1
26	Central Locking Motor RH Rear	3a/M1
27	Central Locking Motor Tailgate	3a/M4
28	Cigar Lighter	2b/G5
29	Clock	2b/G6
30	Coolant Temp. Sensor	1/C5
31	Cooling Fan Motor	1a/A7
32	Cooling Fan Switch	1a/C8
33	Crank Position Sensor	1a/C7
34	Dim/Dip Relay II	2/G4
35	Dim/Dip Relay B	2/G5
36	Dimmer Switch	2/L3
37	Dip Beam Relay F	2/F5
38	Distributor	1a/C2, 1a/D5, 1a/H2, 1a/J7, 4/B5
39	Door Ajar Sender LH Front	3d/F8
40	Door Ajar Sender LH Rear	3d/L8
41	Door Ajar Sender RH Front	3d/F1
42	Door Ajar Sender RH Rear	3d/L1
43	Door Ajar Sender Tailgate	3d/M4
44	EEC IV Module	4/J6
45	Electric Choke	1a/A6, 1a/C3, 1a/F2, 1a/F5
46	Electric Door Mirror	3/E1, 3/E8, 3/F2
47	Electric Mirror Control Switch	3/F2
48	Electric Window Control Switch Front	3a/J4
49	Electric Window Control Switch Rear	3a/K1, 3a/K8
50	Electric Window Motor LH Front	3a/F8
51	Electric Window Motor LH Rear	3a/J8
52	Electric Window Motor RH Front	3a/F1
53	Electric Window Motor RH Rear	3a/J1
54	Electronic Ignition Module	1a/B2
55	Engine Management Relay D	1a/A5, 1a/K5, 4/H2
56	Engine Management Relay M2	1a/K5
57	Engine Management Relay XI	1a/D6, 1a/K2, 1a/G5, 4/G1
58	Engine Temp. Sensor	1a/B7, 1a/F1, 1a/F7, 4/C5
59	ESC 2 Ignition Module	1a/F8
60	Fader Control (4 Way)	5/C4, 5/J4
61	Flasher/Hazard Switch	2a/K4
62	Flasher Lamp LH	2a/A8
63	Flasher Lamp LH Side Marker	2a/E8
64	Flasher Lamp RH	2a/A1
65	Flasher Lamp RH Side Marker	2a/E1
66	Flasher Relay L1	2a/K5
67	Foglamp Front	2a/A2, 2a/A7
68	Foglamp Relay H	2a/E4
69	Foglamp Switch Front	2a/J1
70	Foglamp Switch Rear	2a/J2
71	Fuel Computer	3d/K5
72	Fuel Flow Sensor	3d/C7
73	Fuel Injectors	4/E4
74	Fuel Pump	4/M4
75	Fuel Sender	1/L4, 3d/L5
76	Fuel Shut Off Valve	1a/C3, 1a/J3
77	Glove Box Lamp/Switch	2b/F7
78	Graphic Display Module	3c/H5, 3d/G5
79	Handbrake Warning Switch	1/K5
80	Headlamp Unit LH	2/A6, 3c/A6
81	Headlamp Unit RH	2/A3, 3c/A3
82	Headlamp Washer Pump	3a/C1
83	Headlamp Washer Relay III	2/H2, 3a/F2, 3c/F3
84	Headlamp Wiper Motor	3a/A2, 3a/A6
85	Heated Rear Window	3/M5
86	Heated Rear Window Relay E (PRE 1989)	3/E4
87	Heated Rear Window Timer Relay IV	3/F4
88	Heated Rear Window Switch (PRE 1989)	3/J2
89	Heated Rear Window Switch (POST 1989)	3/K2
90	Heated Windscreen	3/F6
91	Heated Windscreen Relay L3	3/J4
92	Heated Windscreen Switch	3/J3
93	Heated Windscreen Timer Relay L2	3/K4
94	Heater Blower Illumination	2b/F5
95	Heater Blower Motor	3/G6
96	Heater Blower Switch	3/G5
97	High Beam Relay X	2/F4
98	Horn	3/A6, 3/A7

Key to wiring diagrams. Models from 1987 to May 1989

ITEM	DESCRIPTION	DIAGRAM/ GRID REF.	ITEM	DESCRIPTION	DIAGRAM/ GRID REF.
99	Horn Relay C	3/F4	133	Radio Unit	5/C2,
100	Horn Switch	3/L4			5/D5,
101	Hybrid Ignition Module	1a/B7,			5/E8,
		1a/F2			5/K3,
102	Ice Warning Sender	3d/A4			5/K6,
103	Idle Speed Valve	4/D5			5/K8
104	Ignition Coil	1a/C2,	134	Reversing Lamp Switch	2a/D5
		1a/C5,	135	Spark Plugs	1a/D2,
		1a/G2,			1a/D5,
		1a/H6,			1a/J2,
		4/C5			1a/K7,
105	Ignition Relay I	1/H4			4/A5
106	Ignition Switch	1/K1,	136	Speaker LH Door	5/C8,
		3b/L2,			5/D8,
		5/C1,			5/J3,
		5/D3,			5/J6
		5/F7,	137	Speaker LH Front	5/A2,
		5/K7,			5/A5,
		5/L4,			5/A8,
		5/M2			5/G3,
107	Inertia Switch	4/M3			5/G6,
108	Instrument Cluster	1/K3,			5/H8
		1a/M3,	138	Speaker LH Rear	5/F5,
		2/J4,			5/F8,
		2a/J3,			5/M3,
		2b/F2,			5/M6
		3b/K3,	139	Speaker RH Door	5/C3,
		4/K3			5/D6,
109	Instrument Illumination Control	2b/G2,			5/J1,
		3c/J2,			5/J4
		3d/J2	140	Speaker RH Front	5/A1,
110	Interior Lamp Delay Relay VI	2b/E2			5/A3,
111	Interior Lamp Door Switch LH Front	2b/E8			5/A6,
112	Interior Lamp Door Switch LH Rear	2b/J8			5/G1,
113	Interior Lamp Door Switch RH Front	2b/E1			5/G4,
114	Interior Lamp Door Switch RH Rear	2b/J1			5/H6
115	Interior Lamp/Switch Front (High Series)	2b/J3	141	Speaker RH Rear	5/F3,
116	Interior Lamp/Switch Front (Low Series)	2b/J3			5/F6,
117	Interior Lamp/Switch Rear	2b/K3			5/M1,
118	Kickdown Actuator	1/D6			5/M4
119	Kickdown Relay VIII	1/H2	142	Speed Sensor	3d/E4
120	Kickdown Switch	1/J4	143	Starter Motor	1/D5
121	Licence Plate Lamp	2/M3,	144	Stop Lamp Switch	2a/H3,
		2/M6			3b/J3,
122	Light Cluster LH Rear	2/M8,			3c/F5
		2a/M8,	145	Suppressor	1a/J5,
		3c/M8			1a/K4,
123	Light Cluster RH Rear	2/M1,			3/C4,
		2a/M1,			4/E4
		3c/M1	146	TFI Module	4/C8
124	Light Switch	2/L3,	147	Throttle Position Sensor	4/C4
		2a/K3,	148	Trailer Flasher Indicator	2a/H5
		2b/J2,	149	Vacuum Switch	1/G6
		3/L3,	150	Vacuum Valve (From 1988)	1a/A6
		3a/J3,	151	Warning Lamp Cluster	3d/K6
		3c/K4,	152	Windscreen Washer Pump	3a/C1
		3d/J3	153	Wiper Intermittent Relay V	3a/E3
125	Link (Fitted When Manual Trans.)	1/F2	154	Wiper Intermittent Speed Control	3a/G4
126	Low Brake Fluid Sender	1/C3,	155	Wiper Motor Front	3a/E4
		3b/E3	156	Wiper Motor Rear	3a/M6
127	Low Washer Fluid Sender	3d/C1	157	Wiper Switch	3a/H3
128	Luggage Comp. Lamp	2b/L5	158	Wheel Sensor LH Front	3b/B8
129	Luggage Comp. Lamp Switch	2b/M4	159	Wheel Sensor LH Rear	3b/L8
130	Manifold Heater	1a/J1,	160	Wheel Sensor RH Front	3b/B1
		1a/F6	161	Wheel Sensor RH Rear	3b/L1
131	Manifold Temp. Switch	1a/E2			
132	Oil Pressure Switch	1/B6			

13

Key to wiring diagrams (continued). Models from 1987 to May 1989

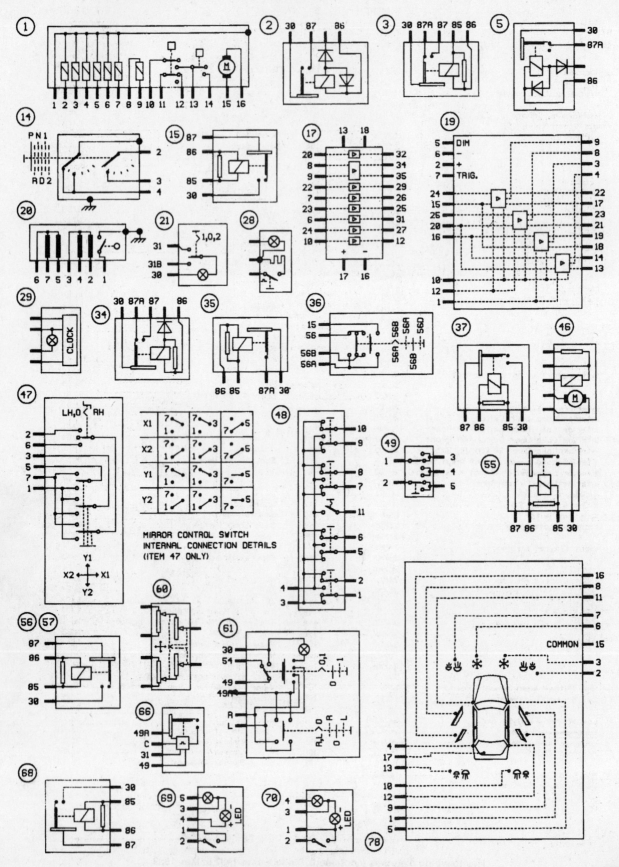

Internal connection details. Models from 1987 to May 1989

H24100

T.M.MARKE

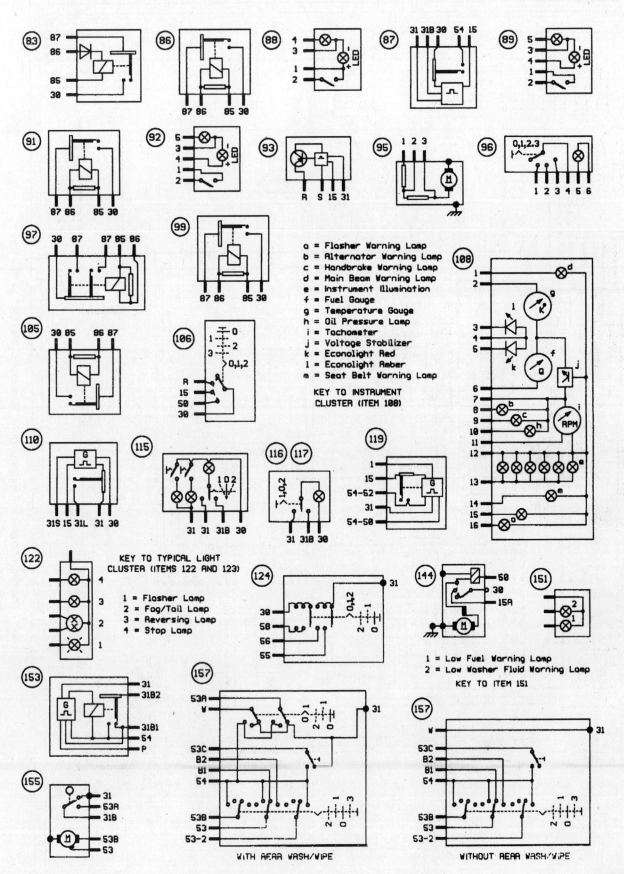

a = Flasher Warning Lamp
b = Alternator Warning Lamp
c = Handbrake Warning Lamp
d = Main Beam Warning Lamp
e = Instrument Illumination
f = Fuel Gauge
g = Temperature Gauge
h = Oil Pressure Lamp
i = Tachometer
j = Voltage Stabilizer
k = Econolight Red
l = Econolight Amber
m = Seat Belt Warning Lamp

KEY TO INSTRUMENT
CLUSTER (ITEM 108)

KEY TO TYPICAL LIGHT
CLUSTER (ITEMS 122 AND 123)

1 = Flasher Lamp
2 = Fog/Tail Lamp
3 = Reversing Lamp
4 = Stop Lamp

1 = Low Fuel Warning Lamp
2 = Low Washer Fluid Warning Lamp
KEY TO ITEM 151

WITH REAR WASH/WIPE

WITHOUT REAR WASH/WIPE

H24101
T.M.MAAKE

Internal connection details (continued). Models from 1987 to May 1989

13

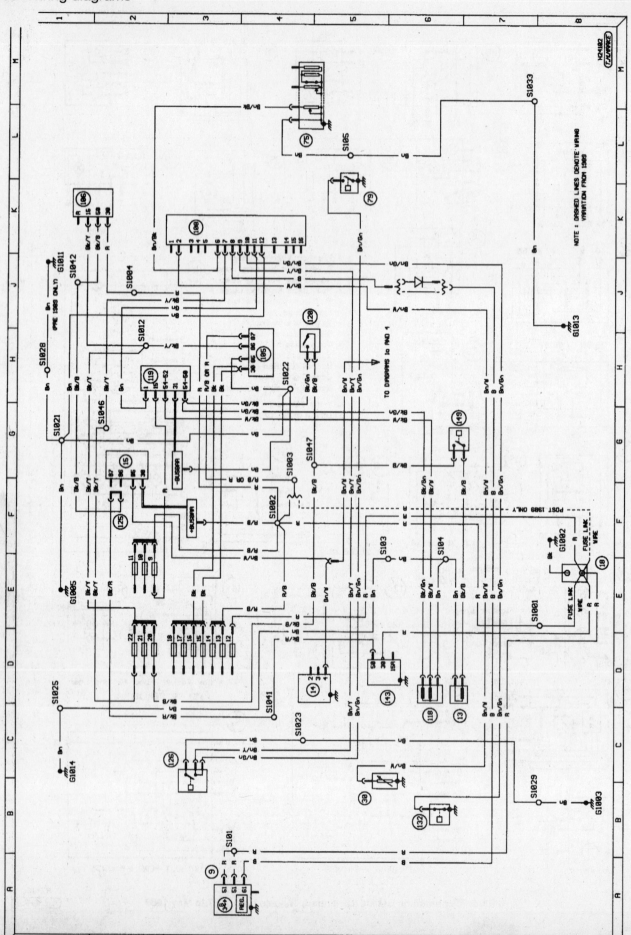

Diagram 1. Starting, charging and warning lamps. Models from May 1987 to May 1989

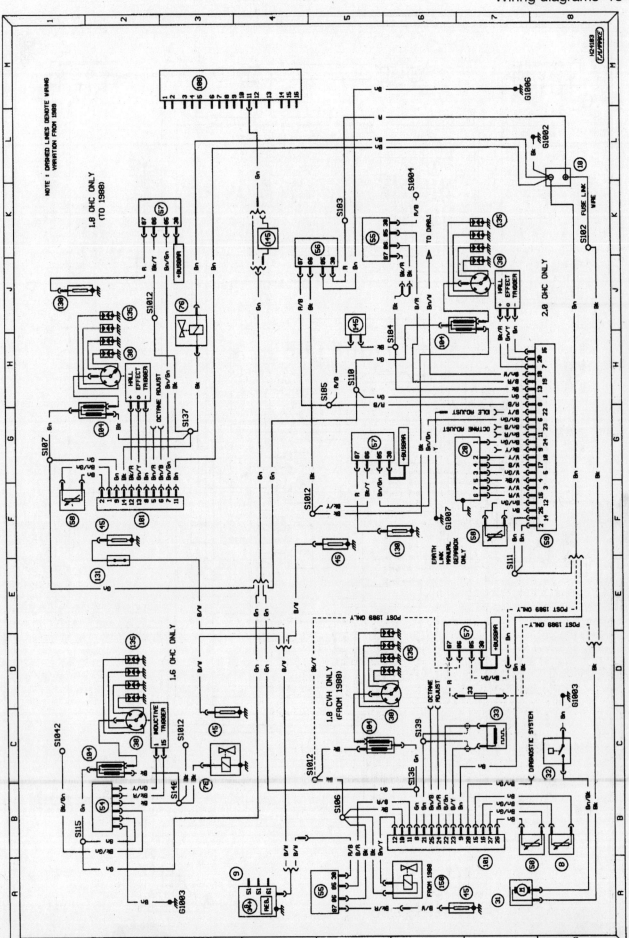

Diagram 1a. Ignition variations. Carburettor models from 1987 to May 1989

13

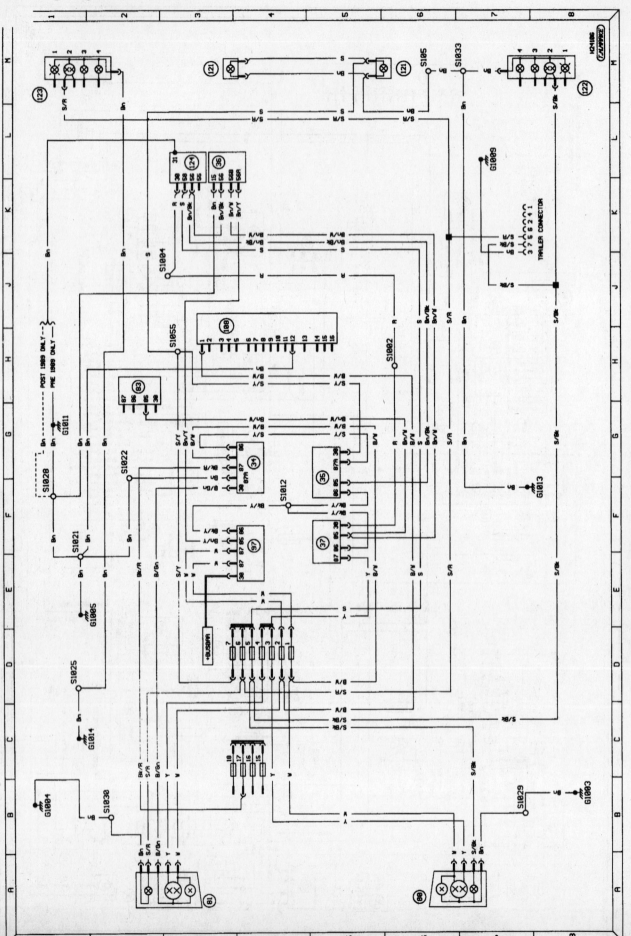

Diagram 2. Exterior lighting - head/sidelamps. Models from 1987 to May 1989

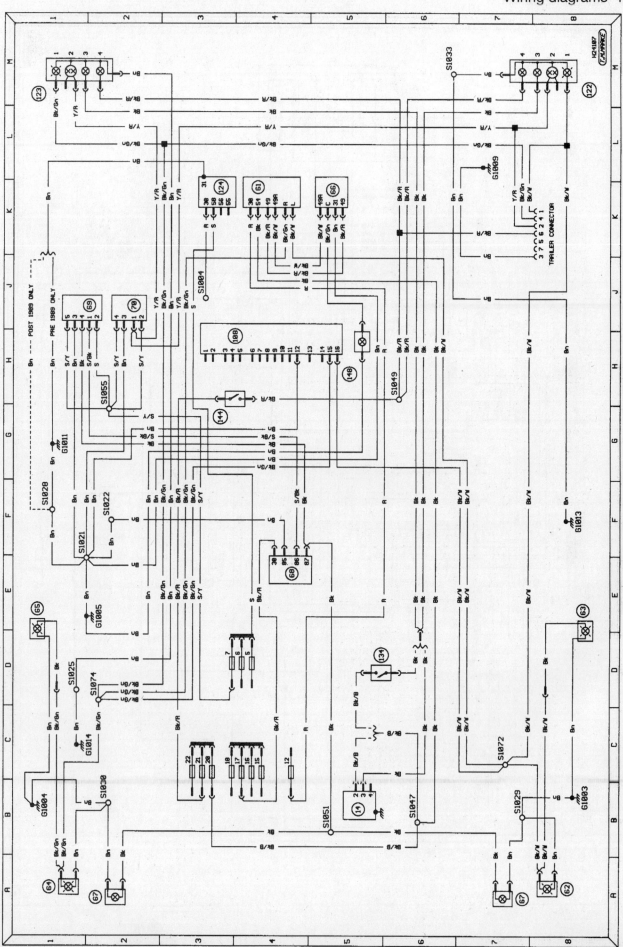

Diagram 2a. Exterior lighting - signal warning lamps. Models from 1987 to May 1989

13

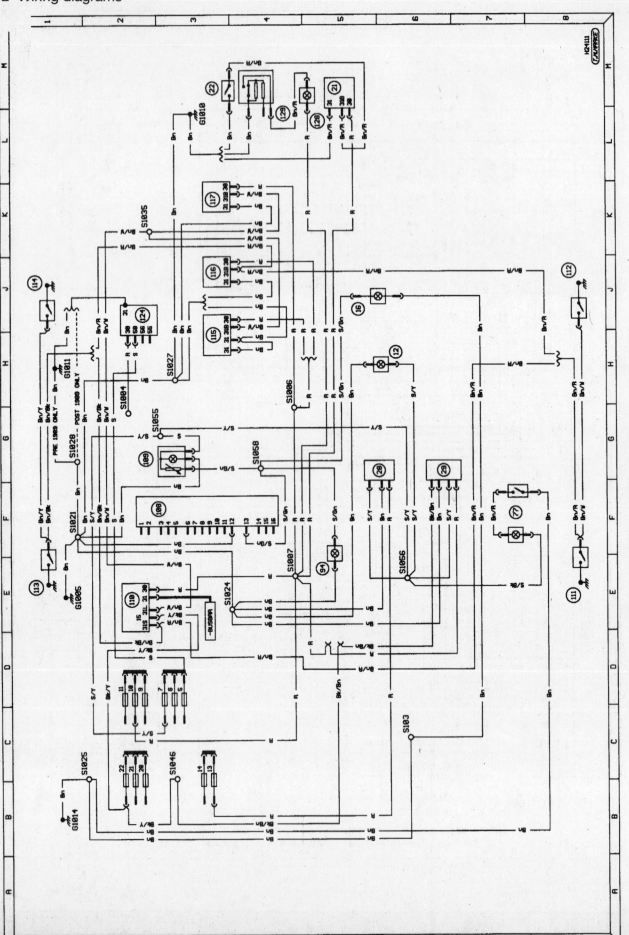

Diagram 2b. Interior lighting. Models from 1987 to May 1989

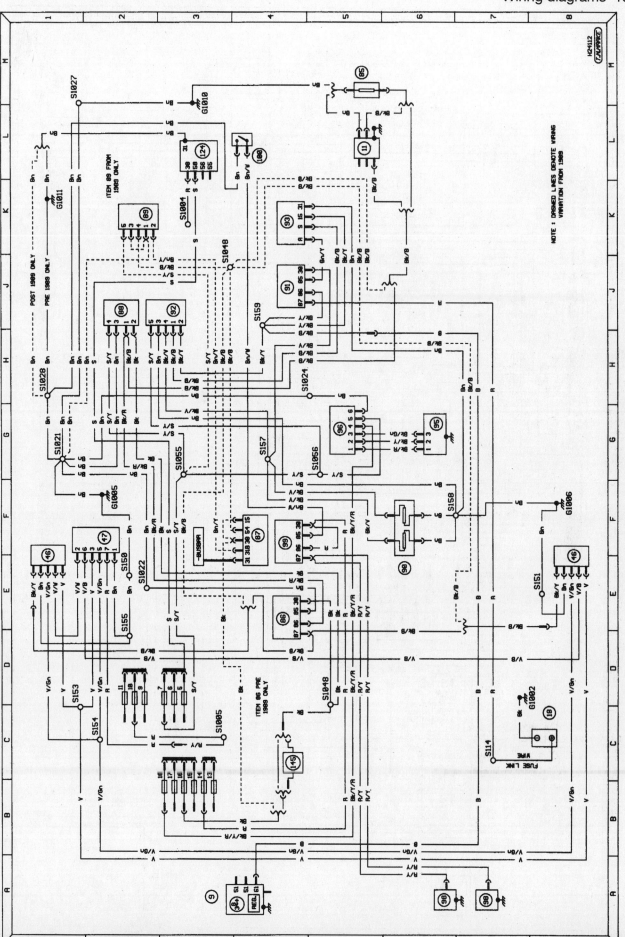

Diagram 3. Ancillary circuits - horn, heater blower, heated mirrors and screens.
Models from 1987 to May 1989

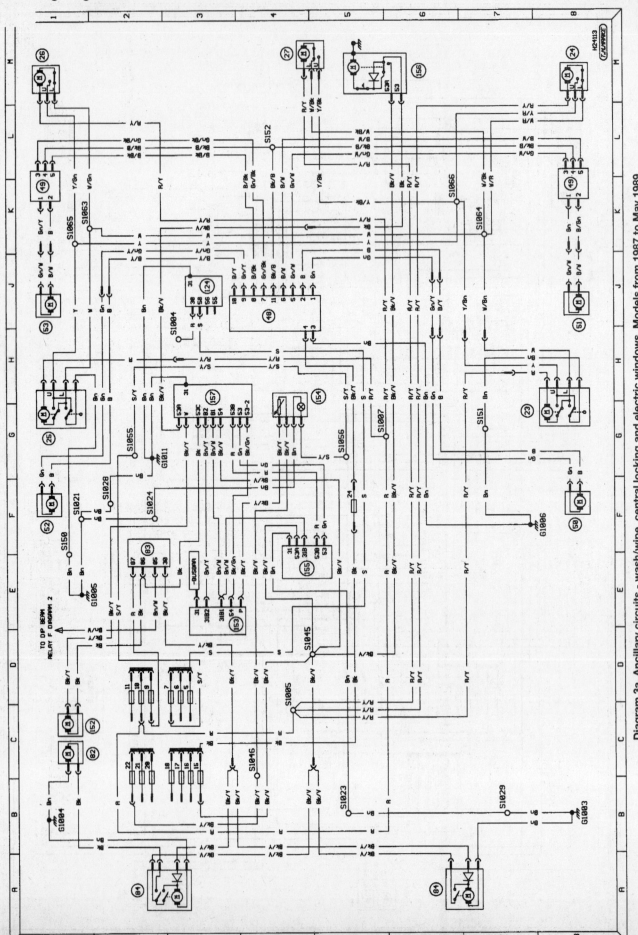

Diagram 3a. Ancillary circuits - wash/wipe, central locking and electric windows. Models from 1987 to May 1989

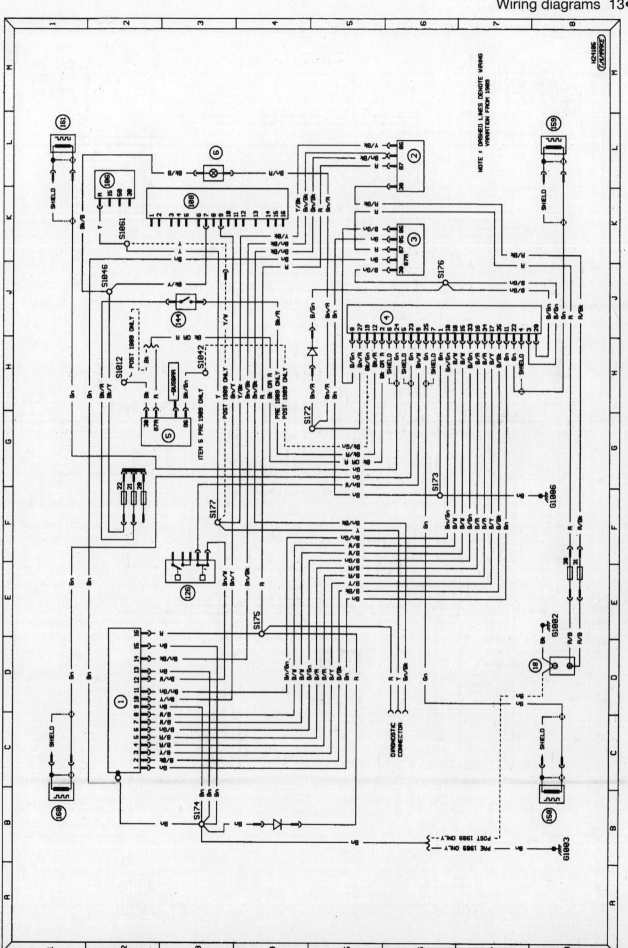

Diagram 3b. Anti-lock braking system. Models from 1987 to May 1989

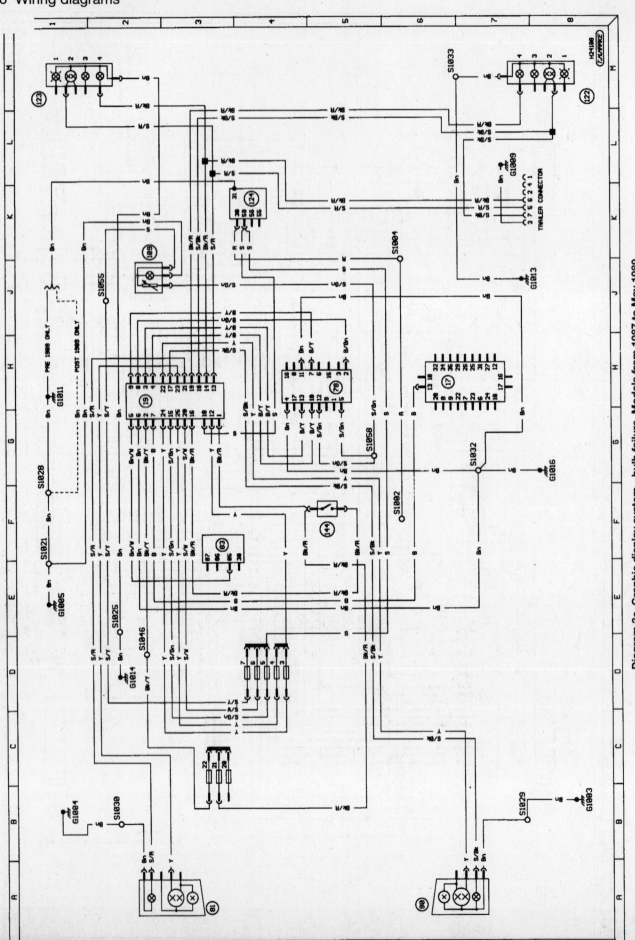

Diagram 3c. Graphic display system - bulb failure. Models from 1987 to May 1989

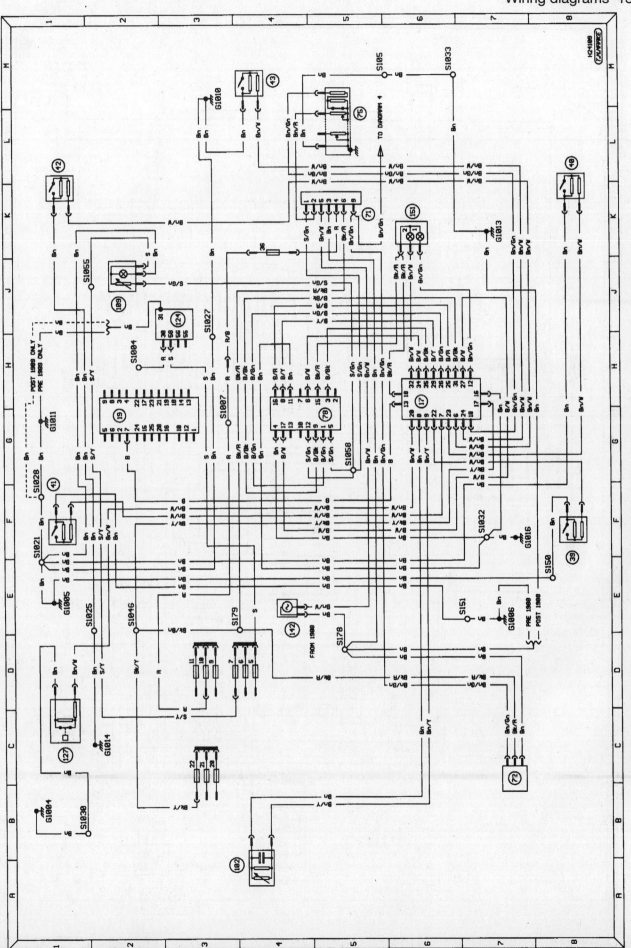

Diagram 3d. Graphic display system - auxiliary warning, door ajar and fuel computer. Models from 1987 to May 1989

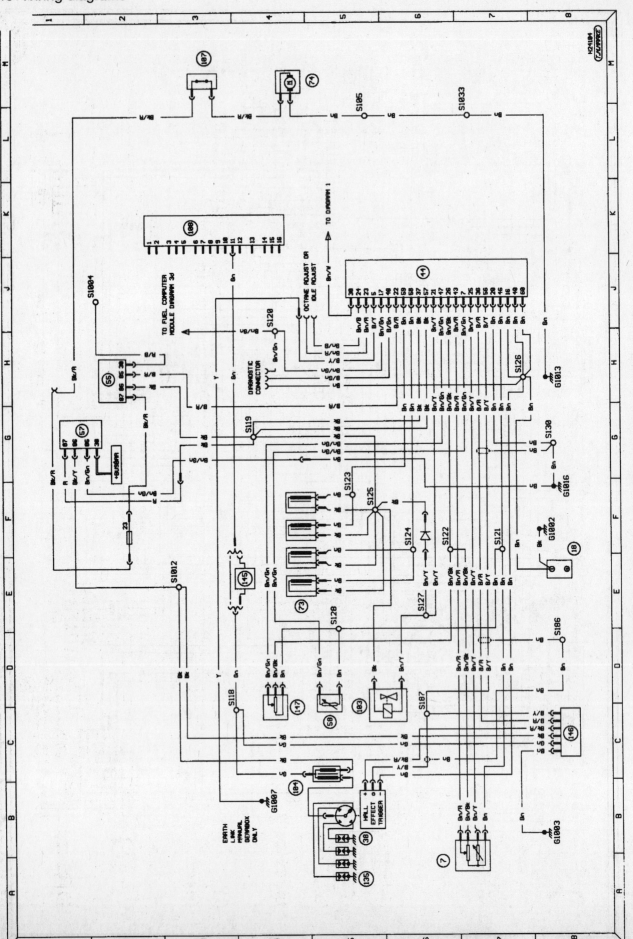

Diagram 4. 2.0 Efi fuel injection and ignition. Models from 1987 to May 1989

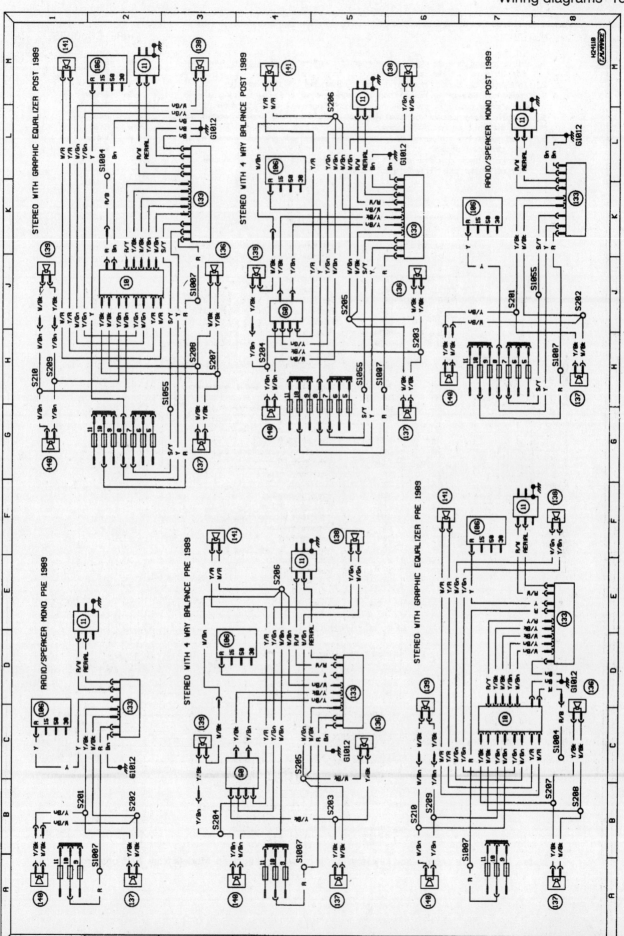

Diagram 5. In-car entertainment. Models from 1987 to May 1989

13

NOTES:

1. All diagrams are divided into numbered circuits depending on function e.g. Diagram 2: Exterior lighting.
2. Items are arranged in relation to a plan view of the vehicle.
3. Items may appear on more than one diagram so are found using a grid reference e.g. 2/A1 denotes an item on diagram 2 grid location A1.
4. Complex items appear on the diagrams as blocks and are expanded on the internal connections page.
5. Feed wires are coloured red (black when switched) and all earth wires are coloured brown.
6. Brackets show how the circuit may be connected in more than one way.
7. Not all items are fitted to all models.

WIRE COLOURS

B Blue
Bk Black
Bn Brown
Gn Green
R Red
Rs Pink
S Grey
V Violet
W White
Y Yellow

FUSE	RATING	CIRCUIT
1	15A	LH Main Beam, LH Driving Lamp
2	15A	RH Main Beam, RH Driving Lamp
3	7.5A	LH Dip Beam
4	7.5A	RH Dip Beam
5	5A	LH Sidelamp
6	5A	RH Sidelamp
7	15A	Instrument Illum., Numberplate Lamp
8	15A	Radio
9	15A	Headlamp Wash
10	7.5A	Interior Lamps, Clock, Door Locking, Mirrors
12	10A	Hazard Warning Lamps, Anti-theft, Door Locking
13	20A	Cigar Lighter, Radio Amplifier
14	10A	Horn
15	15A	Wiper Motors, Washer Pump
16	20A	Heated Rear Window, Heated Mirrors
17	15A	Front Foglamps, Dim/Dip
18	25A	Heater Blower
20	10A	Direction Indicators, Reversing Lamps
21	7.5A	Stop Lamps
22	4A	Control Circuits
23	20A	Fuel Pump
24	30A	Power Windows
30	20A	Anti-lock Brake
31	30A	Anti-lock Brake Pump 1
32	15A	Lambda Sensor
33	30A	Cooling Fan
34	30A	Anti-lock Brake Pump 2
35	1A	EEC V Module
37	1A	Fuel Computer

KEY TO SYMBOLS

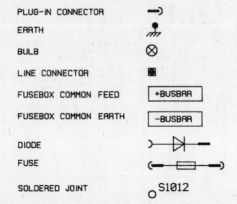

PLUG-IN CONNECTOR
EARTH
BULB
LINE CONNECTOR
FUSEBOX COMMON FEED   +BUSBAR
FUSEBOX COMMON EARTH   -BUSBAR
DIODE
FUSE
SOLDERED JOINT   S1012

Notes, tables, wire colours and key to symbols on wiring diagrams. Models from 1990 onwards

ITEM	DESCRIPTION	DIAGRAM/ GRID REF.
1	ABS Hydraulic Control Unit	3b/C2
2	ABS Main Relay M12	3b/H6
3	ABS Module	3b/G6
4	ABS Pump Relay M13	3b/J6
5	ABS Pump Relay M14	3b/K6
6	ABS Warning Indicator	3b/L3
7	Air Temp. Sensor	1a/G1, 4/B6, 4a/C5
8	Alternator	1/A3, 1a/A4, 3/A3
9	Amplifier (Audio)	5/K6
10	Amplifier/Graphic Equalizer	5/K2
11	Antenna Module	3/L5, 5/C1, 5/C5, 5/K2, 5/K6
12	Anti-theft Module	5a/D2
13	Anti-theft Switch	5a/H2, 5a/H7
14	Ashtray Illumination	2b/H6
15	Auto. Gear Actuator	1/D7
16	Auto. Trans. Inhibitor Switch	1/D4, 2a/B6
17	Auto. Trans. Relay XII	1/F2
18	Auto. Trans. Selector Illumination	2b/J6
19	Auxiliary Warning Module	3c/H6, 3d/G6
20	Ballast Resistor	4/D2, 4a/G8
21	Battery	1/F8, 1a/H8, 2/F7, 2a/G8, 2b/C8, 3/C8, 3a/D8, 3b/D8, 3c/E8, 3d/D8, 4/F8, 4a/F8, 5/D8, 5a/D8
22	Bonnet Switch	5a/A4
23	Bulb Failure Module	3c/H3, 3d/G2
24	Canister Purge Solenoid	4/D3
25	Cargo Space Lamp (Estate Only)	2b/M5, 5a/L6
26	Cargo Space Lamp Switch (Estate Only)	2b/M4, 5a/M3
27	CD Player	5/J5
28	Central Locking Motor LH Front	3a/H8, 5a/H8
29	Central Locking Motor LH Rear	3a/M8, 5a/L8
30	Central Locking Motor RH Front	3a/H1, 5a/H1
31	Central Locking Motor RH Rear	3a/M1, 5a/L1
32	Central Locking Motor Tailgate	3a/M5
33	Cigar Lighter	2b/F6
34	Clock	2b/F7
35	CO Adjuster Potentiometer	4a/C6
36	Coolant Temp. Gauge Sender Unit	1/C6
37	Cooling Fan Motor	1/A5
38	Cooling Fan Relay	1/J6
39	Cooling Fan Switch	1/B5
40	Crank Position Sensor	1a/C6, 1a/H1, 4/D5, 4a/E3
41	Dim/Dip Relay II	2/G3

ITEM	DESCRIPTION	DIAGRAM/ GRID REF.
42	Dim/Dip Relay B	2/F5
43	Dip Beam Relay F	2/E5
44	Dimmer Switch	2/L3
45	Direction Indicator Flasher Relay	2a/K5
46	Direction Indicator/Hazard Switch	2a/K4
47	Direction Indicator Lamp LH	2a/A8
48	Direction Indicator Lamp RH	2a/A1
49	Direction Indicator Side Repeater LH	2a/D8
50	Direction Indicator Side Repeater RH	2a/D1
51	Distributor	1a/C2, 1a/D6, 1a/J2, 4a/D8
52	Door Ajar/Lamp Switch LH Front	3d/F8, 5a/F8
53	Door Ajar/Lamp Switch LH Rear	3d/L8, 5a/K8
54	Door Ajar/Lamp Switch RH Front	3d/F1, 5a/F1
55	Door Ajar/Lamp Switch RH Rear	3d/L1, 5a/K1
56	Door Ajar/Lamp Switch Tailgate (Sapphire & Hatchback Only)	2b/M4, 3d/M4, 5a/L4
57	E.D.I.S. Module	4/E4
58	EEC IV Module	4/K6, 4a/K6
59	Electric Choke	1a/A6, 1a/C3, 1a/E3
60	Electric Door Mirror	3/F1, 3/F8
61	Electric Mirror Control Switch	3/F2
62	Electric Window Control Switch Front	3a/J4
63	Electric Window Control Switch Rear	3a/K1, 3a/K8
64	Electric Window Motor LH Front	3a/F8
65	Electric Window Motor LH Rear	3a/J8
66	Electric Window Motor RH Front	3a/F1
67	Electric Window Motor RH Rear	3a/J1
68	Electronic Ignition Module	1a/B1, 4a/B8
69	Engine Management Relay D	1a/E1, 4/J1, 4a/H1
70	Engine Management Relay XI	4/H1, 4a/G1
71	Engine Temp. Sensor	1a/B6, 1a/G1, 4/B6, 4a/C4
72	ESC 2 Ignition Module	1a/B6
73	Foglamp Front	2a/A2, 2a/A7
74	Foglamp Relay H	2a/E5
75	Foglamp Switch Front	2a/J1
76	Foglamp Switch Rear	2a/J2
77	Fuel Computer	3d/K5
78	Fuel Gauge Sender Unit	1/L4, 3d/L5
79	Fuel Injectors	4/B4, 4a/F4
80	Fuel Pump	1a/F8, 4/M4, 4a/M4
81	Fuel Pump Relay	1a/D7
82	Fuel Rail Temp. Switch	4a/J4
83	Fuel Shut Off Solenoid	1a/B3, 1a/C8
84	Glove Box Lamp/Switch	2b/E7
85	Graphic Display Module	3c/H5, 3d/G5
86	Graphic Equalizer	5/H5
87	Handbrake Warning Switch	1/K5
88	Headlamp Unit LH	2/A6, 3c/A6

13

Key to wiring diagrams. Models from 1990 onwards

ITEM	DESCRIPTION	DIAGRAM/ GRID REF.	ITEM	DESCRIPTION	DIAGRAM/ GRID REF
89	Headlamp Unit RH	2/A3, 3c/A3	131	Lamp Cluster LH Rear	2/M8, 2a/M8, 3c/M8
90	Headlamp Washer Pump	3a/C1	132	Lamp Cluster RH Rear	2/M1, 2a/M1, 3c/M1
91	Headlamp Washer Relay III	3a/F2	133	Lamp Switch	2/L3, 2a/K3, 2b/G3, 3/L3, 3a/K3, 3c/K4, 3d/H3, 5/M3
92	Headlamp Wiper Motor	3a/A2, 3a/A7			
93	Heated Rear Window	3/M5			
94	Heated Rear Window Timer Relay IV	3/C5			
95	Heated Rear Window Switch	3/J3			
96	Heated Washer Jet	3/A1, 3/A8			
97	Heated Windscreen	3/F5			
98	Heated Windscreen Relay L3	3/J5			
99	Heated Windscreen Switch	3/J2			
100	Heated Windscreen Timer Relay L2	3/K5	134	Lamps On Warning Module	2b/G7
101	Heater Blower Illumination	2b/E4	135	Link (Fitted When Manual Trans.)	1/F2
102	Heater Blower Motor	3/G6	136	Low Brake Fluid Sender Unit	1/C3, 3b/D2
103	Heater Blower Switch	3/G5			
104	Heater End Switch	3/F6	137	Low Washer Fluid Sender Unit	3d/C1
105	High Beam Relay X	2/F4	138	Luggage Comp. Lamp (Sapphire/Hatchback)	2b/M5, 5a/L5
106	Horn	3/A7, 5a/A6			
107	Horn Relay C	3/C6	139	MAP Sensor	4/G4, 4a/J4
108	Horn Switch	3/L4	140	Number Plate Lamp	2/M3, 2/M6
109	Hybrid Ignition Module	1a/F3			
110	Ice Warning Sender	3d/A4	141	Oil Pressure Switch	1/B7
111	Idle Speed Solenoid	4a/C5	142	Power Delay Relay M5	4/K5
112	Ignition Coil	1a/C1, 1a/D6, 1a/H2, 4/C5, 4a/B4	143	Radio Unit	5/C3, 5/C7, 5/H2, 5/H8
113	Ignition Relay I	2/G5, 2a/F4, 3/D5, 3a/E5	144	Reversing Lamp Switch	2a/D6
114	Ignition Switch	1/K1, 1a/M1, 2/K2, 2a/K1, 2b/G2, 3/L2, 3a/K2, 3b/K2, 3c/L2, 3d/K2, 4/L1, 4a/L1, 5/M1	145	Spark Plugs	1a/D2, 1a/E6, 1a/J2, 4/C4, 4a/A5
			146	Speaker LH Door	5/B3, 5/B7, 5/J3, 5/K8
			147	Speaker LH Rear	5/D7, 5/L3, 5/L8
			148	Speaker RH Door	5/B1, 5/B5, 5/J1, 5/K5
115	Inertia Switch	1a/E8, 4/M3, 4a/M3	149	Speaker RH Rear	5/D5, 5/L1, 5/L5
116	Instrument Cluster	1/K3, 1a/M3, 2/J3, 2a/H4, 2b/F2, 3b/L3, 4/L3, 4a/K3	150	Speed Sensor	1/H7
			151	Starter Motor	1/C6
			152	Stop Lamp Switch	1/J4, 2a/H4, 3c/F5
117	Instrument Illumination Control	2b/G3, 3c/J2, 3d/J2	153	Suppressor	1a/K5, 4/B5, 4a/E3
118	Intake Air Valve	4/B8	154	Throttle Control Motor	4/B5
119	Interior Lamp Delay Relay VI	2b/D2	155	Throttle Position Sensor	4/B7, 4a/C4
120	Interior Lamp Door Switch LH Front	2b/E8			
121	Interior Lamp Door Switch LH Rear	2b/J8	156	Trailer Flasher Indicator	2a/H5
122	Interior Lamp Door Switch RH Front	2b/E1	157	Vacuum Valve	1a/H3
123	Interior Lamp Door Switch RH Rear	2b/J1	158	Warning Lamp Cluster	3d/K6
124	Interior Lamp/Switch Front (High Series)	2b/J3	159	Washer Pump Front/Rear Screen	3a/C1
125	Interior Lamp/Switch Front (Low Series)	2b/J3	160	Wiper Intermittent Relay V Front	3a/E4
126	Interior Lamp/Switch Rear	2b/K3	161	Wiper Intermittent Relay IX Rear	3a/E2
127	Kickdown Actuator	1/D6	162	Wiper Intermittent Speed Control	3a/H5
128	Kickdown Relay VIII	1/H3	163	Wiper Motor Front	3a/F5
129	Kickdown Switch	1/H4	164	Wiper Motor Rear	3a/M6
130	Lambda Sensor	4/D7, 4a/B6	165	Wiper Switch	3a/H4
			166	Wheel Sensor LH Front	3b/B8
			167	Wheel Sensor LH Rear	3b/M8
			168	Wheel Sensor RH Front	3b/B1
			169	Wheel Sensor RH Rear	3b/M1
			170	Exhaust Pressure Transducer	4/G3

Key to wiring diagrams (continued). Models from 1990 onwards

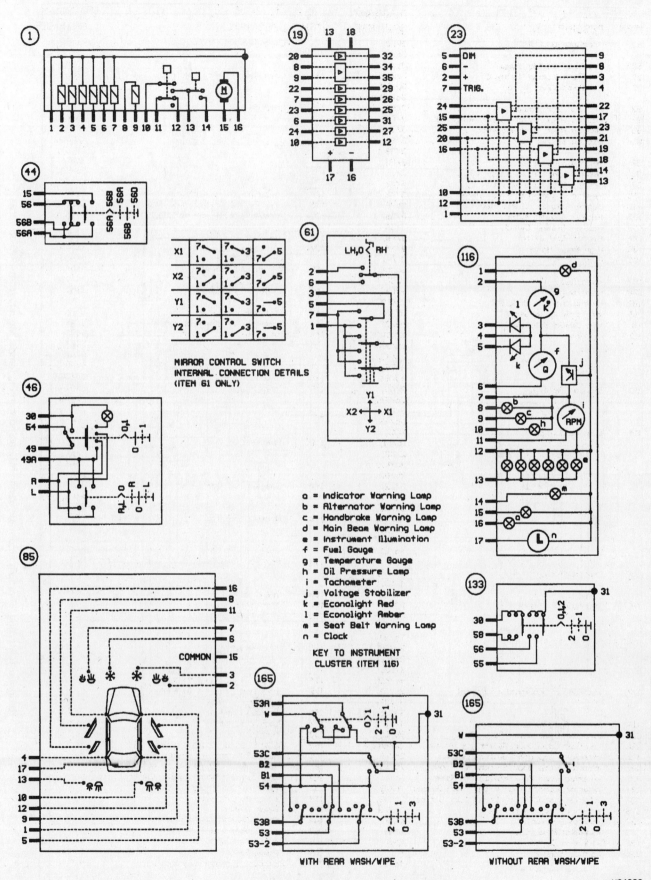

a = Indicator Warning Lamp
b = Alternator Warning Lamp
c = Handbrake Warning Lamp
d = Main Beam Warning Lamp
e = Instrument Illumination
f = Fuel Gauge
g = Temperature Gauge
h = Oil Pressure Lamp
i = Tachometer
j = Voltage Stabilizer
k = Econolight Red
l = Econolight Amber
m = Seat Belt Warning Lamp
n = Clock

KEY TO INSTRUMENT
CLUSTER (ITEM 116)

MIRROR CONTROL SWITCH
INTERNAL CONNECTION DETAILS
(ITEM 61 ONLY)

COMMON

WITH REAR WASH/WIPE

WITHOUT REAR WASH/WIPE

Internal connection details. Models from 1990 onwards

H24303

T.H.MAAKE

13

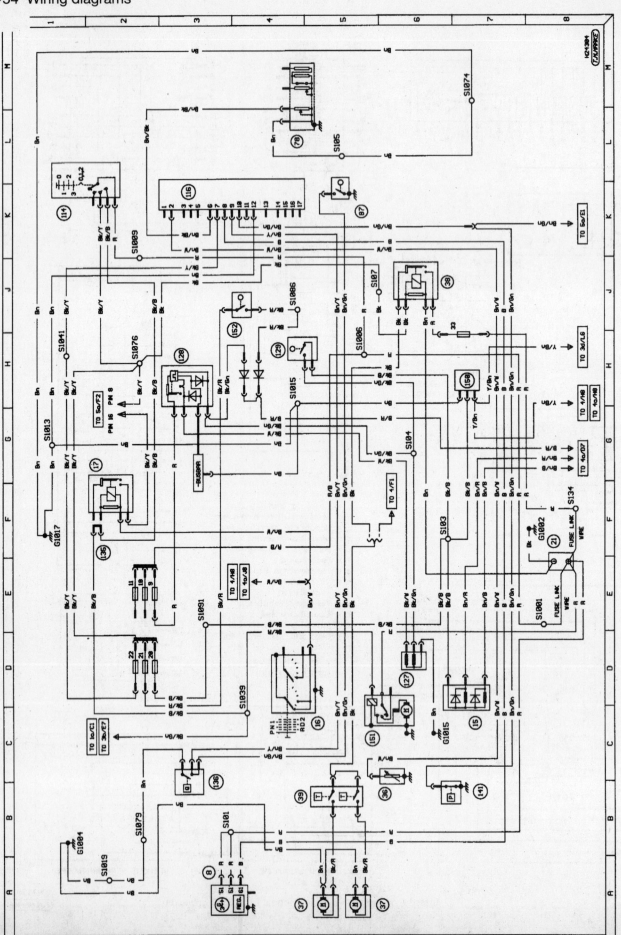

Diagram 1. Starting, charging automatic transmission and warning lamps. Models from 1990 onwards

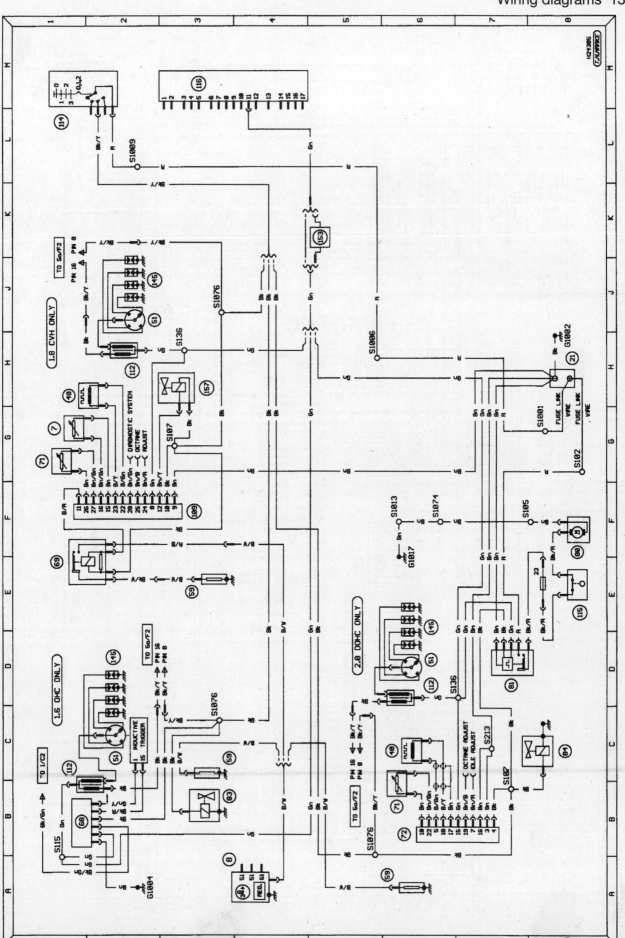

Diagram 1a. Ignition system for all carburettor models. Models from 1990 onwards

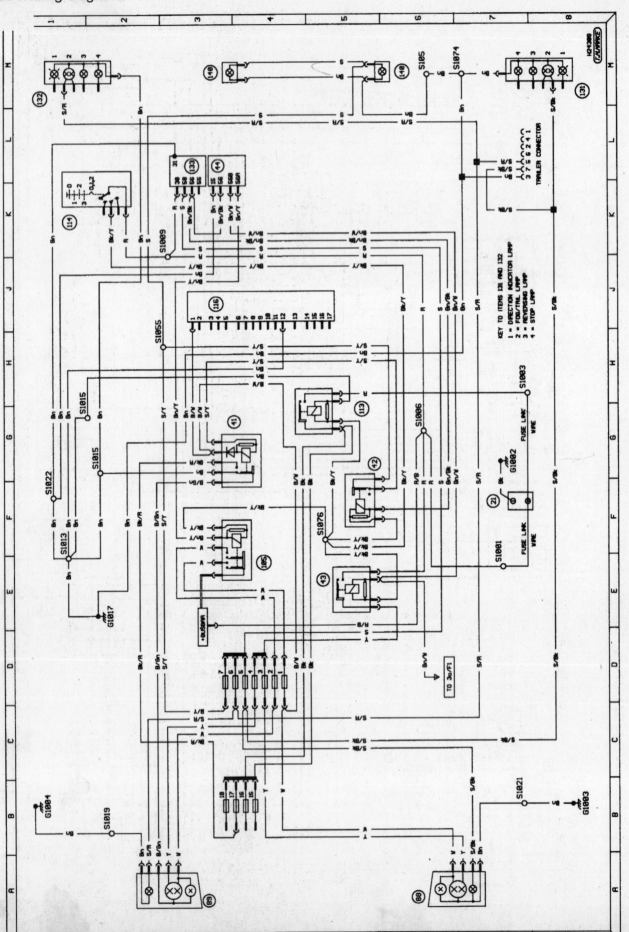

Diagram 2. Exterior lighting - head/sidelamps. Models from 1990 onwards

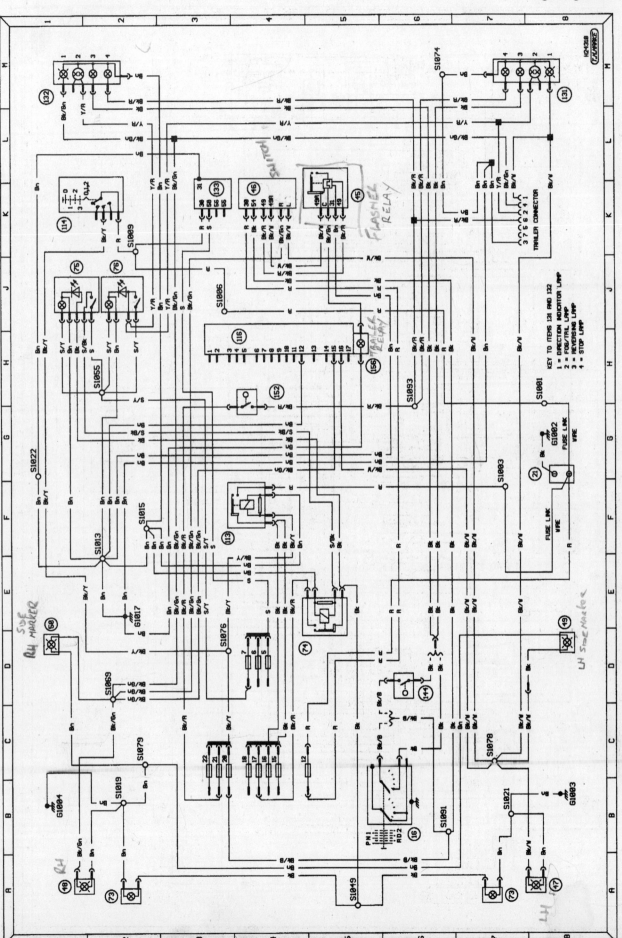

Diagram 2a. Exterior lighting - signal warning lamps. Models from 1990 onwards

KEY TO ITEMS 131 AND 132
1 = DIRECTION INDICATOR LAMP
2 = FOG/TAIL LAMP
3 = REVERSING LAMP
4 = STOP LAMP

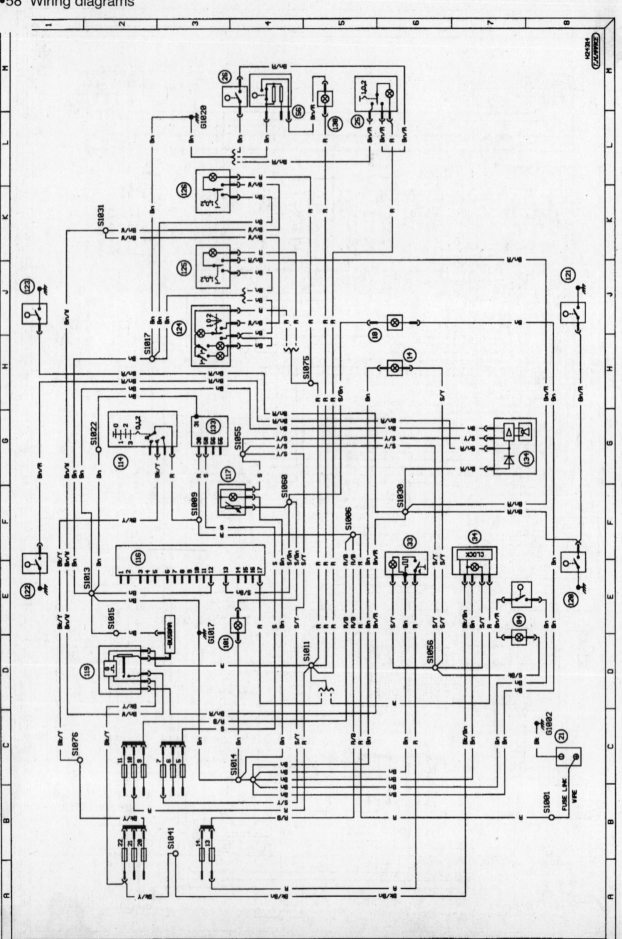

Diagram 2b. Interior lighting. Models from 1990 onwards

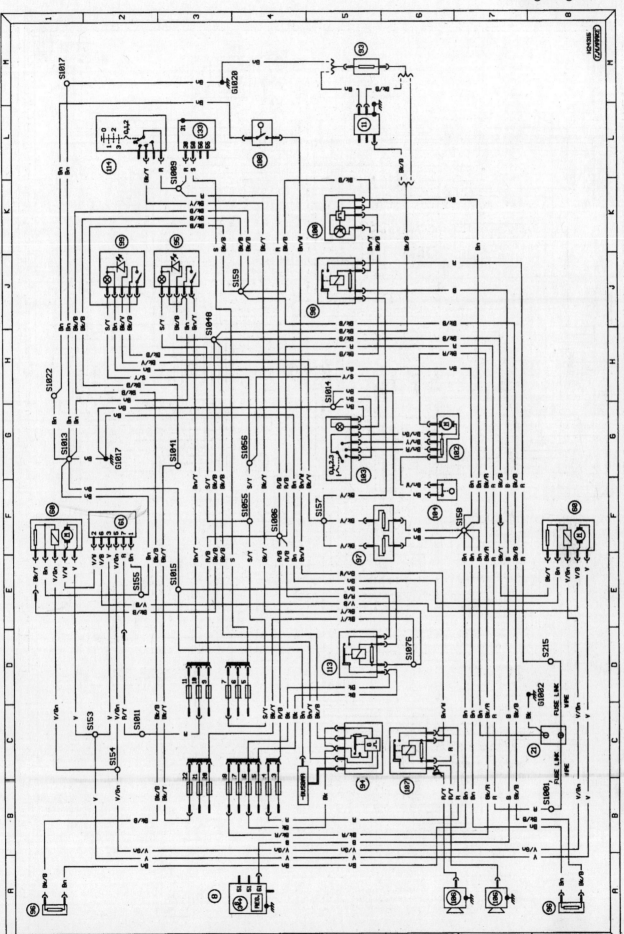

Diagram 3. Ancillary circuits - horn, heater blower, heated mirrors and screens. Models from 1990 onwards

13

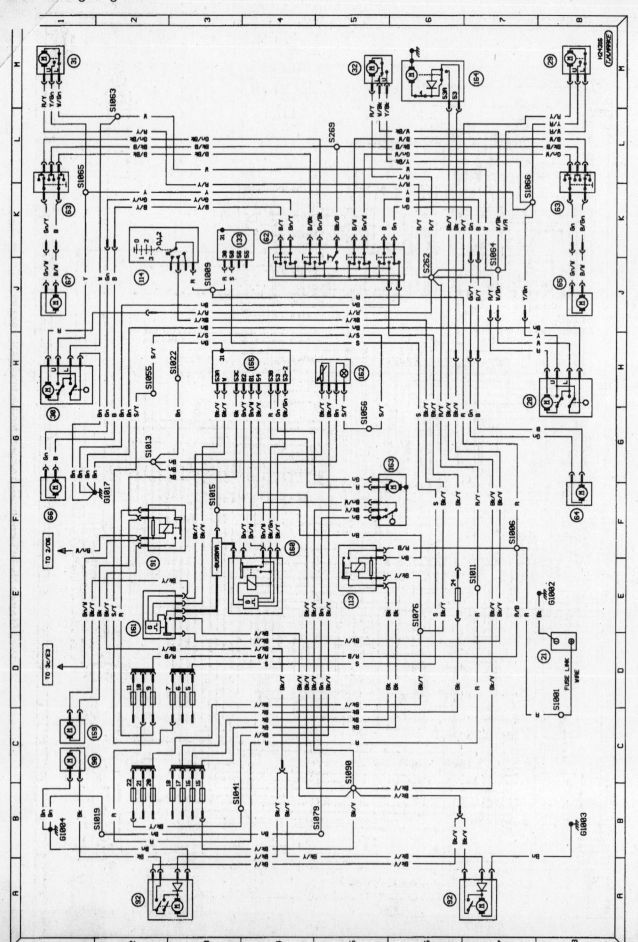

Diagram 3a. Ancillary circuits – wash/wipe, central locking and electric windows. Models from 1990 onwards

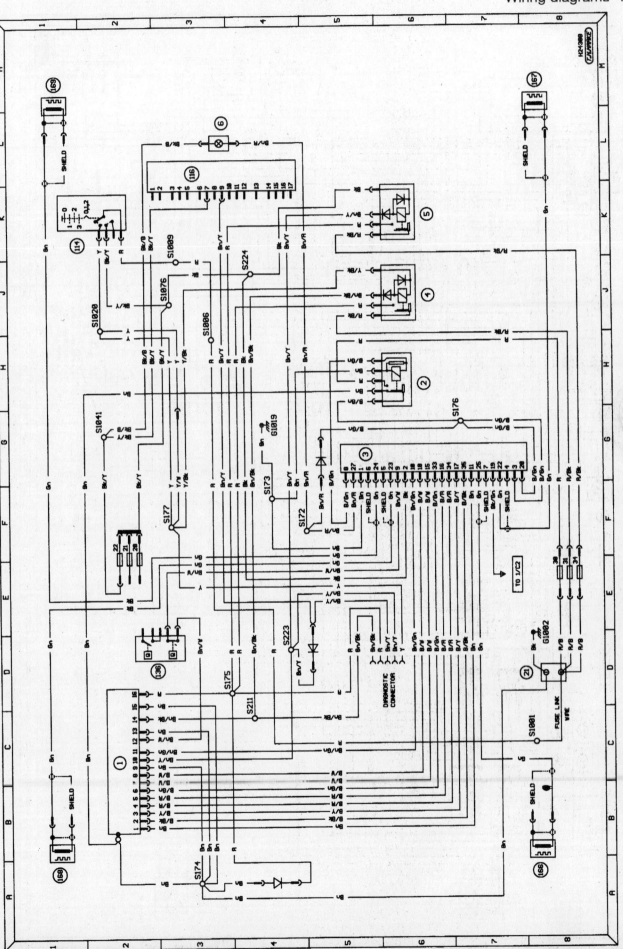

Diagram 3b. Anti-lock braking system. Models from 1990 onwards

13

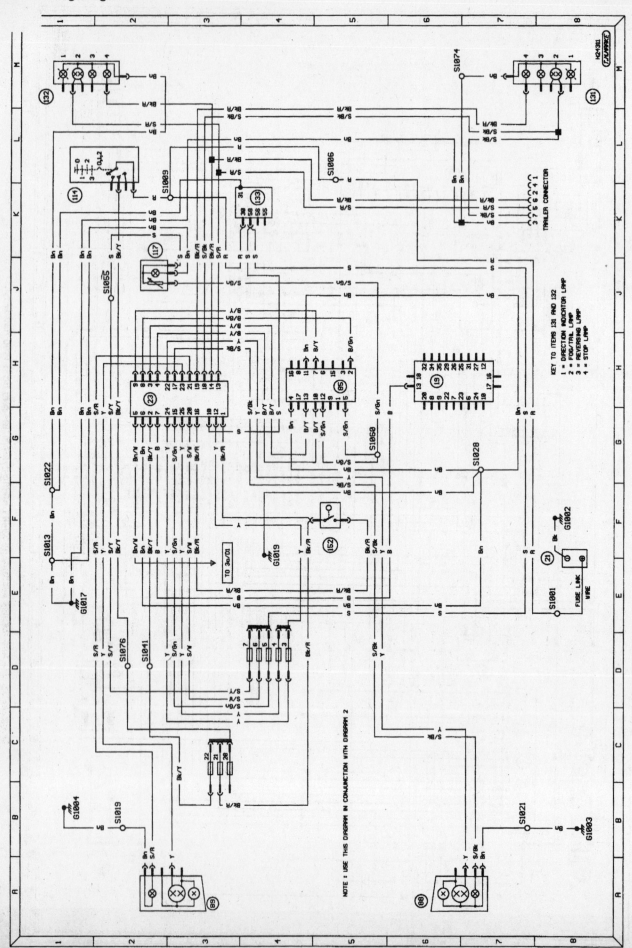

Diagram 3c. Graphic display system - bulb failure. Models from 1990 onwards

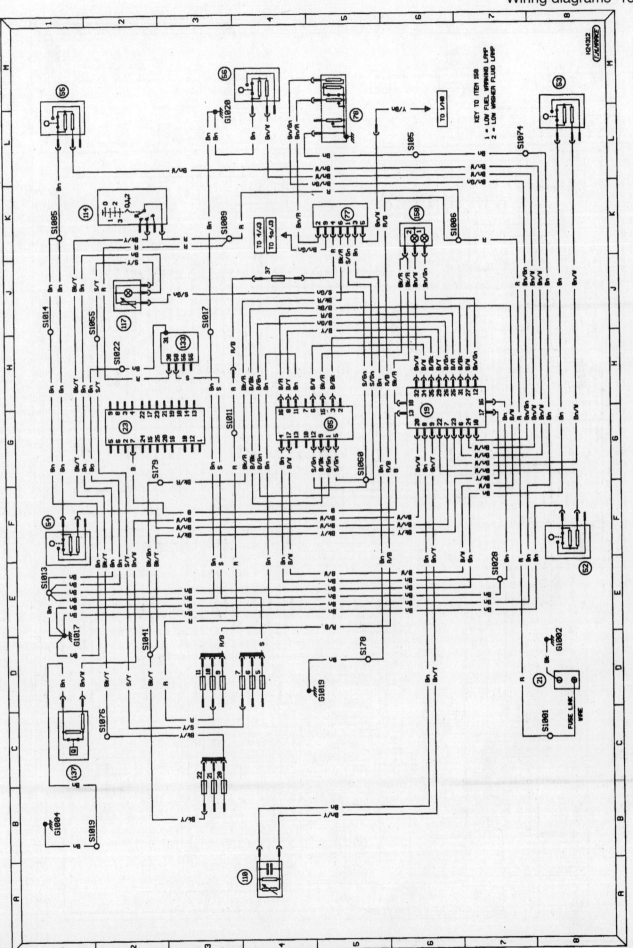

Diagram 3d. Graphic display system - auxiliary warning, door ajar and fuel computer. Models from 1990 onwards

13

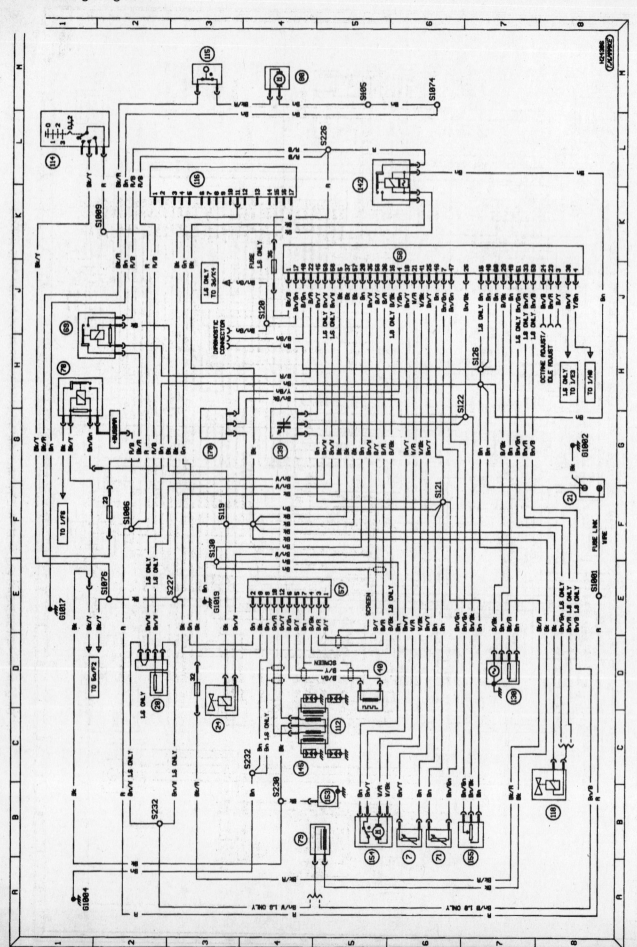

Diagram 4. 1.6 and 1.8 CVH engine Cfi fuel injection and ignition systems. Models from 1990 onwards

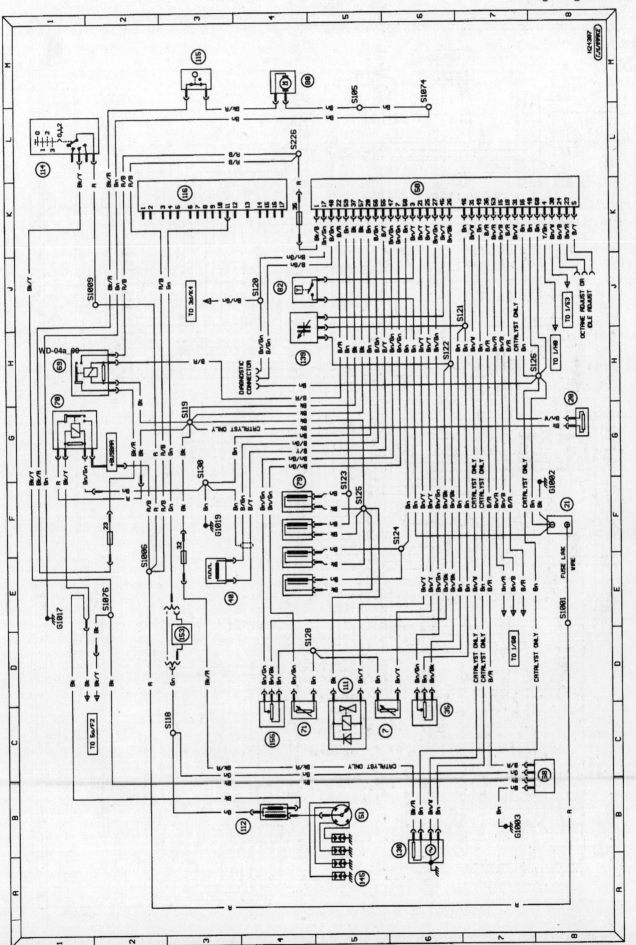

Diagram 4a. 2.0 litre DOHC engine EFI fuel injection and ignition systems. Models from 1990 onwards

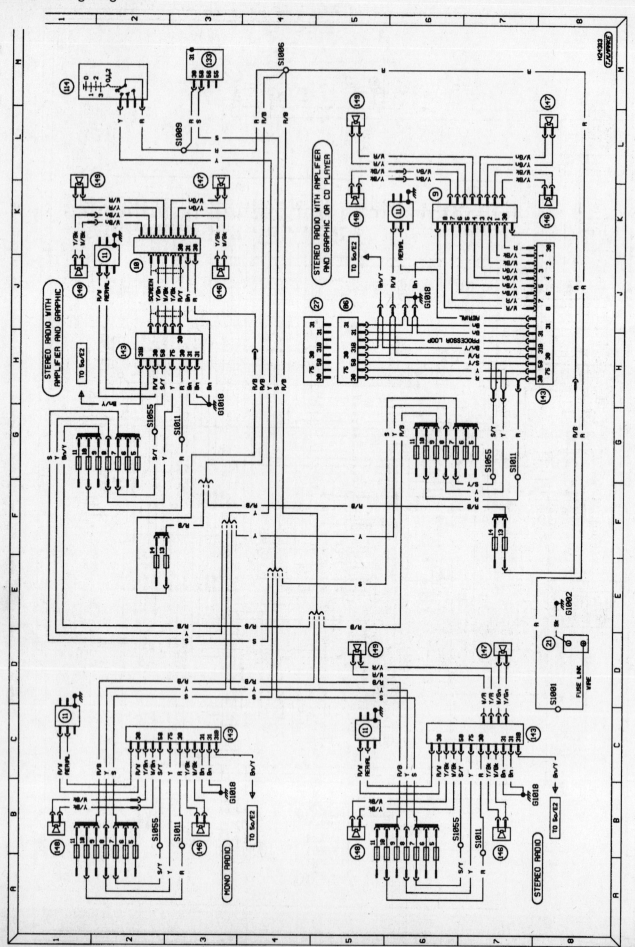

Diagram 5. In-car entertainment. Models from 1990 onwards

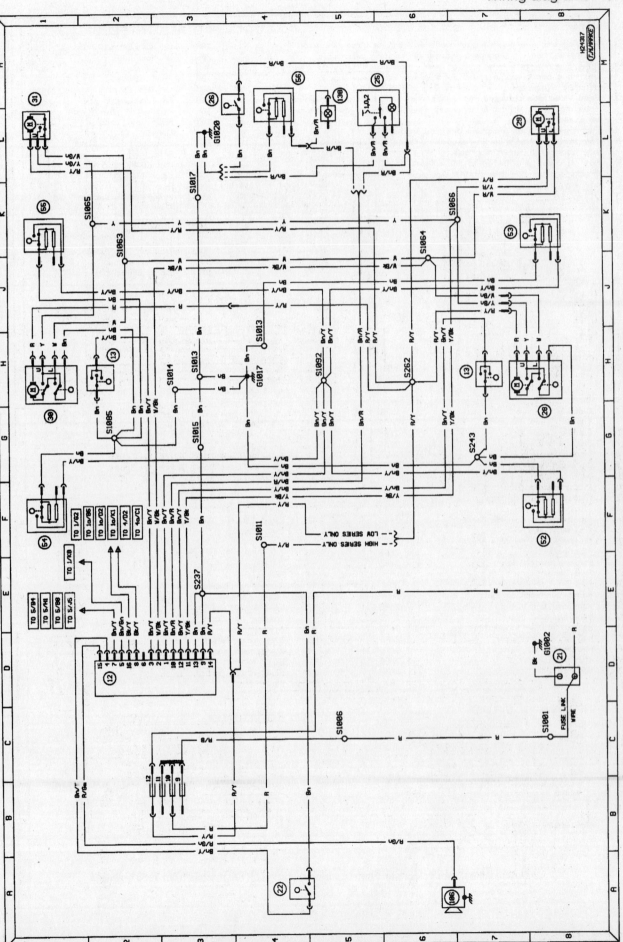

Diagram 5a. Anti-theft alarm. Models from 1990 onwards

13

NOTES:

1. All diagrams are divided into numbered circuits depending upon their function e.g Diagram 2 : Exterior lighting all models.
2. Some components may appear on more than one diagram so their positions are given in coded form in the key below e.g. 2/A1 denotes a component on diagram 2 grid location A1.
3. Feed wires are coloured red (black when switched) and originate from diagram 1. All other diagrams feed from fuse connections or common feeds.
4. Earth wires on all diagrams are coloured brown.
5. The tables below show where common feeds and common earths interconnect between diagrams.
6. Not all items are fitted to all models.
7. Brackets show how the circuit may be connected in more than one way.

Wire Colours

B	Blue	Rs	Pink	
Bk	Black	S	Grey	
Bn	Brown	V	Violet	
Gn	Green	W	White	
R	Red	Y	Yellow	

FUSE	RATING	CIRCUIT
1	20A	LH Main Beam, Dim/Dip
2	20A	RH Main Beam
3	10A	LH Dip Beam
4	10A	RH Dip Beam
5	10A	LH Side Lamps
6	10A	RH Side Lamps
7	10A	Instrument Illumination
8	10A	Rear Fog Lamps
9		Free
10	20A	Interior Lamps, Clock
11		Free
12	10A	Hazard Warning Lamps
13	30A	Cigar Lighter
14	30A	Horn
15	30A	Wiper Motor, Washer Pump
16		Free
17	20A	Dim/Dip
18	30A	Heater Blower
19		Free
20	15A	Flasher, Reversing Lamps
21	15A	Stop Lamps
22	10A	Clock, Brake Indicator
23		Free
24		Free

ITEM	DESCRIPTION	DIAGRAM/ GRID REF.
1	Alternator	1/A3
2	Battery	1/E8
		2/F8
		3/D8
3	Cigar Lighter	3/G5
4	Clock	1/H5
5	Coolant Temp. Sensor	1/C6
6	Dim/Dip Relay II	2/G4
7	Dim/Dip Relay B	2/G5
8	Dimmer Switch	2/L3
9	Dip Beam Relay F	2/F5
10	Distributor	1/D5
11	Electronic Ignition Module	1/C5
12	Flasher/Hazard Switch	2/L4
13	Flasher Lamp LH	2/A8
14	Flasher Lamp LH Side Marker	2/E8
15	Flasher Lamp RH	2/A1
16	Flasher Lamp RH Side Marker	2/E1
17	Flasher Relay 1	2/K5
18	Foglamp Switch Rear	2/J2
19	Fuel Sender	1/L4
20	Fuel Shut Off Valve	1/D6
21	Handbrake Warning Switch	1/K5
22	Headlamp Unit LH	2/A6
23	Headlamp Unit RH	2/A3
24	Heater Blower Illumination	3/E6
25	Heater Blower Motor	3/F6
26	Heater Blower Switch	3/F5
27	High Beam Relay X	2/F4
28	Horn	3/A6

ITEM	DESCRIPTION	DIAGRAM/ GRID REF.
29	Horn Relay C	3/E4
30	Horn Switch	3/J4
31	Ignition Coil	1/D5
32	Ignition Relay I	1/H4
33	Ignition Switch	1/K2
		3/L1
34	Instrument Cluster	1/K3
		2/H3
		3/H3
35	Interior Lamp Door Switch LH Front	3/H8
36	Interior Lamp Door Switch RH Front	3/H1
37	Interior Lamp/Switch	3/K4
38	Licence Plate Lamp	2/M4
		2/M5
39	Light Cluster LH Rear	2/M8
40	Light Cluster RH Rear	2/M1
41	Light Switch	2/L3
		3/K3
42	Low Brake Fluid Switch	1/C3
43	Oil Pressure Switch	1/B6
44	Radio Unit	3/J6
45	Reversing Lamp Switch	2/B6
46	Spark Plugs	1/E5
47	Speaker LH Door	3/M8
48	Speaker RH Door	3/M1
49	Starter Motor	1/E6
50	Stop Lamp Switch	2/H4
51	Windscreen Washer Pump	3/C1
52	Wiper Intermittent Relay V	3/E2
53	Wiper Motor Front	3/F4
54	Wiper Switch	3/K2

COMMON EARTH POINT	DIAGRAM/ GRID REF.
G1002	1/F8
	2/F8
	3/D8
G1005	1/F1
	2/E2
	3/E3
G1006	1/J8
	2/H8
	3/G8

COMMON FEED	DESCRIPTION	DIAGRAM/ GRID REF.
S1003	COMMON BATTERY FEED	1/G2
		2/H5
S1004	COMMON BATTERY FEED	1/J2
		2/J3
		3/J3
S1012	COMMON IGNITION FEED	1/H1
		2/F4

Notes, tables, wire colours and key to wiring diagrams. P100 models from 1988 onwards

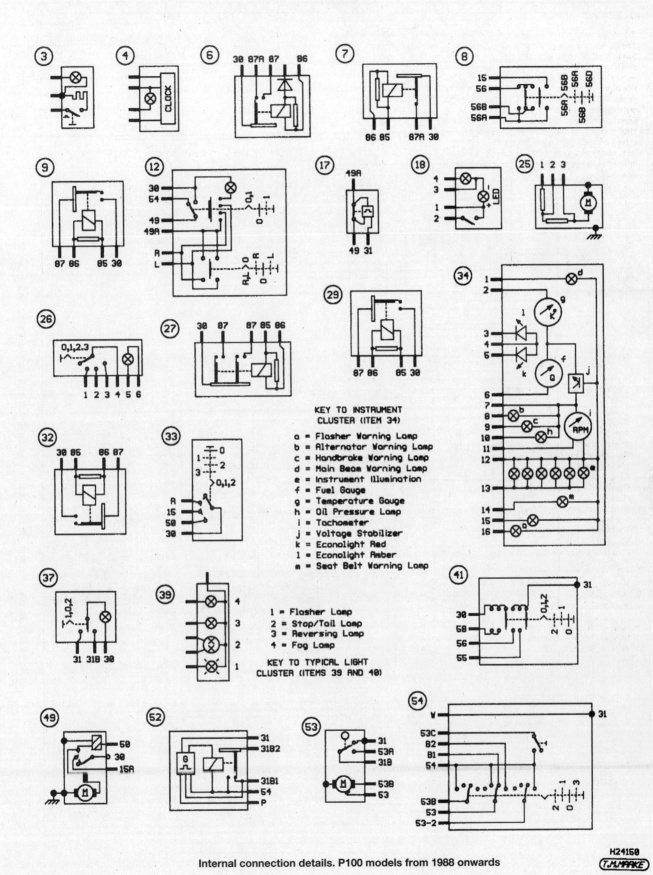

KEY TO INSTRUMENT
CLUSTER (ITEM 34)

a = Flasher Warning Lamp
b = Alternator Warning Lamp
c = Handbrake Warning Lamp
d = Main Beam Warning Lamp
e = Instrument Illumination
f = Fuel Gauge
g = Temperature Gauge
h = Oil Pressure Lamp
i = Tachometer
j = Voltage Stabilizer
k = Econolight Red
l = Econolight Amber
m = Seat Belt Warning Lamp

1 = Flasher Lamp
2 = Stop/Tail Lamp
3 = Reversing Lamp
4 = Fog Lamp

KEY TO TYPICAL LIGHT
CLUSTER (ITEMS 39 AND 40)

Internal connection details. P100 models from 1988 onwards

H24150

T.M.MAAKE

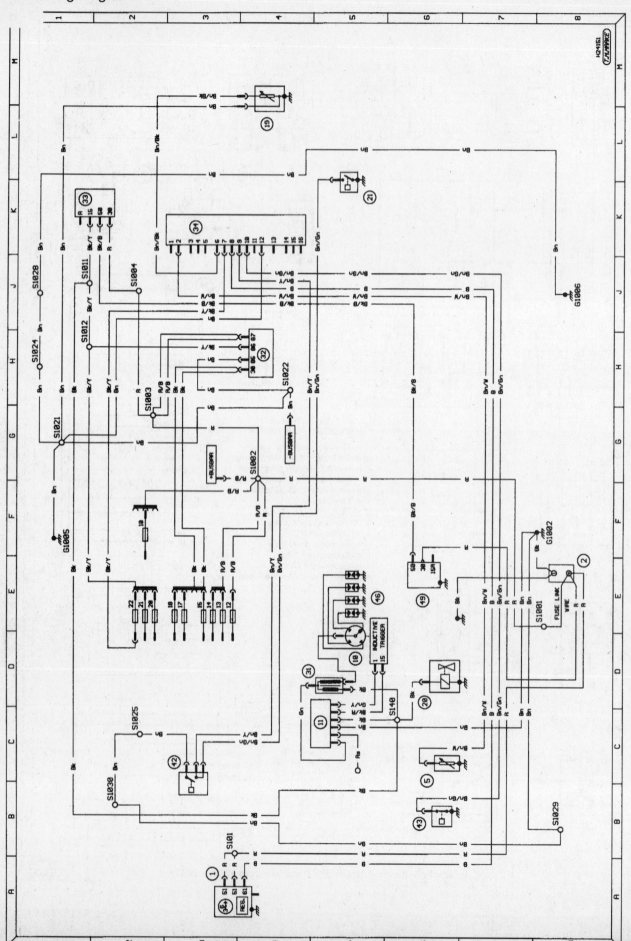

Diagram 1. Starting, charging and ignition. P100 models from 1988 onwards

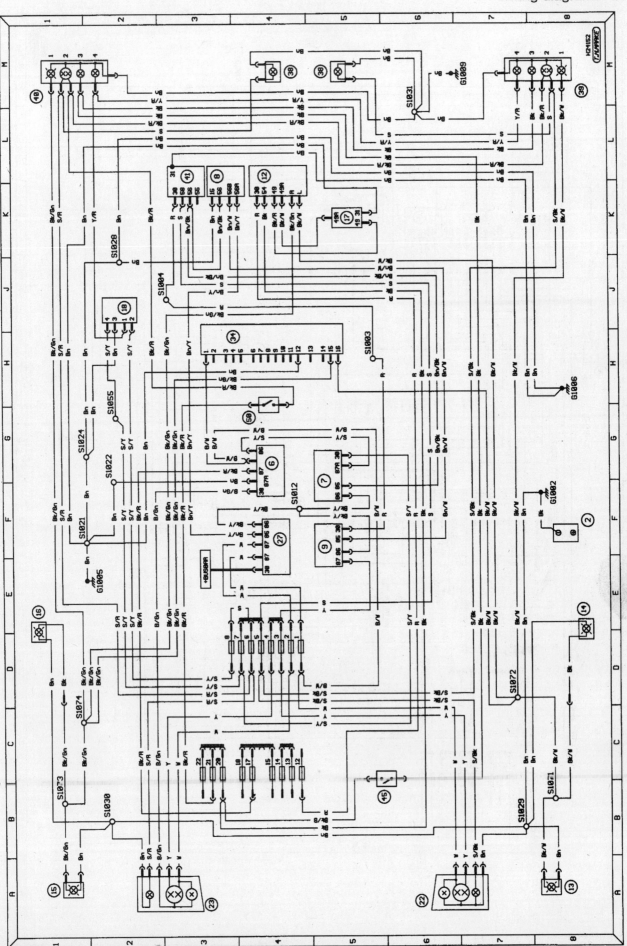

Diagram 2. Exterior lighting. P100 models from 1988 onwards

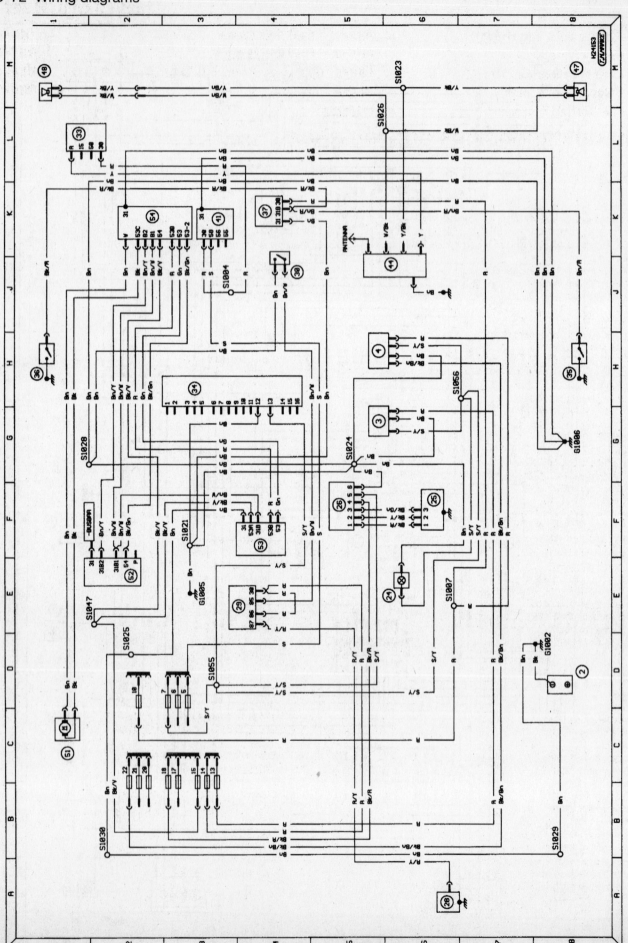

Diagram 3. Ancillary circuits and interior lighting. P100 model from 1988 onwards

General dimensions and weights

Dimensions

Overall length:

Saloon	4467.0 mm (176.0 in)
Hatchback:	
All models up to 1987 except GLS, 2.0iS and Ghia	4407.0 mm (173.6 in)
GLS and 2.0iS models up to 1987	4460.0 mm (175.7 in)
Ghia models up to 1987 and all models from 1987	4425.0 mm (174.3 in)
Estate:	
All models up to 1987 except Ghia	4506.0 mm (177.5 in)
Ghia models up to 1987	4522.0 mm (178.2 in)
All models from 1987	4511.0 mm (177.7 in)
P100	4900.0 mm (193.1 in)

Overall width:

All models up to 1987 except Base, GLS, 2.0iS and Ghia	1867.0 mm (73.6 in)
Base models up to 1987	1821.0 mm (71.7 in)
GLS, 2.0iS and Ghia models up to 1987	1920.0 mm (75.6 in)
All models from 1987 except P100	1694.0 mm (66.7 in)
P100	1920.0 mm (75.6 in)
Saloon models from 1990	1698.0 mm (66.9 in)
Hatchback models from 1990	1694.0 mm (66.7 In)
Estate models from 1990	1720.0 mm (67.8 in)

Overall height:

Saloon:	
All models except GLS	1359.0 mm (53.5 in)
GLS models	1352.0 mm (53.3 in)
Models from 1990	1407.0 mm (55.4 in)
Hatchback:	
All models up to 1987 except GLS and 2.0iS	1420.0 mm (55.9 in)
GLS and 2.0iS models up to 1987	1392.0 mm (54.8 in)
All models from 1987 except GLS	1359.0 mm (53.5 in)
GLS models from 1987	1352.0 mm (53.3 in)
Models from 1990	1407.0 mm (55.4 in)
Estate:	
All models up to 1987 except Base and Ghia	1443.0 mm (56.9 in)
Base models up to 1987	1417.0 mm (55.8 in)
Ghia models up to 1987	1506.0 mm (59.3 in)
Models from 1987	1386.0 mm (54.6 in)
Models from 1990	1428.0 mm (56.3 in)
P100	1520.0 mm (59.9 in)

Weights

Kerb weight†:

Saloon:	
Models before 1990	1025 to 1135 kg (2260 to 2503 lbs)
Models from 1990	1065 to 1240 kg (2343 to 2728 lbs)
Hatchback:	
Models before 1990	1010 to 1145 kg (2227 to 2525 lbs)
Models from 1990	1065 to 1240 kg (2343 to 2728 lbs)
Estate:	
Models before 1990	1065 to 1186 kg (2348 to 2613 lbs)
Models from 1990	1105 to 1190 kg (2431 to 2618 lbs)
P100	1370 kg (3021 lbs)
Maximum gross vehicle weight	Refer to VIN plate
Maximum roof rack load	75 kg (165 lbs)
Minimum towing hitch downward load	25 kg (55 lbs)
Maximum towing hitch downward load	50 kg (110 lbs)

†Exact kerb weights depend upon model and specification

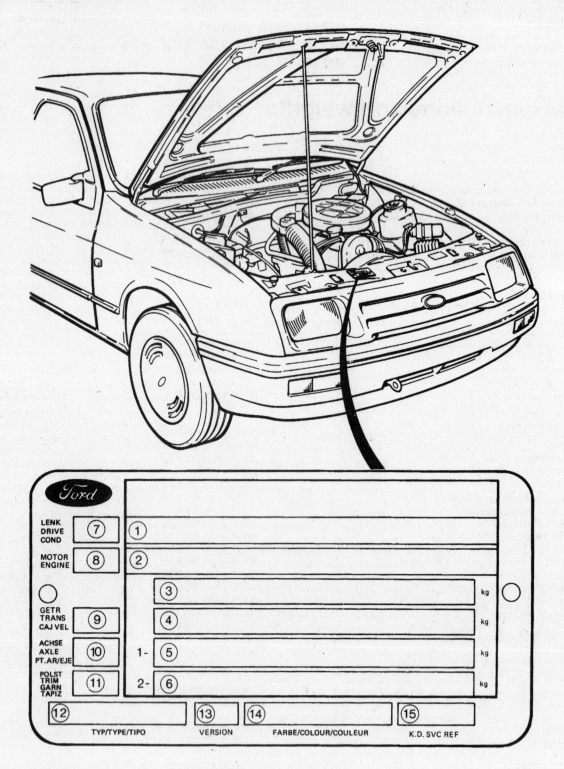

Vehicle identification number (VIN) plate details

1 Type approval number
2 Vehicle identification number (VIN)
3 Gross vehicle weight
4 Gross train weight
5 Permitted front axle loading

6 Permitted rear axle loading
7 LHD or RHD
8 Engine code
9 Transmission code
10 Final drive code

11 Interior trim code
12 Vehicle type number
13 Blank
14 Paint code
15 Blank

Buying spare parts

Spare parts are available from many sources, including maker's appointed garages, accessory shops, and motor factors. To be sure of obtaining the correct parts, it will sometimes be necessary to quote the vehicle identification number. If possible, it can also be useful to take the old parts along for positive identification. Items such as starter motors and alternators may be available under a service exchange scheme - any parts returned should always be clean.

Our advice regarding spare part sources is as follows.

Officially-appointed garages

This is the best source of parts which are peculiar to your car, and which are not otherwise generally available (eg badges, interior trim, certain body panels, etc). It is also the only place at which you should buy parts if the vehicle is still under warranty.

Accessory shops

These are very good places to buy materials and components needed for the maintenance of your car (oil, air and fuel filters, spark plugs, light bulbs, drivebelts, oils and greases, brake pads, touch-up paint, etc). Components of this nature sold by a reputable shop are of the same standard as those used by the car manufacturer.

Besides components, these shops also sell tools and general accessories, usually have convenient opening hours, charge lower prices, and can often be found not far from home. Some accessory shops have parts counters where the components needed for almost any repair job can be purchased or ordered.

Motor factors

Good factors will stock all the more important components which wear out comparatively quickly, and can sometimes supply individual components needed for the overhaul of a larger assembly (eg brake seals and hydraulic parts, bearing shells, pistons, valves, alternator brushes). They may also handle work such as cylinder block reboring, crankshaft regrinding and balancing, etc.

Tyre and exhaust specialists

These outlets may be independent, or members of a local or national chain. They frequently offer competitive prices when compared with a main dealer or local garage, but it will pay to obtain several quotes before making a decision. When researching prices, also ask what "extras" may be added - for instance, fitting a new valve and balancing the wheel are both commonly charged on top of the price of a new tyre.

Other sources

Beware of parts or materials obtained from market stalls, car boot sales or similar outlets. Such items are not invariably sub-standard, but there is little chance of compensation if they do prove unsatisfactory. In the case of safety-critical components such as brake pads, there is the risk not only of financial loss but also of an accident causing injury or death.

Second-hand components or assemblies obtained from a car breaker can be a good buy in some circumstances, but this sort of purchase is best made by the experienced DIY mechanic.

Vehicle identification numbers

Vehicle identification numbers

Modifications are a continuing and unpublicised process in vehicle manufacture, quite apart from major model changes. Spare

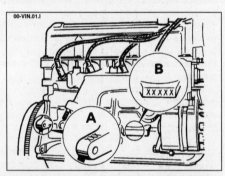

Engine code (A) and engine number (B) locations - SOHC engines

parts lists are compiled upon a numerical basis, the individual vehicle identification numbers being essential to correct identification of the component concerned.

When ordering spare parts, always give as much information as possible. Quote the car model, year of manufacture, body and engine numbers, as appropriate.

The *Vehicle Identification Number (VIN)* plate is mounted on the right-hand side of the body front panel, and may be seen once the bonnet is open **(see illustration)**. Besides the VIN it also carries information on vehicle equipment and permissible loads.

The *engine number* is situated on the cylinder block. On SOHC engines, the number is located on the right-hand side of the cylinder block in front of the engine mounting bracket. On 1.8 litre (R2A) CVH engines, the number is located on the front upper right-hand side of the cylinder block. On 1.6 and 1.8 litre (R6A) CVH engines, the engine number is stamped on the front lower face of the cylinder block, on the alternator side of the timing cover. On DOHC engines, the engine number is stamped on the front face of the cylinder block, below the upper timing chain cover **(see illustrations)**..

Other identification numbers or codes are stamped on major items such as the gearbox, final drive housing, distributor etc. These numbers are unlikely to be needed by the home mechanic.

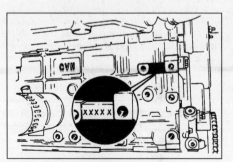

Engine number location - 1.8 litre (R2A) CVH engine

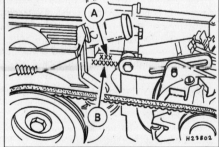

Engine number location - 1.6 litre CVH engine
A Engine code   B Engine number

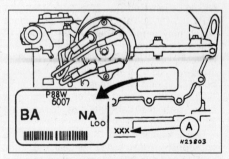

Engine number code sticker and engine number location (A) - DOHC engine

Whenever servicing, repair or overhaul work is carried out on the car or its components, it is necessary to observe the following procedures and instructions. This will assist in carrying out the operation efficiently and to a professional standard of workmanship.

Joint mating faces and gaskets

When separating components at their mating faces, never insert screwdrivers or similar implements into the joint between the faces in order to prise them apart. This can cause severe damage which results in oil leaks, coolant leaks, etc upon reassembly. Separation is usually achieved by tapping along the joint with a soft-faced hammer in order to break the seal. However, note that this method may not be suitable where dowels are used for component location.

Where a gasket is used between the mating faces of two components, ensure that it is renewed on reassembly, and fit it dry unless otherwise stated in the repair procedure. Make sure that the mating faces are clean and dry, with all traces of old gasket removed. When cleaning a joint face, use a tool which is not likely to score or damage the face, and remove any burrs or nicks with an oilstone or fine file.

Make sure that tapped holes are cleaned with a pipe cleaner, and keep them free of jointing compound, if this is being used, unless specifically instructed otherwise.

Ensure that all orifices, channels or pipes are clear, and blow through them, preferably using compressed air.

Oil seals

Oil seals can be removed by levering them out with a wide flat-bladed screwdriver or similar implement. Alternatively, a number of self-tapping screws may be screwed into the seal, and these used as a purchase for pliers or some similar device in order to pull the seal free.

Whenever an oil seal is removed from its working location, either individually or as part of an assembly, it should be renewed.

The very fine sealing lip of the seal is easily damaged, and will not seal if the surface it contacts is not completely clean and free from scratches, nicks or grooves. If the original sealing surface of the component cannot be restored, and the manufacturer has not made provision for slight relocation of the seal relative to the sealing surface, the component should be renewed.

Protect the lips of the seal from any surface which may damage them in the course of fitting. Use tape or a conical sleeve where possible. Lubricate the seal lips with oil before fitting and, on dual-lipped seals, fill the space between the lips with grease.

Unless otherwise stated, oil seals must be fitted with their sealing lips toward the lubricant to be sealed.

Use a tubular drift or block of wood of the appropriate size to install the seal and, if the seal housing is shouldered, drive the seal down to the shoulder. If the seal housing is unshouldered, the seal should be fitted with its face flush with the housing top face (unless otherwise instructed).

Screw threads and fastenings

Seized nuts, bolts and screws are quite a common occurrence where corrosion has set in, and the use of penetrating oil or releasing fluid will often overcome this problem if the offending item is soaked for a while before attempting to release it. The use of an impact driver may also provide a means of releasing such stubborn fastening devices, when used in conjunction with the appropriate screwdriver bit or socket. If none of these methods works, it may be necessary to resort to the careful application of heat, or the use of a hacksaw or nut splitter device.

Studs are usually removed by locking two nuts together on the threaded part, and then using a spanner on the lower nut to unscrew the stud. Studs or bolts which have broken off below the surface of the component in which they are mounted can sometimes be removed using a proprietary stud extractor. Always ensure that a blind tapped hole is completely free from oil, grease, water or other fluid before installing the bolt or stud. Failure to do this could cause the housing to crack due to the hydraulic action of the bolt or stud as it is screwed in.

When tightening a castellated nut to accept a split pin, tighten the nut to the specified torque, where applicable, and then tighten further to the next split pin hole. Never slacken the nut to align the split pin hole, unless stated in the repair procedure.

When checking or retightening a nut or bolt to a specified torque setting, slacken the nut or bolt by a quarter of a turn, and then retighten to the specified setting. However, this should not be attempted where angular tightening has been used.

For some screw fastenings, notably cylinder head bolts or nuts, torque wrench settings are no longer specified for the latter stages of tightening, "angle-tightening" being called up instead. Typically, a fairly low torque wrench setting will be applied to the bolts/nuts in the correct sequence, followed by one or more stages of tightening through specified angles.

Locknuts, locktabs and washers

Any fastening which will rotate against a component or housing in the course of tightening should always have a washer between it and the relevant component or housing.

Spring or split washers should always be renewed when they are used to lock a critical component such as a big-end bearing retaining bolt or nut. Locktabs which are folded over to retain a nut or bolt should always be renewed.

Self-locking nuts can be re-used in non-critical areas, providing resistance can be felt when the locking portion passes over the bolt or stud thread. However, it should be noted that self-locking stiffnuts tend to lose their effectiveness after long periods of use, and in such cases should be renewed as a matter of course.

Split pins must always be replaced with new ones of the correct size for the hole.

When thread-locking compound is found on the threads of a fastener which is to be re-used, it should be cleaned off with a wire brush and solvent, and fresh compound applied on reassembly.

Special tools

Some repair procedures in this manual entail the use of special tools such as a press, two or three-legged pullers, spring compressors, etc. Wherever possible, suitable readily-available alternatives to the manufacturer's special tools are described, and are shown in use. In some instances, where no alternative is possible, it has been necessary to resort to the use of a manufacturer's tool, and this has been done for reasons of safety as well as the efficient completion of the repair operation. Unless you are highly-skilled and have a thorough understanding of the procedures described, never attempt to bypass the use of any special tool when the procedure described specifies its use. Not only is there a very great risk of personal injury, but expensive damage could be caused to the components involved.

Environmental considerations

When disposing of used engine oil, brake fluid, antifreeze, etc, give due consideration to any detrimental environmental effects. Do not, for instance, pour any of the above liquids down drains into the general sewage system, or onto the ground to soak away. Many local council refuse tips provide a facility for waste oil disposal, as do some garages. If none of these facilities are available, consult your local Environmental Health Department for further advice.

With the universal tightening-up of legislation regarding the emission of environmentally-harmful substances from motor vehicles, most current vehicles have tamperproof devices fitted to the main adjustment points of the fuel system. These devices are primarily designed to prevent unqualified persons from adjusting the fuel/air mixture, with the chance of a consequent increase in toxic emissions. If such devices are encountered during servicing or overhaul, they should, wherever possible, be renewed or refitted in accordance with the vehicle manufacturer's requirements or current legislation.

OIL CARE
FOLLOW THE CODE

OIL BANK LINE
0800 66 33 66

Note: It is antisocial and illegal to dump oil down the drain. To find the location of your local oil recycling bank, call this number free.

Introduction

A selection of good tools is a fundamental requirement for anyone contemplating the maintenance and repair of a motor vehicle. For the owner who does not possess any, their purchase will prove a considerable expense, offsetting some of the savings made by doing-it-yourself. However, provided that the tools purchased meet the relevant national safety standards and are of good quality, they will last for many years and prove an extremely worthwhile investment.

To help the average owner to decide which tools are needed to carry out the various tasks detailed in this manual, we have compiled three lists of tools under the following headings: *Maintenance and minor repair*, *Repair and overhaul*, and *Special*. Newcomers to practical mechanics should start off with the *Maintenance and minor repair* tool kit, and confine themselves to the simpler jobs around the vehicle. Then, as confidence and experience grow, more difficult tasks can be undertaken, with extra tools being purchased as, and when, they are needed. In this way, a *Maintenance and minor repair* tool kit can be built up into a *Repair and overhaul* tool kit over a considerable period of time, without any major cash outlays. The experienced do-it-yourselfer will have a tool kit good enough for most repair and overhaul procedures, and will add tools from the *Special* category when it is felt that the expense is justified by the amount of use to which these tools will be put.

Maintenance and minor repair tool kit

The tools given in this list should be considered as a minimum requirement if routine maintenance, servicing and minor repair operations are to be undertaken. We recommend the purchase of combination spanners (ring one end, open-ended the other); although more expensive than open-ended ones, they do give the advantages of both types of spanner.

☐ *Combination spanners:*
  Metric - 8, 9, 10, 11, 12, 13, 14, 15, 17 & 19 mm
☐ *Adjustable spanner - 35 mm jaw (approx.)*
☐ *Spark plug spanner (with rubber insert)*
☐ *Spark plug gap adjustment tool*
☐ *Set of feeler blades*
☐ *Brake bleed nipple spanner*
☐ *Screwdrivers:*
  Flat blade - 100 mm long x 6 mm dia
  Cross blade - 100 mm long x 6 mm dia
☐ *Combination pliers*
☐ *Hacksaw (junior)*
☐ *Tyre pump*
☐ *Tyre pressure gauge*
☐ *Oil can*
☐ *Oil filter removal tool*
☐ *Fine emery cloth*
☐ *Wire brush (small)*
☐ *Funnel (medium size)*

Repair and overhaul tool kit

These tools are virtually essential for anyone undertaking any major repairs to a motor vehicle, and are additional to those given in the *Maintenance and minor repair* list. Included in this list is a comprehensive set of sockets. Although these are expensive, they will be found invaluable as they are so versatile - particularly if various drives are included in the set. We recommend the half-inch square-drive type, as this can be used with most proprietary torque wrenches. If you cannot afford a socket set, even bought piecemeal, then inexpensive tubular box spanners are a useful alternative.

The tools in this list will occasionally need to be supplemented by tools from the *Special* list.

☐ *Sockets (or box spanners) to cover range in previous list (including Torx sockets)*
☐ *Reversible ratchet drive (for use with sockets)*
☐ *Extension piece, 250 mm (for use with sockets)*
☐ *Universal joint (for use with sockets)*
☐ *Torque wrench (for use with sockets)*
☐ *Self-locking grips*
☐ *Ball pein hammer*
☐ *Soft-faced mallet (plastic/aluminium or rubber)*
☐ *Screwdrivers:*
  Flat blade - long & sturdy, short (chubby), and narrow (electricians) types
  Cross blade - Long & sturdy, and short (chubby) types
☐ *Pliers:*
  Long-nosed
  Side cutters (electricians)
  Circlip (internal and external)
☐ *Cold chisel - 25 mm*
☐ *Scriber*
☐ *Scraper*
☐ *Centre punch*
☐ *Pin punch*
☐ *Hacksaw*
☐ *Brake hose clamp*
☐ *Brake/clutch bleeding kit*
☐ *Selection of twist drills*
☐ *Steel rule/straight-edge*
☐ *Allen keys (inc. splined/Torx type)*
☐ *Selection of files*
☐ *Wire brush*
☐ *Axle-stands*
☐ *Jack (strong trolley or hydraulic type)*
☐ *Light with extension lead*

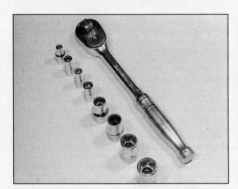

Sockets and reversible ratchet drive

Spline bit set

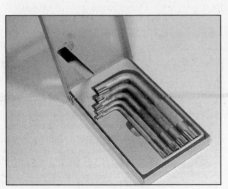

Spline key set

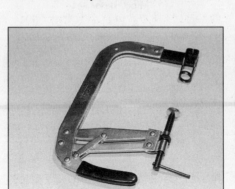

Valve spring compressor

Two- and three legged bearing puller

Special tools

The tools in this list are those which are not used regularly, are expensive to buy, or which need to be used in accordance with their manufacturers' instructions. Unless relatively difficult mechanical jobs are undertaken frequently, it will not be economic to buy many of these tools. Where this is the case, you could consider clubbing together with friends (or joining a motorists' club) to make a joint purchase, or borrowing the tools against a deposit from a local garage or tool hire specialist. It is worth noting that many of the larger DIY superstores now carry a large range of special tools for hire at modest rates.

The following list contains only those tools and instruments freely available to the public, and not those special tools produced by the vehicle manufacturer specifically for its dealer network. You will find occasional references to these manufacturers' special tools in the text of this manual. Generally, an alternative method of doing the job without the vehicle manufacturers' special tool is given. However, sometimes there is no alternative to using them. Where this is the case and the relevant tool cannot be bought or borrowed, you will have to entrust the work to a franchised garage.

☐ Valve spring compressor
☐ Valve grinding tool
☐ Piston ring compressor
☐ Piston ring removal/installation tool
☐ Cylinder bore hone
☐ Balljoint separator
☐ Coil spring compressors (where applicable)
☐ Two/three-legged hub and bearing puller
☐ Impact screwdriver
☐ Micrometer and/or vernier calipers
☐ Dial gauge
☐ Stroboscopic timing light
☐ Dwell angle meter/tachometer
☐ Universal electrical multi-meter
☐ Cylinder compression gauge
☐ Hand-operated vacuum pump and gauge
☐ Clutch plate alignment set
☐ Brake shoe steady spring cup removal tool
☐ Bush and bearing removal/installation set
☐ Stud extractors
☐ Tap and die set
☐ Lifting tackle
☐ Trolley jack

Buying tools

For practically all tools, a tool factor is the best source, since he will have a very comprehensive range compared with the average garage or accessory shop. Having said that, accessory shops often offer excellent quality tools at discount prices, so it pays to shop around.

Remember, you don't have to buy the most expensive items on the shelf, but it is always advisable to steer clear of the very cheap tools. There are plenty of good tools around at reasonable prices, but always aim to purchase items which meet the relevant national safety standards. If in doubt, ask the proprietor or manager of the shop for advice before making a purchase.

Care and maintenance of tools

Having purchased a reasonable tool kit, it is necessary to keep the tools in a clean and serviceable condition. After use, always wipe off any dirt, grease and metal particles using a clean, dry cloth, before putting the tools away. Never leave them lying around after they have been used. A simple tool rack on the garage or workshop wall for items such as screwdrivers and pliers is a good idea. Store all normal spanners and sockets in a metal box. Any measuring instruments, gauges, meters, etc, must be carefully stored where they cannot be damaged or become rusty.

Take a little care when tools are used. Hammer heads inevitably become marked, and screwdrivers lose the keen edge on their blades from time to time. A little timely attention with emery cloth or a file will soon restore items like this to a good serviceable finish.

Working facilities

Not to be forgotten when discussing tools is the workshop itself. If anything more than routine maintenance is to be carried out, some form of suitable working area becomes essential.

It is appreciated that many an owner-mechanic is forced by circumstances to remove an engine or similar item without the benefit of a garage or workshop. Having done this, any repairs should always be done under the cover of a roof.

Wherever possible, any dismantling should be done on a clean, flat workbench or table at a suitable working height.

Any workbench needs a vice; one with a jaw opening of 100 mm is suitable for most jobs. As mentioned previously, some clean dry storage space is also required for tools, as well as for any lubricants, cleaning fluids, touch-up paints and so on, which become necessary.

Another item which may be required, and which has a much more general usage, is an electric drill with a chuck capacity of at least 8 mm. This, together with a good range of twist drills, is virtually essential for fitting accessories.

Last, but not least, always keep a supply of old newspapers and clean, lint-free rags available, and try to keep any working area as clean as possible.

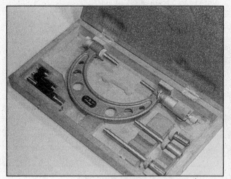
Micrometer set

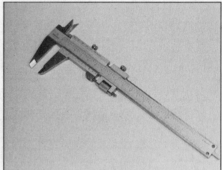
Vernier calipers

Stroboscopic timing light

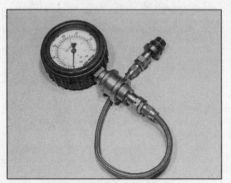
Cylinder compression gauge

Clutch plate alignment set

This is a guide to getting your vehicle through the MOT test. Obviously it will not be possible to examine the vehicle to the same standard as the professional MOT tester. However, working through the following checks will enable you to identify any problem areas before submitting the vehicle for the test.

Where a testable component is in borderline condition, the tester has discretion in deciding whether to pass or fail it. The basis of such discretion is whether the tester would be happy for a close relative or friend to use the vehicle with the component in that condition. If the vehicle presented is clean and evidently well cared for, the tester may be more inclined to pass a borderline component than if the vehicle is scruffy and apparently neglected.

It has only been possible to summarise the test requirements here, based on the regulations in force at the time of printing. Test standards are becoming increasingly stringent, although there are some exemptions for older vehicles. For full details obtain a copy of the Haynes publication Pass the MOT! (available from stockists of Haynes manuals).

An assistant will be needed to help carry out some of these checks.

The checks have been sub-divided into four categories, as follows:

1 Checks carried out **FROM THE DRIVER'S SEAT**

2 Checks carried out **WITH THE VEHICLE ON THE GROUND**

3 Checks carried out **WITH THE VEHICLE RAISED AND THE WHEELS FREE TO TURN**

4 Checks carried out on **YOUR VEHICLE'S EXHAUST EMISSION SYSTEM**

---

1 Checks carried out **FROM THE DRIVER'S SEAT**

Handbrake

☐ Test the operation of the handbrake. Excessive travel (too many clicks) indicates incorrect brake or cable adjustment.

☐ Check that the handbrake cannot be released by tapping the lever sideways. Check the security of the lever mountings.

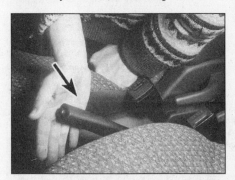

Footbrake

☐ Depress the brake pedal and check that it does not creep down to the floor, indicating a master cylinder fault. Release the pedal, wait a few seconds, then depress it again. If the pedal travels nearly to the floor before firm resistance is felt, brake adjustment or repair is necessary. If the pedal feels spongy, there is air in the hydraulic system which must be removed by bleeding.

☐ Check that the brake pedal is secure and in good condition. Check also for signs of fluid leaks on the pedal, floor or carpets, which would indicate failed seals in the brake master cylinder.

☐ Check the servo unit (when applicable) by operating the brake pedal several times, then keeping the pedal depressed and starting the engine. As the engine starts, the pedal will move down slightly. If not, the vacuum hose or the servo itself may be faulty.

Steering wheel and column

☐ Examine the steering wheel for fractures or looseness of the hub, spokes or rim.

☐ Move the steering wheel from side to side and then up and down. Check that the steering wheel is not loose on the column, indicating wear or a loose retaining nut. Continue moving the steering wheel as before, but also turn it slightly from left to right.

☐ Check that the steering wheel is not loose on the column, and that there is no abnormal

movement of the steering wheel, indicating wear in the column support bearings or couplings.

Windscreen and mirrors

☐ The windscreen must be free of cracks or other significant damage within the driver's field of view. (Small stone chips are acceptable.) Rear view mirrors must be secure, intact, and capable of being adjusted.

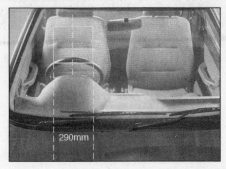

290mm

Seat belts and seats

Note: *The following checks are applicable to all seat belts, front and rear.*

☐ Examine the webbing of all the belts (including rear belts if fitted) for cuts, serious fraying or deterioration. Fasten and unfasten each belt to check the buckles. If applicable, check the retracting mechanism. Check the security of all seat belt mountings accessible from inside the vehicle.

☐ The front seats themselves must be securely attached and the backrests must lock in the upright position.

Doors

☐ Both front doors must be able to be opened and closed from outside and inside, and must latch securely when closed.

2 Checks carried out WITH THE VEHICLE ON THE GROUND

Vehicle identification

☐ Number plates must be in good condition, secure and legible, with letters and numbers correctly spaced – spacing at (A) should be twice that at (B).

☐ The VIN plate (A) and homologation plate (B) must be legible.

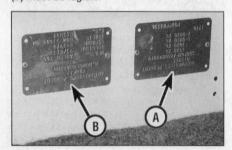

Electrical equipment

☐ Switch on the ignition and check the operation of the horn.

☐ Check the windscreen washers and wipers, examining the wiper blades; renew damaged or perished blades. Also check the operation of the stop-lights.

☐ Check the operation of the sidelights and number plate lights. The lenses and reflectors must be secure, clean and undamaged.

☐ Check the operation and alignment of the headlights. The headlight reflectors must not be tarnished and the lenses must be undamaged.

☐ Switch on the ignition and check the operation of the direction indicators (including the instrument panel tell-tale) and the hazard warning lights. Operation of the sidelights and stop-lights must not affect the indicators - if it does, the cause is usually a bad earth at the rear light cluster.

☐ Check the operation of the rear foglight(s), including the warning light on the instrument panel or in the switch.

Footbrake

☐ Examine the master cylinder, brake pipes and servo unit for leaks, loose mountings, corrosion or other damage.

☐ The fluid reservoir must be secure and the fluid level must be between the upper (A) and lower (B) markings.

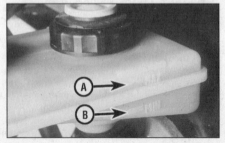

☐ Inspect both front brake flexible hoses for cracks or deterioration of the rubber. Turn the steering from lock to lock, and ensure that the hoses do not contact the wheel, tyre, or any part of the steering or suspension mechanism. With the brake pedal firmly depressed, check the hoses for bulges or leaks under pressure.

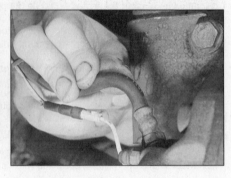

Steering and suspension

☐ Have your assistant turn the steering wheel from side to side slightly, up to the point where the steering gear just begins to transmit this movement to the roadwheels. Check for excessive free play between the steering wheel and the steering gear, indicating wear or insecurity of the steering column joints, the column-to-steering gear coupling, or the steering gear itself.

☐ Have your assistant turn the steering wheel more vigorously in each direction, so that the roadwheels just begin to turn. As this is done, examine all the steering joints, linkages, fittings and attachments. Renew any component that shows signs of wear or damage. On vehicles with power steering, check the security and condition of the steering pump, drivebelt and hoses.

☐ Check that the vehicle is standing level, and at approximately the correct ride height.

Shock absorbers

☐ Depress each corner of the vehicle in turn, then release it. The vehicle should rise and then settle in its normal position. If the vehicle continues to rise and fall, the shock absorber is defective. A shock absorber which has seized will also cause the vehicle to fail.

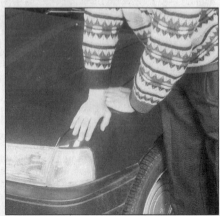

Exhaust system

☐ Start the engine. With your assistant holding a rag over the tailpipe, check the entire system for leaks. Repair or renew leaking sections.

3 Checks carried out WITH THE VEHICLE RAISED AND THE WHEELS FREE TO TURN

Jack up the front and rear of the vehicle, and securely support it on axle stands. Position the stands clear of the suspension assemblies. Ensure that the wheels are clear of the ground and that the steering can be turned from lock to lock.

Steering mechanism

☐ Have your assistant turn the steering from lock to lock. Check that the steering turns smoothly, and that no part of the steering mechanism, including a wheel or tyre, fouls any brake hose or pipe or any part of the body structure.
☐ Examine the steering rack rubber gaiters for damage or insecurity of the retaining clips. If power steering is fitted, check for signs of damage or leakage of the fluid hoses, pipes or connections. Also check for excessive stiffness or binding of the steering, a missing split pin or locking device, or severe corrosion of the body structure within 30 cm of any steering component attachment point.

Front and rear suspension and wheel bearings

☐ Starting at the front right-hand side, grasp the roadwheel at the 3 o'clock and 9 o'clock positions and shake it vigorously. Check for free play or insecurity at the wheel bearings, suspension balljoints, or suspension mountings, pivots and attachments.
☐ Now grasp the wheel at the 12 o'clock and 6 o'clock positions and repeat the previous inspection. Spin the wheel, and check for roughness or tightness of the front wheel bearing.

☐ If excess free play is suspected at a component pivot point, this can be confirmed by using a large screwdriver or similar tool and levering between the mounting and the component attachment. This will confirm whether the wear is in the pivot bush, its retaining bolt, or in the mounting itself (the bolt holes can often become elongated).

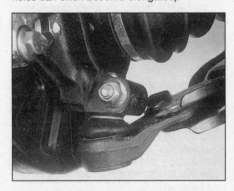

☐ Carry out all the above checks at the other front wheel, and then at both rear wheels.

Springs and shock absorbers

☐ Examine the suspension struts (when applicable) for serious fluid leakage, corrosion, or damage to the casing. Also check the security of the mounting points.
☐ If coil springs are fitted, check that the spring ends locate in their seats, and that the spring is not corroded, cracked or broken.
☐ If leaf springs are fitted, check that all leaves are intact, that the axle is securely attached to each spring, and that there is no deterioration of the spring eye mountings, bushes, and shackles.

☐ The same general checks apply to vehicles fitted with other suspension types, such as torsion bars, hydraulic displacer units, etc. Ensure that all mountings and attachments are secure, that there are no signs of excessive wear, corrosion or damage, and (on hydraulic types) that there are no fluid leaks or damaged pipes.
☐ Inspect the shock absorbers for signs of serious fluid leakage. Check for wear of the mounting bushes or attachments, or damage to the body of the unit.

Driveshafts (fwd vehicles only)

☐ Rotate each front wheel in turn and inspect the constant velocity joint gaiters for splits or damage. Also check that each driveshaft is straight and undamaged.

Braking system

☐ If possible without dismantling, check brake pad wear and disc condition. Ensure that the friction lining material has not worn excessively, (A) and that the discs are not fractured, pitted, scored or badly worn (B).

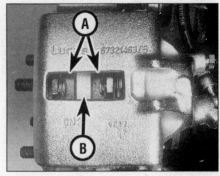

☐ Examine all the rigid brake pipes underneath the vehicle, and the flexible hose(s) at the rear. Look for corrosion, chafing or insecurity of the pipes, and for signs of bulging under pressure, chafing, splits or deterioration of the flexible hoses.
☐ Look for signs of fluid leaks at the brake calipers or on the brake backplates. Repair or renew leaking components.
☐ Slowly spin each wheel, while your assistant depresses and releases the footbrake. Ensure that each brake is operating and does not bind when the pedal is released.

☐ Examine the handbrake mechanism, checking for frayed or broken cables, excessive corrosion, or wear or insecurity of the linkage. Check that the mechanism works on each relevant wheel, and releases fully, without binding.

☐ It is not possible to test brake efficiency without special equipment, but a road test can be carried out later to check that the vehicle pulls up in a straight line.

Fuel and exhaust systems

☐ Inspect the fuel tank (including the filler cap), fuel pipes, hoses and unions. All components must be secure and free from leaks.

☐ Examine the exhaust system over its entire length, checking for any damaged, broken or missing mountings, security of the retaining clamps and rust or corrosion.

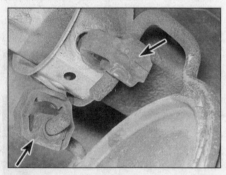

Wheels and tyres

☐ Examine the sidewalls and tread area of each tyre in turn. Check for cuts, tears, lumps, bulges, separation of the tread, and exposure of the ply or cord due to wear or damage. Check that the tyre bead is correctly seated on the wheel rim, that the valve is sound and

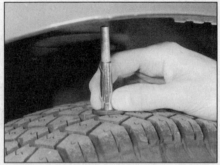

properly seated, and that the wheel is not distorted or damaged.

☐ Check that the tyres are of the correct size for the vehicle, that they are of the same size and type on each axle, and that the pressures are correct.

☐ Check the tyre tread depth. The legal minimum at the time of writing is 1.6 mm over at least three-quarters of the tread width. Abnormal tread wear may indicate incorrect front wheel alignment.

Body corrosion

☐ Check the condition of the entire vehicle structure for signs of corrosion in load-bearing areas. (These include chassis box sections, side sills, cross-members, pillars, and all suspension, steering, braking system and seat belt mountings and anchorages.) Any corrosion which has seriously reduced the thickness of a load-bearing area is likely to cause the vehicle to fail. In this case professional repairs are likely to be needed.

☐ Damage or corrosion which causes sharp or otherwise dangerous edges to be exposed will also cause the vehicle to fail.

4 Checks carried out on YOUR VEHICLE'S EXHAUST EMISSION SYSTEM

Petrol models

☐ Have the engine at normal operating temperature, and make sure that it is in good tune (ignition system in good order, air filter element clean, etc).

☐ Before any measurements are carried out, raise the engine speed to around 2500 rpm, and hold it at this speed for 20 seconds. Allow the engine speed to return to idle, and watch

for smoke emissions from the exhaust tailpipe. If the idle speed is obviously much too high, or if dense blue or clearly-visible black smoke comes from the tailpipe for more than 5 seconds, the vehicle will fail. As a rule of thumb, blue smoke signifies oil being burnt (engine wear) while black smoke signifies unburnt fuel (dirty air cleaner element, or other carburettor or fuel system fault).

☐ An exhaust gas analyser capable of measuring carbon monoxide (CO) and hydrocarbons (HC) is now needed. If such an instrument cannot be hired or borrowed, a local garage may agree to perform the check for a small fee.

CO emissions (mixture)

☐ At the time of writing, the maximum CO level at idle is 3.5% for vehicles first used after August 1986 and 4.5% for older vehicles. From January 1996 a much tighter limit (around 0.5%) applies to catalyst-equipped vehicles first used from August 1992. If the CO level cannot be reduced far enough to pass the test (and the fuel and ignition systems are otherwise in good condition) then the carburettor is badly worn, or there is some problem in the fuel injection system or catalytic converter (as applicable).

HC emissions

☐ With the CO emissions within limits, HC emissions must be no more than 1200 ppm (parts per million). If the vehicle fails this test at idle, it can be re-tested at around 2000 rpm; if the HC level is then 1200 ppm or less, this counts as a pass.

☐ Excessive HC emissions can be caused by oil being burnt, but they are more likely to be due to unburnt fuel.

Diesel models

☐ The only emission test applicable to Diesel engines is the measuring of exhaust smoke density. The test involves accelerating the engine several times to its maximum unloaded speed.

Note: *It is of the utmost importance that the engine timing belt is in good condition before the test is carried out.*

☐ Excessive smoke can be caused by a dirty air cleaner element. Otherwise, professional advice may be needed to find the cause.

Engine

- ☐ Engine fails to rotate when attempting to start
- ☐ Starter motor turns engine slowly
- ☐ Engine rotates, but will not start
- ☐ Engine difficult to start when cold
- ☐ Engine difficult to start when hot
- ☐ Starter motor noisy or excessively-rough in engagement
- ☐ Engine starts, but stops immediately
- ☐ Engine idles erratically
- ☐ Engine misfires at idle speed
- ☐ Engine misfires throughout the driving speed range
- ☐ Engine hesitates on acceleration
- ☐ Engine stalls
- ☐ Engine lacks power
- ☐ Engine backfires
- ☐ Oil pressure warning light illuminated with engine running
- ☐ Engine runs-on after switching off
- ☐ Engine noises

Cooling system

- ☐ Overheating
- ☐ Overcooling
- ☐ External coolant leakage
- ☐ Internal coolant leakage
- ☐ Corrosion

Fuel and exhaust systems

- ☐ Excessive fuel consumption
- ☐ Fuel leakage and/or fuel odour
- ☐ Excessive noise or fumes from exhaust system

Clutch

- ☐ Pedal travels to floor - no pressure or very little resistance
- ☐ Clutch fails to disengage (unable to select gears)
- ☐ Clutch slips (engine speed increases; no increase in vehicle speed)
- ☐ Judder as clutch is engaged
- ☐ Noise when depressing or releasing clutch pedal

Manual gearbox

- ☐ Noisy in neutral with engine running
- ☐ Noisy in one particular gear
- ☐ Difficulty engaging gears
- ☐ Jumps out of gear
- ☐ Vibration
- ☐ Lubricant leaks

Automatic transmission

- ☐ Fluid leakage
- ☐ Transmission fluid brown, or has burned smell
- ☐ General gear selection problems
- ☐ Transmission will not downshift (kickdown) with acceleration
- ☐ Engine will not start in any gear, or starts in gears other than Park or Neutral
- ☐ Transmission slips, shifts roughly, is noisy, or has no drive in forward or reverse gears

Propeller shaft

- ☐ Clunking or knocking noise when taking up drive
- ☐ Vibration when accelerating or decelerating

Final drive and driveshafts

- ☐ Excessive final drive noise
- ☐ Oil leakage from final drive
- ☐ Grating, knocking or vibration from driveshafts

Braking system

- ☐ Vehicle pulls to one side under braking
- ☐ Noise (grinding or high-pitched squeal) when brakes applied
- ☐ Excessive brake pedal travel
- ☐ Brake pedal feels spongy when depressed
- ☐ Excessive brake pedal effort required to stop vehicle
- ☐ Judder felt through brake pedal or steering wheel when braking
- ☐ Pedal pulsates when braking hard
- ☐ Brakes binding
- ☐ Rear wheels locking under normal braking

Suspension and steering systems

- ☐ Vehicle pulls to one side
- ☐ Wheel wobble and vibration
- ☐ Excessive pitching and/or rolling around corners, or during braking
- ☐ Wandering or general instability
- ☐ Excessively-stiff steering
- ☐ Excessive play in steering
- ☐ Lack of power assistance
- ☐ Tyre wear excessive

Electrical system

- ☐ Battery will not hold a charge for more than a few days
- ☐ Ignition/no-charge warning light remains on with engine running
- ☐ Ignition/no-charge warning light fails to come on
- ☐ Lights inoperative
- ☐ Instrument readings inaccurate or erratic
- ☐ Horn inoperative, or unsatisfactory in operation
- ☐ Windscreen/tailgate wipers inoperative, or unsatisfactory in operation
- ☐ Windscreen/tailgate washers inoperative, or unsatisfactory in operation
- ☐ Electric windows inoperative, or unsatisfactory in operation
- ☐ Central locking system inoperative, or unsatisfactory in operation

Introduction

The vehicle owner who does his or her own maintenance according to the recommended service schedules should not have to use this section of the manual very often. Modern component reliability is such that, provided those items subject to wear or deterioration are inspected or renewed at the specified intervals, sudden failure is comparatively rare. Faults do not usually just happen as a result of sudden failure, but develop over a period of time. Major mechanical failures in particular are usually preceded by characteristic symptoms over hundreds or even thousands of miles. Those components which do occasionally fail without warning are often small and easily carried in the vehicle.

With any fault-finding, the first step is to decide where to begin investigations. Sometimes this is obvious, but on other occasions, a little detective work will be necessary. The owner who makes half a dozen haphazard adjustments or replacements may be successful in curing a fault (or its symptoms), but will be none the wiser if the fault recurs, and ultimately may have spent more time and money than was necessary. A calm and logical approach will be found to be more satisfactory in the long run. Always take into account any warning signs or abnormalities that may have been noticed in the period preceding the fault - power loss, high or low gauge readings, unusual smells, etc - and remember that failure of components such as fuses or spark plugs may only be pointers to some underlying fault.

The pages which follow provide an easy-reference guide to the more common problems which may occur during the operation of the vehicle. These problems and their possible causes are grouped under headings denoting various components or systems, such as Engine, Cooling system, etc. The Chapter and/or Section which deals with the problem is also shown in brackets. Whatever the fault, certain basic principles apply. These are as follows:

Verify the fault. This is simply a matter of being sure that you know what the symptoms are before starting work. This is particularly important if you are investigating a fault for someone else, who may not have described it very accurately.

Don't overlook the obvious. For example, if the vehicle won't start, is there fuel in the tank? (Don't take anyone else's word on this particular point, and don't trust the fuel gauge either!) If an electrical fault is indicated, look for loose or broken wires before digging out the test gear.

Cure the disease, not the symptom. Substituting a flat battery with a fully-charged one will get you off the hard shoulder, but if the underlying cause is not attended to, the new battery will go the same way. Similarly, changing oil-fouled spark plugs for a new set will get you moving again, but remember that the reason for the fouling (if it wasn't simply an incorrect grade of plug) will have to be established and corrected.

Don't take anything for granted. Particularly, don't forget that a "new" component may itself be defective (especially if it's been rattling around in the boot for months), and don't leave components out of a fault diagnosis sequence just because they are new or recently-fitted. When you do finally diagnose a difficult fault, you'll probably realise that all the evidence was there from the start.

Engine

Engine fails to rotate when attempting to start

- [ ] Battery terminal connections loose or corroded (Chapter 1).
- [ ] Battery discharged or faulty (Chapter 5).
- [ ] Broken, loose or disconnected wiring in the starting circuit (Chapter 5).
- [ ] Defective starter solenoid or switch (Chapter 5).
- [ ] Defective starter motor (Chapter 5).
- [ ] Starter pinion or flywheel/driveplate ring gear teeth loose or broken (Chapters 2 or 5).
- [ ] Engine earth strap broken or disconnected.

Starter motor turns engine slowly

- [ ] Partially-discharged battery (recharge, use jump leads, or push start) (Chapter 5).
- [ ] Battery terminals loose or corroded (Chapter 1).
- [ ] Battery earth to body defective (Chapter 5).
- [ ] Engine earth strap loose.
- [ ] Starter motor (or solenoid) wiring loose (Chapter 5).
- [ ] Starter motor internal fault (Chapter 5).

Engine rotates, but will not start

- [ ] Fuel pump inertia switch tripped (electric pump) (Chapter 4).
- [ ] Fuel tank empty.
- [ ] Battery discharged (engine rotates slowly) (Chapter 5).
- [ ] Battery terminal connections loose or corroded (Chapter 1).
- [ ] Ignition components damp or damaged (Chapters 1 and 5).
- [ ] Broken, loose or disconnected wiring in the ignition circuit (Chapters 1 and 5).
- [ ] Worn, faulty or incorrectly-gapped spark plugs (Chapter 1).
- [ ] Fuel injection system fault (Chapter 4).
- [ ] Major mechanical failure (eg broken timing chain) (Chapter 2).

Engine difficult to start when cold

- [ ] Battery discharged (Chapter 5).
- [ ] Battery terminal connections loose or corroded (Chapter 1).
- [ ] Worn, faulty or incorrectly-gapped spark plugs (Chapter 1).
- [ ] Fuel injection system fault (Chapter 4).
- [ ] Other ignition system fault (Chapters 1 and 5).
- [ ] Low cylinder compressions (Chapter 2).

Engine difficult to start when hot

- [ ] Air filter element dirty or clogged (Chapter 1).
- [ ] Fuel injection system fault (Chapter 4).
- [ ] Low cylinder compressions (Chapter 2).

Starter motor noisy or excessively-rough in engagement

- [ ] Starter pinion or flywheel/driveplate ring gear teeth loose or broken (Chapters 2 or 5).
- [ ] Starter motor mounting bolts loose or missing (Chapter 5).
- [ ] Starter motor internal components worn or damaged (Chapter 5).

Engine starts, but stops immediately

- [ ] Loose or faulty electrical connections in the ignition circuit (Chapters 1 and 5).
- [ ] Vacuum leak at the throttle body or inlet manifold (Chapter 4).
- [ ] Fuel injection system fault (Chapter 4).

Engine idles erratically

- [ ] Incorrectly-adjusted idle speed (Chapter 4).
- [ ] Air filter element clogged (Chapter 1).
- [ ] Vacuum leak at the throttle body, inlet manifold or associated hoses (Chapter 4).
- [ ] Worn, faulty or incorrectly-gapped spark plugs (Chapter 1).
- [ ] Uneven or low cylinder compressions (Chapter 2).
- [ ] Camshaft lobes worn (Chapter 2).
- [ ] Fuel injection system fault (Chapter 4).

Engine misfires at idle speed

- [ ] Worn, faulty or incorrectly-gapped spark plugs (Chapter 1).
- [ ] Faulty spark plug HT leads (Chapter 5).
- [ ] Vacuum leak at the throttle body, inlet manifold or associated hoses (Chapter 4).
- [ ] Fuel injection system fault (Chapter 4).
- [ ] Distributor cap cracked or tracking internally, where applicable (Chapter 5).
- [ ] Uneven or low cylinder compressions (Chapter 2).
- [ ] Disconnected, leaking, or perished crankcase ventilation hoses (Chapter 4).

Engine misfires throughout the driving speed range

- [ ] Fuel filter choked (Chapter 1).
- [ ] Fuel pump faulty, or delivery pressure low (Chapter 4).
- [ ] Fuel tank vent blocked, or fuel pipes restricted (Chapter 4).
- [ ] Vacuum leak at the throttle body, inlet manifold or associated hoses (Chapter 4).
- [ ] Worn, faulty or incorrectly-gapped spark plugs (Chapter 1).
- [ ] Faulty spark plug HT leads (Chapter 5).
- [ ] Distributor cap cracked or tracking internally, where applicable (Chapter 5).
- [ ] Faulty ignition coil (Chapter 5).
- [ ] Uneven or low cylinder compressions (Chapter 2).
- [ ] Fuel injection system fault (Chapter 4).

Engine hesitates on acceleration

- [ ] Worn, faulty or incorrectly-gapped spark plugs (Chapter 1).
- [ ] Vacuum leak at the throttle body, inlet manifold or associated hoses (Chapter 4).
- [ ] Fuel injection system fault (Chapter 4).

Engine stalls

- [ ] Vacuum leak at the throttle body, inlet manifold or associated hoses (Chapter 4).

☐ Fuel filter choked (Chapter 1).
☐ Fuel pump faulty, or delivery pressure low (Chapter 4).
☐ Fuel tank vent blocked, or fuel pipes restricted (Chapter 4).
☐ Fuel injection system fault (Chapter 4).

Engine lacks power

☐ Fuel filter choked (Chapter 1).
☐ Fuel pump faulty, or delivery pressure low (Chapter 4).
☐ Uneven or low cylinder compressions (Chapter 2).
☐ Worn, faulty or incorrectly-gapped spark plugs (Chapter 1).
☐ Vacuum leak at the throttle body, inlet manifold or associated hoses (Chapter 4).
☐ Fuel injection system fault (Chapter 4).
☐ Brakes binding (Chapters 1 and 10).
☐ Clutch slipping (Chapter 6).

Engine backfires

☐ Vacuum leak at the throttle body, inlet manifold or associated hoses (Chapter 4).
☐ Fuel injection system fault (Chapter 4).

Oil pressure warning light illuminated with engine running

☐ Low oil level, or incorrect oil grade (Chapter 1).
☐ Faulty oil pressure sensor (Chapter 2).
☐ Worn engine bearings and/or oil pump (Chapter 2).
☐ Excessively high engine operating temperature (Chapter 3).
☐ Oil pressure relief valve defective (Chapter 2).
☐ Oil pick-up strainer clogged (Chapter 2).

Note: *Low oil pressure in a high-mileage engine at tickover is not necessarily a cause for concern. Sudden pressure loss at speed is far more significant. In any event, check the gauge or warning light sender before condemning the engine.*

Engine runs-on after switching off

☐ Excessive carbon build-up in engine (Chapter 2).
☐ Excessively high engine operating temperature (Chapter 3).

Engine noises

Pre-ignition (pinking) or knocking during acceleration or under load

☐ Ignition timing incorrect/ignition system fault (Chapters 1 and 5).
☐ Incorrect grade of spark plug (Chapter 1).
☐ Incorrect grade of fuel (Chapter 1).
☐ Vacuum leak at throttle body, inlet manifold or associated hoses (Chapter 4).
☐ Excessive carbon build-up in engine (Chapter 2).
☐ Fuel injection system fault (Chapter 4).

Whistling or wheezing noises

☐ Leaking inlet manifold or throttle body gasket (Chapter 4).
☐ Leaking exhaust manifold gasket (Chapter 4).
☐ Leaking vacuum hose (Chapters 4 and 10).
☐ Blowing cylinder head gasket (Chapter 2).

Tapping or rattling noises

☐ Worn valve gear, timing chain, camshaft or hydraulic tappets (Chapter 2).
☐ Ancillary component fault (water pump, alternator, etc) (Chapters 3, 5)

Knocking or thumping noises

☐ Worn big-end bearings (regular heavy knocking, perhaps less under load) (Chapter 2).
☐ Worn main bearings (rumbling and knocking, perhaps worsening under load) (Chapter 2).
☐ Piston slap (most noticeable when cold) (Chapter 2).
☐ Ancillary component fault (water pump, alternator, etc) (Chapters 3, 5)

Cooling system

Overheating

☐ Auxiliary drivebelt broken or incorrectly adjusted (Chapter 1).
☐ Insufficient coolant in system (Chapter 1).
☐ Thermostat faulty (Chapter 3).
☐ Radiator core blocked, or grille restricted (Chapter 3).
☐ Electric cooling fan or thermostatic switch faulty (Chapter 3).
☐ Viscous-coupled fan faulty (Chapter 3).
☐ Ignition timing incorrect, or ignition system fault (Chapters 1 and 5).
☐ Inaccurate temperature gauge sender unit (Chapter 3).
☐ Airlock in cooling system (Chapter 3).

Overcooling

☐ Thermostat faulty (Chapter 3).
☐ Inaccurate temperature gauge sender unit (Chapter 3).

External coolant leakage

☐ Deteriorated or damaged hoses or hose clips (Chapter 1).
☐ Radiator core or heater matrix leaking (Chapter 3).
☐ Pressure cap faulty (Chapter 3).
☐ Water pump internal seal leaking (Chapter 3).
☐ Water pump-to-block seal leaking (Chapter 3).
☐ Boiling due to overheating (Chapter 3).
☐ Core plug leaking (Chapter 2).

Internal coolant leakage

☐ Leaking cylinder head gasket (Chapter 2).
☐ Cracked cylinder head or cylinder block (Chapter 2).

Corrosion

☐ Infrequent draining and flushing (Chapter 1).
☐ Incorrect coolant mixture or inappropriate coolant type (Chapter 1).

Fuel and exhaust systems

Excessive fuel consumption

☐ Air filter element dirty or clogged (Chapter 1).
☐ Fuel injection system fault (Chapter 4).
☐ Ignition timing incorrect or ignition system fault (Chapters 1 and 5).
☐ Brakes binding (Chapter 10).
☐ Tyres under-inflated (Chapter 1).

Fuel leakage and/or fuel odour

☐ Damaged fuel tank, pipes or connections (Chapters 1 and 4).

Excessive noise or fumes from exhaust system

☐ Leaking exhaust system or manifold joints (Chapters 1 and 4).
☐ Leaking, corroded or damaged silencers or pipe (Chapters 1 and 4).
☐ Broken mountings causing body or suspension contact (Chapter 4).

Clutch

Pedal travels to floor - no pressure or very little resistance

- [ ] Badly stretched or broken cable (Chapter 6).
- [ ] Stripped pawl on pedal (Chapter 6).
- [ ] Broken clutch release bearing or arm (Chapter 6).
- [ ] Broken diaphragm spring in clutch pressure plate (Chapter 6).

Clutch fails to disengage (unable to select gears)

- [ ] Cable free play excessive (Chapter 6).
- [ ] Clutch driven plate sticking on gearbox input shaft splines (Chapter 6).
- [ ] Clutch driven plate sticking to flywheel or pressure plate (Chapter 6).
- [ ] Faulty pressure plate assembly (Chapter 6).
- [ ] Clutch release mechanism worn or incorrectly assembled (Chapter 6).

Clutch slips (engine speed increases, with no increase in vehicle speed)

- [ ] Clutch driven plate linings excessively worn (Chapter 6).

- [ ] Clutch driven plate linings contaminated with oil or grease (Chapter 6).
- [ ] Faulty pressure plate or weak diaphragm spring (Chapter 6).

Judder as clutch is engaged

- [ ] Clutch driven plate linings contaminated with oil or grease (Chapter 6).
- [ ] Clutch driven plate linings excessively worn (Chapter 6).
- [ ] Faulty or distorted pressure plate or diaphragm spring (Chapter 6).
- [ ] Worn or loose engine or gearbox mountings (Chapter 2).
- [ ] Clutch driven plate hub or gearbox input shaft splines worn (Chapter 6).

Noise when depressing or releasing clutch pedal

- [ ] Worn clutch release bearing (Chapter 6).
- [ ] Worn or dry clutch pedal pivot (Chapter 6).
- [ ] Faulty pressure plate assembly (Chapter 6).
- [ ] Pressure plate diaphragm spring broken (Chapter 6).
- [ ] Broken clutch driven plate cushioning springs (Chapter 6).

Manual gearbox

Noisy in neutral with engine running

- [ ] Input shaft bearings worn (noise apparent with clutch pedal released, but not when depressed) (Chapter 7).*
- [ ] Clutch release bearing worn (noise apparent with clutch pedal depressed, possibly less when released) (Chapter 6).

Noisy in one particular gear

- [ ] Worn, damaged or chipped gear teeth (Chapter 7).*

Difficulty engaging gears

- [ ] Clutch fault (Chapter 6).
- [ ] Worn or damaged gear linkage (Chapter 7).
- [ ] Worn synchroniser units (Chapter 7).*

Jumps out of gear

- [ ] Worn or damaged gear linkage (Chapter 7).

- [ ] Worn synchroniser units (Chapter 7).*
- [ ] Worn selector forks (Chapter 7).*

Vibration

- [ ] Lack of oil (Chapter 1).
- [ ] Worn bearings (Chapter 7).*

Lubricant leaks

- [ ] Leaking oil seal (Chapter 7).
- [ ] Leaking housing joint (Chapter 7).*

*Although the corrective action necessary to remedy the symptoms described is beyond the scope of the home mechanic, the above information should be helpful in isolating the cause of the condition, so that the owner can communicate clearly with a professional mechanic.

Automatic transmission

Note: *Due to the complexity of the automatic transmission, it is difficult for the home mechanic to properly diagnose and service this unit. For problems other than the following, the vehicle should be taken to a dealer service department or automatic transmission specialist.*

Fluid leakage

- [ ] Automatic transmission fluid is usually deep red in colour. Fluid leaks should not be confused with engine oil, which can easily be blown onto the transmission by air flow.
- [ ] To determine the source of a leak, first remove all built-up dirt and grime from the transmission housing and surrounding areas, using a degreasing agent or by steam-cleaning. Drive the vehicle at low speed, so that air flow will not blow the leak far from its source. Raise and support the vehicle, and determine where the leak is coming from. The following are common areas of leakage.
  - a) Fluid pan (transmission "sump").
  - b) Dipstick tube (Chapter 1).
  - c) Transmission-to-fluid cooler fluid pipes/unions (Chapter 7).

Transmission fluid brown, or has burned smell

- [ ] Transmission fluid level low, or fluid in need of renewal (Chapter 1).

General gear selection problems

- [ ] The most likely cause of gear selection problems is a faulty or poorly-adjusted gear selector mechanism. The following are common problems associated with a faulty selector mechanism.
  - a) Engine starting in gears other than Park or Neutral.
  - b) Indicator on gear selector lever pointing to a gear other than the one actually being used.
  - c) Vehicle moves when in Park or Neutral.
  - d) Poor gear shift quality, or erratic gear changes.
- [ ] Refer any problems to a Ford dealer, or transmission specialist.

Transmission will not downshift (kickdown) with accelerator pedal fully depressed

- [ ] Low transmission fluid level (Chapter 1).
- [ ] Incorrect selector adjustment (Chapter 7).

Engine will not start in any gear, or starts in gears other than Park or Neutral

- ☐ Faulty starter inhibitor switch (Chapter 7).
- ☐ Incorrect selector adjustment (Chapter 7).

Transmission slips, shifts roughly, is noisy, or has no drive in forward or reverse gears

- ☐ There are many probable causes for the above problems, but the home mechanic should be concerned with only one possibility - fluid level. Before taking the vehicle to a dealer or transmission specialist, check the fluid level and condition of the fluid as described in Chapter 1. Correct the fluid level as necessary, or change the fluid and filter if needed. If the problem persists, professional help will be necessary.

Propeller shaft

Clunking or knocking noise when taking up drive

- ☐ Worn universal joints (Chapter 8).
- ☐ Loose flange bolt (Chapter 8).

Vibration when accelerating or decelerating

- ☐ Worn centre bearing or universal joints (Chapter 8).
- ☐ Bent or distorted shaft (Chapter 8).
- ☐ Deteriorated rubber insulator on centre bearing (Chapter 8)

Final drive and driveshafts

Excessive final drive noise

- ☐ Oil level low, or incorrect grade (Chapter 1)
- ☐ Worn bearings (Chapter 9)
- ☐ Worn or badly adjusted crownwheel and pinion (Chapter 9)
- ☐ Loose or deteriorated final drive mountings (Chapter 9)

Oil leakage from final drive

- ☐ Pinion or output flange oil seal leaking (Chapter 9)

- ☐ Rear cover leaking (Chapter 9)
- ☐ Cover or casing cracked (Chapter 9)

Grating, knocking or vibration from driveshafts

- ☐ Flange screws loose (Chapter 9)
- ☐ CV joints worn (Chapter 9)
- ☐ Driveshaft bent (Chapter 9)

Braking system

Note: *Before assuming that a brake problem exists, make sure that the tyres are in good condition and correctly inflated, that the front wheel alignment is correct, and that the vehicle is not loaded with weight in an unequal manner. Apart from checking the condition of all pipe and hose connections, any faults occurring on the anti-lock braking system should be referred to a Ford dealer for diagnosis.*

Vehicle pulls to one side under braking

- ☐ Worn, defective, damaged or contaminated front or rear brake pads on one side (Chapters 1 and 10).
- ☐ Seized or partially-seized front or rear brake caliper piston (Chapter 10).
- ☐ A mixture of brake pad lining materials fitted between sides (Chapter 10).
- ☐ Brake caliper mounting bolts loose (Chapter 10).
- ☐ Worn or damaged steering or suspension components (Chapters 1 and 11).

Noise (grinding or high-pitched squeal) when brakes applied

- ☐ Brake pad friction lining material worn down to metal backing (Chapters 1 and 10).
- ☐ Excessive corrosion of brake disc - may be apparent after the vehicle has been standing for some time (Chapters 1 and 10).

Excessive brake pedal travel

- ☐ Faulty master cylinder (Chapter 10).
- ☐ Air in hydraulic system (Chapter 10).

- ☐ Faulty vacuum servo unit (Chapter 10).

Brake pedal feels spongy when depressed

- ☐ Air in hydraulic system (Chapter 10).
- ☐ Deteriorated flexible rubber brake hoses (Chapters 1 and 10).
- ☐ Master cylinder mountings loose (Chapter 10).
- ☐ Faulty master cylinder (Chapter 10).

Excessive brake pedal effort required to stop vehicle

- ☐ Faulty vacuum servo unit (Chapter 10).
- ☐ Disconnected, damaged or insecure brake servo vacuum hose (Chapters 1 and 10).
- ☐ Primary or secondary hydraulic circuit failure (Chapter 10).
- ☐ Seized brake caliper piston(s) (Chapter 10).
- ☐ Brake pads incorrectly fitted (Chapter 10).
- ☐ Incorrect grade of brake pads fitted (Chapter 10).
- ☐ Brake pads contaminated (Chapter 10).

Judder felt through brake pedal or steering wheel when braking

- ☐ Excessive run-out or distortion of brake disc(s) (Chapter 10).
- ☐ Brake pad linings worn (Chapters 1 and 10).
- ☐ Brake caliper mounting bolts loose (Chapter 10).
- ☐ Wear in suspension or steering components or mountings (Chapters 1 and 11).

Pedal pulsates when braking hard

- ☐ Normal feature of ABS - no fault

Brakes binding

- ☐ Seized brake caliper piston(s) (Chapter 10).
- ☐ Incorrectly-adjusted handbrake mechanism (Chapter 10).
- ☐ Faulty master cylinder (Chapter 10).

Rear wheels locking under normal braking

- ☐ Seized brake caliper piston(s) (Chapter 10).
- ☐ Faulty brake pressure regulator (Chapter 10).

Steering and suspension

Note: *Before diagnosing suspension or steering faults, be sure that the trouble is not due to incorrect tyre pressures, mixtures of tyre types, or binding brakes.*

Vehicle pulls to one side

- ☐ Defective tyre (Chapter 1).
- ☐ Excessive wear in suspension or steering components (Chapters 1 and 11).
- ☐ Incorrect front wheel alignment (Chapter 11).
- ☐ Accident damage to steering or suspension components (Chapters 1 and 11).

Wheel wobble and vibration

- ☐ Front roadwheels out of balance (vibration felt mainly through the steering wheel) (Chapter 11).
- ☐ Rear roadwheels out of balance (vibration felt throughout the vehicle) (Chapter 11).
- ☐ Roadwheels damaged or distorted (Chapter 11).
- ☐ Faulty or damaged tyre (Chapter 1).
- ☐ Worn steering or suspension joints, bushes or components (Chapters 1 and 11).
- ☐ Wheel bolts loose (Chapter 11).

Excessive pitching and/or rolling around corners, or during braking

- ☐ Defective shock absorbers (Chapters 1 and 11).
- ☐ Broken or weak coil spring and/or suspension component (Chapters 1 and 11).
- ☐ Worn or damaged anti-roll bar or mountings (Chapter 11).

Wandering or general instability

- ☐ Incorrect front wheel alignment (Chapter 11).
- ☐ Worn steering or suspension joints, bushes or components (Chapters 1 and 11).
- ☐ Roadwheels out of balance (Chapter 11).
- ☐ Faulty or damaged tyre (Chapter 1).
- ☐ Wheel bolts loose (Chapter 11).
- ☐ Defective shock absorbers (Chapters 1 and 11).

Excessively-stiff steering

- ☐ Lack of steering gear lubricant (Chapter 11).
- ☐ Seized track rod end balljoint or suspension balljoint (Chapters 1 and 11).

- ☐ Broken or incorrectly adjusted auxiliary drivebelt (Chapter 1).
- ☐ Incorrect front wheel alignment (Chapter 11).
- ☐ Steering rack or column bent or damaged (Chapter 11).

Excessive play in steering

- ☐ Worn steering column universal joint(s) (Chapter 11).
- ☐ Worn steering track rod end balljoints (Chapters 1 and 11).
- ☐ Worn rack-and-pinion steering gear (Chapter 11).
- ☐ Worn steering or suspension joints, bushes or components (Chapters 1 and 11).

Lack of power assistance

- ☐ Broken or incorrectly-adjusted auxiliary drivebelt (Chapter 1).
- ☐ Incorrect power steering fluid level (Chapter 1).
- ☐ Restriction in power steering fluid hoses (Chapter 11).
- ☐ Faulty power steering pump (Chapter 11).
- ☐ Faulty rack-and-pinion steering gear (Chapter 11).

Tyre wear excessive

Tyres worn on inside or outside edges

- ☐ Tyres under-inflated (wear on both edges) (Chapter 1).
- ☐ Incorrect camber or castor angles (wear on one edge only) (Chapter 11).
- ☐ Worn steering or suspension joints, bushes or components (Chapters 1 and 11).
- ☐ Excessively-hard cornering.
- ☐ Accident damage.

Tyre treads exhibit feathered edges

- ☐ Incorrect toe setting (Chapter 11).

Tyres worn in centre of tread

- ☐ Tyres over-inflated (Chapter 1).

Tyres worn on inside and outside edges

- ☐ Tyres under-inflated (Chapter 1).
- ☐ Worn shock absorbers (Chapters 1 and 11).

Tyres worn unevenly

- ☐ Tyres out of balance (Chapter 1).
- ☐ Excessive wheel or tyre run-out (Chapter 1).
- ☐ Worn shock absorbers (Chapters 1 and 11).
- ☐ Faulty tyre (Chapter 1).

Electrical system

Note: *For problems associated with the starting system, refer to the faults listed under "Engine" earlier in this Section.*

Battery will not hold a charge for more than a few days

- ☐ Battery defective internally (Chapter 5).
- ☐ Battery electrolyte level low - where applicable (Chapter 1).
- ☐ Battery terminal connections loose or corroded (Chapter 1).
- ☐ Auxiliary drivebelt worn - or incorrectly adjusted (Chapter 1).
- ☐ Alternator not charging at correct output (Chapter 5).

- ☐ Alternator or voltage regulator faulty (Chapter 5).
- ☐ Short-circuit causing continual battery drain (Chapters 5 and 13).

Ignition/no-charge warning light remains illuminated with engine running

- ☐ Auxiliary drivebelt broken, worn, or incorrectly adjusted (Chapter 1).
- ☐ Alternator brushes worn, sticking, or dirty (Chapter 5).
- ☐ Alternator brush springs weak or broken (Chapter 5).
- ☐ Internal fault in alternator or voltage regulator (Chapter 5).
- ☐ Broken, disconnected, or loose wiring in charging circuit (Chapter 5).

Ignition/no-charge warning light fails to come on

☐ Warning light bulb blown (Chapter 13).
☐ Broken, disconnected, or loose wiring in warning light circuit (Chapter 13).
☐ Alternator faulty (Chapter 5).

Lights inoperative

☐ Bulb blown (Chapter 13).
☐ Corrosion of bulb or bulbholder contacts (Chapter 13).
☐ Blown fuse (Chapter 13).
☐ Faulty relay (Chapter 13).
☐ Broken, loose, or disconnected wiring (Chapter 13).
☐ Faulty switch (Chapter 13).

Instrument readings inaccurate or erratic

Instrument readings increase with engine speed

☐ Faulty voltage regulator (Chapter 13).

Fuel or temperature gauges give no reading

☐ Faulty gauge sender unit (Chapters 4 and 5).
☐ Wiring open-circuit (Chapter 13).
☐ Faulty gauge (Chapter 13).

Fuel or temperature gauges give continuous maximum reading

☐ Faulty gauge sender unit (Chapters 4 and 5).
☐ Wiring short-circuit (Chapter 13).
☐ Faulty gauge (Chapter 13).

Horn inoperative, or unsatisfactory in operation

Horn operates all the time

☐ Horn contacts permanently bridged or horn push stuck down (Chapter 13).

Horn fails to operate

☐ Blown fuse (Chapter 13).
☐ Cable or cable connections loose, broken or disconnected (Chapter 13).
☐ Faulty horn (Chapter 13).

Horn emits intermittent or unsatisfactory sound

☐ Cable connections loose (Chapter 13).
☐ Horn mountings loose (Chapter 13).
☐ Faulty horn (Chapter 13).

Windscreen/tailgate wipers inoperative, or unsatisfactory in operation

Wipers fail to operate, or operate very slowly

☐ Wiper blades stuck to screen, or linkage seized or binding (Chapters 1 and 13).
☐ Blown fuse (Chapter 13).
☐ Cable or cable connections loose, broken or disconnected (Chapter 13).
☐ Faulty relay (Chapter 13).
☐ Faulty wiper motor (Chapter 13).

Wiper blades sweep over too large or too small an area of the glass

☐ Wiper arms incorrectly positioned on spindles (Chapter 1).
☐ Excessive wear of wiper linkage (Chapter 13).
☐ Wiper motor or linkage mountings loose or insecure (Chapter 13).

Wiper blades fail to clean the glass effectively

☐ Wiper blade rubbers worn or perished (Chapter 1).
☐ Wiper arm tension springs broken, or arm pivots seized (Chapter 13).
☐ Insufficient windscreen washer additive to adequately remove road film (Chapter 1).

Windscreen/tailgate washers inoperative, or unsatisfactory in operation

One or more washer jets inoperative

☐ Blocked washer jet (Chapter 1).
☐ Disconnected, kinked or restricted fluid hose (Chapter 13).
☐ Insufficient fluid in washer reservoir (Chapter 1).

Washer pump fails to operate

☐ Broken or disconnected wiring or connections (Chapter 13).
☐ Blown fuse (Chapter 13).
☐ Faulty washer switch (Chapter 13).
☐ Faulty washer pump (Chapter 13).

Washer pump runs for some time before fluid is emitted from jets

☐ Faulty one-way valve in fluid supply hose (Chapter 13).

Electric windows inoperative, or unsatisfactory in operation

Window glass will only move in one direction

☐ Faulty switch (Chapter 13).

Window glass slow to move

☐ Regulator seized or damaged, or in need of lubrication (Chapter 12).
☐ Door internal components or trim fouling regulator (Chapter 12).
☐ Faulty motor (Chapter 12).

Window glass fails to move

☐ Blown fuse (Chapter 13).
☐ Faulty relay (Chapter 13).
☐ Broken or disconnected wiring or connections (Chapter 13).
☐ Faulty motor (Chapter 13).

Central locking system inoperative, or unsatisfactory in operation

Complete system failure

☐ Blown fuse (Chapter 13).
☐ Faulty relay (Chapter 13).
☐ Broken or disconnected wiring or connections (Chapter 13).

Latch locks but will not unlock, or unlocks but will not lock

☐ Faulty switch (Chapter 13).
☐ Broken or disconnected latch operating rods or levers (Chapter 12).
☐ Faulty relay (Chapter 13).

One solenoid/motor fails to operate

☐ Broken or disconnected wiring or connections (Chapter 13).
☐ Faulty solenoid/motor (Chapter 12).
☐ Broken, binding or disconnected latch operating rods or levers (Chapter 12).
☐ Fault in door latch (Chapter 12).

A

ABS (Anti-lock brake system) A system, usually electronically controlled, that senses incipient wheel lockup during braking and relieves hydraulic pressure at wheels that are about to skid.

Air bag An inflatable bag hidden in the steering wheel (driver's side) or the dash or glovebox (passenger side). In a head-on collision, the bags inflate, preventing the driver and front passenger from being thrown forward into the steering wheel or windscreen.

Air cleaner A metal or plastic housing, containing a filter element, which removes dust and dirt from the air being drawn into the engine.

Air filter element The actual filter in an air cleaner system, usually manufactured from pleated paper and requiring renewal at regular intervals.

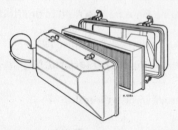

Air filter

Allen key A hexagonal wrench which fits into a recessed hexagonal hole.

Alligator clip A long-nosed spring-loaded metal clip with meshing teeth. Used to make temporary electrical connections.

Alternator A component in the electrical system which converts mechanical energy from a drivebelt into electrical energy to charge the battery and to operate the starting system, ignition system and electrical accessories.

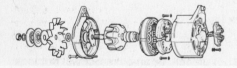

Alternator (exploded view)

Ampere (amp) A unit of measurement for the flow of electric current. One amp is the amount of current produced by one volt acting through a resistance of one ohm.

Anaerobic sealer A substance used to prevent bolts and screws from loosening. Anaerobic means that it does not require oxygen for activation. The Loctite brand is widely used.

Antifreeze A substance (usually ethylene glycol) mixed with water, and added to a vehicle's cooling system, to prevent freezing of the coolant in winter. Antifreeze also contains chemicals to inhibit corrosion and the formation of rust and other deposits that

would tend to clog the radiator and coolant passages and reduce cooling efficiency.

Anti-seize compound A coating that reduces the risk of seizing on fasteners that are subjected to high temperatures, such as exhaust manifold bolts and nuts.

Anti-seize compound

Asbestos A natural fibrous mineral with great heat resistance, commonly used in the composition of brake friction materials. Asbestos is a health hazard and the dust created by brake systems should never be inhaled or ingested.

Axle A shaft on which a wheel revolves, or which revolves with a wheel. Also, a solid beam that connects the two wheels at one end of the vehicle. An axle which also transmits power to the wheels is known as a live axle.

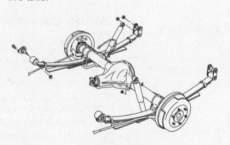

Axle assembly

Axleshaft A single rotating shaft, on either side of the differential, which delivers power from the final drive assembly to the drive wheels. Also called a driveshaft or a halfshaft.

B

Ball bearing An anti-friction bearing consisting of a hardened inner and outer race with hardened steel balls between two races.

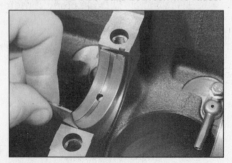

Bearing

Bearing The curved surface on a shaft or in a bore, or the part assembled into either, that permits relative motion between them with minimum wear and friction.

Big-end bearing The bearing in the end of the connecting rod that's attached to the crankshaft.

Bleed nipple A valve on a brake wheel cylinder, caliper or other hydraulic component that is opened to purge the hydraulic system of air. Also called a bleed screw.

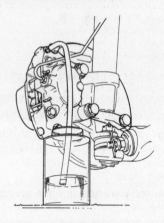

Brake bleeding

Brake bleeding Procedure for removing air from lines of a hydraulic brake system.

Brake disc The component of a disc brake that rotates with the wheels.

Brake drum The component of a drum brake that rotates with the wheels.

Brake linings The friction material which contacts the brake disc or drum to retard the vehicle's speed. The linings are bonded or riveted to the brake pads or shoes.

Brake pads The replaceable friction pads that pinch the brake disc when the brakes are applied. Brake pads consist of a friction material bonded or riveted to a rigid backing plate.

Brake shoe The crescent-shaped carrier to which the brake linings are mounted and which forces the lining against the rotating drum during braking.

Braking systems For more information on braking systems, consult the *Haynes Automotive Brake Manual*.

Breaker bar A long socket wrench handle providing greater leverage.

Bulkhead The insulated partition between the engine and the passenger compartment.

C

Caliper The non-rotating part of a disc-brake assembly that straddles the disc and carries the brake pads. The caliper also contains the hydraulic components that cause the pads to pinch the disc when the brakes are applied. A caliper is also a measuring tool that can be set to measure inside or outside dimensions of an object.

Camshaft A rotating shaft on which a series of cam lobes operate the valve mechanisms. The camshaft may be driven by gears, by sprockets and chain or by sprockets and a belt.

Canister A container in an evaporative emission control system; contains activated charcoal granules to trap vapours from the fuel system.

Canister

Carburettor A device which mixes fuel with air in the proper proportions to provide a desired power output from a spark ignition internal combustion engine.

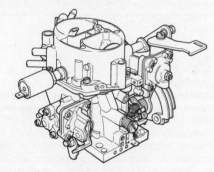

Carburettor

Castellated Resembling the parapets along the top of a castle wall. For example, a castellated balljoint stud nut.

Castellated nut

Castor In wheel alignment, the backward or forward tilt of the steering axis. Castor is positive when the steering axis is inclined rearward at the top.

Catalytic converter A silencer-like device in the exhaust system which converts certain pollutants in the exhaust gases into less harmful substances.

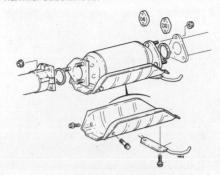

Catalytic converter

Circlip A ring-shaped clip used to prevent endwise movement of cylindrical parts and shafts. An internal circlip is installed in a groove in a housing; an external circlip fits into a groove on the outside of a cylindrical piece such as a shaft.

Clearance The amount of space between two parts. For example, between a piston and a cylinder, between a bearing and a journal, etc.

Coil spring A spiral of elastic steel found in various sizes throughout a vehicle, for example as a springing medium in the suspension and in the valve train.

Compression Reduction in volume, and increase in pressure and temperature, of a gas, caused by squeezing it into a smaller space.

Compression ratio The relationship between cylinder volume when the piston is at top dead centre and cylinder volume when the piston is at bottom dead centre.

Constant velocity (CV) joint A type of universal joint that cancels out vibrations caused by driving power being transmitted through an angle.

Core plug A disc or cup-shaped metal device inserted in a hole in a casting through which core was removed when the casting was formed. Also known as a freeze plug or expansion plug.

Crankcase The lower part of the engine block in which the crankshaft rotates.

Crankshaft The main rotating member, or shaft, running the length of the crankcase, with offset "throws" to which the connecting rods are attached.

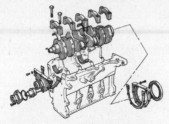

Crankshaft assembly

Crocodile clip See Alligator clip

D

Diagnostic code Code numbers obtained by accessing the diagnostic mode of an engine management computer. This code can be used to determine the area in the system where a malfunction may be located.

Disc brake A brake design incorporating a rotating disc onto which brake pads are squeezed. The resulting friction converts the energy of a moving vehicle into heat.

Double-overhead cam (DOHC) An engine that uses two overhead camshafts, usually one for the intake valves and one for the exhaust valves.

Drivebelt(s) The belt(s) used to drive accessories such as the alternator, water pump, power steering pump, air conditioning compressor, etc. off the crankshaft pulley.

Accessory drivebelts

Driveshaft Any shaft used to transmit motion. Commonly used when referring to the axleshafts on a front wheel drive vehicle.

Driveshaft

Drum brake A type of brake using a drum-shaped metal cylinder attached to the inner surface of the wheel. When the brake pedal is pressed, curved brake shoes with friction linings press against the inside of the drum to slow or stop the vehicle.

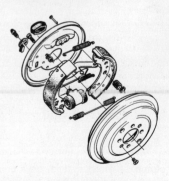

Drum brake assembly

E

EGR valve A valve used to introduce exhaust gases into the intake air stream.

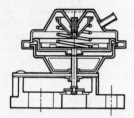

EGR valve

Electronic control unit (ECU) A computer which controls (for instance) ignition and fuel injection systems, or an anti-lock braking system. For more information refer to the *Haynes Automotive Electrical and Electronic Systems Manual.*

Electronic Fuel Injection (EFI) A computer controlled fuel system that distributes fuel through an injector located in each intake port of the engine.

Emergency brake A braking system, independent of the main hydraulic system, that can be used to slow or stop the vehicle if the primary brakes fail, or to hold the vehicle stationary even though the brake pedal isn't depressed. It usually consists of a hand lever that actuates either front or rear brakes mechanically through a series of cables and linkages. Also known as a handbrake or parking brake.

Endfloat The amount of lengthwise movement between two parts. As applied to a crankshaft, the distance that the crankshaft can move forward and back in the cylinder block.

Engine management system (EMS) A computer controlled system which manages the fuel injection and the ignition systems in an integrated fashion.

Exhaust manifold A part with several passages through which exhaust gases leave the engine combustion chambers and enter the exhaust pipe.

Exhaust manifold

F

Fan clutch A viscous (fluid) drive coupling device which permits variable engine fan speeds in relation to engine speeds.

Feeler blade A thin strip or blade of hardened steel, ground to an exact thickness, used to check or measure clearances between parts.

Feeler blade

Firing order The order in which the engine cylinders fire, or deliver their power strokes, beginning with the number one cylinder.

Flywheel A heavy spinning wheel in which energy is absorbed and stored by means of momentum. On cars, the flywheel is attached to the crankshaft to smooth out firing impulses.

Free play The amount of travel before any action takes place. The "looseness" in a linkage, or an assembly of parts, between the initial application of force and actual movement. For example, the distance the brake pedal moves before the pistons in the master cylinder are actuated.

Fuse An electrical device which protects a circuit against accidental overload. The typical fuse contains a soft piece of metal which is calibrated to melt at a predetermined current flow (expressed as amps) and break the circuit.

Fusible link A circuit protection device consisting of a conductor surrounded by heat-resistant insulation. The conductor is smaller than the wire it protects, so it acts as the weakest link in the circuit. Unlike a blown fuse, a failed fusible link must frequently be cut from the wire for replacement.

G

Gap The distance the spark must travel in jumping from the centre electrode to the side

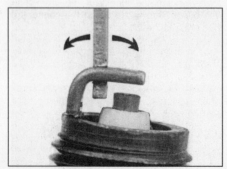

Adjusting spark plug gap

electrode in a spark plug. Also refers to the spacing between the points in a contact breaker assembly in a conventional points-type ignition, or to the distance between the reluctor or rotor and the pickup coil in an electronic ignition.

Gasket Any thin, soft material - usually cork, cardboard, asbestos or soft metal - installed between two metal surfaces to ensure a good seal. For instance, the cylinder head gasket seals the joint between the block and the cylinder head.

Gasket

Gauge An instrument panel display used to monitor engine conditions. A gauge with a movable pointer on a dial or a fixed scale is an analogue gauge. A gauge with a numerical readout is called a digital gauge.

H

Halfshaft A rotating shaft that transmits power from the final drive unit to a drive wheel, usually when referring to a live rear axle.

Harmonic balancer A device designed to reduce torsion or twisting vibration in the crankshaft. May be incorporated in the crankshaft pulley. Also known as a vibration damper.

Hone An abrasive tool for correcting small irregularities or differences in diameter in an engine cylinder, brake cylinder, etc.

Hydraulic tappet A tappet that utilises hydraulic pressure from the engine's lubrication system to maintain zero clearance (constant contact with both camshaft and valve stem). Automatically adjusts to variation in valve stem length. Hydraulic tappets also reduce valve noise.

I

Ignition timing The moment at which the spark plug fires, usually expressed in the number of crankshaft degrees before the piston reaches the top of its stroke.

Inlet manifold A tube or housing with passages through which flows the air-fuel mixture (carburettor vehicles and vehicles with throttle body injection) or air only (port fuel-injected vehicles) to the port openings in the cylinder head.

J

Jump start Starting the engine of a vehicle with a discharged or weak battery by attaching jump leads from the weak battery to a charged or helper battery.

L

Load Sensing Proportioning Valve (LSPV) A brake hydraulic system control valve that works like a proportioning valve, but also takes into consideration the amount of weight carried by the rear axle.

Locknut A nut used to lock an adjustment nut, or other threaded component, in place. For example, a locknut is employed to keep the adjusting nut on the rocker arm in position.

Lockwasher A form of washer designed to prevent an attaching nut from working loose.

M

MacPherson strut A type of front suspension system devised by Earle MacPherson at Ford of England. In its original form, a simple lateral link with the anti-roll bar creates the lower control arm. A long strut - an integral coil spring and shock absorber - is mounted between the body and the steering knuckle. Many modern so-called MacPherson strut systems use a conventional lower A-arm and don't rely on the anti-roll bar for location.

Multimeter An electrical test instrument with the capability to measure voltage, current and resistance.

N

NOx Oxides of Nitrogen. A common toxic pollutant emitted by petrol and diesel engines at higher temperatures.

O

Ohm The unit of electrical resistance. One volt applied to a resistance of one ohm will produce a current of one amp.

Ohmmeter An instrument for measuring electrical resistance.

O-ring A type of sealing ring made of a special rubber-like material; in use, the O-ring is compressed into a groove to provide the sealing action.

O-ring

Overhead cam (ohc) engine An engine with the camshaft(s) located on top of the cylinder head(s).

Overhead valve (ohv) engine An engine with the valves located in the cylinder head, but with the camshaft located in the engine block.

Oxygen sensor A device installed in the engine exhaust manifold, which senses the oxygen content in the exhaust and converts this information into an electric current. Also called a Lambda sensor.

P

Phillips screw A type of screw head having a cross instead of a slot for a corresponding type of screwdriver.

Plastigage A thin strip of plastic thread, available in different sizes, used for measuring clearances. For example, a strip of Plastigage is laid across a bearing journal. The parts are assembled and dismantled; the width of the crushed strip indicates the clearance between journal and bearing.

Plastigage

Propeller shaft The long hollow tube with universal joints at both ends that carries power from the transmission to the differential on front-engined rear wheel drive vehicles.

Proportioning valve A hydraulic control valve which limits the amount of pressure to the rear brakes during panic stops to prevent wheel lock-up.

R

Rack-and-pinion steering A steering system with a pinion gear on the end of the steering shaft that mates with a rack (think of a geared wheel opened up and laid flat). When the steering wheel is turned, the pinion turns, moving the rack to the left or right. This movement is transmitted through the track rods to the steering arms at the wheels.

Radiator A liquid-to-air heat transfer device designed to reduce the temperature of the coolant in an internal combustion engine cooling system.

Refrigerant Any substance used as a heat transfer agent in an air-conditioning system. R-12 has been the principle refrigerant for many years; recently, however, manufacturers have begun using R-134a, a non-CFC substance that is considered less harmful to

the ozone in the upper atmosphere.

Rocker arm A lever arm that rocks on a shaft or pivots on a stud. In an overhead valve engine, the rocker arm converts the upward movement of the pushrod into a downward movement to open a valve.

Rotor In a distributor, the rotating device inside the cap that connects the centre electrode and the outer terminals as it turns, distributing the high voltage from the coil secondary winding to the proper spark plug. Also, that part of an alternator which rotates inside the stator. Also, the rotating assembly of a turbocharger, including the compressor wheel, shaft and turbine wheel.

Runout The amount of wobble (in-and-out movement) of a gear or wheel as it's rotated. The amount a shaft rotates "out-of-true." The out-of-round condition of a rotating part.

S

Sealant A liquid or paste used to prevent leakage at a joint. Sometimes used in conjunction with a gasket.

Sealed beam lamp An older headlight design which integrates the reflector, lens and filaments into a hermetically-sealed one-piece unit. When a filament burns out or the lens cracks, the entire unit is simply replaced.

Serpentine drivebelt A single, long, wide accessory drivebelt that's used on some newer vehicles to drive all the accessories, instead of a series of smaller, shorter belts. Serpentine drivebelts are usually tensioned by an automatic tensioner.

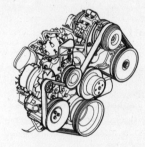

Serpentine drivebelt

Shim Thin spacer, commonly used to adjust the clearance or relative positions between two parts. For example, shims inserted into or under bucket tappets control valve clearances. Clearance is adjusted by changing the thickness of the shim.

Slide hammer A special puller that screws into or hooks onto a component such as a shaft or bearing; a heavy sliding handle on the shaft bottoms against the end of the shaft to knock the component free.

Sprocket A tooth or projection on the periphery of a wheel, shaped to engage with a chain or drivebelt. Commonly used to refer to the sprocket wheel itself.

Starter inhibitor switch On vehicles with an

automatic transmission, a switch that prevents starting if the vehicle is not in Neutral or Park.

Strut See MacPherson strut.

T

Tappet A cylindrical component which transmits motion from the cam to the valve stem, either directly or via a pushrod and rocker arm. Also called a cam follower.

Thermostat A heat-controlled valve that regulates the flow of coolant between the cylinder block and the radiator, so maintaining optimum engine operating temperature. A thermostat is also used in some air cleaners in which the temperature is regulated.

Thrust bearing The bearing in the clutch assembly that is moved in to the release levers by clutch pedal action to disengage the clutch. Also referred to as a release bearing.

Timing belt A toothed belt which drives the camshaft. Serious engine damage may result if it breaks in service.

Timing chain A chain which drives the camshaft.

Toe-in The amount the front wheels are closer together at the front than at the rear. On rear wheel drive vehicles, a slight amount of toe-in is usually specified to keep the front wheels running parallel on the road by offsetting other forces that tend to spread the wheels apart.

Toe-out The amount the front wheels are closer together at the rear than at the front. On front wheel drive vehicles, a slight amount of toe-out is usually specified.

Tools For full information on choosing and using tools, refer to the *Haynes Automotive Tools Manual*.

Tracer A stripe of a second colour applied to a wire insulator to distinguish that wire from another one with the same colour insulator.

Tune-up A process of accurate and careful adjustments and parts replacement to obtain the best possible engine performance.

Turbocharger A centrifugal device, driven by exhaust gases, that pressurises the intake air. Normally used to increase the power output from a given engine displacement, but can also be used primarily to reduce exhaust emissions (as on VW's "Umwelt" Diesel engine).

U

Universal joint or U-joint A double-pivoted connection for transmitting power from a driving to a driven shaft through an angle. A U-joint consists of two Y-shaped yokes and a cross-shaped member called the spider.

V

Valve A device through which the flow of liquid, gas, vacuum, or loose material in bulk may be started, stopped, or regulated by a movable part that opens, shuts, or partially obstructs one or more ports or passageways. A valve is also the movable part of such a device.

Valve clearance The clearance between the valve tip (the end of the valve stem) and the rocker arm or tappet. The valve clearance is measured when the valve is closed.

Vernier caliper A precision measuring instrument that measures inside and outside dimensions. Not quite as accurate as a micrometer, but more convenient.

Viscosity The thickness of a liquid or its resistance to flow.

Volt A unit for expressing electrical "pressure" in a circuit. One volt that will produce a current of one ampere through a resistance of one ohm.

W

Welding Various processes used to join metal items by heating the areas to be joined to a molten state and fusing them together. For more information refer to the *Haynes Automotive Welding Manual*.

Wiring diagram A drawing portraying the components and wires in a vehicle's electrical system, using standardised symbols. For more information refer to the *Haynes Automotive Electrical and Electronic Systems Manual*.

Note: *References throughout this index are in the form - "Chapter number" • "page number"*

Preserving Our Motoring Heritage

< The Model J Duesenberg Derham Tourster. Only eight of these magnificent cars were ever built – this is the only example to be found outside the United States of America

Almost every car you've ever loved, loathed or desired is gathered under one roof at the Haynes Motor Museum. Over 300 immaculately presented cars and motorbikes represent every aspect of our motoring heritage, from elegant reminders of bygone days, such as the superb Model J Duesenberg to curiosities like the bug-eyed BMW Isetta. There are also many old friends and flames. Perhaps you remember the 1959 Ford Popular that you did your courting in? The magnificent 'Red Collection' is a spectacle of classic sports cars including AC, Alfa Romeo, Austin Healey, Ferrari, Lamborghini, Maserati, MG, Riley, Porsche and Triumph.

A Perfect Day Out

Each and every vehicle at the Haynes Motor Museum has played its part in the history and culture of Motoring. Today, they make a wonderful spectacle and a great day out for all the family. Bring the kids, bring Mum and Dad, but above all bring your camera to capture those golden memories for ever. You will also find an impressive array of motoring memorabilia, a comfortable 70 seat video cinema and one of the most extensive transport book shops in Britain. The Pit Stop Cafe serves everything from a cup of tea to wholesome, home-made meals or, if you prefer, you can enjoy the large picnic area nestled in the beautiful rural surroundings of Somerset.

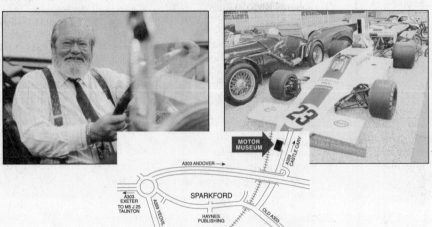

> John Haynes O.B.E., Founder and Chairman of the museum at the wheel of a Haynes Light 12.

< Graham Hill's Lola Cosworth Formula 1 car next to a 1934 Riley Sports.

The Museum is situated on the A359 Yeovil to Frome road at Sparkford, just off the A303 in Somerset. It is about 40 miles south of Bristol, and 25 minutes drive from the M5 intersection at Taunton.
Open 9.30am - 5.30pm (10.00am - 4.00pm Winter) 7 days a week, *except Christmas Day, Boxing Day and New Years Day*
Special rates available for schools, coach parties and outings Charitable Trust No. 292048